SCHIRMER'S GUIDE

TO BOOKS ON MUSIC AND MUSICIANS

SCHIRMER'S GUIDE
to BOOKS on MUSIC and
MUSICIANS

A PRACTICAL BIBLIOGRAPHY

Compiled, with an Introduction and Notes,
by R. D. DARRELL

G. SCHIRMER, Inc.
NEW YORK

CONTENTS

INTRODUCTION

FRAGMENTARY as our knowledge of early history and psychology may
be, there is nothing to contradict—and much to confirm—the notion
that even the earliest deliberate creation of music was almost simul-
taneously accompanied by a sense of need for verbal commentary. It is
extremely doubtful that musical analysis and exegesis are the exclusive
products of later (more sophisticated or effete) times: the first music
commentators and critics probably included the first composers themselves,
but certainly their families and friends.

Commentary actually may have preceded music in achieving written
form: at least it is represented more often in the earliest notated records
chance has preserved for us. And if composition outweighed commentary
in the not-so-dark Middle Ages, perhaps even through the Renaissance and
into the Baroque Era,—the scales balanced again in the late eighteenth
century and probably over-swung in the nineteenth. Nowadays, the unbalance
has become so marked that many observers are seriously concerned over the
apparent lag in musical creation. Even the enormous increase in the
performance, reproduction, and dissemination of music, old and new, which
is so extraordinary a characteristic of the immediate present, scarcely can
match the accompanying multiplication of published and broadcast "words
on music."

Now, the problem of what well may be "too much" music has not escaped
attention, although no one yet seems too sure of what should—or can—be
done about it, but the companion problem of "too much" commentary is seldom
recognized, much less thoughtfully pondered. While it bears heavily on the
musical scholar, educator, and librarian, the lay members of the new mass
audiences usually are unmindful of this problem's very existence, simply for
lack of familiarity with the phenomenal scope of the accumulated literature.
Even musicians—executants, teachers, and students—seldom venture far
outside the narrow areas in this literature that concern them most directly,
lacking time and guidance, if not the urge, to seek unfamiliar paths and wider
horizons.

INTRODUCTION

But for every serious observer of or participant in the musical scene of today, there are pressing, highly practical questions of how to utilize—how even to deal with—the embarrassing wealth of available literature. In the arts, as in the physical world, no region can be colonized successfully or its natural resources tapped profitably until it has been mapped, until roadways make it accessible throughout, and until effective communication systems are built up.

This, of course, is exactly what musicologists and bibliographers have been laboring for many years to accomplish in the realm of literature on music and no one at all familiar with their efforts can fail to marvel at the patience, energy, and skill they have applied to a herculean and too often thankless task. But the endless, progressively more difficult nature of this task, with its consequent stress on increasing specialization, severely limits their effectiveness to ever-narrowing segments both of the field itself and of the potentially interested public.

One of the great general problems of our day is this "well-known tendency of libraries to become clogged by their own volume; of the sciences to develop such a degree of specialization that the expert is often illiterate outside his own minute speciality."[1] More specifically, musical scholars currently proclaim a "large amount of dissatisfaction with existing bibliographical services from the point of view of the subject specialists ... A study of reference works in the field of music (June 1949) concludes that very few works answer the scholar's questions satisfactorily and that the situation as a whole leaves much to be desired."[2]

The musical non-specialist, on the other hand, can muster only wry sympathy with such perturbation, believing (fairly or unfairly) that the scholars' needs are met at least to some extent,—to a very considerable extent, indeed, in comparison with the complete inadequacy of comparable services for the express benefit of himself, or of listeners, musical laymen or middlemen, in general.[3] The needs of the latter, naturally, are less articulate, perhaps less consciously felt, but surely this provides no reliable index to the magnitude or the intensity of the needs themselves.

[1] Norbert Wiener: *Cybernetics—or Control and Communications in the Animal and the Machine.* The Technology Press, John Wiley & Sons, Inc., New York 1948. (p 184.)

[2] *The UNESCO/Library of Congress Bibliographical Survey: Bibliographical Services— Their Present State and Possibilities of Improvement.* Report prepared as a working paper for an international conference on bibliography. Washington, 1950. (pp 14/5.) The study referred to is Manfred F. Bukofzer's *Reference Requirements for the Research Scholar in Music,* a paper read during an institute on music librarianship held at the school of librarianship, University of California, October 29/30, 1948, and published in the Music Library Association *Notes,* Supplement for Members No. 8, June 1949, pp 17/20.

[3] "Music-lovers" is the common term, but a poor one. The ideal term should embrace both musical amateurs and non-executants (listeners)—all those non-professionally interested in more or less serious concert, recorded, and broadcast music.

INTRODUCTION

musicians includes a bibliography of some sort, and various music histories and yearbooks include excellent period-bibliographies.[8]. Collectively, if not always individually, these usually are adequate for most needs of the librarian and scholar, but even when they are both known and accessible to the layman (too often they are neither),[9] they seldom satisfy his dual demand for over-all scope combined with highly detailed information. Seeking further, he is likely to be told flatly that "Music, unlike art, has no index to current periodical literature, nor is there a comprehensive bibliography."[10]

That statement, to be sure, dates from 1947: two years later the Kretzschmar-Myers-Tilly *Music Index—the Key to Current Music Periodical Literature*[11] began to fill one gap, while the lack of *any* comprehensive bibliography—then or now—depends entirely on one's interpretation of "comprehensive."

In its strictest sense, the last such musical bibliography may have been the first: Forkel's *Allgemeine Litteratur der Musik, oder Anleitung zur Kenntniss musikalischer Bücher* (1792) . . . or perhaps Becker's revision of Forkel's work in the *Systematisch-chronologische Darstellung der musikalischen Litteratur von der frühesten bis auf die neueste Zeit* (1836, 1839), later extended by Büchting (1867, 1873) and Eitner (1885).

At any rate, the last reasonably comprehensive work in English probably was James L. Matthew's *The Literature of Music* (1896)—a model critical survey (which can delight anyone lucky enough to pick up a copy), although not designed for easy and complete reference purposes. Even by dint of freely stretching (or squeezing) "comprehensiveness," I know of only two general works available today:[12] Percy A. Scholes's *List of Books About Music*

---

[8] For example, the recent Hinrichsen series, entered in the GUIDE under Yearbooks.

[9] Many are in foreign languages (like the famous Eitner *Quellenlexikon* and Springer-Scheider-Wolffheim *Miscellanea*, entered in Appendix Ib of the GUIDE); many are out-of-print, available only in limited editions, or extremely costly. But even when accessible, their very size and specialization put severe handicaps on their general use by musical laymen.

[10] Mary Neill Barton: *Reference Books—A Brief Guide for Students and Other Users of the Library.* Enoch Pratt Free Library, Baltimore, Maryland, 1947. (p 57.)

[11] The 1949 *Annual Cumulation* (1950) is entered in the GUIDE under Bibliography.

[12] The Gleason-Luper *Bibliography of Books on Music and Collections of Music* (entered in the GUIDE under Bibliography) is scanty both in scope (some 590 titles) and detailed information. Gleason's *Music Literature Outlines* (entered in the GUIDE under Baroque Era and Medieval/Renaissance Era) include bibliographies that are much more extensive, but these of course must be considered specialized. One of the finest works in this field—Eric Blom's *General Index to Modern Musical Literature in the English Language* (Curwen, 1927)—is restricted to the period 1915/1926 and, in any case, now is out-of-print. A remarkable Dutch work has not been completed, as far as I know, and apparently never has been widely circulated outside The Netherlands: Willem Hutschenruyter's *Bijdrage tot de Bibliographie der Muziekliteratur: Deel I—Instrumentale Muziek, Mechanische Muziek, Electrische Muziek, Klokken*, Zeist 1941 (according to the copy I have seen, which has xii, 513, x pages of offset and photostat typescript, but which has been listed elsewhere as published by E. I. Brill, Leiden, 1942-43, Afl. 1-10, 513 p.).

in the English Language (1940)[13] and the National Association of Schools of Music *List of Books on Music* (1935), with six Supplements (1936 to 1948).[14]

The former is a fascinating little book and—to anyone who makes much use of it—a valued, if somewhat eccentric friend, whose idiosyncrasies are easily condoned. But, more objectively considered, it has serious disadvantages. Scholes himself admits frankly (in his preface) that it was compiled in great haste, that it was based primarily on his own library, and that the subject-arrangement was specifically designed to correspond with entries in his *Oxford Companion to Music*.[15] Such factors limit its usefulness, except perhaps as an adjunct to the admirable *Companion* itself, and it is further handicapped by the lack of an author index and (except in rare instances) cross-references and commentary.

The NASM series also has some, if quite different, disadvantages, but its scope and usefulness are far greater. Nearly all the entries are annotated, often at considerable length (in the supplements), and book-prices (omitted in Scholes's *List*) are included. Despite the skimping of some bibliographical details and a decidedly makeshift subject-reference scheme, the series is so good in most respects that if a cumulative edition had been available, the present GUIDE probably never would have been contemplated. Nevertheless, the essential characteristics of the NASM series (its serial publication, its natural school-library orientation, and to a less extent its sketchy treatment of the older entries in the 1935 *List*) unfortunately restrict it to a smaller and more specialized public than its many merits deserve.

The scarcity of existing works in this field (at least of those generally available at reasonable cost), regardless of their individual limitations, is surely fair justification for adding to their number, . . . but is this, in itself, sufficient justification? I was inclined to doubt it at the time the GUIDE was first contemplated; both urge and opportunity to prepare a work of the present character might have been lacking except for a weightier *raison d'être*. The decisive consideration was the apparent need for a bibliography differing

---

[13] Entered in the GUIDE under Bibliography.

[14] Entered in the GUIDE under Bibliography. See also Thompson's *Cyclopedia of Music and Musicians* (entered in the GUIDE under Encyclopedias of Music), which includes an extensive bibliography based on these NASM lists, or at least on the original list and some of the earlier supplements. Unfortunately, in my opinion this collation is unsatisfactory in many respects: annotations have been omitted or revised (seldom for the better) . . . prices have been omitted . . . the typographical scheme is hard on both eyes and mind of the user . . . and, perhaps most importantly, the original arrangement by authors (with separate subject references) has been discarded for a *mélange* in which some books are grouped under subject-headings, while others are entered under their authors' names, and cross-references are entirely lacking!

[15] Entered in the GUIDE under Dictionaries of Music.

in many respects from anything done before—particularly in its general orientation and style: the need for what is best described as a predominantly *practical* bibliography.

Since this may seem at first thought a somewhat odd, or at least superfluous criterion for a type of reference work that always is considered eminently practical (certainly it never is theoretical or speculative in either content or application), and since, moreover, I have made the term something of a shibboleth or touchstone for almost every characteristic feature of the GUIDE, —some explanation is in order.

2. The Notion of "Practicality"

> "It seems very pretty," she said when she had finished it, "but it's rather hard to understand." (You see she didn't like to confess, even to herself, that she couldn't make it out at all.) "Somehow it seems to fill my head with ideas—only I don't exactly know what they are!"
> —CARROLL: *Through the Looking Glass*

Practical considerations obviously are significant factors in planning and producing any book; in a reference work published under commercial rather than eleemosynary auspices, they usually are determining factors. Generally, however, they are taken more or less for granted and submerged in larger questions of *practicability*. It is the latter that most often determine the outcome of the major compromises made in every work: in its scope (where ideal comprehensiveness must be balanced against costs at a point where book size and price seem best matched to the habits and budgets of its potential public) . . . in the time spent on its preparation (where the ideal of infinite research must be balanced against what reasonably unreasonable burdens both publisher and author can bear) . . . in the choice of material to be included or excluded (where readers' and author's appetites for "completeness" must be balanced against their known or presumed tastes and digestive powers) . . .

To be publishable, a book must be practicable, but even successful publication is insufficient proof of its *practicality*,—for that can be determined only after considerable actual use by many readers and then only on the basis of its inherent usefulness, the pertinency and accessibility of its material, and the economy of effort it demands from its readers. The ability of a reference book to pass such severely practical use-tests depends also on the accuracy with which its producers have calculated both intensity and magnitude of a public "demand" and, above all, on the effectiveness with which they have shaped it to meet the essential needs, not only of its potential users, but of its own materials.

INTRODUCTION

Now, it is easy enough to see that the presumed needs of presumed users are primary strategical considerations in planning a book; it scarcely is less evident that tactical working-out considerations should be based on the nature of the materials themselves; but what is the point in endowing these materials with "needs" of their own, much less of endeavoring to meet such hypothetical demands?

What I am trying to do is merely to dramatize a phenomenon familiar to many artists by speaking of an "innate compulsion of related materials to crystallize into their own most natural pattern," or of the "tendency of diversified contents—when isolated in a single book—to organize themselves in their most logical or isomorphic form." Put thus, I'm indulging in anthropomorphic fancy, of course: any actual "need," or tendency, or compulsion is all in the observer's mind. But certainly our minds do seem so constructed that their handling of any multitudinous group of facts is facilitated by first arranging them into some kind of pattern; and out of all possible patterns, the most satisfactory—both to manipulate and to comprehend—invariably seems the one most thoroughly "dictated" by the nature of the specific facts involved.

Granted, this may be a personal fetish, or an over-stretched application of *Gestalt* theory; nevertheless, I've found it to be of practical—indeed essential—value on many occasions and with the most diverse types of materials, from the entire repertory of serious music on records[16] to the component parts and circuits of electronic gear![17]. My only excuse for stressing here what may be a personal obsession is the light it may throw on some of the otherwise perhaps obscure procedures employed in the present work.

Earlier references to "novel" aspects of this GUIDE probably have given, at least by implication, an exaggerated notion of the extent of such features; so far, certainly, they have been mentioned without apologies, possibly with scarcely concealed pride. (Problem children always are the parent's dearest!) Actually, however, there are fewer of them—in the completed work—than one might expect or even than I had braced myself for. Some do remain and must be judged on their own merits, but whatever special pride I may take in them now is primarily in their ability to survive some fairly rigorous tests.

For, while I believe fervently in making virtues out of necessities, I am anxious first to make certain that the necessities are genuine. At any rate,

---

[16] R. D. Darrell: *The Gramophone Shop Encyclopedia of Recorded Music*, first (1936) edition. (Reid's third, completely revised, edition is entered in the GUIDE under Phonograph Records.)

[17] An unsigned series of instruction handbooks for airborne radar equipments, published under joint auspices of the United States War and Navy Departments, 1944/1946.

INTRODUCTION

Such peripheral categories—including some subject-headings introduced for reference purposes only—are prefaced by general notes on their musical relationships, often with definitions or identifications of terms normally unfamiliar to musically minded readers.[20]   And while it is only too easy to confuse a presumed need for information with the urge to impart it, it struck me that comparable explanations also might be of practical worth for many strictly musical subjects of ambiguous, controversial, or popularly misunderstood nature.[21]   (To my own surprise, I found additional justification for this in many standard reference works' inexplicably superficial treatment—or even complete omission—of some such terms.)[22]

Now, I'm keenly aware that informational embellishments of this kind often may be prompted merely by the compiler's urge to enliven his drudgery by reversion to more personal modes of expression (the itch to "spill", as e. e. cummings puts it, his "bright, incalculable soul!").   The overt justification, however, is the enlightenment of both main types of readers—with perhaps not entirely gratuitous information for the non-specialist, for others an explicit avowal of the compiler's intentions and implicit revelation of his personal biases.   But perhaps the most important practical worth of the compiler's taking the reader into his confidence, as it were, lies in the provision of at least some running explanation of his procedures—in selecting among multiple choices in subject-headings, in delimiting the field of a particular subject, and in vindicating his admission or exclusion of certain entries.   And if on occasion there is only a confession of failure to achieve more satisfactory subject terminology, arrangement, or representation (or a concession of sheerly arbitrary, *faute de mieux* actions),—the most inexperienced reader is alerted by the invaluable warning that neither the authority of the printed page nor the most ambitious intentions of its author ever can guarantee omniscience.

In strictly bibliographical details, the GUIDE follows no standard model in its material's arrangement and extent, but combines familiar and original practices in an effort to achieve internal rather than external consistency, as well as maximum economy and practical usefulness of means.   Insofar as possible, sequences and abbreviations are self-explanatory. While no effort has been made to emulate librarians' exact distinctions between what actually appears on a title page and what has been supplied from other sources, I

[20] See, for some representative examples, the General Notes under Dances/Dancing-2, Decibel, Diction (Enunciation), Discographies, Noise, Phonograph Records, Sound Recording and Reproduction, Ultrasonics.

[21] See, for representative examples, the General Notes under Appreciation, Folk (Lore, Music, Songs), Gregorian, Hymns/Hymnody, Instrumentation/Orchestration, Jazz, Musicology, Plainsong, Program Notes, Sight-Playing/Reading/Singing, Tonality/Atonality.

[22] Musicianship and Theory probably are the outstanding examples.

have endeavored, wherever I could,[23] to augment the minimum information required for full and exact identification by additional details—such as list prices, the scope as well as the presence of illustrations and bibliography, and all available edition and reprint data.[24]

The choice of "dictionary style" and combined subject-and-author entries surely is obvious, but perhaps the location of book-entries under subjects rather than authors demands comment. Personally, I always prefer orientation of material by authors, but in this particular field there are over-riding reasons for subject-classification: the specificity of interests exhibited by most music-book readers (whose intense concern with Counterpoint, say, doesn't necessarily imply any marked interest in Chopin, Community Music, or Conducting) and the lamentable fact that most music-book authors are relatively unfamiliar even to the musically minded public (which more often seeks a book *on* such-and-such than *by* so-and-so). Somewhat similar considerations seemed to make a title-index superfluous (the subject is more generally remembered—or sought—than the exact title) and these were reinforced by those of economy, which, of course, also determined the use of cross-references rather than multiple entries.[25]

But the most noticeable exploitation of the general principle of practicality probably is the GUIDE's typographical scheme. Far-sighted readers may be understandably dubious, but the choice of an eight-point type-face, which is almost unavoidable in a work of this kind and extent, provides more significant economies than those of space alone. Normally, no one ever really *reads* a reference book: it is *searched*—and its usefulness depends in large part on the ease with which wanted entries may be located. The present scheme is expressly designed for such scanning and quick-search purposes, not merely in its choice of type-size, but in its use of various type-faces, indentions, and spacing,—for I have an almost obsessive faith in the ability of such "mechani-

[23] Insofar as possible, all entry-data are based on primary sources—*i.e.*, the books themselves. There has been no time yet for statistical computations, but I am sure that well over three-fourths of the actual book-entries are for publications I've personally examined (not read!) ... Quite possibly an exact account will raise the percentage to 85 or even 90.

[24] Considering the unusual extent of such augmented details, it may be wondered why they stop short of supplying index data. The reason is simple: I just didn't realize, early enough, the value of this information and later its inclusion would have made unconscionable demands in source re-examination and type re-setting. Anyway (for such consolation as it may afford), book indices vary so widely in nature that any practicably concise means of treating them well may have been impossible,—and without detailed specifications or evaluations, the mere indication of their presence would be of somewhat dubious usefulness.

[25] Like practically all the GUIDE's general rules, this permits certain exceptions: a few books with both English and foreign text are entered twice (in Appendix I as well as in the main listings); for some prolific authors, at least those represented here by more than two or three works, the usual "see" references in the author entry are augmented by concise title, date, and price data. This abbreviated form is intended only as a special convenience: such books, like all others, are entered in full only under the appropriate subject-headings.

cal" devices to *guide* both eye and mind of the information-seeker. At their best, they not only help him to find what he is looking for more easily and speedily, but also to grasp (with less conscious effort) the relative degree of importance assigned to various classes of materials and the various details of an individual entry.

For similar reasons (together with a preference for highly specific subject-headings and rigorous classifications), I have used as many subject-divisions as the basic materials permit and in many cases made further sub-divisions.[26] Some of the latter obviously are justified by the nature of the materials, while others are primarily of *visual* convenience in that they break up the monotonous flow of uninterrupted book-entries whenever the latter threaten to run over more than (say) two or three full book pages.

The validity of my faith in such optical-psychological aids (at least the effectiveness with which they are exploited here) is subject to use-test, of course, not to argument. All I dare claim in advance for the present typographical scheme is that it has evolved from long deliberation and experimentation. I can only pray that it is able to vindicate itself and eventually atone for whatever preliminary discomfort it may cause any user of the GUIDE.

4. *Apologies/Acknowledgments*

> Certain authors, speaking of their works, say, "My book," "My commentary," "My history," etc. They resemble middle-class people who have a home of their own, and always have "My house" on their tongue. They would do better to say, "Our book," "Our commentary," "Our history," etc., because there is in them usually more of other people's than their own.
> —PASCAL: *Pensées* (Trotter translation)

There remains only the inevitable final ritual of personal inadequacy-and-obligation admissions. But—obstinately practical to the last—I sha'n't indulge in the customary *Mea culpa!* for "any errors that may have crept in." I know too well that errors don't *creep* in: they run, fly, pour, storm, and parachute into any work of this kind! Indefatigably as compiler, editor, and printer root them out, the *n*th proof-reading always will find others—and time inexorably calls a halt to an otherwise endless battle. Anyway, as a book goes to press, it's futile to worry any longer over those annoying, dirty finger-prints of one's collaborating visual, psychological, and typographical gremlins! I can only hope that they will not prove too much of a nuisance and beg the

---

[26] See the list of Major Subject-Headings, p xxxii.

help of keen-eyed readers in reporting them for correction in our files and any possible future supplements or editions.[27]

What still worry me, far more deeply than any self-evident typographical errors, are my own memory-lapses, knowledge-gaps, and judgment-vacillations. Many of these have been spotted and corrected (mostly by grace of the eagle eyes and richly informed mind of my supervising editor); I've caught some others myself, but too late to make any satisfactory amends;[28] the rest remain to be exposed by the GUIDE's users—who will, I sincerely trust, more often find them diverting revelations of the compiler's inadequacies than substantial detriments to the usefulness of the work itself.

But if it's easy to beg forgiveness for any specific entry omission or error, if I have considerable faith in the ability of the "practical" features to plead their own case, I scarcely dare crave absolution for certain other idiosyncrasies that characterize the present book. I like to think that I scorn the customary reference-work canon of strict impersonality out of legitimate distaste for self-conscious solemnity in even the most serious pursuit of knowledge,— but very likely it is merely because some inhere ebullience makes such impersonality not only abhorrent, but imp ssible to me. At any rate, I have made few deliberate attempts to curb what well may be an irrepressible urge to enliven—when given an apt opening—the dreary flow of sheerly factual material. Since all my own notes and commentary are italicized in the GUIDE, perhaps there is no real danger of deception in my lapses into discursiveness, extraneity, or even prejudice. Certainly they serve as additional reminders that the metamorphosis of a critic into a bibliographer never can be quite complete and that even the most earnest bibliographer always is "human, all too human." At best, what I have relished as momentary escape from the otherwise unrelieved drudgery of my task possibly may be welcomed on the same ground by some readers—and at least graciously overlooked, if not excused, by others.

* * * * * * *

Yet all such preoccupation with the expressions of one's own individuality is dangerous insofar as it bolsters the natural tendency of the general public

[27] Please address any corrections or suggestions to the Publication Department, G. Schirmer, Inc., 3 East 43rd Street, New York City 17.

[28] Most of the stylistic inconsistencies (in subject-headings and elsewhere) are less likely to worry readers than they do me, but in any case they're inexcusable. Certain subject-assignments are easily debatable, as is my failure to combine (as I did Instrumentation/-Orchestration) such closely related—and ambiguously separated—subjects as Baton and Conducting, Contemporary Music and Modern Music, Gregorian Chant and Plainsong, etc.

to regard a sizable reference book accredited to a single author, compiler, or editor, as a "one-man" work. The man himself knows better than any reader that this sharp focus of attention is only a dramatic spotlighting, if not actual distortion, of the facts. No matter how distinctively he shapes both general outline and detailed wording, or how thoroughly he infuses it with his own "style,"—any book of this kind is by its very nature an accumulation and crystallization of many talents and many ideas.

A compiler, in particular, is just that: a "plunderer," indeed, according to the Latin derivation, but in any case one who draws his basic materials from others and whose own contribution is largely that of selection, of encouraging these materials to form into their own organic patterns, of revealing them in new perspectives, and—at his best—of giving them fresh illumination.

Indeed, all this is "at best": more often the compiler is one of those "continual plodders," despised by Shakespeare as winning little "save base authority from others' books," or a special victim of man's "remarkable tendency" (noted by Wolfgang Köhler) "to be soothed and satisfied whenever a problem, instead of being solved, has merely been located somewhere." While he can never, even if he wishes, evade sole responsibility for his compilation, still less can he escape the burden of indebtedness (conscious and unconscious) to the labors of many others. And, of course, the more extensive the work, the more "individually" he has attempted to color its contents, the more—and greater—debts he incurs.

In my own case, I am acutely sensible of the inadequacy, if not actual injustice, of the conventional settlement of such debts by a few casual lines of "acknowledgment." I long for a better way to express my deep gratitude for the incalculable help I have drawn upon so freely—and been so freely given. Unfortunately, I can't even begin to specify all these creditors, but among those I best know and remember, I surely must name the following:

§The authors and publishers of the reference books I've thumbed most regularly,—particularly *Baker's Biographical Dictionary of Musicians*,[29] Apel's *Harvard Dictionary of Music*, the National Association of Schools of Music *List* (and supplements) *of Books on Music*, Scholes's *List of Books About Music*, the H. W. Wilson Company's *Cumulative Book Index*, the R. R. Bowker Company's *Publishers Trade List Annual* and *Books in Print*. . .

§The reviewers, compilers, and publishers of music-book notices in many periodicals,—particularly those in *The Musical Quarterly*, Music Library Association *Notes*, and *Publishers' Weekly*. . .

---

[29] Throughout the GUIDE, *Baker's Dictionary* has been used as an authority for the spelling of proper names, except in a few cases (ex. Schoenberg) where a revised form has been endorsed by the musician himself.

INTRODUCTION

§The anonymous compilers (some of whom I've blessed and many others I've cursed on occasion!) of publishers' music-book and general catalogues... Also various publishers' representatives who have been more than ordinarily helpful in providing special information,—particularly Gertrude Borchard of the National Recreation Association, Herbert Coleman of Coleman-Ross, Kathleen Connor of Carl Fischer, Lyle Dowling of the Oxford University Press, J. Fortna of G. Schirmer, Albert G. Hess of Musurgia, Walter Hinrichsen of C. F. Peters and Hinrichsen Edition, Reginald L. McAll of the Hymn Society of America, and Charles Seeger of the Pan American Union...

§The officials and staff-members of various libraries I've consulted, often in quest of information available from no other source,—particularly Richard Appel of the Boston Public Library, Gladys Chamberlain of that unique New York Institution—the 58th Street Music Library, Richard S. Hill of the Music Division of the Library of Congress, and (with a special acknowledgment of his unfailing knowledge, patience, and friendship) Philip L. Miller of the Music Division of the New York Public Library.

§Other personal friends whom I've alternately neglected and exploited outrageously, but on whom I could often depend for specialized information and always for needed advice and encouragement,—particularly Herman Adler, Charlotte and Richard Gilbert, Mary and John Marshall, Ann and Walter Morin, Harvey J. Olnick, Lewis Patlin, Emily and Graydon Walker....

§The officials and staff of the GUIDE's sponsor and publisher, G. Schirmer, Inc.,—above all to my supervising editor, Nathan Broder... but also to many others throughout the Publication Department, the Book Department—which I've haunted and ransacked and distracted for so many months, and the Printing & Production Department—which has labored so valiantly to bring to life on these printed pages even the strangest of my materials and the most seemingly impracticable of my "practical" notions.

—R. D. DARRELL

HOW TO USE
SCHIRMER'S GUIDE TO BOOKS ON MUSIC AND MUSICIANS

BASIC CONSIDERATIONS

The GUIDE may be used most conveniently, as well as most effectively, if you keep in mind exactly what it is and what it tries to do:

1. It is a reference guide to books on music and musicians.

It does not discuss or evaluate composers and their works, but endeavors to provide the most complete possible information on *books*, in English and currently available, which deal with any aspect of music, or with composers (collectively or individually) and their works.

As a general rule, it does not include collections of music itself, unless they also embody considerable text material, and it represents the literature on allied (or peripheral) arts and related subjects only by "samplings"— *i.e.*, selected lists of books most likely to be of interest to listeners and musicians.

2. It is a "practical" bibliography.

It does not include books apparently out-of-print or difficult to obtain in this country—although in many cases reference is made to them, particularly if they are "standard" works (*i.e.*, well known and frequently cited) on their subjects. Books in foreign languages are not entered in the main GUIDE listings, but selections from currently available works in French and German are given in Appendix I, which also includes shorter lists of works in Italian, Spanish, and Latin. Periodical articles are not included at all and as a general rule neither are reprints from scholarly journals, nor private publications of a highly specialized nature intended mainly for the use of musicologists or friends and students of the author.

3. It is directed primarily to musically interested adults.

While of course we hope that the GUIDE will prove extremely useful to librarians and scholars, it has been especially designed for use by *listeners* (*i.e.*, laymen interested in learning more about the music they enjoy in concerts, broadcasts, and recordings), as well as by musical amateurs and professional musicians, teachers, and students.

While it includes books *about* children's musical interests and training, written primarily for parents and teachers, it excludes "juveniles" (*i.e.*, books *for* children), except for a selection of some of the more important books of this type listed in Appendix II.

4. *It is designed to provide maximum information in minimum space.*

The arrangement of entries is in "dictionary style,"—that is, with subjects and authors combined in continuous alphabetical order throughout, thus eliminating the necessity of an index and of skipping among several independently alphabetized classifications. The actual book-entries appear under *Major Subject-Headings* (for a list of these, please see page xxxii), while other subject-headings and the authors' entries provide detailed cross-references to the exact location of the book-entries themselves, plus—in many instances—informative *General Notes*, references to out-of-print "standard" works, specialized bibliographies, etc. In the case of some unusually prolific authors, the usual "see" references are replaced by a condensed listing of their books, together with the subject-headings under which these books are entered in full detail. With this exception, no book normally is listed twice, but of course when an individual book deals with more than one main subject, appropriate cross-references are made to it under each of these subject-headings.

An actual book entry normally includes—besides the full title, sub-title publisher, and date—information on the various editions or reprintings it may have gone through; its illustrations, musical examples, and bibliography, if any; its type of binding, if other than cloth; and in addition, its current (retail) list price. For many books the Compiler has added brief annotations, which (like his *General Notes*) are printed in italics so that they may be clearly distinguished from the factual material in Roman type. For conciseness, much of the bibliographical data in the book entries is given in abbreviated form (please refer to the *Key to Symbols and Abbreviations*, page xxxviii, and to the *Key to Publishers*, page 385). Similarly, a compressed, although not entirely telegraphic, style is used for the annotations.

5. *It is non-critical.*

Insofar as human frailties permit, the inclusion or exclusion of any book on music or musicians is determined by the factors cited in 1., 2., and 3. above,—*not* by what the Compiler may think of its merits. His annotations, too, are not intended as criteria or evaluations, but simply as useful, descriptive information to augment that provided by the books' titles and sub-titles, to indicate more clearly the books' subject-matter, or to clarify confusions arising from changes in titles, publishers, etc. It is impossible, of course, to eliminate all bias from either the choice of entries to be annotated or the wording of the notes themselves, but the Compiler's dominant endeavor has been to achieve as high a degree of objectivity obtainable without lapses into dispiriting prosaicism and the lack of all point or color.

HOW TO FIND A SPECIFIC BOOK

1. *If you already know the exact subject or title—*

Using the first letters of the main subject of the book (*not* those of its actual title, although the main subject usually is the key-word in the title), locate the subject—or the heading closest to it in meaning—in its proper alphabetical order in the GUIDE. Then run down through the book-entries, which are arranged in alphabetical order by their authors' last names, until you find the book you want.

Example: Let's say, to pick at random an example appearing on page 2 of the main GUIDE, you're looking for a book called *The Well-Tempered Accompanist.* The main subject or key-word obviously is "accompanist," so you look under ACC (*not* under WEL, for "well-tempered"). You'll find that while there is no "accompanist" subject-heading, there is one for the extremely close ACCOMPANIMENT. Skipping the "*see also*" cross-references and notes, run down through the book-entries until you find:

> **(ACCOMPANIMENT)**
> Bos, COENRAAD V.
> The well-tempered accompanist: as
> told to Ashley Pettis. Forew Helen
> Traubel. 162 p + 1–p Bos disco-
> graphy, 17 pl (pors, facs), mus ex.
> Presser 1949. **2.50**
> *General & practical advice on a wide variety
> of technical & interpretative problems in
> accompanying German Lieder in particular;
> plus reminiscences of Brahms, Culp, Ger-
> hardt, & other famous composers & singers.*

If you know only the author's name—
Using the first letters of the author's last name, find his entry in its proper alphabetical location. The entry will include one or more "see" references, which direct you to the major subject-headings under which his books are entered in detail.

Examples: If you'd forgotten the title of *The Well-Tempered Accompanist,* but remembered its author's name, you will find under BOS:

> **Bos, Coenraad Valentyn van.** Author.
> See Accompaniment.

If, however, the book is an autobiography, a collection of essays, or other-wise not precisely classifiable by subject, it will be listed directly under the author's name.

Examples:

> **(BERLIOZ-1. Autobiography, Own Writ-ings)**
> (NEWMAN, ERNEST, *ed*)
> Memoirs of Hector Berlioz, from
> 1803 to 1865: comprising his travels
> in Germany, Italy, Russia, & Eng-
> land. Tr Rachel & Eleanor Holmes,
> Annot & translation rev by Ernest
> Newman. xxiii, 533, xiii p, 11 pl
> (pors, etc). Knopf 1932 (1948). **5.00**
> *Probably the most famous of all musical auto-
> biographies, as well as an illuminating picture
> of the man & his times.*

(GRAY, Cecil)
Contingencies and other essays. viii,
199 p, mus ex. Oxford 1947. **4.00**
Outspoken studies & revaluations of Brahms,
Liszt, Bellini, Meyerbeer, Verdi, etc, plus
a revised version of the Gesualdo biography
originally published in "Carlo Gesualdo" by
Gray & Heseltine (1926), but long O/P.

3. *If you have only a general notion of subject or title—*

Often one has a vague recollection of a certain book, but can't recall its exact title or author.   In such cases, the easiest tracing method is to refer to the list of *Major Subject-Headings* (page xxxii), running through it until you find either the subject in mind or one closely allied to it.   If the book sought is not included in this subject's entries, follow the "*see also*" references until you find the specific heading under which the desired book is entered.

Example: Suppose you remember reading or hearing about a book that had something to do with "style" in music and other arts.   In the list of *Major Subject-Headings* there is no entry for Style or Arts, but there is one for Aesthetics.   (If you looked in the GUIDE itself under either Style or Arts, you would find in each case a "*see also:* Aesthetics.")   Turning, then, to Aesthetics, run down through the book entries until you find one that "rings a bell" in your mind:

(AESTHETICS-1. General)
SACHS, CURT
The commonwealth of art: style in
the fine arts, music and the dance.
404 p + 32 pl, mus ex. Norton 1946. **6.00**
The interrelationship of styles & the arts as
expressions of their times.

HOW TO FIND "A BOOK ON ——"

1. *If you're seeking a useful book on some specific subject—*

However valuable the GUIDE may be as a *reference* work for known material, we hope that it may have an even more significant function, that of serving as a *source of suggestions* or "invitation to learning" for the musically interested reader, who may not know in advance what particular book he wants, but who is anxious to find any or several good books on his pet subject.

Such a reader may be a radio listener, who has been stimulated to learn more about Bach's life, say, that he can from any book he now owns or knows... He may be a teacher, giving a course in composition, for which he'd like to consult some books besides those with which he already is familiar,—more recent textbooks, perhaps, than those used in his own student days. . . He may be a student seeking detailed information on handling a baton in conducting, say, or on finger-technique in piano playing, or on the general problems of vocal study. . .

Examples: In such instances as these, turn directly (or via cross-referenced subject-headings) to the particular subject involved and run down through the book entries until you find one or more promising titles:

(BACH-1)

TERRY, CHARLES SANFORD
Bach: a biography. xx, 292 p + 76
pl + 2 charts, 5-p bibl.   Oxford
(1928) 2nd rev ed 1933 (1949).   5.00

A more recent standard work: primarily a record of Bach's career, including much original research, many photographs by the author, and two fold-out genealogical charts.

. . . .

(COMPOSITION)

HINDEMITH, PAUL
The craft of musical composition.
2 v. Associated 1941/2.

V 1: Theoretical part.   Tr Arthur
Mendel. vi, 223 p, 2 fold-out charts,
mus ex. (1937) 1942 (3rd rev ed n d).   4.00

V 2: Exercises in two-part writing.
Tr Otto Ortmann.   viii, 160 p, mus
ex. (1939) 1941.   3.00

English versions of the "Unterweisung im Tonsatz" (1937/9). A noted contemporary composer-pedagogue's re-examination of the tonal elements in music, with analyses of various works according to the new principles derived.

. . . .

(BATON-1. Conducting Techniques)

RUDOLF, MAX
The grammar of conducting: a practical study of modern baton technique. Pref George Szell. xvi, 350 p,
60 diagrs, 467 mus ex.   G. Schirmer
1950.   6.00

A new work that undoubtedly will rank as the standard in its field.   It demonstrates in detail the 6 patterns of beating each of the basic rhythms, with—in an appendix— conductor's analyses, bar by bar, of 11 orchestral pieces, from Bach to Debussy.

. . . .

**(PIANO PLAYING-1.   General, Larger
Aspects & Methods)**

SCHULTZ, ARNOLD
The riddle of the pianist's finger: and
its relationship to a touch-scheme.
xiii, 317 p, 9 diagrs, 1 table, mus ex,
bibl refs.   (1936) C. Fischer repr
1949.   5.00

A method of touch-mechanics based on new theories opposed to those of standard "relaxation" systems, with detailed critical analyses of the teachings of Leschetizky, Matthay,

Breithaupt, & Ortmann. *Originally published*
by the University of Chicago Press (1936).
. . . .

**(SINGING-1.   General, Larger Methods,
etc)**
KAGEN, SERGIUS
On studying singing.   119 p.   Rine-
hart 1950.   **2.00**
"Field of Music" series No 4: a commonsense
survey of the general problems involved, the
natural equipment required, the scope & pur-
pose of related studies, basic procedures, etc.

2.   *If you find it difficult to choose among the available entries—*
With many subjects (such as those of Bach, Piano Playing, and Singing
above), you will find an embarrassment ot riches.   How are you to select
the one or several books best suited to your needs?   Actual examination—
or better yet, study—of the books themselves can provide the only sure
answer. Nevertheless, many significant clues to a satisfactory choice may
be found in the GUIDE entries themselves.

Most important are the title and the sub-title (if any),—while the major
subject-heading and perhaps the sub-category under which a possible choice
is listed provide further clues, particularly if the title itself does not give
a clear indication of the book's exact subject-matter and scope.

The detailed entry data are extremely useful, if you stop to think about
them a bit.   From the stated number of pages, the presence or absence of
illustrations and bibliography, the type of binding (which always is cloth
unless specifically noted as boards or paper), and the list price all serve to
define the book's size and—to some extent at least—its character.   The
date of publication may be a decisive factor, especially when the subject
is one for which you want the most up-to-date treatment.   And with older
books, the number of editions or reprintings often provides a rough index
to their popularity.

The warning symbol (Δ) indicates that a promising book may not be
immediately available in leading musical booksellers' stocks, but that it
must be obtained on special order, or that publication is pending.

The italicized annotations are particularly intended to clarify any ambigui-
ties in the title or sub-title and to augment the information supplied by the
bibliographical data themselves.   And while these notes are non-critical,
they usually do provide helpful hints,—sometimes by calling attention to
the fact that this is a "standard" work or one written by a well-known
authority, sometimes by their more detailed description of the book's
contents.

Few readers like to be *told* what to buy: we believe that what most readers
want is concise and easily accessible *information* on what is available.
What we have tried to provide here is just such basic data, from which
you must then draw your own conclusions and make your own decisions
on which books best meet your individual tastes and needs.

HOW TO WIDEN YOUR MUSICAL HORIZONS

1. *If you're unfamiliar with a particular subject's literature—*
Among the various kinds of useful information sought by readers in general, there is one type that many individuals seem particularly anxious to find. That is some kind of introduction to, or orientation in, a subject that appeals to them, but in which they have done little reading—usually for lack of knowledge about *what* to read. To put the GUIDE to this sort of use, pick out one of the major subjects that particularly interests you, and check through the entire entry under that heading, including the *General Note*, cross- and O/P-references, as well as the actual book listings and annotations. Usually there's a good chance you'll be reminded of the existence of certain books you had once heard about and since forgotten; almost invariably you'll come across others that strike you as unusually enticing.

For further discoveries, check through the various cross-referenced subject-headings on closely related topics. After looking through the Appreciation lists, to cite a popular example, note that the "*see also*" references call your attention such subjects as (among others): Children-2 (including appreciation books for use with children and musical novices). . . Phonograph Records (books dealing with the immense modern repertory of recorded music). . . Program Notes (books of annotations, analyses, and descriptive material on many musical works). . . School Music-2 (books on appreciation and phonograph records especially designed for school use at various age levels). . .

Under the subject in which you're interested, or among the entries under related headings, you'll often find listings or notes on specialized bibliographies that provide vast amounts of additional information, some of it on the out-of-print books, periodical articles, reprints, etc.. that are not included in the GUIDE itself. A number of such works are entered under the subject-heading Bibliography (among them *The Music Index: 1949 Annual Cumulation*, indexing articles on music and musicians from some eighty-one American and foreign periodicals). Many others may be found via the cross-references here (including Magriel's *Bibliography of Dancing: a List of Books and Articles on the Dance and Related Subjects*, and Gleason's *Music Literature Outlines* for the Medieval-Renaissance and Baroque eras).

Whatever your starting point may be, the GUIDE's extensive "*see also*" references can serve as signposts to the many branching paths that will lead you by the easiest routes, first to nearby realms, and eventually throughout the whole world of musical knowledge.

2. *If you've already found an author you particularly admire—*
Look under the name of the author of any book you have especially enjoyed and follow the "see" references to his other available publications, for the chances are good that you'll relish them, too. Or, if you have one of his books, you'll probably find that it contains a bibliography or other references to works by other authors, which he has used or recommends, and these also may be traced easily in the GUIDE.

3. *If you're seeking fresh "adventures" in reading—*

Following some of the search procedures outlined above, or just thumbing through the GUIDE at random, stop to read a bit whenever an unusual subject, author's name, or book-title catches your eye. The *General Note* for the subject or the book-entry's annotation sometimes may serve as a persuasive introduction to works you've never even heard of before, but which may turn out to be exciting and valuable discoveries. More often, perhaps, this kind of "Little-Jack-Horner" dipping will prove less richly rewarding, but it never fails to dredge up fascinating bits-and-pieces of odd, miscellaneous information and curiosity-tickling new names and terms.

For random illustrations of what we mean, here are some heterogeneous Quiz questions that can be answered from an exploration of these pages: What is the difference between Ultrasonics and Supersonics, and which is connected—albeit remotely—with music? Are there any books available on the songs of Birds and on the songs or other sounds of Insects? If you're a Baker Street disciple, you already know that Holmes (Sherlock) was something of a musician, perhaps even a musicologist; but where would you go for a full, scholarly discussion of this aspect of the great detective? And, speaking of musicologists, just what does the term Musicology really mean?

For that matter, isn't your curiosity aroused by the mere existence in the list of *Major Subject-Headings* of such terms as Barbershop, Boxes (music-), Choral Speaking, Color & Music, Health & Music, Metronome, Quizzes, Religion & Music, Stage-Fright, Tests (musical), Whistling, Women & Music?...

Now, of course, the GUIDE is first of all a serious reference work and every endeavor has been made to provide a maximum of useful information in the *General Notes* and references under such important subjects as Church Music, Counterpoint, Folklore, Harmony, History, Opera, Orchestra, School Music, Teaching, and many others. But since there *are* odd aspects to music and since books are written about these too, we do not fear that the GUIDE's seriousness is compromised when such solid fare is enlivened elsewhere by condiments like the perhaps unorthodox, but hopefully provocative, *General Notes* for such major and minor subject-headings as Appreciation, Decibel, Discographies, Fiction, Jazz, Musicianship— Applied & "Theoretical," Noise, Sound Recording & Reproduction, "Theory," Twelve-Tone Technique, etc.

HOW TO PROCEED WHEN YOU REACH A SEEMING DEAD-END

1. *If there is no major heading for the subject you want—*

If the subject in which you're particularly interested does not appear in the list of *Major Subject-Headings* (page xxxii), look for it in its proper alphabetical location in the GUIDE itself. It probably will appear there as a "minor" heading (*i.e.,* followed by notes and references only), but with clues to the most closely related major subjects. If it does not appear at all, try variant forms of the topic, related subjects, and their cross-references.

2. *If you can't find a particular book you know exists—*
When the search of entries under both the book's main subject, or subjects, and the cross-referenced related subject-headings fails to reveal any mention of the book you seek, please consider (before accusing us of omitting it in error) the likelihood of its being out-of-print or its deliberate exclusion for some of the other reasons cited above in *Basic Considerations 1., 2., and 3.*

3. *If you can't interpret an entry's bibliographical data—*
Please consult the *Key to Symbols and Abbreviations* (page xxxviii) and the *Key to Publishers* (page 385). It may be helpful also to refer to those sections of the Compiler's *Introduction* in which he discusses in some detail the system employed for book-entries.

4. *If a particular book is noted "apparently O/P"—*
Most out-of-print books of any consequence and many books "not easily available" (*i.e.*, from American booksellers) may be found for consultation —and sometimes for loan—at the larger public, university, conservatory, and other libraries. Often out-of-print books may be obtained through bookshops specializing in second-hand copies and discontinued publications. Or one may advertise for a copy in the classified columns of various book-trade magazines. If you are convinced of the book's importance, it would be well to write to the original publisher, urging a new edition or reprinting. In some cases, particularly with "standard" works, a re-issue already may be in preparation; in others, receipt of a considerable number of such requests is likely to persuade the publisher that enough demand exists to warrant a new edition or reprint.

5. *If the "see" and "see also" references lead you nowhere—*
Write us a letter calling our attention to an unpardonable blunder! While, of course, some of the *general* references are "circular" (from Appreciation, for example, you're referred to Program Notes; from Program Notes you're referred to Appreciation), we've tried our best to eliminate all "dead-end" and "circular" *specific* references: referring only to those (major) subject-headings under which there are pertinent book-entries or especially significant notes.

* * * * * *

But we sincerely hope you will be led into few, if any, dead-end alleys, either in subjects and individual books, or in orthodox or unorthodox information. We hope that these pages will serve you well as convenient, comprehensive, and concise reference aids; and beyond even this useful function, that they will play the role of a worthily named GUIDE in leading you on to new and rewarding regions throughout the whole wide—and everywhere enticing—world of literature on music and musicians.

MAJOR SUBJECT-HEADINGS

For a general discussion of the use of subject-headings in the GUIDE, please refer to the Introduction (page vii) and to "How to Use *Schirmer's Guide to Books on Music and Musicians*" (page xxiii). A few basic considerations, however, may bear repetition here:

1. The "major" subjects listed below, in bold-face type, are the specific headings under which books actually are entered in the GUIDE. The present list also includes, in light-face type, a few other subject-headings, which are accompanied in the main GUIDE by unusually significant or extensive references or notes; but with these exceptions, the list excludes the many "minor" subject-headings appearing in the GUIDE itself solely for cross-reference purposes.

2. Authors' names are considered as major subject-headings only when they are followed in the GUIDE by one or more actual book-entries,—such as autobiographies, memoirs, collections of essays, or other works unassignable to a specific subject. In the list below, first as well as last names are given for such authors.

3. Composers' and other musicians' names are considered as major subject-headings only when they are followed in the GUIDE by one or more books dealing with their lives or works. Last names only are listed here (although they appear in full in the GUIDE itself), except when closer identification is necessary.

4. Sub-divisions are made in some of the larger categories,—either to segregate books of specialized natures, or sometimes merely to break up unusually extensive lists into more convenient lengths. Similarly, when there are numerous books dealing with an individual composer, the entries often are divided into two or three sub-categories: *e. g.*, 1. Life; 2. Works.; or, 1. Autobiography & Letters. 2. Life. 3. Works. Again, this is primarily for convenience and any implied distinctions between biographies and specialized studies of compositions should not be taken too seriously: most "lives" embody greater or less discussion of the works; many books about a composer's collective or individual works embody some biographical material.

5. The omission of some obviously important subject-headings (and the inclusion of others that may appear to be of no great importance) perhaps will seem less arbitrary when it is remembered that the GUIDE is confined to books in English and currently in-print, and it excludes, as a general rule, highly specialized private publications, reprints of papers from scholarly journals, and collections of music itself. Hence, the presence (or absence) of major subject-headings is determined by the *availablity* of appropriate book-entries in the GUIDE.

It is hoped that the following list of major subject-headings, used with the above considerations in mind, may serve readers as a convenient time-saver, a sort of "guide to the GUIDE," especially in the quick location of actual book-entries pertinent to a specific area of musical or biographical information.

MAJOR SUBJECT-HEADINGS

—A—

Abraham, Gerald
Accompaniment
Acoustics
Acting
Adam

Aesthetics
——1. General
——2. Musical

Africa (music in)/African Music
Aldrich, Richard
Allen, Sir Hugh Percy
Almanacs & Calendars
Amateur Music & Music-Making
America (music in)
American Music
Ancient Music
Anderson, Marian
Anecdotes
Antcliffe, Herbert
Anthologies
Appreciation
Arabia (music in)/Arabian Music
Aristotle
Armstrong, Louis

Arranging
——1. Band, Chorus, & School Orchestra
——2. Dance Band & Orch.

Asiatic Musics
Auber
Augustine
Australia
Autobiographies
Autographs

—B—

Bach Family

Bach, Johann Sebastian
——1. Life
——2. Works

Bagpipes
Baker, Dorothy
Baker, Frank
Bali (music in)/Balinese Music
Ballad/Ballad Opera
Ballet

Band
——1. Brass, Concert, & Military
——2. Drill & Parade Technique

Barber
Barbershop (Ballads, Singing)
Barbirolli
Baroque Era
Bartók
Bassoon

Baton
——1. Conducting Technique
——2. Spinning & Twirling

Bauer, Harold
Beaumarchais
Beecham

Beethoven
——1. Letters, Own Writings
——2. Life
——3. Works

Beggar's Opera
Beissel
Bel Canto
Belgian Music/Belgium (music in)
Berg
Berkshire Festivals

Berlioz
——1. Autobiography & Own Writings
——2. Life & Musical Works

Bibliography (musical)
Birds (& music)
Bizet
Bland
Blom, Eric
Blow
Bonavia, Ferruccio
Borodin
Boston (music in)
Boxes (music—)
Boy Voices

Brahms
——1. Life
——2. Works

Brazil (music in)/Brazilian Music
Breathing
Brian
Britten
Broekman, David

Bruckner
Buck, Sir Percy Carter
Bugle
Bull, Ole
Burleigh, Cecil
Burney
Busoni
Byrd
Byzantine Music

—C—

California (music in)
Campion
Cardus, Neville
Career (musical)
Carillon
Carmichael, Hoagy
Carols
Carreño
Caruso
Casals
Casanova
Chaliapin
Chamber Music
Chanler, Margaret
Chávez
Cherubini
Chevalier

Children (& music)
——1. General
——2. Appreciation, History, Phonograph Records, etc.
——3. Ear-Training, Rhythmic Training, Sight-Singing, etc.
——4. Instruments
——5. Piano Playing
——6. Rhythm Band, Toy Symphony, etc.
——7. Singing, Songs & Speech
——8. "Theory", Elementary Theoretical Studies

China (music in)/Chinese Music

Choir/Choral
——1. General, Choral Singing
——2. Conducting, Training
——3. Choral Music

Chopin
——1. Life
——2. Works

MAJOR SUBJECT-HEADINGS

Choral Speaking
Christiansen
Church Music
Clarinet
Classic Era/Classicism
Colleges/Universities
Colles, Henry Cope
Color (& music)
Community Music

Composers (Collective
  Studies)
——1. Standard
——2. Contemporary
——3. National Schools
    a) American
    b) Austrian, Czech,
      German
    c) English (British)
    d) French, Italian
    e) Russian

Composition
Concerto
Condon, Eddie
Conducting
Conductors
Contemporary Music
Cook, Ida
Copland
Copyright (musical)

Counterpoint
——1. Larger Works, Spe-
    cialized Studies
——2. Shorter Methods

Couperin Family
Covent Garden
Cowboy Music
Crist
Criticism (musical)
Crosby
Cugat, Xavier
Czechoslovakia (music in)
  /Czech Music

—D—

Damrosch Family
(The) Dance (General)
Dance Bands

Dances/Dancing
——1. Educational
——2. Country,   Folk,
    National, Regional,
    Round, Square, etc.
——3. Ballroom & Social

Dann
Davies

Debussy
——1. Criticism & Letters
——2. Life & Works

Decibel
Delibes
Delius
Denmark (music in)/Dan-
  ish Music
Dictation
Diction (Enunciation)
Dictionaries of Music
Dictionaries of Musical
  Terms
Discographies
Documents (musical)
Dominican Republic (mu-
  sic in)
Donizetti
Drama
Drinker, Henry S.
Dryden
Dukas
Duncan
Dunn
Duparc
Dvořák

—E—

Ear-Training
Eastman School of Music
Education (Music-)
Einstein, Alfred
Elgar
Elizabethan Music
Ellington
Encyclopedias of Music
England (music in)
English Music
Erskine, John
Eurhythmics
Europe
Examinations (musical)
Expression

—F—

Facsimiles
Falla
Fauré
Fellowes, Edmund Horace
Ffrangcon-Davies
Film Music
Films (General)
Finck, Henry
Finn
Fiorello
Flotow

Flute
Foldes, Lili
Folklore

Folksongs
——1. Various Sources
——2. American only

Form
Foster
Franck
French Horn
French Language
French Music
Fugue

—G—

Galli-Curci
Gatti-Casazza
Gaviniés
German Language
German Music/Germany
  (music in)
Gershwin
Gilbert & Sullivan
Gilmore
Gluck
God Save the King
Godowsky
Goethe
Gounod
Grainger
Gray, Cecil
Gregorian (Chant, Music)
Grieg
Griffes
Guadagnini Family
Gundry
Guthrie, Woody
Gypsy Music

—H—

Hager
Haggin, B. H.
Hammerstein
Hammond Organ

Handel
——1. Life
——2. Works

Handy, William Christo-
  pher
Hanslick
Harding, Rosamond
Harmonica

Harmony
——1. General & Specialized Studies
——2. Methods, including Harmonic Analysis
Harp
Harris, Roy
Haydn
Hayes
Health & Music (Musical Therapy)
Hearing
Heine
Heiner, Marie Hays
Heinsheimer, Hans W.
Historical Collections of Music
History (of Music)
——1. General, Large Works
——2. Over-all Studies
——3. Short Histories, Outlines, etc.
——4. Special Periods
——5. Specialized Studies
Hoffmann
Holmes, Sherlock
Holst
Horne, Lena
Hughes, Adella Prentiss
Hughes, Spike
Humor
Huneker, James Gibbons
Hungarian Music/Hungary (music in)
Hutchinson Family
Hymns/Hymnody
——1. General, Handbooks, Hymnals, Specialized Studies
——2. Hymn Stories & Hymn Writers

—I—

Improvisation/Extemporization
India (music in/)Indian Music
Indians (American) (music of)
Industry (music in)
Insects (music of)
Instrumentation/Orchestration
Instruments
Interpretation
Interpreters
Ireland (music in)/Irish Music

Ireland, John
Italian Language
Italian Music/(Italy (music in)
Ives, Burl

—J—

Japan (music in)/Japanese Music
Java (music in)/Javanese Music
Jazz
Jefferson
Jewish Music & Musicians
Joyce, Eileen

—K—

Karg-Elert
Karsavina, Tamara
Keyboard Harmony
Keyboard Instruments & Music
Koussevitzky
Kramer, A. Walter
Kreisler
Kreutzer

—L—

Lambert, Constant
Lamond, Frederic
Lane
Lanier
Latin Language
Latin America (music in)/ Latin-American Music
Lawes
Lawrence, Marjorie
Lehmann, Lotte
Lemare, Edwin Henry
Letters (of musicians)
Libraries (of music)
Lind
Liszt
Literature & Music
Lomax, John Avery
Luther, Martin/Lutheran Music

—M—

MacDowell
Madrigal

Mahler
Mann, Thomas
Mannes, David
Manuscript (musical)
March
Martinu
Mason, Daniel Gregory
Mason, Lowell
Masonic Music
Mass
Massenet
"Master Musicians" (series)
Matthay
Mattheson
McCormack
Medieval/Renaissance Eras
Melody
Melody-Writing
Memorization/Memory (musical)
Mendelssohn
——1. Letters, Own Writings
——2. Life
——3. Works
Metronome
Mexican Music/Mexico (music in)
Mezzrow, "Mezz"
Miaskovsky
Mickiewicz
Milhaud
Military Music
Milton, John (the elder)
Minstrels/Minstrelsy
Miscellanies
Mode/Modality
Modern Music
Modulation
Monody/Monophony
Monteverdi
Mörike
Morton, Jelly Roll
Motet
Mozart
——1. Letters
——2. Life
——3. Works
"Musical Pilgrim" (series)
Musicianship — Applied & "Theoretical"
Musicology
Mussorgsky
Myers, Rollo H.

—N—

Naboukov
National Music/Nationalism (in music)

Sight-Playing & Reading
Sight-Singing
Sinatra
Singers

Singing
——1. General, Larger
Methods, etc.
——2. Shorter Methods,
Specialized Studies,
etc.
——3. Popular

Skilton
Slezak, Leo
Smetana
Smyth, Dame Ethel
Solfège/Solfeggio
Song(s)
Songbooks
Song Translations
Songwriting
Sorabji, Kaikhosru
Sound Recording & Re-
production
Sousa
Spain (music in)/Spanish
Music
Spalding, Albert
Speech
Stage-Fright
Stanislavski, Constantin
Star-Spangled Banner
Stein, Gertrude
Still, William Grant
Stoeckel
Stokowski, Leopold
Stradivari
Strauss Family
Strauss, Johann, Jr.
Strauss, Richard

Stravinsky
——1. Own Writings
——2. Life & Works

String Instruments
String Playing
String Quartet
Surette, Thomas Whitney
Swarthout, Gladys
Sweden (music in)/Swed-
ish Music
"Symphonia" (series)
Symphony
Symposia
Szigeti, Joseph

—T—

Taste
Tauber
Taubman, Howard
Taylor, Deems

Taylor, Robert Lewis
Tchaikovsky
——1. Own Writings &
Life
——2. Works
Teachers
Teaching
——1. Pedagogy, Audio-
Visual Methods
——2. Music Teaching in
General
——3. Piano Teaching
Television
Tempo
Terry, Sir Richard R.
Tests (musical)
Theatre
Themes

"Theory" (musical)
——1. General & Over-all
Surveys
——2. Rudiments: Larger
Works
——3. Rudiments: Small-
er Works
——4. Specialized Studies
& Miscellanies

Thibaud, Anton Friedrich
Thomson, Virgil
Thursby
Timing
Tonality/Atonality
Toscanini
Tovey, Sir Donald Francis
Toye, Francis
Transposition
Trapp Family
Trombone
Troubadours/Trouvères
Trumpet
Twelve-Tone Technique

—U—

Ultrasonics
d'Urfey

—V—

Variation
Vaughan Williams
Verdi
——1. Life
——2. Works
Vibrato
Vienna (music in)
Viola/Viola Playing

Violin (The Instrument,
History, Manufacture,
Repairs, Varnish, etc.)
Violin Music
Violin Playing
Violinists
Violoncello Playing
Vivaldi
Vocal Music
Voice
Volpe, Arnold

—W—

Wagner, Friedelind

Wagner, Richard
——1. Own Writings, Au-
tobiography, Cor-
respondence, etc.
——2. Life & Theories
——3. Musical Works
(Collective & Indi-
vidual Studies, Li-
brettos, etc.)

Wales (music in)/Welsh
Music
Walter, Bruno
Walton
Waltz
Warfield, Frances
Waters, Ethel
Watts, Isaac
Weber
Wechsberg, Joseph
Weingartner
Westrup, Jack Allan
Whistling
Whithorne
Whittaker, William Gillies
Who's Who (musical)
Willson, Meredith
Wind Instruments
Winn, Edith Lynwood
Wolf, Hugo
Women (& music)
Wood, Sir Henry
Worcester Music Festival
"World of Music" (series)

—Y—

Yearbooks
Ysaÿe

—Z—

Zweig, Stefan

KEY TO SYMBOLS & ABBREVIATIONS

(Used in Schirmer's Guide book listings)

Δ   special order, limited edition, in preparation, etc.

Note: When this special symbol is placed above a book's price, it serves as a warning that the book itself is a limited edition or some other publication not normally carried in musical booksellers' stocks, but which presumably is available on special order. When the symbol appears in lieu of a book's price, it indicates that no price has yet been set for the book (or that none is known to us), or that the American price has not yet been determined for an imported publication.

abr	abridged; abridgment
acc	accompanied by; accompaniment
app	appendix
App I	Foreign language booklists
—— Ia	Books in French
—— Ib	Books in German
—— Ic	Books in Italian
—— Id	Books in Spanish
—— Ie	Books in Latin
App II	Juvenile book lists
—— IIa	Juvenile biographies
—— IIb	Miscellaneous juveniles
arr	arranged; arranger
aug	augmented
b&w(s)	black-and-white reproduction(s)
bds	boards
bibl	bibliography
bk	book
c	circa
cent	century
chap	chapter
col	color, (-ed)
coll(s)	collected, (-ion); (-s)
comp(s)	compiler(s); compiled by
corr	corrected
diagr(s)	diagram(s)
ea	each
ed(s)	editor(s), (-ion); edited by
enl	enlarged

esp	especially
ex	example
fac(s)	facsimile(s)
flex	flexible binding
forew	foreword
frontis	frontispiece
illus	illustrated by, (-ions), (-or)
incl	including
inst(s)	instruments
intro	introduction
mim	mimeographed
mus ex	musical examples
n d	no date
no	number
O/P	out of print
op(p)	opus; opera
orch	orchestra, (-ted)
p	pages
photo(s)	photograph(s)
photolith	photo-lithographed
pl	plates
pop ed	popular edition
por(s)	portrait(s)
pr	printing; imprint
pref	preface
pseud	pseudonym
pub	publisher, (-ed)
ref(s)	reference(s)
repr	reprint; reprinting
repro	reproduced; reproduction
rev	revised
sel	selected by; selection
spir	spiral binding
supp(s)	supplement(s)
TO/P	temporarily out of print
tr	translated by, (-or)
univ	university
unp	unpaged
v	volume(s)

Warning: All book list-prices quoted herein are based on the latest, most authentic information available to us, but of course they are subject to change without notice. Prices in parentheses and all imported book prices are particularly subject to change and should be read as approximations only.

SCHIRMER'S GUIDE TO BOOKS ON MUSIC AND MUSICIANS

—A—

Abbot, Waldo. Author. See Radio.

Abbott, Lawrence. Author. See Harmony
–1.

ABC (of Music)

See:

Appreciation	Ear-Training
Children (esp 3 & 8)	Sight-Singing
Dictionaries of Terms	Theory (esp 2 & 3)

ABILITY (Musical)

See:

Examinations	Teaching
Psychology	Tests

Abrahall, C. H. Author. See Joyce.

Abraham, Gerald. Author, Editor.

Design in music. vii, 55 p, paper.
Oxford 1949.   1.00
*A collection of essays originally pub in the
Hallé Society magazine, England.*

See also:

Beethoven–3. Quartets (1942).	1.00
Borodin. Biography (1927).	4.00
Chopin–2. Musical style (1939).	2.75
Composers–3e. 8 Soviet (1943).	1.25
——. Masters of Russian music, by Calvocoressi & Abraham (1936).	4.50
Grieg. Symposium (1948).	3.00
History–4. 100 years (1938/49).	3.25
Modern Music. This stuff (1933/9).	1.40
Mussorgsky. Biography, by Calvocoressi, ed Abraham.	2.50
——. Boris Godounov (1948).	.60
Rimsky-Korsakov. Biog (1945/9).	1.00
Russian Music. On (1939).	3.75
——. Studies in (1935).	5.00
Schubert–2. Music of (1947).	3.00
Sibelius. Music of (1947).	3.00

Tchaikovsky–1. Biography (1944/9).	1.00
——. Miniature biography (1938).	.40
Tchaikovsky–2. Music of (1946).	3.00

A CAPPELLA MUSIC

See:

Choir/Choral	Elizabethan Music
Church Music	History
Composers (& under individual names)	Madrigal
	Medieval/Renaissance

ACCOMPANIMENT

See also:

Arranging–2 (Wilson)	Keyboard Instruments
Choir/Choral–2	Organ Playing (esp Demarest)
Church Music	Piano Playing
Composition (esp Kitson)	Plainsong (esp Arnold. Springer)
Conducting	
Dance Music (esp Heynssen)	Progr....ues
	Score-Reading
Gregorian Chant	Song
Instrumentation	Songwriting

*Note: Apart from Arnold's book (now back
in print), the works included here are primarily concerned with the practical aspects of
accompanying.   There is additional discussion of song accompaniments to be found
in some books on individual song composers
(e.g. Schubert).*

*Standard works apparently O/P (or not easily
available in this country) include those by
Buck, Durand (in French), Lindo, Richardson, etc.*

ARNOLD, F. T.
The art of accompaniment from a
thorough-bass as practised in the
17th & 18th centuries.   xxi, 918 p,
mus ex. Oxford 1931 (1949).   45.00
*A monumental standard study: authoritative
not only on its specialized subject, but on
many interpretative aspects of 17th- & 19th-
century music.*

1

Bos, Coenraad V.
The well-tempered accompanist: as
told to Ashley Pettis. Forew Helen
Traubel. 162 p + 1-p Bos discography, 17 pl (pors, facs), mus ex.
Presser 1949.　　　　　　　　　2.50
*General & practical advice on a wide variety
of technical & interpretative problems in
accompanying German Lieder in particular;
plus reminiscences of Brahms, Culp,
Gerhardt & other famous composers &
singers.*

David, Elizabeth Harbison
I played their accompaniments. vi,
246 p, illus. Appleton 1940　　　2.50
Reminiscences of Schumann-Heink & others.

Fétis, F. J.
Treatise on accompaniment from score
on the organ or pianoforte. T. Alfred
Whittingham.　　56 p, 40-p mus ex.
Reeves n d.　　　　　　　　　　(2.75)
*Super-title: "How to play from score." Origi-
nally published in French in 1829.*

Moore, Gerald
The unashamed accompanist. ix, 84
p. Macmillan 1944 (3rd pr 1946).　1.50
*Advice (on Lieder acc in particular) by a
noted concert & recording pianist.*

Winn, Cyril
Do you accompany? 31 p, mus ex,
paper. Curwen 1929.　　　　　　1.00
*Practical suggestions "for those who love to
to do it as well as those who have to do it."*

Acker, Helen. Author.
See App IIa (juvenile biographies).

ACOUSTICS

*Note: Many musicians & most listeners tend
to restrict this field to architectural or auditorium acoustics only, but of course it actually
embraces all physical (& many psychological
& psycho-physiological) aspects of music
in its larger realm as the science of sound.
Indeed, the need for a better understanding of
acoustic principles on the part of the professional & lay musical public is the major
theme of Redfield's book below. The other
books listed include only a few standard works,
plus all those available that are especially
concerned with musical acoustics. For others
on related subjects—*

See also:
Decibel	Radio
Film Music	Radio Music
Films	Scale
Hearing	Sound Rec & Repro
History	Stokowski
Instruments	Theatre (esp Burris-
Organ (esp Smith)	Meyer & Cole)
Phonograph	Ultrasonics
Psychology	Vibrato

*Standard works (particularly concerned with
music) apparently O/P include those by
Buck, Jeans, Lloyd, Miller, Wood, etc.*

(American Standards Association)
Proposed American standard acoustical terminology.　　47 p, paper.
American Standards Assn, N. Y.,
1949.　　　　　　　　　　　　1.00
*Some 500 tentative basic definitions (revisions
of the 1942 standards), sponsored—for trial
& study—by the Acoustical Society of
America & Institute of Radio Engineers.*

Bartholomew, Wilmer T.
Acoustics of music. xvi, 242 p, illus,
8-p bibl. Prentice 1942 (3rd pr
1946).　　　　　　　　　　　　4.00
*Relating the physical science to the æsthetic
resources of music & its performance.*

Broadhouse, John
Musical acoustics: the phenomena
of sound as connected with music.
xii, 436 p, 104 figs, tables, mus ex,
brief bibl. Reeves (1881) 4th ed
1926; Scribner repr (1950).　　　4.00
Super-title: "The student's Helmholtz."

Culver, Charles Aaron
Musical acoustics. xiv, 215 p, illus.
Blakiston (1941) rev 2nd ed 1947.　3.00
Carleton College course for music students.

Geralton, James. See App IIb (juvenile).

Hamilton, Clarence G.
Sound and its relation to music. 150
p, illus, chap bibls. Ditson 1912.　1.50
*"Music Students Library."　Compact state-
ment of physical laws underlying music.*

Hector, Luther Grant (& others)
Physics for arts & sciences. viii, 731
p, illus. Blakiston 1949.　　　　5.50
*Originally pub (in part) as "Electronic
physics" 1943.　Sound & music discussed,
p 317/360.　Co-authors: H. S. Lein & C. E.
Scouten.*

Helmholtz, Hermann
　(See also Broadhouse above.)
On the sensations of tone as a physiological basis for the theory of
music.　Tr Alexander J. Ellis. xix,
576 p, illus.　Smith 6th ed 1948.　12.50
*The pioneer & still classic work in this field.
Originally pub in German, 1862; reprinted
here from the 2nd English ed of 1885.*

Jeans, (Sir) James
Science and music.　x, 258 p, 10 pl,
64 b&ws, 1-p bibl. Cambridge 1937
(1947).　　　　　　　　　　　2.75

A standard work by a noted scientist, written especially for laymen & musicians, on acoustical fundamentals; with chapters on harmony & discord, the concert room, & hearing.

KNUDSEN, VERN O. & HARRIS, C. M.
Acoustical designing in architecture.
x, 457 p, 222 illus, tables. Wiley 1950.　7.50
Superseding an earlier standard work, "Architectural acoustics" (1932) by Knudsen alone. Non-mathematical treatment of all acoustical aspects of room, studio, & hall design.

MCLACHLAN, N. W.
The new acoustics: a survey of modern development in acoustical engineering.　vi, 166 p, illus, diagrs, 2-p bibl.　Oxford 1936.　3.00

MATZKE, HERMANN.　See App Ib.

MORSE, PHILIP MCCORD
Vibration and sound.　xix, 469 p, illus, 1–p bibl.　McGraw (1936) 2nd ed 1948.　6.00
Basic mathematical theory; "International Series in Pure & Applied Physics."

OLSON, HARRY F.
Elements of acoustical engineering. xviii, 539 p, illus. Nostrand (1940) 2nd rev ed 1947 (1948).　7.50
Electrical, mechanical, & acoustical system analogies; detailed studies of loudspeakers, microphones, speech, noise, hearing.

RAYLEIGH, LORD (JOHN WM. STRUTT)
The theory of sound.　2 v in 1: xliii, 480, xvi, 504 p, diagrs, 2-p bibl. Dover repr 1945　5.95
Reprint of the 2nd ed, 1894/1929, of a standard reference work originally pub in 1877; historical intro by Robert Bruce Lindsay.

REDFIELD, JOHN
Music: a science and an art.　307, xxiii p, 5 pl, mus ex. Knopf 1928 (7th pr 1949).　3.75
Same, Tudor repr 1949.　1.98
An urgent plea, aimed particularly at musicians & listeners, for approaching music from the scientific as well as the artistic side. The last section deals with possibilities of future improvements of the present weaknesses in musical & instrumental resources.

RICHARDSON, EDWARD GICK
Sound: a physical text-book.　vii, 344 p, illus, diagrs, bibl refs. (1927) Longmans 4th ed 1947.　5.00
A standard British work, originally pub by Edward Arnold, London, in 1927.

ACTING

See also:

Career	Singing
Drama	Speech
Films (esp Pudovkin)	Stanislavski
Lehmann	Television
Opera–1 (esp Shea)	Theatre
Radio (esp Cott)	

Note: The books included here are only a sampling of the available literature, most of which contains little material on acting in opera.

BEHNKE, (*Mrs.*) KATE EMIL-
Speech and movement on the stage. Forew Clemence Dane.　xi, 196 p, 8 pors, 2-p bibl. Oxford 1930.　3.00
Chapter 13, p 152/9, "Music & the actor."

COLE, TOBY (*comp.*)
Acting: a handbook of the Stanislavski method.　Intro Lee Strasberg. x. 223 p, illus.　Lear 1948.　3.00

COLE, TOBY & CHINOY, HELEN KRICH (*eds*)
Actors on acting: the theories, techniques, & practices of great actors of all times as told in their own words. xiv, 596 p, 26–p bibl.　Crown 1949.　5.00
A symposium, with a history of the theatre, some 150 biographies, & 2000-title bibl.

STANISLAVSKI, CONSTANTIN
An actor prepares.　Tr Elizabeth Reynolds Hapgood.　Intro John Gielgud.　xx, 295 p, diagrs. (1936) Theatre Arts 1948.　3.00
New edition for the 50th anniversary of the Moscow Art Theatre.
Building a character.　Tr Elizabeth Reynolds Hapgood.　Intro Joshua Logan.　xx, 292 p.　Theatre Arts 1949.　3.50
Sequel to "An actor prepares." Chap 11 (p 78/103) is on Diction & Singing; chap 11 (p 177/216) on Tempo-Rhythm in Movement.

ADAM, Adolphe

See also:

Appreciation	Opera
French Music	Phonograph Records
History	Program Notes

BEAUMONT, CYRIL W.
The ballet called Gisella.　viii, 140 p, 47 photos.　Beamont, London Δ (1944), rev ed 1945.　(6.50)

POSNER, SANDY
Giselle: the story of the ballet.　95 p, illus incl 4 col pl (Joyce Millen). Black (1945) 5th ed 1949 via Trans-atlantic.　.75
"Ballet Pocket Library" series.

Adami, Giuseppe. Editor.
See App Ib (German), App Ic (Italian).
Adkins, Hector Ernest. Author.
See Band–1.
Adler, Guido. Author.
See App Ib (German books).
Adler, Kurt. Editor. See Songbooks.

ADVICE (Musical)

See:

Appreciation	School Music
Children	Singing
Piano Playing	Teaching, etc

AESTHETICS

1. General 2. Musical

General Note: As acoustics embraces all scientific aspects of music, so aesthetics embraces all artistic aspects within its larger realm of "beauty" in general. For convenience, the lists here are divided into two sub-categories: 1. books dealing with aesthetics in general, in which music is considered only as one of the arts; 2. books dealing primarily with musical aesthetics. The first list is only a sampling of the large available literature—thought to be particularly useful to musicians & listeners. The second is curtailed only because of the lack of pertinent in–print publications.

AESTHETICS (1. General)

DEWEY, JOHN
Art as experience. viii, 355 p, 9 pl.
Minton 1934. 5.00
Analyses of the æsthetic experience & of the various arts in terms of Dewey's well-known whole analysis of experience.

DUDLEY, LOUISE, & FARICY, AUSTIN
The humanities: applied æsthetics.
xiii, 600 p, illus, mus ex, 2–p bibl.
McGraw 1940. 4.50
Applied æsthetics, including considerable material on music.

FEIBLEMAN, JAMES KERN
Aesthetics: a study of the fine arts in theory & practice. xi, 463 p.
Duell Sloan 1949. 5.00
Objectivist, philosophical approach to a theory embracing the arts; including "Music as an element in the universe" (p 336/352).

FINKELSTEIN, SIDNEY
Art and society. 288 p, 8 p. illus.
International Pubs. Co., N. Y., 1947. 3.25
The layman's relationship to the arts (including music). Marxian approach.

GREENE, THEODORE MEYER
The arts and the art of criticism.
xxx, 690 p, illus, bibl refs. Princeton
1940 (rev ed) (1948). 7.50

A philosophic approach. Includes R. D. Welch's supplementary essay, "The expressed content of Beethoven's third symphony."

HARAP, LOUIS
Social roots of the arts. 192 p.
International Pubs., N. Y., 1949. 3.25
Relationships between the arts (incl music) & social forces; Marxian point of view.

HOSPERS, JOHN
Meaning and truth in the arts. viii, 252 p, bibl. North Carolina 1946. 4.00
Redefinitions & clarifications of "meaning," "reality," & "truth" in the arts.

OGDEN, ROBERT MORRIS
The psychology of art. xviii, 291 p, 97 illus (photos, b&ws by H. E. Baxter, mus ex, etc), bibl refs. Scribner 1938. 4.00
A study based on a Carnegie Foundation grant: including sections on aesthetics, music (p 41/81), poetry, visual art, & eurhythmics (p 259/277).

RADER, MELVIN M. (ed)
A modern book of esthetics. Anthology. xxxv, 504 p. Holt 1935. 3.60
Essays by various authors illustrating diverse æsthetic theories.

RICHARDS, I. A., OGDEN, C. K., WOOD, JAMES
The foundations of æsthetics. x, 92 p, illus. Lear (1925) 2nd ed 1948. 2.75

SACHS, CURT
The commonwealth of art: style in the fine arts, music and the dance.
404 p + 32 pl, mus ex. Norton 1946. 6.00
The interrelationship of styles & the arts as expressions of their times.

SANTAYANA, GEORGE
The life of reason: or the phases of human progress. V 4: Reason in art.
ix, 230 p. Scribner (1905) 1928. 2.75
Chapter 4, p 44/67, is on music.

SCHILLINGER, JOSEPH
Mathematical basis of the arts. x, 696 p, illus. Philosophical 1948. 15.00
A method of rhythmical design that "links the arts of music, science, & space."

VINCI, LEONARDO DA
Paragone: a comparison of the arts.
Tr & intro Irma A. Richter. xiii, 112 p, 12 sepia pl, b&ws, bibl refs.
Oxford 1949. 5.50

Excerpts from the MS notes, originally included in "The literary works of Leonardo da Vinci" (1939). Italian text with parallel English translation.

WIER, ALBERT E.
Thesaurus of the arts. 690 p, 28-p
bibl. Putnam 1943.   5.00
Same, Tudor repr 1949.   1.98
*Architecture, ballet, drama, literature, music,
painting, screen, sculpture, etc.*

AESTHETICS (2. Musical)

See also:

Appreciation	Poetry
Criticism	Program Notes
History	Psychology
Jefferson	Stravinsky-1
Literature	Tovey (esp "A musi-
Musicology	cian talks")
Philosophy	

*Standard works apparently O/P include those
by Busoni, Hanslick, Pratt, Schoen, etc.*

BRELET, GISÈLE. See App Ia.

FERCHAULT, GUY. See App Ia.

McEWEN, JOHN B.
The foundations of musical æsthetics:
or, the elements of music. 124 p, mus
ex, 2-p bibl. Kegan Paul (1917), via Δ
Curwen (5th pr, n d).   (1.00)
*"Music Lover's Library" series: a Scottish
composer's approach to the problems of sound,
temperament, tonality, scales, form, the
rhythm of contrapuntal music, etc.*

PIGUET, J.-CLAUDE. See App Ia.

SEASHORE, CARL E.
In search of beauty in music: a
scientific approach to musical æsthetics. xvi, 389 p, illus. Ronald 1947. 4.50
*Seashore's summing-up of his many years of
experimental investigation, particularly in
the field of musical psychology.*

SCHERCHEN, HERMANN
On the nature of music. Regnery
1950, in prep.   4.50
*Great music in the cultural & spiritual life of
the last centuries.*

SILBERMANN, ALPHONS
Of musical things: the æsthetics of
music. Forew Eugene Goossens.
116 p, bds. Grahame Book Co., Δ
Sydney, Australia, 1949.   (2.00)
9 lectures, with record-references.

Affelder, Paul. Author.
See Phonograph records.

AFRICA (Music in)/AFRICAN MUSIC

See also:

Ancient Music	Instruments
Arabia (music in)	Jazz
Dance (esp Sachs)	Negro Music
Folklore	Negro Spirituals
Folksongs	Schweitzer-1 & 2

*Note: The best-known works on African music
& instruments apparently are O/P (or not
easily available in this country). These include books by Hornbostel, Kirby, Krehbiel,
etc., and in particular the extensive annotated
bibliography, "African Native Music"
(1936), compiled by Douglas H. Varley.*

*The controversial question of African contri-
butions to American jazz is considered pro &
con in several of the more important books
on jazz.*

CARRINGTON, JOHN F.
Talking drums of Africa. 96 p, 12
illus (photos, b&ws, map, mus ex),
2½-p bibl. Carey Kingsgate Press, Δ
London, 1949.   (1.50)
*Drum language, signals & signalling, African
musical instruments.*

HERMAN, JULIUS
Music of South African life in its
relation to the culture of Europe.
183 p. Juta & Co., Cape Town, 1926 Δ
(1949?)   (2.25)

TRACEY, HUGH
Chopi musicians: their music, poetry,
& instruments. x, 180 p, 15 pl, 7
diagrs, mus ex, map, 2-p bibl. Oxford 1948.   4.75
*A study of the Portuguese East African tribe,
famous for its xylophone orchestras.*

Ngoma: an introduction to music
for Southern Africans. xi, 91, xxi p,
illus (photos, b&ws). Longmans Δ
1948.   (2.85)
*An exposition of African music and a plea
for its future development, with photographs
of native dancers & instruments.*

TUCKER, A. N.
Tribal music and dancing in the
southern Sudan: at social & ceremonial gatherings. 57 p, 61 mus Δ
ex. Reeves n d (1933).   (4.25)
Descriptive account from personal observation.

AGILITY

See:

Piano Playing	Violin Playing
Singing	Etc.

Aguilera, Francisco. Editor.
See Latin America.

Aitken, Geraldine L. Author.
See Children-5.

ALABAMA (Music in)

See: Folklore, Folksongs-2 (esp Arnold).

ALAIN, Jehan
See: esp App Ia (Gavoty).

Alaleona, Domenico. Author. See App Ic.

ALBÉNIZ, Isaac
See: esp App Ia (Collet).

Appreciation	Piano Music
Composers	Program Notes
History	Spanish Music
Phonograph Records	

ALBINONI, Tomaso
See: esp App Ic (Giazotto).

Albus, Harry James. Author.
See App IIa (Anderson, Bach juveniles).
Alchin, Carolyn Alden. Author.
See: Ear-Training, Harmony–2, Keyboard
Harmony.
Aldanov, Mark (pseud of Mark Aleksandro-
vich Landau). Author. See Beethoven–2.
Aldous, Donald W. Author.
See Sound Rec & Repro.
Aldrich, Putnam. Author.
See Bach–2, Ornamentation.

ALDRICH, Richard
Note: Other Aldrich books apparently are O/P.
Concert life in New York, 1902-1923.
Ed & index by Harold Johnson. xvii,
795 p.   Putnam 1941   5.00
*From the scrapbooks of a noted critic of a
"golden age" of music in America.*

Musical discourse: from the New
York Times. 305 p. (Oxford 1928)
via C. Fischer.   3.00
*Essays on program music, folksong, The
Beggar's Opera, Shakespeare & Music,
Wagner & Brahms, Berlioz today, Patti, etc.*

Translator. See Singing–1 (Lehmann).

Alexander, Van. Author. See Arranging–2.
Alexanian, Diran. Author.
See Violoncello Playing.
Alford, Violet. Editor. See Dances–2.
Allen, Jules Verne. Author.
See Cowboy Music.
Allen, J. Worth. Author.
See School Music–3.
Allen, Warren Dwight. Autnor.
See History–1, March.
Allchin, Basil C. Author.
See Ear-Training.
Allen, Edward Heron. Catalogued under
Heron-Allen.

ALLEN (Sir) Hugh Percy
See also: England (music in), History.

BAILEY, CYRIL
Hugh Percy Allen. viii, 170 p, illus.
Oxford 1948.   (*A memoir.*)   2.50

ALLIED ARTS & TECHNIQUES
See:

Acting	Painting/Pictures
Aesthetics	Philosophy
Ballet	Poetry
Dance	Psychology
Drama	Radio
Education	Sound Rec & Repro
Films	Television
Literature	

*Note: In addition, many books on "Appreci-
ation" & History (of music) lay special stress
on the correlation of music with other arts.*

Allison, Muryl. Co-author (with Wadley).
See Children–1.

ALMANACS & CALENDARS
See also: Contemporary Music (Slonimsky),
Yearbooks.
*Note: Most biographies of composers (&
especially all those in the "Master Musicians" series) include chronologies or calendars of material pertinent to their subject.*

CRAWFORD, REBEKAH (*ed*)
Musical messages for every day in
the year: a musician's birthday book.
Unp (378 p), 12 illus. G. Schirmer
1897 (1915).   2.00
A yearbook with dates & quotations.

HENDERSON, WILLIAM & ZUCKER, PAUL.
Music lovers' almanac. Unp (394 p),
illus. Doubleday 1943.   3.95
Day-by-day anniversaries, 1st performances.

MOORE, ELIZABETH C.
An almanac for music-lovers. xiii,
382 p, illus (Lyle Justis). Holt 1940. 2.50

(PETERS EDITION)
Peters edition music calendar 1950.
Unp (54 p), illus (pors & facs), paper.
Peters 1949.   1.50
*The illustrations in this year's issue are
devoted entirely to Bach & the Bach family:
portraits, music facsimiles, etc.*
*Note: The 1951 Peters Edition calendar was
published in November 1950.*

Altmann, Wilhelm. Compiler.
See Orchestral Music.

ALTO (Voice)
See:

M. Anderson	School Music–3
Boy Voices	Schumann-Heink
Children–7	Singing
Choir/Choral	Voice
Church Music	

Alton, Robert. Author. See Violin

AMATEUR MUSIC & MUSIC-MAKING

See also:

Appreciation	Folklore
Barbershop	Folksongs
Children	Operetta
Choir/Choral	Rorke
Community Music	School Music
Fellowes	Songbooks

Note: For self-help instruction books in various executant techniques, see Leeming below, also Piano Playing–4, Singing, etc.

BARTON, FREDERICK B.
Music as a hobby: how to have fun with music as a performer & as a listener. ix, 159 p. Harper (1941), rev ed 1950.   2.50
Breezy, inspirational approach to amateur music-making & to musical appreciation.

BOWEN, CATHERINE DRINKER
Friends and fiddlers. x, 261 p. Little Brown 1935 (11th pr 1947).   2.50
Informal sketches of amateur musicians and their families.

JOHNSON, GERALD W.
A little night-music: discoveries in the exploitation of an art. x, 125 p, illus (R. Q. Yardley). Harper 1937   2.00
The trials & rewards of a flute-playing newspaper man (& those of his friends).

LEEMING, JOSEPH
It is easy to make music: how to play all the popular instruments. 208 p, illus (Jeanne Bendick). Watts 1948, via Crown.   3.00

SCHAUFFLER, ROBERT HAVEN
Fiddler's folly and encores. 156 p, illus (Fritz Eichenberg). Holt 1942 (3rd pr 1945).   2.00
Two short novels, plus briefer pieces from "Fiddler's luck" below.
Fiddler's luck: the gay adventures of a musical amateur. 275 p. Island (1920) 6th rev ed 1941.   2.00

SHERA, F. H.
The amateur in music. 78 p, 3-p bibl, bds. Oxford 1939.   1.25
Plato to Roger North; some 18th-century & notable 19th-century musical amateurs.

SPAETH, SIGMUND
Music for fun. xiii, 259 p, illus. Whittlesey 1939.   2.25
Same, Blakiston repr 1945.   1.00

Amberg, George. Author. See Ballet.
Ambrose, Kay. Author. See Ballet.

AMERICA (Music in)
See also: esp American Music.
Also:

Aldrich	Mannes
Ballet	Mason
Boston	Negro Music
California	Opera–1 & 4
Christiansen	Philharmonic
Church Music	Philadelphia
Colleges	Pilgrims
Damrosch Family	Psalms/Psalmody
(The) Dance	Publishers
Dann	Puritans
Education	School Music–2
Erskine	Sheet Music
Finn	Songs
Folklore	(Mattfeld & Davis)
Folksongs–2	Stokowski
History	Taubman
Hutchinson Family	Thomson
Jefferson	Worcester
Latin America	Yearbooks

Standard works apparently O/P include those by Lahee, Mathews, Zanzig, etc.

CARPENTER, PAUL S.
Music: an art & a business. Pref Helene C. Carpenter & Lawrence N. Morgan. ix, 246 p, 7-p bibl. Oklahoma 1950.   3.75

Provocative attacks on the music industry, unions, & educational systems, especially for failing to support American composers.

CLARK, KENNETH S.
Municipal aids to music in America: an exposition & analysis of the findings in a survey made by the National Bureau for the Advancement of Music. 297 p, photos. National Bureau for the Advancement of Music 1925, via National Recreation Assn.   2.00

Reports on "Our European heritage," "What cities might do," "Permissive legislation," & "Some typical musical systems."

COVEY, CYCLONE
Of music and of America singing. Chap 9 (pp 490/552) in "Seeds of Liberty: the genesis of the American mind," by Max Saville. xix, 587, xxxi p, illus. Knopf 1948.   6.50

DANIEL, OLIVER
Music in America.
Crowell, in prep.   △

EATON, QUAINTANCE (ed)
Musical U. S. A.: how music developed in the major American cities. 206 p, some 100 illus. Allen Towne 1949, via Crown.   1.98

"Historical panorama" by various writers, mostly dealing with specific cities or regions; the outgrowth of a series of articles originally pub in "Musical America."

EWEN, DAVID
Music comes to America.   295 p.
Allen Towne (1942) rev ed 1947, via
Arco.   3.50
A history of our musical culture.

MACDOWELL, TREMAINE
American studies.   vii, 96 p.   Minneapolis 1948.   1.50
*Includes a discussion of the place of music
in studies of American civilization.*

SCHIAVO, GIOVANNI ERMENEGILDO
Italian-American history: v I.   604,
xxxv p, pors.   7–p bibl.   Vigo Press, △
N. Y., 1947.   10.00
*Book 1 is devoted to a discussion of Italian
music & musicians in the United States;
book 2 to a dictionary of musicians' biographies and bibliography.   An appendix, xxxv
p, includes biographical sketches & portraits
of the publication's sponsors.   (V 2 of this
work is devoted to "The Italian contribution
to the Catholic Church in America ")*

SONNECK, O. G.
Early concert life in America (1731-
1800).   339 p. (1907) Musurgia pho- △
tolith repr 1949.   10.40
Reprint ed of a standard work.

WHITLOCK, E. C. & SAUNDERS, R.D. (eds)
Music and dance in Texas, Oklahoma,
& the Southwest.   232 p + advts,
many photos (pors).   Musical Research, Hollywood, 1950.   4.00
*Brief articles by the editors, Schoenberg,
Sorantin, & Dunkley; biographical sketches
of local musicians (p 139/232); lists of
colleges & schools, civic activities, etc.*

American Guild of Organists.
See Organ Playing, Organists.

AMERICAN MUSIC
See also: esp America (music in).
Also:

Appreciation	Negro Music
Barbershop	Negro Spirituals
Composers (esp 3a, &	Opera–3
under individuals)	(esp Hipscher)
Contemporary Music	Popular Music
Cowboy Music	(esp Spaeth)
Folklore	Phonograph Records
Folksongs–2	Program Notes
History	School Music
Indians (American)	Sheet Music
Jazz	Songs
Koussevitzky	(Mattfeld & Davis)
Latin America	Songbooks
National Music	Yearbooks

*Note: Standard works apparently O/P (or not
easily available) include those by Cowell,
Elson, Mason, etc.*

BRITTON, ALLEN P. (comp)
A bibliography of early sacred
American music.   Musurgia 1951,
pending.   △
*"Musurgia Studies in Musicology," series A,
v 8 (on subscription only).*

ELSON, LOUIS C.
National music of America and its
sources.   Additions by Arthur Elson.
367 p, illus.   Page (1899) rev ed
1946.   2.50

GOLDMAN, R. F. & SMITH, ROGER (eds)
Landmarks of early American music,
1760-1800.   103 p, 7 facs, music,
3–p bibl, paper.   G. Schirmer 1943.   1.50
*A collection of 32 psalm-tunes, hymns,
patriotic songs & marches, with historical &
biographical notes.*

GORDON, PHILIP
The availability of contemporary
American music for performing groups
in high schools & colleges.   xiii, 144
p, 14–p annot bibls.   Teachers College
1950.   2.75
*"Contributions to Education" No. 961: a
detailed statistical & analytical study.*

HARWELL, RICHARD B.
Confederate music.   xi, 184 p, 5 pl
(facs), 8–p bibl.   North Carolina
1950   3.50
*Songs, composers, & music publishing in the
South during the War between the States;
with a checklist of some 648 titles and a
chapter on "Dixie & its rivals."*

HOWARD, JOHN TASKER
Our American music: 300 years of
it.   xxii, 841 p, 32 pl, 51–p bibl.
Crowell (1931) 3rd rev ed 1946 (1948). 6.00
*Probably the most extensive work on both
music in America & American music itself.*

KŘENEK, ERNST   See App Ib.

ROSENFELD, PAUL
An hour with American music.   179
p.   Lippincott 1929.   1.00
*Discussions of Jazz, Spirituals, and various
composers, especially Harris & Varèse.*

SONNECK, O. G. & UPTON, W. T. (comps).
A bibliography of early secular
American music (18th century).   xvi,
617 p. (1905) Library of Congress △
rev & enl 1945 (1949), via GPO.   2.00
*A standard reference work, covering some
1100 titles, for historians & bibliographers.
Originally by Sonneck alone, the 1945 ed is
practically a new work by Upton.*

AMERICAN MUSICIANS

See:

America (music in)	Dictionaries of Music
American Music	Encyclopedias of Mus.
Composers (esp 3a &	Who's Who
under individuals)	Yearbooks

Also under the names of individuals.

American Standards Association. Publisher. See Acoustics.

Amey, Ellen. Author. See Piano Playing–2.

Amillet, Paul. Author. See App Ia.

ANALYSIS (Musical)

See: esp Program Notes.

Also:

Appreciation	Fugue
Chamber Music	Harmony
Church Music	Opera
Composers (& under	Piano Music
individual names)	Song
Composition	Symphony
Concerto	Theory
Counterpoint	Violin Music
Form	Vocal Music

ANCIENT MUSIC

General Note: "Ancient" here is used to embrace the period up to, but not including, the Medieval & Renaissance eras.

See also:

Africa (music in)	Byzantine Music
Anthologies (Davison-	Greek Music
Apel, Gleason)	History
Arabia (music in)	Instruments
Aristotle	Jewish Music
Asiatic Musics (note)	Medieval/Renaissance

Standard works apparently O/P include those by Galpin, Langdon, Wallaschek, etc.

ENGEL, CARL (1818-1882)
Music of the most ancient nations: particularly of the Assyrians, Hebrews, & Egyptians, with special reference to discoveries in Western Asia & in Egypt. xii, 380 p, illus, mus ex. (1864) Reeves repr 1910.   8.50
A standard early work.

GALILEI, VINCENZO. See App Ic.

GALPIN, FRANCIS W.
The music of the Sumerians, Babylonians, and Assyrians: described & illustrated from original sources. xv, 110 p, 12 pl, mus ex, 12-p bibl refs. Cambridge 1937.   6.00
A standard work, describing various instruments, the place of music in ritual & civil life, cuneiform notation, etc, with musical examples, including one complete hymn.

GEVAERT, FRANÇOIS AUGUSTE. See App Ia.

PARKHURST, H. E.
The beginnings of the world's music. vii, 70 p, illus, paper. C. Fischer 1915. *(An essay.)*   .75

SACHS, CURT
See also: App Ib (ed Bücken: Sachs.)
The rise of music in the ancient world, east and west. 324 p, 8 pl, mus ex. Norton 1943.   6.75
Explorations in musical archeology, with special attention to oriental systems, up to the beginnings of medieval music: "Europe and the road to major & minor." Until a good, separate book on oriental music in general comes along, the material on that subject here is probably the most extensive and authoritative available.

SCHNEIDER, MAX F. *(ed)*. See App Ib.

SMITH, HERMANN
The world's earliest music, traced to its beginning in ancient lands. xv, 362 p, illus. Reeves n d (1904).   6.00

Ancis, S. Author. See Modulation.

Andersen, Arthur Olaf. Author. See:

Children–8. Short lessons in musical theory (1926). 2 v, each	.75
——. Teacher's manual (1926).	1.50
Counterpoint–2. Strict & Free (1931).	1.50
Harmony–2. Lessons in (1923/ 1938). 3 v, complete.	4.95
Instrumentation. Practical orchestration (1929).	3.50

Anderson, Arvid C. Author.
See Composers–1.

Anderson, Emily. Editor. See Mozart–1.

ANDERSON, Marian

See also: Negro Music, Singers.
Also: App IIa (Albus juvenile).

VEHANEN, KOSTI
Marian Anderson: a portrait. 270 p, photos. Whittlesey 1941.   3.50
By the singer's accompanist for 10 years, in collaboration with George J. Barnett.

Anderson, Virgil A. Author. See Speech.

Anderson, William Robert. Author. See:

Brahms. Introduction to (1949).	1.00
Elgar. Introduction to (1949).	1.00
Haydn. Miniature biog. (1939).	.40
Rachmaninoff. Concerti (1946).	.50
Sight-Singing. Rhythmic (1933).	.50

Co-author (with McKinney). See:
Appreciation. Discovering music
(1934/1949).   4.75
——. How to listen (1943/1947).   1.00
History–2. Music in (1940).   5.50

Andersson, Otto. Author. See Instruments.
Andral, Marie-Marguerite. Co-author
(with Marcel-Dubois). See Dances–2 (ed
Alford).
Andrews, Edward Deming. Author.
See Folklore.
Andrews, Hilda. Author. See Terry.
Andrews, H. K. Author. See Harmony–2.
Andriessen, Hendrik. Author. See Franck.

ANECDOTES

See also: Humor, Miscellanies (esp Slonimsky).

*Also under the names of individual composers
& musicians for anecdotes included in biographies, autobiographies, reminiscences, etc.*

*Note: Collections apparently O/P include
those by Ewen, Gates, Schelling, etc.*

KAUFMANN, HELEN L.
The little book of music anecdotes.
xii, 275 p, illus. Grosset 1948.   .75
"Little Music Library" series, pocket size.

Angelis (Rev) Michael de. Author.
See Latin.
Angell, Warren M. Author. See Singing–2.
Anger, J. Humphrey. Author.
See Harmony–2.

ANGLICAN CHANT

See: Church Music, Psalms/Psalmody–1
(esp Brown).

Angoff, Charles (*pseud* of Richard W.
Hinton).
Author.   See Composers–1, App IIa.
juvenile biography: Stradivari).
Annett, Thomas. Author.
See School Music–1.

ANNOTATIONS

See: esp Program Notes.
Also:

Appreciation
Chamber Music
Church Music
Composers (& under
  individuals)
Concerto
Contemporary Music
Opera

Operetta
Organ Music
Piano Music
Sonata
Song
Symphony
Violin Music
Vocal Music

d'ANNUNZIO, Gabriele. See App Ia
(Tosi, ed, d'Annunzio-Debussy correspondence, in French).

Anson, H. V. Author.
See Theory–4 (Dyson, ed).

ANTCLIFFE, Herbert

Short studies in the nature of music.
245 p. Kegan Paul & Dutton 1920,   △
via Curwen.   (1.50)

*Six essays on the nature of music, program
music, form, religious emotion, etc.*

ANTHEIL, George

See: American Music, Composers–2 & 3a,
Contemporary Music.

*Note: Both Pound's "Antheil & the theory of
harmony" (1927) & Antheil's own "Bad boy
of music" (1945) apparently are O/P.*

ANTHEMS

See:

Choir/Choral–3
Church Music

National Music
  (Nettl)
Vocal Music

ANTHOLOGIES

*General Note: Anthology-collections of music
itself are not, as a general rule, listed in this
guide, although some exceptions are made (e.g.
the Davison-Apel, Gleason, & Parrish-Ohl
works below), where the material itself is of
special significance and the books themselves
are generally available at comparatively modest
prices. However, such famous historical
collections as the various "Denkmäler"
series, & those edited by Einstein, Riemann,
Pedrell, etc, are omitted, since they are either
O/P or not easily available in this country.*

*Please refer to the general note under Sym-
posia and for some of the more important
anthologies devoted to specialized subjects see
also:*

Acting (Cole &
  Chinoy)
Aesthetics–1 (Rader)
American Music
  (Goldman & Smith)
Composers–1 (Foss)
Counterpoint–2 (Sod-
  erlund)
Criticism (Demuth)
Documents (Nettl)
Folksongs
Jazz (Ramsey, Tole-
  dano)

Letters (Norman &
  Shrifte)
Miscellaneous
Negro Spirituals
Organ Music (esp
  Klein, Schweigert)
Piano Music (Apel,
  Sachs)
Poetry (ed Boas)
Program Notes (Bald-
  win)
Schweitzer–1
Songbooks

See also: App IIa (juveniles by Kinscella,
Schauffler, & others).

COOKE, JAMES FRANCIS
Great men and famous musicians on
the art of music: a series of intimate
discussions.   Intro J. L. Long.   446
p, illus, mus ex. Presser 1925.   2.25

DAVISON, A. T. & APEL, WILLI (eds)
Historical anthology of music: 200
examples of oriental, mediæval, &
renaissance music to 1600.   xi, 258
p, music (209 p).   Harvard (1946)
rev ed 1949.   8.00
Including original & translated texts, com-
mentary, & bibliographical references.
Historical anthology of music, v 2:
examples of baroque, rococo, & pre-
classical music.   viii, 303 p, music
(276 p), bibl refs. Harvard 1950.   10.00
A continuation to about 1780: some 128 works
by composers from Peri to Hopkinson, with
commentary & text translations.

FABRICANT, N. D. & WERNER, H. (eds)
A caravan of music stories by the
world's great authors.   Intro Karl
Krueger. x, 312 p.   Fell 1947.   3.50
26 stories by Chehhov, Hardy, Hecht, Joyce,
Mann, Mansfield, & others.

GLEASON, HAROLD (ed)
Examples of music before 1400. xi,
117 p, frontis, repro music, paper.
Crofts (1942) 2nd ed 1945.   4.00
Some 100 compositions exemplifying both
monodic (beginning with Greek & Hebrew
chants) & polyphonic music (mostly 13th &
14th century English, French, & Italian).

JACOBS, ARTHUR (comp)
A music lover's anthology.   Intro
Sir Malcolm Sargent.   240 p, 8 pors
(Milein Cosman), 6–p bibl of sources.
Winchester Pubs., Winchester, Eng-   Δ
land, 1948.   (3.75)
A collection of writings on music from the
time of Byrd, plus original essays by Christo-
pher Hassall ("Music & English Poetry") &
Scott Goddard ("The Prospect Before Us")

NETTEL, REGINALD (comp)
To soothe a savage breast.   236 p.
Evans Bros., London, 1950.   (3.50)
"A series of opinions on music & life . . . in-
tended for those who have a good eye for
English prose & an ear for music." Some 47
authors are represented, grouped under the
heads, "The Golden Age," "The Age of
Reason," & "The Romantic Age."

PARRISH, CARL & OHL, JOHN F. (eds)
Masterpieces of music before 1750:
an anthology of musical examples
from Gregorian chant to J. S. Bach.
Norton 1951, in prep.   5.00

SCHERING, ARNOLD (ed)
History of music in examples—
Geschichte der Musik in Beispielen:
dreihundertfünfzig Tonsätze aus
neun Jahrhunderten.   viii, 481 p,
music, + 36–p unbound booklet.
(B & H 1931) Broude repr 1950.   15.00

A standard collection recently restored to
print: music only, except for a 4-p introduc-
tion and separate booklet of notes, bibl refs,
& indices; title pages in English & German;
text in German—which of course is little or
no handicap to the fruitful use of the work
even by non-German readers.

ANTHROPOLOGY (& music)

See:
Ancient Music   Musicology (esp)
Folklore   General Note)
History   Philosophy (Howes)
Instruments

ANTIQUITY (Music of)
See: Ancient Music, History.

Antrim, Doron Kemp. Editor.
See Dance Bands.

Apel, Willi, Author, editor. See:
Anthologies. Davison & Apel: His-
torical anthology, v 1 (1946/1949).   8.00
———. Same, v 2 (1950).   10.00
Dictionaries of Music.   Harvard
dictionary (1944).   7.50
French Music.   Secular (1949).   12.50
Notation. Of polyphonic music
(1945/1949).   8.00
Organ. Early history (1948).   1.00
Piano Music.   Masters of the key-
board (1947).   5.00

APPALACHIANS.
See: esp Folksongs–2 (Sharp).

Appel, Livia. Compiler. See Bibliographies.
Appenzeller, Else. Author. See App Ib.

APPLIED MUSICIANSHIP
For a general note on the respective scopes &
referenced subject-headings of the fields of
applied & theoretical musicianship, please
see under Musicianship.

APPRECIATION
General Note: Like "that blessed word, Meso-
potamia," "appreciation" is a magic term, so
elastic & omnipotent that it may be—and
sometimes is—applied to practically any book

*on music except a technical manual. Here,
however, it has been restricted as far as possible
to books designed to enhance the non-pro-
fessional listener's over-all enjoyment of
music. Only the best-known available works
are listed below, while others that can be
classified more rigorously (e.g. under Program
Notes) may be found in the following categories in particular:*

See also: esp Children–2, Program Notes,
School Music–2.

Also:

Aesthetics–1 & 2	Organ Music
Amateur Music	Philosophy
Chamber Music	Phonograph Records
Composers (& under	Piano Music
individuals)	Piano Playing–1
Concerto	(Cohen)
Contemporary Music	Psychology
Criticism	Radio Music
Education	Song
Film Music	Stokowski
Miscellanies	Symphony
Opera	Violin Music
Orchestra	

Also: App IIb (Kinscella, Skolsky).

BACHARACH, A. L. (*ed*)
The musical companion: a compendium for all lovers of music. 751 p,
frontis fac, mus ex, tables. Gollancz △
(1934) 15th ed 1946. (4.25)
*Includes the "ABC of music" by W. R.
Anderson, & sections on orchestra, opera,
chamber, instrumental, & vocal music, etc.,
by Blom, Bonavia, Dent, Evans, Harrison,
Hussey & Toye.*
*Note: For an abridged American edition
(1935/48), see under Erskine below.*

BERNSTEIN, MARTIN
An introduction to music: with analyses of representative works &
musical examples. 448 p, illus
Prentice (1937) 2nd ed 1951. 5.65

CLIFFE, CEDRIC
The making of music: how to recognize & understand orchestral music.
335 p. Cassell 1949. 3.00
*Folksy British approach for listeners to the
machine (orchestra & its instruments), music
(in various forms), & its makers.*

COPLAND, AARON
What to listen for in music. xii, 281
p, mus ex. Whittlesey 1939. 3.50
*A composer's explanations of composers'
materials & the use they make of them.*

DARNTON, CHRISTIAN
You and music. x, 180 p, paper.
Penguin (1940) rev ed 1945. .35

DICKINSON, EDWARD
The education of a music lover. xi,
293 p, 3–p bibl. Scribner 1911
(1937). O/P
*One of the earliest books "for those who study
or teach the art of listening." (Just gone O/P.)*

ERB, J. LAWRENCE
Music appreciation for the student:
a handbook for amateur & music-
student. xv, 239 p. G. Schirmer
1926 (1941). 3.00

ERSKINE, JOHN (*ed*)
A musical companion: a guide to the
understanding & enjoyment of music.
xvi, 516, xxxii p + chart, mus ex.
(1935) Tudor repr 1948. 2.98
*Originally pub 1935 by Knopf; an American
edition, somewhat abridged & with an added
section on music in the U. S. A. by Olga
Samaroff Stokowski, of the British book listed
under Bacharach above.*

FELDMAN, HARRY ALLEN
Music and the listener. 205 p.
Dutton 1939. 2.50

FINNEY, THEODORE M.
Hearing music: a guide to music
appreciation. x, 354 p, mus ex.
Harcourt 1941. 4.00
*The listener's technique, music as literature,
& "independent" listening.*

GOLDBECK, FREDERICK
The perfect conductor: listening to
music with your eye. xx, 202 p, 17
diagrs, 65 mus ex. Pellegrini 1951. 3.50

HAGGIN, B. H.
Music for the man who enjoys
"Hamlet." 128, ii p, mus ex. Knopf
1944 (3rd pr 1945) 2.75
*Thematic & harmonic analyses with phono-
graph-record references to works by Beethoven,
Mozart, & Schubert in particular.*

HAMILTON, CLARENCE G.
Music appreciation: based upon
methods of literary criticism. 396
p, 24 pors, 28 b & ws, mus ex. Ditson
1920. 2.50
"Music Students Library" series.

HARRISON, SIDNEY
Music for the multitude. 336 p.
Macmillan (1940) rev ed 1948. 2.50
*Stressing the development of music in relation
to its social & political setting.*

JOHNSON, WILLIAM W.
Intelligent listening to music: a
guide to enjoyment & appreciation
for all lovers of music. 191 p. Pitman
(1935) 3rd ed 1943. 2.50

KAUFMANN, HELEN L.
The little guide to music appreciation. x, 309 p. Grosset (1940)
1947.   .75
*"Little Music Library" series, pocket size.
A revision of material originally pub in "You
can enjoy music" (1940) & later in "Home
book of music appreciation" (1942).*

KREHBIEL, H. E.
How to listen to music: hints &
suggestions to untaught lovers of
the art. xv, 361 p, 12 pl, mus ex.
Scribner (1896) 1931).   2.50

LEWIS, LEO RICH
The ambitious listener. 96 p, paper.
Ditson 1929.   .75

MACMAHON, DESMOND
The road to music: a guide-book for
the listener who wishes to understand the art of music. 77 p, illus,
mus ex, bds. W. Paxton & Co., London, 1949.   1.00

MANUEL, ROLAND & TAGRINE, N. See App
Ia.

MAREK, GEORGE R.
The Good Housekeeping guide to
musical enjoyment. viii, 342 p, 24
pors, 16 photos. Rinehart 1949.   3.50
*Breezy, inspirational articles, including a
chapter on "What books should I read?"*

MASON, DANIEL GREGORY
From song to symphony: a manual
of music appreciation. 243 p, illus,
mus ex. Ditson 1924.   1.50
*Second-year text for a "study course in music
understanding."*

A guide to music: for beginners &
others. V 5 "Appreciation" series.
243 p, illus. Gray 1909 (1937).   2.00
*For other volumes in this series, see Surette &
Mason below.*

MCKINNEY, HOWARD D.
Music and man: a general outline of
a course in music appreciation based
on cultural backgrounds.   405 p,
illus. American 1948.   3.00
*Contemporary American music & "back-
grounds for listening." A textbook with
discussion topics & recommended works to
hear.*

MCKINNEY, H. D. & ANDERSON, W. R.
Discovering music: a course in music
appreciation. xx, 490 p, illus, mus
ex, chap bibls. American (1934)
rev ed 1949.   4.75

*Textbook, including a chart of the arts
against the background of history.*
How to listen to good music. 302 p.
Garden City repr 1947.   1.00
*Originally pub by Rutgers as "The challenge
of listening" (1943).*

MOORE, DOUGLAS
From madrigal to modern music: a
guide to musical styles. 354 p, mus
ex, bibl. Norton 1942.   5.00
*Analyses of representative works with phono-
graph-record references.*

Listening to music. xi, 301 p, mus
ex. Norton (1932) rev enl ed 1937. 4.00

RORKE, J. D. M.
The latch-key to music. 36 p, mus
ex. Oxford 1942.   .70
*Simple & direct advice on cultivating the
ability to "think" music.*

SAMAROFF-STOKOWSKI, OLGA
The listener's music book. 293 p,
mus ex. Norton 12th pr 1947.   3.50
*Originally (1935) "The layman's music
book." An outgrowth of the late Mme
Samaroff's layman's course in music understanding.*

SCHOLES, PERCY A.
The listener's guide to music: with a
concert-goer's glossary.   110 p,
illus. Oxford (1919) 1947.   2.00

Music appreciation: its history and
technics. Ed Will Earhart. xix, 398
p. Witmark 1935.   4.00
*American ed of the book titled in England
"Music, the child, & the masterpiece."*

SKOLSKY, SYD. (See also App IIb.)
Evenings with music. 382 p, illus,
mus ex. Dutton 1944 (4th pr 1945) 3.00
Make way for music. 138 p. Dutton
1946.   2.50
*Both books include programs of recorded
music (Columbia recordings exclusively).*

SPAETH, SIGMUND
The art of enjoying music.   viii,
246 p, bds. (1933) Permabooks 1949. .35
*Condensed popular ed of a book pub by
McGraw-Hill 1933 & repr by Garden City
in 1938.*

At home with music. xi, 366 p, 15
col pl. Doubleday 1946.   3.95
*Includes an appendix, "Your radio-phono-
graph" by Frank Freimann.*

The common sense of music. 375 p, illus, mus ex. Liveright 1924 & later pr. *School ed.* 2.00

Music for everybody. 128 p, bds. (1934) Sentinel 2nd ed 1945. .60

SPALDING, WALTER RAYMOND
Music: an art & a language. 350 p. Schmidt (1920) rev ed 1939. *Now available only together with 4 v of supplementary music.* *Complete:* 7.50

STRINGHAM, EDWIN JOHN
Listening to music creatively. xx, 479 p, mus ex. Prentice (1943) rev ed 1946 (5th pr 1947). 5.35
Stressing romantic & post-romantic music, and integration of music with other arts.

SURETTE, T. W. & MASON, D. G.
The appreciation of music. xi, 222 p, mus ex. Gray 1907 (16th pr n d). 2.00
V 1 of an "Appreciation of music" series of which v 2/5 are by Mason alone:

V 2: Great modern composers. (See Composers—1).

V 3: Short studies in great masterpieces. (See Program Notes).

V 4: Music as a humanity & other essays. (See under Mason in general alphabetical list).

V 5: A guide to music. (See above, Mason).

ULRICH, HOMER
The education of a concert-goer. xviii, 257 p, mus ex, 7–p bibl. Dodd Mead 1949. 4.00
An explanation of the "mechanical" side of music—its performance, distribution, programming, etc—from the professional musician's point of view; plus the usual discussion of musical forms, styles, etc.

WELCH, ROY DICKINSON
The appreciation of music. xvii, 216 p, mus ex. Harper (1927) rev ed 1945. 2.50
Emphasizing the fundamental materials of music, composers' methods, & common forms.

ZANZIG, AUGUSTUS D.
Roads to music appreciation: a guide to listener & to teacher or leader. 36 p, 5–p bibl, paper. National Recreation Assn (1939), rev ed 1948. .35

APPROACH TO MUSIC

See: esp Appreciation

Also:
Children
School Music

Teaching
Theory

APTITUDE (Musical)/APTITUDE-TESTS

See:
Children
Examinations
Psychology

School Music
Teaching
Tests

ARABIA (Music in)/ARABIAN MUSIC

See also:
Ancient Music
Asiatic Musics
  (note only)
History

Instruments
Jewish Music
Oriental Music
  (note only)

Note: A standard work by Ribera apparently is O/P, and in addition to the Farmer works listed below there are other monographs by or edited by him, which are O/P or in several cases available only in limited editions—originally privately published, later (around 1946) taken over by Hinrichsen. Other standard works apparently O/P (or not easily available) include those by Christianovitsch (in French), Kiesewetter (in German), etc.
The 6th installment of the "Bibliography of Asiatic Musics," referred to above, is devoted to Moslems in general & Arabic-speaking peoples ("Notes" for March 1949).

DANIEL, SALVADOR FRANCESCO
Music and musical instruments of the Arab: with introduction on how to appreciate Arab music. Ed H. G. Farmer. xii, 272 p, illus, mus ex, △ 3–p bibl. Reeves n d (1914/5?). (5.50)
Originally "La musique arabe" (1863); with a 36–p memoir of Daniel & 92–p of notes.

D'ERLANGER, RODOLPHE. See App Ia.

FARMER, HENRY GEORGE
Ghosts: an excursus on Arabic musical bibliographies. 8 p, paper. Hin- △ richsen n d (1946?). 1.00
An article on apocryphal musical treatises, originally published in "Isis" (1945/6).

Historical facts for the Arabian musical influences on musical theory: studies of the music of the Middle Ages. xii, 376 p, mus ex, bibl refs. △ Reeves n d (1930). (7.50)

The minstrelsy of "The Arabian Nights": a study of music & musicians in the Arabic "Alf Laila wa Laila." 53 p+12 pl, paper. Hinrichsen △ n d (1945). 4.50

FARMER, HENRY GEORGE (*ed & tr*)
Sa'adyah Gaon on the influence of music. xi, 109 p, facs, mus ex, 3–p △ bibl, paper. (1943) Hinrichsen 1946. 10.00
Translation with notes of parts of the final chapter of "Kitab al-amanat" by a Jewish philosopher who died in 1042.

ROBSON, JAMES (*ed & tr*)
Ancient Arabian musical instruments. Including notes on the instruments by H. G. Farmer. 19, xxiii p, facs, bibl refs. (1938) Hinrichsen n d (1946). △   5.00
As described by Al-Mufaddal ibn Salama (9th century) in the unique Istanbul MS of the "Kitab al-malahi."

Arbeau, Thoinot (pseud of Jean Tabourot). Author. See Dance.

ARCHITECTURE (& Music)
See: Acoustics, Theatre.

ARGENTINA (Music of)
See: Latin America.
Note: Pamphlets by Luper & Videla-Rivero (Pan-American Union) apparently are O/P.

ARISTOTLE. Author.
See also:
Ancient Music   History
Greek Music   Medieval/Renaissance

On the art of poetry. Tr S. H. Butcher. With a supplement: On (Book 8, chaps 5/7, of "Politics"). Tr Ben Jamin Jowett. Tr cor, ed, & intro by Milton C. Nahm. xvii, 51 p, bibl. Liberal Arts Press, N. Y., 1948.   .40
"Little Library of Liberal Arts" series.
Works. The Oxford Translation. Ed J. A. Smith & W. D. Ross. V 7: Problems (Problemata). Tr E. S. Forster. Oxford 1927.   5.00
One of the earliest detailed studies of musical theory.

Arlton, Alexander V. Author. See Birds.
Arma, Paul. Author. See App Ia.
Armitage, Merle. Author.
See Dance, Graham.

ARMSTRONG, Louis
See also: Jazz, Popular Music
Note: Armstrong's own "Swing that music" (1936) apparently is O/P.

GOFFIN, ROBERT
Horn of plenty: the story of Louis Armstrong. Tr James F. Bezou. iii, 304 p, frontis por. Allen Towne 1947.   3.00
Life & work of the great Negro trumpeter.

ARMSTRONG, LOUIS
Autobiography. Prentice in prep.   △

PANASSIÉ, HUGUES. See App Ia.

Armstrong, Lucille. Editor. See Dances-2
Armstrong, Thomas. Author.
See R. Strauss.

ARNE (Dr) Thomas Augustine
See:
England (music in)   History
English Music   Phonograph Records
Note: Books on Arne by Cummings & Langley apparently are O/P.

Arnold, Byron. Author. See Folksongs-2.
Arnold, Elliott. Author.
See Romberg. App IIa. (Sibelius, juvenile).
Arnold, Frank Thomas. Author.
See Accompaniment.
Arnold, John Henry. Author.
See Plainsong.
Arnold, Melvin. Co-author (with Joy).
See Schweitzer-2.
Arnold, William Harkness. Author.
See French Language.
Arnstein, Helen. Co-author (with Horne & Moss). See Horne.
Aronson, Maurice. Author. See Godowsky.

ARRANGING
1. **Band, Chorus, & School Orchestra**
2. **Dance Band & Orchestra**
Note: The second sub-category is confined to books dealing with popular music or jazz arranging only.
See also: Instrumentation, Transposition.

ARRANGING (1. Band, Chorus, & School Orchestra)
See also:
Band-1   Organ Playing
Choir/Choral   (esp Ellingford)
Film Music (esp   School Music-3
   Skinner)

DEUTSCH, MAURY
Arranging: a startling new approach for composers & arrangers. 3 v: 30, 31, 31 p, mus ex, typescript repro, paper. Author, N. Y., 1948.   3.00
Concise technical notes, primarily on "American-style" arranging for radio, films, & dance bands. One of a series of hand-books: see also Instrumentation, Psychology, & Theory-4 (Deutsch).

LAKE, M. L.
The American band arranger: a self-instructor for mastering the essential principles of practical & artistic arranging for military band. 44 p, paper. C. Fischer 1920.   1.25

LEIDZÉN, ERIK
An invitation to band arranging.
vi, 195 p, mus ex. Presser 1950.   **5.00**

SKEAT, WILLIAM J. (*& others*)
The fundamentals of band arranging:
a text book for students. Co-authors
Harry F. Clarke & Russell V.
Morgan. 88 p, bibl, paper. Fox 1938   2.00

WHITE, WILLIAM C.
Military band arranging: a practical
course for schools & private study.
72 p, mus ex. C. Fischer 1934.   2.00

WILSON, HARRY ROBERT
Choral arranging: for schools, glee
clubs, & publication, a complete
guide for the problems of choral
arranging for all types of voice combinations & for all kinds of choral
groups. . . . 123 p, mus ex. Robbins
1949.   3.50
Includes notes on choral accompaniments &
texts, preparation of MSS, etc.

YODER, PAUL
Arranging method for school bands.
Ed Jay Arnold. 191 p, mus ex, paper.
Robbins 1946.   3.00

ARRANGING (2. Dance Band & Orches-tra)

See also: Dance Band.

ALEXANDER, VAN
First arrangement: an introductory
method of arranging for the modern
orchestra. 64 p, paper. Capitol
Songs, Inc., N. Y., 1946.   2.00

CESANA, OTTO
Course in modern dance arranging.
King 1940.   2.00

Voicing the modern dance orchestra.
112 p. King, 1946.   4.00

DIAMANTE, CARLOS
Arranging Latin-American music
authentically: a reference & guide
to typical Latin-American dance
forms with examples of forms scored
for orchestra. 39 p, illus, mus ex.
King Brand Pubs, N. Y., 1948   **1.75**

ELLIS, NORMAN
Instrumentation and arranging for
the radio & dance orchestra. xxviii,
193 p. G. Schirmer (1936) 1937.   3.50
Instrumentation, scoring for special effects,
arranging for publication, etc.

JACOBS, DICK
Arranger-aid. 8 p, paper. Bregman
1940. (*Charts & mus ex only.*)   .50

MILLER, GLENN
Glenn Miller's method for orchestral
arranging. 116 p. Mutual Society,
Inc., N. Y., 1943.   3.00
Includes 2 inserts: complete sample scores
in manuscript reproduction.

OLIVER, SY
Self-instructor arranging course. Ed
Dick Jacobs. 104 p, mus ex, paper.
Embassy Music Corp., N. Y., 1949.   2.50
Practical workbook: modern dance-band arr.

WARRINGTON, JOHNNY
Modern harmony for the dance-band
arranger. 24 p, paper. Bregman
1948.   1.00

Tonal color and effects: for the
dance band arranger. Ed Dick
Jacobs. 24 p, photo, mus ex, paper.
Bregman 1949.   1.00

WEIRICK, PAUL
Dance arranging: a guide to scoring
music for the American dance orchestra. xii, 154 p. Witmark (1934)
rev enl ed 1937.   3.00
The rev ed includes new chapters on "swing,
microphone technique, rhumba," etc.

ART/THE ARTS

See:

Aesthetics	Painting/Pictures
Literature	Poetry

Also: General note under Allied Arts &
Techniques.

ARTICULATION

See:

Diction	Speech
Pronunciation	Voice
Singing	

ART-SONG

See:

Singing	Vocal Music
Song	

Also: under individual song composers
(Brahms, Schubert, Schumann, R. Strauss,
etc.).

Arts Enquiry (The). Sponsors.
See England (music in).

Arvey, Verna. Author.
See (The) Dance, Still.

ASCAP (American Society of Composers, Authors, & Publishers)

See: esp Composers–3a (McNamara)

Also:

America (music in)	Copyright
American Music	Yearbooks

Ashton, Joseph Nickerson. Author.
See Church Music.
Ashton, Winifred. Catalogued under Dane,
Clemence (*pseud*).

ASIATIC MUSICS

*Note: An extensive bibliography (compiled by
Richard A. Waterman, William Lichten-
wanger, Virginia Hitchcock Herrmann,
Horace I. Poleman, & Cecil Hobbs) currently
is being published in instalments in "Notes",
the quarterly journal of the Music Library
Association. Sections that have appeared
to date (beginning with the December 1947
issue) are headed: "General," "Southwest
Asia (General, Ancient Civilizations, Jews:
Ancient & Modern, Christians, Moslems),"
"India," "Southwest Asia (General, Burma.
Siam, Indo-China, Malaya & Malay
Archipelago, Philippine Islands)," "Central
East Asia (General, Japan, Korea, China),"
"Central Asia & Siberia."*

*Presumably the complete series eventually
will be re-published in book form, but no
definite announcement has yet been made.*

Atlantis Buch der Musik.
See App Ib (Hamel).

ATONALITY.

See: Tonality/Atonality.

AUBER, Daniel-François-Esprit

See also:

Composers-1	Opera-1 (esp Crosten)
French Music	Phonograph Records
History	

DENT, EDWARD J. (*tr*)
Fra Diavolo: a comic opera in 3
acts. French words by Eugene
Scribe. English version. xvi, 63 p,
paper. Oxford 1944.   .80

Auda, Antoine. Author. See App Ia.

AUDIENCE

See:

Psychology	Theatre
Stage-Fright	

Audio Devices. Publisher.
See Sound Rec & Repro.

AUDIO ENGINEERING

See:

Acoustics (esp Olson)	Phonograph
Decibel	Phonograph Records
Instruments	Radio
(esp Lewer)	Sound Rec & Repro

AUDIO-VISUAL (Aids, Materials, Methods)

See: Teaching-1.

AUDITION

See:

Career	Singing
Radio (esp Cott)	

Audsley, George Ashdown. Author.
See Organ, Organ Playing.

AUER, Leopold. Violinist, author.

See:

History	Violinists
Violin Playing	

*Note: An autobiography & two books on violin
playing apparently are O/P.*

Auer, Max. Author. See App Ib.

AUGUSTINE (Saint) (Augustine Aurelius)

Writings of Saint Augustine. V 2.
459 p. Cima Pub. Co., N. Y., 1948.   4.00
*V 6 in the series "Fathers of the Church, a
new translation," including (p 151/379) "On
music," tr Robert Catesby Taliaferro—pre-
viously available only in mimeographed form,
pub 1939 in the "St. John's Program" series.*

KNIGHT, W. F. JACKSON
St. Augustine's De Musica: a synopsis. v, 125 p, bibl refs. Orthological △
Institute, London, 1949.   (3.75)
*A valuable abstract of "On Music," based on
the text of the Migne edition and providing
a reliable idea of the Augustinian theories
for those who find the complete treatise heavy
& confusing going.*

Aulich, Bruno. Author. See String Quartet.

AURAL (Culture, Harmony, Training)

See:

Children-3	Sight-Playing & Reading
Dictation	Sight-Singing
Ear-Training	Solfège/Solfeggio
Score-Reading	Theory

AUSTRALIA (Music in)

MORESBY, EMILY ISABELLE
Australia makes music. Forew Bernard Heinze. x, 197 p, 20 photos,
b&ws, 1-pbibl. Longmans 1948 (1950).   3.50
*Informal history with personal reminiscences,
including lists of choral societies, doctors
of music, recordings of Australian compositions, etc. . .*

AUSTRIA (Music in)

See:

Composers-1 & 3b	History
Dances-2 (Armstrong)	Vienna

Ausubel, Nathan. Editor. See Folklore.

AUTOBIOGRAPHIES

Besides the famous autobiographies of Berlioz, Rimsky-Korsakov, & Wagner (the third unfortunately is O/P), many musicians have written the story of their own lives. For some of the available autobiographies, reminiscences, & memoirs, see:

Armstrong	Mannes
Bauer	Mason
Beecham	Mezzrow
Berlioz–1	Neel
Cardus	Rimsky-Korsakov
Carmichael	Rolland
Chanler	Rorke
Chevalier	Schweitzer–1.
Condon	Smythe
Cugat	Sorabji
Erskine	Sousa
B. Ives	Spalding
Fellowes	Stanislavski
Finn	Szigeti
Foldes	Toye
Gatti-Casazza	F. Wagner
Heiner	Walter
Heinsheimer	Warfield
Horne	Weingartner (App Ib)
Hughes	Waters
L. Lehmann	Willson
Lemare	Wood
Lomax	

See also: (App Ia):

Chevalier	Jaques-Dalcroze
Coppola	Milhaud
Durand	Thibaud

Also (App Ib):

Busch	Krenek
Chaliapin	Slezak
Hofmann	Weingartner
Kahl	

AUTOGRAPHS

General Note: Reproduced autographs frequently are included in composers' collected letters & in biographies.

See also: Facsimiles, Manuscript.

(HARROW REPLICA, No. 1)
The autographs of three masters: Beethoven, Schubert, & Brahms. Unp (5 p). Heffer 1942.　　　3.50
Beethoven's "Ich liebe dich," Schubert's sketch of a piano-sonata Andantino, & the signature of Brahms.

MAGNAT, G. E.　See App Ia.

WINTERNITZ, EMANUEL
Musical autographs: from Monteverdi to Hindemith. 150 p facs, 206 p text. Bittner, in prep.　　△

Avery, Elizabeth.　Author.　See Speech.

AYRE

See:

Campion	Madrigal
Elizabethian Music	(esp Fellowes)
England (music in)	Medieval/Renaissance
English Music	Song
History	Vocal Music

Note: The standard work, Peter Warlock's "The English ayre" (1926) is O/P.

Ayrton, Michael.　Author.
See Purcell (Mandinian).

—B—

Bacchelli, Riccardo di. Author.
See App Ic.

BACH

General Note: The available literature is divided into the following sub-categories:
Bach Family
Bach, Carl Philipp Emanuel
(references only)
Bach, Johann Christian (note only)
Bach, Johann Sebastian
  1. Life   2. Works

BACH FAMILY

Note: Standard works apparently O/P (or not easily available) include those by Bitter (in German), Terry, etc.

GEIRINGER, KARL
A history of the Bach family.
(In prep for 1951)   △

MÜLLER-BLATTAU, JOSEPH. See App Ib.

REESER, EDUARD
Sons of Bach. Tr W. A. G. Doyle-
Davidson. 63 p, 21 pl (pors & facs),
mus ex, ½-p bibl, bds. Continental
n d (1947).   2.50
"Symphonia" series of illustrated mono-graphs: Carl Philipp Emanuel, Johann Christian, Johann Christoph, & Wilhelm Friedemann Bach; with lists of editions & recordings.

BACH, Carl Philipp Emanuel

Author. See Keyboard Instruments.
See (for material about C. P. E. Bach):
Appreciation   History
Bach Family   Keyboard Instruments
J. S. Bach-1   & Music
Chamber Music   Phonograph Records
Composers-1   Piano Music
Concerto   Program Notes
Note: Standard works apparently O/P (or not easily available) include those in German by Cherbuliez, Schenker, Schmid, Vrieslander etc.

BACH, Johann Christian

See: Bach Family, J. S. Bach-1.
Note: Terry's biography (1929) is O/P.

BACH, Johann Sebastian   (1. Life)

General Note: Most biographies of course also discuss the works in more or less detail, but the books specifically devoted to studies of the works themselves, collectively or individually, are listed under 2. Works.

See also:
Almanacs/Calendars   History
  (Peters Calendar)   Keyboard Instruments
Appreciation   & Music
Baroque Era   Luther
Church Music   Organ
Composers-1   Program Notes

Also: All IIa (juveniles by Albus, Goss, Wheeler, Wheeler & Deucher).

Note: Standard works apparently O/P (or not easily available) include those by Boughton, Parry, Spitta (but see note-entry below), Terry ("Bach: the historical approach", 1930), Van Loon, etc; those in French by Gérold, Tiersot, etc; those in German by Bitter, Dahms, Hitzig, Moser, Steglich, Wolfrum, etc.

BESCH, HANS. See App Ib.

BLUME, FRIEDRICH
Two centuries of Bach: an account
of changing taste. Tr Stanley
Godman. 85 p, bibl refs. Oxford 1950. 2.00
A study of the "rediscovery" of Bach and his influence on music in the last 200 years. Originally in German (1947): "J. S. Bach im Wandel der Geschichte."

BUHRMAN, T. SCOTT
Bach's life: chronologically as he
lived it. 54 p, 7 pl. Organ Interests
1935.   3.75
With stop-lists of Bach's organs.

CART, WILLIAM. See App Ia (in French).

CHERBULIEZ, A. E. See App Ib (in German)

DAVID, HANS T. & MENDEL, A. (*eds*)
The Bach reader: a life of Johann
Sebastian Bach in letters & docu-
ments. 431 p, 22 pl (por, etc) + 15
facs, mus ex, 12–p annot bibl.
Norton 1945.   7.50
A standard collection of all the significant source materials: including Bach's own writings, pertinent documents, early critical

estimates, etc; plus a reprint of Forkel's "Life of Bach" in the Stephenson translation, p 295/356.

FIELD, LAURENCE N.
Johann Sebastian Bach: the musician's musician. xi, 166 p, 1 por, 1 fac, 1–p bibl. Augsburg 1943 (6th pr 1947). 1.50

FISCHER, EDWIN. See App Ib.

FORKEL, JOHANN NIKOLAUS. See App Ib.
Note: In addition to the facsimile of the first German edition (listed in App Ib), Forkel's "Bach" is included (in Stephenson's translation) in the David & Mendel "Bach Reader" above.

GEIRINGER, KARL
The lost portrait of J. S. Bach. Unp (12 p incl 8–p text), col frontis por+ 2 pors, paper. Oxford 1950. 1.00
A 4-color reproduction of a rediscovered pastel by Gottlieb Friedrich Bach; portraits of C. P. E. & Johann Ambrosius Bach: with a genealogical table and notes by Geiringer.

GRACE, HARVEY
Bach: 22 p, cover por, paper. Novello n d (1939). .40
Miniature biography ("great musicians").

GREW, EVA MARY & SYDNEY
Bach. xiv, 239 p, 8 pl (por, facs, etc), 3–p bibl. Dent 1947; Pellegrini 1949. 2.50
"Master Musicians" series, with the usual calendar, personalia, & catalogue of works; plus a genealogy of the Bach family.

GURLITT, WILIBALD. See App Ib.

HOELTY-NICKEL, THEODORE (ed)
The little Bach book. 162 p, 8 pl. Valparaiso 1950. (Symposium.) 3.00
Essays by Buszin, Nettl, Rosenwald, et al.

MATTHAEI, KARL (ed). See App Ib.

MEYER, MARIE ANTOINE. See App Ia.

MEYNELL, ESTHER
Bach. 140 p, frontis por, 2–p bibl. (1933) Wyn 1949. 1.00
"Great Musicians" series, originally published in the "Great Lives" series by Duckworth, London, 1933.

The little chronicle of Magdalena Bach. 245 p. (1925) E. C. Schirmer 1940 (1950). 2.50
A fictional biography of Bach, originally published anonymously by Chatto & Windus

(& Doubleday) in 1925. Purportedly written by Bach's second wife, Anna Magdalena, it often is assumed to be authentic—as apparently by the publishers of the German edition (see App Ib), who omit Mrs Meynell's name entirely!

MÜLLER VON ASOW, HEDWIG & E. H. (eds).
See App Ib (Bach's letters, in German).

PEYSER, HERBERT F.
Johann Sebastian Bach. vi, 58 p, 7 illus (pors, etc), 1 mus ex, bds. Grosset 1950. .50
"N. Y. Philharmonic-Symphony Society Musical Biographies" series: presumably a revision of a booklet published for members of the society in 1945.

PIRRO, ANDRÉ. See App Ia.

RAUPACH, HANS (ed). See App Ib.

SCHALLENBERG, E. W.
Joh. Seb. Bach. Tr. W. A. G. Doyle-Davidson. 63 p, 17 pl, 3–p mus ex, ½–p bibl, bds. Continental n d (1947). 2.50
"Symphonia" series of extensively illustrated monographs.

SCHWEITZER, ALBERT
J. S. Bach. Pref C. M. Widor; tr Ernest Newman. 2 v: xvi, 428; vii, 498 p, 5 pl, mus ex. (1911) Black, via Macmillan 1923 (1950). 8.00
A standard work, originally written in French, 1905; published in an enlarged German edition in 1908 (for a 1947 reprint see App Ib); first translated into English in 1911.

SPITTA, PHILIPP. See App Ib.
Note: Spitta's monumental standard biography (original German edition, 1873/80) unfortunately is represented today only by the greatly abridged German edition of 1935, listed in App Ib. An off-set reproduction, or re-issue, of the 3-volume English translation by Bell & Fuller Maitland (Novello 1884/5, 2nd ed 1899; O/P for some years) is rumored to be in preparation, but no definite information is available.

STEGLICH, RUDOLF. See App Ib.

TERRY, CHARLES SANFORD
Bach: a biography. xx, 292 p + 76 pl + 2 charts, 5–p bibl. Oxford (1928) 2nd rev ed 1933 (1949). 5.00
A more recent standard work: primarily a record of Bach's career, including much original research, many photographs by the author, and two fold-out genealogical charts.

BACH, Johann Sebastian (2. Works)

See also:

Appreciation	Mass
Bach–1	Orchestral Music
Baroque Era	Organ Music
Chamber Music	Phonograph Records
Choir/Choral–3	Piano Music
Church Music	Program Notes
Composers–1	Song(s)
Concerto	Themes
Counterpoint–1	Timing
Fugue	Trumpet (Menke)
Keyboard Instruments	Violin Music
& Music	Vocal Music

Note: Standard works apparently O/P (or not easily available) include those by Hannam, Hull, Iliffe, Pirro, Terry, Whittaker, etc; also those in German by Hauptmann, Landshoff, Schering, Schreyer, Werker, etc.

See the note under the author entry for Henry S. Drinker for information on Drinker's translations of Bach choral texts.

ALDRICH, PUTNAM
Ornamentation in J. S. Bach's organ works. 61 p, frontis fac, 39 mus ex, bibl refs. Coleman 1950. 2.00
A detailed study, claimed to be the first based exclusively on sources accessible to Bach.

BOULT, ADRIAN C. & EMERY, WALTER
The St Matthew Passion: its preparation & performance. 75 p, 1 fac, mus ex, 1–p bibl, bds. Novello 1949. 1.40
Practical notes on rehearsal & performance details, the continuo & solo parts, etc.

DAVID, HANS THEODORE
J. S. Bach's "Musical Offering:" history, interpretation, & analysis. xi, 190 p, 13 pl (facs), mus ex, bds. G. Schirmer 1945. 3.00
A study supplementing the author's edition of the music itself: including a description of the various editions and a discussion of ornament interpretation, as well as a fascinatingly detailed history & technical analysis of the work.

DICKINSON, A. E. F.
The art of J. S. Bach. 254 p, 5 pl (pors, fac, etc), 42 mus ex, 1–p bibl. (1936) Hinrichsen rev ed 1950. 3.00
Re-issue of a study originally published by Duckworth, London, in 1936.

DUFOURCQ, NORBERT. See App Ia.

FLORAND, FRANÇOIS. See App Ia.

FULLER MAITLAND, J. A.
Bach: the keyboard suites. 64 p, mus ex, paper. Oxford 1925. 1.00
Bach's "Brandenburg Concertos." 47 p, mus ex, paper. Oxford 1929 (1945). 1.00

The "48": Bach's Wohltemperirtes Clavier. 2 v: 38, 38p, mus ex, paper. Oxford 1925. 2.00
All three works above are in the "Musical Pilgrim" series of analyses.

GANNETT, KENT (comp)
Bach's harmonic progressions: (1000 examples). v, 51 p, music. Ditson 1942. 1.00
Except for a 2-p introduction, this consists of music only: one-bar examples of Bach's progressions, drawn from the chorales, & transposed to C major or A minor.

GRACE, HARVEY
The organ works of Bach. Intro Ernest Newman. xvi, 319 p, mus ex. Novello 1922 (1950). 3.50
A standard, specialized study, with detailed notes on the music, its registration & phrasing, etc, plus a collation-table of the Novello, Peters, & Augener editions.

GRAY, CECIL
The forty-eight preludes and fugues of J. S. Bach. viii, 148 p, mus ex. Oxford 1938 (2nd pr 1948). 1.75
Critical analysis of each work, with general observations on the "48" as a whole.

HUBER, ANNA GERTRUD. See App Ib.

KELLER, HERMANN. See App Ib.

KIRKPATRICK, JOHN (ed)
6 Brandenburg Concerti. Unp (178- △ p facs). Peters 1950. 25.00
A facsimile edition of Bach's manuscript, reproduced in its original size, with a foreword by Kirkpatrick, a preface in German by Peter Wackernagel and in condensed English translation by Anthony Brun.

Inventionen und Sinfonien. Unp (iv △ + 64–p facs). Peters 1948. 7.50
A facsimile edition of the 2- & 3-part Inventions, from Bach's 1723 MS (Pr. Staatsbibl. Berlin P. 610), with a 1-p foreword.

KURTH, ERNST. See App Ib.

MACPHERSON, STEWART
Bach's forty-eight preludes and fugues: a commentary. 2 v: 107, 79 p, mus ex, paper. Novello n d (1934). (3.50)
Novello "Primers" Nos 111/2.

MANN, WILLIAM
Introduction to the music of Bach. 80 p, mus ex. Dobson 1950. 1.00

NEUMANN, WERNER (comp)
Joh. Seb. Bach's handbook of cantatas. 202 p, paper. B & H 1947, via Associated 1950. 3.00

Except for its awkwardly phrased English cover & title pages, this detailed catalogue is in German (see also App Ib), but that is little handicap to its use as a reference work even by those who know little German. It covers all the sacred & secular cantatas, with titles, voice registers, instrumentation, Bach Gesellschaft references, etc, for each aria & chorus.

PAYNE, MAY DE FOREST (*comp*)
Melodic index to the works of Johann Sebastian Bach. xvi, 101 p, mus ex. G. Schirmer 1938.   3.00
A complete index of themes (in music reproduction), arranged by melodic design.

RIEMANN, HUGO
Analysis of J. S. Bach's Wohltemperirtes Clavier (48 preludes & fugues). Tr J. S. Shedlock. 2 v: xix, 168; 210 p, mus ex, flex. Augener 1890 (7th pr n d).   3.00

SAMPSON, BROOK
A digest of the analyses of Bach's celebrated 48 fugues from the Well-Tempered Clavier. ? p, some 1600 mus ex, 46 tables. Vincent n d (1905) via Reeves.   Δ (6.50)
Outline analysis of each of J. S. Bach's 48 fugues (in "Das wohltemperirte Clavier"). 36 p, mus ex, paper. Vincent n d, via Reeves.   (1.50)

SCHMIEDER, WOLFGANG (*ed*)
Thematisch-systematisches Verzeichnis der musikalischen Werke von Johann Sebastian Bach: Bach-Werke Verzeichnis (BWV). xxiv, 748 p, mus ex, bibl refs. B & H 1950.   15.00
Received too late for proper entry in App Ib, but in any case worthy of notice here as an invaluable reference work even for non-German readers. It includes complete thematic indices, notes on the autograph scores & published editions, bibliographical references, chronological sketch, etc.

SMEND, FRIEDRICH. See App Ib.

TAYLOR, STAINTON DE B.
The chorale preludes of J. S. Bach: a handbook. Forew W. G. Whittaker. xii, 126 p, mus ex. Oxford 1942 (1944).   1.75
For organists primarily: combining & augmenting original analyses by Grace, Schweitzer, Spitta, & Pirro, and including notes on Bach's organs.

TERRY, CHARLES SANFORD
Bach: the cantatas and oratorios. 2 v: 52, 38 p, mus ex, paper. Oxford 1925.   2.00

Bach: the mass in B minor. 47 p, mus ed 1931 (4th pr 1949).   1.00
Bach: the passions. 2 v: 56, 80 p, mus ex, paper. Oxford 1926.   2.00
All three works above are in the "Musical Pilgrim" series of analyses.
Bach's orchestra. xv, 250 p, illus, mus ex, tables, 3-p bibl refs. Oxford 1932 (1949).   7.00
A detailed, standard study of Bach's instrument usage & characterization and the effects of local & contemporary conditions (of cantata performance, etc) on his instrumentation.

THIELE, EUGEN. See App Ib.

TOVEY, DONALD FRANCIS
A companion to "The Art of Fugue" (Die Kunst der Fuge). 79 p, mus ex. Oxford 1931 (1949).   2.00
An analysis to enable students to verify their own analyses; a supplement to Tovey's edition of the music itself.

(UNESCO DISCOGRAPHY)
The works of Johann Sebastian Bach: general discography. Intro Hans David. Archives of Recorded Music UNESCO, in prep.   Δ
In preparation for 1951 publication, first in French, later in English.

WACKERNAGEL, PETER (*ed*). See App Ib.
  (*See also Kirkpatrick above.*)

WILKINSON, CHARLES W.
How to play Bach's 48 preludes and fugues: a guide for the use of piano students. ix, 135 p. Reeves n d (1939).   Δ (3.00)

WILSON, STEUART
Bach's St Matthew Passion. Hinrichsen in prep for 1951.   Δ
Miniature "Survey" series M-9.

BACH, Wilhelm Friedemann
See:
Bach Family   History
J. S. Bach–1   Phonograph Records

Bacharach, Alfred Lewis. Editor.
See Appreciation, Composers–1, English Music.
Bachelin, Henri. Co-author (with Cellier). See App Ia.
Bachner, Louis. Author. See Singing–1.
Backus, Edythe N. Editor.
See Libraries.
Bagar, Robert Conti. Author.
See Wagner–3. (With Biancolli). See Opera–3. Program Notes.

BAGPIPES

See also:

History	Ireland (music in)
Instruments	Scotland (music in)

Note: A bibliography by Askew (1932) and works by Malcolm and Manson apparently are O/P (or not easily available).

FLOOD, WILLIAM H. GRATTAN
The story of the bagpipe: its history, origin of reed pipes, the pipes of ancient Celtic Ireland & Wales, the Scottish scene & Scottish melodies, changes from the 16th to 19th centuries.   xx, 237 p, 26 illus, mus ex, △ 2–p bibl. Scott 1911, via Reeves   (4.00)
In the "Story of Music" series; now O/P in the Scribner American edition.

Bailey, Albert Edward. Author.
See Hymns/Hymnody–2.
Bailey, Bertha Wingert. Co-author (with Jones). See Theory–2.
Bailey, Cyril. Author. See Allen.
Bailey, Dorothy Seyl. Author.
See Piano Playing–4.
Bainton, Roland H. Author.
See Luther.
Bairstow, (Sir) Edward Cuthbert.
Author.   See Counterpoint–1, Form. (With Greene). See Singing–2.
Bakaleinikoff, Vladimir. Author.
See Instruments, School Music–3.
Bakeless (Mrs) Katherine Little. Author.
See App IIa & IIb (juveniles).

BAKER, Dorothy

Young man with a horn. 243 p.
Houghton 1938.   2.75
Same. 184 p, paper. Signet repr
1945 (1949).   .25
A novel of life among jazz musicians, inspired by the life of Bix Beiderbecke.

BAKER, Frank

Full score. 344 p. Coward 1942.   2.50
Life of a fictional composer: Harrison Bate.

Baker, Theodore. Author, editor.
See Dictionaries of Music, Dictionaries of Terms, Counterpoint–2.
Bakker, M. G. Co-author (with Kempers).
See Opera–1.

BALAKIREV, Mily Alexeievitch

See:

Appreciation	Phonograph Records
Composers–3e	Program Notes
History	Russian Notes

Baldwin, Lillian Luverne. Author.
See Program Notes.
Baldwin, Samuel Atkinson. Author.
See Organists.
Balet, Jan. Author, illus. See App IIb.
Balfoort, Dirk J. Author.
See Stradivari.

BALI (Music in)/BALINESE MUSIC

See also:

Asiatic Musics	Instruments
(note only)	Oriental Music
History (esp 2, Sachs)	(note only)

Note: The bibliography of Asiatic Musics, referred to above, includes a Balinese section in its 9th installment: Music Library Association "Notes," December 1949 issue.

COVARRUBIAS, MIGUEL
Island of Bali.   xv, 417 p, illus (drwgs author, photos Rose Covarrubias). Knopf 1937.   7.50
Includes a discussion of Balinese instruments & music, p 206/20.

McPHEE, COLIN
(*See also App IIb.*)
Dance in Bali.
Auvergne 1950 in prep.   1.50
A house in Bali. x, 234 p + 44–p photos, mus ex. Day 1946.   4.00
A musician's account of life in Bali in the 30's, modern Balinese music & musicians, the gamelan orchestra, etc; with photographs by the author.

Ball, John Jr. Author.
See Phonograph Records.

BALLAD/BALLAD OPERA

General Note: Many ballad books are collections or studies of folksongs or quasi-folk-songs, or of ballad texts only. Only a sampling of the more generalized literature is listed here.

See also: Folklore, Folksongs (esp 2, Niles).

Also:

Appreciation	Minstrels/Minstrelsy
Barbershop	Opera
Beggar's Opera	Phonograph Records
Cowboy Music	Popular Music
England (music in)	Song(s)
Foster	Songbooks
History	Vocal Music

Note: Gagey's "Ballad opera" (1937) is O/P.

NORTHCOTE, SYDNEY
The ballad in music.   124 p, 4–p bibl. Oxford 1942.   2.50
Historical & critical survey of the ballad in music & poetry, including Maurice Brown's

ballad index with list of available (British) recordings.

WELLS, EVELYN KENDRICK
The ballad tree: a study of British & American ballads, their folklore, verse, & music; together with 60 traditional ballads & their music. ix, 370 p, 17 pl (pors, facs, etc), music (tunes only), 8–p bibl. Ronald 1950. 4.50
An over-all survey from the time of the Robin Hood ballads, with an analysis of the various elements that contribute to ballads' "universal, timeless" appeal.

Ballard, Elizabeth Flanders. Co-editor (with Flanders & others). See Folksongs–2.

BALLET

General Note: The enormous literature on this subject, a considerable part of which is of comparatively recent (and much of it British) origin, presents an insoluble problem to the musical bibliographer. Obviously, nearly all of it has some musical pertinence, occasionally even musical importance; just as obviously, however, music itself is seldom, if ever, the object of much direct attention. In any case, space exigencies would forbid any extensive or perhaps even representative listings. We have tried to include most of the available books of particular musical interest and for the rest to attempt no more than a sampling, omitting most of the "picture-books," specialized studies, etc.

See also: esp (The) Dance, Dance Music.

America (music in)	Modern Music
American Music	Nijinsky
Appreciation	Opera (esp 3 Mason)
Contemporary Music	Pavlova
Covent Garden	Phonograph Records
Duncan	Program Notes
England (music in)	Russia (music in)
English Music	Russian Music
French Music	Waltz
History	Yearbooks
Karsavina	

Also: Composers, and under the names of individual ballet composers & composers whose works have been adapted to ballets, esp:

Adam	Ravel
Britten	Respighi
Chávez	Rimsky-Korsakov
Chopin–2	Roussel
Copland	Schoenberg
Debussy–2	Schumann–2
Delibes	Strauss, J.
de Falla	Stravinsky–2
Lambert	Tchaikovsky–2
Prokofiev	Vaughan Williams
Purcell	Walton

Also: App IIb (juveniles by Marie-Jeanne and Streatfeild).

Those who wish to investigate the subject further will do well to consult Paul Magriel's remarkably comprehensive "Bibliography of dancing," 1936, & supplement, 1941. See (The) Dance (Magriel).

AMBERG, GEORGE
Art in modern ballet. ix, 115 p, some 200 pl (8 col). Pantheon 1946.   15.00
Drawings & paintings, plus index & data on some 833 ballets from 1909 to 1945.

Ballet in America: the emergence of an American art. xx, 244 p, some 91 photos. Duell Sloan 1949.   6.00
Same. 221 p, 12–p photos, paper. Mentor cheap ed 1949.   .35
Includes a 150-year chronology & 2 original ballet libretti: "Fancy Free" & "Laurie makes up her mind" from "Oklahoma."

AMBROSE, KAY
The ballet-lover's companion: aesthetics without tears for the ballet-lover. xii, 80, iii p, illus. Knopf 1949.   1.95
The ballet-lover's pocket book: technique without tears for the ballet-lover. 65 p, illus. Knopf 1945 (1947).   1.50
Both booklets with the author's drawings illustrating various steps & techniques.

BEAUMONT, CYRIL W.
Complete book of ballets: a guide to the principal ballets of the 19th & 20th centuries. xxiv, 900 p, 95 pl. (1937) Grosset repr 1949.   2.98
A standard work, originally published by Putnam (1937), with program & biographical notes for some 200 ballets.

Dancers under my lens: essays in ballet criticism. 160 p, 15 photos. Beaumont 1949.   4.50
Contributions to "Ballet" magazine, 1946/8, plus earlier essays from "Dancing World" & "Dance Journal," 1922/35.

A primer of classical ballet (Cecchetti method) for children. 60 p, 9 pl (Eileen Mayo), flex. Beaumont 1933 (7th pr 1949).   1.50
Same. A second primer. 65 p, 8 pl (Eileen Mayo), flex. Beaumont 1935 (6th pr 1950).   1.50
Same. A third primer, with dances by Eleanor Banks, Margaret Craske, & others. 61 p, mus ex, flex. Beaumont 1941 (repr 1949).   1.50

The Sadler's Wells Ballet: a detailed account of works in the permanent repertory, with critical notes. 214

p + 49–p photos. Beaumont
(1946), rev enl ed 1947. **3.75**
Studies of some 30 ballets.
Note: See also Gautier below for a work trans-
lated by Beaumont. These of course are only
a few of the many ballet books written, edited,
or translated by Beaumont, many of which
are published by his own firm in London, and
most of which are currently available.

BRADLEY, LIONEL
Sixteen years of Ballet Rambert. 82
p, 74 photos, b&ws (Hugh Steven-
son). Hinrichsen 1946. **4.00**
"Survey" series S-4. The complete repertory
of the oldest English ballet company, with
indices of composers, choreographers, dancers,
& designers represented.

DAVIDSON, GLADYS
Stories of the ballets. xvi, 486 p,
1 col pl, 19 b&w pl. T. Werner
Laurie, London, 1949. **3.50**
"Romantic stories" of some 77 ballets by
some 33 choreographers.

FRANKS, A. H.
Approach to the ballet. xii, 300 p,
102 illus. Pitman 1948. **5.00**
Ballet history, technique, stories, & present
status, stressing British activities.

GABRIEL, JOHN
Ballet school. Forew Tamara
Karsavina. 128 p, photos. (1947)
Pitman 1948. **8.50**
Photographs & descriptions of steps &
movements, posed by famous dancers.

GAUTIER, THÉOPHILE
The romantic ballet as seen by
Théophile Gautier: being the notices
of all the principal performances of
ballet given at Paris during the years
1837–1848. Tr Cyril Beaumont. 87
p, 14 pl. Beaumont 1932 (1947). **3.00**
Ballet reviews from "La Presse," "Le Moni-
teur," "Le Figaro," etc, dealing with such
noted dancers as Cerito, Essler, Grahn, Grisi,
Pierrot, Taglioni, et al.

GIBBON, MONK
The "Red Shoes" ballet: a critical
study. 95 p, 4 col pl, 47 pl. Saturn
Press, London, 1948, 3rd ed n d, via
Auvergne 1949. **5.75**
A detailed study of the famous film ballet,
with 2 chapters on "The ballet & its music,"
p 42/8, and material on the composer, Brian
Easdale, Beecham & the London Philhar-
monic, as well as on Shearer, Massine,
Helpmann, etc.

GREGOR, JOSEPH. See App Ib.

GRANT, GAIL
The technical manual and dictionary
of classical ballet. Pref Florence
Rogge. 87 p, illus (author). Kamin
1950. **3.00**
Definitions & descriptions in dictionary
style, from Adage, Adagio to Voyagé.

HASKELL, ARNOLD L.
Ballet: a complete guide to appreciation, history, aesthetics, ballets,
dancers. 217 p, 16–p pl + b&ws
(Kay Ambrose), paper. Penguin
(1938) rev ed 1949. **.35**
"Pelican" pocket-book A-122.

Ballet panorama: an illustrated
chronicle of three centuries. 120 p,
158 pl (4 col). Batsford (1938) 3rd
rev ed 1948. **2.75**
An extensively illustrated survey, with em-
phasis on the romantic movement & Russian
ballet.

Note: See also England—music in, for "Since
1939," which includes a section by Haskell
on ballet, as well as others on films, music,
& painting. In addition to the books above
& the yearbooks below, Haskell has written or
edited many others on various ballet subjects.

HASKELL, ARNOLD L. (*ed*)
The ballet annual, 1950: a record
& year book of the ballet. 148 p, col
frontis, some 138 photos, 5 b&ws,
5–p bibl (Cyril Swinson). Black
1950, via Macmillan. **4.50**
Review of the year's ballet events, with em-
phasis on British activities. Of the earlier
issues in this series (begun in 1947), Nos 2
(1948) & 3 (1949) apparently still are
available, $6.00 each.

Sadler's Wells ballet books. Lane
n d (1949).
No 1. See Tchaikovsky-2 (ed
Haskell: The sleeping beauty).
No 2. Job and The rake's progress.
48 p + 13–p photos, mus ex, paper. **.50**
Essays on the ballets (music by Vaughan
Williams & Gavin Gordon respectively) by
Frank Howes, Geoffrey Keynes, James Laver,
& Joan Lawson.

No 3. Hamlet and Miracle in the
Gorbals. 46 p + 13–p photos, mus
ex, paper. **.50**
Essays on the ballets (music by Tchaikovsky
& Arthur Bliss respectively) by Michael
Benthall, Eric Blom, Clemence Dane, Arnold
L. Haskell, & M. H. Middleton.

Carnaval, Le Spectre de la rose, and Les Sylphides. 40 p + 13-p photos, mus ex, paper.   .50

Essays on the ballets (music by Schumann, Weber, & Chopin respectively) by Stewart Deas, Arnold L. Haskell, & Lincoln Kirstein.

LAWRENCE, ROBERT
The Victor book of ballets and ballet music. xviii, 531 p, some 200 photos, some 400 mus ex, 5-p discography. S & S 1950.   5.00

A companion work to the Victor books of concertos (see Concerto: Veinus), operas (see Opera–3: Biancolli & Bagar), symphonies (see Symphony: O'Connell), and overtures & tone poems (see Program Notes: O'Connell).

MANCHESTER, P. W. & MORLEY, IRIS
The rose and the star: ballet in England & Russia compared. 95 p, 53 photos (Morley). (1949) Macmillan 1950.   2.75

Originally published in London by Gollancz. Informal dialogue discussions on training, repertory, classical ballets, & criticism; with comparisons on British & Russian productions of "Giselle," "The Sleeping Beauty," & "Swan Lake," in particular.

MICHAUT, PIERRE. See App Ia.

NOBLE, PETER (ed)
British ballet. Forew Margot Fonteyn. 358 p, some 90 photos, b&ws (Sheila Graham), 3-p bibl. Skelton Robinson n d (1949?).   4.00

Articles by the editor, Beaton, Beaumont, Bliss, Bradley, Haskell, Helpmann, Williamson, et al; plus a reference section & biographical index.

PALMER, WINTHROP BUSHNELL
Theatrical dancing in America: the development of the ballet from 1900. 159 p, 20 photos, 3-bibl. Ackerman 1945 via Beechhurst.   3.00

Dance criticism "from a social point of view" on "The American Revolution" (Duncan, Shawn, St Denis, Graham, Humphrey, Weidman) & "Russian Ballet" (Mordkin, Pavlova, Diaghileff, Nijinsky, Fokine, et al.).

POSNER, SANDY & ROBERTSON, M. E.
Ballet pocket library (series). Illus (Joyce Millen). Newman Wolsey & Black, London, via Transatlantic 1947/50.

Stories & descriptions of individual ballets. For the four booklets by Posner, see under: Adam ("Giselle"), Delibes ("Coppélia"), Stravinsky–2 ("Petrouchka"), & Tchaikov-

sky–2 ("The sleeping princess"). *For the six booklets by Robertson, see the Robertson entries below and also under Respighi ("La boutique fantasque") & Tchaikovsky–2 ("Le lac des cygnes").*

ROBERT, GRACE
The Borzoi book of ballets. xvii, 362, xxiii p, + 59 photos. Knopf 1946 (1947).   5.00

Introduction on Ballet in the U. S., followed by descriptions & data on some 68 ballets from "The afternoon of a faun" to "Voices of spring," plus a glossary of ballet terms.

ROBERTSON, MARION E.
Le beau Danube and Le tricorne: stories of the ballets. 96 p, illus (Joyce Millen) incl 4 col pl. Newman Wolsey, London, 1947, via Transatlantic.   .75

"Ballet Pocket Library" series. Descriptions of the ballets to music by J. Strauss & Manuel de Falla respectively.

Checkmate and The rake's progress: Stories of the ballets. 95 p, illus (Joyce Millen) incl 4 col pl. Black 1949, via Transatlantic 1950.   .75

"Ballet Pocket Library" series. Descriptions of the ballets to music by Arthur Bliss & Gavin Gordon respectively.

Hamlet and Miracle in the Gorbals: stories of the ballets. 95 p, illus (Joyce Millen) incl 4 col pl. Black 1949, via Transatlantic 1950.   .75

"Ballet Pocket Library" series. Descriptions of the ballets to music by Tchaikovsky & Arthur Bliss respectively.

L'Oiseau de feu and Shéhérazade: stories of the ballets. 95 p, illus (Joyce Millen) incl 4 col pl. Newman Wolsey, London, 1947, via Transatlantic.   .75

"Ballet Pocket Library" series. Descriptions of the ballets to music by Stravinsky & Rimsky-Korsakov respectively.

SEVERN, MERLYN (photographer)
Ballet in action. With intro essay & critical notes by Arnold L. Haskell. xxiv, 128 p, some 200 photos (sequences). Lane 1938 (1947).   7.50

Sadler's Wells ballet at Covent Garden: a book of photographs. 80 p. Lane 1947.   4.00

Two of the best-known ballet "picture-books." The former illustrates sequences from some 40 ballets; the latter (which has no text) illustrates sequences from "Sleeping beauty," "Miracle in the Gorbals," "The Rake's

Progress," "Symphonic Variations," &
"Adam Zero."

SEYMOUR, MAURICE (*photographer*)
Ballet: 101 photographs. Forew
Leonide Massine. Unp (224 p).
Pellegrini 1947.   10.00
Another popular "picture-book," with notes.

SITWELL, SACHEVERELL (*ed*)
The romantic ballet from contemporary prints.   12 p + 16 col pl.
Batsford 1948.   1.50
*Batsford "Colour Books" No 1: introduction
& notes by Sitwell. Presumably this is based
on an earlier, larger work: "The romantic
ballet in lithographs of the time," by Beaumont & Sitwell (Faber, 1938).*

SLONIMSKY, JURI (*& others*)
The Soviet ballet. xii, 285 p, some
100 photos. Philosophical 1947.   **4.75**
*Essays by various writers, with biographical
sketches of the leading dancers.*

STOKES, ADRIAN
Russian ballets. 213 p, 16 photos.
(1935) Dutton 1936 (1946).   **3.50**
*Studies of some 8 works in detail, with notes
on some 6 others. Originally published by
Faber & Faber, London. Note: Another work
by Stokes apparently is still available:
"Tonight the ballet," Faber & Faber 1934,
Dutton 1935, $2.00.*

WILLIAMSON, AUDREY
Ballet renaissance.   Pref Robert
Helpmann. 163 p, photos.   (1948)
Transatlantic 1949.   **4.50**
The ballet in London, 1945-1947.

Contemporary ballet. xi, 184 p +
64–p photos.   (1946) Macmillan
1950.   **3.75**
*Historical background & contemporary scene,
with studies of various British companies.
Originally published by Rockliff, London.*

BALLET DANCERS
See:
Ballet   Nijinsky
(The) Dance   Pavlova
Duncan

Ballwebber, Edith. Author. See Dances–3.
Batzell, Winton James. Author.
   See History–2.
Bampton, Ruth.   Author. See Theory–3.

BAND
   1.   Brass, Concert, Military Band
   2.   Drill & Parade Technique

BAND (1. Brass, Concert, Military)

See also:

America (music in)	History
American Music	Instrumentation
Appreciation	(esp Lang)
Arranging–1	Instruments
Bassoon	March
Bugle	Military March
Children–5	Orchestra
Clarinet	Phonograph Records
Community Music	Sax/Saxophone
Conducting (esp	School Music–3
Wright)	Sousa
Dance Band	Trombone
Flute	Trumpet
French Horn	Wind Instruments
Gilmore	

*Note: Standard works apparently O/P (or not
easily available) include those by Clappé,
Eberle, Giles, E. F. Goldman ("Amateur band
guide," 1926), R. F. Goldman ("The band's
music," 1938), Hind, Russell & Elliott,
Vincent, Wright, etc.*

ADKINS, HECTOR ERNEST
Treatise on the military band: instrumentation, arranging, training,
& conducting. ix, 253 p, 58 pl, diagrs,
mus ex. Boosey (1931) rev ed 1945.   **7.50**
An extensively detailed, practical study.

COOK, KENNETH (*ed*)
"Oh, listen to the band'": a brass
band miscellany. Intro Henry Geehl.
96 p, cartoons, mus ex, 1–p bibl,
paper.   Hinrichsen 1950.   1.50
*Presumably this is the same as the book an-
nounced variously as "Brass Band Parade"
& "The Bandsman's Everything Within."*

GALLO, STANISLAO
The modern band: a treatise on wind
instruments, symphony band, &
military band. 2 v. Birchard 1935.
V 1: Wind instruments—technique,
notation, tone color, & use in band
& orchestra; Band instruments. 165
p, illus, tables, mus ex.   3.50
V 2: Score examples. 101 p, music
only.   2.50

GOLDMAN, EDWIN FRANKO
Band betterment: suggestions &
advice to bands, bandmasters, &
band-players. ix, 193 p, 6 photos.
C. Fischer 1934 (1948?).   5.00
*A wealth of practical advice by one of the best-
known American bandmasters.*

GOLDMAN, RICHARD FRANKO
The concert band. ix, 246 p, 11 illus,
6–p bibl. Rinehart 1946.   3.00
*"Field of Music" series, v 1: history, instru-
ments, music, the bandmaster, etc.*

BAND (2. Drill & Parade Technique)
See also: Baton–2.

DALE, CARROLL R.
Fundamentals of drill for marching bands, drum corps, pep squads, & other marching units. vi, 99 p, illus. Gamble 1940. **1.75**

DVORAK, RAYMOND FRANCIS
The band on parade. ix, 115 p, illus. C. Fischer 1937. **3.00**
Includes lists of suitable music.

HINDSLEY, MARK HUBERT
Band at-ten-tion!: drill master's & drum major's edition. 93 p, illus. Gamble 1932. **1.75**
Note: Gamble-Hinged Music Co, Chicago, also publishes a "Marching maneuver" series (1935 & later), by Hindsley & others. **10** *booklets, paper, $1.00 each.*

HUBER, LOUIS JOSEPH
Let's all cheer: a collection of cheers, yells, animated formations for school bands, & cardograms to promote pep at athletic contests. 165 p, paper. Northwestern Press, Minneapolis, 1948. **1.00**

JOHNSTON, LAWRENCE
Parade technique: a practical manual for the marching band. 60 p, illus, paper. Belwin 1944. **1.25**

RIGHTER, CHARLES BOARDMAN
Gridiron pageantry: the story of the marching band for bandsmen, directors, & football fans. 75 p, illus, paper. C. Fischer 1941. **1.50**

Banister, Henry Charles. Author.
Note: Banister's lectures ("Interludes," ed Macpherson, 1898) apparently are O/P, as are his various musical textbooks.

Banke, Cécile de. Author.
See Choral Speaking.
Banks, Louis. Author. See Voice.

BANTOCK, (Sir) Granville
See:

Choir/Choral–3	Phonograph Records
Composers–3c	Program Notes
England (music in)	Song(s)
English Music	Vocal Music

Note: A study by H. O. Anderton (1925) apparently is O/P.
Editor. See Folksongs–1.

Baranoski, Stephen. Author.
See Hammond Organ.

BARBER, Samuel
See also:

Appreciation	Contemporary Music
American Music	Phonograph Records
America (music in)	Program Notes
Composers–2 & 3a	Symphony
Concerto	

BRODER, NATHAN
Samuel Barber.
G. Schirmer in prep. △
"Schirmer's Contemporary Composers" series: biography, list & analyses of works, bibliography, & discography.

BARBERSHOP (Ballads, Singing)
See also:

Amateur Music	Popular Music
Community Music	Songbooks

MARTIN, "DEAC"
Keep America singing. 148 p, illus. Society for the Preservation & Encouragement of Barber Shop Quartet Singing in America, Detroit, 1948. **2.50**
A record of the society's first 10 years.

SPAETH, SIGMUND
Barber shop ballads and how to sing them. Intro Ring Lardner. xvi, 125 p, illus, music. Prentice 1940. **1.96**
Superseding an earlier collection published by Simon & Schuster in 1925.

BARBIROLLI, John
See also:

Conductors	Interpreters
England (music in)	Phonograph Records

RIGBY, CHARLES
John Barbirolli: a biographical sketch. 191 p, illus. John Sherratt △ & Son, Altrincham, England, 1948. **(3.25)**
An uncritical biography with photographs.

Barbour, Harriot Buxton. Author (with Freeman). See Children–2, App IIb.
Barjansky, Serge. Author.
See String Playing.
Barker, Frank Granville. Author.
See Opera–1.
Barlow, Harold. Compiler (with Morgenstern). See Themes.
Barnard, Elizabeth. Author (with Davies). See Children–3.
Barnard, Floyd P. Co-author (with Jones). See Theory–2.
Barne, Kitty. Author.
See Orchestra, App IIb.
Barnes, A. F. Author. See Harmony–2.
Barnes, Edward Shippen. Compiler, author. See Choir/Choral–3, Modulation.
Barnes, Grace. Author. See Speech.

Barnes, William Harrison. Author.
See Organ.
Barnett, David. Author.
See Education, Teaching–2.

BAROQUE ERA

General Note: This is roughly the period of the 17th century and the first half of the 18th, —the bridge between the Renaissance and the so-called "modern" Classic & Romantic eras,—and of which the outstanding musical spokesmen are Monteverdi, Schütz, Buxtehude, Purcell, Bach & Handel.

See also:

Accompaniment (Arnold)	History
Anthologies (esp Davison & Apel, v 2)	Keyboard Instruments & Music
Appreciation	Opera–1
Chamber Music	Orchestral Music
Choir/Choral–3	Organ Music
Church Music	Phonograph Records
Classic Era	Piano Music
Composers–1 (& under individual names)	Program Notes
	Theatre (Scholz)
Concerto	Violin Music
	Vocal Music

Note: Standard works apparently O/P (or not easily available) include Sacheverell Sitwell's "Southern baroque art" (1931), etc; and those in German by Flemming, Nettl, Tintelnot, Wellesz, etc.

BUKOFZER, MANFRED F.
Music in the baroque era: from Monteverdi to Bach. xvi, 489 p, 12 pl (pors, facs, etc), 105 mus ex, 27-p bibl. Norton 1947.   6.75
"Norton History of Music" series: the first extensive study in English of this period, with scholarly discussions of its music & men, plus a list of music editions.

CLERCX, SUSANNE. See App Ia.

GLEASON, HAROLD (*comp*)
Music literature outlines. Series 2: Music in the baroque. viii, 158 p, chap bibls, typescript repro, paper. Levis Music Stores, Rochester, N. Y., 1950.   3.00
A guide to the study of music through the early, middle, & late baroque and the rococo periods in Italy, the Netherlands, Germany, Austria, France, Spain, & England, with separate sections on Bach & Handel. Special reading lists, book & periodical bibliographies, lists of representative music & recordings. (For No 1 in this series, see Medieval-Renaissance.)

HAAS, ROBERT MARIA. See App Ib (ed Bücken).

LIESS, ANDREAS. See App Ib.

Barrett, William Alexander. Co-author with Stainer). See Dictionaries of Terms.
Barrows, Sarah T. Author (with Pierce).
See Voice.
Barry, Phillips. Co-editor (with Flanders, Ballard, & Brown). See Folksongs–2.
Barth, Herbert. Editor. See App Ib.
Bartholomew, Edward Fry. Author.
See Psychology.
Bartholomew, Wilmer Tillett. Author.
See Acoustics.
Bartlett, Ella Herbert. Author.
See App IIa (Foster & Herbert juveniles).
Bartlett, Hazel. Compiler.
See Bibliography.

BARTÓK, Béla

See also:

Appreciation	Hungarian Music
Chamber Music	Modern Music
Composers–2	Orchestral Music
Concerto	Phonograph Records
Contemporary Music	Piano Music
Folklore	Program Notes
History	String Quartet

Author. See Folklore (a book on Yugoslav folk music, in prep), and App Ia (a booklet in French on folk-music collecting). Bartók's noted book on Hungarian Folk music (English translation, 1931) unfortunately is O/P at present.

DILLE, DENIJS
Béla Bartók. Dobson in prep.   Δ
"Contemporary Composers" series; originally published in Flemish, 1939.

HARASZTI, EMIL
Béla Bartók: his life and works. Tr Dorothy Swainson & the author. 104 p, frontis por, mus ex, 1-p bibl. Lyrebird 1938.   6.75
One of the earliest extended studies, originally published in Hungarian, 1930. Includes a catalogue of works.

SEIBER, MÁTYÁS
The string quartets of Béla Bartók. 24 p, mus ex, paper. Boosey 1945.   .60
Analytical notes for the six string quartets, plus a 2-p list of Bartók's works.

STEVENS, HALSEY
Bartók. Oxford in prep.   Δ

Barton, Frederick Bushnell. Author.
See Amateur Music.
Barzun, Jacques. Author.
See Berlioz–2, Romantic Era, Wagner–2.

BASIC MUSICIANSHIP

See:

Children (esp **3 & 8**)	Sight-Singing
Ear-Training	Solfège/Solfeggio
School Music	Theory–2 & 3

BASS (Double) (String)

See:

Instrumentation　　　　String Instruments
Instruments　　　　　　(esp Watson)
Orchestra

BASSES (Figured) (Thorough)

See:

Accompaniment　　　　Harmony
　(esp Arnold)　　　　History
Baroque Era　　　　　Keyboard Instruments
Composition　　　　　& Music

BASSOON

See also:

Band–1　　　　　　Instruments
History　　　　　　Orchestra
Instrumentation　　Wind Instruments

LANGWILL, LYNDESAY G.
The bassoon and double bassoon: a
short illustrated history of their
origin, development, & makers. 40
p, 11 pl, 2–p bibl, paper. Hinrichsen
n d (1948?).　　　　　　　　　　　1.25

*"Miniature Survey" series M-24: a concise,
authoritative survey, including material originally published in the "Proceedings of the
Musical Association," Leeds, England,
1939/42.*

Bathurst, Effie Geneva. Co-author (with
Murray). See School Music–1.

BATON

1. Conducting Technique
2. Spinning & Twirling

BATON (1. Conducting Technique)

See also:

Band　　　　　　　Conductors
Choir/Choral–2　　Orchestra
Conducting　　　　School Music–3 & 4

EARHART, WILL
The eloquent baton. vii, 93 p,
diagrs, mus ex. Witmark 1931 (5th
pr 1946).　　　　　　　　　　　　1.75

OTTERSTEIN, ADOLPH W.
The baton in motion: a photographic
presentation of the technic of conducting, together with material for
practice, with an added section on
vocal conducting. 59 p, photos
(Dwight Bentel), music, 1–p annot
bibl, paper. C. Fischer (1940) rev
aug ed 1942.　　　　　　　　　　1.25

RUDOLF, MAX
The grammar of conducting: a practical study of modern baton tech-

nique. Pref George Szell. xvi, 350 p,
60 diagrs, 467 mus ex. G. Schirmer
1950.　　　　　　　　　　　　　6.00

*A new work that undoubtedly will rank as the
standard in its field. It demonstrates in
detail the 6 patterns of beating each of the
basic rhythms, with—in an appendix—
a conductor's analyses, bar by bar, of 11
orchestral pieces, from Bach to Debussy.*

SCHMID, ADOLF
The language of the baton. vii,
123 p, photos, diagrs, mus ex.
G. Schirmer 1937.　　　　　　　3.00

*Practical directions with some 100 musical
examples, 107 diagrams, & 13 photographs.*

STOESSEL, ALBERT
The technic of the baton: a handbook for students of conducting.
Pref Walter Damrosch. 102 p,
photos, diagrs, mus ex, 1–p bibl,
paper. C. Fischer (1920) aug ed
1928.　　　　　　　　　　　　　1.50

WATERS, FRED E.
Practical baton technique for student
conductors. 30 p, diagrs, paper.
Gamble 1939.　　　　　　　　　1.00

BATON (2. Spinning & Twirling)

See also: Band–2.

BENNER, CHARLES W. & PAINTER, PAUL
The art of baton spinning: presenting the rudimental organization of
baton spinning & twirling, incorporating the Benner system of baton
pedagogy. 2 v: 64 p each, illus,
paper. Gamble 1938.　　　　　　3.00

The underhand technique in baton
twirling. 32 p, illus, paper. Gamble
2nd rev enl ed (ed C. J. Duncan)
1940.　　　　　　　　　　　　　1.00

*The latter book is Volume 2 of a "Baton
Twirling" series, edited by Painter & Benner,
and including other books by Bennett,
Duncan, & McAllister, Black, & the editors.*

LEE, ROGER L.
The baton: twirling made easy. 98
p, illus, paper. Boosey n d (1949).　1.50

How to twirl a baton. 28 p, illus
(Charles Deaton), paper. Ludwig
(1936) rev ed 1939.　　　　　　1.00

BAUER, Harold

See also: Interpreters, Pianists.

Harold Bauer: his book. 306 p,
photos, mus ex. Norton 1948.　　3.75

*Reminiscences of the noted pianist's long
career abroad and in the United States.*

Bauer, Marion Eugénie. Author. See:
Children–2. How music grew, by
Bauer & Peyser (1925/39). **5.00**
Contemporary music. 20th-century
music (1933/47). **5.00**
——. Summary of above (1935). **.25**
History–2. Music through the ages,
by Bauer & Peyser (1932/46). **5.00**
Quizzes. Musical questions (1941). **2.75**
Theory–2. Music is a language
(1951, in prep). △

Bauer, Robert. Compiler.
See Phonograph Records.
Bauman, Alvin. Author.
See Sight-Singing & Reading.

BAX, (Sir) Arnold E. Trevor
See:

Appreciation	English Music
Chamber Music	History
Choir/Choral–3	Phonograph Records
Composers–2 & 3c	Piano Music
Contemporary Music	Program Notes

*Note: An autobiography, "Farewell, my
youth" (1942), apparently is O/P (or not
easily available in this country).*

Baxter, Harry. Co-author (with Larson).
See Wind Instruments.
Bayard, Samuel, Preston. Editor.
See Folklore.
Bayton-Power, Henry. Author.
See Composition:
Beach, Frank Ambrose. Author.
See Operetta.
Beaufils, Marcel. Author. See App Ia.

BEAUMARCHAIS, Pierre A. C. Caron de
See also:

History	Mozart–3 (Crozier,
Literature	Dent)
Mozart–1 & 2	Opera
	Rossini (esp Dent)

LEMAÎTRE, GEORGES
Beaumarchais. viii, 362, xi p, por
2–p bibl, bds. Knopf 1949. **4.00**
*A study of the fabulous career of the versatile
Frenchman best known (musically) as the
author of "The barber of Seville" & "The
marriage of Figaro." English translations
of the opera libretti for these works are listed
under Mozart–3 (Dent) & Rossini (Dent).
In addition, various editions of the French
texts are available, some published in this
country (by Oxford, Holt, etc) for school use.*

Beaumont, Cyril William. Author, translator, publisher. See Adam, Ballet,
Tchaikovsky–2 (Sedgewick)

BE-BOP
See: Jazz (esp Heather, **Griffin**).

Beck, Earl Clifton. Author.
See Folklore.
Beck, Georges. Author, compiler.
See App Ia.
Beck, Jean-Baptiste & Louise. Authors.
See App Ia.
Bedrock, Gerald Stares. Author.
See Keyboard Instruments & Music.
Bédier, Joseph. Author. See Wagner–2.

BEECHAM, (Sir) Thomas
See:

Ballet (esp Gibbon)	Interpreters
Conductors	Philharmonic
England (music in)	Phonograph Records

*Note: An autobiography, "A mingled chime"
(1943), is O/P, at least in this country, but
a second autobiographical volume is announced
"in preparation" in England. Also O/P
(or not easily available) are studies of Beecham
by Geissmar and Smythe.*

BEETHOVEN, Ludwig van
1. **Letters, Own Writings**
2. **Life**　3. **Works.**

BEETHOVEN (1. Letters, Own Writings)
See also:

Autographs	Fascsimiles
(Harrow Replica)	Letters

*Note: Standard collections of the letters
apparently O/P (or not easily available)
include those edited by Kalischer (English tr
Shedlock), Kastner (in German), Kerst, etc.*

BEETHOVEN, LUDWIG VAN. See App Ib.

HÜRLIMANN, MARTIN (ed). See App Ib.

KOPP, TILLY (ed). See App Ib.

KRUSEMAN, PHILIP (ed)
Beethoven's own words, compiled &
annotated. Tr Herbert Antcliffe.
59 p, frontis por, 1–p bibl. Hinrichsen 1947. **2.50**
*"Miniature Survey" series M-23. Brief
excerpts from the "Konversationshefte,"
"Heiligenstadt Testament," & various
marginal notes by Beethoven.*

PROD'HOMME, J. G. (ed). See App Ia.

REICH, WILLI (ed). See App Ib

SONNECK, O. G. (ed)
Beethoven's letters in America:
fac-similes with commentary; in
commemoration of March 26, 1827.

xxix, 213 p, 35 facs.   (Beethoven Association, N. Y., 1927) N. Y. Public Library via G. Schirmer.   10.00
Interleaved facsimiles of 35 letters owned by Americans, with transcripts, translations, background notes, etc.

BEETHOVEN (2. Life)

See also:

Appreciation	History
Classic Era	Opera
Composers-1	Program Notes
Documents	Symphony
Goethe	Vienna

Also: App IIa (Goss, Wheeler juveniles).

Note: Standard works apparently O/P (or not easily available) include those in English, or English translations, by Bekker, Carpenter, Closson (but see App Ia for French ed), Crowest, Grace, Herriot, Hévésy (but see App Ia for French ed), Newman, Nohl (but see App Ia for French ed), Riezler, Rolland (but see App Ia & Ib for French & German eds), Schindler, Specht, Thayer (but see note under Thayer entry below), Wagner, etc.

Also those in German by Bücken, Kalischer, Lenz, Marx, Nottebohm, Schiedermair, Wegeler & Ries, etc.

ALDANOV, MARK
The tenth symphony. Tr Gregory Golubeff. viii, 149 p. Scribner 1948.   2.75
A "symbolical novelette" of the Viennese scene, Beethoven, & Razumovsky.

BÜCKEN, ERNST. See App Ib.

BUENZOD, EMANUEL. See App Ia.

BURK, JOHN N.
The life and works of Beethoven. viii, 483 p, mus ex. (1943) Modern Library repr 1946.   1.25
A standard short biography, with program notes on the works; originally published by Random House, 1943.

CHANTAVOINE, JEAN. See App Ia.

CLOSSON, ERNEST. See App Ia.

HÉVÉSY, ANDRÉ DE. See App Ia.

HOFMANNSTHAL, HUGO VON. See App Ib.

HÜRLIMANN, MARTIN. See App Ib.

D'INDY, VINCENT
Beethoven: a critical biography. Tr Theodore Baker. v, 127 p, 16 pl (pors, facs, etc), 4 foldout tables. Boston 1913 (repr n d).   2.50
A standard study of Beethoven's productive life history in terms of an examination of his most characteristic works. Originally published in French in 1911.

KING, GEORGE S.
Ludwig van Beethoven. Hinrichsen in prep for 1951.   △
"Miniature Survey" series M-11.

KOBALD, KARL. See App Ib.

LUDWIG, EMIL
Beethoven: life of a conqueror. Tr George Stewart McManus. xiii, 356 p, 9 pl (pors, facs), Putnam 1943 (1948).   4.00
A popular, romantic biography.

MACARDLE, DONALD W. (ed). See Thayer below.

McNAUGHT, WILLIAM
Beethoven. 28 p, cover por, paper. Novello n d (1940).   .40
Miniature biography ("great musicians").

NOHL, WALTHER. See App Ib.

NOLI, FAN S.
Beethoven and the French revolution. 117 + 6 p, 3–p bibl. International Universities Press, N. Y., 1947.   2.50
A highly individual, controversial study of Beethoven as an ultra-revolutionary.

PAAP, WOUTER
Ludwig van Beethoven. Tr W. A. G. Doyle-Davidson.   64 p, 18 pl (pors, facs, etc), mus ex, bds. Continental n d (1947).   2.50
"Symphonia" series of illustrated monographs; a brief study of the life & works— the symphonies in particular.

PROD'HOMME, J. G. See App Ia.

PRYCE-JONES, ALAN
Beethoven.   119 p, frontis por, 1–p bibl. (1933) Wyn 1948.   1.00
"Great Musicians" series, originally published by Duckworth ("Great Lives"), 1933.

RAU, HERIBERT
Beethoven: a biographical romance. Tr S. E. Randolph. 332 p.   Ditson 1908.   2.00

ROLLAND, ROMAIN. See App Ia & Ib.

SCHAUFFLER, ROBERT HAVEN
Beethoven: the man who freed music. xxviii, 693 p, 30 pl, 6–p bibl. (1929) Tudor repr 1947.   2.49
A popular, romanticized biography & study of Beethoven's creative processes; originally published in 2 volumes by Doubleday.

SCHRADE, LEO
Beethoven in France: the growth of

an idea. xi, 271 p, 14–p bibl. Yale
1942.   3.00
*A study of the reciprocal influences of
Beethoven's music & intellectual France.*

SCOTT, MARION M.
Beethoven. viii, 343 p, 8 pl (pors,
facs, etc), mus ex, 10-p bibl. Dent
1934, cor repr 1947; Pellegrini 1949. 2.50
*"Master Musicians" series, with the usual
calendar, personalia, catalogue of works.*

SMOLLE, KURT. See App Ib.

SONNECK, O. G. (*comp*)
Beethoven: impressions of contemporaries. vii, 231 p, 16 pors. G. Schirmer
1926 (2nd pr n d).   4.00
*Informal impressions of Beethoven's visitors,
compiled & annotated by Sonneck.*

SULLIVAN, J. W. N.
Beethoven: his spiritual development. xi, 262 p. Knopf 1927 (4th
pr 1947).   3.00
Same. 144 p, paper. Mentor repr
1949.   .35
*A noted mathematician's illuminating study
of Beethoven's music as an expression of his
personal vision of life.*

THAYER, ALEXANDER WHEELOCK
The life of Ludwig van Beethoven.
Ed. Krehbiel. 3 v. 1921   Δ
*Note: This is the best-known standard bi-
ography. Originally published in German,
1866/79, it is currently O/P in the rev 3rd
edition published by The Beethoven Association, New York. However, an extensively
revised & expanded new version is in preparation by Donald W. MacArdle.*

TURNER, W. J.
Beethoven: the search for reality.
343 p, frontis, mus ex. Dent (1927)
cheap ed 1933 (1945).   2.00
*A standard study of the man and his music,
especially notable for its analysis of the
composer's character & his artistic ideals.*

VALENSI, THÉODORE. See App Ia.

ZERKAULEN, HEINRICH. See App Ib.

BEETHOVEN (3. Works)
*Note: Standard works apparently O/P (or not
easily available) include those in English, or
in English translations, by Behrend, Blom,
Elterlin, Marliave, Marx, Walker, Weingartner, etc.
Also those in French by Herwegh, Prod'-
homme, etc; in Italian by Bruers, etc; in*

*German by Haas, Helm, Mersmann, Notte-
bohm, Riemann, Schering, Seyfried, etc.*

See also:

Appreciation	Phonograph Records
Autographs	Piano Music
Chamber Music	Program Notes
Choir/Choral–3	Rolland
Classic Era	Song(s)
Composers–1	String Quartet
Concerto	Symphony
Facsimiles	Themes
History	Timing
Opera	Violin Music
Orchestral Music	Vocal Music

ABRAHAM, GERALD
Beethoven's second-period quartets.
79 p, mus ex, paper. Oxford 1942
(1943).   1.00
*"Musical Pilgrim" series of analyses: Op
59, 74, & 95. For companion booklets, see
below: Fiske, Hadow.*

BERLIOZ, HECTOR
A critical study of Beethoven's nine
symphonies: with a few words on his
trios & sonatas, a criticism of
"Fidelio," & an introductory essay
on music. Tr Edwin Evans Sr. xii,   Δ
165 p, frontis por.   Reeves n d
(1913?).   (2.50)
*A famous study, temporarily O/P in England,
but scheduled for early re-issue.*

COVIELLO, AMBROSE
Difficulties of Beethoven's pianoforte sonatas: an analysis of common
faults in performance with suggestions for their cure. Several volumes:
each 25/29 p, mus ex, paper. Oxford
1933/5.
Performance analyses of individual sonatas:
1. C major, Op. 2, No. 3.   .50
2. C minor, Op, 10, No. 1 . O/P?
3. C minor, Op. 13. O/P?
4. D major, Op. 10, No 3.   .50
5. A major, Op. 2, No 2.   .50
6. G major, Op. 31, No 1.   .50
7. A flat major, Op. 26   .50
8. F minor, Op. 2, No 1. O/P?

DENT, EDWARD J. (*tr*)
Fidelio, or Wedded Love: an opera
in two acts. Words adapted from
the French of J. N. Bouilly by
J. F. Sonnleithner & F. Treitschke.
English version.   xvi, 37 p, paper.
Oxford 1938.   .80
The libretto, with prefatory notes.

EVANS, EDWIN, *Sr.*
Beethoven's nine symphonies: fully
described & analyzed. 2 v. Reeves
n d (1923/4?).   Δ
V 1: Nos 1/5. xxiii, 381 p, tables,
mus ex. 1923.   (5.00)

V 2: Nos 6/9. xix, 372 p, tables, mus ex. 1924? (5.00)
Immensely detailed musical analyses.

FISCHER, KURT VON. See App Ib.

FISKE, ROGER
Beethoven's last quartets. 79 p, mus ex, paper. Oxford 1940. 1.00
"Musical Pilgrim" series of analyses: from Op 127. For companion booklets, see Abraham (above) & Hadow (below).

GIRARD, RENÉ. See App Ia.

GROVE, GEORGE
Beethoven and his nine symphonies. vii, 407 p, mus ex, 1–p bibl. (1896) Oxford & Novello 1948. 5.00
Reprint of the 2nd rev edition (1896) of an early, standard work, long O/P.

HADOW, W. H.
Beethoven's Op 18 quartets. 64 p, mus ex, paper. Oxford 1926. 1.00
"Musical Pilgrim" series of analyses. For companion booklets, see Abraham, Fiske.

HARDING, H. A.
Analysis of form: as displayed in Beethoven's 32 pianoforte sonatas, with a description of the form of each movement. iv, 67 p mus ex, paper. △ Novello (1895) new ed 1901. (2.00)
Novello "Primer" No 34.

HOWES, FRANK
Beethoven: notes & analysis of symphonies 2 & 3, piano concertos 4 & 5, violin concerto, & "Heiligenstadt Testament". 45 p, mus ex, paper. Oxford 1933. 1.00
"Musical Pilgrim" series of analyses.

JOHNSTONE, J. ALFRED
Notes on the interpretation of 24 famous piano sonatas of Beethoven. 205 p, frontis por, 2–p bibl. Reeves △ n d (1927). (3.00)
Super-title: A helpful guide for the student.

KASTNER, RUDOLF
Beethoven's piano sonatas: a descriptive commentary in the light of Schnabel's interpretations . . . Tr Gerald Abraham. 55 p, paper. △ Reeves n d (1935). (1.00)
Super-title: Beethoven's sonatas and Artur Schnabel. Includes a biographical sketch of Schnabel.

KELBERINE, ALEXANDER
The four famous pianoforte sonatas of Ludwig van Beethoven: an essay

in analysis . . . 59 p, mus ex, paper. J. Fischer 1939. 1.00
Analyses of the "Pathétique," "Moonlight," "Waldstein," & "Appassionata" sonatas.

MASON, DANIEL GREGORY
The quartets of Beethoven. x, 294 p, frontis fac, 21 mus ex. 3–p annot bibl. Oxford 1947. 5.00
An objective, detailed critical study.

MILNE, A. FORBES
Beethoven's pianoforte sonatas. 2 v: 66, 68 p, mus ex, paper. Oxford 1925/28. 2.00
"Musical Pilgrim" series of analyses, covering 12 sonatas only.

NIEVERGELT, EDWIN. See App Ib.

PIAZZA, H. (*printer*)
Beethoven's sonata appassionata, Op 57. Unp (44 p). (L'Edition d'Art H. Piazza, Paris & The Beethoven Association, N. Y., n d) △ N.Y.Public Library via G. Schirmer. 10.00
A facsimile reproduction, prepared & printed by H. Piazza in a limited de luxe edition, of the complete original MS.

REINECKE, KARL
The Beethoven pianoforte sonatas: letters to a lady. Tr E. M. Trevenen Dawson. 142 p, mus ex, paper. Augener n d (1897). 2.50
Analyses in the form of letters, dated from 1894 to 1897, to a pianist friend.

SHAW, H. WATKINS
Beethoven's fifth concerto for pianoforte ("The Emperor"): a guide. 24 p, mus ex, bibl notes, paper. Hinrichsen 1946. .50
"Miniature Survey" series M-4. The booklet includes an outline of concerto principles & a list of recordings.

SHEDLOCK, JOHN S.
Beethoven's pianoforte sonatas: the origin & respective values of various readings. 51 p, mus ex, paper. Augener n d (1918). 1.00

SHEPHERD, ARTHUR
The string quartets of Ludwig van Beethoven historic & analytic commentaries. 91 p, mus ex. Author, Cleveland, 1935. 2.00

TEETGEN, ALEXANDER
Beethoven's symphonies: critically discussed. Pref John Broadhouse. 118 p, mus ex. Reeves (1879) 2nd △ ed 1915. (2.00)

THOMAS, THEODORE & STOCK, FREDERICK
Talks about Beethoven's symphonies analytical essays with diagrams.
Ed Rose Fay Thomas.   xiii, 218 p,
mus ex.   Ditson 1930.   2.50

TOVEY, DONALD FRANCIS
Beethoven: Pref Hubert J. Foss.
vii, 138 p, mus ex. Oxford 1945.   3.00
An analysis of Beethoven's methods of composition; Tovey's last work, left unfinished at his death in 1936.

A companion to Beethoven's pianoforte sonatas: bar-to-bar analysis.
xiv, 301 p, 1 illus, mus ex.   Royal
Schools of Music, London, 1931
(repr 1947).   5.00

WELLESZ, EGON
Introduction to the music of Beet- △
hoven. Dobson in prep.   1.00

WESTERBY, HERBERT
Beethoven and his piano works
(sonatas, concertos, variations, etc):
descriptive & analytic aid to their
understanding & rendering.   xii,
114 p, 3 pl (por, facs), 43 mus ex. △
Reeves n d (1931).   (2.25)
The Beethoven section from the author's "Piano works of the great composers."

BEGGAR'S OPERA
See also:
Ballad   Operetta
England (music in)   Phonograph Records
History   Poetry (ed Boas)
Opera   Song(s)

Note: Standard works apparently O/P (or not easily available) include those by Gagey ("Ballad opera", 1937), Schultz ("Gay's beggar's opera," 1923), etc. The list below includes only one representative recent edition of the opera text itself; others probably are available, especially in England.

GAY, JOHN
The beggar's opera.   136 p, illus
(Mariette Lydis). Heritage 1948.   4.50

KIDSON, FRANK
The beggar's opera: its predecessors
& successors.   109 p, frontis por, 7
illus (facs, etc).   Cambridge 1922. 1.25
A standard work, including a study of the music (John Christopher Pepusch) and its sources, p 64/79.

Begun, Semi Joseph. Author.
See Sound Recording & Reproduction.
Behnke, Emil. Author. See Voice.

Behnke, (Mrs) Kate Emil-. Author.
See Acting, Speech.
Note: Other books by Mrs Behnke—on singing, speech, & voice—apparently are O/P (or not easily available).

BEIDERBECKE, Bix
See:
D. Baker   Phonograph Records
Jazz   Popular Music

BEISSEL, Johann Conrad
KLEIN, WALTER CONRAD
Johann Conrad Beissel: mystic
& martinet, 1690–1768.   Forew
Richard H. Shryock. ix, 218 p, 5-p
bibl notes. Pennsylvania 1942.   2.25
"Pennsylvania Lives" series. A study of the singular "Vorsteher" of the Seventh Day Baptist monastic order & the Erphrate Cloisters, where much music was composed & published.

Bekker, Paul. Author. See Form.
Note: Numerous other books by Bekker apparently are O/P.

BEL CANTO
See also:
History   Opera
Italy (music in)   Singing
Note: Hermann Klein's "The bel canto" (1923) apparently is O/P.

MACHABEY, ARMAND. See App Ia.

REID, CORNELIUS L.
Bel canto: principles and practices.
211 p, mus ex, 4-p bibl.   Coleman
1950.   4.50

BELGIAN MUSIC/BELGIUM (Music in)
See also: Franck, History, Sax.

BRAGARD, ROGER. See App Ia.
LEIRENS, CHARLES
Belgian music. 40 p, 9 illus, paper.
Belgian Information Center, 630
5th Ave, N. Y., 1943.   △
A brief outline booklet: "Art, Life, & Science in Belgium" No 1. Apply to the Belgian Information Center.

Belgodère-Johannes, V. Author.
See App Ia.

BELL(S)/BELL-RINGING
See:
Carillon   History
Children-4   Instruments

Bell, Clair Hayden. Author. See Hager.
Bell, Leslie R. Author.
See Children–3.
Bellasis, Edward. Author.
See Cherubini.

BELLINI, Vincenzo
See: esp App Ic (Cavazzuti: "Bellini a Londra," in Italian).
Also:
History　　　　　　　Opera
Italian Music　　　　Phonograph Records

Note: Standard works apparently O/P (or not easily available) include those by Lloyd (in English); Pougin (in French); and in Italian by Amore, della Corte, Fraccardi, Parodi, Pizzetti, etc.

BELLMAN, Carl Mikael
Note: Van Loon's & Castagnetta's "The last of the troubadours" (1939) is O/P.

Bender, James Frederick. Compiler, author. See Pronunciation, Speech. Co-author (with Fields). See Speech.
(A) Benedictine of Stanbrook. Author. See Plainsong.
Benedictines of Solesmes. Editors. See Gregorian Chant.
Benét, Laura. Author. See App IIa (Lind juvenile).
Benn, Christopher. Author. See Mozart–3.
Benner, Charles Wallace. Author, co-editor (with Painter). See Baton–2.
Benoit, Camille. Author. See Wagner–3.
Benson, Barbara Elna. Author. See Industry.
Benthall, Michael. Author. See Ballet (ed Haskell).
Berberova, Nina. Author. See App Ia.

Berezowsky, Alice. Author.
Note: "Duet with Nicky" (Nicolai Berezowsky), 1943, is O/P.

BERG, Alban
See also:
Appreciation　　　　　Phonograph Records
Chamber Music　　　　Schoenberg
Composers–2　　　　　Tonality/Atonality
Concerto　　　　　　　Twelve-Tone
History　　　　　　　　　Technique
Modern Music　　　　　Vienna
Opera

REICH, WILLI
Alban Berg. Dobson in prep.　　△
"Contemporary Composers" series. Presumably based on Reich's biography in German (1937), written in collaboration with Theodor Wiesengrund-Adorno & Ernst Krenek.

Bergel, Kurt. Editor.
See App Ib (Schweitzer).
Berger, Arthur. Author. See Copland.
Bergmann, Leola Nelson. Author.
Bergmann, Ludwig. Author.
See Ultrasonics.
Bergmann, Walter George. Editor.
See Community Music.
Berkley, Harold. Author.
See Violin Playing.
Berkovits, George. Editor.
See App Ib (Editor & others).

BERKSHIRE FESTIVALS
See also:
America (music in)　　　Koussevitzky
Boston (music in)　　　　Yearbooks

HOWE, M. A. DEWOLFE
The tale of Tanglewood: scene of Berkshire muscal festivals.　Intro Koussevitzky. 101 p, photos, bds.
Vanguard 1946.　　　　　　　2.75

BERLIN, Irving
See: esp App IIa (Ewen juvenile).
Also:
America (music in)　　　Phonograph Records
American Music　　　　　Popular Music
Opera–3 (McSpadden)　　Songs (Mattfeld &
Operetta　　　　　　　　　　Davis)

Note: Alexander Woolcott's "Story of Irving Berlin" (1925) is O/P.

BERLINER, Emile
See:
Acoustics　　　　　　　Radio
Phonograph　　　　　　Sound Rec & Repro
Note: Wile's "Emile Berliner: maker of the microphone" (1926) apparently is O/P.

BERLIOZ, Hector
1. Autobiography, Own Writings
2. Life & Musical Works

BERLIOZ, Hector
(1. Autobiography, Own Writings)

(EVANS, EDWIN, SR, tr)
Mozart, Weber, and Wagner: with various other essays on musical subjects.　Tr Edwin Evans, Sr.　xiv, 216 p, frontis fac, 4 pors.　Reeves n d (1918?).　　　　　　　　(2.50)
Super-title (cover only): "A charming book of musical essays."　The 3rd volume of "Mid realms of song" ("A travers chants").　For Nos 1 & 2, see Beethoven–3 & Gluck.

(HOPKINSON, CECIL, comp)
A bibliography of the musical and

literary works of Hector Berlioz. Edinburgh (Scotland) Bibliographical Society 1950. △

No data are yet available on this work, except that it has been issued in a limited edition at £5, 5s, and in an ordinary edition at £3, 3s.

NEWMAN, ERNEST (*ed*)
Memoirs of Hector Berlioz, from 1803 to 1865: comprising his travels in Germany, Italy, Russia, & England. Tr Rachel & Eleanor Holmes. Annot & translation rev by Ernest Newman. xxiii, 533, xiii p, 11 pl (pors, etc). Knopf 1932 (1948).   5.00
Same. Tudor repr 1935 (1947).   2.98
Probably the most famous of all musical autobiographies, as well as an illuminating picture of the man & his times.

Author. See also:
Beethoven-3. 9 symphonies (1913) (2.50)
Conducting. The conductor (1915).   .60
Gluck. And his operas (1915).   (2.25)
Instrumentation. Treatise, enl & rev R. Strauss (1905/48).   7.50
——. Treatise, abridged   1.50

Notes: The Beethoven & Gluck books above are temporarily O/P, but are scheduled for early re-issue. . . . The dates given in parentheses above of course are those of the translated versions. . . . Newman's edition of "Evenings in the orchestra" (1929) apparently is O/P.

BERLIOZ
(2. Life & Musical Works)
See also:

Appreciation	Orchestral Music
Band-1	Paganini
Choir/Choral-3	Phonograph Records
Composers-1	Program Notes
Conducting	Romantic Era
French Music	Sax/Saxophone
History	Song(s)
Instrumentation	Symphony
Liszt	Themes
Mass	Timing
Opera	Vocal Music
Orchestra	

Note: Standard works apparently O/P (or not easily available) include those in English by Turner, Wotton, etc; in German by Pohl, Schrader, etc; in French by Cocquard, Ernst, Hippeau, Jullien, Masson, Prod'homme, Tiersot, etc.

BARZUN, JACQUES
Berlioz and the romantic century. 2 v: xv, 573; 511 p, 18 pl (pors), annot 74-p bibl & discography. Little Brown 1950.   12.50

The first large-scale work in English and a powerful plea for a re-valuation of one of the most controversial of all composers. The biographical sections are interwoven with critical essays on the works and on program music, romanticism, etc. The appendices include (in addition to the extensive annotated bibliography & discography) a chronology, list of errors in the scores, an index of misconceptions about Berlioz, a detailed criticism of Boschot's biography, etc, as well as a 53-p general index.

BOSCHOT, ADOLPHE. See App Ia.

DANISKAS, J.
Hector Berlioz. Tr W. A. G. Doyle-Davidson. 62 p, 21 pl (pors, facs, etc), mus ex, ½-p bibl, bds. Continental n d (1947).   2.50
"Symphonia" series of illustrated monographs, including a table of Berlioz's works.

ELLIOT, J. H.
Berlioz. ix, 243 p, 8 pl (pors, facs, etc), mus ex, 2-p bibl. Dent 1938 (1946).   2.50
"Master Musicians" series with the usual calendar, personalia, & catalogue of works. Presumably to be issued shortly in this country by Pellegrini & Cudahy.

GANZ, A. W.
Berlioz in London. Pref Sir Thomas Beecham. 222 p + 15 pl (pors, facs, etc). Quality Press Ltd., London, 1950.   3.75
An account of the five visits between 1847 & 1855, largely in Berlioz's own words; plus some hitherto unpublished correspondence between Berlioz & Henriette Smithson.

LOCKSPEISER, EDWARD
Berlioz. 16 p, cover por, paper. Novello n d (1939).   .40
Miniature biography ("great musicians").

POURTALÈS, GUY DE. See App Ia.

WOTTON, TOM S.
Hector Berlioz: four works. **52 p,** mus ex, paper. Oxford 1929.   1.00
"Musical Pilgrim" series of analyses: "Symphonie fantastique," "La Captive," and the overtures to "Benvenuto Cellini", & "Le Corsaire." The same author's more extensive study, "Hector Berlioz" (1935), apparently is O/P.

Berman, Eleanor Davidson. Author. See Jefferson.
Bernard, Robert. Author. See App Ia.

BERNERS, (Baron)
(Gerald Hugh Tyrwhitt-Wilson)
See:

Ballet	English Music
Composers–2 & 3c	Phonograph Records
Contemporary Music	Piano Music

Note: An autobiography, "First childhood" (1934), apparently is O/P (or not easily available in this country).

Bernstein, Martin. Author.
See Appreciation, Score-Reading.
Berr, Albert. Author. See App Ib.
Berry, Cecilia Ray. Compiler.
See Folksongs–2.
Bertensson, Sergei. Co-author (with Leyda).
See Mussorgsky, Rachmaninoff.
Bertrand, Paul. Author. See App Ia.
Besch, Hans. Author. See App Ib.
Bessaraboff, Nicholas. Author.
See Instruments.
Besseler, Heinrich. Author.
See App Ib (ed Bücken).
Best, Clarence J. Author.
See School Music–1.

BETHLEHEM BACH CHOIR
See: America (music in), Choir/Choral.
Note: Raymond Walter's "Bethlehem Bach Choir" (1918) is O/P.

Biancolli, Louis. Author.
See Tchaikovsky–2.   Co-author (with Bagar). See Opera–3.   Program Notes.

BIBLE (Music of the)
See: esp Jewish Music.
Also:

Ancient Music	Church Music
Asiatic Musics	Facsimiles
(note only)	(esp Deutsch)

BIBLIOGRAPHY (Musical)
See also: Libraries, Literature.
General Note: Musical bibliographies are discussed at some length in the compiler's introduction to this Guide, pages vii ff.

The books listed below probably are the only generally available works in this field (and in English) that deal with books on music & musicians, rather than collections of music itself. But of course most musical biographies and works on specialized subjects include bibliographies of various lengths & degrees of importance. Some of these are detailed lists of "sources consulted"; some are no more than cursory "related reading" lists. In the present Guide entries, the presence of a bibliography is indicated by the abbreviation

"bibl," usually prefixed by the number of pages the bibliography occupies. (Ex: "5-p bibl.") Critically annotated bibliographies are indicated by "annot bibl"; bibliographical references in the form of footnotes or end-of-chapter lists are indicated by "bibl refs" or "chap bibls."

Also included in the present Guide are a number of whole-book bibliographies dealing with specialized, individual subjects. For some of the more important of these, see —

Africa (note only, Varley)	History–1 (Strunk)
	Hofmeister (note)
American Music (Britton, Sonneck & Upton)	Industry (note only, Beckett & Fairley)
Arabian Music (Farmer)	Italian Music (Vogel, Einstein, note)
Asiatic Musics (note only)	Jewish Music (Sendry, Yasser)
Baroque Era (Gleason)	Latin America (Boggs, Thompson)
Berlioz–1 (Hopkinson)	Libraries (Myers)
Community Music (Nat. Recr. Assn.)	L. Mason (H. L. Mason)
Conducting (note only) Grosbayne)	Medieval/Renaissance (Gleason)
(The) Dance (Magriel)	Poe (Evans)
Education (Larson)	Radio (Broderick, Cooper, Rose)
Film Music (Nelson & Rubsamen)	Songs (Mattfeld & Davis)
Folklore (Felton, Haywood, Tully & Rael)	Rolland (Starr)
Health (Soibelman)	Yearbooks (Hinrichsen)
Hearing (Miller)	

In addition, extensive subject bibliographies are included in most of the larger Dictionaries & Encyclopedias of music.

Note: Among the more important pertinent works in English, apparently O/P (or not easily available) are Eric Blom's "A general index to modern musical literature in the English language" (Curwen 1927), the Library of Congress's "(Class M) Music and books on music" (GPO 1917), and the WPA Writers' "Bio-bibliographical index of musicians in the U. S. A. from colonial times" (Pan-American Union & Library of Congress 1941).

APPEL, LIVIA *(comp)*
Bibliographical citation in the social sciences and the humanities: a handbook of style for authors, editors, & students. 32 p, paper. Wisconsin (1940) 3rd ed 1949.   .75

BARTLETT, HAZEL *(comp)*
Catalogue of early books on music (before 1800) supplement: books acquired by the Library [of Congress] 1913–1942, with a list of books on music in Chinese & Japanese. iv, 143 p. Library of Congress (via GPO) 1944.   1.00
A supplement to the Gregory & Sonneck work below. The Chinese list is compiled & annotated by K. T. Wu (p 121/31), the Japanese

list by Shio Sakanishi (p 132/3). There is also a list of books from the Dayton C. Miller Collection (p 137/43).

EITNER, ROBERT.　See App Ib.

GLEASON, HAROLD & LÜPER, A. T. (comps)
A bibliography of books on music and collections of music: selected from works in the English language, generally available in the United States, with emphasis on those recently published, together with certain other standard works.　47 p, min, paper.　Compilers (Eastman School of Music), Rochester, N. Y. 1948.　　　　　　　　　　　1.75
Some 590 titles arranged in 8 categories (general comprehensive works, history & criticism, biography, etc.)

GOFF, FREDERICK R.
Early music books: in the rare books division of the Library of Congress. 16 p, illus, facs (some col), paper. Library of Congress 1949.　　　△
Reprinted from "Notes," December 1948. Apply to the Library of Congress.

GREGORY, J. (comp) & SONNECK, O. G. (ed)
Catalogue of early books on music (before 1800).　312 + 2 p.　Library of Congress (via GPO) 1913.　　　.60
Prepared by Julia Gregory under the direction of Sonneck, who also contributes a prefatory note. Entries are in the detailed style of the Library of Congress catalogue cards. For a supplement to this work, see Bartlett above.

KRETZSCHMAR, FLORENCE (& others, eds)
The music index: 1949 annual cumulation.　308 p.　Information Service　△ Inc, Detroit, 1950.　　　　　　25.00
Co-editors: Kurtz Myers & H. Dorothy Tilly. The first cumulative volume of a new monthly dictionary-catalogue of articles on music & musicians in some 81 American & foreign periodicals. Immensely detailed and elaborately cross-referenced.

(LIBRARY OF CONGRESS)
Music subject headings used on printed catalog cards of the Library of Congress.　Library of Congress (via GPO) 1950/1, in prep.　　　△
A long-awaited bibliographic style manual.

(NATIONAL ASSN OF SCHOOLS OF MUSIC)
List of books on music (1935) and six supplements (1936, 1939, 1941, 1943, 1946, 1948).　57, 14, 30, 31, 35, 39, & 63 p respectively, paper.　△
Complete set:　　　　　　　　1.25
Apply directly to Dr Burnet C. Tuthill, Mem-

phis College of Music, 1822 Overton Park, Memphis 12, Tennessee. Except for the original 1935 list, the entries are copiously (& in many cases critically) annotated. The original list, plus some of the earlier supplements, at least, is also the basis of the bibliography included in Thompson's "International cyclopedia of music & musicians," p 2298/2380 in the current 5th edition. (See Encyclopedias of Music.)

SCHOLES, PERCY A. (comp)
A list of books about music in the English language.　Prepared as an appendix to "The Oxford companion to music."　64 p.　Oxford 1940.　　　.75
Based largely on the author's own library & classified according to categories used in the "Companion" itself. This list was included in the 2nd edition of the "Companion" (see Dictionaries of Music), but has been omitted from later editions & now is available only separately. Presumably a revised version of the List is in preparation, but there has been no definite announcement.

SPRINGER, HERMANN: SCHNEIDER, MAX; & WOLFFHEIM, WERNER.　See App Ib.

WEIGL, BRUNO (ed).　See App Ib.

BILLINGS, William

See:

America (music in)	Hymns/Hymnody
American Music	Psalms/Psalmody
Choir/Choral-3	(MacDougall)
Composers-3a	Puritans

Bicchieri, Rocco.　Designer, compiler. See Instrumentation.

Bickham, George, Sr.　Penman, engraver. See Facsimiles.

Bigelow, Arthur Lynds.　Author. See Carillon.

Bigelow, Earl R.　Author (with others). See Form, Theory-2 (Cookson).

BIOGRAPHIES (of Musicians)

General Note: Biographies of individual musicians are entered under the individual names. (For a check-list of musicians represented by book entries, please refer to the list of Major Subject-Headings.)

See also:

Appreciation	History
Composers	Who's Who
Dictionaries of Music	Yearbooks
Encyclopedias of Music	App IIa (juveniles)

Also: "Great Lives" series, "Master Musicians" series, "Schirmer's Contemporary Composers" series, "Symphonia" series, & the Novello series below.

BIOGRAPHIES ("GREAT MUSICIANS" SERIES)

Note: This is a series of miniature biographies (actually biographical sketches), uniform in (paper-cover) format, edited by William McNaught, & prepared by various authors.

For the individual booklets, see ——

Bach–1	Liszt
Beethoven–2	Mendelssohn–2
Berlioz–2	Mozart–2
Brahms–1	Purcell
Chopin–1	Rossini
Debussy–2	Schubert–1
Dvořák	Schumann–2
Elgar	Tchaikovsky–1
Gluck	Verdi–1
Handel–1	Wagner–2
Haydn	Weber

BIRDS (& Music)

Note: Standard works apparently O/P (or not easily available) include those by Brand, Garstang, Saunders, Witchell, etc.

See also: App IIb (Mason juvenile).

ARLTON, ALEXANDER V.
Songs and other sounds of birds. xi, 195 p, mus ex, bibl. Author, Parkland, Washington, 1949. △ 5.00

MATHEWS, F. SCHUYLER
Field book of wild birds and their music: a description of the character & music of birds . . . with songs reproduced in musical notation. xxxv, 262 p, 53 pl (some col), mus ex. Putnam 1904 (& later eds). 3.95

Birge, Edward Bailey. Author & co-author (with McConathy, et al.). See School Music–1.

BISPHAM, David (Scull)

See:

America (music in)	Opera
History	Singers

Note: The autobiographical "A Quaker singer's recollections" (1920) is O/P.

BIZET, Georges

See also:

Appreciation	Phonograph Records
Ballet	Program Notes
Composers–1	Song(s)
French Music	Themes
History	Timing
Merimée (note)	Vocal Music
Opera	

Note: Standard works apparently O/P (or not easily available) include those by Parker, etc; in German by Istel, Voss, Weissmann, etc; in French by Bellaigue, Brancour, Delmas, Galabert, Gauthier-Villars, Landormy, etc.

COOPER, MARTIN
Bizet: Carmen. 31 p + 8 pl, 1–p bibl, mus ex, paper. Boosey 1947. .60
Georges Bizet. 136 p, 1–p bibl, mus ex. Oxford 1938. 2.50
The booklet is in the "Covent Garden Operas" series; the larger work is a biography, including a critical discussion of Bizet's compositions.

CURTISS, MINA
The life and times of Georges Bizet. In prep. △

DEAN, WINTON
Bizet. x, 262 p, 8 pl (pors, facs, etc), 2–p bibl, mus ex. Dent 1948. 2.50
"Master Musicians" series, with the usual calendar, personalia, & catalogue of works. Presumably to be issued shortly in this country by Pellegrini & Cudahy.
Introduction to the music of Bizet. 61 p, mus ex. Dobson 1950. (1.00)

NIETZSCHE, FRIEDRICH. See App Ib.

Blancké, Wilton Wallace. Author (with Speck). See Theory–2.

BLAND, James A.

See also: America (music in), Negro Music.

DALY, JACK
A song in his heart: the life & times of James A. Bland. Winston in prep. 3.00
The story of the composer of "Carry me back to old Virginny," etc, illustrated with contemporary prints.

Blasis, Carlo. Author. See (The) Dance.
Bleeker, James W. Author. See Theory–3.
Blegen, Theodore Christian. Editor (with Ruud). See Folksongs–1.
Blesh, Rudi (Rudolph Pickett). Author. See Jazz.

BLISS, Arthur (Edward Drummond)

See: esp Ballet (ed Haskell, Posner: "Miracle in the Gorbals," "Checkmate").

Also:

Choir/Choral–3	English Music
(esp Manners)	History
Composers–2 & 3c	Phonograph Records
Contemporary Music	Program Notes

BLITZSTEIN, Marc

See:

American Music	Opera
Composers–2 & 3a	Phonograph Records
Contemporary Music	Program Notes

BLOM, Eric

A musical postbag.   x, 318 p, 16
illus (Leo Hardy).   Dent (1941) 4th △
ed 1949.   (3.50)
*A collection of musical essays, originally
published in the Birmingham "Post" in the
1930's, by a noted British critic.*

Author, compiler.   See also:

Ballet.   Ed Haskell: Hamlet &
Miracle in the Gorbals, including
an essay by Blom (1949).   .50
Composers–1.   Some great (1944).   2.00
Dictionaries of Music.   Everyman's
dictionary of music (1946/8).   3.50
England.   Music in (1942/7).   (.35)
Mozart–2.   Biography (1935).   2.50
Mozart–3.   Ed Crozier: Cosl fan
tutte, incl Blom essay (1945).   .50
Schubert–1.   Miniature biog (1938).   .40
Tchaikovsky–2.   Orch works (1927).   1.00

*Note: Blom's "General index to modern mu-
sical literature" (1927) and numerous other
books apparently are O/P (or not easily available in this country).*

BLOW, John

See also:

Choir/Choral–3   History
Church Music   Purcell
English Music   Restoration Era

SHAW, HAROLD WATKINS
John Blow, doctor of music.   10 p,
paper.   Hinrichsen n d (1946?).   1.25
*A miniature biography, originally published
in the "Musical Times," 1937.*

BLUES

See: esp Negro Music, Negro Spirituals.
Also:

America (music in)   Morton
Folklore   Phonograph Records
Folksongs–2   Popular Music
Handy   Songbooks
Jazz   Ethel Waters
Mezzrow

Blume, Friedrich.   Author.
See Bach–1, App Ib (ed Bücken).   Editor.
See App Ib.
Blumenfeld, Harold.   Translator.
See Praetorius (note).
Boas, Frederick Samuel.   Editor.
See Poetry.
Boggs, Ralph Steele.   Compiler.
See Folklore.
Bohman, Esther L.   Author (with Dillon).
See Libraries.

BOITO, Arrigo

See: esp Ic (Nardi biog, in Italian).
Also:

Appreciation   Opera
Composers–1   Phonograph Records
History   Program Notes
Italian Music   Verdi

*Note: Standard works apparently O/P (or not
easily available) include those in Italian by
Ballo, Boccardi, Pompeati, etc.*

BOLIVIA (Music in)
See: Latin America.

Boll, André.   Author.   See App Ia.

BONAVIA, Ferruccio

Musicians in Elysium.   125 p, illus
(Beatrice MacDermott).   Secker
1949.   (1.50)
*The Italian-British critic's amusing imagin-
ary dialogues between Wagner & Rossini,
Mozart & Don Giovanni, J. Strauss & Tchaikovsky, Beethoven & Napoleon, etc.*

Author.   See also:
Mozart–2.   Miniature biog (1938).   .40
Rossini.   Miniature biog (1941)   .40
Verdi–1.   Biography (1930/47).   (2.50)
Verdi–2.   Rigoletto (1947).   .60

Bonavia-Hunt, Noel Aubrey.   Author.
See Organ.
Boni, Margaret Bradford.   Editor.
See Folksongs–1.
Bonsall, Elizabeth Hubbard.   Author.
See Hymns/Hymnody–2.

BOP
See: Jazz (esp Griffin, Feather).

Borch, Gaston Louis Christopher.
Author.   See Instrumentation.
Borgeaud, Henri.   Editor.
See App Ia (Debussy correspondence)
Borland, John Ernest.   Author.
See Instruments, School Music–1.

BORODIN, Alexander Porfirievitch

See also:

Appreciation   Phonograph Records
Ballet   Program Notes
Chamber Music   Rimsky-Korsakov
Composers–1 & 3e   Russian Music
History   String Quartet
Opera   Symphony
Orchestral Music   Themes

Note: The Stassov-Habets "Borodin & Liszt"

(1893/6) apparently is O/P, as are several works on Borodin by Russian authors.

ABRAHAM, GERALD
Borodin the composer and his music, a descriptive & critical analysis of his work & study of his value as an art-force. 205 p, 5 pors, mus ex. Reeves n d (1927). (4.00)

Borowski, Felix. Co-author, editor (with Upton). See Opera-3, Program Notes.
Borren, Charles van den.
Catalogued under Van den Borren, Charles.
Bory, Robert. Editor. See App Ia.
Bos, Coenraad Valentyn van. Author.
See Accompaniment.
Boschot, Adolphe. Author. See App Ia.
Bostelmann, Louis J. Author.
See Violin Playing.

BOSTON (Music in)

See also:

America (music in)	Koussevitzky
Boston Symphony	H. T. Parker
History	Publishing

HUMPHREY, MARTHA BURNHAM
An eye for music: drawings & text. 108 p, illus. H. M. Teich & Co (Algonquin Press), Boston, 1949. 3.50
Rehearsal sketches with informal notes on the Boston Symphony, Koussevitzky, Symphony Hall visitors, "Pops", Esplanade & Tanglewood concerts, etc.

JOHNSON, H. EARLE
Musical interludes in Boston, 1795-1830. Forew Otto Kinkeldey. xvii, 366 p, 6 pl. Columbia 1943. 6.00
"Columbia Studies in Musicology" No 5: a continuation of Sonneck's studies on concert life in America, with contemporary documentation (lists of publishers & publications, teachers, programs, etc).

Symphony Hall, Boston. Intro M. A. DeWolfe Howe. vii, 431 p + 4 photos. Little Brown 1950. 6.00
An anecdotal history of music in America for the last 50 years in terms of a famous auditorium & the artists who have appeared there. The appendices include lists of orchestras, conductors, & soloists; works performed by the Boston Symphony; data on the new organ, etc.

BOSTON SYMPHONY ORCHESTRA

See:

America (music in)	History
Berkshire Festivals	Koussevitzky
Boston (music in)	Orchestra

Note: M. A. DeWolfe Howe's history of the orchestra (1914, rev ed 1931) currently is O/P, as are the collections of Philip Hale's program notes (1935/39).

Bosworth, Harriette Dexter. Author.
See Teaching-3.
Botkin, Benjamin Albert. Editor.
See Folklore.
Botsford, Florence Hudson. Editor.
See Folksongs-1.
Bouchor, Jean. Author. See App Ia.
Boult, (Sir) Adrian Cedric. Author.
See Bach-2, Conducting.
Bouvet, Charles. Author. See App Ia.

BOW/BOWING

See:

Instruments	Viola/Viola Playing
String Instruments	Violin
String Playing	Violin Playing
String Quartet	Violoncello Playing

Note: Standard works apparently O/P (or not easily available) include those by Balfour, Saint George, Wunderlich (in German), etc.

Bowen, Catherine Drinker. Author.
See Amateur Music, Tchaikovsky-1.
Bowen, York. Author.
See Piano Playing-2.
Bowman, Edward Morris. Author.
See Children-1. Editor. See Theory-2 (Weitzmann).

BOXES (Music-)

MOSORIAK, ROY
The curious history of music boxes. 242 p, 40 pl. Lightner Publishing Co., Chicago, 1943. 5.00

BOY VOICES

See also:

Children-7	School Music-4
Choir/Choral-1 & 2	Singing
Community Music	Voice

Note: Among the numerous works on this subject, apparently O/P (or not easily available), are those by Curwen, Fleming, Ivemey, Martin, Stubbs, etc.

JOHNSON, CLAUDE ELLSWORTH
The training of boys' voices. vii, 70 p, frontis, mus ex. Ditson (1906) enl ed 1935. 1.25
"Music Students Library" series.

MELLALIEU, W. NORMAN
The boy's changing voice. 34 p, mus ex, paper. Oxford 1935 (3rd pr 1947). .50
Practical notes for boys' choir leaders.

MOODY, CHARLES H.
The choir-boy in the making: a
practical & concise treatise on the
training of choristers. 44 p, mus ex.
Oxford (1923) 2nd ed 1939 (2nd pr
1944). .75

NICHOLSON, SIDNEY H.
Boys' choirs. 21 p, mus ex, paper.
(1922) via C. Fischer. .40
*"Festival Booklet" No 9, originally published
by Paterson, Scotland.*

NOBLE, T. TERTIUS
The training of the boy chorister.
24 p, mus ex, paper. G. Schirmer
1943. .50
*Training methods used with the choir of
St. Thomas Church, New York City.*

STOCKS, H. C. L.
The training of boy choristers. 30
p, mus ex, paper. Musical Opinion
1931. .50

Boyd, Charles Newell. Author (with Earhart). See Theory–2. Co-editor (with Pratt).
See Dictionaries of Music (Grove, sup v).

Boyd, Morrison Comegys. Author.
*Note: The fine "Elizabethan music & mu-
sical criticism" (1940) unfortunately has
just been announced O/P.*

Boyd, Neva L. Author (with Dunlavy).
See Dances–2.
Boyden, David Dodge. Author.
See History–3.
Boys, Henry. Author.
See Britten (Britten & others).
Bozza, Eugène. Compiler. See App Ia.
Bradley, Lionel. Author. See Ballet.
Bradley, Vincent. Author.
See Sight-Playing & Reading.
Bragard, Roger. Author. See App Ia.
Bragers, Achille Pierre. Author.
See Gregorian Chant.

BRAHMS, Johannes
1. Life   2. Works

BRAHMS (1. Life)
See also:

Appreciation	Letters
Autographs (Harrow	Program Notes
Replica)	Romantic Era
Composers–1	Schumann
History	

Also: App IIa (juveniles by Deucher, Goss
& Schauffler).

*Note: Standard works apparently O/P (or not
easily available) include collections of letters
ed by Litzmann, Kalbeck, etc; biographies in
English or English translations by Colles,
Deiters, Dietrich, Erb, Fuller Maitland,
Henschel, Lee, Pulver, Schauffler, Specht, etc;
in German by Kalbeck, Laux, Reimann, etc.*

CULSHAW, JOHN
Brahms: an outline of his life &
music. Pref Alec Robertson. 31 p.
mus ex, paper. Hinrichsen n d
(1947?). 1.25
"Miniature Survey" series M–19.

GEIRINGER, KARL
Brahms: his life and work. Tr H.
B. Weiner & Bernard Miall. xv,
383 p, 11 pl, mus ex, 5–p bibl. Oxford (1936) 2nd rev ed 1947. 5.00
*An enlarged edition, with 40 new letters, of a
standard biography first published in German
in 1934.*

HILL, RALPH
Brahms. 143 p, frontis por, 2-p bibl.
(1941) Wyn 1948. 1.00
*"Great Musicians" series, originally pub-
lished in the "Great Lives" series, Duckworth,
London, 1941.*

LANDORMY, PAUL. See App Ia.

LATHAM, PETER
Brahms. ix, 230 p, 8 pl (pors, facs,
etc), mus ex, 2–p bibl. Dent 1948;
Pellegrini 1949. 2.50
*"Master Musicians" series (superseding an
earlier biography by Erb), with the usual
calendar, personalia, catalogue of works.*

MAY, FLORENCE
The life of Brahms. Intro Ralph
Hill. 2 v: xv, 699 p, 13 pl (pors, etc),
2 facs. (1905) 2nd rev ed Reeves
n d (1948?). 10.00
*Originally published by Arnold, London;
revised & enlarged by the author (a pupil of
Brahms) for a German edition of 1911.*

NIEMANN, WALTER
Brahms. Tr Catherine Alison Phillips. xiii, 492 p, 8 pl (pors, etc), 6–p
bibl. Knopf 1929 (6th pr 1947). 4.00
*A standard study of the man & his music,
originally published in German in 1920. A
Tudor repr (1929) apparently in O/P.*

OREL, ALFRED. See App Ib.

REFARDT, EDGAR. See App Ib.

REHBERG, PAULA & WALTER. See App Ib.

ROBERTSON, ALEC
Brahms. 16 p, cover por, paper.
Novello n d (1939).   .40
Miniature biography ("great musicians").

WIDMANN, JOSEF VIKTOR. See App Ib.

BRAHMS (2. Works)

See also:

Appreciation	Program Notes
Chamber Music	Song(s)
Choir/Choral-3	String Quartet
Composers-1	Symphony
Concerto	Themes
Orchestral Music	Timing
Phonograph Records	Violin Music
Piano Music	Vocal Music

Note: Standard works apparently O/P (or not easily available) include those in English or English translations by Colles, Drinker (see note under Drinker entry below), Friedländer, Harrison, Mason, Murdoch, etc; in German by Barth, Brand, Burckhardt, Knoor & Riemann, Krause, Nagel, etc.

ANDERSON, W. R.
Introduction to the music of Brahms.
84 p, mus ex. Dobson 1949.   1.00
A brief analytical survey, with concise catalogue of works & list of recordings.

BROWNE, PHILIP AUSTIN
Brahms: the symphonies. **72 p, mus ex,** paper. Oxford 1933.   1.00

COLLES, H. C.
The chamber music of Brahms. 64 p, mus ex, paper. Oxford 1933.   1.00
Both works above are in the "Musical Pilgrim" series of analyses. For a companion booklet, see Lee below.

DRINKER, HENRY S.
The chamber music of Johannes Brahms. 130 p, 6 pors, 2–p bibl notes. Elkan 1932.   1.25
Originally prepared as program notes for the Brahms centenary at Philadelphia.

Note: For information on the Drinker translations of Brahms's vocal works, see the note under the author-entry for Drinker.

EVANS, EDWIN, Sr
Historical, descriptive, and analytical account of the entire works of Johannes Brahms; treated in the order of their opus number, preceded by a didactic section, and followed by copious tables of reference; specially designed for the use of concert-goers, pianists, singers, & students. **4 v.** Reeves 1912/36.

V 1: Handbook to the vocal works of Brahms. xviii, 599 p, frontis por, tables. 1912 (1950).   (7.50)

V 2: Handbook to the chamber & orchestral music of Brahms: 1st series (to Op 67 inclusive). viii, 304 p, mus ex, tables. N d (1933, repr 1950).   (6.00)

V 3: Handbook to the chamber & orchestral works of Brahms: 2nd series (Op 68 to the end). xi, 351 p, mus ex, tables. N d (1935, repr 1949).   (6.00)

V 4: (originally scheduled for V 2): Handbook to the pianoforte works of Brahms: comprising the complete solo works, works for piano & orchestra, also works for piano duet and organ, works as applicable to pianoforte solo. xv, 327 p, mus ex, tables, 7–p bibl. N d (1936, repr 1950).   (6.00)

One of the (if not the) most extensive & exhaustive series of musical analyses in the available literature. The four volumes cover the complete works in individual, detailed rhythmic, thematic, & formal analysis,— occupying over 1500 text pages and embodying over 1000 examples in music notation.

LEE, E. MARKHAM
Brahms's orchestral works. **45 p, mus ex,** paper. Oxford 1931.   1.00
"Musical Pilgrim" series of analyses: overtures, serenades, variations, & violin concerto. For companion booklets on the symphonies & chamber works, see above, Browne & Colles respectively.

MASON, DANIEL GREGORY
The chamber music of Brahms. xii, 276 p, frontis por, 3 facs, mus ex, brief bibl. (Macmillan 1933) Edwards repr 1950.   3.50
Listed O/P above, this standard analytical study has just been reprinted.

Brand, Erick D. Author.
See Instruments.
Brandl, Willy. Author. See App Ib.

BRASS INSTRUMENTS

See:

Band-1	Sax/Saxophone
Bugle	Trombone
Instrumentation	Trumpet
Instruments	Wind Instruments
Orchestra	

Bray, Mabel E. Co-author (with McConathey & others). See School Music-1.

BRAZIL (Music in)/BRAZILIAN MUSIC

See also: Latin America.

Note: Pertinent works apparently O/P (or not easily available) include Almeida's "Historia da musica brasileira" (1926), and pamphlets by Andrade, Siqueira Coutinho, Luper, etc.

CORRÊA DE AZEVEDO, LUIS HEITOR
Brief history of music in Brazil. (Text in Portuguese & English) tr Elizabeth M. Tylor & Mercedes de Moura Reis. vi, 92 p, map, 7–p bibl, paper. Pan American Union 1948. .75

"Pan American Music" series No 16: a concise over-all survey, with notes on individual Brazilian composers & their works.

HOUSTON-PERET, ELSIE (*ed*). See App Ia ("Chants populaires du Brésil").

BREATHING

See also:

Health	Speech
Singing	Voice

Note: Pertinent works apparently O/P (or not easily available) include those by Dodds, Kofler, Myers, etc.

KELLOG, IRWIN
Why breathe?: a handbook of illustrated exercises for correct breathing. 62 p, illus, paper. G. Schirmer (1927) 1939. .60

Brée, Malwine. Author.
See Piano Playing–1.
Bregman, Adolph. Co-editor (with Coleman). See Folksongs–2.
Brelet, Gisèle. Author. See App Ia.
Brennecke, Ernest, Jr. Author.
See Milton.
Brent-Smith, Alexander. Author.
See Schubert–2.
Breuer, Katharina. Author.
See Dances–2 (Alford, ed).
Brewster, Mela Sedillo. Author.
See Dances–2.

BRIAN, Havergal

NETTEL, REGINALD
Ordeal by music: the strange experience of Havergal Brian. ix, 147 p, frontis por, 3 facs. Oxford 1945. 3.25
The biography of a little-known British composer & writer on music.

Bridge, (Sir) John Frederick. Author.
See Counterpoint–2.

Note: Several other books by Bridge, including the autobiographical "A Westminster pilgrim" (1918), apparently are O/P (or not easily available in this country).

Briggs, G. A. Author.
See Sound Rec & Reproduction.
Brindejont-Offenbach, Jacques. Author.
See App Ia.
Brink, Carol Ryrie. Author.
See Hutchinson Family.

BRITAIN (Music in)

See: England (music in)

BRITISH MUSEUM

See: Bibliography, England, Libraries.

Note: We have no availability data on various catalogues and accession-lists published by the British Museum.

BRITISH MUSIC

See: English Music.

General Note: Although of course there is an exact distinction between (Great) Britain and England, it is not always observed in books dealing with music & musicians. And while the general tendency in Great Britain today is to use "British" where "English" probably would have been used in the past, Americans are more accustomed to the latter term.

Britt, (Rev) Matthew. Author.
See Hymns/Hymnody–1.

BRITTEN, Benjamin

See also:

Appreciation	Modern Music
Choir/Choral–3	Opera
(esp Manners)	Phonograph Records
Composers–2 & 3c	Program Notes
Contemporary Music	Song(s)
English Music	Vocal Music

BRITTEN, BENJAMIN (*& others*)
The rape of Lucretia: a symposium. △
101 p, illus. Lane 1948. (7.50)

A commemorative publication, with reproductions of John Piper's stage designs, photographs of the original production, and discussions of the opera by Britten, Piper, Henry Boys, & Eric Crozier.

CROZIER, ERIC (*ed*)
Benjamin Britten: Peter Grimes. 55 p, frontis por, fac, 11 pl (designs by Kenneth Green), mus ex, paper. Lane 1945 (1946). .50
"Sadler's Wells Opera Books" No 3: introduction by Britten and essays by E. M. Forster ("George Crabbe: the poet & the

man"), *Edward Sackville-West ("The musical & dramatic structure"), & Montague Slater ("The story of the opera").*

KELLER, HANS
Britten: Rape of Lucretia & Albert Herring. 35 p + 8 pl, mus ex, paper. Boosey 1947. .60
Albert Herring: analytical guide. 19 p, mus ex, paper. Boosey 1949. .25
The latter pamphlet is an extract from the booklet above, one of the "Coveni Garden Operas" series.

STUART, CHARLES
Britten: Peter Grimes. 35 p + 8 pl, mus ex, paper. Boosey 1947. .60
"Covent Garden Operas" series.

WHITE, ERIC WALTER
Benjamin Britten: a sketch of his life & work. 109 p, frontis por, mus ex, 2–p bibl, paper. Boosey 1948. △
A first, short biography, available in England (price 7/6), but for some reason apparently restricted (1949/50) from sale in the U.S.A.

Britton, Allen P. Compiler.
See American Music.

BROADCASTING
See: esp Radio, Radio Music.
Also:
Acoustics   Sound Rec & Repro
Appreciation   Television

Broadhouse, John. Author.
See Acoustics, Organ, Violin.
Brock, Earl E. Author.
See Hymns/Hymnody–2.
Brockway, Wallace. Author.
See Liszt. (With Weinstock). See Composers–1, Opera–1.
Broder, Nathan. Author.
See Barber. Editor. See Schirmer's Contemporary Composers Series. Translator (with Mendel). See Mozart–2 (Einstein).
Broderick, Gertrude G. Compiler.
See Radio.

BROEKMAN, David
The shoestring symphony. 247 p. S & S 1948. 2.75
The lively misadventures of a composer in Hollywood during the depression era.

Bronarski, Ludwik. Author. See App Ia.
Brook, Donald. Author. See:
Composers–2. Gallery (1946). 4.25
Composers–3d. 5 French (1947). 4.50
Composers–3e. 6 Russian (1947). 3.50

Conductors. Gallery (1945/6). 3.50
Opera–3. Companion (1947). 4.25
Pianists. Masters of the keyboard (1946). 3.50
Singers. Of today (1949). 3.75
Violinists. Of today (1948/9). 3.00

Brooks, B. Martin. Author (with Brown).
See School Music–1.
Brower, Harriette. Author.
See Children–5, Piano Music, App IIa.
Brown, Calvin Smith. Author.
See Literature.
Brown, George. Co-editor (with Flanders).
See Folksongs–2.
Brown, Harry A. Co-author (with Brooks).
See School Music–1.
Brown, Jean Parkman. Author.
See Children–3.
Brown, Ralph Morse. Author.
See Singing–1.
Brown, Ray F. Editor.
See Psalms/Psalmody.
Brown, William Earl. Author.
See Singing–2.
Browne, Philip Austin. Author.
See Brahms–2.
Bruce, Robert. Author.
See Songwriting.

BRUCKNER, Anton
See also:
Appreciation   Mahler
Choir/Choral–3   Phonograph Records
Church Music   Program Notes
Composers–1 & 3b   Symphony
  (esp Newlin)   Vienna
History   Walter

Note: Pertinent works apparently O/P (or not easily available) include a booklet in English by Engel; and books in German by Decsey, Göllerich & Auer, Gräflinger, Schwebsch, Kurth, Orel, etc.

AUER, MAX. See App Ib.

BRUCKNER, ANTON (letters). See App Ib.

FARGA, FRANZ. See App Ib.

GRÜNINGER, FRITZ. See App Ib.

LAUX, KARL. See App Ib.

MACHABEY, ARMAND. See App Ia.

ODERMATT, HERMANN. See App Ib.

REFARDT, EDGAR. See App Ib.

VASSENHOVE, LÉON VAN. See App Ia.

WOLFF, WERNER
Anton Bruckner: rustic genius. Intro Walter Damrosch. 283 p, frontis

por, fac, silhouettes (Otto Böhler), mus ex, 2–p bibl. Dutton 1942.   **4.00**
The first full-length biography in English; including a chronology & analyses (but no complete catalogue) of the works. For a revised version in German, see App Ib.

Brunold, Paul. Author. See Couperin.
Bruyer, José. Author. See App Ia.
Buchanan, Fannie Rebecca. Author. See App IIb (juvenile).
Buchanan, Walter. Author. See Solfege/Solfeggio.

BUCK, (Sir) Percy Carter

The scope of music. 135 p, 5 illus, 40 mus ex, 3–p bibl. Oxford (1924) 2nd ed 1938 (3rd pr 1945).   **2.00**
Ten lectures on aesthetics, music criticism, appreciation, psychology, etc.
Author, editor. See also:
Harmony–2. Unfigured (1911).   **1.75**
History–1. Oxford, intro v & v 1 & 2, ed Buck (note only).
History–3. History (1929/47).   **(1.35)**
Psychology. For musicians (1944).   **2.00**
Note: Several other books by Buck apparently are O/P (or not easily available).

Bücken, Ernst. Author, editor. See App Ib.
Buday, George. Author. See Dances–2 (Alford, ed).
Budge, Helen. Author. See Harmony–1.
Buenzod, Emanuel. Author. See App Ia.

BUGLE

See also:
Band–1	School Music–3
Instruments	Trumpet
Military Music	Wind Instruments

CANTY, DANIEL J.
Bugle signals, calls, & marches for Army, Navy, Marine Corps, Revenue Cutter Service, & National Guard. iii, 68 p, mus ex, paper. Ditson 1927.   **.50**

SAFRANEK, V. F.
Complete instructive manual for field trumpet and drum: containing the signal calls used in the United States Army, Navy, Marine Corps, Revenue Cutter, National Guard, & Boy Scouts Service, together with words to trumpet calls, & all necessary information. xvi, 135 p, illus, mus ex, paper. C. Fischer (rev ed 1918) newly rev 1942.   **.75**

Buhrman, Thomas Scott Godfrey. Author. See Bach–1.
Bukofzer, Manfred F. Author. See Baroque Era, Medieval/Renaissance (Bukofzer, Kantorowicz), Rounds.
Bulber, Francis Gerard. Author. See Teaching–2.

BULL, (Dr) John

See:
Church Music	History
Elizabethan Music	Keyboard Instruments
English Music	& Music

Note: Leigh Henry's "Dr John Bull" (1937) apparently is O/P (or not easily available in this country).

BULL, Ole Bornemann

See also:
History	Violin Music
Norway (music in)	Violinists

Also: App IIa (Acker, Headland juveniles).

SMITH, MORTIMER
The life of Ole Bull. ix, 220 p, illus. Princeton 1943 (2nd pr 1947).   **3.00**

The first full-length biography in English: originally published for the American-Scandinavian Foundation, and including a note on Bull's violins & a bibliographical note.

BÜLOW, Hans Guido von

See:
History	Pianists
Liszt	Wagner

Note: English translations of von Bülow's memoirs & letters apparently are O/P.

Burch, Gladys. Author. See App IIa & IIb (juveniles).
Burchenal, Elizabeth. Editor, compiler. See Dances–2.
Burgess, Francis. Author. See Plainsong.
Burgin, Miron. Editor. See Latin America.
Buritt, William Nelson. Author. See Singing–2.
Burk, John Naglee. Author. See Beethoven–2. Editor. See Wagner–1.
Burke, Cassie. Author (with Meierhoffer & Phillips). See School Music–2.
Burkert, Otto. Compiler. See App Ib (Weigl, ed).

BURLEIGH, Cecil

See also: American Music, Composers–3a.

HOWARD, JOHN TASKER
Cecil Burleigh. 32 p, frontis **por,**
mus ex, paper. C. Fischer 1929.   .25
List of works & brief analyses.

Burlin, (Mrs) Natalie Curtis.
Catalogued under Curtis, Natalie.

BURMA (Music in)/BURMESE MUSIC
See: India (music in).
*Note: The bibliography of Asiatic Musics
(see note under Asiatic Musics) contains a
section on Burma in its 8th installment,
Music Library Association "Notes" for
December 1949.*

BURNEY, Charles
See also: England (music in), History.
*Note: Dr Burney's own celebrated "General
history of music" (1789, repr 1935) apparently is O/P (or not easily available in this
country).*

SCHOLES, PERCY A.
The great Dr Burney: his life, his
travels, his works, his family, & his
friends. 2 v: xxxix, 379; xiv, 438 p,
46 pl, 62–p bibl. Oxford 1948.   19.00
*A truly encyclopaedic study of the historian
& of the times in which he lived.*

Burns, Samuel Thompson. Author.
See School Music–4.
Burrell, (Hon. Mrs.) Mary. Collector.
See Wagner–1 (ed Burk).
Burris-Meyer, Harold. Author (with Cole).
See Theatre.
Burrowes, John Freckleton. Author.
See Piano Playing–2.
Burrows, Raymond. Compiler (with Red-
mond). See Themes.
Burton, Jack. Compiler.
See Popular Music.
Busch, Carl. Co-author (with McCray).
See Conducting.
Busch, Fritz. Author. See App Ib.
Bush, Alan Dudley. Author.
See Counterpoint–1.
Bush, Margaret. Editor.
See App IIa (Gilbert & Sullivan juvenile).

BUSINESS (Music-)
See: esp Career.
Also:

America (music in)	Publishing
(esp Carpenter)	Singing–3
Appreciation	Teaching–2
(esp Ulrich)	(esp Gibbin)

BUSONI, Ferruccio (Benvenuto)
See also:

Appreciation	Opera
Composers–2	Phonograph Records
Concerto	Pianists
Contemporary Music	Piano Music
History	Program Notes

*Note: Pertinent works apparently O/P (or not
easily available in this country) include
those in German by Bekker, Leichtentritt,
Nadel, Selden-Goth, etc; in Italian by Guer-
rini, Santelli, etc; also the English translation of Busoni's own booklet, "Towards a
new esthetic of music" (1911).*

BUSONI, FERRUCCIO
Ferruccio Busoni: letters to his wife.
Tr Rosamond Ley. 319 p, 8 pl.
Longmans 1938.   6.00
*A comprehensive selection from more than
800 letters from the composer-pianist to his
wife. The collection appeared originally in
German (edited by Schuh) in 1935.*

DENT, EDWARD J.
Ferruccio Busoni: a biography. xv,
368 p, 24 pl, mus ex. Oxford 1933.   O/P
*The standard biography in English, includ-
ing a list of Busoni's repertory as a pianist
and a catalogue of his compositions.
Note: Apparently just gone O/P (late 1950),
but surely only temporarily.*

Bussler, Ludwig. Author.
See Form (Cornell), Harmony–2, Theory–3.
Buttree, Julia M. (Seton). Author.
See Indians (American).

BUXTEHUDE, Dietrich
See:

Appreciation	Keyboard Instruments
Bach–1	& Music
Baroque Era	Organ Music
Choir/Choral–3	Phonograph Records
Church Music	Program Notes
Composers–1	

*Note: Pertinent works apparently O/P (or not
easily available in this country) include those
in German by Crusnick, Jimmerthal, Stahl,
etc; Hagen (in Danish), Pirro (in French),
etc.*

Buzzi-Peccia, Arturo. Author.
See Singing–2.

BYRD, William
See also:

Appreciation	History
Baroque Era	Keyboard Instruments
Choir/Choral–3	& Music
Church Musi	Madrigal
Composers–1	Medieval/Renaissance
Elizabethan Music	Phonograph Records
English Music	Program Notes

FELLOWES, EDMUND H.
William Byrd. xi, 271 p, 9 pl (pors,
facs, etc), mus ex, bibl refs. Oxford
(1936) 2nd ed 1948.   4.50

*Revision of a standard work, first published
in 1936, and itself an expansion of "Byrd:
a short account," published in 1923 for the
Byrd tercentenary.*

Byrnes, Aquinas. Editor.
See Hymns/Hymnody–1.
Bytovetski, Pavel L. Author.
See Violin Playing.

BYZANTINE MUSIC

See also:

Ancient Music	Jewish Music
Asiatic Musics	Mass
(note only)	Medieval/Renaissance
Church Music	Monophony
Gregorian Chant	Notation
History	Plainsong
Hyms/Hymnody–1	Psalms/Psalmody

*Note: Standard works apparently O/P (or not
easily available) include those by Hoëg (in
French); Tardo and Tiby (in Italian), Tillyard (in English), Wellesz (in German), etc.*

*Not included in the lists below are the fac-
similes & transcriptions issued in the "Monumenta Musicae Byzantinae" series, edited by
Hoëg, Tillyard, & Wellesz, and published by*

*Munksgaard in Copenhagen, Denmark.
However, for a subsidiary volume, see the first
Wellesz entry below.*

HATHERLEY, STEPHEN G.
A treatise on Byzantine music.   vi, △
162 p, 208 mus ex. Reeves 1892.   (6.25)

*An early study of Eastern music in general,
including analyses of some 50 Greek, Russian,
Turkish, & Egyptian examples.*

WELLESZ, EGON
Eastern elements in western chant:
studies in the early history of ecclesi-
astical music. xvi, 212 p, 6 pl, mus
ex, bibl refs, paper. Byzantine Institute via Oxford 1947.   7.50

*"Monumenta Musicae Byzantinae: subsi-
dia", V 2, No 1, American series. A scholarly
work, including a list of reference MSS, and
dealing with Greek hymns in the Mass &
Office of the Western Church, the structure of
Byzantine melody, etc.*

A history of Byzantine music and
hymnography. xiii, 358 p, 6 pl,
music, 11–p bibl. Oxford 1949.   8.50

*A scholarly, comprehensive work by an out-
standing authority, who here synthesizes a
vast amount of research in various related
fields. It includes chapters on notation, the
"pagan background," the structure of Byzantine melodies, etc.*

—C—

Cabos, Francine. Author. See App Ia.

CACCE
See:

History   Madrigal
Italian Music   Medieval/Renaissance

Note: W. Thomas Marrocco's anthology of "14th-century Italian cacce" (1942) is O/P.

Cain, Noble. Author. See Choir Choral–1.

CALENDARS (Musical)
See: Almanacs/Calendars.

CALIFORNIA (Music in)
See also:

America (music in)   Folklore
Dances–2 (esp Czar-   Folksongs–2
   nowski)   History

Note: Rodriguez's & De Segurola's "Music & dance in California" (1940) apparently is O/P.

DA SILVA, OWEN (*ed*)
Mission music of California: a collection of old California mission hymns & masses, transcribed & edited. Accompaniments & chirography Arthur M. Bienbar; mission sketches Paul A. Moore; intro John Steven McGroarty. xv, 132, 2 p, 11 pl, music, 2–p bibl. Lewis 1941.   7.50

GAGEY, EDMOND W.
The San Francisco stage: a history based on annals compiled by the research department of the San Francisco Federal Theatre. xv, 264 p, illus. Columbia 1950.   3.50
Covering minstrel shows & operas, as well as vaudeville, the legitimate drama, & the careers of many noted actors.

SAUNDERS, RICHARD DRAKE (*ed*)
Music and dance in California and the west. 285 p + 26–p advts, many photos (pors). Bureau Musical Research, Hollywood, 1948.   4.50
Brief articles by Schoenberg, Stravinsky, Antheil, et al.; sections on opera, films, dance, teaching, etc; biographical sketches of local musicians, p 163/280.

Calvé, Emma. Author. See App Ia.
Note: An autobiography, tr Gilder (1922), apparently is O/P.

Calvocoressi, Michael D. Author. See:
Composers–3e. Masters of Russian
music, with Abraham (1936).   4.50
Debussy–2. Miniature biog (n d).   .40
Mussorgsky. Biography (1946).   2.50
Russian Music. A survey (1944).   (.35)
Note: Calvocoressi's reminiscences ("Musician's gallery," 1933), and books on musical criticism (1923), musical taste (1925), etc, apparently are O/P (or not easily available).

Campa, Arthur Leon. Author. See Folklore.

CAMPANOLOGY
See: Carillon.

Campbell, Leroy B. Author. See Piano Playing–2.
Campbell, Olive Arnold. Collector (with Sharp). See Folksongs–2.
Campion, Charles Thomas. Translator, compiler. See Schweitzer–1 & 2.

CAMPION (Campian), Thomas
See also:

Elizabethan Music   History
England (music in)   Madrigal
English Music   Poetry

KASTENDIECK, MILES MERWIN
England's musical poet, Thomas Campion. 203 p, frontis fac, mus ex, 3–p bibl. Oxford 1938.   3.50
A standard study of the Elizabethan poet-composer, with considerable material on the relationship between music & poetry in Campion's and other ages.

CANADA (Music in)/CANADIAN MUSIC
See:

America (music in)   Folklore
American Music   Folksongs–1 & 2
Composers–3a (esp   History
   Saminsky)

Cannon, Beekman Cox. Author. See Mattheson.

CANON

See: Counterpoint, Fugue, Rounds.

Note: Standard works apparently O/P (or not easily available) include those by Jode (in German), Ziehn, etc. However, most books on counterpoint & fugue include at least some material on canon.

CANTATA

See:

Appreciation
Choir/Choral-3
Church Music
Composers (& under
   individual names)

History
Phonograph Records
Program Notes
Vocal Music

Note: Standard works apparently O/P (or not easily available) include those by Schmitz (in German), Upton, etc.

Canty, Daniel. J. Author. See Bugle.
Capell, Richard. Author. See Opera–1.
Capri, Antonio. Author. See App **Ic**.

CARDUS, Neville

Author.   See also Composers–1.

Autobiography. 288 p, illus. Collins △
1947.   3.50
The life-story of the noted British music critic & sportswriter.

CAREER (Musical)

See also:

America-music in
   (esp Carpenter)
Appreciation
   (esp Ulrich)
Colleges
Criticism (Thompson)
Education
Erskine ("What is
   music")

Film Music
Radio
Radio Music (esp
   LaPrade)
Singing–3
Songwriting
Teaching–2 (esp
   Gibbin)
Television

Note: Pertinent works apparently O/P (or not easily available) include those by Anderson, Patterson, Tapper, Taubman, etc.

DENIS, PAUL
Your career in show business. Forew
Abel Green. 240 p, illus, bibl, bds.
Dutton 1948.   3.00

ELKIN, ROBERT (*ed*)
Your musical career. 256 p. Wm. Earl △
Co., Bournemouth, England, 1950. (3.75)

FEINGOLD, S. NORMAN
Scholarships, fellowships, and loans.
254 p, bibl. Bellman Pub Co, Boston,
1949.   6.00
Subsidies in various fields, incl music.

JOHNSON, HARRIETT
Your career in music. Intro Olga

Samaroff Stokowski.   319 p, illus.
Dutton 1944 (4th pr 1946).   3.00
Written in collaboration with Vocational Guidance Research, Evelyn Steele, director.

JONES, CHARLES REED (*ed*)
Your career in motion pictures,
television, & radio. 255 p. Sheridan
1949.   2.98
Personal advice from some 29 stars, including Frank Sinatra ("Start singing," p 92/8), Dimitri Tiomkin ("The musical director,' p 168/76), Gene Autry, Bob Hope, et al.

CARILLON

General Note: Under this heading, the listings include available books on bells, bell-ringing, campanology, chimes, etc. However, see also Children–4 for Coleman's "Book of bells," & Organ for Perkins's "The organ and bells of Westminster Abbey."

Standard works apparently O/P (or not easily available) include those by Lefévere, Morris, Price, Rice, Walters, Young, etc.

BIGELOW, ARTHUR LYNDS
Carillon: an account of the Class
of 1892 bells at Princeton, with notes
on bells & carillons in general. x,
75 p + 12-p photos + 16-p list of
carillons in the U. S. & Canada.
Princeton 1948.   2.00
The Princeton carillon; the origin & development of bells & carillons; the carillon in America.

English type of carillonic bells:
their history & music. 70 p, por,
music (p 25/69), typescript repro,
paper.   Schulmerich Electronics,
Sellersville, Penna, 1949.   2.00

MAHRENHOLZ, CHRISTHARD. See App Ib.

PEERY, PAUL D.
Chimes and electronic carillons:
modern tower bells. xi, 146 p, illus,
music, 4-p bibl. Day 1948.   3.75
Primarily about electronic bells (except for the extensive bibliography). Includes arrs of 31 hymns, 3 chimes, 8 bugle calls.

PRICE, PERCIVAL
Campanology, Europe 1945–47: a
report on the condition of carillons
on the continent of Europe as a result
of the recent war. vii, 161 p, paper.
Michigan 1948.   1.25

Carlin, Benson. Author. See Ultrasonics.
Carmer, Carl. Author, editor.
See Folksongs–2.

51

CARMICHAEL, Hoagy (Hoagland Howard)
See also: Jazz, Popular Music.
The stardust road.   156 p, illus.
Rinehart 1946.   3.00
Reminiscences of early jazz & jazzmen by the composer of "Stardust."

Carner, Mosco.   Author.   See:
Dvořák.   Miniature biog (1941).   .40
Harmony-1.   Study of 20th-century harmony, v 2 (1942 4).   2.50
Waltz.   The waltz (1948).   2.50
Also: Puccini, ed Crozier. (*The "Bohème" & "Mme Butterfly" booklets include essays by Carner, among others.*)

Carnett, Ellis L.   Author.
See Choir/Choral-2.

CAROLS
See also:

Folklore	Medieval/Renaissance
Folksongs-**1** & **2**	Minstrels Minstrelsy
History	Songbooks

Note: In addition to the Dearmer & Maus collections listed below, there are numerous other publications of carol music only.

COBBOLD, JOAN
Carol Christmas: music edition.   80 p, illus, music, paper. Oxford 1941.   **1.25**
A carol play (based on carols from the Oxford book below) with suggestions for appropriate scenery, costumes, etc.

DEARMER, PERCY (& *others, eds*)
Oxford book of carols: music edition.
xxix, 491 p, music. Oxford 1928 (18th pr 1949).   3.50
A standard collection: the music & texts of some 200 carols, edited with notes by Dearmer, Vaughan Williams, & Martin Shaw.

DUNCAN, EDMONSTOUNE
Story of the carol.   xii, 253 p, illus (facs, etc), mus ex, 20–p bibl & list of carol collections. Scott 1911, via Reeves.   (4.00)
"Music Story" series; formerly available via Scribner in the U. S. A.; including chronology, glossary, & biographical indices.

GREENE, RICHARD LEIGHTON (*ed*)
The early English carols.   cxlv, 461 p, frontis fac, 26–p annot bibl.
Oxford 1935.   10.00
A scholarly study, dealing with carol texts (only) up to the year 1550.

MAUS, CYNTHIA PEARL (*ed*)
Music section of "The world's great Madonnas." Evelyn Lysle Fielding, music collaborator. vi, 90 p, music, bds. Harper 1948.   1.50
Some 62 Christmas songs from an anthology of pictures, music, etc, published 1947.

MOTTINGER, ALVINA H. (*ed*)
Christmas carols: their authors & composers; a collection of favorite carols compiled and with biographical & historical annotations. 95 p, music, paper. G. Schirmer 1948.   1.00
Some 44 carols, words & music, with notes on their origins, composers, & arrangers.

NILES, JOHN JACOB (*ed*)
The Anglo-American carol study book: containing English carols in their early traditional form & surviving versions traditional in the United States. 44 p, music, bibl refs, paper. G. Schirmer 1948.   .75
"American Folk-Song" series, Set 26: eight carols in 2 or 3 versions each, with notes.

RICKERT, EDITH (*ed*)
Ancient English Christmas carols: MCCC to MDCC.   345 p, illus. (1910) Oxford 1925.   2.75
"Medieval Library" series: a scholarly study of carols of the Nativity, Divine Mystery, & Yuletide Festivity. Texts only.

VAN LOON, H. W. & CASTAGNETTA, GRACE
Christmas carols: illustrated & done into simple music.   64 p, col illus, music, paper. S & S (1937) rev ed 1950.   1.00
20 carols, arranged by Grace Castagnetta, with notes & illustrations by Van Loon.

WASNER, FRANZ (*ed*)
The Trapp book of Christmas songs: selected & arranged for voice & piano.   128 p, col illus (Agathe Trapp), music, bds. Pantheon 1950.   3.50
Carols in many languages, with English translations, as sung by the Trapp Family Choir, arranged with notes by the Trapp Family's musical director.

WHEELER, OPAL. See App IIb (juvenile).

Carpenter, Paul Simons. Author.
See America (music in).
Carr, Raymond Norman. Author.
See School Music-3.
Carré, John Franklin. Author.
See Teaching-3.

CARREÑO, (Maria) Teresa

See also:
History   Piano Playing
Pianists   Women

Note: Carreño's own "Possibilities of tone color by artistic use of the pedal" (1919) apparently is O/P (or not easily available).

MILINOWSKI, MARTA
Teresa Carreño: "by the grace of God." xvi, 410 p, illus. Yale 1940 (2nd pr 1941).   3.50
Vassar College 75th anniversary publication: a standard biography of the great pianist.

Carrillo, Julián. Author. See App Id.
Carrington, John F. Author.
See Africa (music in).

Carse, Adam von Ahn. Author. See:
Conducting. Orchestral (1929).   2.50
Instrumentation. Practical hints on orchestration (1919?).   1.00
Orchestra. The orchestra (1949).   2.50
———. In the 18th century (1940)   3.75
———. The orchestra from Beethoven to Berlioz (1948).   7.50
School Music–3. Conducting school orchestra (1924).   .50
Wind Instruments. Musical (1939). (7.50)

Note: Several other books by Carse apparently are O/P (or not easily available).

Cart, William. Author. See App Ia.
Caruso, Dorothy. Author. See E. Caruso.

CARUSO, Enrico

See also:
America (music in)   Opera
Gatti-Casazza   Singers
History   Singing
Interpreters   Phonograph Records

Note: Caruso's own "How to sing" (1913) apparently is O/P, as are books about him by Fucito & Beyer, Key & Zirato, Marafioti, Petriccioni (in Italian), etc.

CARUSO, DOROTHY
Enrico Caruso: his life and death. 303 p, illus (photos & caricatures). S & S 1945.   2.75
A biography by the famous tenor's widow, including material from his letters, & a list of phonograph recordings. This book apparently supersedes a biography ("Wings of song"), 1928, by Dorothy Caruso & Torrance Goddard.

CASALS, Pablo (Pau)

See also:
History   Violoncello Playing
Interpreters   (esp Alexanian)
Phonograph Records

LITTLEHALES, LILLIAN
Pablo Casals. 232 p, 10 photos, 1 fac, mus ex. Norton (1929) rev & enl ed 1948.   3.75
Including new chapters on Casals's political activities, the reasons for his concert retirement, & a discography.

TOBEL, RUDOLF VON. See App Ib.

CASANOVA, Giacomo

See also:
Classic Era   Italy (music in)
Da Ponte (note)   Mozart
History   Opera
Note: Despite his highly tenuous link with Mozart, the "great lover" would have no place in the present Guide save for the fact that the Nettl entry below deals as much with the music of Casanova's time as with the man.

NETTL, PAUL
The other Casanova: a contribution to 18th-century music & manners. xii, 293 p, 16 pl (pors, facs, etc), 3–p bibl. Philosophical 1950.   3.75
An attempt to view the history of music from the perspective of Casanova's "Memoirs," including considerable material on Mozart, Da Ponte, and many musicians, dancers, & actors. Presumably a revision of the author's "Musik und Tanz bei Casanova" (1927).

Case, Edmund Wallace. Author.
See Teaching–2.
Castagnetta, Grace. Arranger (with Van Loon). See Carols.

CATECHISMS OF MUSIC

See:
Gregorian Chant   History
(Hügle)   Theory–3

CATHEDRAL MUSIC

See:
Byrd   English Music
Choir/Choral–3   History
Church Music (esp   Organ Music
  Fellowes)   Organists (West)
Composers (& under   Plainsong
  individual names)   Purcell
Elizabethan Music   Terry
Note: Bumpus's "History of English cathedral music" (1908) apparently is O/P.

CATHOLIC CHURCH MUSIC

See: esp Church Music (esp Nemmers, Society of St Gregory, & Weinmann).

Also:

Choir/Choral–3	Latin Language
Composers (& under	Mass
individual names)	Organ Music
Gregorian Chant	Palestrina
History	Plainsong

Cauchie, Maurice. Compiler.
See Couperin (Brunold).

Cavazzuti, Pietro. Author. See App Ic.

CEBOTARI, Maria
See: esp App Ib (Mingotti biog in German).
Also: Opera, Singers, Phonograph Records.

Cellier, Alexandre. Author (with Bachelin).
See App Ia.

CEMBALO
See:

History	Keyboard Instruments
Instruments	Piano

Cerminara, Gina. Author.
See Italian Language.

Cesana, Otto. Author. See:

Arranging–2. Course in modern	
dance arranging (1938).	2.00
——. Voicing the modern dance	
orchestra (1946).	4.00
Counterpoint–2. Modern (1940).	3.00
Harmony–2. Modern (1939).	3.00

CHABRIER, (Alexis-) Emmanuel
See:

Appreciation	Orchestral Music
Ballet	Phonograph Records
French Music	Piano Music
History	Program Notes
Opera	Vocal Music

Note: Works apparently O/P (or not easily available) include those, in French, by Desaymard, Martineau, Servières, etc.

Chadwick, George Whitefield. Author.
See Harmony–2, H. Parker.

Chaffin, Lucien Gates. Author.
See Songwriting.

Chailley, Jacques. Author (with Challan).
See App Ia.

CHALIAPIN (Shaliapin), Feodor
See:

History	Phonograph Records
Interpreters	Singers
Opera	App IIa (Acker)

Note: Two volumes of memoirs, in English translations (1926 & 1932), apparently are O/P (or not easily available), but see App Ib for Chaliapin's "Meine Jugend," in German.

Challan, Henri. Co-author (with Chailley).
See App Ia.

Chalupt, René. Author. See App Ia.

CHAMBER MUSIC
See also:

Appreciation	Phonograph Records
Composers (& under	Program Notes
individual names)	String Quartet
History	Violin Music
Keyboard Instruments	
& Music	

Note: Standard works apparently O/P (or not easily available) include those by Altmann (catalogue in German), Dunhill, Kilburn, Meyer, Stratton & Frank, etc.

COBBETT, WALTER WILSON (*ed*)
Cobbett's cyclopedic survey of chamber music. Pref W. H. Hadow. 2 v: xii, 585 p; 641 p, frontis, mus ex, 9–p bibl. Oxford 1929/30. △
A standard reference work, which has been O/P for some years (last price $42.00), but which happily is scheduled for early re-issue.

COHN, ARTHUR
Chamber music: a comprehensive guide. Farrar 1951, in prep. 6.00

KING, A. HYATT
Chamber music. 72 p, 7 col pl, 33 b&w illus, bibl, bds. Chanticleer 1948. 2.50
"World of Music" series No. 3; an over-all survey, particularly notable for its many well-chosen illustrations.

ROWEN, RUTH HALLE
Early chamber music. 188 p, mus ex, 8–p bibl. Columbia 1949. 3.50
A scholarly study covering the period from around 1600 to the early 1700's.

TOVEY, DONALD FRANCIS
Essays in musical analysis: chamber music. Ed Hubert J. Foss. viii, 217 p, mus ex. Oxford 1944 (1945). 2.75
A supplementary volume to the "Essays in musical analysis" devoted to orchestral & choral works (see Program Notes). This is based on Tovey's notes from 1900 to 1936, and was completed after his death by Foss. Some piano works are included.

ULRICH, HOMER
Chamber music: the growth & practice of an intimate art. xvi, 430 p, mus ex, charts, 8–p bibl. Columbia 1948. 6.00
The historical development of forms & styles; and studies of the chamber works of various major composers. It includes a 21-p list of published scores & phonograph recordings.

CHAMBER ORCHESTRA

See esp App Ia (Pincherle: "L'Orchestre de chambre," 1948).

Also:

Appreciation	Orchestra
Chamber Music	Orchestral Music
Composers (& under	Phonograph Records
individual names)	Program Notes

Chamberlain, Mabel. Co-author (with MacMahon). See School Music–4.

Champigneulle, Bernard. Author. See App Ia.

Chandler, Anna Curtis. Author (with Cypher). See Teaching–1.

CHANGE-RINGING

See: Carillon.

CHANLER, Margaret

Memory makes music. xi, 171 p. Stephen-Paul 1948 (via Greenberg). 2.50

Reminiscences of Brahms, Liszt, Verdi, Wagner, musical life in Rome & the U.S.A., by Mrs. Winthrop Chanler, friend of many musicians and the mother of the American composer, Theodore Ward Chanler.

CHANSON DE ROLAND

See: Troubadours/Trouvères.

CHANT/CHANTING

See:

Byzantine Music	Plainsong
Choir/Choral	Psalms/Psalmody
Church Music	(esp Brown)
Gregorian Chant	

Chantavoine, Jean. Author. See App Ia.

CHANTEY

See: Sea Shanties & Songs.

Chao-Mei-Pa. Author. See China (music in).

Chapple, Stanley. Author. See Harmony–2, Keyboard Harmony. Co-author (with Trotter). See Children–8.

CHARPENTIER, Marc-Antoine

See: App Ia (Crussard biog in French).

Chase, Ann Hastings. Editor. See Dances–2.

Chase, Gilbert. Author, editor. See Latin America, Radio Music.

Note: Chase's "Music of Spain" (1941) and several other books on Latin-American music apparently are O/P (or not easily available).

Chase, Richard. Compiler. See Dances–2.

CHÁVEZ, Carlos

See also:

American Music	Latin America
Appreciation	Mexican Music
Composers–3a	Phonograph Records
Contemporary Music	Program Notes

Note: Chávez's own "Toward a new music" (1937) apparently is O/P.

Carlos Chávez: catalogue of his works. Pref Herbert Weinstock. xxxii, 15 p, frontis por, fac, 5–p bibl, paper. Pan American Union 1944. .50

Chen, Chin-Hsin Yao & Shih-Hsiang. Editors. See China (music in).

Cherbuliez, Antoine-Elisée. Author. See App Ib.

CHERUBINI, (Maria) Luigi

See also:

Appreciation	Opera
Composers–1	Phonograph Records
History	Program Notes

Note: Standard works apparently O/P (or not easily available) include those by Epine (in French), Hohenemser, Schemann, & Wittmann (in German). Cherubini's own "Treatise on counterpoint & fugue" is O/P, at least in the English translations.

BELLASIS, EDWARD
Cherubini memorials illustrative of his life. xv, 429 p, frontis por, mus △ ex. (1874, 1905). Reeves 1912. (3.25)

CROWEST, FREDERICK J.
Cherubini. viii, 115 p, mus ex. △ Sampson Low 1890, via Reeves. (1.80)

CHEVALIER, Maurice

The man in the straw hat: my story. Tr Caroline Clark. viii, 245 p, 33 photos. Crowell 1949. 3.50

The music-hall star's autobiography. See also App Ia for what presumably is the original French version, "Ma route et mes chansons" (1946).

Chickering, Geraldine Jencks. Co-editor (with Gardener). See Folksongs–2.

Chidester, Gerald R. Co-author with Prescott). See School Music–3.

CHILDREN (and Music)

General Note: For books designed particularly for children's own use, see App IIa (juven-

iles). The books listed below are primarily intended for parents & teacher, although of course many of them may be enjoyed—as well as profitably used—by older children and, in some cases at least, by adult beginners in music.

The available literature is so large & varied that for convenience it has been divided here into the following sub-categories:

1. **General**
2. **Appreciation, History, Phonograph Records.**
3. **Ear-Training, Sight-Singing, Rhythmic Training, etc.**
4. **Instruments.**
5. **Piano Playing.**
6. **Rhythm Band, Toy Symphony, etc.**
7. **Singing, Songs, Speech, etc.**
8. **"Theory," Elementary Theoretical Studies.**

See also: esp App IIa & b (juveniles).
Amateur Music　　　　School Music
Education　　　　　　Teaching

CHILDREN (1. General)

Note: Pertinent works apparently O/P (or not easily available) include those by Austin, Macpherson, de Rusette, Stinson, Tapper, Thorn, etc.

COLEMAN, SATIS N.
(*See also Children-3 & 4.*)
Your child's music. 180 p. Day 1939 (1942). 　　　　　　2.00
Cover sub-title: "A guide to the musical development of children of all ages & degrees of musical ability."

GORDON, DOROTHY
All children listen. 128 p. George W. Stewart, N. Y., 1942. 　　1.50
A study of children's radio programs.

KNAPP, IDA C.
The child's unfoldment through music: a collection of teaching methods & materials to be used with pre-school children. 57 p, mus ex, paper. Willis 1947. 　1.00

KREVIT, WILLIAM
Music for your child. viii, 128 p, illus (Marc Simont), 4-p bibl. Dodd 1946. 　　　　　　2.50
A practical handbook for parents, including lists of recommended books & records.

LAWRENCE, SIDNEY J.
Everyone's musical, psychologically

speaking. 167 p, illus (Roland Roy-craft). Summy 1946. 　　　2.50
Studies & case-histories in teacher-parent-child relationships.

NEWMAN, ELIZABETH
How to teach music to children: a creative plan of awakening & leading children into music, with a graded system of lessons & material. xii, 141 p, illus, mus ex, 3-p bibl, paper. C. Fischer 1925. 　　1.50

PERKINS, CLELLA LESTER
How to teach music to children. vii, 216 p, music, 1-p bibl. Hall McCreary 1936. 　　　　　1.75
Singing, rhythm band, elementary theory, etc, with lists of materials.

ROSSMAN, FLOY ADELE
Pre-school music: a guide to parents. Forew C. M. Tremaine. 26 p, mus ex, 2-p annot bibl, paper. National Bureau for the Advancement of Music 1940, via National Recreation Assn, N. Y. 　　　　　　.15

SHEEHY, EMMA DICKSON
There's music in children. 120 p, photos, chap bibls. Holt 1946. 　2.25
Fostering the 2-to-6-year-old's natural interest in musical activities. The chapter on "radio & phonograph" includes a 6-p selection of useful recordings.

SHIELDS, ELIZABETH McE.
Music in the religious growth of children. 128 p, mus ex. Abingdon 1943. 　　　　　　　1.50

TAYLOR, FREDERICK A.
So we're going to have music lessons. 20 p, illus (Richard K. Moll), paper. Humphries 1947. 　　　　.50
For a companion work, addressed to children rather than to their parents, see App IIb for Taylor's "So you're going to take music lessons."

CHILDREN (2. Appreciation, History, Phonograph Records, etc.)
See also:
Appreciation　　　Phonograph Records
Composers　　　　Program Notes
History　　　　　School Music-2
Also: Ballet (Beaumont primer).
Also: App IIb (juveniles by Barbour & Freeman, Buchanan, Cooke, Kinscella, Skolsky, Macy.
Note: Pertinent works apparently O/P (or not easily available) include those by Clarke, Hudson, Sutton, etc.

BARBOUR, H. B. & FREEMAN, W. S.
The children's record book. 186 p,
3–p bibl. Durrell 1947, via Crown.　2.00
*Classified lists of recommended recordings
for children from 6 months to 16 years.
Supersedes the same authors' "How to teach
children to know music," 1942.*

BAUER, MARION & PEYSER, ETHEL
How music grew: from prehistoric
times to the present day.　Intro
William J. Henderson. xix, 647 p,
some 60 illus, mus ex, 5–p bibl.
Putnam (1925) rev ed 1939.　5.00
*Over-all story-history, especially designed
for younger readers.*

BRUXNER, MERVYN
Letters to a musical boy.　viii, 176
p, illus (Barbara Greg), 3–p bibl.
Oxford 1940.　2.50

*Informal "appreciation" lessons, including
composers date-chart, Italian glossary, etc.*

CRUNDEN, MARJORIE MORSE (*comp*)
Disc adventures for tiny, 'tween
and 'teen agers. 34 p, paper. College
Women's Club of Montclair, N. J.,
1949.　.40
*A classified basic record list for the children's
record loan library, Glen Ridge, New Jersey,
Free Public Library.*

EISENBERG, PHILIP & KRASNO, HECKY
A guide to children's records: a
complete guide to recorded stories,
songs, & music for children.　195 p.
Crown 1948.　2.00
*"Growing up with records" & annotated lists
of discs for various age groups (2 to 15).*

HARTSHORN, W. C. & LEAVITT, H. S.
The world of music: making friends
with music: The pilot, teacher's
book 1. vi, 195 p, mus ex. Ginn
1940.　3.20
Same series: The mentor, teacher's
book 2. vii, 328 p, mus ex. Ginn
1940.　3.56
*Aids for teachers using the Ginn & Co.
"World of music" series of songbooks.*

KEITH, ALICE & SHEPHERD, ARTHUR
Listening in on the masters: a course
in music appreciation for home,
school, & club, with radio & record
illustrations. iii, 126 p, illus, mus
ex, paper. Birchard 1926.　.40
*Prepared for school use with the Cleveland
Orchestra's children's concerts.*

KINSCELLA, HAZEL GERTRUDE
History sings: backgrounds of
American music. xv, 560 p, illus,

map. University Pub Co, Lincoln,
Nebraska, 1948, 1951 rev in prep.　2.00

LYNCH, VIRGINIA & HAMILTON, E. V.
Music and musicians. viii, 201,
12 p, illus. Allyn 1939 (1946).　2.00
Appreciative approach to musical forms, etc.

McGEHEE, THOMASINE C.
People and music: a textbook in
music appreciation. vi, 398, 8 p,
illus, mus ex. Allyn 1929 (1947).　1.75
My musical notebook. 194 p, illus,
mus ex, paper. Allyn 1932 (1940).　1.00
*Formerly "My musical measure": a work-
book, with blanks to be filled in, for use with
"People and music" above.*

SCHOLES, P. A. & EARHART, W. C.
The complete book of the great
musicians: comprising books 1, 2,
& 3. 435 p, illus, mus ex. Oxford
rev ed 1931.　3.50
*"A course in appreciation for younger
readers." Also issued in 3 separate volumes,
but apparently no longer available in this
form (at least in the U. S. A.).*

SEYMOUR, HARRIET AYER
Home music lessons: how to find
your musical self. 48 p, illus mus
ex. C. Fischer 1930.　1.00
*Inspirational approach; with a list of recom-
mended (RCA Victor) records.*

STORR, MURIEL
Music for children: first steps in
appreciation. xii, 195 p, diagrs,
mus ex, 3–p bibl. (1924) E. C.
Schirmer n d.　2.50
*Written in collaboration (part 2) with A.
E. F. Dickinson; originally pub in England
by Sidgwick & Jackson.*

WILLIAMS, WYNDHAM G.
Looking and listening: an introduction to musical appreciation. 48 p,
illus (Keith & Norman Roberts),
mus ex, brief bibl, bds.　John
Murray, London, 1948, via Transatlantic 1950.　.85
*Mainly pictures & diagrams, with straight-
forward, informative captions, dealing with
musical fundamentals, instruments, etc.*

CHILDREN (3. Ear-Training, Sight-Singing, Rhythmic Training, etc.)

See also:

BERNARD, ELIZABETH & DAVIES, M. G.
Playing with sounds: the first 4
years of pitch training . . . 44 p,
mus ex, paper. Curwen 1939.   1.40
*Games & songs to teach pitch & tonality;
introduction to staff notation.*

BELL, LESLIE R.
The chorister: theory & sight read-
ing for vocalists, Book 1. ix, 118 p,
W. J. Gage, Toronto, 1947.   1.25
Mainly unison songs, with notes.

BROWN, JEAN PARKMAN
Intervals, chords, and ear-training
for young pianoforte students. 110
p, mus. Ditson 1897.   1.25
"Music Students Library" series.

COLEMAN, SATIS N.
  (*See also Children–1 & 4.*)
First steps in playing and composing:
a music book for children. 73 p,
illus. Day (1926) rev ed 1930.   1.25
*Music-making with glasses, bowls, etc; exer-
cises in a special notation, with blanks to be
filled in. "Creative Music" series.*

DILLER, ANGELA & PAGE, KATE STEARNS
A pre-school music book. v, 68 p,
mus ex, paper. G. Schirmer 1936.   .75
*Preparation for group work with children
from about 2 1/2 to 5 years old.*

GAYNOR, JESSIE L.
Elements of musical expression: the
major mode. 82 p, mus ex, Summy
1907.   1.50
Ear-training & dictation through 4th grade.

GEST, ELIZABETH
  (*See also Children–8.*)
Keyboard harmony for juniors. 56
p, mus ex, paper. Ditson (1931) new
enl ed 1936.   .75

HARDY, T. MASKELL
Mental effect: a basis for singing at
sight from either notation, with
practical hints on teaching the subject to children. Forew Percy Buck.
63 p, 8 illus (Jack Fairhurst), mus
ex, paper. Curwen n d (1927?).   (.90)
*Teaching tone-thinking and the use of both
ordinary & tonic sol-fa notations.*

HARRIS, CUTHBERT
Ear training: first steps. mus ex,
paper. Schmidt 1926.   .75

HARRIS, E. F. & SIMS, M. L.
Learning to listen: lessons in the
elements of music & ear-training for

children. vii, 144 p, mus ex, paper.
G. Schirmer 1929.   1.50
Writing books (4) for above. Each: .50

HOOD, MARGUERITE V. & SCHULTZ, E. J.
Learning music through rhythm. xi,
180 p, music, 3–p annot bibl. Ginn
1949.   3.20
Rhythmic methods, primary & int. grades.

HUGHEY, FANNIE E.
Color music for children: a guide
for mothers & teachers of young
children.   Intro E. R. Kroeger.
xii, 235 p, illus & mus ex in color.
G. Schirmer 1912.   3.00
*Learning staff notation via colors, with
sections on calisthenics & piano technique.*

WADLEY, FREDERICKA & ALLISON, M.
Discovering music: a guide for teach-
ing music to pre-school children . . .
58 p, music, bds. Boston n d.   1.25
*Songs & games, with notes based on the
Schlieder principles of music education.*

WATERMAN, ELIZABETH
ABC of rhythmic training: a course
in the correlation of music & movement. 148 p, music. Summy (1927)
rev ed n d.   3.60
First to fourth grade material.

CHILDREN (4. Instruments)
(Other than Piano—for which see Children
5; and Rhythm Band Toy Symphony—for
which see Children–6)
See also:

Appreciation	Instruments
Children–1 & 2	Orchestra
Community Music	Recorder
Instrumentation	School Music–3

Also: App IIb (juveniles by Commins,
Dushkin, Freeman, Gest, MacPhee, Posell).

*Note: Pertinent books apparently O/P (or not
easily available) include those by Coleman
("Creative music in the home," 1939, & "The
drum book," 1931/42), de Rusette, etc.*

COLEMAN, SATIS N.
  (*See also Children–1 & 3.*)
Bells and bell ringing: a unit on the
making & playing of bells. Unp
(27 p), illus, mus ex (special notation), paper. Day 1938.   .35
The book of bells. vii, 177 p, illus,
music. (1928) Day 1938.   2.75
The marimba book: how to make
marimbas & how to play them. 106 p,

illus, mus ex. Day (1926) rev ed
1930. **1.25**
The psaltery book. 80 p, illus, mus
ex (special notation), bds. Oscar
Schmidt, Jersey City, N. J., (1928)
1937. **1.50**
*Note: Although primarily for children, Mrs
Coleman's books also may be used profitably
by adult beginners in music.*

HUNTINGTON, HARRIET E.
Tune up: the instruments of the
orchestra & their players. Photos by
the author. Forew Ernest LaPrade.
Unp (77 p). Doubleday 1942. **2.50**

LACEY, MARION
Picture book of musical instruments.
55 p, illus (Leonard Weisgard).
Lothrop 1942. **2.00**
*Note: Although the two picture books above are
primarily for children, they are included here
for their general usefulness.*

LAPRADE, ERNEST
Alice in orchestralia. Forew Walter
Damrosch. 171 p, illus (col frontis
& b&ws by Carroll C. Snell). (1925)
Garden City repr 1945 (1948). **1.50**
*A children's classic: introduction to the
orchestra & its instruments in story form,
with an appendix on instruments & orchestra
builders, and specimen (Damrosch) children's
orchestral programs.*

SCOTT, M. M.
What can I play?: a book about
musical instruments. Forew M. E.
Waddell. 95 p, illus. Quality Press,
London, 1944 (1945). **2.00**

WINN, EDITH L.
First steps in violin playing: an introductory text book for young children. xiii, 125 p, illus, mus ex, chap
bibls. C. Fischer (1908) rev ed 1925. **2.50**
Super-title: "The child violinist."

ZANZIG, AUGUSTUS D.
(*See also Children–6.*)
How to make and play a shepherd's
pipe. Forew Jennie Cossitt. 32 p,
illus, music, paper. National Recreation Assn (1939) 3rd ed 1950. **.35**
With lists of music & sources of supply.

CHILDREN (5. Piano Playing)
See also: Piano Playing, Teaching–3.
*Note: The list below is, of course, only a
sampling of the large literature of introductory piano methods, most of which, however, contain little actual text.*

AITKEN, GERALDINE L.
Music before lessons begin: an out-
line of simple & natural experiences
in music. Intro H. A. Seymour. iii,
59 p, music, paper. C. Fischer 1930/1. **1.00**
*For children 2 to 6. A supplement to
Seymour's "Home music lessons" (see
Children–2 above).*

BOWMAN, EDWARD MORRIS
Master lessons in piano playing:
letters from a musician to his nephew.
Intro Albert Ross Parsons. 151 p,
illus, mus ex. Presser 1911. **1.50**

BROWER, HARRIETTE
How a dependable piano technic was
won: a story. 71 p, illus, mus ex,
paper. Ditson 1929. **.75**
"Pocket Music Student" series.

DARDENELLE, LOUISE
"Harmony first" method for the
piano. 96 p, music, charts, paper.
Paul-Pioneer, N. Y., 1936. **1.25**

FISK, BEATRICE HATTON
Keyboard fundamentals for beginners.
82 p, photos (Howard K. Fisk),
music, paper. Boston 1947. **1.25**

FREEDMAN, JULIAN
Teaching piano to your child. 48
p, col illus (André Dugo). Lothrop
1948. **2.00**
*Simplified approach, using colored notes on
a "junior staff."*

MATTHAY, TOBIAS
The child's first steps in piano-forte-
playing. 23 p, illus, mus ex, paper.
Williams 1912 via Boston. **.75**

MELLICHAMP, NELL V.
How to begin: a hand-book for
teachers of piano. 16 p, mus ex,
paper. Willis 1929 (1930). **.50**

RABINEAU, LAURETTA B.
Invitation to music: a piano book
for everyone. 46 p, music, paper.
Boston 1947. **1.50**
*Mainly music & exercises to be filled in, with
5-p appendix of teaching material.*

SMITH, MONA (*comp*)
Applied principles of Schmitz training
for children. unp (9 p), paper. C.
Fischer 1942. **.30**

WILLIAMS, JOHN M.
What to teach at the very first
lessons. vi, 63 p, keyboard chart,
mus ex, paper. Presser 1925. **.60**

CHILDREN
(6. Rhythm Band, Toy Symphony, etc.)

See also: Children-3 & 4, Community Music (esp Bergman).

DILLER, ANGELA & PAGE, KATE S.
How to teach the rhythm band. 23 p, illus, mus ex, paper. G. Schirmer 1928 (1930). .35

GREENFIELD, MARJORIE H.
Drums and triangles: 100 graded percussion band exercises for beginners. xiii, 62 p, mus ex, paper. Curwen n d (1930?). (1.20)

RUSETTE, LOUIE E. DE
The children's band. **67 p,** paper. Curwen n d. (1.00)

STICKLE, MARY L.
The toy symphony: teacher's manual. v, 24, frontis, diagr, mus ex, paper. Birchard 1930. .75
Instructions for playing by the rote method; accompanying an instrumental book ($1.25) of song & toy-symphony orchestrations.

SUMMERFIELD, HATTIE
Slingerland rhythm. vi, 47 p, illus, music, paper. Boston 1930. 1.00

VANDEVERE, J. LILIAN
The toy symphony orchestra: its organization & training. 22 p, illus, paper. .50
Practical handbook with graded material.

Note: In addition to the Stickle and Vandevere books above, C. C. Birchard & Co, Boston, publishes a special catalogue of toy-symphony scores, "picture" scores, & operettas with toy-symphony accompaniments.

VOTAW, LYRAVINE
Rhythm band direction. 43 p, illus, mus ex, paper. Ludwig n d. 1.00

ZANZIG, AUGUSTUS D.
(*See also Children-4.*)
Starting and developing a rhythm band. 24 p, mus ex, paper. National Recreation Assn 1937 (1948). .35
Straightforward advice, with lists of recommended scores & recordings, and information on making & buying instruments.

CHILDREN (7. Singing, Songs, Speech)
See also: esp Boy Voices.

Choir/Choral	Song(s)
Cowboy Music	Songbooks
Folksongs-1 & 2	Speech
School Music-4	Vocal Music
Singing	Voice

Note: Cushing's "Children's song index" (Wilson 1936) apparently is O/P. Numerous elementary singing methods (especially those with little or no text) are not listed.

EMRICH, MARION & KORSON, GEORGE (eds)
The child's book of folklore. xv, 240 p, illus (John O'Hare Cosgrove II), music (tunes only). Dial 1947. 3.00
A standard collection of American songs, games, riddles, tales, rhymes, etc, primarily children from six to twelve.

FIELD, (Rev) JUSTIN
The simplicity of plainsong. Pref Rev Felix Couturier. x, 37, p, diagrs, mus ex, paper. J. Fischer 1931. .50
Children's lessons in plainsong singing.

FINN, WILLIAM JOSEPH
Child voice training in ten letters. 44 p, mus ex, paper. FitzSimons 1944. 1.00

HARDY, T. MASKELL
How to train children's voices: specially written for school teachers & conductors of ladies' choirs. 90 p, mus ex, paper. Curwen n d (19th ed, 1947?). (1.00)
Voice-production exercises for children. 64 p, music, paper. Curwen 1911. (*Sequel to above.*) (1.35)

HOWARD, FRANCIS EDWARD
The child-voice in singing: treated from a physiological & a practical standpoint, and especially adapted to schools & boy choirs. 138 p, mus ex. Novello (1896) rev ed 1898 (1923). 1.50
The pioneer—and still a standard—work in this field.

JACOBS, RUTH KREHBIEL
The successful children's choir. 63 p, 2-p bibl, paper. Choir Publications, Los Angeles, (1939) 3rd rev enl ed 1948, via FitzSimons. 1.50
A popular, practical handbook, including lists of suggested choir materials.

SEEGER, RUTH CRAWFORD
American folk songs for children: in home, school, & nursery school. Pref Lilla Belle Pitts. 190 p, illus (Barbara Cooney), music. Doubleday 1948. 4.00
Some 95 songs, with 36-p prefatory material on the utilization of folk music for children, and 6-p classified indices.

Animal folk songs for children: traditional American songs. 80 p,

illus (Barbara Cooney), music.
Doubleday 1950. 2.50
*Some 43 songs (34 freshly notated) with 4-p
introduction & 2-p list of sources.*

WILKINS, JOSEPH F. (*comp*)
Index of songs for young singers.
49 p, spir. Allen Press, Lawrence,
Kansas, 1948. 3.00
Classified lists with descriptive notes.

WOOD, ALICE L.
Sound games: speech correction for
your very young. vii, 103 p. Dutton
1948. 1.50

(WPA WRITERS, *comps*)
The Spanish-American song and
game book. Compiled by workers of
the writers' program, music program,
& art program of the Work Projects
Administration in the state of New
Mexico. Forew Charles Ethrige
Minton. xvi, 87 p, illus, music.
Barnes 1942 (3rd pr 1945). 3.00
*Mostly singing games, with directions, and
texts in English & Spanish.*

CHILDREN (8. "Theory," Elementary Theoretical Studies)

See also:

Children-3	Harmony
Composition	Notation
Dictionaries of Terms	Theory-2 & 3

Also: App IIb (Loofbourow juveniles).

ANDERSEN, ARTHUR OLAF
Short lessons in musical theory for
school children. 2 v. FitzSimons
1926.

V 1: 48 p, mus ex, paper. 3rd pr. .75
V 2: 47 p, mus ex, paper. 2nd pr. .75
Teacher's manual for above. 64 p. 1.50

CUMBERLAND, GLADYS
A short primer in the elements of
music: 100 easy questions with the
answers, & a series of test papers.
32 p, paper. Schmidt 1924. .40

CURWEN, (*Mrs*) J. SPENCER
The teacher's guide to Mrs Curwen's
pianoforte method: being a practical
course of the elements of music. viii,
388, 10 p, mus ex. Curwen (1886)
(16th ed 1913) 29th ed n d. (4.00)

DINGLEY-MATHEWS, BLANCHE
Conversation lessons for the beginner
in music presenting rhythm, melody,
harmony, & notation step-by-step.
60 p, mus ex, paper. Church (1905?)
1915. 1.00

EDWARDS, RUTH & SIMON, ERIC
First steps in music. 32 p, mus ex,
paper. Marks 1948. .60
*Mainly exercises in elementary theory. Cover
subtitle: "A new approach to music for
beginners of all ages."*

GEST, ELIZABETH
(*See also Children–3.*)
What every junior should know
about music: for class & individual
work, or club meetings. 44 p, illus,
mus ex, paper. Boston 1936. .60
*Workbook, mainly definitions, with blank
staves to be filled in.*

HAMILTON, ANNA HEUERMANN
Composition for beginners: a practical course in original composition
from the simplest possible beginning
... 93 p, mus ex, bds. Presser 1922. 1.25

HOUSE, L. MARGUERITTE
My music book: books 1 & 2. 48; 48
p, illus (Frederic H. Kock), mus ex,
paper. Schmitt 1937/40. 1.00
Workbooks with blanks to be filled in.

MOY, EDGAR (*comp*)
60 writing lessons in musical theory.
2 v: 16, 16 p, paper. Mills 1934
(1943). .70

PELTERSON, BERTHA K.
50 practical lessons in elements of
musical notation. Forew George
H. Gartlan. 102 p, mus ex, paper.
Hinds 1926. .54

RANKS, H. W. & MORGAN, H. B. NOHAVEC
Composing your own music: progressive steps to composing music, a
workbook for classes in creative
music. 32 p, paper. Schmitt 1939. .50

REEVER, GRACE & KURTZ, MARION
Music fun: theory and appreciation.
3 books: each 63 p, illus (Elaine
Ends), paper. Kenworthy Ed. Service, Buffalo, 1940 (23rd pr n d). 1.17
Same (by Kurtz only): Teacher's
manuals. 3 books, each 61 p, illus,
mus ex, paper. Kenworthy Ed.
Service 1948 1.17

ROBYN, LOUISE & HANKS, HOWARD
The Robyn harmony: a junior course
in written harmony, keyboard harmony, & ear training. 3 v, paper.
Ditson 1936/8.

V 1: iv 56 p, mus ex. 1936. O/P?
V 2: iv, 59 p, mus ex. 1936. .75
V 3: iv, 40 p, mus ex. 1938. .75

*Note: The works above, by Moy, Pelterson,
Ranks & Morgan, Reever & Kurtz, Robyn &
Hanks, are all workbooks, with blank staves
to be filled in.*

SHEPHARD, FRANK H.
Children's harmony: treating of
scales, keys, intervals, simple chords,
& chord-connections, and the training of perceptive powers. 89 p, mus
ex, paper, G. Schirmer 1896 (1924). .75
*Pt 1 of "Harmony simplified" (see Har-
mony-2).*

SLONIMSKY, NICOLAS
The road to music. ix, 178 p, illus,
mus ex. Dodd Mead 1947. 2.75
*While this book is the outgrowth of a series
of articles on the children's page of "The
Christian Science Monitor," it is suitable
both in style & comprehensiveness for use by
adults anxious to obtain a first grounding
in the basic principles of musicianship.*

TROTTER, YORKE & CHAPPLE, STANLEY
Yorke Trotter principles of musicianship for teachers & students. xv,
80 p, mus ex, paper. Bosworth 1933. 2.50

VILLE, MARA
Music made easy: a work book. 50
p, illus, mus ex, paper. Presser 1948. .50

CHILE (Music in)/CHILEAN MUSIC
See: Latin America
Also: App Id (Viu: "Músicos modernos de
Chile," 1944).

CHIMES
See: Carillon.

CHINA (Music in)/CHINESE MUSIC
See also:

Ancient Music (esp	Folksongs-1
Sachs)	History
Asiatic Musics	Instruments
(note only)	Oriental Music
Bibliographies (esp	(note only)
Bartlett)	Songbooks
Folklore	

*Note: Standard works apparently O/P (or not
easily available) include those by van Aalst,
Gulik, Levis, Soulié de Morant (in French),
etc. For an extensive bibliography see that
noted under the Asiatic Musics reference
above. The 11th & 12th installments of
this bibliography (Music Library Association
"Notes" for June & September 1950) were
devoted to China.*

CHAO-MEI-PA
The yellow bell: a brief sketch of the
history of Chinese music. 61 p,

frontis por, illus, mus ex, 2-p bibl.
Author, Baldwin, Maryland, 1934. 1.25
*Originally published in French, 1932, as
"La cloche jaune."*

CHEN, S. H. & C. H.
The flower drum and other Chinese
songs. Forew Pearl S. Buck; pref
Henry Cowell. 64 p, illus, music,
1-p bibl, paper. Day 1944. 2.00
*17 old and new songs, with commentary & a
guide to Chinese pronunciation.*

GRANET, MARCEL
Festivals and songs of ancient China:
including love songs of the Shih
Ching. Tr E. D. Edwards. ix, 281
p. Dutton 1932. 6.00
*"Broadway Oriental Library" series origi-
nally published in French, 1919; no music,
but many song texts.*

GREEN, G. P.
Some aspects of Chinese music: &
some thoughts & impressions on art
principles in music. 149 p. Reeves △
n d (1913?). (1.65)

Ching, James. Author.
See Piano Playing-1, Stage Fright.
Chinoy, Helen Krich. Co-editor (with
Cole). See Acting.
Chissell, Joan. Author.
See Schumann-2.
Chochum, Corinne. Author. See Dances-2

CHOIR/CHORAL
*General Note: For convenience the available
literature is divided into the following three
sub-categories:*

1. **General, Choral Singing**
2. **Conducting, Training, etc.**
3. **Choral Music**

See also:

Amateur Music	Instrumentation
Boy Voices	(esp Forsythe)
Children-7	Phonograph Records
Choral Speaking	Plainsong
Church Music	Program Notes
Community Music	School Music-4
Composers (& under	Sight-Singing
individual names)	Singing
Gregorian Chant	Vocal Music
History	

CHOIR/CHORAL (1. General, Choral Singing)
See also: Singing (esp-2, Taylor).
*Note: Standard works apparently O/P (or not
easily available) include those by Grace, Mees,
Nicholson, Staton, Stubbs, Venables, etc.*

CAIN, NOBLE
Choral music and its practice. xii,
190 p, diagrs, 6–p bibl. Witmark
(1932) rev ed 1942.   **2.50**
The emphasis is on a cappella singing.
Appendices include lists of unacc. choral
scores & recommended books.

CHRISTIANSEN, F. MELIUS
School of choir singing: a one-year
course in singing for older & newer
choirs. 90 p, mus ex. Augsburg 1932. **1.00**

DAVIES, H. WALFORD
Church choirs. 20 p, mus ex, paper.
Paterson 1924, via C. Fischer.   **.40**
"Festival Booklets" series No. 1.

EARHART, WILL
Choral technics: a course integrating
sight singing, vocal training, choral
repertory, & musical understanding.
viii, 103 p, music. Witmark 1937
(3rd pr n d).   **1.75**
A standard work, with many musical
examples.

EHMANN, WILHELM. See App Ib.

FINN, WILLIAM JOSEPH
(*See also Choir/Choral–2.*)
An epitome of some principles of
choral technique. 16 p, mus ex,
paper. Birchard 1935.   **.30**

LORENZ, ELLEN JANE
The choir singer's manual.   23 p,
diagrs, mus ex, paper. Lorenz 1946.   **.50**

RAUGEL, FÉLIX. See App Ia.

SMALLMAN, JOHN & WILCOX, E. H.
The art of a cappella singing: with 16
representative works, containing
instruction for singers in choral
groups to promote an artistic ensemble, & analysis of the compositions for technique, interpretation,
& appreciation.   vii, 197 p, music.
Ditson 1933.   **2.00**

STOESSEL, ALBERT
The choralist's double dozen: 24
"case method" exercises for small
& large choirs. Pref Caroline Beeson
Fry.   iv,   21 p,   music,   paper.
Birchard 1931.   **.50**

CHOIR/CHORAL (2. Conducting, Train-ing)

Note: Standard works apparently O/P or not
easily available) include those by Jacobs,
Manchester, Phillips, Richardson, Roberts,
etc.

See also:
Accompaniment   Organ Playing
Arranging–1 (Wilson)   Organists
Choir/Choral–1 & 3   School Music–4
Christiansen   (esp Burns)
Conducting   Teaching–2
Finn

ANTCLIFFE, HERBERT
The choirmaster: a practical guide
to organizing & conducting choirs
& choral societies.   Intro Sir Henry
Coward. 78 p, diagrs, 2–p bibl, bds.
Paxton & Co, London, n d.   **1.00**
Includes lists of choral music.

CARNETT, E. L.
The technique of conducting. 88 p,
music, paper.   Broadman 1948.   **.75**
Primarily for conducting church music for
choral groups—hymns, in particular.

CHRISTY, VAN A.
(*See also Choir/Choral–3.*)
Glee club and chorus: a handbook of
organizing, conducting, & maintaining glee club & choral organizations,
with selected, graded, & classified
lists of octavo music & texts.   viii,
149 p, illus, bds. G. Schirmer 1940.   **3.50**
A standard guide-book for the choral director,
with detailed, classified tables of recommended
musical materials.

COLEMAN, HENRY
The amateur choir trainer.   Forew
Harvey Grace. xvi, 143 p, mus ex,
5–p annot bibl, paper. Oxford 1932
(5th pr 1945).   **1.50**
Choral conducting for women's insti-
tutes.   32 p, diagrs, mus ex, paper.
Oxford 1932 (1942).   **.40**
Youth club choirs. xi, 108 p, diagrs,
mus ex, flex.   Oxford 1950.   **1.25**
Practical handbooks on their specialized
subjects, with suggested materials.

COWARD, HENRY
Choral technique and interpretations
for choral conductors & choirmasters.
333 p, 2 pl, mus ex. Gray n d (1914?) **4.50**

DAVISON, ARCHIBALD T.
Choral conducting. x, 73 p, diagrs,
mus ex. Harvard 1940 (5th pr 1948)   **2.00**
A standard work, outlining methods of the
former conductor of the Harvard Glee Club.

EDESON, DONALD J. S.
The training of Catholic choirs: a
short treatise for choirmasters &
organists. 63 p, mus ex, 1½–p bibl,
paper.   Cary & Co., London, 1934,
via E. C. Schirmer.   **1.25**

FINN, WILLIAM JOSEPH
(*See also Choir/Choral–1.*)
The art of the choral conductor.
V 1: choral technique. viii, 292 p,
mus ex. Birchard 1939.   4.00
The conductor raises his baton. Pref
Leopold Stokowski. x, 302 p, mus
ex. Harper 1944.   3.75
*Two standard works by the director of the
noted Paulist Choir: Father Finn.*

FUHR, HAYES M.
Fundamentals of choral expression.
xi, 103 p, 2–p bibl. Nebraska 1944.   2.00
*Practical advice on organizational as well as
interpretative problems.*

GRACE, HARVEY
The training and conducting of
choral societies. 70 p, illus, paper.
Novello n d (1938?).   (1.25)
Novello "Primer" series 113.

HJORTSVANG, CARL
The amateur choir director: a handbook. 127 p, diagrs, mus ex. Abingdon 1941.   1.50

HOGGARD, LARA G.
Improving music reading in the
choral rehearsal. ii, 25 p, mus ex,
typescript repro, paper. Shawnee
Press 1947 (1949?).   .50
*Training methods demonstrated in the Fred
Waring Music Workshops.*

JONES, ARCHIE N.
Techniques in choral conducting.
136 p, diagrs, mus ex, 2–p bibl. C.
Fischer 1948.   3.00
*The appendices include a glossary, recom-
mended anthems, community song collections,
choral recordings, & interpretative analyses.*

KRONE, MAX T.
Expressive conducting. iv, 92 p,
illus, mus ex, paper. Kjos 1945.   1.50
*Primarily choral, with recommended songs
for community singing.*

NORDIN, DAYTON W. (*ed*)
The choirmaster's workbook: v 2.
277 p, tables, spir. Augustana 1949.   2.25
*Pocket-size handbook with church-year calen-
dars for 1949/52. Volume 1 (1947) is O/P.*

PETERSON, PHEBE LEWIS
A junior choir manual: a practical
guide & instruction book for choir
directors & church music committees
48 p, paper. Lorenz 1937.   .50

STAPLES, H. J.
The choirmaster and organist: a

manual. 159 p. Epworth Press,
London, 1939 (2nd pr 1941).   1.50

THOMAS, KURT. See App Ib.

TOOP, AUGUSTUS
The organist and his choir. 64 p,
mus ex, paper. Musical Opinion
1925.   1.00

WODELL, FREDERICK W.
Choir and chorus conducting: a
treatise on the organization, management, training, & conducting of
choirs, choral societies, & other vocal
ensembles. 266 p, diagrs, mus ex.
Presser (1901) 12th ed 1931.   2.25
*Includes questions, for classroom use, on the
subject matter of each chapter.*

WOODGATE, LESLIE
The choral conductor. Intro Sir
Malcolm Sargent. viii, 80 p, mus
ex, paper. Ascherberg 1949.   1.25
*A guide to choral performances, with lists of
works & "Messiah" performance-notes.*
The chorus master. 41 p, diagrs, mus
ex, paper. Ascherberg 1944 (3rd pr
1945).   2.00
A guide to directing choral rehearsals.

CHOIR/CHORAL (3. Choral Music)
See also:

Choir/Choral–1 & 2	Hymns/Hymnody
Church Music	Madrigal
Composers (& under	Mass
individual names)	Motet
Composition (esp	Phonograph Records
Davison)	Plainsong
Gregorian Chant	Psalms/Psalmody

*Note: Pertinent works apparently O/P (or not
easily available) include those by Drinker
(see special note under author entry for Henry
S. Drinker), Thompson & Dickinson, etc.*

BARNES, EDWARD SHIPPEN (*comp*)
Choirmasters' and chorus conductors'
guide: a systematic classification of
church & chorus music in octavo
form. 180 p, paper. Boston n d
1949?). *Classified lists.*   .25

CHRISTY, VAN A.
(*See also Choir/Choral–2.*)
Evaluation of choral music: methods
of appraising the practical value of
choral compositions with reference
to music generally available in the
United States. x, 107 p, 18 tables,
2½–p bibl. Teachers College 1948.   2.15
"Contributions to Education" No. 885.

DAVID, HANS THEODORE (*ed*)
The art of polyphonic song: com-

positions of the 16th & 17th centuries, for 2 to 8 parts. English tr Willis Wager. 111 p, music, bds. G. Schirmer 1940.   2.00

A collection of music, but included here since it also embodies an introduction on the interpretation of polyphonic music, plus detailed notes on the compositions.

HOLCOMB, CLIFFORD A.
Methods and materials for graded choirs. xii, 137 p, 3–p bibl, paper. Boardman 1948.   .50

LOCKE, ARTHUR WARE (*comp*)
Selected list of choruses for women's voices. x, 237 p, paper. (1927) Smith College 2nd rev enl ed 1946.   3.75
Smith College Monograph No. 2.

MANNING, ROSEMARY
From Holst to Britten: a study of modern choral music. vii, 80 p, mus ex, paper. Workers' Music Assn, London, 1949.   (1.50)
Notes on choral works by Bliss, Boughton, Britten, Bush, Holst, Ireland, Lambert, Rubbra, Tippett, Vaughan Williams, & Walton.

RHEA, LOIS & RAYMOND
Choral program planning. 88 p, paper. Southern 1947.   1.00
Graded list & classified index of works.

CHOPIN, Frédéric
1. Life   2. Works

CHOPIN (1. Life)
See also:

Appreciation	Program Notes
Composers–1	Romantic Era
History	Sand
Poland (music in)	

Also: App IIa (Wheeler juveniles).

Note: Standard works apparently O/P (or not easily available) include the letters, ed Opienski, and books by Bidou, Finck, Ganche (in French), Hoesick (in Polish), Huneker, Jachimecki (in French), Karasowski, Leichtentritt (in German), Murdoch, Niecks, Pourtalès (but see App Ia), Uminska & Kennedy, Weissmann (in German), etc.

BRONARSKI, LUDWIK. See App Ia.

CHERBULIEZ, A. E. See App Ib.

COATES, HENRY
Chopin. ? p, cover por, paper. Novello n d.   .40
Miniature biography ("great musicians").

CORTOT, ALFRED. See App Ia.

GIDE, ANDRÉ
Notes on Chopin. Tr Bernard Frechtman. 126 p, mus ex. Philosophical 1949.   3.75
Extracts from Gide's journals on Chopin & music in general. See also App Ia for the original French edition of 1948.

HEDLEY, ARTHUR
Chopin. viii, 214 p, 8 pl (pors, facs, etc), mus ex, 3–p bibl. Dent 1947, Pellegrini 1949.   2.50
"Master Musicians" series, with usual calendar, catalogue of works, etc. This work, embodying the results of latest Polish research, replaces an earlier biography in this series by J. Cuthbert Hadden (1921).

LISZT, FRANZ
Frédéric Chopin. Tr John Broadhouse. viii, 240 p, frontis. Reeves & Scribners (1901) rev ed 1913.   4.00
Available again after having been O/P during the war years. See also App Ib for a German translation.

MAINE, BASIL
Chopin. 128 p, frontis por, bibl. (1933) Wyn 1949.   1.00
"Great Musicians" series; originally published in London, 1933, without the present 3–p catalogue of works.

MIZWA, STEPHEN P. (*ed*)
Frédéric Chopin, 1810–1849. xviii, 108 p, col frontis. 35 pl (pors, facs, etc). Macmillan 1949.   3.00
A centennial publication under the auspices of the Kosciusko Foundation. It includes life-story by Mizwa, articles by Chasins, Conrad, Downes, Hanson, Jarecki, Paderewski; excerpts from unpublished letters to Delfina Potocka; & an extensive catalogue of works compiled by Bronislaw Sydow.

POURTALÈS, GUY DE. See App Ia.

REHBERG, PAULA & WALTER. See App Ib.

SCHALLENBERG, E. W.
Frédéric Chopin. Tr M. Smedts. 57 p, 23 illus (pors, facs), bibl, bds. Continental n d (1948/9?).   2.50
"Symphonia" series of extensively illustrated brief biographies.

TARNOWSKI, COUNT
Chopin: as revealed by extracts from his diary. Tr Natalie Janotha; ed J. Tangueray. 69 p, 8 pors Reeves n d (1905).   △   (1.65)

WEINSTOCK, HERBERT
Chopin: the man and his music. x, 336, xxii p, 9 pl (pors, facs), 6–p annot bibl. Knopf 1949.   5.00

First of the special centennial releases. Includes a detailed analysis of the works, and an appendix of documents & genealogical data.

WIERZYNSKI, CASIMIR
The life and death of Chopin. Tr Norbert Guterman; pref Artur Rubinstein. xvi, 444 p + 12–p pl, 5–p bibl. S & S 1949.   3.95

A centennial biography by a Polish poet & musicologist with special emphasis on Chopin's early life & Polish backgrounds, and excerpts from the Potocka correspondence.

CHOPIN (2. Works)

See also:

Appreciation	Piano Music
Ballet (esp Haskell)	Piano Playing
Composers–1	Poland (music in)
Concerto	Program Notes
Phonograph Records	Themes
Piano Playing	Vocal Music

Note: Standard works apparently O/P (or not easily available) include those by Dunn, Ganche (in French), Johnson, Kelley, Kleczinski, Leichtentritt (in German), etc.

ABRAHAM, GERALD
Chopin's musical style. xiii, 116 p, mus ex. Oxford 1939 (3rd pr 1946). 2.75

Studies of the "evolution of a musical personality, Chopin's mature style (1831/40), & the last phase (1841/49)."

JONSON, G. C. ASHTON
A handbook to Chopin's works: giving a detailed account of all the compositions of Chopin, short analyses for the piano student, & critical quotations from the writings of well-known musical authors . . . 287 p, tables, 9–p annot bibl. Reeves △ (1905), 3rd ed n d.   (4.50)

Detailed program notes rather than technical analyses, plus biographical sketch, & chronological lists of works.

PANIGEL, ARMAND (& others, comps)
The works of Frederic Chopin: general discography prepared under the supervision of Armand Panigel. Intro & notes Marcel Beaufils. 253 p + 8 pl (pors, facs), paper. Revue Disques, Paris, 1950. △

The first volume in the series of "Archives of Recorded Music UNESCO." Co-compilers: Claude Galtat, Jean Germain, Antoine

Goltea, & Henry-Jacques. For the original French edition (1949), see App Ia (Panigel). The present English translation (translator unnamed) is a limited edition, but negotiations are now in progress for American publication of this and other works in preparation in the monumental UNESCO series.

PORTE, JOHN F.
Chopin, the composer and his music: an analytic critique of famous traditions & interpretations as exhibited in the playing of great pianists, past & present. 193 p, frontis por. Reeves △ 1935.   (2.50)

Super-title: "The why & how of playing Chopin."

CHORAL SPEAKING

See also: Poetry, Speech, Voice.

Note: The works listed are only a sampling of the considerable literature, much of which is published by The Expression Company, Magnolia, Massachusetts.

BANKE, CÉCILE DE
The art of choral speaking. Intro Charles Swain Thomas. 227 p, diagrs. Baker's Plays, Boston, 1937. 1.75

GULLAN, MARJORIE
Choral speaking. xii, 91 p. Expression (1931) 3rd rev ed 1936.   2.25

The speech choir: with American poetry & British ballads for choral reading. xix, 284 p. Harper 1937.   2.50

KEPPIE, ELIZABETH E.
The teaching of choric speech. 149 p. Expression 1937.   2.25

CHORALE(S)

See:

Bach–1 & 2	Church Music
Choir/Choral–3	Luther

Note: Collections of music only (chorales by Bach & others) are not listed here.

CHORD(S)

See:

Acoustics	Harmony (esp Budge)
Children–3 & 8	Scales
Composition	Theory (esp 4)

Chorley, Henry Fothergill. Author.
See National Music.

Note: Chorley's "Recollections" (1862) & other larger works apparently are all O/P.

CHRISTIANSEN, Frederick Melius

See also: Choir/Choral–1 (for Christiansen's own book on choral singing).

BERGMANN, LEOLA NELSON
Music master of the middle west:
the story of F. Melius Christiansen
& the St. Olaf choir. v, 230 p, illus.
Minnesota 1944.   2.50

CHRISTMAS
See: Carols, Folklore, Songbooks.

Christy, Van Ambrose. Author.
See Choir/Choral–2 & 3.

CHROMATICISM
See:

Composition	Monophony
Harmony	Scale
History	Theory

Chujoy, Anatole. Editor.
See (The) Dance.

Church, Norval L. Co-author (with
Dykema). See School Music–3.

CHURCH MUSIC
See also:

Accompaniment	History
America (music in)	Hymns/Hymnody
American Music	Jewish Music
(esp Britton)	Latin Language
Ancient Music	Luther
Asiatic Musics	L. Mason
(note only)	Mass
Augustine	Medieval/Renaissance
Bach	Mode/Modality
Baroque Era	(esp Perfield)
Byrd	Organ Music
Byzantine Music	Organ Playing
California (music in)	Organists
Carillon	Phonograph Records
Children–1 (esp	Pilgrims (music of)
Shields)	Plainsong
Choir/Choral	Program Notes
Community Music	Psalms/Psalmody
Composers (& under	Puritans (& music)
individual names)	Religion (& music)
Elizabethan Music	Terry
England (music in)	Vocal Music
Fellowes	Watts
Gregorian Chant	

*General Note: Here, if ever, there should be
opportunity for several distinct sub-categories,
into which the enormous literature on
this subject could be conveniently divided.
Unfortunately, however, a large part of the
literature is O/P, many other publications
are eliminated from the present lists by reason
of their highly specialized nature or the fact
that they are not easily or generally available;
and of the remaining works that can be listed
here, many cannot be fitted accurately into
specific sect or other sub-categories.*

*So, after several fruitless attempts to develop
sub-classification schemes that would be both
accurate & useful, they have been abandoned*

*entirely. We have fallen back on one basic
list of available publications, but wherever
possible we have tried to augment the titles &
sub-titles with descriptive notes that will give
the prospective reader at least some notion
of the individual work's particular scope
& denominational point of view (if it is
restricted to one).*

*Note: Standard works apparently O/P (or not
easily available) include those of Arnold,
Curwen, Douglas, Engel, Gastoué (in French),
Gilbert, Hadow, Hughes, Lorenz, Nicholson,
Ninde, Predmore, Richardson, Stewart, Terry,
Whitley, etc.*

*Of these, a special note might be made on the
late Canon Wilfred Douglas's "Church music
in history & practice" (Scribner 1937), for
it is an extremely useful over-all survey &
general introduction to the whole subject. A
reprint or new edition is badly needed.*

ASHTON, JOSEPH N.
Music in worship: the use of music
in church worship. 232 p. Beacon
(1943) 4th ed 1947.   3.00
*An interdenominational survey, distinguish-
ing between music's function in liturgical
& non-liturgical services.*

BLUME, FRIEDRICH.   See App Ib (ed
Bücken).

CLOKEY, JOSEPH W.
In every corner sing: an outline of
church music for the layman. 86 p,
1–p bibl, paper. Morehouse-
Gorham Co, N. Y., 1945 (1946).   .50
*Primarily from the Protestant point of view.
The same publishers also provide a supplement: a list of choir & organ music for the
small choir, 8 p, mim, paper, 35c.*

DAVIES, WALFORD & GRACE, HARVEY
Music and worship. xi, 255 p, mus
ex, 3–p annot bibl. Gray 1935.   2.50
*A standard work, primarily from the Church-
of-England point of view.*

DAVISON, ARCHIBALD T.
Protestant church music in America.
ix, 182 p, mus ex. E. C. Schirmer
1933 (4th pr 1948).   3.00
*A standard work, dealing with the attitudes
& conditions affecting Protestant church
music, as well as with the theory & substance
of the music itself.*

DICKINSON, EDWARD
Music in the history of the western
church: with an introduction on
religious music among primitive &
ancient peoples. ix, 426 p, mus ex,
5–bibl. Scribner 1902.   4.00

Perhaps "the" standard, comprehensive, historical survey.

FELLOWES, EDMUND H.
English cathedral music from Edward VI to Edward VII. ix, 268 p, mus ex. Methuen (1941) 4th ed 1948.   4.50
An authoritative survey of a musically rich specialized subject. The appendix includes examples of cathedral weekly music lists.

The office of the Holy Communion as set by John Merbecke. 42 p, mus △ ex (in 2 colors). Oxford 1949.   4.00
A limited edition of "At the Communion" from "The booke of common praier noted" (1550), together with biographical notes, and studies of Merbecke's notation & the modern revival of his (Anglican) service.

Tudor church music: appendix with supplementary notes. 55 p, paper. Oxford 1948.   5.00
Appendix to the definitive 10-volume "Carnegie" edition of Tudor church music.

GARDNER, G. L. H. & NICHOLSON, S. H. (eds)
A manual of English church music: with an appendix bringing it up to date. viii, 232 p, mus ex, tables. Society for Promoting Christian Knowledge, London (1923) rev ed 1932, via Macmillan.   2.50
Includes articles by various writers & a list of English church-music composers.

GERBERT, MARTIN (ed). See App Ie.

HOELTY-NICKEL, THEODORE (ed)
The musical heritage of the church. 127 p, paper. Valparaiso 1946.   .50
A symposium (from the Lutheran point of view), with essays by Bichsel, Buszin, Rosenwald, Sanderson, Schrade, Stelzer.

HOFFMANN, HANS. See App Ib.

KETTRING, DONALD D.
Steps toward a singing church. 342 p. Westminster 1948.   4.50
A study in organizing & maintaining the (Protestant) church choral program. The appendix includes mimeographed forms, statistical tables, and a list of anthems.

NEMMERS, ERWIN ESSER
Twenty centuries of Catholic church music. Forew Rev Carlo Rossini. xvii, 213 p, 11 pl, 4 tables, chap bibls. Bruce 1949.   4.00
An attempt at a scholarly survey by a non-musicologist. The appendix includes a glossary & the "Motu Proprio on sacred music."

NININGER, RUTH
Growing a musical church. xiii, 157 p, 2-p bibl, paper. Broadman 1947.   .75
One of a series of Baptist Sunday School Board church music publications.

PARKER, (Mrs) ALVIN A. (& others, eds).
Church music and musical life in Pennsylvania in the 18th century. 3 v in 4: 1182 p, 410 pl, 15-p bibls. Society of Colonial Dames, Phila- △ delphia, 1926/47.   21.00
An extensive specialized study including numerous facsimiles of early MSS & scores. The first two volumes are edited by Mrs Parker, v 3 by May A. Leach, & v 4 by William Lichtenwanger.

PARRY, W. H.
Thirteen centuries of English church music: an introduction to a great national tradition. 64 p, illus, mus ex. Hinrichsen 2nd enl ed 1946.   1.50
Historical summary from the 7th century to the present, with biographical notes, for the general reader.

PATTERSON, FLOYD
Pioneering in church music: the organization & development of a state-wide church music program among Baptists in Texas.   92 p, tables, paper. Baylor 1949.   1.00

PHILLIPS, CHARLES HENRY
The singing church: an outline history of the music sung by choir & people. 279 p, 9 illus, 61 mus ex, 6-p bibl. Faber 1945 (3rd pr 1946).   6.00
From the English point of view, covering the era from pre-Reformation services to the present. Includes glossary & history charts.

PRATT, WALDO SELDEN
Musical ministries in the church: studies in the history, theory, & administration of sacred music. 213 p, 9-p bibl. G. Schirmer (1901) 3rd ed 1923.   1.50
A standard work (from the Protestant point of view) on American church music. It includes a history of English hymnody.

(PROTESTANT EPISCOPAL CHURCH, U. S. A., JOINT COMMISSION ON CHURCH MUSIC)
The choral service: the liturgical music for morning & evening prayer; the Litany & the Holy Communion ...xx, 102 p, music. Gray (1927) rev ed n d.   2.00
Title on cover only: "The choral service: a manual for clergy & organist."

PUSHEE, RUTH
Music in the religious service. 91 p,
3½-p bibl. Revell 1938.   1.00

RICHARDS, G. DARLINGTON
The voluntaries and their place in
the church service.   26 p, paper.
G. Schirmer 1911.   .25
*Brief essays on general principles; types of
suitable preludes, offertories, & postludes;
and the value of extemporizing.*

ROBERTSON, ALEC
Sacred music. 72 p, 4 col pl, 26 b&ws
(facs, etc), mus ex. Chanticleer 1950.   2.50
*"World of Music" series No 11: a hand-
somely illustrated over-all survey.*

ROUTLEY, ERIK
The church and music: an enquiry
into the history, the nature, & the
scope of Christian judgment on music.
255 p, bibl refs + 1-p bibl note. △
Duckworth 1950.   (2.75)
*The story of Christian thought about music,
with special reference to Augustine's "De
Musica" & the achievements of the 19th
century (incl the Schenker theories).*

SHAW, MARTIN
The principles of English church
music composition. 48 p, mus ex,
paper. Musical Opinion 1921.   1.00

SIMS, W. HINES
Instrumental music in the church. x,
132 p, 1-p bibl, paper. Broadman
1947.   .75
*Use of the organ, piano, & orchestra in the
Baptist Sunday School Board church-music
course series; with lists of materials.*

(SOCIETY OF ST GREGORY OF AMERICA)
The white list of the Society of Saint
Gregory of America, with a selection
of Papal documents & other informa-
tion pertaining to Catholic church
music. 95 p, paper.   St Gregory
Society, N. Y., 4th aug ed 1947.   1.00
Prepared by the Society's music committee.

STUBBINGS, G. W.
A dictionary of church music. 128 p.
Epworth Press, London, 1949; Philosophical 1950.   3.75
*Dictionary style: short explanations of the
principal technical terms & most important
topics, from A Cappella to Wind Pressure.*

SWARM, PAUL (ed)
Guideposts for the church musician:
a manual workbook to help those
desiring to improve church music.
Associate ed Val Jayne; pref Ernest

C. Witham. Unp (some 244 p), 7-p
illus, bibl refs, loose-leaf bind. Church
Music Foundation, Decatur, Ill.,
1949.   10.00
Handbook of classified, practical notes.

SWISHER, WALTER SAMUEL
Music in worship. 83 p, mus ex, chap
bibls, paper. Ditson 1929.   .75
*"Pocket Music Student" series, with notes on
the hymn, choir & organ, the function of the
service prelude & anthem, etc.*

URSPRUNG, OTTO. See App Ib (ed Bücken).

WEINMANN, KARL
History of church music: an outline
history of Catholic church music from
its origins to the Motu Proprio of
Pope Pius X, 1903.   vii, 216 p, 6-p
bibl. (Pustet n d, 1910) McLaughlin
& Reilly repr n d (1948?).   2.75
*Anonymous English translation of a standard
work, originally in German, 1906.*

WOLFE, P. A. & DICKINSON, H. A. & C.
The choir loft and the pulpit: 52
complete services of worship. 124 p,
paper. Gray 1943.   1.50
Mainly lists of (Protestant) material.

CIVILIZATION (Music &)
See: Aesthetics, History, Philosophy.

CIVIL WAR (& Music)
See:

America (music in)	History
American Music	Popular Music
(esp Harwell)	Sheet Music
Folklore	Songbooks
Folksongs-2	

CLARINET
See also:

Band-1	Instruments
Chamber Music	Orchestra
Concerto	Wind Instruments
Instrumentation	

DUNBAR, RUDOLPH
Treatise on the clarinet (Boehm
system). 141 p, illus, mus ex. John
E. Dallas & Sons, London, 1939 (7th
pr 1947).   3.50

FOSTER, LEVIN WILSON
A directory of clarinet music. 128 p,
paper. Author, Pittsfield, Massachusetts, 1940.   3.00

STUBBINS, WILLIAM H.
Applied musical theory for the
clarinetist. George Wahr, Ann Arbor,
Michigan, 1951 in prep.   3.00

The study of the clarinet: an intro- duction to the problems of clarinet playing. 155 p, illus, chart. music, typescript repro, paper. George Wahr Pub Co, Ann Arbor, Michigan, 1940 (1948). 3.00

WILLAMAN, ROBERT The clarinet and clarinet playing: a text for beginners, advanced players, listeners. 241 p, frontis por, illus (Stanley P. Cook), mus ex. Author, Salt Point, N. Y., 1949. 3.75

Clarke, Kenneth Sherman. Author. See America (music in), Industry. **Clarke, A. Mason.** Author. See Violinists. **Clarke, Harry F.** Co-author (with Skeat & Morgan). See Arranging–1. **Clarke, Hugh Archibald.** Author. See Counterpoint–2, Dictionaries of Terms. Harmony–2.

CLASS METHODS
See:

Children	School Music
Choir/Choral	Singing
Education	Teaching
Piano Playing	Violin Playing

CLASSIC ERA/CLASSICISM
See also:

Aesthetics	Orchestral Music
Appreciation	Organ Music
Baroque Era	Phonograph Records
Chamber Music	Piano Music
Choir/Choral–3	Program Notes
Church Music	Romantic Era
Composers–1 (& under	Song(s)
individual names)	Symphony
History	Tonality/Atonality
Instrumentation	Variation
Musicology	Vienna
Opera	Violin Music
Orchestra	Vocal Music

General Note: Although to the man in the street "classical" music is everything outside the province of popular music & jazz, and although "classicism" strictly implies the presence of certain qualities that may be found to a greater or less extent in serious music of all periods, the "classic era" term is used here in its familiar, restricted musical sense of the period lying between (& merging with) the Baroque & Romantic eras,—in particular the period of the Viennese classical school of composers led by Haydn, Mozart, & Beethoven, and sharing Schubert (& perhaps Brahms) with the Romantic Era.

The composers & music of this period are of course the subjects of an enormous literature, but curiously enough there is as yet only one

entry (in English) to be listed here rather than under some of the closely allied subject- headings suggested as cross-references above:

BÜCKEN, ERNST. See App Ib (Handbuch der Musikwissenschaft, v 4).

LANG, PAUL HENRY Music in the classic era. Norton in prep. △

V 5 of the "Norton History of Music" series, of which Lang is also the general editor (see History–1).

CLAUDEL, Paul *See:* App Ia (Samson's biog in French).

CLAVECIN/CLAVICHORD
See: esp App Ib (Neupert's "Das Klavi- chord," in German).
Also:

Appreciation	History
Baroque Era	Keyboard Instruments
Chamber Music	& Music (esp Ken-
Elizabethan Music	yon)
Instruments	Piano

CLAVILUX
See: Color (& music), Instruments.

CLEMENS, Jacobus ("non Papa") *See:*

Choir/Choral–3	History
Church Music	Medieval/Renaissance
Composers–1	(esp Lowinsky)

Clercx, Susanne. Author. See App Ia.

CLEVELAND (Music in) *See:* America (music in), A. Hughes.

Cliffe, Cedric. Author. See Appreciation. **Clinton-Baddeley, Victor Clinton.** Author. See Poetry. **Clippinger, David Alva.** Author. See Sight-Singing, Singing–2. **Clokey, Joseph Waddell.** Author. See Church Music, Plainsong. **Closson, Ernest.** Author. See Piano, also App Ia. **Clough, F. F.** Compiler (with Cuming). See Phonograph Records.

CLUBS (Musical)
See:

Amateur Music	School Music–1
America (music in)	Yearbooks
Community Music	

Note: Elson's "Music club programs from all nations" (1906/28) apparently is O/P.

Coar, Birchard. Author.
See Conductors, French Horn.
Coates, Henry. Author.
See Chopin, Palestrina.
Cobbett, Walter Wilson
See Chamber Music.
Cobbold, Joan. Author. See Carols.
Coeuroy, André (Jean Belime). Author.
Editor. See App Ia.
Cohen, Harriet. Author.
See Piano Playing–1.
Cohn, Arthur. Author.
See Chamber Music.
Cole, Edward Cyrus. Co-author (with Burris-Meyer). See Theatre.
Cole, Natalie Robinson. Author.
See School Music–1.
Cole, Toby. Compiler, editor.
See Acting.
Coleman, Arthur P. & Marion M.
Authors. See Mickiewicz (note only).
Coleman, Henry. Author.
See Choir/Choral–2.
Coleman, (Mrs) Satis Narrona Barton.
Author. See Children–1, 3, & 4. Editor
(with Bregman). See Folksongs–2.

COLERIDGE-TAYLOR, Samuel

Note: A "memory sketch" by Coleridge-Taylor's widow (1944) and a life & letters by Sayers (1925/27) both apparently are O/P (or not easily available in this country).

Colin, Charles. Author. See Trumpet.
Collaer, Paul. Author. See App Ia.
Collan, Anni. Co-author (with Heikel).
See Dances–2 (ed Alford).

COLLEGES/UNIVERSITIES

See also: Education, School Music.
Note: Standard works apparently O/P (or not easily available) include Dickinson's "Music & the higher education", 1915 (O/P at Scribner's, New York, but still listed in the Reeves catalogue in London), Jeffers's "Music for the general college student" (1944), & Welch's "The study of music in the American college" (1925).

JONES, VINCENT
Music education in the college. vi,
220 p, diagrs, tables, mus ex, 13–p
bibl. Birchard 1949.   3.00
A recent over-all survey, with specimen lessons at various levels.

KAHO, ELIZABETH E.
Analysis of the study of music literature in selected American colleges. △
74 p, bibl. Teachers College 1950.   2.35

"Contributions to Education" No 971, based on a poll of some 432 institutions, which were queried about the compositions used in their courses or considered essential to the training of musicians.

(MUSIC SUPERVISORS NATIONAL CONFERENCES RESEARCH COUNCIL)
Survey of college entrance credits
and college courses in music. Fore.
C. M. Tremaine. ix, 209 p, 3 diagrs,
tables. National Bureau for the
Advancement of Music 1930, via
National Recreation Assn.   2.00
The attitude of the colleges toward music and a detailed tabulation of data.

THOMPSON, RANDALL
College music: an investigation for
the Association of American Colleges.
Forew Robert L. Kelly. xviii, 279 p,
2 pl. Macmillan 1935.   2.75
A standard, extensively documented study of the place of music in 30 liberal arts colleges for the academic year 1932/3, with a suggested program for development.

COLLES, Henry Cope

Essays and lectures. With a memoir
of the author by H. J. C. vii, 224
p, frontis por, mus ex. Oxford 1945. 3.75
Shorter writings of the London "Times" critic, with a memoir by his widow.

On learning music and other essays.
68 p, paper. Oxford 1940.   .50

Author, editor. See also:
Brahms–2. Chamber music (1933).   1.00
Davies, Walford. Biog (1942).   2.50
Dictionaries of Music. Grove's,
ed Colles. 6-v 4th ed & sup v.   37.50
History–1. Oxford v 7 (note).   △
History–2. Growth of music (1912;
3 v in 1, 1939).   5.00
History–5. Parry Evolution, rev
Colles, 1930.   (2.50)

Note: Several other books by Colles apparently are O/P (or not easily available).

Collet, Henri. Author. See App Ia.
Collinson, Francis M. Author.
See Instrumentation/Orchestration.

COLOMBIA (Music in)

See: Latin America.

COLOR (& Music)

Note: Pertinent works, dealing mainly with so-called "color music," apparently O/P (or not easily available) include those by Karwoski & Odbert, Rimington, etc.

See also:

Aesthetics	Children–3 (Hughey)
Acoustics	Psychology

KLEIN, ADRIAN BERNARD
Coloured light: an art medium; being the 3rd ed enlarged of "Colour-Music." xxx, 287 p, 23 pl, 20 diagrs, 10-p bibl. (1926) Technical Press, London, 1937, via Anglobooks 1950. 6.25

The standard work on the subject—one that has fascinated some æstheticians, at least one composer (Scriabin), and many inventors —of whom the best known probably is Thomas Wilfred, who has demonstrated a "color-organ" called the "Clavilux."

COLORATURA

See: esp App Ia (Machabey: "Le bel canto").

Also:

History	Singers
Interpreters	Singing
Opera	Voice
Ornamentation	Vocal Music

Colson, Percy. Author. See Massenet.
Commins, Dorothy Berliner. Author. See App Ib (juveniles).

COMMUNITY MUSIC

See also:

Amateur Music	Folksongs
Band–1	Operetta
Children	School Music
Choir/Choral	Songbooks
Folklore	Teaching

Note: Van de Wall's "The music of the people" (1938) apparently is O/P (or not easily available).

In addition to the NRA, Frieswyck, & Zanzig entries below, the National Recreation Association, 315 Fourth Avenue, New York City 10, publishes or distributes many pamphlets, song sheets, specialized music lists, etc (plus a magazine, "Recreation") of marked value to everyone engaged—or interested—in various aspects of community music.

BERGMAN, WALTER G. (& others)
Practical music for all: a symposium. Intro Christopher le Fleming; conclusion H. Watkins Shaw. 95 p, paper. Hinrichsen n d (1948?). 1.75
Hinrichsen "Survey" series S-8: brief chapters by various authors on percussion bands, recorders, bamboo pipes, brass bands, piano classes, amateur opera, choral singing, & amateur orchestras.

FRIESWYK, SIEBOLT H.
Forty approaches to informal singing: varied approaches to the art of conducting informal singing, with suggested musical material. 30 p, mus ex, 3–p bibl, paper. National Recreation Assn (1939) 3rd ed 1948. .35
How to improve group singing.

(MUSIC EDUCATORS NATIONAL CONFERENCE)
Music for everybody: a report & pictorial review. Intro Claude B. Smith. 52, xii p, photos, paper. MENC 1950. 1.00
Pictures & reports on community activities, prepared by the Committee on School-Community Music Relations & Activities.

(NATIONAL RECREATION ASSN)
Annotated bibliography for music leaders in camp, playground, recreation center. 8 p, typescript repro, paper. National Recreation Assn 1948. .15
A regularly revised list of useful material.

(PLAYGROUND & RECREATION ASSOCIATION OF AMERICA)
Community music: a practical guide for the conduct of community musical activities. 193 p, diagrs, chap bibls. (1920) Birchard 1926. 1.50
A standard work, with stories of American songs, carols, singing games, etc.

WILSON, HARRY ROBERT
Lead a song!: a practical guide to the organization & conducting of informal group singing. iii, 114 p, diagrs, mus ex, bibl refs. Hall McCreary 1942. 1.50
A standard, comprehensive collection of useful directions, with an 11-p annotated section of "Sources of Songs".

ZANZIG, AUGUSTUS D.
Community and assembly singing: a complete guide to general singing in the community, school, church, club, camp, & home. 64 p, paper. Witmark 1933. .75
Music and men: a manual for planning & developing musical activities in communities near training or manufacturing centers—of army, navy or industry. 30 p, 2–p bibl, paper. National Recreation Assn (1941) 2nd ed 1942. .15
Starting and maintaining a community orchestra. Forew Ernest

LaPrade. 50 p, paper. National
Recreation Assn 1940.   .35
*Standard booklets of practical advice &
directions by an authority in this field.*

"COMPANIONS"

*Note: Books titled or sub-titled musical
"companions" are usually more or less
"popularized" hand- or guide-books.*

See:

Appreciation (Bach-	Mozart-3
arach, Erskine)	(Hutchings)
Ballet (Ambrose)	Program Notes
Dictionaries of Music	Program Notes
(Scholes)	(Bagar & Biancolli)
Miscellanies	

COMPETITIONS

See: Examinations, School Music, Tests.

*Note: For information on State & National
school-music competition festivals, consult
the Music Educators National Conference,
64 East Jackson Blvd, Chicago 4, the distributors of graded music lists, etc, published
by the National School Band, Orchestra, &
Vocal Associations.*

COMPOSERS (Collective Studies)

*General Note: Most books on music are
primarily concerned with composers: besides
the numerous biographies & critical studies
(listed in the present Guide under the name of
the individual composer concerned), many
books on specialized subjects deal as much
with the men involved as with their particular
musical works or techniques under discussion.*

*The present subject-heading, however, is re-
served for books dealing in general (either
explicitly or implicitly) with two or more composers as such. Most of the books listed in
this category actually are collections of short
biographies or biographical sketches or "story-
lives"; many of them include at least some
material on their subjects' compositions; a
few are critical studies of the music only of
a selected group of composers—often those
of a special national school or historical
period.*

*For convenience, the following sub-categories
are employed:*

1. Standard Composers

*(The older, "famous" composers of the Baro-
que, Classic, & Romantic eras; sometimes
with a few earlier, usually with a few "modern"
writers thrown in for good measure. But in
general the span is roughly from Bach &
Handel to Debussy & Richard Strauss.)*

2. Contemporary Composers

3. National Schools

a) **American** (in some cases including
Latin-American & Canadian composers)

b) **Austrian, Czech, German**

c) **English (British)**

d) **French, Italian**

e) **Russian**

*In many cases, of course, there is only a
slight distinction (if any) between a book
dealing with, say, Contemporary Composers
and one on Contemporary Music, or American
Composers and American Music.*

COMPOSERS (1. Standard Composers)

See also: under the names of individuals.

Also:

Appreciation	"Master Musicians"
Baroque Era	series
Biographies ("Great	Medieval/Renaissance
Musicians" series)	"Musical Pilgrim"
Chamber Music	series
Church Music	Opera
Classic Era	Orchestral Music
Concerto	Organ Music
Criticism	Phonograph Records
Dictionaries of Music	Piano Music
Documents	Program Notes
Encyclopedias of Mu-	Romantic Era
sic	Song(s)
"Great Musicians"	Symphony
series	Variation
History	Violin Music
Letters	Vocal Music

Also: App IIa (juvenile biographies).

*Note: Pertinent works apparently O/P (or not
easily available) include those by Coeuroy
(in French), Detheridge, Dole, Downes, Elson,
Ewen, Gilman, Hadow, Huneker, Jell, Land-
dowski (in French), Mason, Parry, Rolland,
Salazar (in Spanish), Sollitt, Upton, etc.*

ANDERSON, ARVID C.
Masters of music. 192 p, pors.
Review & Herald Pub Assn, Washington, D. C., 1948.   2.25
17 composers, Bach to Sibelius.

ANGOFF, CHARLES
Fathers of classical music. viii, 164
p, illus (La Verne Reiss), 4–p bibl.
Beechhurst 1947.   3.00
*"The growth of opera & birth of the sym-
phony" in terms of composers from Monteverdi to Bach, Handel, & Haydn.*

BACHARACH, ALFRED LEWIS (ed)
Lives of the great composers. 3 v,
paper. (1935) Pelican 1942 (1947).
V 1: From Byrd to Mozart &
Haydn: the classics. 190 p.   .35
V 2: Beethoven & the romantics.
220 p.   .35

V 3: Brahms, Wagner, & their contemporaries. 191 p.   .35
Sketch biographies by various writers; originally published in one volume by Gollancz in England & by Dutton in the U. S. A.
The music masters: including "Lives of the great composers." V 1: From the 16th century to the time of Beethoven. 366 p. Pilot 1942 (1948). 3.50
A new & more extensive series of biographical sketches, which includes those in the "Lives" series above, plus many additions. The present volume contains pieces on ⎸some 38 composers by some 19 writers. Three other volumes are in preparation.

BLOM, ERIC
Some great composers.   120 p. Oxford 1944.   2.00
15 biographical sketches from Purcell to Tchaikovsky & Dvořák.

BOSCHOT, ROBERT. See App Ia.

BROCKWAY, WALLACE & WEINSTOCK, H.
Men of music: their lives, times & achievements. Intro Deems Taylor. xvi, 649 p, 22 pl (pors). S&S (1939) rev enl ed, 9th pr, 1950.   5.00
Studies of some 22 composers from Palestrina to Sibelius & Stravinsky, with a list of recommended phonograph recordings. The current revision adds a chapter on Berlioz.

BRUXNER, MERVYN
Bach and Handel. *(Min. Survey M-10.)* Hinrichsen in prep.   Δ

BUENZOD, EMMANUEL. See App Ia.

CARDUS, NEVILLE
Ten composers. 166 p. Cape 1945.   2.00
Schubert, Wagner, Brahms, Mahler, Strauss, Franck, Debussy, Elgar, Delius, Sibelius.

EHINGER, HANS. See App Ib.

ELSON, ARTHUR
Modern composers of Europe: being an account of the most recent musical progress in the various European nations, with some notes on their history, & critical & biographical sketches of the contemporary musical leaders in each country. viii, 355 p, 32 pors. Page (1904) rev ed 1922 (1925).   2.50
The title's "modern" is that of 1904: most of the many composers discussed are of the late 19th century.

ENGEL, CARL
Alla breve: from Bach to Debussy. xx, 286 p, bds. G. Schirmer 1921.   2.00
Biographical sketches of some 20 composers.

EWEN, DAVID
Composers of yesterday: a biographical & critical guide to the most important composers of the past. viii, 488 p, 212 pors, 6–p bibl. Wilson 1937.   5.00
230 biographical sketches; lists of works.
Note: For "From Bach to Stravinsky," ed Ewen, see History–5.

FOSS, HUBERT J. *(ed)*
The heritage of music. 2 v: 265; iv, 263 p, mus ex. Oxford 1927 & 1934. 5.00
Essays by Fellowes, Terry, Whittaker, & others. V 1 runs from Palestrina to Franck & Ravel; v 2 from Byrd to Hugo Wolf.

GOETSCHIUS, PERCY
Masters of the symphony. x, 393 p, mus ex. Ditson 1929 (1936).   2.50
5th-year textbook of a "study course in music understanding." Includes a few modern composers and an "epilogue on American symphonists."

GRAF, MAX
From Beethoven to Shostakovich: the psychology of the composing process. 474 p, mus ex. Philosophical 1947.   4.75
Freudian analysis of the sources of musical imagination & the work of musical fantasy.

GROVE, *(Sir)* GEORGE
Beethoven, Schubert, Mendelssohn.   Δ
Macmillan in prep.   5.50
The most noted of Grove's own contributions to the dictionary that bears his name, given separate publication inasmuch as they are to be replaced in the forthcoming 5th edition of Grove's (see Dictionaries of Music).

KAUFMANN, HELEN L.
Stories of 100 great composers. xvi, 239 p. Grosset 1943.   .75
Pocket-size "Little Music Library" series.

LACROIX, JEAN *(ed)*. See App Ib.

LEONARD, RICHARD ANTHONY
The stream of music: the story of music in terms of the great men who made it. xiii, 454 p, 8 pors. Doubleday 1943 (1946).   5.00
17 biog sketches, Bach to Stravinsky.

MASON, DANIEL GREGORY
Beethoven and his forerunners. xxxvi, 352 p, mus ex, 4–p bibl. Macmillan (1940) rev ed 1930.   3.00
Palestrina, Haydn, Mozart, Beethoven; with studies of "Periods of musical history," & "The principles of pure music."

Great modern composers. Biographical section by Mary L. Mason. viii, 228 p, mus ex. Gray 1916.　　2.00

A study of romanticism & realism in terms of some 14 composers from Schubert to Strauss & Debussy.

Note: Mason's "From Grieg to Brahms" (1902, 1936) and "The romantic composers" (1906, 1930) both apparently are O/P.

MATTHEWS, W. S. B.
The masters and their music: a series of illustrative programs, with biographical, esthetical, & critical notations, designed as an introduction to music as literature. xi, 248 p, 11 pors. Presser 1898.　　2.00

"Appreciative" approach to various composers from Bach to Liszt, plus a few such "modern masters" (1898) as Brahms & MacDowell.

MEYER, MARIE ANTOINE. See App Ia.

PARRY, C. HUBERT
Studies of great composers. vi, 376 p, frontis por. Kegan Paul & Curwen △ (1886, 20th ed 1934), 24th ed n d.　(2.25)

Biographical studies of 11 composers, Palestrina to Wagner.

PITROU, ROBERT. See App Ia.

ROLLAND, ROMAIN. See App Ia.

RUTZ, HANS. See App Ib.

SCHERCHEN, HERMANN. See App Ib.

THOMAS, HENRY & DANA LEE
Forty famous composers. viii, 437 p, pors (Gordon & Campbell Ross). Halcyon 1948.　　1.49

Bach to Shostakovitch, with brief lists of their major compositions. Apparently this is an enlarged version of the same authors' "Living biographies of great composers," Garden City 1940, Halcyon repr 1947.

ZIMMERMANN, CURT. See App Ib.

COMPOSERS (2. Contemporary Composers)

Note: Pertinent works apparently O/P (or not easily available) include those by Ewen, Mason, Pannain, Rosenfeld, etc.

See also: under individual names.

Also: App IIa (juvenile biographies).

Also:

Appreciation	Piano Music
Ballet	Popular Music
Chamber Music	Program Notes
Composers-3	Schirmer's "Contem-
Concerto	porary Composers"
Contemporary Music	series
Jazz	Symphony
Modern Music	Violin Music
Opera	Vocal Music
Orchestral Music	Who's Who
Organ Music	Yearbooks
Phonograph Records	

BROOK, DONALD
Composers' gallery: biographical sketches of contemporary composers. 218 p, 41 pl. Rockliff 1946.　　4.25

22 British, 18 other contemporaries.

COPLAND, AARON
Our new music: leading composers in Europe & America. xiv, 305 p. Whittlesey 1941 (1948).　　4.00

A standard work, in which a leading American composer writes about his contemporaries (& himself), including a discussion of the "new musical media" & a selected list of phonograph recordings.

EWEN, DAVID (ed)
The book of modern composers. Intro Nicolas Slonimsky. x, 586, xv p, chap bibls & 2-p general bibl. Knopf (1942) 2nd rev enl ed 1950.　　6.00

A miscellany in which 31 composers, from Sibelius to Gershwin, are the subjects of a biographical sketch, a "personal note" & a critical estimate (by various authors), usually plus a statement by the composer himself. There are also lists of principal works, selected recordings, & books. The present 2nd edition adds Britten & Piston to the original group of 29 represented, brings some material on the others up-to-date, but omits the portraits included before.

Note: Ewen's "Composers of today" (1934) & "20th century composers" (1937) both apparently are O/P.

GRAY, CECIL
A survey of contemporary music. 266 p. Oxford (1924) 2nd ed 1928 (4th pr 1947).　　4.00

A standard, if highly provocative, series of studies of the special contributions to contemporary music by the works of Strauss, Delius, Elgar, Debussy, Ravel, Stravinsky, Scriabin, Schoenberg, Sibelius, Bartók, Busoni, Van Dieren, and a group of "minor" composers.

MELLERS, WILFRID
Studies in contemporary music. 216 p, 66 mus ex. Dobson 1947.　　2.50

The French tradition (Satie, Fauré, Debussy, Roussel, Koechlin);Central European (Mahler, Wellesz, Kodály); British (Holst, Rubbra, Rawsthorne, Bax, Tovey, Harty, Bridge).

THOMPSON, OSCAR (*ed*)
Great modern composers. x, 383 p.
Dodd Mead 1941 (4th pr n d).   3.00
33 composers, from Bartók to Villa-Lobos, by 18 authors, in studies (with lists of major works) reprinted with revisions from the "International cyclopedia of music & musicians' (see Encyclopedias of Music).

SCHUH, WILLI. See App Ib.

COMPOSERS (3. National Schools)
a) American Composers

(In some books Latin-American & Canadian composers also are included.)
See also: under the names of individuals.

Also:

America (music in)	National Music
American Music	Opera-3
Appreciation	(esp Hipscher)
Ballet	Phonograph Records
Composers-1 & 2	Popular Music
History	Program Notes
Jazz	Schirmer's "Contem-
Koussevitzky	porary Composers"
Latin America (esp	series
Slonimsky)	Who's Who
Modern Music	Yearbooks

Also: App IIa (juvenile biographies).

Note: The Hughes & Elson "American composers" (1900/11) apparently is O/P.

EWEN, DAVID (*ed*)
American composers today: a biographical & critical guide. 265 p, pors, bibl refs. Wilson 1949.   4.00
A "who's who" of some 187 composers, including Europeans now resident in the U.S.A.& major Latin-American composers. There are brief lists of principal works, phonograph recordings, & books.

GALT, MARTHA CAROLINE
Know your American music: a handbook. 86 p, paper. National Federation of Women's Clubs, Ithaca, N.Y., (1943) 3rd pr 1946.   1.25
Mainly classified lists of compositions.

HOWARD, JOHN TASKER
Our contemporary composers: American music in the 20th century. With the assistance of Arthur Mendel. xv, 447 p, 14 pors, 2-p bibl. Crowell 1941
1941 (5th pr 1948).   4.00
A companion work to the author's "Our American music" (1931/46) (see American

Music). A standard, extensive survey of composers of various types & schools, plus lists of works, recordings, awards, etc.
Note: See also Howard's booklet-studies of contemporary American composers, listed individually under Burleigh, Crist, Dunn, Kramer, Lane, Russell, Skilton, Whithorne.

MCNAMARA, DANIEL I. (*ed*)
The ASCAP biographical dictionary of composers, authors, & publishers. vii, 483 p. Crowell 1948.   5.00
Biographical data on some 1870 composers & lyric writers (with lists of representative works), plus information on some 300 music publishers.

OSBURN, MARY HUBBELL
Ohio composers and musical authors. 238 p, frontis. Author, Columbus, Ohio, 1942.   2.00

REIS, CLAIRE R.
Composers in America: biographical sketches of contemporary composers with a record of their works. xvi, 399 p. Macmillan (1930) rev enl 4th ed 1947.   5.00
A standard reference work on some 330 composers (including several of foreign birth, now resident in this country), cataloguing all their major works with performance data, running time, publisher, recordings, etc.

SAMINSKY, LAZARE
Living music of the Americas. 284 p, mus ex. Howell Soskin via Crown 1949.   3.00
Highly individual & controversial evaluations of Copland, Hanson, Harris, Ives, Schuman, Sessions, Thomson, & many others, plus the leading composers of Canada, Brazil, Cuba, Mexico, Colombia, & Chile.

COMPOSERS
(3b. Austrian, Czech, German)
See also: under the names of individuals.
Also:

Appreciation	Opera
Composers-1 & 2	Phonograph Records
Contemporary Music	Program Notes
Czechoslovakia	Twelve-Tone Tech-
History	nique
Modern Music	Vienna
National Music	

KAHL, WILLI (*ed*). See App Ib.

NEWLIN, DIKA
Bruckner, Mahler, Schoenberg. x, 293 p, mus ex, 6-p bibl. Columbia 1947 (2nd pr 1947).   3.50
A student of Schoenberg maintains the thesis

that he is the heir (via Bruckner & Mahler) of the Viennese classical tradition.

REFARDT, EDGAR. See App Ib.

RUTZ, HANS. See App Ib.

SUERMONDT, R. P.
Smetana and Dvořák. 59 p, illus, mus ex, bds. Continental n d (1948/9?).   2.50
"Symphonia" series of extensively illustrated brief studies.

COMPOSERS (3c. English, British)
See also: under the names of individuals.
Also:

Appreciation	English Music
Ballet	History
Choir/Choral–3	Madrigal
(esp Manners)	Modern Music
Church Music	National Music
Composers–1 & 2	Opera
Contemporary Music	Phonograph Records
Elizabethan Music	Program Notes
England (music in)	Yearbooks

Note: Pertinent works apparently O/P (or not easily available) include those by Baptie, Barrett, Bridge, Flood, Holbrooke, etc.

TOVEY, DONALD FRANCIS
Some English symphonists: a selection from "Essays in musical analysis." 80 p, mus ex. Oxford 1941.   1.75
16 studies, including those of works by Elgar, Parry, Somerville, Vaughan Williams, & Walton, from the "Essays" (see Program Notes).

COMPOSERS (3d. French, Italian)
See also: under the names of individuals.
Also:

Appreciation	Italian Music
Ballet	Modern Music
Composers–1 & 2	National Music
Contemporary Music	Opera
French Music	Phonograph Records
History	Program Notes

Note: Pertinent works apparently O/P (or not easily available) include those by Coeuroy (in French), Dumesnil (in French), Ferris, Hargrave, Hervey, Hill, Oulmont (in French), Streatfeild, etc.

BROOK, DONALD
Five great French composers. xi, 216 p, photos. Rockliff 1947.   4.50
Berlioz, Franck, Saint-Saëns, Debussy, Ravel; with lists of their works.

LALO, PIERRE. See App Ia.

MACHABEY, ARMAND. See App Ia.

PIZZETTI, ILDEBRANDO. See App Ic.

SHERA, F. H.
Debussy and Ravel. 58 p, mus ex, paper. Oxford 1925.   1.00
"Musical Pilgrim" series. A study of their use of technical devices, plus analyses of several well-known works for orch & piano.

COMPOSERS (3e. Russian)
See also: under the names of individuals
Also:

Appreciation	National Music
Ballet	Opera
Composers–1 & 2	Phonograph Records
Contemporary Music	Program Notes
History	Russian (music in)
Modern Music	Russian Music

Note: Pertinent works apparently O/P (or not easily available) include those by Montagu-Nathan, Sabaneyeff, etc.

ABRAHAM, GERALD
(*See also Calvocoressi below.*)
Eight Soviet composers. 102 p, mus ex. Oxford 1943 (4th pr 1946).   1.25
Shostakovitch, Prokofiev, Khatchaturian, Knipper, Shebalin, Kabalevsky, Szerzhinsky, Shaporin.

BROOK, DONALD
Six great Russian composers. x, 193 p, 33 pl. Rockliff 1946 (2nd pr 1947).   3.50
Glinka, Borodin, Mussorgsky, Tchaikovsky, Rimsky-Korsakov, Scriabin.

CALVOCORESSI, M. D. & ABRAHAM, G.
Masters of Russian music: biographical studies of the great Russian composers. 511 p. Knopf 1936.   4.50
Sketches of some 14 composers, including Dargomyzhsky, Glazounov, Liadov, Liapunov, Scriabin, Serov, & Taneiev, as well as the better-known names.

MOISENKO, RENA
Realist music: 25 Soviet composers. Forew Sir Adrian Boult. 277 p, 12 illus (pors, etc), mus ex, 4–p bibl. Meridian Books, London, 1949.   (3.00)
The theory & application of Socialist music, with biographical sketches of 25 composers from Alexandrov to Zhelobinsky. This book apparently supersedes the author's "20 Soviet composers," a booklet published by the (London) Workers' Music Assn, 1943.

SEROFF, VICTOR I.
The mighty five: the cradle of Russian national music. 280 p, 7 pl, 12–p bibl. Allen Towne 1948, via Crown 1949.   4.00
The fabulous story of the "Five": Balakirev, Mussorgsky, Borodin, Cui, & Rimsky-Korsakov. (For a French version see App Ia.)

COMPOSITION

General Note: Helm's illuminating article on this subject in the "Harvard Dictionary of music" stresses the wide variety of material contained in books bearing the word "composition" in their titles. Many are little more than musical primers or elementary "theory" books, while others are primarily text-books on Harmony or Form. On the other hand, some books on specific theoretical subjects (Helm cites Prout's "Applied forms" in particular) have as much, if not more, useful material on composition itself than many of the explicitly titled Composition books.

The present lists, however, are confined to publications that do contain the term "composition" in their titles, or that clearly deal with composition in general. But reference certainly should be made to some of the other allied subject-headings listed below, especially Form, Melody Writing, & Songwriting.

See also:

Children–3	Improvisation
Church Music (esp	Instrumentation
Shaw)	Melody Writing
Counterpoint	Ornamentation
Film Music (esp	Radio Music
Eisler, Skinner)	Songwriting
Form	Theory
Harmony	Variation

Note: Standard works apparently O/P (or not easily available) include those by Corder, Czerny, Dunstan, Evans, McEwen, Parry, Riemann (in German), Stainer, etc.

BAYTON-POWER, HENRY
How to compose music: a simple guide to the composition of melodies & to their effective harmonization. xi, 86 p, mus ex, bds. Pitman 1937.   **2.50**
Elementary approach for the novice.

DAVISON, ARCHIBALD T.
The technique of choral composition. xiii, 206 p, 241 mus ex. Harvard 1945 (2nd pr 1946).   **3.00**
A standard work on its specialized subject, called by the author an essay in "chorestration."

DORIAN, FREDERICK
The musical workshop. xvi, 368 p, 17 pl (facs, etc), 29 mus ex, 12–p bibl refs & notes. Harper 1947.   **4.00**
Not itself a "method," but a historical & analytical study of composers' own methods in the use of "inspiration, craft, & synthesis."

HILL, ALFRED
Harmony and melody: & their use in the simple forms of music together

with special instruction in the composition of school music.   96 p. Schmidt n d (1927?).   **1.50**

HINDEMITH, PAUL
The craft of musical composition. 2 v. Associated 1941/2.
V 1: Theoretical part. Tr Arthur Mendel. vi, 223 p, 2 fold-out charts, mus ex. (1937) 1942 (3rd rev ed n d).   **4.00**
V 2. Exercises in two-part writing. Tr Otto Ortmann. viii, 160 p, mus ex. (1939) 1941.   **3.00**
English versions of the "Unterweisung im Tonsatz" (1937/9). A noted contemporary composer-pedagogue's re-examination of the tonal elements in music, with analyses of various works according to the new principles derived.

D'INDY, VINCENT (ed SÉRIEYX). See App Ia. ("Cours de composition musicale").

KITSON, C. H.
The elements of musical composition. iv, 144 p, mus ex. Oxford 1936.   **1.50**
Six lectures on accompanied vocal writing. viii, 64 p, mus ex. Oxford 1930 (1949).   **1.25**
Practical advice on writing for chorus, soloists, & orchestra, with notes on texture, thematic development, & climaxes.

MCHOSE, ALLEN I.
Basic principles of the technique of 18th-century composition.   Crofts △ in prep.   **(3.50)**.

MESSIAEN, OLIVIER. See App Ia.

NORDEN, HUGO
An introduction to homophonic composition. 16 p, mus ex, paper. Humphries 1941.   **.50**
Practical notes on writing études for non-keyboard instruments.

SCHILLINGER, JOSEPH
The Schillinger system of musical composition. Overture Henry Cowell; intro & glossary Arnold Shaw & Lyle Dowling. 2 v: xxiv, 1640 p, diagrs, tables, mus ex. C. Fischer 1946.   **30.00**
An elaborately mathematical approach to the various problems & techniques of composition; originally written in the form of a correspondence course (1941) and prepared for the present publication by Shaw & Dowling.

SCHLIEDER, FREDERICK W.
Lyric composition through improvisation: first year's training in formal musical self-expression. 262 p, mus ex. Birchard 1927 (1935).   **3.00**

Fundamental laws of rhythm, melody, & harmony applied to a basic form of composition.

Lyric composition through improvisation: A second presentation & use of pianistic harmonic chordations available for creative musical expression. 67 p, mus ex, typescript repro, paper, spir. Schlieder Book Foundation, Decatur, Illinois, 1946.   4.50

A companion work in the "Schlieder Creative Harmony" series, this dealing with concordant intervals & "broken-chord figures applied to inharmonic associates."

SCHOENBERG, ARNOLD
  (*See also, under Schoenberg author entry: "Style and idea".*)

Models for beginners in composition. 2 v: I, Music examples; II, Syllabus & glossary. 24, 25 p, mus ex, paper. G. Schirmer 1942.   2.00

Ear-training, development of a sense of form, the coordination of melody & harmony, and an understanding of the technique & logic of musical construction—all based on the procedures of Bach, Beethoven, & other great composers.

STAINER, JOHN
Guide to beginners in composition. vi, 140 p, mus ex, paper. Presser n d (1880?).   1.00

CONCERT "COMPANIONS"

See: Appreciation, Program Notes (also note under "Companions").

CONCERT HALLS

See:

Acoustics	Italy (music in)
America (music in)	Queen's Hall
Covent Garden	Theatre
England (music in)	Vienna

CONCERTO

See also:

Appreciation	Phonograph Records
Composers (& under	Piano Music
individual names)	Program Notes (esp
Form	Tovey v 3)
History	Themes (esp Burrows
Mozart-3 (Girdle-	& Redmond)
stone, Hutchings)	Timing
Orchestral Music	Violin Music (esp
Organ Music	Swalin)

CULSHAW, JOHN
The concerto. 72 p, 4 col pl, 31 b&ws (pors, facs, etc), mus ex, bibl note. Chanticleer 1950.   2.50

"World of Music" series No 10: an exten-

sively illustrated monograph on the history & characteristics of the concerto form.

VEINUS, ABRAHAM
Victor book of concertos. xxv, 450 p, 500 mus ex. S & S 1948   3.95

Analyses of 130 concertos of various types available on RCA Victor records, with a glossary & 10-p discography. A companion work to the "Victor books" of the Ballet, Opera, Overtures & Tone Poems (see Program Notes), and Symphony.

Note: An earlier work by Veinus, "The concerto" (Doubleday 1944), is O/P.

CONDON, Eddie

See also: Jazz.

CONDON, EDDIE & SUGRUE, THOMAS
We called it music: a generation of jazz. 341 p, photos. Holt 1947.   3.00

The guitarist's autobiography, with jazz history "narrations" by Sugrue, an appendix on Chicago dance-bands by John Swingle, & a list of Condon recordings since 1927.

CONDUCTING

See also: esp Baton-1.

Also:

Band-1	Interpreters
Choir/Choral-2	Orchestra (esp Carse)
Conductors	Repertory (Swan)
Dance Band	School Music-3 & 4
History	Score-Reading
Instrumentation	Stokowski
Interpretation	Timing

Note: A bibliography by Benjamin Grosbayne is not generally available. Standard works apparently O/P (or not easily available) include those by Schoeder, Schünemann (history, in German), Wagner, etc.

BERLIOZ, HECTOR
The orchestral conductor: theory of his art. 21 p, diagrs, mus ex, paper. C. Fischer n d (1915?).   .60

Originally published in French, 1855; included as a supplement in various editions of the "Treatise on instrumentation" (see Instrumentation/Orchestration). No translator is named in the present edition, but one published by Reeves in London (1917) is credited to John Broadhouse.

BOULT, (*Sir*) ADRIAN C.
Handbook on the technique of conducting. 45 p, 2 photos, 25 diagrs, paper. Hall (1920) 7th rev ed 1949.   1.50

A booklet (mostly on single-sided pages) of concise practical directions.

CARSE, ADAM
Orchestral conducting: a textbook
for students & amateurs. iv, 100 p,
illus, mus ex, 1–pf bibl. Augener 1929
(3rd pr 1935).   2.50
With a section on orchestral instruments.

DOLMETSCH, RUDOLPH
The art of orchestral conducting. 46 p,
illus (T. L. Poulton), mus ex, paper.
Bosworth 1942.   1.50

CROGER, T. R.
Notes on conductors and conducting:
also the organizing & conducting of
amateur orchestras. 76 p, illus.
Reeves n d (1907?) 6th pr n d   (2.00)

GEHRKENS, KARL W.
Essentials in conducting. ii, 184 p,
diagrs, mus ex, 2–p bibl. Ditson
1919.   1.75
*"Music Students Library" series; a standard
shorter work.*

Twenty lessons in conducting. 63 p,
diagrs, mus ex, paper. Ditson 1930.   .75
"Pocket Music Student" series.

INGHELBRECHT, D. E. See App Ia.

KENDRIE, FRANK ESTES
Handbook on conducting and orchestral routine: for the prospective conductor of either chorus or orchestra.
45 p, diagrs, mus ex, 2–p bibl. Gray
1930.   1.25

LEWIS, JOSEPH
Conducting without fears: a helpful
handbook for the beginner. 2 v,
paper. Ascherberg 1942/45.
V 1: Conducting—a general survey.
55 p. 1942 (4th pr 1945). Via Sam
Fox, N. Y.   1.00
V 2: Choral & orchestral conducting.
76 p, tables. 1945.   2.50
*Informal advice, on organization as well as
interpretative problems, especially for the
novice conductor or amateur & school choruses
& orchestras.*

McCRAY, WALTER & BUSCH, CARL
Principles of conducting. 45 p, illus,
mus ex, paper. FitzSimons 1930.   .75

RUDOLF, MAX. See Baton–1 ("The grammar of conducting").

SCHERCHEN, HERMANN
Handbook of conducting. Tr M. D.
Calvocoressi; forew Edward J. Dent.
xi, 243 p, mus ex. Oxford 1933 (6th
pr 1949).   3.50
Probably the standard modern work, notable

*in particular for its "severely practical"
approach, exhaustively detailed analyses of
specific compositions, and its wealth of
examples from the works of modern (as well
as older) composers.*

VAN HOESEN, KARL
Handbook of conducting. 118 p,
photos, diagrs, mus ex, 1–p bibl,
paper. Crofts (1939) rev ed 1950.   3.00
"Eastman School of Music" series No 8.

WEINGARTNER, FELIX
On conducting. Tr Ernest Newman.
56 p, mus ex, paper. Kalmus n d
(1933).   .75
*A standard essay, originally published in
German, 1895, and here reprinted from the
Breitkopf & Härtel ed of 1906, which was
translated from the 3rd German ed of 1905.*

WILSON, ROBERT BARCLAY
The technique of orchestral conducting. Forew Dan Godfrey. 51 p,
diagrs, mus ex. Macmillan 1937.   .65

WOOD, (*Sir*) HENRY
About conducting. Pref note Hubert
Foss. 124 p, illus (frontis por, facs,
charts, etc). Sylvan 1945.   3.00
*Informal notes & practical advice by the late
conductor of the London "Proms."*

WRIGHT, DENIS
The brass band conductor: a handbook for students. Forew Sir Adrian
Boult. 93 p, illus, mus ex, 3–p annot
bibl. Duckworth 1948.   2.00
*The mechanics, the conductor's musical
qualities, the conductor in action.*

CONDUCTORS
See also:

Conducting	Philharmonic
History	Phonograph Records
Interpreters	Who's Who
Orchestra	Yearbooks

Also under the names of individuals:

Barbirolli	Mannes
Beecham	Neel
Berlioz	Sousa
Christiansen	Stokowski
Damrosch	Toscanini
Finn	Volpe
Gilmore	Walter
Koussevitzky	Weingartner
Lambert	Wood

*Note: Pertinent works apparently O/P (or
not easily available) include those by Beecham
(memoirs, 1943), Ewen ("The man with the
baton," 1936), Geissmar ("Two worlds of
music," Beecham & Furtwängler, 1946),
Schliessmann ("Dirigenten von Gestern und
Heute," 1928), etc.*

BROOK, DONALD
Conductors' gallery: biographical
sketches of well-known orchestral
conductors, including notes on the
leading symphony orchestras, & a
short biography of the late Sir Henry
Wood.   xii, 188 p, 45 pl (pors &
orchs).   Rockliff 1945 (4th pr 1947).   3.50
*Sketches of 32 British conductors, with notes
on leading British orchestras.*

BUSCH, FRITZ.   See App Ib.

COAR, BIRCHARD
The masters of the classical period
as conductors.   vii, 126 p, mus ex,
6–p bibl, paper.   Author, De Kalb,
Illinois, 1949.   2.50
Bach, Handel, Haydn, Mozart, & Beethoven.

EWEN, DAVID
Dictators of the baton.   x, 310 p, 33
pors, 2–p bibl.   (1943) Ziff-Davis
2nd ed 1948, via Prentice 1950.   3.50
*Biographical sketches of 33 American (&
visiting) conductors, with historical notes &
a list of 25 major American orchestras.*

FURTWÄNGLER, WILHELM.   See App Ib.

SHORE, BERNARD
The orchestra speaks.   218 p, 2 pl.
Longmans 1938 (14th pr 1946).   3.00
*Studies of 14 conductors, mostly British,
plus a chapter on contemporary composer-
conductors; written by the first violist of the
BBC Symphony.*

WEINGARTNER, FELIX.   See App Ib.

CONFEDERATE STATES (Music in)
See: American Music (Harwell).

Conger, Katherine.   Compiler.
See Singing–1.
Conklin, Maurice.   Author.
See Singing–2.

CONTEMPORARY MUSIC
See also: esp Composers–2, & under the
names of such individual composers as—

Barber	Pizzetti
Bartók	Prokofiev
Berg	Russell
Britten	Schoenberg
Chávez	W. Schuman
Copland	Shostakovitch
Crist	Sibelius
Dunn	Skilton
Harris	Sorabji
Ireland	Stravinsky
Kramer	D. Taylor
Lane	Thomson
D. G. Mason	Vaughan Williams
Miaskovsky	Walton

Also: esp Modern Music.

Appreciation	Radio Music
Ballet	Schirmer's "Contem-
Choir/Choral–3	porary Composers"
(esp Manners)	series
Dance Music	Tonality/Atonality
Film Music	Twelve-Tone Tech-
History	nique
Monophony (Partch)	Yearbooks
Phonograph Records	(esp Myers)
Program Notes	

*Note: Pertinent works apparently O/P (or not
easily available) include those by Chávez
("Towards a new music," 1937), Cowell
("New musical resources," 1930), Foulds,
Salazar (several books in Spanish), Saminsky
("Music of our day," 1939), Schwerké, etc.*

BAUER, MARION
Twentieth century music: how it
developed, how to listen to it.   xiv,
463 p, mus ex, 8–p bibl.   Putnam
(1933) rev ed 1947.   5.00
*An expansion (from 18 to 23 chapters) of a
general survey endorsed by the National
Federation of Music Clubs.*

A summary of twentieth century
music.   39 p, paper.   Putnam 1935.   .25
*A supplement pamphlet for textbook use of
"Twentieth century music" above.*

DYSON, GEORGE
The new music.   152 p, mus ex, bds.
Oxford (1924) 2nd ed 1926 (4th pr
1948).   3.00
*A searching analysis of contemporary musical
values, techniques, and specific problems in
melody, rhythm, texture, & architecture.*

ERPF, HERMANN.   See App Ib.

LE ROUX, MAURICE.   See App Ia.

LIESS, ANDREAS.   See App Ib.

MERSMANN, HANS.   See App Ib.

MOOSER, R. A.   See App Ia.

SALAZAR, ADOLFO
(See also App Id.)

Music in our time: trends in music
since the romantic era.   Tr Isabel
Pope.   367 p, mus ex, 7–p bibl.
Norton 1946.   6.75
*Originally in Spanish:"La música moderna,"
1944. A study of the parallel developments
of music & society in the disentanglement
of the "modernist" from the Romantic world.*

SLONIMSKY, NICOLAS
Music since 1900: an encyclopedic
survey of modern music (1900–1948).
lxiii, 759 p.   (1937) Coleman 3rd rev
enl ed 1949.   7.50

Current revision of a standard reference work: a "descriptive chronology" of musical events since the turn of the century. It includes a "tabular view of stylistic trends" and a section of significant letters & documents (among them the recent Soviet declarations of a new musical policy). The new edition's expanded index (p 713/759) lists references by major compositions as well as by composers' names.

WÖRNER, KARL H. See App Ib.

Conway, Marmaduke P. Author.
See Organ playing.

COOK, Ida
We followed our stars. 246 p + 17 photos (by the author). Morrow 1950.   3.50
Reminiscences of a British author of light fiction, who (with her sister) must rank as the most fervent opera "fan" & star-worshipper on record. There is much material on Galli-Curci, Ponselle, & refugee-work among European artists during the last war.

Cook, Kenneth. Editor. See Band–1.
Cooke, Charles. Author.
See Piano Playing–4.
Cooke, Donald Edwin. Author, illustrator.
See App IIa (Dukas).

Cooke, James Francis. Author. See:
Anthologies. Great men & famous musicians (1925).   2.25
Europe. Musical travelogues (1934).   3.00
History–2. Standard (1910/36).   1.50
Memory. How to memorize (1948).   1.50
Pianists. Great pianists on piano playing (1913).   3.00
Singers. Great singers on singing (1921).   2.25
See also: App IIb (juveniles).

Cookson, Frank B. Editor.
See Theory–2, Form (Bigelow).
Coon, Oscar. Compiler, editor.
See Dictionaries of Terms, Theory–3.
Cooper, Isabella Mitchell. Compiler.
See Radio.
Cooper, Martin. Author.
See Bizet, Opéra-Comique, Opera–1.
Cooper, Page. Co-author (with Wagner).
See F. Wagner.
Coopersmith, Jacob Maurice. Author.
See Dominican Music.

COPLAND, Aaron
See also:

America (music in)	Film Music
American Music	Orchestral Music
Appreciation	Phonograph Records
Ballet	Piano Music
Chamber Music	Program Notes
Composers–2 & 3a	Radio Music
Contemporary Music	

Author. See:
Appreciation. What to listen for in music (1939).   3.50
Composers–2. Our new music (1941).   4.00

BERGER, ARTHUR
Aaron Copland. G. Schirmer in prep. △
"Schirmer's Contemporary Composers" series; biography, list & analyses of works, bibliography, & discography.

SMITH, JULIA
Note: An authorized biography is announced as "in preparation."

Coppola, Piero. Author. See App Ia.

COPYRIGHT (Musical)
See also: Radio Music, Songwriting.

KNIGHT, GEORGE MORGAN, Jr.
How to internationally copyright your brainchild (including U. S. copyright information). 48 p, mim, bds. Knight Pub Co, Leonardtown, Maryland, 4th ed (ed Leta S. Bender) 1948.   1.00

NICHOLSON, MARGARET
A manual of copyright practice for writers, publishers, & agents. x, 255 p, 1–p bibl. Oxford 1945.   3.00
Outline history of copyright law, 49 problematical aspects of the subject, examples of actual forms used, etc.

SHAFTER, ALFRED M.
Musical copyright. Intro John Henry Wigmore. xix, 667 p, mus ex. Callaghan & Co, Chicago, (1932) 2nd rev ed 1939.   12.00
Evolution of musical copyright, its practical features, infringement, international aspects, tables of U. S. & foreign cases.

(U. S. LIBRARY OF CONGRESS, COPYRIGHT OFFICE)
Catalogue of copyright entries: published music (series); unpublished music (series).   △
Note: Although this monumental series is hardly suited for normal entry here, it certainly deserves passing mention, especially since

the volumes devoted to published music in recent years have been revised in content & style in a manner to make them even more useful than in the past as musicological as well as copyright reference works. For prices of current issues (and of earlier volumes still in-print), address the Copyright Office, Library of Congress, Washington 25, D. C.

Corbett, Geoffrey. Author. See Gundry.

CORELLI, Arcangelo
See:

Appreciation	Italian Music
Baroque Era	Phonograph Records
Concerto	Program Notes
History	Violin Music
Italy (music in)	

Note: Marc Pincherle's biography, in French (1933), apparently is O/P.

Corle, Edwin. Editor.
See Stravinsky-2.
Cornell, John Henry. Author. See Form

CORNET
See:

Band-1	Instruments
Bugle	Trumpet
Instrumentation	Wind Instruments

Corrêa de Azevedo, Luis Heitor. Author. See Brazil (music in).
Corrodi, Hans. Author. See App Ib.
Corte, Andrea della. Author. See App Ia & App Ic.
Cortot, Alfred. Author. See Piano Playing-1, App Ia.

COSTA RICA (Music in)
See: Latin America.

Cott, Ted. Author. See Quizzes, Radio.

COUNTERPOINT

1. **Larger Works, Specialized Studies**
2. **Shorter Methods**

General Note: The distinction between these two sub-categories is not too strongly marked in some cases and should not be taken too seriously: primarily it is a convenience for separating the more extensive or specialized books on the subject from the profusion of short "methods" or instruction books for class or individual use. Many of these "methods" are little more than series of exercises to be worked out by the student.

See also:

Bach	Harmony
Baroque Era	History
Composition	Medieval/Renaissance
Ear-Training (esp	Palestrina
Gingrich)	Theory
Form	Twelve-Tone Tech-
Fugue	nique

COUNTERPOINT
(1. Larger Works, Specialized Studies)

Note: Standard works apparently O/P (or not easily available) include those by Bellermann (in German), Cherubini, Schenker (in German), etc.

BAIRSTOW, EDWARD C.
Counterpoint and harmony. x, 408 p. mus ex. Macmillan (1937) 2nd ed 1945 (1949).   3.50
A textbook in the simultaneous study of strict counterpoint & contrapuntal harmony, diatonic discords, chromatic harmony.

BUSH, ALAN
Strict counterpoint in Palestrina style: a practical text-book. Forew John Ireland. 27 p, mus ex, paper. Williams n d (1948?).   2.50

DUBOIS, THÉODORE. See App Ia.

FUX, JOHANN JOSEPH
Steps to Parnassus: the study of counterpoint. Tr Alfred Mann, with collaboration of John St. Edwards. 156 p, mus ex. Norton 1943.   3.50
The celebrated "Gradus ad Parnassum," first published in 1725, long O/P in an earlier (& inadequate) English translation, 1886.

GOETSCHIUS, PERCY
  (*See also Counterpoint-2.*)
Counterpoint applied in the invention, fugue, canon, & other polyphonic forms: an exhaustive treatise on the structural & formal details of the polyphonic or contrapuntal forms of music. ix, 318 p, mus ex. G. Schirmer 1902 (1949).   3.50
A sequel to the same author's "Homophonic forms of musical composition" & companion work to his "Larger forms of musical composition" (see Form).

JEPPESEN, KNUD
Counterpoint: the polyphonic vocal style of the 16th century. Tr & intro Glen Haydon. xviii, 302 p, mus ex. Prentice 1939 (2nd pr 1949).   5.00
Originally in Danish, 1931; later in German, 1935. A standard work that includes an outline history of contrapuntal theory, as well as elaborate analyses of canons, masses, motets,

etc, but which is also widely used as a text-book of counterpoint based primarily on the practice of Palestrina.

KITSON, C. H.
(See also Counterpoint–2.)
The art of counterpoint. viii, 344 p,
mus ex. Oxford (1907) 2nd ex 1924
(1947).   4.00
A standard British textbook, covering both 16th-century & "modern" counterpoint.
Applied strict counterpoint. 100 p,
mus ex. Oxford 1916 (1949).   1.75
Carrying strict counterpoint beyond its purely grammatical aspects (as in "The art of counterpoint"), including material on hymn-tunes & their simple treatment, counterpoint on a chorale, madrigal & motet writing.

KŘENEK, ERNST
Studies in counterpoint: based on the
twelve-tone technique. ix, 37 p, mus
ex, paper. G. Schirmer 1940.   1.50
An eminent practitioner of the twelve-tone technique describes its elementary principles as he has applied them in his own works.

KURTH, ERNST. See App Ib.

MCHOSE, ALLEN I.
The contrapuntal harmonic tech-
nique of the 18th century. Forew
Howard Hanson. xvi, 433 p, mus ex.
Crofts 1947.   7.00
"Eastman School of Music" series. A study of the evolution of Bachian polyphony, with some 800 examples, mostly Bach chorales.

MERRITT, ARTHUR TILLMAN
Sixteenth-century polyphony: a basis
for the study of counterpoint. xvii,
215 p, mus ex, 3–p bib. Harvard
1939 (4th pr 1949).   3.50
An analytical study of the "single line" (plainsong) & contrapuntal technique, with special emphasis on the Palestrina style.

MORRIS, R. O.
(See also Counterpoint–2.)
Contrapuntal technique in the 16th
century. xi, 74 p + 49–p mus ex.
Oxford 1922 (1944).   3.00
An analytical study contrasting the "academic" rules of Fux, Rockstro, et al., with the actual techniques of the great polyphonic composers, especially those of the Elizabethan & earlier British schools. There is special emphasis on 16th-century "rhythmical freedom & subtlety" and on the "workings of the old modal system."

PISTON, WALTER
Counterpoint.   235 p, mus ex.
Norton 1947.   5.25

One of the more extensive, recent American textbooks, based largely on the practice of Bach & later composers. A companion work to the same author's "Harmony."

PORTER, QUINCY
A study of sixteenth century counterpoint: based on the works of Orlando
di Lasso. 40 p, diagrs, mus ex, paper.
Loomis & Co, Boston, (1940) 3rd ed
1948.   1.50
Detailed analyses of 2– & 3–part works by Lassus, as used in courses at the New England Conservatory of Music.

RUBBRA, EDMUND
Counterpoint. Hutchinson in prep.   Δ
Announced as "not a textbook, but a survey of ways in which counterpoint can be a vitalizing force in music."

SODERLUND, GUSTAVE FREDERIC
Direct approach to counterpoint in
16th-century style.   Intro Howard
Hanson. x, 133 p, mus ex. Crofts
1947.   3.50
"Eastman School of Music" series. A formulation of rules based on statistical analyses of great composers' polyphonic works.

SODERLUND, GUSTAVE FREDERIC (*comp*)
Examples illustrating the development of melodic line & contrapuntal
style, from Greek melody to Mozart.
52 p, music, paper. Crofts 1932 (3rd
pr 1945).   2.50
Examples of Gregorian chant and
works by Orlando Lassus & Giovanni
Pierluigi   Palestrina   for   use   in
classes of counterpoint. 171 p, music,
paper. Crofts 1937 (3rd ed 1946). 5.00
Both works in the "Eastman School of Music" series and exceptions (owing to their special usefulness to students of counterpoint) to our usual rule of omitting collections of music.

SPALDING, WALTER
Tonal counterpoint: studies in part-
writing. viii, 258 p, mus ex. Schmidt
1904 (1932).   2.50
A standard older American textbook.

COUNTERPOINT (2. Shorter Methods)

Note: Standard works apparently O/P (or not easily available) include those by Ayres, Gladstone, Jadassohn, Juon (in German), Kessler, Macpherson, Pearce, Richardson, Richter, Riemann, Rockstro, etc.

ANDERSEN, ARTHUR OLAF
Strict and free counterpoint.   viii,
84 p, mus ex. Birchard 1931.   1.50

BAKER, THEODORE
A manual of counterpoint: forming a sequel to Prof. Oscar Paul's "Manual of harmony." 132 p, mus ex, bds. G. Schirmer 1887.   2.00
The Paul manual itself (in German 1880, in English 1885) apparently is O/P.

BRIDGE, J. FREDERICK
Complete exposition of the rules of strict counterpoint. vii, 84 p, mus ex, paper. Presser n d (1878?).   1.00
Same: Counterpoint. 88 p, mus ex. Ditson 1878.   1,25
Same, paper covers.   .90
"Music Students Library" series.
Double counterpoint and canon. ix, 127 p, mus ex, paper. Gray 1881.   1.50

CESANA, OTTO
Course in modern counterpoint. unp (11 p), mus ex, paper, spir. King 1940 (1947).   3.00

CLARKE, HUGH A.
Counterpoint strict and free, double counterpoint, imitation, fugue, & canon. 112 p, mus ex. Presser 1901 (1929).   1.25

GOETSCHIUS, PERCY
(See also Counterpoint–1.)
Exercises in elementary counterpoint. 169 p, mus ex. G. Schirmer 1910 (1938).   3.00

JACOB, GORDON. See Theory–4 (ed Dyson).

KANITZ, ERNEST
A counterpoint manual: fundamental techniques of polyphonic music writing. vii, 65 p, mus ex, mim, paper. Birchard 1948.   2.00
A workbook outline of rules & examples for "strict" counterpoint based on the practices of Bruckner, Reger, etc, & "free" counterpoint in the most advanced styles.

KITSON, C. H.
(See also Counterpoint–1.)
Counterpoint for beginners. 114 p, mus ex. Oxford 1927 (10th pr 1946).   1.50
Through counterpoint in 3 parts.
Invertible counterpoint and canon. 96 p, mus ex. Oxford 1928 (2nd pr 1947).   2.00

KOECHLIN, CHARLES
A summary of the rules of counterpoint: with examples in 2, 3, & 4 parts. Tr Ernest Quinan. 137 p, frontis por, mus ex, paper. Heugel, Paris, 1927.   5.25

LAUTNER, LOIS & KENT, CHARLES
Two-part 16th century counterpoint: a first year course. iv, 119 p, mus ex, typescript repro, paper. Homeyer, Boston, 1948.   2.50
A course prepared for use at the New England Conservatory of Music.

LOVELOCK, WILLIAM
Free counterpoint (complete). 110 p, mus ex, paper. A. Hammond & Co., London. 1949.   (3.00)
Exercises in 2, 3, & 4 parts, and counterpoint on a chorale.

LYTLE, VICTOR VAUGHN
The theory and practice of strict counterpoint. xiv, 222 p, mus ex, 2–p bibl. Ditson 1940.   1.75
"Music Students Library" series.

MOKREJS, JOHN
Natural counterpoint: (the original point system). 62 p, mus ex, paper. Summy 1941.   1.00

MORRIS, R. O.
(See also Counterpoint–1.)
Introduction to counterpoint. 55 p, mus ex, paper. Oxford 1944 (1945).   1.00
Outline of strict counterpoint, with modifications based on 18th-century practice.

OREM, PRESTON WARE
The art of interweaving melodies: a first method of counterpoint for students of all ages. 162 p, mus ex, bds. Presser 1937.   1.25

PEARCE, CHARLES W.
Students' counterpoint. xx, 93 p, mus ex. G. Schirmer 1926 (rev ed, 19th pr n d).   1.75
A manual of strict counterpoint with an appendix of 48 cantus firmi exercises.

PROUT, EBENEZER
Counterpoint—strict and free. xiv, 259 p, mus ex. Augener 1890 (16th pr n d).   4.25
Additional exercises, melodies, & unfigured basses for harmonizing. viii, 74 p, exercises only. Augener 1890 (10th pr n d).   2.30
Double counterpoint and canon. xi 248 p, mus ex. Augener 1891 (9th pr n d).   4.25
Standard old-style British textbooks.

SMITH, LEO
Elementary part writing. 150 p, mus ex. Harris Co, Oakville, Ontario, 1939.   1.50

Exercises in Grade 3 harmony, Grade 4 counterpoint, & 2-part writing, with sample Canadian examination questions.

TAPPER, THOMAS
First year counterpoint: 2 & 3 voices. iv, 106 p, mus ex. Schmidt 1913 (1935).   1.50

THIMAN, ERIC H.
Practical free counterpoint. 66 p, mus ex, paper. Curwen n d (1947). (1.50)
2- & 3-pt counterpoint, melodic style, and harmonic vocabulary.

VOGLER, JULIUS
A modern method of counterpoint. 18 p, mus ex, paper. Briegel 1935.   .50

WRIGHT, FRANK
The essentials of strict counterpoint. Pref T. Tertius Noble. 42 p, mus ex, paper. Author, Brooklyn, N. Y., 1935.   2.00

YORK, FRANCIS L.
Counterpoint simplified: a textbook in simple strict counterpoint. viii, 149 p, mus ex. Ditson 1907.   1.50
"Music Students Library" series.

COUPERIN FAMILY

See also:

Appreciation	Keyboard Instruments
Baroque Era	& Music
Church Music	Organ Music
Composers-1	Phonograph Records
French Music	Program Notes
History	Vocal Music

Note: Standard works apparently O/P (or not easily available) include those by Bouvet (in French), Quittard (in French), etc.

BRUNOLD, PAUL
François Couperin. Tr J. B. Hanson. 77 p, 5 pors, 2 facs, paper.

CAUCHIE, MAURICE (*comp*)
Thematic index to the works of François Couperin. 133 p, mus ex, paper.

Both works above, boxed: Lyrebird, Paris, 1949.   7.50
Observations on Couperin & his music, with a catalogue of works & notes on available recordings. Available only with Cauchie's thematic index, which is also issued by The Lyrebird Press, noted as the publishers of Couperin's complete works.

MELLERS, WILFRID
François Couperin: and the French classical tradition. 412 p + 9 pl (pors, etc), mus ex, 6-p bibl. (Dobson 1950) Roy 1951, in prep.   6.00

Announced as the 1st comprehensive study in English, with a complete thematic index.

TIERSOT, JULIEN.   See App Ia ("Les Couperin," in French).

Courlander, Harold. Author.
See Folklore.
Courvoisier, Karl. Author.
See Violin Playing.
Coussemaker, Edmond de. Editor.
See App Ie.
Covarrubias, Miguel. Author, illustrator.
See Bali (music in), Mexico (music in).

COVENT GARDEN

See also:

Ballet	History
"Covent Garden	Opera
Opera Books" Series	Purcell (Mandinian)
England (music in)	

SHAWE-TAYLOR, DESMOND
Covent Garden. 72 p, 7 col pl, 28 b&ws. Chanticleer 1948.   2.50
"World of Music" series No 4: an extensively illustrated history from the first theatre in 1732 to the present day.

"COVENT GARDEN OPERA BOOKS"

Note: This is a series of paper-covered booklets, published, under the general editorship of Anthony Gishford, by Boosey & Hawkes.

For individual entries, see:

Bizet (Cooper)	R. Strauss (Pryce-
Britten (Keller,	Jones)
Stuart)	Verdi-2 (Bonavia,
Massenet (Colson)	Fisher, Hussey)
Mozart-3 (Lee)	Wagner-3 (Geissmar,
Mussorgsky	Redlich, Wellesz)
(Abraham)	

Covert, William Chalmers. Editor.
See Hymns/Hymnody-1.
Covey, Cyclone. Author.
See America (music in).
Coviello, Ambrose. Author.
See Beethoven-3, Matthay, Piano Playing-1.

Coward, (Sir) Henry. Author.
See Choir/Choral-2.

Note: Other books by & about Coward apparently are O/P (or not easily available).

COWBOY MUSIC

See also:

America (music in)	Folklore
American Music	Folksongs-2
California (music in)	Lomax
Dances-2	Songbooks

Note: Pertinent works apparently O/P (or not easily available) include those by Larkin "Singing cowboy," 1931), etc.

ALLEN, JULES VERNE
Cowboy lore. xvi, 164 p, illus (Ralph J. Pereida), music. Naylor Co, San Antonio, Texas, "7th Lucky Horse-shoe" ed 1950.   2.50
Includes the music of various cowboy songs, arr Mrs. G. Embry Eitt.

LOMAX, JOHN A. (*comp*)
Songs of the cattle trail and cow camp. Forew William Lyon Phelps. xx, 189 p, 78 illus. (1919) Duell Sloan rev illus ed 1950.   3.00
A standard collection (texts only); originally published by Macmillan, now illustrated with period drawings & sketches by noted western artists.

LOMAX, JOHN A. & ALAN (*eds*)
Cowboy songs and other frontier ballads. Music ed: Edward N. Waters. xxxviii, 431 p, music (tunes only). Macmillan (1910) rev enl ed 1945.   5.00
A standard collection of words & music, with extensive documentation.

SHAW, LLOYD
Cowboy dances: a collection of western square dances. Forew Sherwood Anderson. Appendix: (33) cowboy dance tunes arr Frederick Knorr. 417 p, some 144 photos, diagrs, music. Caxton (1939) rev ed ((11th pr) 1949. 5.00
Some 75 dances with complete calls, explanations, & illustrations, plus glossary & list of recordings.

COWELL, Henry Dixon
See:
American Music   History
Composers-2 & 3a   Phonograph Records
Note: Cowell's own "New musical resources" (1930) and his symposium, "American composers on American music" (1937), both apparently are O/P.

Crabshaw, Cyril M. Author.
See Schubert-2.
Cramer, Edward E. Author.
See Violin Playing.
Crawford, Alethea Brinckerhoff. Author. (with Rebekah Crawford). See App IIa.
Crawford, Rebekah. Editor.
See Almanacs. Co-author (with Alethea Crawford). See App IIa (juveniles).
Crawford, Phyllis. Co-compiler (with Sears). See Song(s).

CREATION (Musical)
See:
Aesthetics   Composition
Amateur Music   Philosophy
Children-3 & 8   Psychology

Creedy, E. J. Author. See Scale.
Crews, Albert R. Author. See Radio.

CRIST, Bainbridge
See also:
American Music   Vocal Music
Composers-3a
For a book by Crist, see Songwriting.

HOWARD, JOHN TASKER
Bainbridge Crist. 35 p, frontis por, mus ex, paper. C. Fischer 1929.   .25
List of works with brief analyses.

Crite, Allan Rohan. Illustrator.
See Negro Spirituals.

CRITICISM (Musical)
General Note: Nearly as elastic a term as "appreciation," "criticism" at its widest stretch might include almost every book on music & musicians except technical manuals & "methods." For such "criticism" of music, see particularly Appreciation, Composers (and under the names of individual composers), under the names of individual critics, Program Notes, etc. The list of books below, however, is confined—with the exception of the Demuth anthology—to those about music criticism.

See also:
Aesthetics-1 (esp   Miscellanies (esp
  Greene) & 2   Slonimsky)
History   Musicology
Note: Pertinent works apparently O/P (or not easily available) include those by Boyd, Calvorcoressi ("Principles & methods of musical criticism," 1923), Kolodin, Simon, etc.

DEMUTH, NORMAN (*comp*)
An anthology of musical criticism. xxvii, 397 p, 15-p bibl. Eyre & Spottiswoode, London, 1947.   3.00
A pocket-size "treasury" of many apt examples, ranging all the way from Thomas Morley on the subject of Dunstable to Constant Lambert on "Atonalism."

FRENCH, RICHARD F. (*ed*)
Music and criticism: a symposium. viii, 181 p. Harvard 1948.   3.00
The major addresses presented at the Harvard Symposium on Music Criticism, May 1947,

by Archibald T. Davison, E. M. Forster, Roger Sessions, Edgar Wind, Olga Samaroff-Stokowski, Virgil Thomson, Otto Kinkeldey, Paul H. Lang, & Huntington Cairns.

GRAF, MAX
Composer and critic: two hundred years of musical criticism. 331 p. Norton 1946.   4.00
The only available history of music criticism, confined to that published in periodicals & newspapers, rather than critical material & attitudes embodied in music encyclopedias, histories, biographies, etc.

MACHABEY, ARMAND. See App Ia.

OLIVER, ALFRED RICHARD
The encyclopedists as critics of music. viii, 227 p, 12–p bibl. Columbia 1947.   3.00
A scholarly study of the articles on music in the famous "Encyclopédie" (Paris 1751–77), dealing with the history of opera in France from Lully to Gluck, the musical "wars" of the 18th century, the reforms of Rameau, etc.

THOMPSON, OSCAR
Practical musical criticism. viii, 178 p. Witmark 1934.   2.50
Experienced advice on the profession, the appraisal of music & performances, the writing, & the life of a music critic.

CRITICS (Musical)

Note: For collected critical essays, or memoirs by—and books about—noted critics, see under the names of individuals, among them:

Abraham	Parker
Aldrich	Rolland
Berlioz–1 & 2	Rosenfeld
Blom	Schumann–1
Cardus	Sorabji
Debussy–1	Stravinsky–1
Einstein	Taubman
Gray	Taylor
Haggin	Thomson
Hanslick	Tovey
Huneker	Toye
Lambert	Wagner–1
D. G. Mason	Westrup
Myers	Whittaker
Newman	

Croger, T. R. Author. See Conducting.

CROONING

See:

Crosby	Sinatra
Popular Music	Singing–3
Radio Music	

Note: Bowly's "Modern style singing (crooning)" apparently is O/P.

CROSBY, Bing (Harry Lillis)
See also:

America (music in)	Popular Music
Film Music	Radio Music
Jazz	Singing–3

Note: A biography of Crosby by his brother, Ted, apparently is O/P.

MIZE, J. T. H.
Bing Crosby and the Bing Crosby style: Crosbyana through biography, photography, discography. xiv, 15, 170 p, illus. Academy of American Music, Chicago, 1946.   3.00

ULANOV, BARRY
The incredible Crosby. xiii, 336 p, illus. Whittlesey 1948.   3.50
With 16-p photos & 25-p discography.

Crosfield, Domini. Author.
See Dances–2 (ed Alford).
Cross, Joan. Author.
See Opera–3 (ed Crozier).
Cross, Milton. Author. See Opera–3.
Crossley-Holland, Peter. Editor.
See Wales (music in).
Crosten, William L. Author. See Opera–1.

Crowest, Frederick James. Author.
See Cherubini.
Note: Numerous other books by this prolific British author apparently are O/P (or not easily available in this country).

Crozier, Eric. Editor, author.
See "Sadler's Wells Opera Books" series (ed Crozier); also Britten, Mozart–3.
Crunden, Marjorie Morse. Compiler.
See Children–2.
Crussard, Claude. Author. See App Ia.

CRYS

See: Folklore, Folksongs, History.
Note: Bridge's "The old cryes of London" (1921) apparently is O/P.

CUBA (Music in)/CUBAN MUSIC

See: Cugat, Popular Music, Latin America.
Also: Composers–3a (Ewen, Saminsky).

CUGAT, Xavier
See also: Dance Bands, Popular Music.

Rumba is my life. 210 p, illus (Cugat). Didier 1948.   3.50
Memoirs, with his own caricatures, of the noted band leader, who specializes in Latin-American dance music.

CUI, Cesar Antonovitch
See:

Composers-3e	Program Notes
History	Rimsky-Korsakov
Phonograph Records	Russian Music

Culshaw, John. Author.
See Brahms-1, Concerto, Rachmaninoff.
Culver, Charles Aaron. Author.
See Acoustics.
Cumberland, Gladys. Author.
See Children-8.
Cuming, G. J. Co-compiler (with Clough).
See Phonograph Records.
Cummings, William Hayman. Author.
See Purcell, Theory-3.
Cundiff, Hannah Matthews. Co-author
(with Dykema). See School Music-1.

CURIOSITIES (of Music)
See: Miscellanies.
*Note: L. C. Elson's book with this title
(actually dealing with ancient music) is O/P.*

Curtis, Mina. Author. See Bizet.

Curtis, Natalie (Mrs Paul Burlin). Editor.
See Negro Spirituals.
*Note: Several other books by Curtis (includ-
ing "Songs and tales from the dark continent,"
1920) apparently are O/P.*

Curwen, Annie J.
(Mrs J. Spencer Curwen).
Author. See Children-8, Teaching-2.
Cutter, Benjamin. Author.
See Harmony-2, Kreutzer.

Cuvelier, André. Author. See App Ia.

CYCLOPEDIAS
See: Dictionaries of Music, Encyclopedias
of Music.

Cypher, Irene Fletcher. Co-author (with
Chandler). See Teaching-1.
Czarnowski, Lucile K. Author.
See Dances-2.
Czech, Stan. Author. See App Ib.

CZECHOSLOVAKIAN MUSIC
See also:

Appreciation	History
Composers-1 & 3b	Martinu
Dances-2 (ed Alford:	National Music
Lubinová)	Phonograph Records
Dvořák	Program Notes
Folklore	Smetana
Folksongs-1	Songbooks

*Note: A pamphlet by Jan Lowenbach, "Czecho-
slovak music: the voice of a people" (1943),
no longer seems generally available in this
country. Possibly it still can be imported
from Orbis Publishing House, Prague XIII,
Stalinova 46, Czechoslovakia.*

NEWMARCH, ROSA
The music of Czechoslovakia. Pref
Sir Henry Wood; forew Eduard
Benes. viii, 244 p, frontis. Oxford
1942 (1943).   3.00
*A history of what used to be called Bohemian
music, discussing minor composers (or perhaps
those merely less well known to Americans),
as well as Dvořák & Smetana.*

—D—

Dadachanji, Serozh. Co-author (with Gopal). See Dances–2.
Dale, Benjamin James. Author. See Theory–4 (ed Dyson).
Dale, Carroll R. Author. See Band–2.
Daly, Jack. Author. See Bland.
Daly, William H. Author. See Orchestra.
Damais, Emile. Co-author (with Boll). See App Ia.

DAMROSCH FAMILY

FINLETTER, GRETCHEN DAMROSCH
From the top of the stairs. 252
p. Little Brown 1946.   2.50
Reminiscences of the family & its friends, by one of Walter Damrosch's daughters.

Damrosch, Frank. Author.
See Sight-Singing, Teaching–2.
Note: L. P. & R. P. Stebbins's "Frank Damrosch, let the people sing" (1945) apparently is O/P.

DAMROSCH, Walter Johannes

See: America (music in), Conductors.
Note: Dr. Damrosch's "My musical life" (1923, 1930) apparently is O/P.

DANCE/DANCES/DANCING

General Note: For convenience, book-listings (which in some cases are samplings only of the large available literature) are arranged in the following categories:

The Dance (General)
Dance Bands
Dance Music
Dancers (cross-references only)
Dances/Dancing
  1. Educational
  2. Country, Folk, National, Regional, Round, Square, etc.
  3. Ballroom & Social

(The) DANCE (General)

See also:

America-music in (Whitlock & Saunders)	Dance Music Dances–1, 2, & 3 History
Ballet	Libraries (esp Moore)
California (Saunders)	Yearbooks

Note: Only a sampling of the large available literature is included here. For a detailed survey, please see Magriel's "Bibliography of dancing" listed below.

Pertinent works that might have been included, except that they apparently are O/P (or not easily available) include those by H'Doubler, Kinney, Kirstein, La Meri, Martin, etc.

ARBEAU, THOINOT
(*pseud* of Tabourot, Jean)
Orchesography: a treatise in the form of a dialog whereby all may easily learn & practice the honorable exercise of dancing. Tr Mary Stewart Evans. 212 p, illus, bibl. Kamin 1948.   10.00
A new edition of one of the first books on dancing (1588), first translated into English (& pub) by Beaumont, London, 1925.

ARMITAGE, MERLE
Dance memoranda. Ed Edwin Corle. 57 p, some 250 illus. Duell Sloan 1947.   6.00
Notes & pictures dealing with Stravinsky, Diaghilev, Nijinsky, Pavlova, Duncan, etc.

BLASIS, CARLO
An elementary treatise upon the theory & practice of the art of dancing. Tr Mary Stewart Evans. 55 p + 15–p pl (facs) & frontis. Kamin 1944.   2.50
A standard work of historical importance (1820), by a famous dancer

CHUJOY, ANATOLE (*ed*)
The dance encyclopedia. Intro Anton Dolin; forew Lincoln Kirstein. xv, 546 p, 11–p bibl. Barnes 1949.   7.50
Articles, biographical sketches, etc, arranged in dictionary style, and including a 12–p discography by Manning Solon.

DENBY, EDWIN
Looking at the dance. 448 p, 9 pl. Pellegrini 1949.   4.00
Some 168 articles, mostly from the New York "Herald Tribune" (1937/47), by one of the leading American dance critics.

EVANS, EDWIN, *Jr*
Music and the dance: for lovers of

the ballet. 192 p, frontis por. Jenkins,
London, n d (1948).   2.50
*A collection of essays by the noted British
writer on music, together with an appreciation
of Evans by Ninette de Valois & a memoir
by Dyneley Hussey.*

HORST, LOUIS
Pre-classic dance forms.   Forew
Henry Gilford. x, 170 p, illus, music,
Dance Observer, N. Y., 1937 (1940).   2.00

LLOYD, MARGARET
The Borzoi book of modern dance.
xxiii, 356, xxvi p, 49 photos, 2–p bibl.
Knopf 1949.   5.00
*A history of the modern dance, with studies
of outstanding dancers from Isadora Duncan
to Dunham, Tamiris, et al., of today.*

MAGRIEL, PAUL (*comp*)
A bibliography of dancing: a list of
books & articles on the dance &
related subjects.   229 p, 199 facs.
Wilson 1936.   4.75
Same, 4th cumulated supplement,
1936–1940.   104 p, paper. Wilson
1941.   1.85
*A standard reference work: exhaustive,
classified listings of all types of published
material on various aspects of the dance.*

MAGRIEL, PAUL (*ed*)
Chronicles of the American dance.
xii, 268 p, 118 illus (pors, facs).
Holt 1948.   5.00
*13 articles, mostly from "Dance Index"
magazine, by E. D. Andrews, William Boli-
tho, George Freedley, Baird Hastings, Robert
Horan, Lillian Moore, Carl Van Vechten,
& Marian Hannah Winter.*

MARTIN, JOHN
The dance: the story of the dance
told in pictures & text.   160 p, 266
photos. Tudor 1946.   3.75
*The basic Dance, Dance for the sake of the
dancer, As spectacle (ballet), As means of
communication, In the technological era.*

SACHS, CURT
World history of the dance.   Tr
Bessie Schönberg. xii, 469 p, 32 pl,
mus ex, 6–p bibl. Norton 1937.   7.50
*A standard work, originally published in
German, 1933, tracing the development of
the dance throughout the world & throughout
the ages.   Chapter 5 is devoted to dance
music in particular.*

SPENCE, LEWIS
Myth and ritual in dance, game, &
rhyme. x, 202 p, 37 pl, 6–p bibl.
Watts, London, 1947; via Transatlantic 1949.   3.75

VAGANOVA, AGRIPPINA
Fundamentals of the classic dance
(Russian ballet technique).   Tr &
ed Anatole Chujoy. 132 p, 118 illus,
paper. Kamin 1946.   3.50
*By a noted Russian ballerina & teacher,
originally published in Russian, 1934. Also
available in a British edition (Black, 1948)
as "Basic Principles of Classical Ballet,"
with an introduction by Ninette de Valois.*

VAILLAT, LÉANDRE. See App Ia

DANCE BANDS

See also:

Armstrong	Jazz
Arranging–2	Mezzrow
D. Baker	Morton
Carmichael	Negro Music &
Condon	Musicians
Conducting	Popular Music
Crosby	Who's Who
Cugat	Yearbooks
Ellington	

*Note: Pertinent works apparently O/P or not
easily available) include those by Noble,
Specht, Wilson, etc.*

ANTRIM, DORON K. (*ed*)
Secrets of dance-band success. 87 p,
photos. Mills 1936.   1.00
*As outlined by Dorsey, Ellington, Lombardo,
Madriguera, Whiteman, & others.*

GRAHAM, ALBERTA POWELL
Strike up the band!: bandleaders of
today.   160 p, 4–p bibl. Nelson
1949.   2.00
*Sketches, written primarily for youngsters,
of some 35 leaders of the "pioneer," "transition," & "modern" eras; from Armstrong
through Goodman to Woody Herman &
Lionel Hampton.*

SIMON, GEORGE T. See App IIb (juvenile).

WHITEMAN, PAUL & LIEBER, LESLIE
How to be a band leader.   160 p,
photos. McBride (1941) 1948.   2.50
*The practical requirements for ambitious
boys, plus sketches of the careers of Ellington,
Goodman, Kenton, Monroe, et al.*

DANCE MUSIC

See also:

Appreciation	Jazz
Ballet (esp Lawrence)	Phonograph Records
(The) Dance	Popular Music
Dances–1, 2, 3	Program Notes
Folklore	Waltz
History	

*Note: Standard works apparently O/P (or not
easily available) include Evelyn Porter's
"Music through the dance" (1937), etc.*

ARVEY, VERNA
Choreographic music: for the dance.
523 p, 25 illus (pors, facs, etc), mus
ex, chap bibls & 9–p bibl. Dutton
1941.   6.00
*An extensive survey of all types of music used
for or inspired by dancing.*

HEYNSSEN, ADDA
Modern dance accompaniment: relationship of music & dance. 13 p,
music, paper. Curwen 1948.   .90
*Illustrative musical examples with brief notes
on the problems of shape, patterns, etc.*

NETTL, PAUL
The story of dance music. Pref
Martha Graham. xiii, 370 p, mus
ex, 6–p bibl. Philosophical 1947.   4.75
*An over-all historical survey, of unorthodox
musicological approach, and with emphasis
on 17th- to 19th-century dance music.*

DANCERS

See:

Ballet	History
(The) Dance	Nijinski
Duncan	Pavlova

DANCES/DANCING (1. Educational)

See also:

Children–1	Eurhythmics
Community Music	School Music
Dances–2	Teaching

Also: Ballet (Beaumont primer).
*Note: Only a sampling of the considerable
available literature is listed below.*

DRIVER, ANN
Music and movement. Pref L. P.
Jacks. vi, 122 p, illus (Molly Mac
Arthur, mus ex. Oxford 1936 (5th
pr 1949).   1.50
*A British educator on the utilization of rhyth-
mic activities, music appreciation through
movement-design, etc.*

HUGHES, DOROTHY
Rhythmic games and dances: basic
activities for elementary grades.
iv, 186 p, diagrs, 97–p music. American 1942.   2.65
*Dance-games for children, with instructions,
music (piano scores), & notes.*

JONES, RUTH W. & DeHAAN, MARGARET
Modern dance in education: techniques & dances. 88 p, illus, paper,
spir. Teachers College 1948.   1.75
*Teachers College also issues a companion
publication: Deborah Hunt Jennings's*

"*Music for modern dance,*" *42 p, music only,
paper, 1950.*

JORDAN, DIANA
The dance as education. 84 p. Ox-
ford 1938.   1.50
Aesthetic, gymnastic, & rhythmic dancing.

LADD, VALERIA GIBSON
Rhythm and the Noyes technique.
155 p, 199 illus (author). W. J. △
Clark, N. Y., 1949.   6.50
Based on Florence Fleming Noyes principles.

LA SALLE, DOROTHY (*comp*)
Rhythms and dances for elementary
schools: grades 1 to 8. xx, 168 p,
photos, music. Barnes 1926.   4.00

RADIR, RUTH
Modern dance for the youth of
America: a text for high school &
college teachers. xiii, 337 p, illus
(Ray Gough), chap bibls. Barnes
1944 (4th pr 1948).   3.00
*Includes suggestions for creative work in
movement, rhythm, space, & pantomime.*

ROGERS, FREDERICK RAND (*ed*)
Dance: a basic educational technique; a functional approach to the
use of rhythmics & dance as prime
methods of body development & control, and transformation of moral &
social behavior. xx, 351 p. illus
(photos & diagrs), 17–p annot bibl.
Macmillan 1941.   4.75
*Articles by some 20 writers, including Moses
Smith on "Music & dance," p 94/9.*

SHURR, GERTRUDE & YOCOM, R. D.
Modern dance: techniques & teaching. 191 p, 81 pl. Barnes 1949.   3.75
*Dance warm-ups, techniques, & exercises,
with detailed instructions & photographs.*

STECHER, WILLIAM A. & MUELLER, G. W.
Games and dances for exercise &
recreation. xi, 392 p, diagrs, music,
1–p sports bibl. Presser (1926) 1941.   3.00
*Especially for recreation directors, camp
leaders, school & kindergarten teachers.*

WHITLOCK, VIRGINIA BENNETT
Come and caper: creative rhythms,
pantomimes, and plays, with music
by various composers. Pref Rebecca
J. Coffin. x, 134 p, illus, music (sel
& ed Nothera Barton), bds. G.
Schirmer 1932.   3.00
*Music with extensive notes & illustrations
on the rhythmic & interpretative activities
developed for 1st-to-8th grade children at the
Lincoln School of Teachers College, Columbia
University, New York.*

DANCES/DANCING (2. Country, Folk, National, Regional, Round, Square, etc.)

General Note: Almost no other category in the present Guide impales the editor more awkwardly on a double-horned dilemma. In the first place, the subject-heading itself is highly debatable: "Folk Dances" might well be considered a preferable choice. But we were reluctant to use it, because elastic as the term "folk" may be, it seems to us that it is stretched well beyond the breaking point in most pertinent publications, few of which make any attempt to distinguish between authentic folk material and dances better characterized as "national," "regional," etc. Moreover (and this was the deciding factor), it seemed to us that both the primary appeal and the practical usefulness of these books are to dancers rather than to folklorists.

The dilemma's other and equally sharp horn is how much of the large available literature should be sampled here and on the basis of what criteria. Most pertinent books are primarily collections of music itself and while nearly all of them include considerable text, the latter usually consists only of performing instructions, costume descriptions, and the like. In the end, we have made a purely arbitrary selection, trying to include at least the best-known & most recent publications, and perhaps favoring those that deal with American square dances—currently enjoying a popular revival.

We have no information on the current availability of a "Bibliography of folk dances, games, & singing games, folk songs & near folk songs, etc," compiled by Margaret Van Voorhees & Mabel Spizzy-Anderson, and published in mimeographed form by the University of Hawaii, Honolulu, 1941. But for another bibliography, see under Minneapolis Public Library below.

See also:
Children–6 & 7   Indians (American)
Community Music   Latin America
Cowboy Music   National Music
(The) Dance   Phonograph Records
Dances–1   School Music–1 & 2
Folklore   Wales (music in)
History   (esp Williams)

ALFORD, VIOLET (*ed*);
Handbooks of European national dances (series). Each: 40 p, 4 col pl, map, music (arr Ferdinand Rauther), bibl. Chanticleer 1948/50.

A series published under the auspices of the Royal Academy of Dancing & the Ling Physical Education Society (England). Volumes issued to date, listed in alphabetical order by authors, include:

Armstrong, Lucille.   Dances of Portugal (1948).   1.50

——. Dances of Spain: Part 1, South, Center, Northwest (1950).   1.50

Breuer, Katharina.   Dances of Austria (1948)   1.50

Buday, George. Dances of Hungary (1950)   1.50

Crosfield, Domini. Dances of Greece (1948)   1.50

Heikel, Yngvar & Collan, Anni. Dances of Finland (1948).   1.50

Lorenzen, Poul & Jeppesen, Jeppe. Dances of Denmark (1950).   1.50

Lubinová, Mila. Dances of Czechoslovakia (1949).   1.50

Marcel-Dubois, Claudie & Andral, Marie-Marguerite.   Dances of France: Part 1, Brittany & Bourbonnais (1950).   1.50

Salvén, Erik.   Dances of Sweden (1949).   1.50

Van der Ven-ten Bensel, Elise. Dances of the Netherlands (1949).   1.50

Witzig, Louise.   Dances of Switzerland (1949).   1.50

BOYD, NEVA L. & DUNLAVY, TRESSIE M. Old square dances of America. 96 p, paper. FitzSimons 1932 (4th pr 1949?).   .75

BREWSTER, MELA SEDILLO
Mexican and New Mexican folk dances. 47 p, charts, music, spir. New Mexico (1937) 2nd rev ed n d.   1.50

BURCHENAL, ELIZABETH (*ed*)
American country-dances, v I: 28 contra-dances, largely from the New England states.   xvi, 63 p, illus, music (piano accs by Emma Howells Burchenal), bds. G. Schirmer 1918.   3.00

Folk-dances and singing games: 26 folk-dances . . viii, 83 p, illus, music, bds. G. Schirmer (1909) rev ed 1933 (1938).   3.00

Dances of the people: a second volume of folk-dances & singing games, containing 28 folk-dances . . . Intro Joy Elmer Morgan. ix, 78 p, illus, music, bds. G. Schirmer (1913) rev ed 1934 (1942).   3.00

Folk-dances from old homelands: a third volume of folk-dances & singing games, containing 33 folk-dances. x, 85 p, illus, music. G. Schirmer 1922.   3.00

The three books above comprise a series of representative dances (U. S. A., Great

Britain, & various European countries), with music & detailed notes & instructions.

Other Burchenal publications include:

Folk-dances of Denmark. 1915.

Folk-dances of Finland. 1915 (1943).

Folk-dances of Germany. 1938.

National dances of Ireland.

Three old American quadrilles.

Folk-dance music. Ed Burchenal & C. Ward Crampton. 1908 (1938).

CHASE, ANN HASTINGS (*ed*)
The singing caller: a book on the square dance, with calls & music. 78 p, illus, music, paper. Association 1944 (2nd pr 1947). **1.50**

CHASE, RICHARD (*comp*)
Hullabaloo: and other singing folk games. 57 p, illus (Joshua Tolford), music (piano arrs Hilton Rufty). Houghton 1949. **2.00**

Old songs and singing games. xii, 52, music, paper. North Carolina 1938. **.75**

CHOCHEM, CORINNE
Jewish holiday dances. Poems by Alfred Hayes, photos by Slavko Vorkapich, music arr Trudi Rittman. Forew Darius Milhaud. 87 p, Behrman House, N. Y., 1948. **5.00**

CHOCHEM, CORINNE & ROTH, MURIEL
Palestine dances!: folk dances of Palestine. 64 p, illus (drwgs Moses Soyer, photos John Mills Jr), music. Behrman House, N. Y., 1941 (1946). **3.00**

CZARNOWSKI, LUCILE K.
Dances of early California days. 159 p, illus, music, 2–p bibl. Pacific 1950. **5.00**
39 dances (mostly of Spanish or Mexican origin) with variants; early Californian social setting; typical festival programs.

DOLMETSCH, MABEL
Dances of England and France from 1450 to 1600: with their music & authentic manner of performance. xii, 163 p, 9 pl (facs, etc), music, 1–p bibl. Routledge 1949. **9.00**
A reconstruction, from contemporary treatises, of the authentic manner of dancing the basse-danse, English measure, branle, pavan, galliard, volta, coranto, & Allemande.

DUGGAN, ANNE SCHLEY (& others)
(*See also Dances-3.*)
The folk dance library. 5 v: illus, maps, music, bibl. Barnes 1948. **15.00**
Co-authors: Jeanette Schlottmann & Abbie Rutledge. The individual titles are:

V 1: The teaching of folk dance.
V 2: Folk dances of Scandinavia.
V 3: Folk dances of European countries.
V 4: Folk dances of the British Isles.
V 5: Folk dances of the U. S. & Mexico.

DUNHAM, KATHERINE
Journey to Accompong. ix, 162 p, illus (Ted Cook). Holt 1946. **2.50**
The noted dancer-anthropologist's day-by-day field notes on native dancing & dancers in the Maroon village of Accompong in Jamaica, British West Indies.

DURLACHER, ED (*comp*)
Honor your partner: 81 American square, circle, & contra dances with complete instructions for doing them. 286 p, photos (Ira Zasloff), music arr Ken Macdonald). Devin 1949. **7.50**

FOX, GRACE I. & MERRILL, KATHLEEN G.
Folk dancing in high school and college. ix, 89 p, illus (Charlotte St. John), music, 1–p bibl. Barnes 1944. **3.00**

GOPAL, RAM & DADACHANJI, SEROZH
Indian dancing. 96 p+ 42–p photos. △
Phoenix 1951, in prep. **(4.80)**
History of the origins and explanation of the movements & gestures of the 4 schools: Bharata Natyam, Kathakali, Kathak, & Manipuri; with a biographical sketch of Gopal (a noted Indian dancer).

HERMAN, MICHAEL (*comp*)
Folk dances for all. xii, 99 p, illus (drwgs Ben Stein, photos Gjon Mili), music, paper. Barnes & Noble 1947. **1.00**

JOHNSON, EDITH
Regional dances of Mexico. vii, 78 p, illus (Louise Remund), music, 2–p bibl. Banks Upshaw, Dallas, Texas, 1935 (4th pr n d). **2.00**

KENNEDY, DOUGLAS
England's dances: folk dancing today & yesterday. Intro Ralph Vaughan Williams. 158 p, 20 illus + map, 4–p bibl. Bell 1949. **1.75**
A survey by the director of the English Folk Dance and Song Society.

KIRKELL, MIRIAM H. & SCHAFFNIT, IRMA K.
Partners all—places all!: 44 enjoyable square & folk dances for everyone. 129 p, illus (Deidre Baird), music, 1–p bibl. Dutton 1949. **3.95**

KRAUS, RICHARD G.
Square dances of today: and how to teach & call them. Forew Charley Thomas. ix, 130 p, 49 illus (Carl Pfeufer), music (arr Charles Leonhard), 1–p annot bibl. Barnes 1950. **3.00**

A general survey of the square-dance revival, with detailed instructions for some 64 dances (with music for 31 of them), plus lists of records, periodicals, & schools.

LA MERI
Spanish dancing. Forew Walter Terry. xii, 188 p, photos, 3-p bibl. Barnes 1948. **5.00**
A detailed study, based on the author's first-hand experience, of regional traditions & techniques, and technical terminology.

LEAF, EARL
Isles of rhythm. Forew Katherine Dunham. xii, 211 p, photos (author). (1948) Blue Ribbon repr 1949. **1.00**
Primarily a pictorial record of West Indian dance cultures; originally pub by Barnes.

LOVETT, BENJAMIN B. (*comp*)
"Good morning:" music, calls, & directions for old-time dancing as revived by Mr & Mrs Henry Ford. 124 p, illus, music, paper. Henry Ford, Dearborn, Michigan (1926) 4th ed 1943. **.75**

MADDOCKS, DURWARD
Swing your partners: a guide to modern country dancing. 111 p, illus, bds, spir. Stephen Daye, Brattleboro, Vermont, (1941), rev 2nd ed 1950. **1.50**

MANNERS, ZEKE
American square dances: with calls illustrations, & music. 36 p, photos, music, paper. Robbins 1948. **.60**

MAYO, MARGOT
The American square dance. 120 p, illus (Selma Gorlin), music, bibl. Sentinel (1943) rev enl ed 1948. **1.25**

MELLOR, HUGH
Welsh folk dances: an inquiry, with notation of certain dances. 91 p, illus, music, paper. Novello 1935. △ **(1.50)**

(MINNEAPOLIS PUBLIC LIBRARY, MUSIC DEPARTMENT, *comp*)
An index to folk dances and singing games. xiv, 202 p. American Library Assn, Chicago, 1936. **1.00**
Same, supplement. 112 p, paper. American Library Assn 1949. **1.25**

OWENS, LEE
American square dances of the west and southwest. 182 p, illus, music (arr Viola Ruth). Pacific Books, Palo Alto, Calif, 1949. **3.50**
Detailed "off-floor" & "on-floor" instructions, with a 3-p section on "How to play the music," by Viola Ruth.

REYES-TOLENTINO, FRANCISCA S. (*ed*)
Philippine national dances. x, 371 p, illus, diagrs, music. Silver 1946. **3.00**
50 dances with native background material, based on research sponsored by the University of the Philippines.

ROHRBOUGH, LYNN (*ed*)
Play party games. 32 p, music (tunes only), paper. Coöperative Recreation Service, Delaware, Ohio, 1930 (1932). **.25**
27 dances & singing games with directions.

RYAN, GRACE LAURA (*comp*)
Dances of our pioneers. Forew Elmer D. Mitchell. 196 p, illus (Brooks Emerson), music (arr Robert T. Benford). Barnes 1926 (5th pr 1939?). **4.00**

SHAW, LLOYD
The round dance book: a century of waltzing; with over 100 old-time American round dances & circle mixers. Forew Thomas Hornsby Ferril. 443 p, illus. music. Caxton Printers 1948. **5.00**
Waltzes, polkas, mazurkas, schottisches, etc; with a "discussion of old books" (p 25/48) & lists of recommended recordings.

SPREEN, HILDEGARD L.
Folk-dances of South India. With the assistance of R. Ramani. Forew Marie Buck. xvi, 134 p, illus, music, 1-p bibl, bds. Oxford (1945) 2nd ed 1948. **3.75**
A detailed technical guide, with music in Indian & European notations, song-texts in Tamil & English translations.

TOLMAN, BETH & PAGE, RALPH
The country dance book: the old-fashioned square dance, its history, lore, variations, & its callers. 192 p, illus (F. W. P. Tolman), music, 1-p bibl (1937) via Barnes 1949. **2.75**
Originally published by The Countryman Press, Weston, Vermont, and Farrar & Rinehart, N. Y.

DANCES/DANCING (3. Ballroom & Social)

Note: Only a sampling of the large available literature is listed below.
See also: Cugat, Popular Music.

BALLWEBBER, EDITH
Group instruction in social dancing. Intro Mary Jo Shelly. x, 131 p, illus (Peg Sidle). Barnes 1938. **3.00**

DUGGAN, ANNE SCHLEY
(*See also Dances–2*).
The complete tap dance book. xliii,
100 p, illus, music (Esther Allen
Bremer & Sally Tobin Dietrich).
Barnes 1947.　　　　　3.50
*A combined edition of "Tap dances" (1932)
& "Tap dances for school & recreation"
(1935).*

HOSTETLER, LAWRENCE A.
Walk your way to better dancing.
xiii, 263 p, illus (photos, diagrs).
Barnes 1942 (5th pr 1949?).　　　3.00
*The same author's "Art of social dancing"
(1930 & later eds) apparently is O/P.*

MARSH, AGNES LEWIS & LUCILE
Textbook of social dancing: with
complete plans for dance parties. ix,
143 p, illus. (1933) J. Fischer 2nd
enl ed 1935.　　　　　3.50
*Originally published by the Buckingham
Marsh Press, Bridgeport, Connecticut.*

MURRAY, ARTHUR
How to become a good dancer. Intro Paul Whiteman. x, 191 p, illus
(photos, diagrs). S & S (1938) rev
ed 1947 (19th pr n d).　　　　2.75

WRIGHT, ANITA PETERS & DEXTER
How to dance. xi, 219 p, illus (Betty
Randolph Bean), bds (1942) Perma
Giants repr 1949.　　　　.95
Originally pub by The Garden City Press.

Dane, Clemence (*pseud* of Winifred Ashton):
Author. See Ballet (ed Haskell), Mozart–3
(ed Crozier).
Danhauser, Adolphe-Léopold. Author.
See App Ia & App Id.
Daniel, Oliver. Author.
See America (music in).
Daniel, Salvatore Francesco. Author.
See Arabia (music in).
Daniélou, Alain. Author.
See India (music in), Scales.

DANISH MUSIC
See: Denmark (music in)/Danish Music.

Daniskas, John. Author. See Berlioz–2.

DANN, Hollis
See also: Education, School Music.
Author. See School Music–4.

DEJARNETTE, REVEN S.
Hollis Dann: his life & contribution
to music education. xii, 157 p, 5
illus. Birchard 1940.　　　　2.00
Study of a leading American music educator.

Dannreuther, Edward. Author, editor.
See History–1 (Oxford v 6, note only).
*Note: Dannreuther's other books apparently
are O/P, at least in this country.*

DA PONTE, Lorenzo
See: esp Mozart–1, 2, & 3 (esp Benn, Croz-
ier, Dent).
Also:
Casanova　　　　　History
Classic Era　　　　Opera
*Note: The memoirs of Da Ponte (librettist
of "Così fan tutte," "Don Giovanni," & "Le
Nozze di Figaro") apparently are O/P both
in the original 4-v edition (1823/7) & the
1929 reprint.*

Dardenelle, Louise. Author.
See Children–5.
Darlington, Marwood. Author.
See Gilmore.
Darington, William Aubrey. Author.
See Gilbert & Sullivan.
Darnton, Christian. Author.
See Appreciation.
Dart, Thurston. Author.
See Appreciation.
Da Silva, (Rev) Owen Francis. Editor.
See California (music in).
Daubeny, Ulric. Author
See Wind Instruments.
Davenport, Marcia. Author. See Mozart–2.
Davey, Henry. Author. See History–3.
David, Elizabeth Harbison. Author.
See Accompaniment.

David, Hans Theodore. Author, editor.
See:
Bach–1.　　Bach reader (1945), ed
David & Mendel　　　　7.50
Bach–2.　　Musical offering (1945).　3.00
Choir/Choral–3.　　Art of polyphonic
song (1940).　　　　2.00

Davidson, Gladys. Author. See Ballet.
*Note: Several collections of opera stories
apparently are O/P (or not easily available).*

Davies, Majorie C.　　Co-author (with
Barnard). See Children–3.

DAVIES (*Sir*) (**Henry**) **Walford**
See also: England (music in), History.
Author. See Choir/Choral–1, Church Music.

COLLES, H. C.
Walford Davies: a biography.　203
p, illus, mus ex.　Oxford 1942 (3rd
pr 1943).　　　　2.50
*Life & works of the late Master of the King's
Musick, including a chronology & catalogue.*

Davis, Arthur Kyle, Jr. Editor.
See Folksongs–2.

Davis, Arthur Paul. Author. See Watts.

Davis, Ellen L. Co-compiler (with Matt-feld). See Song(s).

Davis, Ennis. Author. See Education.

Davis, George. Author. See Radio Music.

Davis, Hallowell. Editor, also co-author (with Stevens). See Hearing.

Davison, Archibald Thompson. Author, editor. See:

Anthologies. Historical, v l, Davison
& Apel (1946/9).   8.00

———. Same, v 2 (1950).   10.00

Choir/Choral–2. Choral conducting
(1940).   2.00

Church Music. Protestant church
music in America (1933).   3.00

Composition. Technique of choral
composition (1945).   3.00

Day, Cyrus Lawrence. Editor.
See Dryden, d'Urfey.

DEAFNESS

See:

Hearing	Speech (esp Potter)
Heiner	Warfield

Deakin, Irving. Author.
See App IIa (Prokofiev juvenile).

Dean, Winton. Author. See Bizet.

Dearmer, Percy. Editor.
See Carols, Hymns/Hymonody–1.

Deas, Stewart. Author.
See Ballet (ed Haskell), Hanslick.

DEBUSSY, (Achille-) Claude
1. Criticism & Letters
2. Life & Works

DEBUSSY (1. Criticism & Letters)

Monsieur Croche, the dilettante
hater. Tr B. N. Langdon Davies.
Forew Lawrence Gilman. xiv, 212
p, frontis por. (1928) Lear 1948.   **2.75**
*Debussy's articles on music (1901/1914),
originally published in book form in 1921;
O/P for some years in the present English
translation (Viking 1928) until re-printed
by Lear. The collection provides notable
illumination, not only on the composers liked
& disliked, but on Debussy himself as man &
artist.*

See also (for Debussy's letters, in French):
App Ia (Debussy, Durand, Tosi); also (for
a discussion of Debussy's critical theories):
Debussy–2 (Vallas).

DEBUSSY (2. Life & Works)

See also:

Appreciation	Opera
Chamber Music	Orchestral Music
Composers– 1 & 3d	Phonograph Records
Contemporary Music	Piano Music
French Music	Program Notes]
History	Song(s)
Modern Music	Vocal Music

Also: App IIa (Harvey, juvenile biog.)

*Note: Standard works apparently O/P (or not
easily available) include those by Cortot,
Dumesil ("How to play & teach Debussy,"
1932), Gilman, Liess (in German), Thompson, Vallas (biog, 1933, but see App Ia for
French ed), etc; also works in French by
Coeuroy, Laloy, Koechlin, Suarès, etc.*

CALVOCORESSI, M. D.
Debussy. 14 p, cover por, paper.
Novello n d.   .40
Miniature biography ("great musicians").

DUMESNIL, MAURICE
Claude Debussy: master of dreams.
326 p, frontis por. Washburn 1940.   2.50
*Reminiscences & anecdotes by a Debussy
student, who was also a close family friend.*

JANKÉLÉVITCH, VLADIMAR. See App Ia.

KETTING, PIET
Claude-Achille Debussy. Tr W. A.
G. Doyle-Davidson. 58 p, 15 pl
(pors, facs, etc), 1–p bibl, mus ex,
bds. Continental n d (1947).   2.50
*"Symphonia" series of extensively illustrated
brief studies, including a catalogue of
Debussy's works.*

LOCKSPEISER, EDWARD
Debussy. xii, 292 p, 8 pl (pors, fac),
mus ex, 7–p bibl. Dent (1936) 2nd
rev ed 1944; Pellegrini 1949.   2.50
*"Master Musicians" series, with usual calen-
dar, personalia, & catalogue of works.*

Introduction to the music of △
Debussy. Dobson, in prep.   1.00

MYERS, ROLLO H.
Debussy. 125 p, frontis por, 1–p
bibl. (1948) Wyn 1949.   1.00
*"Great Musicians" series, originally pub-
lished by Duckworth, London, 1948.*

SCHAEFFNER, GEORG. See App Ib.

SCHMITZ, E. ROBERT
The piano works of Claude Debussy.
Forew Virgil Thomson. xix, 236
p + 12–p pl (pors, fac, etc), 1–p
bibl. Duell Sloan 1950.   5.00
*Brief general commentary and extensive
technical analyses of the piano-solo compositions, with many individual notes on performance & interpretative details.*

STROBEL, HEINRICH. See App Ib.

VALLAS, LÉON (*See also App Ia.*)
The theories of Claude Debussy,
musicien français. Tr Marie O'Brien.
xiii, 189 p, illus (frontis por & fac).
Oxford 1929. 2.00
An analytical study of Debussy's views on
music in general, criticism, education, French
music, Wagner, etc, as expressed in his critical
articles, a 5-p list of which is included. Origi-
nally published in French, 1927.

DECIBEL

General Note: The decibel (abbreviated db) is
a ratio unit of changes in energy, in common
acoustical & electronic use for the measure-
ment of intensities. Although still foreign
to most musicians & listeners, it is likely
to become more familiar & more widely used,
especially to those concerned in any way with
radio broadcasting & sound recording. Event-
ually, it well may be adapted to serve as a
more exact scale of performance loudness
levels than the p & f indications, upon which
music has depended so long, but only for lack
of anything better.

The layman should be reminded, however, that
properly used the decibel refers to changes
of intensity or power, rather than absolute
values, unless a specific zero reference level
is stated.

See also:
Acoustics   Sound Rec & Repro
Hearing   (esp Mills)

LLOYD, L. S.
Decibels and phons: a musical analogy. 20 p, diagrs, paper. Oxford
1923. .50
A simple explanation in musical terms of the
distinction between decibels & the closely
related units for subjective loudness measure-
ments—phons.

RAO, V. V. LAKSHAMANA
Decibel notation: its application to
radio & acoustics. xvi, 179 p, illus,
tables, diagrs, 4–p bibl. Chemical
1946. 3.75
A standard, detailed technical study.

Decsey, Ernst. Author. See App Ib.

DEFINITIONS OF TERMS (Musical)
See:
Dictionaries of Music   Encyclopedias
Dictionaries of Terms   Theory–2 & 3

DeHaan, Margaret. Co-author (with Jones)
See Dances–1.

DeJarnette, Reven S. Author. See Dann.
De Lamater, Eric. Author.
See Wind Instruments.
Delaunay, Charles. Compiler. See Jazz.

DELIBES, (Clément-Philibert-) Léo
See also:
Appreciation   History
Ballet   Opera
Composers–1   Phonograph Records
French Music   Program Notes

Note: Standard works apparently O/P (or not
easily available) include those in French by
de Curzon, Guiraud, etc.

POSNER, SANDY
Coppélia: the story of the ballet.
96 p, illus incl 4 col pl (Joyce Millen).
Black (1945) 4th ed 1947, via Trans-
atlantic. .75
"Ballet Pocket Library" series.

DELIUS, Frederick
See also:
Appreciation   History
Composers–2 & 3c   Opera
Contemporary Music   Phonograph Records
English Music   Program Notes

Note: Pertinent works apparently O/P (or not
easily available) include Clare Delius's mem-
ories of her brother (1935), a study by Philip
Heseltine (Peter Warlock) (1923), & an essay
by Robert H. Hull (1928).

FENBY, ERIC
Delius as I knew him. viii, 234 p +
7–p music + 3–p index, frontis por,
mus ex. (Bell 1936) Quality Press,
London, 1948. 2.50
A study by the composer-amanuensis & friend
of Delius's last years.

HUTCHINGS, ARTHUR
Delius: a critical biography. ix, 193
p, 10 photos (ports, etc), mus ex,
1–p bibl. Macmillan 1948. 3.75
Includes an "appreciation" of Delius's
music, a catalogue of his works, and a
(British) discography to 1946.

DELVINICOURT, Claude
See: App Ia (Landowski: "L'Oeuvre de
Claude Delvincourt").

Demarest, Clifford. Author.
See Organ Playing.
Demuth, Norman. Author, compiler. See:
Criticism. Anthology (1947). 3.00
Franck. Biography (1949). 4.75
Gounod. Introduction to the music
of (1950) in prep. 1.00

Ravel. Biography (1947).   2.50
Roussel. A study (1947).   3.75

Denby, Edwin. Author. See (The) Dance.
Dengler, Clyde R. Author.
See Singing–2.
Denis, Paul. Author. See Career.

DENMARK (Music in)/DANISH MUSIC

See also:

Dances–2 (ed Alford: Lorenzen & Jeppe- sen)	Folksongs–2 History Phonograph Records
Folklore	

KAPPEL, VAGN
Contemporary Danish composers
against the background of Danish
musical life and history. Tr O. A.
Hansen. 116 p, 18 pl (facs, etc),
paper. Danske Selskab, Copenhagen
(1948) 2nd rev ed 1950.   (1.50)

Information on Danish music history & musi-
cal organizations, with biographies of 14
composers (from Carl Nielsen to Niels Viggo
Bentzon) contributing to the formation of the
contemporary nationalist school, plus lists
of available recordings of Danish music.

Dennis, Charles Maschel. Co-author (with
Nicoll). See Singing–2.

Densmore, Frances. Author.
See Indians (American)
Note: Miss Densmore's extensive & authori-
tative writings on American Indian music
have largely appeared in specialized publica-
tions of the Bureau of American Ethnology
(Smithsonian Institute, via GPO); the South-
west Museum, Los Angeles; The Museum of
the American Indian, New York; & offprints,
etc, via the author, Red Wing, Minnesota.

Dent, Edward Joseph. Author. See
Busoni. Biography (1933).   7.50
Handel–1. Biography (1934/48).   1.00
Mozart–3. Mozart's operas: a criti-
cal study (1913/48).   4.75
——. Crozier, ed: Così fan tutte
(1945). Includes a Dent essay.   .50
Opera–1. Foundations of English
opera (1928).   3.50
——. Opera (1940).   (.35)
Purcell. Mandinian: The fairy
queen (1947). Incl. a Dent essay.   (6.30)
Shakespeare. Granville-Barker:
Studies (1934). Incl Dent essay.   3.75
Theatre. A theatre for everybody
(1945).   (4.50)

Translator. For the Dent series of English
translations of opera librettos, see Opera–2,
also individual listings under:

Auber	Mozart
Beethoven–3	Rossini
Donizetti	Tchaikovsky–2
Flotow	Verdi–2
Gluck	Weber

Note: Several other books by Dent apparently
are O/P (or not easily available).

DE RESZKE, Jean

See:

History	Singers
Opera	Singing–2 (Teyte)

Note: Clara Leiser's "Jean de Reszke and the
great days of opera" (1934) apparently is
O/P.

Desfossés, Beatrice. Author. See Speech.
Deswert (de Swert), Jules. Author
See Violoncello Playing.
Dethier, Jean V. Author.
See Harmony–2.
Deucher, Sybil. Author & co-author (with
Wheeler). See App IIa (juvenile biogra-
phies):

Bach	MacDowell
Brahms	Mozart
Grieg	Schubert
Haydn	

Deutsch, Leonhard. Compiler.
See Folksongs–1, Sight-Playing.
Deutsch, Maury. Author. See Arranging–1,
Instrumentation, Psychology, Theory–4.
Deutsch, Otto Erich. Author, editor.
See Facsimiles, Schubert–1, "World of
Music" series.
Dewey, John. Author. See Aesthetics–1.

DIAGHILEV, Sergei P.

See:

Ballet	Karsavina
(The) Dance	Russian Music
History	Stravinsky

Note: Pertinent works apparently O/P (or not
easily available) include those by Beaumont,
Haskell, Lifar, etc.

Diamante, Carlos. Author.
See Arranging–2.

DIATONIC HARMONY

See: Harmony.

Dichter, Harry. Compiler.
See Sheet Music.

DICKENS, Charles

Note: Lightwood's "Charles Dickens and
music" (1912) apparently is O/P.

Dickinson, Alan Edgar Frederic. Author.
See Bach–2, Mozart–3, Vaughan Williams.
Co-author (with Storr). See Children–2.
Note: Several other works by A. E. F. Dickinson apparently are O/P.

Dickinson, Clarence. Author.
See Organ Playing. Co-author (with Wolfe & Helen A. Dickinson). See Church Music.

Dickinson, Edward. Author.
See Appreciation, Church Music.
Note: Several other works apparently are O/P (or not easily available).

Dickinson, George Sherman. Author.
Note: Several books by G. S. Dickinson, including "The pattern of music" (1939), apparently are for limited distribution only (at Vassar College), or O/P.

Dickinson, Helen A. Co-author (with Wolfe & Clarence Dickinson). See Church Music.

DICTATION

General Note: There is an obviously close relationship between this subject and Ear-Training & Sight-Singing: many of the musical exercises included in all such books may be used interchangeably.

See also:
Children–3　　　　　Sight-Singing
Ear-Training　　　　Solfège/Solfeggio
Keyboard Harmony　Theory–2 & 3
　(esp McHose &
　White)

Note: Pertinent works apparently O/P include the White & Jones "Harmonic dictation" (1932), among others.

McHOSE, ALLEN IRVINE
Teachers' dictation manual. x, 183 p, mus ex, typescript repro. Crofts 1948.　　　　　　　　　　　　　　3.00
"Eastman School of Music" series; exercises in rhythmic, melodic, harmonic, & harmonic counterpoint dictation.

ORTMANN, OTTO
Problems in the elements of ear dictation. 95 p, diagrs, mus ex, paper. Peabody Conservatory, Baltimore, 1934.　　　　　　　　　　1.00
"Research Studies in Music," No. 2.

WHITE, BERNICE
Melodic dictation. xii, 141 p, mus ex. American 1935.　　　　　　3.50
Same, Teacher's supplement. iii, 59 p, music, paper. American 1935.　　.75

DICTION (ENUNCIATION)

General Note: Only a sampling (of particular musical interest) of the large available literature is listed below. Perhaps it isn't needless to add that the term "diction" is a popular misnomer: the books themselves deal with problems of enunciation, pronunciation, inflection, etc, rather than with the actual choice of words.

See also:
Choral Speaking　　　　Pronunciation
French Language　　　　Singing
German Language　　　　Song(s)
Italian Language　　　　Speech
Latin Language　　　　　Voice

HAWN, HENRY GAINES
Diction for singers and composers. 172 p, diagrs, mus ex. Presser (1900) rev ed 1911 (1928).　　　　　　2.00

ROGERS, CLARA KATHLEEN
Clearcut speech in song. viii, 102 p, mus ex, 1–p bibl, paper. Ditson 1927.　　　　　　　　　　　　　　.75

"Pocket Music Student" series.

English diction: a text book for singers & speakers. 2 v.
V 1: The voice in speech: a a practical system for the improvement of defective voices, & the attainment of perfect diction in both speech & song. 123 p, paper. Ditson 1915.　1.25
V 2: Song and speech. xi, 105 p, mus ex, paper. Ditson 1912.　　1.25
Volume 2 was published first as "English diction: in song & speech." Volume 1 was written later to meet the need for a more generalized introduction to the subject.

RUSSELL, LOUIS ARTHUR
English diction for singers and speakers. vi, 81 p, mus ex. Ditson 1905.　　　　　　　　　　　　　1.25
"Music Students Library" series.

WARING, FRED
Tone syllables. 7 p, 2 diagrs, mus ex, paper. Shawnee Press, N. Y., rev ed 1948.　　　　　　　　　△
Outline of rules for a method of enunciation in choral singing; supplied with the Waring series of choral editions.

DICTIONARIES OF MUSIC

General Note: The distinction between dictionary and encyclopedia is not always observed in book titles: Grove's, for example, has become in the course of time much more of a true encyclopedia than a dictionary. For convenience, however, entries have been classified in accordance with their familiar titles, except in the case of the Scholes "Companion," which is actually a dictionary, hence entered below.

See also:

Dictionaries of Musical   History
Terms   Encyclopedias

For some specialized dictionaries, see:

America–music in   Latin America (Slon-
(Schiavo)   imsky)
Composers–3a   Russian Music (Vodar-
(McNamara)   sky-Shareff)
Hammond Organ   Themes (Barlow &
(Irwin)   Morgenstern)
                     Violin (Emery)

Note: Standard works apparently O/P (or not easily available at the present time in this country) include those by Baltzell, Dunstan, Fétis (in French), Hull, Moser (in German), Riemann (in English & German), etc.

APEL, WILLI
Harvard dictionary of music. x, 833 p, illus, mus ex, subject bibls. Harvard 1944 (6th pr 1950).   7.50
The only standard work devoted to all aspects of music *only—i. e., no biographical data on* musicians *are included, except incidentally. Various authorities have collaborated in providing articles on their own special fields. An enormous range of subjects is covered, many of them in considerable detail.*

ARMA, PAUL & TIENTOT, Y.   See App Ia.

BAKER, THEODORE
Baker's biographical dictionary of musicians. xiii, 1298 p, subject bibls. G. Schirmer (1900) 4th rev enl ed 1940 (3rd pr with 1949 supplement).   7.50
The exact converse of the Apel work above, a standard reference book of biographical data, completely revised by Gustave Reese, Gilbert Chase, Robert Geiger, & others. The current printing includes the Slonimsky supplement listed below.

(SLONIMSKY, NICOLAS)
Supplement 1949 to Baker's biographical dictionary of musicians. 95 p (pp 1224/1298), paper. G. Schirmer 1949.   .75
Available separately for owners of earlier printings of Baker's dictionary above. In addition to the new & augmented entries, it includes a 2–p introduction & 5–p errata list.

BLOM, ERIC (*comp*)
Everyman's dictionary of music. xiii, 706 p. (1946) McKay n d (1948).   3.50
American edition of a recent British work containing some 10,000 concise entries.

GERSTBERGER, KARL.   See App Ib.

GROVE, GEORGE (& COLLES, H. C., *ed*)
Grove's dictionary of music and musicians. Macmillan 4th rev ed 1940 (1946).   37.50

First published in England, 1878–1889, the celebrated "Grove's" has been revised, enlarged, & widely used over the years, until today it is probably the most familiar standard musical reference work in English. In the course of its evolution, however, the arrangement of volumes & editions has become exceedingly confusing: the present so-called 4th edition comprises the 5–v main dictionary (3rd rev ed 1927, repr 1946) and an American Supplement (2nd ed), plus a Supplementary Volume, as outlined below:

V 1: A–C.   xxxiii, 773 p, 20 pl, mus ex, subject bibls.

V 2: D–J.   xxv, 800 p, 19 pl, mus ex, subject bibls.

V 3: K–O.   xxv, 787 p, 16 pl, mus ex, subject bibls.

V 4: P–SON.   xxv, 840 p, 22 pl, mus ex, subject bibls.

V 5: SONG–Z.   xxv, 791 p, 17 pl, mus ex, subject bibls.

(PRATT, W. S. & BOYD, C. H., *Am eds*)
(V 6:) American Supplement. vii, 438 p, 16 pl, subject bibls. (1920) rev enl ed 1928 (1946).
(6–volume set only.)   30.00

(COLLES, H. C., *ed*)
Grove's dictionary of music and musicians: supplementary volume. xvi, 688 p, 35 pl, mus ex, subject bibls. 1940 (1944).   7.50
The supplementary volume, available separately, brings the 6–v set above up-to-date to 1940. In addition to new articles, it contains many augmentations of earlier entries & constant references back to the main dictionary.

Notes: 1) For a separate publication of Grove's own articles on Beethoven, Schubert, & Mendelssohn, see Composers–1. 2) A completely revised 5th edition of Grove's is in preparation, under the general editorship of Eric Blom, but apparently it will not be ready for several years.

SCHOLES, PERCY
The Oxford companion to music: self-indexed & with a pronouncing glossary. lix, 1160 p, col frontis, 12 pors, some 1200 illus, mus ex. Oxford (1938) 8th rev ed 1950.   14.50
The most extensive "one-man" dictionary, particularly notable for its many, if small-sized illustrations: portraits, instruments, facsimiles, etc. A book list (included in the 2nd English edition, but not in later English or American editions) is available separately: see Bibliography (Scholes). The current 8th

edition embodies minor corrections in the main text and a new appendix of added material on some 90 musicians.

SCHUH, WILLI & REFARDT, E. See App Ib.

DICTIONARIES OF MUSICAL TERMS

General Note: Works in this category are confined to books (or for the most part, booklets) devoted primarily to concise definitions, usually with guides to pronunciation. For more extended definitions, historical surveys, etc, reference should be made to standard Dictionaries & Encyclopedias of Music.

See also:

Appreciation	History
Children–8	Notation
Dictionaries of Music	Pronunciation
Encylopedias	Theory–2 & 3

In addition to the entries below, undoubtedly there are others still in-print. But since a large proportion of these dictionaries of terms cover much the same ground, our listings have been confined as far as possible to the best-known & most widely distributed publications.

BAKER, THEODORE
A dictionary of musical terms: containing upwards of 9,000 English French, German, Italian, Latin & Greek words & phrases used in the art & science of music, carefully defined, & with the accent of foreign words marked; preceded by rules for the pronunciation of Italian, German, & French. vi, 257 p, mus ex. G. Schirmer (1895) 21st ed 1923.   2.00
A standard work, with a supplementary English-Italian vocabulary for composers, & an appendix of 700 additional words & phrases.

A pronouncing pocket-manual of musical terms. xviii, 256 p, mus ex, paper. G. Schirmer (1933) rev & aug ed 1947.   .50
Pocket edition of the dictionary above, including the elements of notation & biographical dates of noteworthy musicians.

CLARKE, HUGH A.
Pronouncing dictionary of musical terms. 124 p, mus ex. Presser 1896.   1.25

Same, pocket size, paper covers.   .30

COON, OSCAR (ed)
Pocket standard dictionary of musical terms: giving concise definitions of the terms & phrases in general use in music, together with a treatise on the elements of music. xv, 94 p, mus ex. C. Fischer 1905.   .50

Same, paper covers.   .30

ELSON, LOUIS C.
Elson's music dictionary: containing the definition & pronunciation of such terms & signs as are used in modern music . . xi, 306 p, mus ex. Ditson 1905 (1933).   1.75
With a list of foreign composers & artists, list of popular errors in music, a short English-Italian musical vocabulary.

Elson's pocket dictionary: the important terms used in music with their pronunciation & definition— together with the elements of notation & a biographical list of over 700 noted names in music. xii, 195 p, paper. Ditson 1909.   .40

FOSS, HUBERT
The concertgoer's handbook. 259 p, 5-p annot bibl. Sylvan 1946.   3.25
A different type of concise reference book, directed to listeners rather than students, and covering a wide variety of musical subjects in brief explanatory notes, arranged alphabetically in dictionary style.

GEHRKENS, KARL WILSON
Handbook of music terms. 103 p, mus ex, bibl, paper. Ditson 1927.   .75
"Pocket Music Student" series. Not in dictionary style, but including definitions grouped under such headings as Notation, Musical Elements, Forms, Acoustics, Italian Terms, Instruments, Voices, etc.

GORDON, HAMILTON ADAIR
Pocket dictionary of musical terms. With additions by Henry Marx. 40 p, paper. Robbins 1947.   .25

HEROLD, HUGO & NOATZSCH, RICHARD. See App Ib.

KAUFMAN, HELEN L.
The little dictionary of musical terms. vii, 277 p, mus ex. Grosset 1947.   .75
Pocket-size "Little Music Library" series.

MATHEWS, W. S. B. & LIEBLING, E. (eds)
Mathews & Liebling pronouncing and defining dictionary of music. 264 p, mus ex. Church (1896) rev ed 1925.   1.25
With supplementary English-Italian vocabulary & list of prominent composers & artists.

MIGOT, GEORGES. See App Ia.

SCHOLES, PERCY A.
The Scholes music handbook: being a complete book of reference giving both meaning & pronunciation of the technical words found in programs & in program notes. Ed for

American readers by Will Earhart.
xxx, 101 p. Witmark 1935.   **1.50**
*American edition of "The Radio Times music
handbook" (England). Like the Foss work
above, it is directed to listeners rather than
students, and not in dictionary style or covering all terms, but a classified list of some 887
term-explanations that the author considers
"first aid to the puzzled listener."* (The
British version is currently in its 4th edition:
Oxford, London, 1950.)

STAINER, JOHN & BARRETT, W. A.
Dictionary of musical terms. Compressed by K. M. Ross. 96 p, mus
ex, paper. Novello n d.   **(1.75)**
*Novello "Primers" No. 21: an abbreviated
edition of a standard work first published in
1876 (London), but O/P currently.*

DICTIONARIES (Rhyming)

See: Songwriting (Lewis, Wood).

Dietrich, Fritz. Author. See App Ib.

DIEREN, Bernhard van. Catalogued under
Van Dieren, Bernard.

Dike, Helen. Author. See App IIb.
Dille, Denijs. Author. See Bartók.

Diller, Angela. Author. See
Children–3. Pre-school music book,
Diller & Page (1936).   .75
Children–6. How to teach the
rhythm band, Diller & Page (1928).   .35
Keyboard Harmony. Course, in 4
v (1936/49).   4.75
Theory–2. 1st theory book (1921).   3.00
Also: App IIa (Verdi, Wagner juveniles).

Dillon, Josephine K. Co-author (with
Bohman). See Libraries.

D'INDY, Vincent. Catalogued under Indy.

Dingley-Mathews, Blanche. Author.
See Children–8, Ear-Training.

DIRECTING/DIRECTORS

See:
Choir/Choral–2   Dance Band
Conducting   Orchestral
Conductors   School Music–3 & 4

DISCOGRAPHIES

See:
Children–2   Phonograph Records
Chopin–2 (ed Panigei)   School Music–2
Jazz (Delaunay,   Unesco (note only)
   Smith)

*General Note: Discography is the inevitable
term fabricated to provide record cataloguers
with a single word corresponding to book cataloguers' "bibliography." Except for some
specialized works (children's & jazz records),
book-length discographies are listed under
Phonograph Records in the present Guide.
However, most recent books on every kind of
musical subject properly include discographies of some length—usually selected lists of
pertinent or especially recommended phonograph recordings. The usefulness of these
lists is of course largely dependent (apart
from the care with which they are compiled)
on the date & place of publication: older lists
are likely to be out-of-date; those in foreign
books are likely to include European releases
only.*

DISCRIMINATION (Musical)

See:
Aesthetics   Psychology
Appreciation   Tests

DISEASES (Musical)

See: Health.

Dobrzynski, Boris. Author.
See Stravinsky–2.

DOCTORS (and Music)

See: Health.

DOCUMENTS (Musical)

*General Note: Many books on individual
composers & various historical eras re-
produce or discuss pertinent original documents. Recently, however, several books
on individual composers have been devoted
exclusively to the presentation & annotation
of strictly documentary material. See esp:*
Bach–1 (David &   & Bertensson)
   Mendel)   Schubert–1 (Deutsch)
Moussorgsky (Leyda

See also:
Composers (& under   Facsimiles
   individual names)   History
Contemporary Music   Letters
   (Slonimsky)   Musicology

NETTL, PAUL
The book of musical documents.
Pref Carleton Sprague Smith, xiv,
381 p, 24 pl. Philosophical 1948.   5.00
*A highly miscellaneous anthology of docu-
ments (mostly in brief excerpts) pertaining to
musical history, modeled on Hermann
Unger's "Musikgeschichte in Selbstzeugnis-
sen" (1928).*

Doerflinger, William Main. Compiler.
See Sea Shanties & Songs.

Doisy, Marcel. Author. See App Ia.
Dolejsi, Robert. Author.
See Viola/Viola Playing.
Dolmetsch, Arnold. Author.
See Interpretation.
Dolmetsch, Mabel. Author. See Dances–2.
Dolmetsch, Rudolph. Author.
See Conducting.

DOMINICAN REPUBLIC (Music in)
See also: Latin America.

COOPERSMITH, J. M.
Music and musicians of the Dominican Republic. Forew Charles Seeger.
Spanish tr María Hazera & Elizabeth M. Tylor. 146 p, 5 pl (4 pors,
10 photos, map), mus ex, 6–p bibl,
2–p discography, paper. Pan American Union 1949.   1.25

No. 15 in the music series, Division of Mu-
sic & Visual Arts, Pan American Union,
Washington, D. C. The text is given in
Spanish ("Música y Músicos de la República
Dominicana"), as well as in English, and
includes a historical survey as well as a study
of the folklore, instruments, dances, etc, based
on a field trip made in 1944.

Donington, Robert. Author.
See Instruments.

DONIZETTI, Gaetano
See also:
Appreciation   Italy (music in)
Composers–1   Opera
History   Phonograph Records
Note: Pertinent works apparently O/P (or not
easily available) include those in Italian by
Barblan, Cametti, Caversazzi, Cicconetti,
Donati-Petteni, Franccaroli, Gabrielli, Ga-
vazzeni, etc.

DENT, EDWARD J. (*tr*)
Don Pasquale: a comic opera in 3
acts. Words & music by Donizetti;
English version. 62 p, paper. Oxford 1946.   .80

ZAVADINI, GUIDO. See App Ic (biography
in Italian).

Doorly, Charles C. Author.
See Sight-Singing.
Dorf, Richard H. Author.
See Sound Recording & Reproduction.
Dorian, Frederick. Author.
See Composition, Interpretation.
Doring, Ernest N. Author.
See Guadagnini Family, Stradivari.
Dorsey, Jane. Co-author (with Avery &
Sickles). See Speech.

Dossert, Deane. Author. See Singing–2.
Doty, Ezra William. Author. See Form.

DOUBLE BASS
See:
Instrumentation   Orchestra
Instruments   String Instruments

Douel, Jean. Author. See App Ia.
Douglas, Alan. Author.
See Instruments.

DOUNIS, D. C.
See: Violin Playing (Leland).

Douty, Nicholas. Author. See Singing–2.
Downes, Edward. Author.
See Program Notes.
Downes, Olin. Editor (with Siegmeister).
See Folksongs–2.
Note: Several books by Downes ("The lure of
music," "Symphonic broadcasts," etc) appar-
ently are O/P.

Downing, William B. Author.
See Singing–2.

DRAMA
General Note: Only a sampling (of particular
musical interest) of the large available litera-
ture is listed here.
See also:
Acting   Television
Opera   Theatre
Radio   Wagner

ELLIS-FERMOR, UNA
The frontiers of drama. vii, 154 p.
Oxford (1945) 2nd ed 1946.   3.00
A discussion of means by which the art form
may transcend its normal limitations.

GAGEY, EDMOND M.
Revolution in American drama. viii,
315 p. Columbia 1947.   3.75
Developments since 1912, including some dis-
cussion of operettas & musical comedies.

DRAMA (MUSIC–)
See:
Appreciation   Opera
History   Wagner

Drew, William Sydney. Author.
See Singing–2.
Drinker, Henry Sandwith. Author, compiler, translator. See Brahms–2.
Note: Numerous other works by Drinker, in-
cluding a catalogue of the Drinker choral
library and translations of Bach choral texts,
song-texts of Brahms, Medtner, Schumann,

Wolf, etc, are privately printed for specialized distribution only. For information, address The Association of American Choruses, Drinker Choral Library, c/o Westminster Choir College, Princeton, N. J.

Drinker, Sophie. Author. See Women.
Driver, Ann. Author. See Dances–1.

DRUM(S)

See:

Band	Instruments
Bugle	(esp Mason)
Children–4 & 6	Orchestra
Instrumentation	

Note: P. R. Kirby's "The kettle drum" (1930) apparently is O/P.

DRYDEN, John

See also:

England (music in)	Poetry
English Music	Purcell
Handel	Restoration Era
History	Song(s)

DAY, CYRUS LAWRENCE (*ed*)
The songs of John Dryden. xvi, 199 p, 25 music facs. Harvard 1932.　2.50
Reproductions & discussions of 25 settings of Dryden poems; a companion work to the author's "Songs of Thomas d'Urfey."

Dubin, Al. Author. See Songwriting.
Dubois, Théodore. Author. See App Ia.
Dudley, Louise. Author (with Faricy). See Aesthetics–1.

DUFAY, Guillaume

See:

Anthologies	History
Choir/Choral–3	Madrigal
Church Music	Mass
Composers–1	Medieval/Renaissance
French Music	Phonograph Records

Note: Standard works apparently O/P (or not easily available) include a study by Van den Borren (in French, 1926) and J. & C. Stainer's "Dufay & his contemporaries" (1893, 1898). A reprint of the latter, however, is rumored to be in preparation.

Dufourcq, Norbert. See App Ia.
Duggan, Anne Schley. Author. See Dances–2 & 3.

DUKAS, Paul

See:

Appreciation	History
Composers–2	Phonograph Records
French Music	Program Notes

Also: App IIa (juveniles by Cooke, Rostron)

Author. See App Ia (Dukas: "Les écrits de Paul Dukas sur la musique").

Dumesnil, Maurice. Author. See Debussy–2.
Dumesnil, René. Author. See App Ia.
Dunbar, Rudolph. Author. See Clarinet.

DUNCAN, Isadora

See also: Ballet, (The) Dance.　.
Note: An autobiography ("My life," 1928) apparently is O/P (or not easily available).

MAGRIEL, PAUL (*ed*)
Isadora Duncan. vii, 85 p, some 60 photos, 7–p bibl. Holt 1947.　　3.50
Critical essays (largely from "Dance Index" magazine) by Craig, Macdougal, Martin & Van Vechten, plus a chronology.

Duncan, William Edmonstoune. Author. See Carols, Minstrels/Minstrelsy.
Note: Several other books by Duncan apparently are O/P (or not easily available).

Dunham, Katherine. Author. See Dances–2.
Dunham, Rowland W. Author. See Organ Playing.
Dunhill, Thomas Frederick. Author. See Mozart–3.
Dunk, John L. Author. See Scale.
Dunkley, Ferdinand Luis. Author. See Voice.
Dunlap, Orrin Elmer, Jr. Author. See Television.
Dunlavy, Tressie M. Co-author (with Boyd). See Dances–2.
Dunn, George E. Compiler. See Gilbert & Sullivan.

DUNN, James Philip

See also:

America (music in)	Composers–3a
American Music	

HOWARD, JOHN TASKER
James P. Dunn. 13 p, frontis por, mus ex, paper. J. Fischer 1925.　　.25
Catalogue of works & brief analyses.

Dunstan, Ralph. Author. See Harmony–2, Theory–3.
Note: Several other books by Dunstan apparently are O/P (or not easily available).

DUPARC, Henri

See also:

Appreciation	Phonograph Records
Composers–1 & 2	Song(s)
French Music	Song Translations
History	Vocal Music

NORTHCOTE, SYDNEY
The songs of Henri Duparc. 122 p,
2 pors, 1 fac, mus ex, 1–p bibl. Dobson 1949; Roy 1950.　　　　3.50
The first study in English: a biographical sketch with quotations from Duparc's correspondence, detailed analyses of 14 songs, & 2–p discography.

Dupré, Marcel. Author. See App Ia.
Durand, Jacques. Author. See App Ia.
Durlacher, Ed. Compiler. See Dances–2.
Dushkin, David. Author. See App IIb.

DVOŘÁK, Antonín
See also:

Appreciation	Orchestral Music
Chamber Music	Phonograph Records
Composers–1 & 3b	Piano Music
(esp Suermondt)	Program Notes
Concerto	Themes
Czechoslovakia	Timing
History	Violin Music
Opera	Vocal Music

Also: App IIa (Judson, Purdy, & Van Straaten juveniles).

Note: Standard works apparently O/P (or not easily available) include those by Abraham, Fischl, Hoffmeister, Sirp (in German), Sourek & Stefan (in German), Stefan (in English & German), etc.

CARNER, MOSCO
Dvořák.　14 p, cover por, paper.
Novello n d (1941).　　　　.40
Miniature biography ("great musicians").

KULL, HANS. See App Ib

KVET, J. M.
Note: Kvet's sketch of Dvořák's personality & work, once announced in preparation for Hinrichsen's "miniature survey" series, now is indefinitely postponed.

ROBERTSON, ALEC
Dvořák.　viii, 234 p, 9 pl (pors, facs, etc), mus ex, 2–p bibl.　Dent 1945 (1947); Pellegrini 1949.　　2.50
"Master Musicians" series, with the usual calendar, personalia, & catalogue of works.

Dvorak, Raymond Francis. Author. See Band–2.

Dykema, Peter William. Author. See:
School Music–1.　New handbook, Dykema & Cundiff (1923/39).　　3.50
—.　Teaching & administration, Dykema & Gehrkens (1941).　　4.40
School Music–3.　Band training manual, Church & Dykema (1939).　1.00
—. Orchestra training manual, Church & Dykema (1930/4).　　.60
Tests.　K–D music tests, Kwalwasser & Dykema (1930).　　2.25

Dyson, George. Author, editor. See:
Contemporary Music.　The new music (1924/6).　　3.00
Ear-Training: Allchin: Aural training, ed Dyson (1940).　　1.00
History–5. Progress of music (1932). 2.00
Theory–4: Dyson, ed: Harmony, Counterpoint, & Improvisation, by Dale, Jacob, & Anson; 2 v (1940). 4.25

—E—

EAR (Musical)

See: esp Ear-Training, Hearing.

Acoustics   Psychology
Appreciation   Sound Rec. & Repro.

Earhart, Will. Author, editor. See:

Appreciation. Music appreciation,
by Scholes, ed Earhart (1935).   4.00

Baton–1. Eloquent baton (1931).   1.75

Children–2. Book of great musicians,
by Scholes & Earhart (1931)   3.50

Choir/Choral–1. Technics (1937)   1.75

Dictionaries of Terms. Scholes music
handbook, ed Earhart (1935).   1.50

Ear-Training. Music to the listening ear (1932).   2.00

School Music–1. Meaning & teaching of music (1935)   4.00

Theory–2. Elements of music, by
Boyd & Earhart (1938). 2 v.   3.00

Theory–3. Music theory for piano
students, by Hamilton, Goetschius,
Marshall, & Earhart (1924/30). 2v.   2.00

EARLY MUSIC

See:

Ancient Music   Gregorian Chant
Arabian Music   History
Church Music   Jewish Music
Baroque Era   Medieval/Renaissance
Elizabethan Music   Troubadours/
Greek Music   Trouvères

EAR-TRAINING

*General Note: In its larger aspects this
important branch of training in elementary
applied musicianship embraces the closely
related subjects of Dictation, Sight-Playing &
Reading, Sight-Singing, & Solfège. Wisely
breaking down the arbitrary barrier once
erected between the applied & "theoretical"
fields, most modern books on harmony &
theory emphasize ear-training and include
more or less specific ear-training material,
just as many of the books listed here include
considerable material on harmony & theory.*

*Since all books listed below include musical
examples, the usual "mus ex" is omitted from
the bibliographical data. The note, "Exercises," indicates that the book contains little
text and is devoted primarily to musical
exercises for ear-training purposes.*

See also:

Children–3 & 8   Score-Reading
Dictation   Sight-Playing &
Harmony   Reading
Hearing   Sight-Singing
Keyboard Harmony   Solfège-Solfeggio
Psychology   Theory
Rhythm

*Standard works apparently O/P include those
by Alchin, Jadassohn, Lawton, Macmillan,
Macpherson & Read, Oakey, Robinson,
Shinn, Trotter, Wood, etc.*

ALCHIN, CAROLYN A.
Ear training for teacher and pupil.
ix, 136 p. Ditson 1904 (1932).   1.50
"Music Students Library" series; exercises.

ALLCHIN, BASIL C.
Aural training. 40 p, paper. Novello
n d (1940).   1.00
*No 1 in "Musicianship for Students" series,
ed Dyson. For No 2, see Theory–4 (Dyson).*

DINGLEY-MATTHEWS, BLANCHE
Harmonic ear training and theory:
to hear & understand. ix, 262 p.
Church 1926. (1st-year course.)   2.00

EARHART, WILL
Music to the listening ear. xiv, 173
p. Witmark 1932.   2.00
*Text for a course combining ear-training,
dictation, & appreciation.*

GINGRICH, IRVING
Contrapuntal ear-training: and advanced course for music schools &
colleges. 127 p. FitzSimons (1932)
rev ed 1938. (Exercises.)   2.50

HEACOX, ARTHUR E.
Ear-training: a course of systematic
study for the development of musical
perception. 117 p, flex. Presser
1898. (Exercises.)   1.00

HINDEMITH, PAUL
Elementary training for musicians.
xiii, 237 p. Associated 1946.   4.00
*A handbook of sight-reading, ear-training,
& notation, with each chapter divided into
"Action in time" (meter & rhythm), "Action
in space" (pitch), & "Combined action."*

JOHNSON, FREDERICK
Exercises in ear training. 34 p, paper.
Wood 1938. (Exercises.)   .75

SCHOLES, PERCY A.
The beginner's guide to harmony:
being an attempt at the simplest
possible introduction to the subject,
based entirely on ear-training. 62 p.
Oxford (1922) 2nd ed 1924 (1939). 1.25

SHINN, FREDERICK G.
Examination aural tests: & how to
study for them. 102 p, flex. Augener
1924 (4th pr 1937). 2.00
*"In preparation for the tests given in the
examinations of the Associated Board & in
the diploma examinations of the R.A.M. &
the R. C. W."*

WEDGE, GEORGE A.
Ear-training and sight-singing: applied to elementary musical theory:
a practical & coördinated course for
schools & private study. vi, 174 p.
G. Schirmer 1921. 3.00

Advanced ear-training and sight-
singing: as applied to the study of
harmony: a continuation of the practical & coördinated course for schools
& private study. vi, 323 p+2 charts.
G. Schirmer 1922. 4.00
*Together these 2 books form a standard,
extensive work on practical musicianship
from the basic elements through triads, 7th &
9th chords, chromatic alterations, modulation
& embellishment.*

WRIGHT, FRANK & NOBLE, T. TERTIUS
Ear training tests: clarifying the use
of the material of harmony. (*Exercises.*) 32 p, stiff paper. Gray 1936. 2.00

EASTMAN SCHOOL OF MUSIC.
See: America (music in).
*Note: For information about bulletins of the
Eastman School festivals of American music
& for Charles Riker's history of the school's
first quarter century (1948), apply to the
Eastman School of Music of the University
of Rochester, N. Y.*
*For some of the publications issued in the
Eastman School of Music series, see:*

Anthologies (Gleason)	(McHose, Soderlund)
Bibliographies (Glea-	Dictation (McHose)
son & Luper)	Keyboard Harmony
Composition	(Mc Hose & White)
(McHose)	Organ Playing
Conducting	(Gleason)
(Van Hoesen)	Sight-Singing
Counterpoint-1	(McHose & Tibbs)

Eaton, Quaintance. Editor.
See America (music in)

ECUADOR (Music in). See Latin America.

Edeson, Donald Joseph Scott. Author.
See Choir/Choral-2.

Edgerly, Beatrice. Author.
See Instruments.

EDITIONS OF MUSIC (Historical) ("Denkmäler")
*Please see the general notes under Anthologies
& Historical Collections of Music.*

EDUCATION (Music—)
*General Note: No books on education in
general are listed here. Those that are listed
are confined, insofar as possible, to the wider
aspects of music-education, as distinguished
from books devoted primarily to music in
schools (School Music), to practical aspects
of music-teaching in general (Teaching), and
to instruction in various specialized subjects.*

See also:

Appreciation	Mason
Children–1	Musicology
Colleges	School Music–1
Community Music	Psychology
Dann	Teaching–1
Erskine	Teaching–2
Mannes	(esp Murphy)

*Standard works apparently O/P (or not easily
available) include those by Barnes, Carroll,
Davison, Hunt, Lavignac, McEachern,
Mursell, Smith, etc.*

BARNETT, DAVID
Living with music. 62 p, mus ex.
Stewart 1944. 1.50
*Based on experience (Thomas School) in
developing innate musical talents.*

They shall have music. 108 p, mus
ex. Stewart 1944. 1.50
*Musical activities in colleges, schools, &
communities.*

DAVIS, ENNIS
More than a pitch-pipe: the human,
professional, & business relations
of the music educator to his school
& community. Pref. P. W. Dykema,
forew G. Gildersleeve. ix. 177 p.
Birchard 1941. 2.00
*Practical & psychological aspects of success-
ful work in music-education.*

FARNSWORTH, CHARLES HUBERT
The why and how of music study: for
parents & teachers. v, 71 p, paper.
Ditson 1927. .75
*"Pocket Music Student" series. Discovering
& applying musical talent.*

HALE, NOEL V.
Education for music: a skeleton plan
of research into the development of
the study of music as part of the
organized plan of general education.
xix, 243 p. Oxford 1947. 3.75

LARSON, WILLIAM S. (*ed*)
Bibliography of research studies in
music education. 132 p, paper.
Music Educators' National Conference, Chicago, 1949. 2.00
*Some 1600 titles, 1932–1948; superseding
a 1944 publication ed Arnold M. Small.*

MORGAN, HAZEL NOHAVEC (*ed*)
Music education source book: a
compendium of data, opinion, &
recommendations, compiled from the
reports of investigations, studies, &
discussions conducted by the MENC
curriculum committees during the
period 1942–1946, & a selection of
pertinent material from current
releases of the organization. xiii,
256 p, 6–p bibl. Music Educators'
National Conference, Chicago, 1947. 3.50

MURSELL, JAMES L.
Education for musical growth. viii,
343 p, chap bibls. Ginn 1948. 3.75
*Concepts, avenues, & a development pro-
gram for the process of "becoming musical."*
Human values in music education.
388 p, chap bibls. Silver 1934. 3.00
The philosophical aspects.

SHAW, HAROLD WATKINS (*ed*)
Musical education: a symposium.
259 p, mus ex. Hinrichsen n d
(1947?). 2.50
*Hinrichsen "Survey" series S-3. Includes
articles by Barbirolli, Bullock, Hill, Northcote,
& Westrup.*

WATSON, JACK MCLAURIN
The education of school music
teachers for community music leader-
ship. ix, 91 p. Teachers College
1948. 2.10
*Teachers College series of "Contributions to
education," No. 948.*

EDUCATION (Physical)

See:
Dances-1 & 2   School Music
Eurhythmics   Teaching

EDUCATORS

See:
Dann   Mason
Erskine   Parker
Mannes   Surette

Edwards, Ruth. Author (with Simon).
See Children-8.
Ehinger, Hans. Author. See App Ib.
Ehmann, Wilhelm. Author. See App Ib.

EINEM, Gottfried. See App Ib (Rutz).

EINSTEIN, Alfred.
Greatness in music. Tr César Saer-
chinger. vii, 299 p. Oxford (1941)
rev ed 1945. 3.75
*Studies of questionable & unquestionable great-
ness, and the esoteric & historical conditions
for greatness, stimulated by a chapter in
Burkhardt's "Observations on world history."*
Author, editor. See also:
History–2. Short (1936/47). 4.00
Italian Music. Vogel bibliography,
rev Einstein (note). △
Madrigal. Golden age (1942). 1.25
——. Italian (1949). 3 v. 30.00
Mozart–2. Character & work (1945). 5.00
Mozart–3. Köchel index (1937/47). 12.50
Romantic Era. Music in (1947). 6.00
Schubert–1. Musical portrait (1950). 5.00
*Note: Einstein's "Gluck" (1936) & several
works in German apparently are O/P.*

Eisenberg, Philip. Author.
See Children–2.
Eisenstein, Serge M. Author. See Films.
Eisler, Hanns. Author. See Film music.
Eitner, Robert. Author, compiler.
See App Ib.
Ekman, Karl. Author. See Sibelius.

ELECTRICITY & MUSIC

See:
Acoustics (esp Olson)   Organ
Decibel   (esp Whitworth)
Film Music   Phonograph
Hammond Organ   Phonograph Records
Instruments   Radio Music
 (esp Douglas, Lewer)   Sound Rec & Repro
                        Stokowski

ELEMENTARY MUSICIANSHIP/ELE-MENTS OF MUSIC

See:
Appreciation   Ear-Training
Children (esp 3 & 8)   Sight-Singing
Dictionaries of Terms   Theory (esp 2 & 3)

ELGAR, (Sir) Edward

See also:
Appreciation   History
Composers-2 & 3c   Phonograph Records
English Music   Program Notes
*Note: Standard works apparently O/P (or
not easily available in this country) include
those by Dunhill, Maine, Newman, Porte,
Reed, Shera, etc.*

ANDERSON, W. R.
Introduction to the music of Elgar.
70 p, mus ex. Dobson 1949. 1.00
A brief outline-study with record list.

(ELGAR, EDWARD)
Falstaff: analytical essay by the
composer. 16 p, paper. Novello
n d (1933). .50

My friends pictured within: the
subjects of the Enigma Variations as
portrayed in contemporary photographs & Elgar's manuscript. Unp
(35 p), illus (pors & facs), paper.
Novello n d (1946). 3.00

JOSE, EVERARD
The significance of Elgar. 29 p,
frontis. Heath 1934. 1.00

MCNAUGHT, WILLIAM
Elgar. 22 p, cover por, paper.
Novello n d (194?). .40
Miniature "Biographies of Great Musicians."

POWELL, (*Mrs*) RICHARD
Edward Elgar: memories of a vari-
ation. xiii, 98 p, 8 illus, 4 facs.
Oxford (1937) 2nd ed 1947. 4.25
Reminiscences by the "Dorabella" of the
Intermezzo in the Enigma Variations. (A 3rd
ed, on which we have no data, was announced
by Methuen, London, in 1949.)

REED, WILLIAM HENRY
Elgar. viii, 227 p, 8 pl, mus ex,
1–p bibl. Dent (1939) rev ed 1934
(1946). Via Pellegrini 1949. 2.50
"Master Musicians" series, including the
usual calendar, catalogue of works, "per-
sonalia," etc.

WESTBROOK, FRANCIS B.
Elgar's "Dream of Gerontius."
Hinrichsen in prep for 1951. △
"Miniature Survey" series M-12.

ELIZABETHAN MUSIC
See also:

Campion	Fellowes
Choir/Choral–3	History
Church Music	Keyboard Instruments
Byrd	Madrigal
Counterpoint	Medieval/Renaissance
(esp Morris)	Milton
England (music in)	Poetry (esp Pattison)
English Music	

Note: Glyn's "Elizabethan virginal music &
its composers" (1924) apparently is O/P.

(After this section was type-set, the Boyd
work below unfortunately went O/P also;
the entry is left here for reference purposes
only.)

BOYD, MORRISON COMEGYS
Elizabethan music and musical crit-
icism. xii, 363 p. 8 illus, mus ex,
25–p bibl. Pennsylvania 1939. O/P
A standard scholarly work on Tudor &
Jackobean music. The bibliographies cover

contemporary music collections & treatises, as
well as modern books on Elzabethan music.

(HARROW REPLICA)
Parthenia, or The Maydenhead of the
first musike that ever was printed
for. the virginalls. unp (34), frontis,
music. Heffer 1942. 12.50
Facsimile reproduction of the original 1612/3
publication; pieces by Byrd, Bull, & Gibbons.

Elkan, Ida. Author. See Sight-Playing.
Elkin, Robert. Author.
See Career, Philharmonic, Program Music,
Queen's Hall
Ellingford, Herbert F. Author.
See Masonic Music, Organ Music.

ELLINGTON, Duke (Edward Kennedy)
See also: Jazz, Popular Music.

ULANOV, BARRY
Duke Ellington. x, 322 p, 16–p
photos. Creative Age 1946. 3.00
Biographical study of the Negro dance-band
leader & composer; includes a 34–p dis-
cography of Ellington records.

Ellinwood, Leonard Webster. Editor.
See Hymns Hymnody–1.
Elliott, Godfrey Monroe. Editor.
See Films.
Elliott, John Harold. Author.
See Berlioz–2.
Ellis, Alexander John. Author, translator.
See Acoustics (Helmholtz).
Ellis, Norman. Author. See Arranging–2.
Ellis, William Ashton. Author, translator.
See Wagner–2 (Glasenapp).
Ellis-Fermor, Una. Author. See Drama.
Elson, Arthur. Author.
See Composers–1, Encyclopedia of Music.
Elson, Louis Charles. Author. See:
American Music. National (1899). 2.50
Dictionaries of Terms. Elson's
(1905). 1.75
——. Elson's pocket (1909). .40
Theory–2. Theory (1890/1935). 2.70
Note: Numerous other books by Elson & by
his son, Arthur, apparently are O/P.

Elwin, Verrier. Author.
See India (music in).

EMBELLISHMENTS. See Ornamentation.

Embs, Anton H. Co-author (with Mc-
Conathy, Howes, & Fouser). See Harmony–2.
Emery, Frederic Barclay. Author.
See Violin.
Emery, Stephen Albert. Author.
See Harmony–2.

Emery, Walter. Co-author (with Boult).
See Bach–2.

Emil-Behnke, Kate. Catalogued under
Behnke.

Emrich, Marion Vallat. Editor
See Children–7.

ENCYCLOPEDIA BRITANNICA
See: Tovey ("Articles on music from the
Encyclopedia Brittanica").

ENCYCLOPEDIAS OF MUSIC
*General Note: The distinction between En-
cyclopedias & Dictionaries of music is not
always accurately maintained in publishers'
titles: the Pratt book below, for example, might
well be considered a dictionary. However, for
convenience, classifications are made on the
basis of familiar title usage.*

See also:

Dance (Chujoy)	Phonograph Records
Dictionaries of Music	(Reid)
English Music	
(Palmer)	

*Standard works apparently O/P (or not easily
available in this country) include those by
Abert (in German), De Bekker & Parkhurst,
Champlin & Apthorp, Lavignac & Laurencie
(in French), Riemann (in German), etc.*

BLUME, FRIEDRICH *(ed)* See App Ib.

EITNER, ROBERT. See App Ib.

ELSON, ARTHUR
The book of musical knowledge: the
history, technique, & appreciation
of music, together with the lives of
the great composers. ix, 609 p, illus,
mus ex. (1915, rev ed 1934) Tudor
repr 1946.   2.98
*Evolution of music, great composers, musical
form, instruments, special topics, & important terms. Originally published in 1915 by
Houghton Mifflin*

HUGHES, RUPERT
(TAYLOR, D. & KERR, R., *eds)*
Music lovers' encyclopedia: containing a pronouncing & defining dictionary of terms, instruments, etc.,
including a key to the pronunciation
of 16 languages, many charts; an
explanation of the construction of
music for the uninitiated, a pronouncing biographical dictionary,
the stories of the operas, & numerous
biographical & critical essays by distinguished authorities. xxv, 887 p
— 2 charts. (1903) Garden City rev
ed 1939 (1947).   2.49
*Completely revised & newly ed by Deems
Taylor & Russell Kerr (1939).*

PRATT, WALDO SELDEN
The new encyclopedia of music and
musicians. ix, 970 p, illus, bibls.
Macmillan (1924) rev ed 1929 (1948).   6.00
*Dictionary style in 3 sections: Definitions
& descriptions, Biographies, Places, insti-
tutions, & organizations; with appendices,
Bibliographical notes, Persons before 1700:
Operas & oratorios since 1900, additional
death dates.*

SCHUH, WILLI *(ed)* See App Ib.

THOMPSON, OSCAR *(ed)*
The international cyclopedia of music
and musicians. xvi, 2380 p, bibls.
Dodd Mead (1938) 5th ed rev & enl
(ed Nicolas Slonimsky) 1949.   16.00
*The most extensive 1-volume encyclopedia.
Includes appendices: Plots of operas, 145 p;
Pronunciations of names & titles; bibliography, 282 p (based on the National Association of Schools of Music "List of books on
music").*

ENCYCLOPEDISTS. See Criticism (Oliver).

Engel, Carl (1818-1882). Author.
See Ancient Music.

Engel, Carl (1883-1944). Author.
See Composers–1.
*Note: Engel's book of essays, "Discords
Mingled" (1931), currently is O/P.*

England, Paul. Author. See Opera–3.

ENGLAND (Music in)
*General Note: Under Britain (Music in) &
British Music, we noted the reasons of ex-
pediency for classifying pertinent books under
the often less exact headings, England (music
in) & English Music, which are more familiar
to American readers.*

See also:

Ballet	History
Berlioz–2 (Ganz)	Masonic Music
Church Music	Neel
Conductors (Brook)	Philharmonic
Covent Garden	Queen's Hall
Dances–2	Shaw
(esp Dolmetsch)	Watts
Elizabethan Music	Year books
English Music	(Hinrichsen)

*Standard works apparently O/P (or not easily
available in this country) include those by
Crowest, Galloway, Grace, Hueffer, etc.*

(ARTS ENQUIRY—"PEP")
Music: a report on musical life in
England. 224 p, tables. Political &   △
Economic Planning, London, 1949.   (4.50)
*A report on various aspects of music in Eng-
land, sponsored by the Dartington Hall
Trustees & published on behalf of the Arts
Enquiry (3rd in a series on the arts).*

BLOM, ERIC
Music in England. 288 p, paper.
Pelican (1942) rev ed 1947.   .35
A concise musico-sociological survey.

LAFONTAINE, HENRY CART DE
The king's musick: a transcript of
records relating to musick & musicians, 1460–1700. xii, 522 p. No- △
vello 1909.   (3.75)
*Excerpts from the Lord Chamberlain's
Records.*

MELLERS, WILFRID H.
Music and society: England and the
European tradition. 230 p + chart,
8 pl, 1–p bibl. Dobson (1946, 160 p),
2nd rev enl ed 1950; Roy 1951.   3.50
*Re-issue, just announced, of a discussion of
the relationships between music & civilization,
especially in England from the 16th to the 20th
centuries; with an added chapter on American
music.*

NETTEL, REGINALD
Music in five towns, 1840–1915: a
study of the social influence of music
in an industrial district. Intro Frank
Howes. x, 120 p. Oxford 1944.   3.50
The orchestra in England: a social
history. 296 p, illus. Cape 1946
(2nd pr 1948).   3.00
*Growth of the classical orchestra, the Phil-
harmonic & Nationalist periods.*

RUSSELL, THOMAS
Music. 64 p, bds. Lane 1947.   1.00
*A brief survey, No 2 in the "New Develop-
ments" series edited by Jack Lindsay.*
The Proms. 72 p, 4 col pl, 33 b&ws.
Parrish & Co., London, 1949.   △
*"World of Music" series No 9, but not an-
nounced (at least yet) for American issue by
Chanticleer.   An extensively illustrated sur-
vey of the famous popular-concerts through
"bombs, bankruptcy, & broadcasting."*

SCHOLES, PERCY A.
The mirror of music, 1844–1944: a
century of musical life in Britain as
reflected in the pages of the "Musical
Times."   2 v: xix, 523; xvii, 438 p,
118 pl. Oxford 1947.   17.50
*A detailed survey of a century's musical life
& activity covered by a famous periodical.*

VAN DEN BORREN, CHARLES
The sources of keyboard music in
England. Tr James E. Matthew. vii,
378 p, mus ex. Oxford 1915 (1948).   7.00
*A detailed study of 16th-century & early 17th-
century virginalists & their music. Originally
pub in France in 1912.*

WALKER, ERNEST
A history of music in England. viii,
386 p, mus ex. Oxford (1907) 2nd ed
1924.   4.50
Up to the close of the 19th century.

ENGLISH MUSIC

See also:

Appreciation	Folklore
Chamber Music	History
Choir/Choral–3	Madrigals
(esp Manners)	Masonic Music
Church Music	Opera–1 (esp Dent)
Composers–1, 2, & 3c	Poetry (esp Boas,
(& under individual	Pattison)
names)	Program Notes
Elizabethan Music	Rounds (Bukofzer)
England (music in)	Year books
Film Music	(Hinrichsen)

*Note: Standard works apparently O/P (or
not easily available in this country) include
those by Anderton, Chappell, Crowest, Davey,
Fuller Maitland, Hadow, Harris, Hayes,
Maine, Pulver, Scholes, Westrup, Young, etc.*

BACHARACH, A. L. (*ed*)
British music in our time. 256 p,
mus ex, paper. Pelican 1946 (1951).   .35
*Essays, mainly on specific British composers,
by various British writers.*

MYERS, ROLLO H.
Music since 1939. 48 p, 26 photos,
paper. Longmans 1948.   .50
*"Arts in Britain" series No 7, stressing war-
time activities of British musicians.*

MYERS, ROLLO H. (*& others*)
Since 1939: ballet, films, music, paint-
ing. 184 p + 11 col pl & 77 b&ws.
Phoenix House, London, 1949.   (3.00)
*Besides the Myers survey (listed separately
above), this larger book includes similar
brochures by Arnold Haskell (ballet), Dilys
Powell (films) & Robin Ironside (painting).*

PALMER, RUSSELL (*comp*)
British music: an encyclopedia of
British musicians.   Forew Malcolm
Sargent. 283 p, 42 photos, 2–p bibl.
Skelton Robinson 1947.   △
Biographical index; 3–p discography.

WESTRUP, J. A.
British music. 42 p, 11 photos, 2–p
bibl, paper. Longmans (1943), rev
ed 1949.   .50
*"Life & Thought" series, published for The
British Council: a concise survey, including
a 7-p selected discography.*

ENJOYMENT (Musical)

See:

Aesthetics	Psychology
Appreciation	

ENUNCIATION
See: esp Diction.
Also: Pronunciation, Speech, Voice.

Erb, John Lawrence. Author.
See Appreciation.

Erlanger, (Baron) Rudolphe d'. Author.
See App Ia.

Erpf, Hermann. Author. See App Ib.

ERSKINE, John
The memory of certain persons. 439
p. Lippincott 1947. 4.00

My life as a teacher. 249 p. Lippincott 1948. 3.50

*An autobiography, 1879-1946, & the first of
several supplementary books dealing in more
detail with specialized aspects of a many-
faceted career in education & music. The
2nd of these, Erskine's "musical autobiography," including a history of the Juilliard
School of Music, has just been announced:*
My life in music. viii, 283 p, frontis
por. Morrow 1950. 3.50

What is music? 212 p, mus ex, 4-p
annot bibl. Lippincott 1944. 3.00

*An unclassifiable book, half of which is devoted
to answering the title's question, and touches
on aesthetics, philosophy, & theory; the
second half of which discusses various types
of careers in music.*
Author. See also:
App IIa. Mendelssohn (juvenile). 2.75
Note: "The complete life" apparently is O/P.
Editor. See:
Appreciation. Musical companion,
American edition (1935/48). 2.98

Eschman, Karl Henry. Author.
See Modern Music.

ESSAYS
*Note: In general, collections of essays on
music (unless they have a specific major
subject) are listed under their authors' names.*
See esp:

Abraham	Myers
Aldrich	Newman
Berlioz-1	Rolland
Colles	Rorke
Debussy-1	Sampson
Finck	Schumann-1
Gray	Sorabji
Harding	Taylor
Lambert	Thomson
MacDowell	Tovey
Mann	Westrup
Mason	Whittaker

ESSENTIALS OF MUSIC. See Theory.

ESTHETICS. See Aesthetics.

EURHYTHMICS
*Note: Eurhythmics is a system of musical
training largely based on physical movement.
It is closely associated with the name of its
principal exponent, Émile Jaques-Dalcroze.*

See also:

Aesthetics-1 (esp	Rhythm
Ogden)	App Ia (Jaques-
Children-3	Dalcroze)
Dances-1	

*Note: Other books by Jaques-Dalcroze in
English editions apparently are O/P or not
easily available in this country.*

JAQUES-DALCROZE, ÉMILE
(Jaques-Dalcroze method of eurhythmics) Rhythmic movement. 2 v,
vii, 64 p; iii, 96 p 20 music, illus,
mus ex, paper. Novello 1920/1. 6.00

*V 1: Development of the rhythmic & metric
sense of the instinct for harmonious &
balanced movements & of good motor habits.
V 2: Bars of 6 to 9 beats & a chapter on the
application of rhythmic movement to pianoforte technique.*

PENNINGTON, JO
The importance of being rhythmic: a
study of the principles of Dalcroze
eurhythmics applied to general education & to the arts of music, dancing,
& acting. Intro Walter Damrosch.
xi, 142 p, illus (drwgs Paul Thevenaz;
photos Edwin F. Townsend). Putnam 1925. 2.00
*Based on & adapted from Jaques-Dalcroze's
"Rhythm, music & education."*

EUROPE
See also:

Belgium	History
Czechoslovakia	Italy
England	Russia
France	Vienna

COOKE, JAMES FRANCIS
Musical travelogues: little visits to
European musical shrines for the
casual traveller, the music lover, the
student, & the teacher. 333 p, illus.
Presser 1934. 3.00

Evans, Edwin (Senior). Author. See:
Beethoven. 9 Syms. (1923/4). 10.00
Brahms-2. Handbooks to the works
of, 4 v (1912/1936). 25.00
Organ Playing. Technics (1937). 4.00
Plainsong. Modal acc. (1911). 2.25
Wagner-2. Wagner's teachings by
analogy (1915). 2.50
*Note: Various other books by Evans appar-
ently are O/P (or not easily available).*

Evans, Edwin (Junior). Author. See:
Dance–1. Music and (1948).   2.50
Opera–1. Crozier, ed: Opera in
English (1945).   .50
Schumann–2. Miniature biography.   .40
Stravinsky. Firebird etc. (1933).   1.00
Tchaikovsky–1. Biog. (1906/1935).   2.50
Note: A collection of essays, "The margin of music" (1924) apparently is O/P.

Evans, May Garrettson. Author.
See Poe, Theory–3.
Evans, Willa McClung. Author.
See Lawes.
Evetts, Edgar T. Author.
See Singing Voice.

EVOLUTION OF MUSIC
See: esp History–5 (Parry).

Ancient Music	History
Appreciation	Medieval/Renaissance
Harmony (esp Kitson)	

Note: Standard works apparently O/P include those by Casella, Combarieu, Glyn, Kryzhanovsky, etc.

Ewen, David. Author, editor. See:
America (music). Music comes to
America (1942/47).   3.50
Composers–1. Of Yesterday (1937).   5.00
Composers–2. Modern (1942/50).   6.00
Composers–3a. American (1949).   4.00
Conductors. Dictators (1943/48).   3.50
History–5. Bach to Stravinsky
(1933).   4.00
Interpreters. Living (1940).   5.00
———. Men & women who make
music (1939/1949).   3.00
Popular Music. Men of (1944/49).   3.00
Program Notes. Music for the
millions (1944/50).   2.98
———. Same, Mentor abr repr (1950).   .35
Toscanini. Story of (1951).   2.50
Yearbooks. American music (1948).   6.00
App IIa (Berlin, Gershwin, Haydn, &
Strauss Family juveniles).
Note: Numerous other books by Ewen, including "Musical Vienna" (1939), written in collaboration with Frederic Ewen, apparently are O/P.

Ewen, Frederic. Editor. See Heine.

EXAMINATIONS (Musical)
See also: School Music, Tests.

Note: Standard works apparently O/P include those by Antcliffe, Colles, Wright, etc.

FIELDEN, THOMAS
Marks and remarks: musical examinations & their problems. 101 p, mus
ex. (1937) Williams rev ed 1948.   (2.00)
British usage: piano examinations & aural tests only; appendix added to original ed.

EXOTIC MUSIC
See:

African Music	Chinese Music
Ancient Music	History
Arabian Music	Oriental (note only)

EXPERIENCE (Musical)
See:

Aesthetics	Philosophy
Appreciation	Psychology
Children	

Expert, Henry. Editor.
See Historical Collections of Music (note only).

EXPRESSION
See also:

Aesthetics	Piano Playing
Children–3	Psychology
Conducting	Singing
Harding	Violin Playing
Interpretation	

Note: Standard works apparently O/P include those by Kobbé, Lussy, Vandercook, etc.

FERGUSON, DONALD N.
On the elements of expression in music. iii, 114 p, mus ex, mim, paper.
Minnesota (1944) 1948.   1.50
Aesthetic problems; form & content in isolation & relation; music as metaphor.

SORANTIN, ERICH
The problem of musical expression:
a philosophical & psychological study.
vi, 122 p, mus ex, flex. Marshall &
Bruce Co., Nashville, Tenn., 1932.   2.00
In 2 parts, theorectical & analytical; the latter examines melodic & rhythmic figures.

EXTEMPORIZATION
See: Improvisation/Extemporization.

Exton, William, Jr. Author.
See Teaching–1.

EYE-TRAINING
See:

Sight-Reading &	Sight-Singing
Playing	Score-Reading

—F—

Fabricant, Noah Daniel. Editor (with Werner). See Anthologies.

FACSIMILES

General Note: Most biographies and many specialized studies include facsimile reproductions of manuscript scores, letters, programs, or other documents. Others appear in every well illustrated Encyclopedia or History of music.

We do not have full information on the standard pertinent works apparently O/P (or not easily available), but one of them that should be mentioned is "An old Saint Andrews music book" (MS Wolfenbüttel 1677), edited by James Houston Baxter (Oxford 1931).

See also:

Autographs	individual names)
Bach–2 (esp Kirkpatrick)	Elizabethan Music (Harrow)
Beethoven–1 (Sonneck)	Handel–2 (Harrow)
Beethoven–3 (Piazza)	Letters
Composers (& under	Songbooks
	(ed Walker)

BACH, J. S. See App Ib.

BECK, JEAN & LOUISE (*eds*). See App Ia.

COUSSEMAKER, EDMOND (*ed*). See App Ie.

FORKEL, JOHANN NIKOLAUS. See App Ib.

GERBERT, MARTIN (*ed*). See App Ie.

(HARROW REPLICAS)

No. 2. Purcell and Handel in Bickham's Musical Entertainer. 23 pl, 2–p notes (Otto Erich Deutsch). △ Heffer 1942.   10.00
From the 1736/40 London publication: title page volume 1, 14 songs by or associated with Purcell & Handel, and a page written by Willington Clark, engraved by Bickham.

No. 5. Selected plates from the Universal Penman engraved by George Bickham, the elder. 24 pl, 3–p notes (O. E. Deutsch) Heffer △ 1943.   10.00
Examples of the 18th-century penmasters' art from various issues of the "Universal Penman," published from 1733 to 1760.

No. 6. Encomium musices: by Phillippe Galle, Jean van der Straet, & Johannes Bochius. 18 pl, 4–p note △ (O. E. Deutsch) Heffer 1943.   10.00
Reproductions of plates originally engraved at Antwerp around 1600, illustrating Biblical episodes involving musical instruments.

No. 7. St. Cecilia's album. 43–p facs, 8–p notes (O. E. Deutsch). △ Heffer 1944.   7.50
Album-leaf manuscript and autographs by 43 composers, from d'Albert to Wolf.

LARSEN, JENS PETER (*ed*). See App Ib.

LEWIS, HENRY (*ed*)
Music: B. M. additional MS. 14905. xii + some 120–p facs. △ Hinrichsen 1936.   10.00
Facsimile reproduction of "one of the earliest British musical manuscripts": "Musica neu Beroriaeth," ascribed by the editor to around 1100 (a date strongly questioned by Reese & other authorities).

SCHÜNEMANN, GEORG (*ed*). See App Ib.

Faelton, Reinhold. Author.
See Piano Playing–2.

Failoni, Sergio. Author. See App Ic.

Fairfield, John Houghton. Author. See Violin.

FALLA, Manuel de

See also:

Appreciation	Piano Music
Ballet	Program Notes
Composers–2	Spain—music in
Contemporary Music	Themes
History	Timing
Orchestral Music	Vocal Music
Phonograph Records	

Note: Roland Manuel's biography in French, 1930, apparently is O/P (or not easily available).

PAHISSA, J. See App Id (biog in Spanish).

TREND, J. B.
Manuel de Falla and Spanish music. xvii, 184, vi p, mus ex. Knopf (1929) new ed 1934.   2.50
A study of the man & his work, with analyses, and English translations of the seven "Popular Spanish Songs".

Farga, Franz. Author.
See Violin, also App Ib.
Faricy, Austin. Co-author (with Dudley).
See Aesthetics–1.

Farmer, Henry George. Author, editor, translator. See:
Arabia (music in). Ghosts (1946?).   1.00
——. Historical facts for Arabian influences (1930).   (7.50)
——. Minstrelsy of "The Arabian Nights" (1945).   4.50
——. Sa'adyah Gaon on the influence of music (1943/6).   10.00
Instruments. Glen col. (1945).   1.00
——. Turkish instruments in the 17th century (1937).   5.00
Military Music. Title (1950)   2.50
——. Rise & development (1912).   (3.75)
Organ. Of the ancients (1931).   (10.00)
Scotland (music in). History of music in Scotland (1947).   5.00
——. In medieval Scotland (1930).   (1.50)
——. Music in 18th-century Scotland (1946).   1.00
——. Music making (1950).   5.00
Note: Numerous other works by Farmer apparently are O/P, or—especially in the case of various privately printed or highly specialized books & papers—not easily available in this country.

Farnsworth, Charles Hubert. Author.
See Education.
Farnsworth, Paul Randolph. Author.
See Taste.

FARRAR, Geraldine
See:

History	Phonograph Records
Interpreters	Singers
Opera	

Note: Two books of memoirs & a study by Wagenknecht apparently are O/P.

Faulkner, Anne Shaw (Mrs. Marx E. Oberndorfer). Author.
See School Music–2.
Faure, Gabriel (*not* the composer). Author.
See App Ia.

FAURÉ, Gabriel (-Urbain)
See also:

Appreciation	Piano Music
Chamber Music	Program Notes
Composers–2	Song(s)
French Music	Song Translations
History	Vocal Music
Phonograph Records	

Note: Pertinent works apparently O/P (or not easily available) include those in French by Bruneau, Dujet, Fauré-Frémiet, Jankélévitch, Servières, etc.

FAURE, GABRIEL. See App Ia.

KOECHLIN, CHARLES
(*See also App Ia.*)
Gabriel Fauré (1845–1924). Tr Leslie Orrey.   viii, 98 p, frontis por, 1–p bibl. Dobson 2nd rev ed 1946.   2.50
A study by a composer-friend, originally published in French in 1927, and listed in a new edition (1949) in App Ia.

ROSTAND, CLAUDE. See App Ia.

SUCKLING, NORMAN
Fauré. vii, 229 p, 10 pl (pors, fac, etc). mus ex, 1–p bibl. Dent 1946.   2.50
"Master Musicians" series, with the usual calendar, personalia, & catalogue of works. An American reprint (Pellegrini) has not yet been announced.

FAUST
See: esp App Ia (Ferchault, Guy: Faust—une légende et ses musiciens).
Also:

Berlioz	Phonograph Records
Goethe	Program Notes
Liszt	Romantic Era
Mann	Wagner
Opera	

Faville, Mildred. Author.
See School Music–2.
Favre-Lingorow, Stella. Author.
See App Ib.
Fay, Harry F. Author.
See Ornamentation.
Feather, Leonard. Author. See Jazz.
Feiblemen, James Kern. Author.
See Aesthetics–1.
Feingold, S. Norman. Author.
See Career.
Feldman, Harry Allen. Author.
See Appreciation.

FELLOWES, (Rev) Edmund Horace
Memoirs of an amateur musician.
viii, 220 p, 8 pl. Methuen 1946   3.75
Canon Fellowes' reminiscences deal not only with his notable career as an editor & authority on Elizabethan music, but also with his activities as an amateur musician, lecturer, librarian, & tennis player.
Author, editor. See also:
Byrd. Biography (1923/48).   4.50
Church Music. English cathedral music (1941/8).   **4.50**

——. Office of the Holy Communion as set by Merbecke (1949).   4.00

——. Tudor church music—appendix with notes (1948).   5.00

Madrigal. English madrigal (1925).   2.00

——. English madrigal composers (1921/48).   5.00

——. English madrigal school—guide (1913).   1.25

——. English madrigal verse, ed Fellowes (1920/9).   5.00

Note: A biography of Gibbons (1925) and several other books by Fellowes apparently are O/P (or not easily available in this country).

Felton, Harold W. Editor. See Folklore.
Fenby, Eric. Author. See Delius.
Ferchault, Guy. Author. See App Ia.

Ferguson, Donald Nivison. Author. See:
Expression. Elements of (1944/8).   1.50
History–2. History of musical thought (1935/48).   6.50

——. Short history (1943).   5.50

Piano Music. Piano music of 6 great composers (1947).   5.00

Ferguson, Howard. Co-author (with Morris). See Sight-Playing & Reading.

Fern, Leila. Catalogued under Thompson, Lelia Fern.

FESTIVALS (Musical)

See:

America (music in)	School Music–1
England (music in)	(esp Moore)
History	Worcester
	Yearbooks

Also: App Ib (Tenschert: "Salzburg").

Note: W. A. Fisher's book on American festivals & D. Stoll's on European festivals apparently are O/P (or not easily available).

Fétis, Francois-Joseph. Author.
See Accompaniment.

Note: Numerous other books by Fétis apparently are O/P (or not easily available), at least in English translations.

Février, Henri. Author. See App Ia.

FFRANGCON-DAVIES, David Thomas

Note: The noted Welsh baritone's own "Singing of the future" (1905), long O/P as a separate publication, was included in the biography below, which itself has just been announced O/P as we go to press.

FFRANGCON-DAVIES, MARJORIE David Ffrangcon-Davies his life & work. (The singing of the future.)

Intro Ernest Newman. xxi, 192 p, 6 pl. Lane 1938.   O/P

A biography by the singer's daughter.

Ffrangcon-Davies, Marjorie. Author.
See David Ffrangcon-Davies above.

FICTION (Musical)

See:

Anthologies (Fabri-	Holmes, Sherlock
cant & Werner)	Mann
Bach–1 (Meynell)	Rolland
D. Baker	Tchaikovsky–1
Beethoven–2	(K. Mann)
(Aldanov)	App Ib (Bücken)

Also: App IIb (juvenile fiction)

Barne	Marie-Jeanne
Gronowicz	Simon
Kinscella	Streatfeild

Note: Perhaps it is unkind to add that a good many biographies of musicians (and not only the juveniles in App IIa) blend a considerable amount of fiction with their facts!

Field, Justin. Author.
See Children–7.

Field, Laurence N. Author.
See Bach–1.

"FIELD OF MUSIC" (Series)

This is a new series of books on various aspects of music, published in uniform format by Rinehart & Company, and edited by Ernest Hutcheson. For the volumes issued to date, see:

Band–1 (Goldman)	Singing–1 (Kagen)
Program Notes	Violin Music (Letz)
(Seaman)	Vocal Music (Kagen)

Fielden, Thomas. Author.
See Examinations, Piano Playing–1 & 2.

Note: Fielden's "Music and character" (1932?) apparently is O/P (or not easily available).

Field-Hyde, F. C. Author.
See Singing–1 & 2.

Fielding, Evelyn Lysle. Co-editor (with Maus). See Carols.

Fields, Victor Alexander. Author.
See Singing–1, Speech.

FIGURED BASS

See:

Accompaniment	History
(esp Arnold)	Keyboard Harmony
Baroque Era	Keyboard Instruments
Harmony	& Music (esp Bach)

Fillebrown, Thomas. Author. See Voice.

FILM MUSIC

See also:

Acoustics (esp Olson)	History
Career	Sound Recording &
Contemporary Music	Reproduction
Films (General)	Stokowski

Note: Pertinent works apparently O/P (or not easily available) include those by Erdmann & others (in German), Poirier (in French), Sabaneev, etc.

EISLER, HANNS
Composing for the films.   xi, 165 p, mus ex.   Oxford 1947.   3.00
A controversial study stemming from a Film Music Project begun in 1940. It includes an analysis of Eisler's score, in 12-tone technique, "14 ways to describe rain."

HUNTLEY, JOHN
British film music.   Forew Muir Mathieson.   247 p, 24 illus.   Skelton Robinson n d (1947).   O/P
With contributions by Vaughan Williams & Louis Levy, and a biographical index of British composers, directors, "recordists," etc. (Just announced out-of-print.)

LEVY, LOUIS
Music for the movies.   Forew Sydney Box.   viii, 182 p, 9 photos.   Sampson Low 1948.   3.00
The conductor's memoirs, with informal notes on recording music for British films.

LONDON, KURT
Film music: a summary of the characteristic features of its history, aesthetics, technique, & possible developments.   Tr Eric S. Bensinger; forew Constant Lambert.   280 p, illus, mus ex.   Faber (1936) new ed in prep.   △
One of the earliest & most extensive books on the subject; O/P for some years, but scheduled for early re-issue in a new ed.

NELSON, R. U. & RUBSAMEN, W. H. (comps)
Literature on music in films and radio.   59 p, paper.   California 1946.   1.25
"Hollywood Quarterly" V 1 supplement: Annual Communications Bibliography. Also reprinted in Hinrichsen's Yearbook 1949/50 (see Yearbooks).

SKINNER, FRANK
Underscore.   v, 292 p, 17 photos (Peter Gowland & Herb Carlton), mus ex, bds.   Skinner Music Co, Hollywood, Calif., n d (1950).   3.00
A detailed study of writing, arranging, & recording a complete film score: a combination instruction book & personal narrative, with actual score examples, timing sheets, etc, of the score for "The Irishman."

FILMS (General)
General Note: Only a sampling (of some musical interest) of the large available literature is listed below.

See also:

Acting	History
Film Music	Teaching-1

EISENSTEIN, SERGEI M.
Film form: essays in film theory, Ed & tr Jay Leyda.   xi, 279 p, illus, 5–p bibl.   Harcourt 1949.   4.50
A freshly translated, authorized collection of the noted director's writings on film theory (including the integration of sound into the film-pattern) from 1928 to 1945.

The film sense.   Ed & tr Jay Leyda. xii, 288 p + fold-out sheet (9 photos, 14 b&ws, mus ex), 6–p bibl, 8–p Eisenstein bibl.   Harcourt (1942), rev ed 1947.   4.00
A standard work, with considerable material on music, including a study of audio-visual sequences in "Alexander Nevsky."

ELLIOTT, GODFREY MONROE (ed)
Film and education: a symposium on the role of the film in the field of education.   xi, 597 p.   Philosophical 1948.   7.50
Articles on various aspects of the use of films in education by 37 contributors.

LINDGREN, ERNEST
The art of the film: an introduction to film appreciation.   xiv, 242 p, 32 photos, 2–p bibl.   Allen 1948.   4.50
Includes a chapter on film music, p 141/153.

PUDOVKIN, V. I.
Film technique and film acting: the cinema writings of V. I. Pudovkin. Tr Ivor Montagu, intro Lewis Jacobs. xviii, 204, 11, 153 p. (1930/5).   Lear repr 1949.   3.75
One-volume reprint of two books (originally published in these translations in England, 1930, rev 1933 & 1935), including a series of lectures delivered at the State Institute of Cinematography, Moscow.

FINCK, Henry Theophilus
Musical progress: a series of practical discussions of present day problems in the tone world.   xvi, 422 p.   Presser 1923.   2.00
A miscellany, mainly from "Etude" magazine.
Author.   See also:
Interpreters.   Success in music (1909/-36).   3.00
Note: Several other books by Finck apparently are O/P (or not easily available).

FINCK, Hermann
Note: The British conductor-composer's "My melodious memories" apparently is O/P.

FINGERS/FINGERING

See:

Organ Playing
Piano Playing–1 (esp Schultz)
Also: App Ia (Jarosy).

Piano Playing–2 & 3
Violin Playing
Violoncello Playing

Finkelstein, Sidney. Author.
See Aesthetics–1, Jazz.
Finlan, Leonard. Co-author (with Manser).
See Speech.

FINLAND (Music in)/FINNISH MUSIC

See:

Dances–2 (ed Alford: Heikel & Collan)
Folklore

History
Sibelius

Finletter, Gretchen Damrosch. Author.
See Damrosch Family.

FINN, (Father) William Joseph

Sharps and flats in five decades: an autobiography. x, 342 p. Harper 1947. 3.75

Informal memoirs & views on church music by the founder of the Paulist choristers.

Author See also:

Children–7. Child voice training in 10 letters (1944). 1.00
Choir/Choral–1. Epitome of some principles (1935). .30
Choir/Choral–2. Art of the choral conductor (1939). 4.00
——. The conductor raises his baton (1944). 3.75

Finney, Ross Lee. Author.
See Harmony–1.
Finney, Theodore Mitchell. Author.
See Appreciation, History–2.

FIORILLO, Federigo

See also: Violin Music, Violin Playing.

WINN, EDITH L.
How to study Fiorillo: a detailed descriptive analysis of how to practice these studies, based upon the best teachings of representative, modern violin playing. vi, 74 p, mus ex. C. Fischer (1910) 1937. 1.00

Fisch, Samuel. Author. See App Ib.
Fischer, Edwin. Author. See App Ib.
Fischer, Kurt von. Author. See App Ib.
Fisher, Trevor. Author. See Verdi–2.
Fisher, William Arms. Author, editor.
See Folksongs–1, Publishers/Publishing.

Note: Other books by Fisher apparently are O/P, but numerous collections of music only, edited by him, are generally available.

Fisk, Beatrice Hatton. Author.
See Children–5.
Fiske, Roger. Author. See Beethoven–3.
Fitzgibbon, Henry Macaulay. Author.
See Flute.

FITZWILLIAM VIRGINAL BOOK

See:

Elizabethan Music
England (music in)
English Music

History
Keyboard Instruments & Music

Note: A 2-v reprint of the music itself, ed Fuller Maitland & Barclay Squire (Breitkopf & Härtel 1899), is currently available from Broude Brothers, New York, $37.50.

FLAGSTAD, Kirsten

See:

Interpreters
Opera
Phonograph Records

Singers
Wagner–2 (esp Gilman)

Flagg, Marion. Author.
See School Music–1;
Flanders, Helen Hartness. Editor (with Ballard, Brown, & Barry). See Folksong–2.
Fleischmann, Aloys. Editor.
See Ireland (music in).
Flesch, Karl. Author. See Violin Playing.
Fletcher, Alice Cunningham. Author.
See Indians (American).
Fletcher, Harvey. Author. See Hearing.
Flint, Edward W. Author. See Organ.
Flood, William Henry Grattan. Author.
See Bagpipes, Ireland (music in).
Florand, François O. P. Author.
See App Ia.

FLORIDA (music in)

See: Folksongs–2 (esp Morris).
Also: America (music in), Folklore, Arnold Volpe.

FLOTOW, Friedrich von

See also:

Composers–1
History

Opera
Phonograph Records

DENT, EDWARD J. (*tr*)
Martha: a romantic comic opera in 4 acts. German words by W. Friedrich. English version. xviii, 67 p, paper. Oxford 1941. .80

Flower, Newman. Author.
See Handel–1, Schubert–1.

FLUTE

See also:

Chamber **Music**
Concerto
History
Instrumentation
Instruments

Orchestra
Phonograph Records
Recorder
Wind Instruments

Note: Standard works apparently O/P (or not easily available) include those by Boehm, Chapman, Hotteterre (in French), Miller, Welch, etc.

DUSHKIN, DAVID. See App IIb (juvenile).

FITZGIBBON, H. M.
The story of the flute: being a history of the flute & everything connected with it. 12, xvi, 292 p, illus mus ex, 4–p bibl. Reeves (1913) 2nd aug ed 1928.   Δ   (3.50)
Long O/P in the Scribner ed of 1914.

ROCKSTRO, RICHARD SHEPHERD
A treatise on the construction, the history, and the practice of the flute: including a sketch of the elements of acoustics & critical notices of 60 celebrated flute-players. xli, 664 p, 67 illus, mus ex. Rudall Carte (1890) rev ed 1928, via Boosey.   Δ   (9.00)
A standard, but somewhat antiquated work.

F-M (Frequency Modulation)
See: Radio (esp Siepmann).

FOKINE, Michel
See: Ballet, (The) Dance,
Note: Books on Fokine and his ballets, by Beaumont and Kirstein, apparently are O/P (or not easily available in this country).

Foldes, Andor. Author.
See Piano Playing–1.

FOLDES, Lili
Two on a continent. 254 p. Dutton 1947.   3.00
The American adventures of a Hungarian newspaper woman and her pianist-husband, Andor Foldes.

FOLK (LORE, MUSIC, SONGS)

General Note: Few other musical subjects involve the cataloguer in as many or as controversial problems as those clustered like barnacles on all facets of "folk" music. And the basic problems are further complicated here by the exigencies of a "practical" bibliography designed primarily for use by non-specialists. An immense literature exists, but the publications generally available today comprise on one hand a comparatively few books (mostly of a highly specialized nature), and on the other innumerable collections of music itself—much of which is of highly questionable folk authenticity.

Our present "solution" of these problems is evasive and quite arbitrary, to be justified if at all solely on pragmatic grounds. We dodge the question of authenticity entirely, taking titles that include or imply the term "folk" at their face value (except in the case of folk dances, for which see Dances-2). And for convenience we employ the following sub-categories:

Folklore
(Books about folklore & folk music in general; books dealing with folksong collecting, analysis; books dealing with instrumental folk music or both instrumental tunes & folk-songs.)

Folksongs (1. Various Sources)
(A sketchy sampling only of folksong collections, particularly those with some accompanying text devoted to background & source materials, representing songs of various nationalities, or to individual nationalities other than American.)

Folksongs (2. American only)
(A substantially complete selection of available books dealing with American folksongs of various types or American translations & variants of foreign folksongs, plus some of the better-known collections of folksongs that are accompanied by considerable text devoted to background & source materials.)

(Folk Dances See Dances-2.)

Readers who wish to pursue the subject further are referred to the article on Folk Song, p 274/6, in the Harvard Dictionary of Music (see Dictionaries of Music, Apel) and the articles on Folk Music—A General Survey, p 559/583, & Folk Music in America, p 584/607 in the International Cyclopedia of Music and Musicians, 5th ed (see Encyclopedias of Music, ed Thompson). Also to the works cited as references in these articles, and to those cited in the bibliographies of many of the works listed below.

FOLKLORE

See also:

Ballad
Children-7 (Emrich & Korson)
Cowboy Music
Dances-2
Gypsy Music
Folksongs-1 & 2
Guthrie

B. Ives
Jazz
Lomax
Minstrels/Minstrelsy
Negro Music
Negro Spirituals
Popular Music
Sea Shanties & Songs

Also: National Music, and under—

Africa	Ireland
America	Italy
Arabia	Japan
Asiatic Musics	Java
(Note only)	Jewish Music
Bali	Latin America
Belgium	Mexico
Brazil	Oriental Music
China	(Note only)
Czechoslovakia	Poland
Dominican Republic	Russia
England	Scotland
France	Spain
India	Sweden
Indians (American)	Wales

Note: Among many standard works apparently O/P (or not easily available in this country) a few might be singled out for mention here: Béla Bartók's "Hungarian folk music" (1931) Buchanan's "American folk music" (1939), Dankert's "Das europäische Volkslied" (1939), Martinengo-Cesaresco's "Essays in the study of folk songs" (1886), Tiersot's "L'Histoire de la chanson populaire en France" (1889), etc.

ANDREWS, EDWARD D.
The gift to be simple: songs, dances, & rituals of the American Shakers. xi, 170 p, illus, music (tunes only), 4–p bibl. Augustin 1940.　　5.50
Including some 17 reproductions of old prints and some 79 tunes.

AUSUBEL, NATHAN (ed)
A treasury of Jewish folklore: stories, traditions, legends, humor, wisdom, & folk songs of the Jewish people. xxiv, 741 p, music (tunes only). Crown 1948.　　4.00
A companion work (in general style & format) to the Botkin works below; includes some 75 religious & secular songs.

BARTÓK, BÉLA & LORD, ALBERT B. (eds)
(*See also App Ia.*)
Serbo-Croatian folk songs: texts & transcriptions of 75 folk songs . . . Columbia 1951 in prep.　　8.50

BAYARD, SAMUEL PRESTON (ed)
Hill country tunes: instrumental folk music of southwestern Pennsylvania. xxvii, unp (128 p), 2 photos, 5–p bibl, music (tunes only). American Folklore Society, Philadelphia, 1944.　　3.00

BECK, EARL CLIFTON;
Lore of the lumber camps. xii, 348 p, 15 illus, 2–p bibl, music (tunes only). Michigan 1948.　　3.75
A revised version of the author's "Songs of the Michigan Lumberjacks" (1941). Some 118 song texts are given, with tunes for 16.

BOTKIN, B. A. (ed);
A treasury of American folklore: stories, traditions, & ballads of the people. Forew Carl Sandburg. xxvii, 932 p, music (tunes only). Crown 1944 (16th pr 1948).　　3.50
Same, rev & abridged ed: The pocket treasury of American folklore. 424 p, 2–b bibl, paper. Pocket Books 1950.　　.25
A treasury of New England folklore: stories, ballads, & traditions of the Yankee people. xxvi, 934 p, music (tunes only). Crown 1947 (2nd pr 1949).　　4.00
A treasury of Southern folklore: stories, ballads, traditions, & folkways of the people of the South. Forew Douglas Southall Freeman. xxiv, 776 p, music (tunes only). Crown 1949.　　4.00
All three works above are similar in style & format: grab-bag miscellanies of tales, anecdotes, curious customs, games, etc. Each contains from 50 to 100 songs (words & tunes only).
Note: Botkin also edited "Folk-say: a regional miscellany," 4 volumes (University of Oklahoma Press, 1929/32), of which v 2, 3, & 4 are listed as currently available.

CAMPA, ARTHUR LEON
Spanish folk poetry in New Mexico. 224 p, 4–p bibl. New Mexico 1946.　　3.00

COURLANDER, HAROLD
Haiti singing. 273 p, illus, music (tunes only). North Carolina 1939.　　3.50
An approach to Haitian social & religious life via folk melodies & rhythms.

FELTON, HAROLD W. (ed)
Legends of Paul Bunyan. Forew James Stevens. xxi, 418 p, illus, some col (Richard Bennett), 29–p bibl. Knopf 1947.　　5.00
A collection of tales, primarily for young people, plus an extensive bibliography of works in various forms relating to the legends of the fabulous folk hero.

HAYWOOD, CHARLES (comp)
A bibliography of North American folklore and folksong. xxx, 1292 p, maps. Greenberg 1951.　　27.50
A comprehensive, annotated listing of some 40,000 entries in two main groups: "The American people north of Mexico, including Canada" & "The American Indian."

HENSEL, WALTHER. See App Ib.

KENNEDY-FRASER, MARJORY
Lowland Scots song: its interpretation. 20 p, mus ex, paper. Paterson 1922, via J. Fischer.　　.40

"Festival Booklet" No. 7. Title on cover only: "Scots folk song."

KORSON, GEORGE (*ed*)
Coal dust on the fiddle: songs & stories of the bituminous industry. xvi, 460 p, frontis, music (tunes only), 4–bibl. Pennsylvania 1943.   3.50

Minstrels of the mine patch: songs & stories of the anthracite industry. xii, 332 p, frontis, music (tunes only), 5–p bibl. Pennsylvania 1938 (2nd pr 1943).   3.00

Pennsylvania mining-industry folklore. Pennsylvania songs and legends. 474 p, 1 illus, music (tunes only). Pennsylvania 1949.   5.00
An authoritative state folklore symposium, with contributions by the editor & 13 other writers; an outgrowth of the Pennsylvania Folk Festival, organized in 1936.

LACHMANN, ROBERT. See App Ib (ed Bücken).

LEACH, MARIA & FRIED, JEROME (*eds*)
Funk & Wagnalls standard dictionary of folklore, mythology, & legend.

V 1: A–I. ix, 531 p. Funk 1949.   7.50
V 2: J–Z. 534/1196 p. Funk 1950.   7.50
Some 8,000 entries, including many on folksongs & other musical subjects.

METFESSEL, MILTON
Phonophotography in folk music: American Negro songs in new notation. Intro Carl E. Seashore. x, 181 p, 68 illus (photos, photograms), 2–p bibl. North Carolina 1928.   3.00
"Social Study" series. Transcriptions & analyses of folk-singers' actual vocal lines via sound-wave phonophotographic recordings. Particularly important for the authoritative illumination it throws on intonation, vibrato, etc.

SCHINDLER, KURT
Folk music and poetry of Spain and Portugal (Música y poesía popular de España y Portugal). xxx, 370, 127 p, frontis por, music (tunes only), paper. Hispanic Institute, New York, 1941.   10.00
An extensive standard study: with text in English & Spanish; some 1000 musical examples.

SHARP, CECIL J.
English folk song: some conclusions. Pref Maud Karpeles. 143 p, 2–p bibl, mus ex. Novello (1907) 2nd ed 1936.   (2.25)

TOOR, FRANCES
A treasury of Mexican folkways: the customs, myths, folklore, traditions, beliefs, fiestas, dances, & songs of the Mexican people. xxxii, 566 p, illus (10 col pl, 100 drwgs by Carlos Merida, 170 photos), music (tunes only). Crown 1947.   5.00
A collection similar in general style to those by Ausubel & Botkin above.

TULLY, MARJORIE F. & RAEL, J. B. (*comps*)
An annotated bibliography of Spanish folklore in New Mexico & Southern Colorado. 124 p, paper. New Mexico 1950.   1.00
Revised & enlarged version of a master's thesis (Tully) to include some 702 entries up to December 1948.

FOLKSONGS (1. Various Sources)

See also:

Appreciation	Negro Spirituals
Ballad	Phonograph Records
Carols	Popular Music
Children–2 & 7	Rounds
Chinese Music	School Music–4
Folklore	Sea Shanties & Songs
Folksongs–2	Song(s) (esp Sears)
Haydn (ed Geiringer)	Songbooks
Latin America	Voice (esp Westerman)
National Music	Vocal Music

Note: Surprisingly enough, this sub-category, which should be packed with many entries, turns out to have extremely few legitimate candidates, largely since most pertinent publications are collections of music only (with little or no accompanying text), or else foreign publications whose current availability is difficult to determine.

Accordingly, we have stretched some of our usual rules in order to give at least a few representative samplings. But these are by no means comprehensive *samplings: many collections undoubtedly are available if one takes the trouble to search for them, especially via foreign sources of supply. Again the interested reader is advised to consult the cross-references under Folk above, the other sources of information cited there, journals of various folksong societies, etc.*

One further comment: examples of actual music appearing in the books listed below (and under Folksongs–2) may be given either as tunes only (i.e., without accompaniment, but of course with the accompanying song texts), or as harmonized arrangements with piano or other accompaniment. The former are characteristic of almost all scholarly works; the latter of works designed for a more general public. For practical purposes folksong accompaniments often are advantageous, but it always should be remembered that these are not part of the authentic source-material, but additions & arrangements designed for popular convenience, and whose musical value is dependent on the taste & skill of the arranger. In general, folk specialists reject all accompaniments, at least in theory; in practice, even purists will concede the usefulness of accompaniments provided by such authorities as Sharp, Botsford, Tiersot, et al. Unfortunately, however, not all folksong arrangers command comparable taste & talent.

BANTOCK, (*Sir*) GRANVILLE (*ed*);
100 folksongs of all nations: for medium voice. xxxvii, 175 p, 1 por, 9–p bibl, music, paper. Ditson 1911.   3.50
"Musicians Library" series, with considerable introductory material & notes.

BLEGEN, THEODORE C. (*ed*)
Norwegian emigrant songs and ballads. Translations by Martin B. Ruud. 350 p, music (harm Gunnar J. Malmin). Minnesota 1936.   3.00
Some 50 songs, collected on a research project under a Guggenheim fellowship grant.

BONI, MARGARET BRADFORD (*ed*)
Fireside book of folk songs. 323 p, col illus (Alice & Martin Provensen, music (arr piano Norman Lloyd). S. & S. 1947.   5.00
One of the most popular general-public collections: 147 American, English, Irish, & Scottish songs, including traditional & quasi-folk airs.

BOTSFORD, FLORENCE HUDSON (*ed*)
Botsford collection of folk-songs: with English versions by American poets. Intro Carl Engel. 3 v, bds. (1922) G. Schirmer 1930/3.   10.50
Same, paper covers.   7.50
V 1: The Americas, Asia, and Africa. x, 219 p, music, bds. 1930.   3.50
Same, paper covers.   2.50
V 2: Northern Europe. ix, 246 p, music, bds. 1931.   3.50
Same, paper covers.   2.50
V 3: Southern Europe. vii, 292 p, music, bds. 1933.   3.50
Same, paper covers.   2.50
With the exception of Engel's 3–p introduction, "A reason for folk-song" (in v 1), and acknowledgment pages in each volume, there is no accompanying text. However, the wide scope of the contents, the use of superior song-text translations, and the musical significance of the entire work warrant an exception to our general rule of excluding collections of music only.

DEUTSCH, LEONHARD (*comp & arr*)
A treasury of Slovak folk songs. 127 p, illus (Joseph Cincik), music. Crown 1950.   5.00
Note: Published under the sponsorship & general editorship of Rev. John L. Lach; introductions by Monsignore Milos K. Mlynarovich & Adam P. Lesinsky; explanatory notes by Francis Hrusovski; English verses by Willard R. Trask.

FISHER, WILLIAM ARMS (*ed*)
60 Irish folksongs: for high voice. xii, 201 p, 1 pl, music, paper. Ditson 1915.   3.50
"Musicians Library" series, with notes.

HOUSTON-PERET, ELSIE (*ed*). See App Ia.

LUMPKIN, B. G. & McNEIL, N. L. (*comps*)
Folksongs on records: issue 3, cumulative, including essential material in 1 & 2. 98 p, 6½–p bibl, paper. A. Swallow, Denver, Colorado, 1950.   △   2.00

RUBIN, RUTH (*ed*)
A treasury of Jewish folksong. 224 p, illus (T. Herzl Rome), music (piano arrs Ruth Post), ½–p bibl. Schocken 1950.   4.50
Some 110 cradle, children's, love, work, holiday, partisan, & Israeli songs, with notes & a pronunciation guide. The texts are in Yiddish or Hebrew, with English translations.

SHARP, CECIL J.
100 English folksongs: for medium voice. xlv, 235 p, music, paper. Ditson 1916.   3.50
"Musicians Library" series. A standard collection of 29 ballads, 66 songs, & 5 accumulative songs, with a 4–p introduction & 29 pages of background & source notes.

TIERSOT, JULIEN *ed*)
60 folksongs of France: for medium voice. xxiv, 159 p, music, paper. Ditson 1915.   3.50
"Musicians Library" series. A standard collection by a French authority (editor of many French folksong publications), with a 6–p introduction and 10 pages of notes in French & English.

FOLKSONGS (2. American only)

Note: While the listings below are more comprehensive than those in Folksongs-1 above, it should be stressed again that they are only samplings of the enormous literature. However, an effort has been made to secure a substantially complete selection of available publications that include considerable accompanying text—i.e., those generally considered as "books," rather than collections of music only.

A most useful reference work in this category (unfortunately no longer in print, but available for consultation at many libraries) is the Library of Congress, Music Division, "Check list of recorded songs in the English language in the archive of American folk song to July 1940," (1942). Another valuable work apparently O/P (or not easily available) is Mellinger Edward Henry's "Bibliography for the study of American folksongs" (Mitre Press, London, 1937)

Again (please refer to the note under Folksongs-1) note should be made of the distinction between musical examples in the form of unharmonized tunes ("tunes only") and those provided with piano or other accompaniments.

ARNOLD, BYRON (ed)
Folksongs of Alabama. xiii, 193 p, illus (pors), music (tunes only), 1-p bibl & bibl refs. Alabama 1950.   4.50
Some 153 songs from some 45 collectors, with notes & biographical sketches.

BERRY, CECILIA RAY (comp)
Folk songs of old Vincennes. Intro & notes Joseph Médard Carrière. 95 p, music. FitzSimons 1946.   2.00
Songs with French & English texts.

CARMER, CARL
America sings: stories & songs of our country's growing. 243 p, illus (Elizabeth Black Carmer), music (arr Edwin John Stringham). Knopf 1942 (1950).   5.00
Songs of the rivers of America. xi, 196 p, illus, music (arr Albert Sirmay). Farrar 1942.   4.00

COLEMAN, SATIS N. & BREGMAN, A. (eds)
Songs of American folks. 128 p, illus (Alanson Hewes), music (arr Coleman). Day 1942.   2.50
47 songs with background material.

DAVIS, ARTHUR KYLE, JR. (ed)
Folk-songs of Virginia: a descriptive index & classification of material collected under the auspices of the Virginia Folklore Society. lxiii, 389 p. Duke 1949.   4.00

No music, but some 2454 versions of variants of 974 folksong listings, and an 11-p list of phonograph recordings, particularly notable for its rigorous classification scheme. A quasi-supplement to the work below.
Traditional ballads of Virginia: collected under the auspices of the Virginia Folklore Society. xviii 634 p, 9 illus, bibl refs, music (tunes only). Harvard 1929.   3.00
A collection of texts & variants, with some music, confined to ballads figuring in the famous Child collection.

DOWNES, OLIN & SIEGMEISTER, ELIE
A treasury of American song. 412 p, music. (1940) Knopf 2nd ed rev & enl 1943.   7.50
Some 200 songs of various periods & types; piano arrangements, notes, & record lists.

FLANDERS, HELEN HARTNESS (& others, eds)
The new Green Mountain songster: traditional folk songs of Vermont, collected, transcribed, & edited. xx, 278 p, illus (facs), music (tunes only). Yale 1939.   3.50
Co-editors: Elizabeth Flanders Ballard, George Brown, Phillips Barry. The work includes elaborate notes & a 2-p Barry bibliography.

GARDNER, E. E. & CHICKERING, G. J. (eds)
Ballads and songs of southern Michigan. xviii, 501 p, music (tunes only), 4-p bibl. Michigan 1939.   3.50

GRAY, ROLAND P. (ed)
Songs and ballads of the Maine lumberjacks: with other songs from Maine. xxi, 191 p. Harvard 1924.   2.50
Texts only, no music.

HENRY, MELLINGER EDWARD (ed)
Folk-songs from the southern highlands. xvi, 460 p, illus, music (tunes only), bibl refs. Augustin 1938.   6.00

HUDSON, ARTHUR PALMER
Folksongs of Mississippi and their background. xii, 321 p, 7-p bibl. North Carolina 1936.   5.00
No music; texts & background material only.

JACKSON, GEORGE PULLEN (ed)
American folk music for high school and other choral groups. Unp (80 p), illus, music (arr Charles Faulkner Bryan), paper. Birchard 1947.   1.25
25 songs (piano accs); 6-p intro & notes.
Note: Mr. Jackson's well-known "Spiritual folk-songs of early America" (1937), "Down-east spirituals and others of olden times" (1934), "White and Negro spirituals" (1944),

& *"White spirituals in the southern uplands"* (*1933*), all apparently are O/P.

KOLB, SYLVIA & JOHN HARRISON (*eds*)
A treasury of folk songs. xv, 240 p, music (tunes only) 6½–p bibl, paper.
Bantam 1948.   .25
Title on cover only: "Frankie and Johnny & Ninety Others." Pocket song collection, with a 3½-p record list.

LINSCOTT, ELOISE HUBBARD (*ed*)
Folk songs of old New England. Intro James W. Carpenter. xiii, 337 p, music, 19–p bibl refs. Macmillan 1939.   5.00

LOMAX, JOHN A. & ALAN (*eds*)
American ballads and folk-songs. Forew George Lyman Kittredge. xxxix, 625 p, music (tunes only), 9–p annot bibl. Macmillan 1934 (1947).   6.00
Our singing country: a second volume of American ballads & folk songs. xxxiv, 416 p, music (tunes only, ed Ruth Crawford Seeger), 6–p bibl. Macmillan 1941.   6.50
Companion standard works.
Folk song U. S. A.: the 111 best American ballads, collected, adapted, & arranged. xvi, 407 p, music (arr Charles & Ruth Crawford Seeger), 10–p annot bibl. Duell Sloan 1948.   6.00
The last of John A. Lomax's folksong books, designed (with piano arrangements & generous background material) for the widest possible audience.

MORRIS, ALTON C. (*ed*)
Folksongs of Florida. Forew Arthur Palmer Hudson. xvi, 463 p, music (tunes only, transcribed by Leonhard Deutsch), 6–p bibl. Florida 1950.   7.50
Some 243 songs, 167 tunes, 17 drawings.

NILES, JOHN JACOB (*ed*) (*See also: Carols.*)
The Anglo-American ballad study book: containing 8 ballads in current tradition in the United States of America. 38 p, music, bibl refs, paper. G. Schirmer 1945.   .75
"American Folk-Song" series No. 24; with introductory remarks, texts, & notes.
The shapenote study book. 19 p, music, paper. G. Schirmer 1950.   .60
Same series, No. 27: 8 hymns from "The Sacred Harp" (1844) & "The Southern Harmony" (1835), with notes.

OWENS, WILLIAM (*ed*)
Texas folk songs. 302 p, music, 8–p bibl. University Press, Dallas, 1950. 5.00

A collection of ballads, mostly of Southern rather than Western derivation, gathered from Texan singers & arr Willa Mae Kelly Koehn.

RANDOLPH, VANCE (*ed*)
Ozark folksongs. Collected & edited for the State Historical Society of Missouri by Floyd C. Shoemaker & Frances G. Emberson. 4 v. Missouri State Historical Society, Columbia, △
Missouri   15.00
V 1: British ballads and songs. 439 p, illus, music (tunes only), 9–p bibl. 1946.
V 2: Songs of the south and west. 436 p, illus, music (tunes only). 1948.
V 3: Humorous and play-party songs. 399 p, illus, music (tunes only). 1949.
V 4: Religious songs and other items. 455 p, 8 pors, music (tunes only). 1950.
A monumental regional collection of some 883 songs & variants, available only as a complete set directly from the Missouri State Historical Society.

SANDBURG, CARL (*comp*)
The American songbag. xxiii, 495 p, illus, music. Harcourt 1927 (1946).   4.95
One of the best-known popular collections: some 280 songs, ballads, & ditties, with piano accompaniments by various composers.
New American songbag. 109 p, music. Broadcast Music, N. Y., 1951.   2.50
A sequel-collection of new & old songs, announced for publication on Sandburg's 73rd birthday, 6 January 1951.

SCARBOROUGH, DOROTHY
A song catcher in southern mountains: American folk songs of British ancestry. xvi, 496 p, illus (Paul Laune), music (tunes only). Columbia 1937.   4.50
Songs and song-collecting.

SHARP, CECIL (*collector*)
(*See also Folksongs–1.*)
English folk songs from the southern Appalachians: comprising 273 songs & ballads with 968 tunes, including 38 tunes contributed by Olive Dame Campbell. Ed Maud Karpeles. 2 v: xxxvii, 436 p; xi, 411 p, frontis map, music (tunes only), 4–p bibl. Oxford (1917) 1932.   16.00
A monumental standard collection.

SMITH, REED (*ed*)
South Carolina ballads: with a study of the traditional ballad today. xii, 174 p, music (tunes only), 1–p bibl refs. Harvard 1928.   3.00

Mostly texts, with some musical examples and historical commentary.

THOMAS, JEAN & LEEDER, JOSEPH A.
The singin' gatherin': tunes from the southern Appalachians. xii, 113 p, 30 photos, music (harmonized by Walter Kob). Silver 1939.   **2.50**
With commentary on the songs & associated activities: dancing, dramatizing, & reading; plus the script of a folk-festival play in 19 episodes.

WHEELER, MARY
Steamboatin' days: folk songs of the river packet era. x, 121 p, illus, music (tunes only). Louisiana 1944.   **2.95**

WHITFIELD, IRÈNE THÉRÈSE
Louisiana French folk songs. xiv, 159 p, music (tunes only), 4–p bibl. Louisiana 1939.   **3.00**
"Romance Language Series No. 1." Includes songs of 3 types: Louisiana-French, Acadian, or Cajun-French, Negro-French or Creole dialect.

Foote, Arthur. Author.
See Modulation, Piano Playing–2. Co-author (with Spalding). See Harmony–2.

Forchhammer, Theophil. Co-compiler (with Kothe). See App Ib (Weigl).

Forkel, Johann Nikolaus. Author.
See App Ib (Bach, in German).
Note: While the English edition of Forkel's "Bach" is no longer in-print as a separate publication, it is included—in the Stephenson translation of 1808/20—in David & Mendel's "Bach Reader" (see Bach–1).

FORM

General Note: For all its familiarity and common use, this is an extremely ambiguous term, which may mean (as the Harvard Dictionary of Music points out) either "form in music" or "form(s) of music." Form in the first sense often is discussed in various types of books on music, but perhaps particularly in those classified in the present Guide under the subject-headings Aesthetics, Psychology, & Philosophy. The second sense usually is that implied in most books on musical "form" —i.e., those listed below, although a few of them also touch on the larger aspects of form in general.

See also:

Abraham ("Design")	Modern Music
Aesthetics–1 & 2	(esp Eschman)
Beethoven–3	Philosophy
(esp Harding)	Program Notes
Composers (& under	Psychology
individual names)	Theory
Composition	Tonality/Atonality
History	

Also: such specific "forms" as—

Carol	Rounds
Concerto	Sonata
Fugue	Song(s)
Madrigal	Symphony
March	Variation
Opera	**Waltz**

Note: Standard works apparently O/P (or not easily available) include those by Anger, Arensky, Glyn, Martens (in German), Pauer, Roberts, Salazar (in Spanish), Statham, Stöhr (in German), Tobel (in German), etc.

BAIRSTOW, EDWARD
The evolution of musical form. 119 p, mus ex. Oxford 1943 (3rd pr 1945).   **2.45**
An analytical study rather than a textbook.

BEKKER, PAUL
The story of music: an historical sketch of the changes in musical forms. 277 p, 10 pors. Norton 1927.   **3.50**
The development of a series of lectures on the history of "change in music".

BIGELOW, EARL R. (& *others*)
Form in melody. xi, 131 p, mus ex, paper. FitzSimons 1949.   Δ
Creative-analytical theory of music, bk 2.
Co-authors: Frank B. Cookson, Arrand Parssons, John D. Ramaley— with Bigelow, all of the Northwestern Univ. School of Music.

BÜCKEN, ERNST.   See App Ib

CORNELL, J. H.
The theory and practice of musical form: on the basis of Ludwig Bussler's "Musikalische Formenlehre." 260 p, mus ex. G. Schirmer 1883.   **3.50**
With composition exercises.

DOTY, E. W.
The analysis of form in music. v, 97 p, paper, spir. Crofts 1947.   **1.50**
Homophonic forms in the classical & romantic eras; workbook with staves for exercises.

GOETSCHIUS, PERCY
The homophonic forms of musical composition: an exhaustive treatise on the structure & development of musical forms, from the simple phrase to the song-form with "trio." xviii, 236 p, mus ex. G. Schirmer 1898 (1926).   **3.00**
The larger forms of musical composition: an exhaustive explanation of the variations, rondos, & sonata designs, for the general student of musical analysis, & for the special student of structural composition. ix, 231 p, mus ex. G. Schirmer 1915 (1943).   **2.50**

Two standard works. The latter is a sequel to the former and also to the same author's Applied Counterpoint (See Counterpoint–1).
Lessons in music form: a manual of analysis of all the structural factors & designs employed in music composition. vii, 146 p, mus ex. Ditson 1904 (1932).　　　　　　1.50
"Music Students Library" series.

HARRIS, CUTHBERT
The student's short course in musical forms. 30 p, mus ex, paper. Schmidt (1932) aug ed 1945.　　　　　　1.00

JADASSOHN, S.
Manual of musical form. Tr Edwin Barber. 156 p, mus ex, paper. B & H 1892.　　　　　　2.50

LEHMANN, F. J.
The analysis of form in music. 65 p, mus ex. Comings 1919.　　　　　　1.75

LEICHTENTRITT, HUGO. See App Ib.
Note: An English translation, rev & enl, is in preparation: Harvard 1951, $6.50.

MACPHERSON, STEWART
Form in music: with special reference to the designs of instrumental music. xii, 279 p, mus ex, paper. Williams (1908) rev ed 1930.　　　　　　3.50
Studies in phrasing and form: including a new supplement, "Some thoughts on the fundamentals of musical rhythm." 167 p, mus ex, paper. Williams (1911) rev ed 1932 (via Wood).　　　　　　2.00

MORRIS, R. O.
The structure of music. xiii, 124 p, mus ex. Oxford 1935 (4th pr 1947).　　1.25
Students' concise outline of harmonic & contrapuntal forms, with an appendix on vocal forms & the symphonic poem.

MURPHY, HOWARD A.
Form in music for the listener. Forew Peter W. Dykema. xxii, 225 p, mus ex, 4–p bibl. RCA (1945) 2nd rev ed 1948.　　　　　　2.00
"Appreciative" approach; with glossary & record (RCA Victor only) lists.

PAUER, ERNST
Musical forms. 186 p, mus ex. Ditson 1878.　　　　　　2.00
"Music Students Library" series.

PROUT, EBENEZER
Musical form. xii, 257 p, mus ex. Augener 1893 (14th pr n d).　　　　4.25
Applied forms. xii, 307 p, mus ex. Augener 1895 (11th pr n d).　　　　4.25

Two standard, if somewhat antiquated works. The latter (a sequel to "Musical form") is especially notable for its usefulness as a textbook in musical composition.

TAPPER, THOMAS
First year analysis (musical form). iv, 118 p, mus ex. Schmidt 1914 (1944).　　　　　　1.50

TOBIN, J. RAYMOND
How to understand musical form. 99 p, mus ex, paper. Boosey 1949.　　2.00
A conversational (dialogue) discussion of varied aspects & problems of musical form.

Forster, Edward Morgan. Author.
See Britten (ed Crozier), Criticism (ed French).

Forster, S. A. Co-author (with Sandys).
See Violin.

Forsyth, Cecil. Author.
See Instrumentation/Orchestration. Co-author (with Grimson). See Violin Playing.

Foss, Hubert James. Editor, author.
See Composers–1, Dictionaries of Terms, Tovey, Vaughan Williams.
Note: A book of essays, "Music in my time" (1933) apparently is O/P (or not easily available in this country).

Foster, Levin Wilson. Author.
See Clarinet.

FOSTER, Stephen Collins
See also:

America (music in)	Phonograph Records
American Music	Song(s)
Appreciation	Songbooks
Composers–1 & 3a	Vocal Music

Also: App IIa (juveniles by Bartlett, Higgins, Purdy, Wheeler).

Note: Among the pertinent works apparently O/P is the Milligan biography (1920), while numerous reprints of papers & specialized studies are not generally available.
Collections of music only are not listed. The one exception that might have been made ("A treasury of Stephen Foster," 1946, ed John Tasker Howard) is currently "remaindered" and apparently is not scheduled for reprinting.

HOWARD, JOHN TASKER
Stephen Foster: America's troubadour. xv, 445 p, col frontis, 28 pl (pors, facs, etc), 28–p bibl (comp Fletcher Hodges, Jr). (1934) Tudor repr 1945.　　　　　　1.98
A standard biography, originally published by Crowell (1934).

MORNEWECK, EVELYN FOSTER
Chronicles of Stephen Foster's family: illustrated from contemporary paintings, photographs, & prints. 2 v: xxi, ix, 767 p, illus. Pittsburgh 1944. Boxed.   5.00
Authentic documentation largely based on letters collected by Stephen Foster's brother, Morrison, father of the present author.

WHITTLESEY, W. R. & SONNECK, O. G. (*comps*)
Catalog of first editions of Stephen C. Foster (1826–1864). 79 p. Library of Congress, via GPO 1915.   .40
Title catalogue with full descriptions (prepared for Library of Congress cards), plus author, publisher, & first-line indices.

Fouser, Charles Elliott. Co-author (with McConathy & others). See Harmony –2.

Fowles, Ernest. Author.
See Keyboard Harmony.

Fox, Grace I. Author (with Merrill).
See Dances–2.

Fox Strangways, Arthur Henry. Author.
See India (music in).
Note: Fox Strangways's biography of Cecil Sharp (1933) and other books, including several collections of song translations, apparently are O/P (or not easily available).

Fracht, Jack Albert. Author
(with Robinson). See Singing–2.

FRANCE (Music in)

See: esp French Music.

Ballet	Folklore
Berlioz–1	Folksongs–1
Dances–2	History
(esp Dolmetsch)	Minstrels/Minstrelsy
Debussy–1	Opera
Dictionaries of Music	Rolland
Encyclopedias of	Troubadours
Music	Yearbooks

Also: App Ia (Dumesnil, René "La musique en France entre les deux guerres").

FRANCK, César (-Auguste)

See also:

Appreciation	Piano Music
Chamber Music	Program Notes
Composers–1 & 3d	Song(s)
Concerto	Symphony
French Music	Teachers
History	Themes
Organ Music	Timing
Phonograph Records	Vocal Music

Note: Standard works apparently O/P (or not easily available) include those by d'Indy and Lynn; Haag (in German), and those in French by Coquard, Emmanuel, Tournemire, etc.

ANDRIESSEN, HENDRIK
César Franck. Tr W. A. G. Doyle-Davidson. 60 p, 12 pl (pors, etc), short bibl, bds. Continental 1947.   2.50
"Symphonia" series of extensively illustrated brief studies, with list of works.

DEMUTH, NORMAN
César Franck. 228 p, 9 illus (pors, facs, etc), 1–p bibl, mus ex. (Dobson 1949) Philosophical 1949.   4.75
A recent British study of the man & his music; including an unusually detailed catalogue of published & unpublished works.

DUFOURCQ, NORBERT. See App Ia.

GRACE, HARVEY
The organ works of César Franck. 37 p, mus ex, paper. Novello 1948.   .90
Based on a 1923 "Music Times" article.

HORTON, JOHN
César Franck. 66 p, mus ex, paper. Oxford 1948.   1.00
"Musical Pilgrim" series: a brief sketch of Franck's career & work, plus analyses of some of his major compositions.

KUNEL, MAURICE. See App Ia.

VAN DEN BORREN, CHARLES. See App Ia.

Franckenstein (Sir) George. Editor.
See "World of Music" Series.
Frank, Paul L. Author.
See Romantic Era/Romanticism.

FRANKO, Sam
Note: A book of memoirs, "Chords and discords" (1938), apparently is O/P.

Franks, A. H. Author. See Ballet.
Franz, Frederick. Author.
See Metronome.
Fray, Jacques. Author (with Saperton).
See Piano Playing–4.
Frayne, John George. Author (with Wolfe).
See Sound Recording & Reproduction.
Freedman, Julian. Author.
See Children–5.
Freeman, Larry (Graydon LaVerne). Author. See Popular Music.
Freeman, Warren Samuel. Co-author (with Barbour). See Children–2. Co-author (witn Leavitt). See School Music–2. Author. See App IIb, & (with Whittaker) App IIa.
Freemantel, Frederic (Freemantle, Frederic Charles). Author. See Singing–2, Speech.
French, Richard Frederic. Editor.
See Criticism.

FRENCH HORN

See also:

Band-1	Orchestra
Instruments	Wind Instruments
Instrumentation	

COAR, BIRCHARD
The French horn. viii, 99 p, 8 pl,
mus ex, 8–p bibl, paper, typescript
repro. Author, De Kalb, Illinois,
1947.   **3.00**

*History & development, technical consider-
ations, principles of teaching, suggestions
for performers of concertos, list of works.*

FRENCH LANGUAGE

See also:

Diction	Pronunciation
Dictionaries of Terms	(Jones)
	Singing

*Note: Laird-Brown's "Singers' French"
(1926) apparently is O/P.*

ARNOLD, WILLIAM HARKNESS
French diction for singers and
speakers. v, 120 p, mus ex. Ditson
1912.   **1.50**

"Music Students Library" series.

THURWANGER, CAMILLE
French musical diction: an ortho-
logic method for acquiring a perfect
pronunciation in the singing & speaking of the French language, for the
special use of English-speaking
people. iv, 106 p, mus ex. (1910)
via Coleman.   **2.00**

*Originally published in 1910 by G. Schirmer,
New York, & Novello, London.*

FRENCH MUSIC

See also:

Appreciation	Opera-2 & 3
Ballet	Orchestral Music
Chamber Music	Organ Music
Composers-1, 2, & 3d	Phonograph Records
(also under individ-	Piano Music
ual names)	Program Notes
Concerto	Rolland
Dances-2	Song(s)
(esp ed Alford)	Symphony
Debussy-1	Troubadours
Folklore	Violin Music
History	Vocal Music
Opera-1 (esp Crosten)	

*Note: Standard works apparently O/P (or
not easily available) include those by Hargrave, Hervey, Hill, Jean-Aubry, Lasserre,
Locke, etc; also (in French) by Coeuroy, La
Laurencie, Tiersot, etc.*

APEL, WILLI (ed)
French secular music of the 14th
century. Forew Paul Hindemith.
xii, 39 p, 8 pl (facs), 133–p music, bibl Δ
refs, paper. Medieval 1950.   **12.50**

*A scholarly achievement in filling some of
the gaps in musical knowledge between
Machaut & Dufay: some 81 works (ballades,
virelais, & rondeaux), with detailed notes.
The literary texts are edited by Robert W.
Linker & Urban T. Holmes, Jr. The com-
positions include the complete (preserved)
works of Solage, "Trebor," & Jacob de
Senleches, and the complete French works of
Matheus de Perusia & Anthonello de Caserta.*

BOLL, ANDRÉ & DAMAIN, ÉMILE. See App
Ia.

CHAMPIGNEULLE, BERNARD. See App Ia.

DUFOURCQ, NORBERT. See App Ia.

DUMESNIL, RENÉ. See App Ia.

GAUDEFROY-DEMOMBYNES, J. See App Ia.

LANDORMY, PAUL. See App Ia.

Frere, Walter Howard. Author.
See Hymns (Hymnody ("Hymns Ancient &
Modern," historical introduction).

FRESCOBALDI, Girolamo

See:

Appreciation	Madrigal
Baroque Era	Medieval/Renaissance
Composers-1	Organ Music
History	Phonograph Records
Italy (music in)	Program Notes
Keyboard Music	

*Note: Standard works apparently O/P (or not
easily available) include those in Italian by
Bennati, Berenzi, Ronga, Sostegni, etc.*

Fried, Jerome. Co-editor (with Leach).
See Folklore.

Frieswyck, Siebolt Henry. Author.
See Community Music.

Friskin, James. Author.
See Piano Playing-2.

Fröhlich, Joseph. Author. See App Ib.

Fröschels, Emile. Author (with Jellinek).
See Speech.

Fry, George. Author. See Violin.

Fryberger, Agnes Moore. Author.
See School Music-2.

FUGUE

See also:

Appreciation	History
Bach-2	Phonograph Records
Choir/Choral-3	Piano Music
Composition	Organ Music
Counterpoint	Theory
Form	

*Note: Standard works apparently O/P (or not
easily available) include those by Kitson,
Knorr (in German), Marchant, Müller-
Blattau (in German), etc.*

GÉDALGE, ANDRÉ. See App Ia.

HIGGS, JAMES
Fugue. iv, 115 p, mus ex, 2 charts,
paper. Gray n d.   **1.50**
Originally a Novello "primer."

KITSON, C. H.
The elements of fugal construction.
76 p, mus ex. Oxford 1929 (2nd pr
1948).   **2.50**
*A standard short method, presenting the basic
principles of fugal writing.*

OLDROYD, GEORGE
The technique and spirit of fugue:
an historical study. Forew Stanley
Marchant. viii, 220 p, mus ex. Oxford 1948.   **4.00**
*Historical & preparatory survey, rather than
a "method"; based particularly on Bach's
work & including detailed analyses. In effect,
a "prelude" to the study of fugal composition.*

OREM, PRESTON WARE
Manuel of fugue: including canon,
imitation, & double counterpoint.
72, p, mus ex, bds. Presser 1939.   **.75**

PROUT, EBENEZER
Fugue. xi, 258 p, mus ex. Augener
1891 (11th pr n d.).   **4.25**
Fugal analysis: a companion to "Fugue." viii, 257 p, mus ex. Augener
1896 (6th pr n d).   **4.25**
*Two standard older works. The latter is
mainly a collection of fugues (in various
styles) put into score & analyzed.*

RICHARDSON, A. MADELEY
Helps to fugue-writing, based on
Bach's "Das wohltemperirte Klavier." Forew Rubin Goldmark. 90 p,
mus ex, paper. Gray 1930   **2.00**

Fuhr, Hayes M. Author.
See Choir/Choral–2.
Fuller-Maitland, John Alexander. Author.
See Bach–2, History–1 (Oxford v 4).

*Note: Numerous other books by Fuller-Mait-
land, including an autobiography, apparently
are O/P (or not easily available).*

FUN (Musical)
See:

Amateur Music	Community Music
Anecdotes	Humor
Anthologies	Miscellanies
Children	Quizzes (Cott)

FUNCTIONAL MUSIC
See: esp App Ia (Landowski).
Also:

Amateur Music	Health
Children	History
Community Music	Industry
Composers–2	Modern Music
Contemporary Music	Radio Music
Film Music	School Music

FUNDAMENTALS (of Music)
See: esp Theory.
Also:

Children–8	Sight-Playing & Read-
Dictionaries of Terms	ing
Ear-Training	Sight-Singing
Musicianship (note	Solfège/Solfeggio
only)	Teaching–2

FURTWÄNGLER, Wilhelm
See Conductors, Phonograph Records.
Author. See App Ib ("Gespräche").

FUTURE (of Music)/
FUTURISM (Musical)
See:

Aesthetics	Philosophy
Composers–2	Tonality/Atonality
Contemporary Music	Twelve-Tone
Modern Music	Technique

*Note: Dent's "Terpander, or music of the
future" (1927) apparently is O/P.*

FUX, Johann Joseph
See: History, also App Ib (Liess's biography
in German).
Author. See Counterpoint–1.

—G—

Gabriel, John. Author. See Ballet.

GABRILOVITCH, Ossip
Note: Clara Clemens's "My husband Gabrilo-witsch" (1938) apparently is O/P.

Gagey, Edward McAdoo. Author.
See California (music in), Drama.

Gaisberg, Frederick William. Author.
See Phonograph Records.

Gajard, (Dom) Joseph. Author.
See Plainsong.

Gál, Hans. Author.
See Score-Reading, Vienna.

Galambos, Robert. Co-compiler (with Miller, & others). See Hearing.

Gale, Albert & Martha Brockway.
Arranger & co-author (with the Krones).
See Indians (American).

Galilei, Vincenzo. Author. See App Ic.

GALLI-CURCI, Amelita
See also: Opera, Singers, Singing.

LE MASSENA, C. E.
Galli-Curci's life of song. 336 p,
photos. Paebar 1945.   3.75
With a list of roles & 4-p discography.

Gallo, Stanislao. Author. See Band–1.

Galpin, (Rev) Francis Willam. Author.
See Ancient Music, Instruments.

Galt, Martha Caroline. Author.
See Composers–3a.

Gambler, Eugene. Author. See Singing–2.

GAMES
See: Dances—1 & 2, Folklore.

Gangoly, Ordhendra Coomar. Author.
See India (music in).

Gannett, Kent. Compiler. See Bach–2.

Ganz, A. W. Author. See Berlioz–2.

Gardner, Carl E. Author.
See Harmony–2, Theory–3.

Gardner, Emelyn Elizabeth. Editor.
See Folksongs–2.

Gardner, George Lawrence Harter.
Author. See Church Music.

Gardner, Maurice. Author.
See Instrumentation.

Gariel, Edoardo. Author.
See Harmony–2 (also App Id).

Garland, Wallace Graydon. Author.
See Songwriting.

Garroway, Will. Author.
See Piano Playing–1.

Gartlan, George H. Co-author (with Damrosch & Gehrkens). See Sight-Singing.

Gassner, Jerome. Author. See Mass.

Gatti, Guido Maria. Author.
See Pizzetti.

GATTI-CASAZZA, Giulio
See also: Opera–1 & 4.
Memories of the opera. Pref Howard Taubman. xii, 326 p, illus. Scribner 1941.   3.50
Memoirs of the Metropolitan's director, 1908–1935, originally pub serially (in part) in the "Saturday Evening Post," 1933.

Gaudefroy-Demombynes, Jean. Author.
See App Ia.

GAUTIER, Judith
See: App Ib (Wagner correspondence, in German, ed Schuh).

Gautier, Théophile. Author. See Ballet.

GAVINIÉS, Pierre
See also: Violin Music, Violin Playing.

WINN, EDITH L.
How to study Gaviniés: a book for advanced violin students who wish to perfect their bowing, technic, & the higher positions. x, 128 p, mus ex. C. Fischer 1913 (1923).   1.00

Gavoty, Bernard. Author. See App Ia.

GAY, John. *See:* Beggar's Opera.

Gaynor, Jessie L. Author.
See Children–3.

Gédalge, André. Author. See App Ia.

Gehrkens, Karl Wilson. Author. See:
Conducting. Essentials (1919).   1.75
——. 20 lessons in (1930).   .75
Dictionaries of Terms. (1927).   .75
School Music–1. Intro. (1919).   2.00
——. Music in grade schools (1934).   2.50
——. Music in junior high (1936).   2.50
Theory–2. Fundamentals (1924).   1.50

——.   Notation & terminology (1920).   2.20

Co-author (with Damrosch & Gartlan). See: Sight-Singing.   Exercises (1925).   3.00
Co-author (with Dykema).   See: School Music–1.   Teaching & administration of high school music (1941).   4.40

Geiringer, Karl.   Author, editor.   See:
Bach Family.   History, in prep.   △
Bach–1.   Lost portrait (1950).   1.00
Brahms–1.   Life & work (1936/47).   5.00
Haydn.   Creative life (1941/6).   5.00
——.   Folksong cat., in prep.   △
Instruments.   Musical (1940/5).   4.50

Geisel, Victor George.   Co-author (with Goldsmith). See Sound Rec & Repro.

Geissmar, Bertha.   Author.   See Wagner–3.
Note: Other books by Geissmar, memoirs and on Beecham & Furtwängler, apparently are O/P (or not easily available in this country).

Genest, Emile.   Author.   See App Ia.

GENIUS (Musical)

See:

Aesthetics	Philosophy
Einstein (Greatness in music)	Psychology
	Tests

Georgii, Walter.   Author.   See App Ib.
Geralton, James.   Author.   See App IIb.
Gerbert (von Hornau), Martin.   Editor. See App Ie.

GERMAN, (Sir) Edward

See: Composers–3c, English Music.
Note: W. H. Scott's biography (1932) apparently is O/P.

GERMAN LANGUAGE

See also:

Diction	Pronunciation
Dictionaries of Terms	(esp Jones)

WILCKE, EVA
German diction in singing.   Tr. Arthur Edward Smith.   Rev & ed Bainbridge Crist.   150 p, illus, mus ex.   Dutton 1930   2.50
Includes a discussion of the physiology of the voice & of phonetics in general.

GERMAN MUSIC/GERMANY (Music in)

See:

Appreciation	History
Chamber Music	National Music
Composers—1, 2, 3g	Opera
(& under names of	Piano Music
individuals)	Program Notes
Choir/Choral–3	Song
Concerto	Symphony
Contemporary Music	Violin Music
Europe	Vocal Music

Also: App Ib (Schiedermair: "Musik am Rheinstrom").
Note: Moser's history (in German), Fay's "Music study in Germany," and many other works apparently are O/P (or not easily available in this country).

Gérold, Théodore.   Author.   See App Ia.

GERSHWIN, George

See also:

American Music	Phonograph Records
Appreciation	Piano Music
Composers–3a	Popular Music
Jazz	Program Notes

Note: A symposium ed by Armitage & Isaac Goldberg's biography apparently are O/P.

CHALUPT, RENÉ.   See App Ia (In French)

EWEN, DAVID.   See App IIa (juvenile).

GERSHWIN, GEORGE
George Gershwin's song-book: special piano arrangements, ed & rev Herman Wassermann.   126 p, frontis, music.   S & S (1932) 1941.   3.00
Music only, except for the composer's 2–p introduction.   A reprint (omitting the Alajalov illustrations & the record lists) of the original 1932 edition.

Gerstberger, Karl.   Author.   See App Ib.
Gerson, Robert A.   Author.
See Philadelphia.
Gescheidt, Adelaide.   Author.
See Singing–2.
Gest, Elizabeth.   Author.
See Children–3 & 8, also App IIb.

GESUALDO, Don Carlo

See:

History	Madrigal (Einstein)
Italian Music	Medieval/Renaissance

Note: The Gray & Heseltine "Carlo Gesualdo" (1926) is O/P, but a revised version of the biographical section is included in Cecil Gray's "Contingencies."   See Gray.

Gevaert, François-Auguste.   Author.
See Instrumentation, also App Ia.
Ghéon, Henri.   Author.   See App Ia.
Giazotto, Remo.   Author.   See App Ic.
Gibbin, Leonard Douglas.   Author.
See Teaching–2.
Gibbon, Monk.   Author.   See Ballet.

GIBBONS, Orlando

See:

Choir/Choral–3	English Music
Church Music	History
Elizabethan Music	Madrigal

Note: Fellowes's biography (1925) is O/P, but just announced for 1951 re-issue.

Gibbs, George A., Jr. Author. See:
Harmony–2. Modern (1938).   **2.00**
Piano Playing–3. Harmonizing mel-
odies at sight (1941).   **1.00**
——. Chord construction (1937).   **1.25**
Theory–4. Modern musical problems
analyzed (1946).   **1.50**

Giddings, Thaddeus Philander. Author.
See School Music–1. Co-author (with
Maddy). See School Music–3.

Gide, André. Author.
See Chopin–1 (also App Ia).

Geigling, Giuseppe. Author. See App Ib.

Gieseking, Walter. Co-author (with Leimer).
See Piano Playing–2.

Gilbert, J. M. Author. See App Ia.

GILBERT, (Sir) William Schwenk
See: Gilbert & Sullivan, below.

GILBERT & SULLIVAN
See also:
Appreciation   Operetta
Composers–1   Phonograph Records
English Music   Themes
History   Vocal Music
Also: App IIa (Bush, Purdy, Wheeler).
*Note: The collections of texts & the selection
of words & music listed below of course are
only a sampling of the large available litera-
ture. Standard works about G & S and
their operettas, apparently O/P (or not
easily available in this country), include
those by Bassuk, Dunhill, Godwin, Goldberg,
Halton, Rickett & Hoogland, etc.*

Words and music of the best-loved
Gilbert & Sullivan operas. Intro
Alan Pitt Robbins. 191 p, illus
(Gilbert), 38–p music, paper. Avon
1950.   **.25**
*Pocket-size publication of "Pinafore,"
"Pirates of Penzance," & "Mikado" libretti,
with music (piano & voice) for the best-
known airs.*

DARLINGTON, W. A.
The world of Gilbert & Sullivan:
a key to the Savoy operas. Intro
Brooks Atkinson. xiii, 209 p, 17 pl
(pors, facs, etc). Crowell 1950.   **3.50**
*A British G & S enthusiast writes informally
but illuminatingly about the famous pair,
with explanations of allusions to contemporary events & situations, and an index to
all characters in the operettas.*

DUNN, GEORGE E. *(comp)*
A Gilbert & Sullivan dictionary.
175 p. (1936) Oxford 1937.   **2.50**
*Originally published by Allen & Unwin.
Dictionary-style entries from "Abudah" to*

*"Zorah," including all characters, obscure
terms & phrases, 1st-performance information, etc.*

GILBERT, W. S.
The best-known works of W. S. Gilbert.
232 p, illus (drwgs by Gilbert).
(Hartsdale House 1932) Halcyon
repr 1950.   **.69**
*Libretti of "Pinafore," "Pirates of Penz-
ance," & "Mikado," plus the "Bab Ballads."*
The complete plays of Gilbert &
Sullivan. 711 p, illus (drwgs by
Gilbert). Modern Library n d (1936).   **2.45**
*Modern Library "Giants" G-25: the libretti
of all 14 Gilbert & Sullivan operettas.*
The plays and poems. Pref Deems
Taylor. lx, 1218 p, illus (drwgs by
Gilbert). Random 1947.   **3.50**
*Complete texts of the 14 G & S operas, plus
3 other Gilbert plays & the "Bab Ballads."*

PEARSON, HESKETH
Gilbert and Sullivan: a biography.
319 p, 3 illus, bibl. Hamish Hamil-   △
ton, London, (1935) 4th pr 1949.   **2.50**
*Reprint of a standard work, originally pub-
lished in 1935 by Hamilton in London & by
Harper & Brothers in the United States.*

TAYLOR, DEEMS *(ed)*
A treasury of Gilbert & Sullivan:
the words & the music of 102 songs
from 11 operettas. 405 p, illus
(Lucille Corcos), music (arr Albert
Sirmay). S & S 1941.   **6.00**
*Songbook with 11 col & 100 b&w illustra-
tions.*

Gildersleeve, Glenn. Author. See Tests.

Gilman, Lawrence. Author.
See Wagner–3.
*Note: All of the noted American critic's
other books apparently are O/P.*

GILMORE, Patrick Sarsfield
See also:
America (music in)   History
Band–1   Military Music
DARLINGTON, MARWOOD
Irish Orpheus: the life of Patrick S.
Gilmore, bandmaster extraordinary.
130 p, 8 illus (pors, facs, etc). Oliver-
Maney-Klein Co, Philadelphia, 1950.   **2.50**
*A quasi-juvenile "story" of the leader of
Gilmore's Band of 19th-century fame & the
claimant composer of "When Johnny Comes
Marching Home."*

Giltay, J. W. Author.
See String Instruments.

Gingrich, Irving. Author.
See Ear-Training.
Ginzkey, Franz Karl. Editor. See App Ib.
Gipson, Richard McCandless. Author.
See Thursby.

GIPSY MUSIC
See: Gypsy Music.

Girdlestone, Cuthbert Morton. Author.
See Mozart–3 (also App Ia).
Givler, Robert Chenault. Compiler.
See Theory–4.
Glasenapp, Carl Friedrich. Author.
See Wagner–2.
Glasson, T. Bath. Author.
See Sight-Singing.
Gleason, Harold. Author, editor. See:

Anthologies. Examples of music
before 1400 (1942).   4.00

Baroque Era. Music in (literature
outlines, II) (1950).   3.00

Bibliography. Books on music, by
Gleason & Luper (1948).   1.75

Medieval/Renaissance. Music in 2.50
(literature outlines, I) (1949).

Organ Playing. Method (1940/9).   5.50

GLEE CLUB
See:

Amateur Music	Colleges
Arranging–1 (esp	Community Music–4
Wilson)	School Music–4
Choir/Choral–2	Songbooks
(esp Christy)	

Glenn, Mabelle. Co-author (with Mursell).
See Psychology.

GLINKA, Michail Ivanovitch
See:

Appreciation	Phonograph Records
Composers– 1 & 3e	Program Notes
History	Russian Music
Opera	Themes

*Note: The Montagu-Nathan biography
(1916) apparently is O/P.*

GLUCK, Christoph Willibald (Ritter von)
See also:

Appreciation	Phonograph Records
Composers–1	Program Notes
History	Themes
Opera	Vocal Music

*Note: Standard works apparently O/P (or not
easily available) include those by Cooper,
Landormy (in French), Marx (in German)
Newman, Riedel (in German), Tenschert (in
German), Tiersot (in French), etc.*

*Also O/P, but possibly due for re-issue, is
Einstein's biography (1936) in the "Master
Musicians" series.*

BERLIOZ, HECTOR
Gluck and his operas: with an account of their relation to musical
art.   Tr Edwin Evans, Sr. xiv, △
167 p, frontis por. Reeves 1914.   (2.25)
*A standard study, temporarily O/P, but
scheduled for early re-issue.*

CORTE, ANDREA DELLA. See App Ic.

DENT, EDWARD J. (*tr*)
Orpheus: an opera in 3 acts. Original
Italian words by Ranieri de Calza-
bigi. English version. xxviii, 21 p,
paper. Oxford 1941.   .80
The libretto in English, with notes.

HOWES, FRANK
Gluck.   16 p, cover por, paper.
Novello n d.   (.40)
Miniature biography ("great musicians").

PROD'HOMME, J.-G. See App Ia.

GOD SAVE THE KING
(British National Anthem)
Note: Cummings's study (1902) is O/P.

SCHOLES, PERCY A.
God save the king: its history &
romance. 62 p, illus, mus ex, paper.
Oxford 1942.   .85

Goddard, Scott. Author.
See Mozart–3, Weber.
Godet, Robert. Author, editor.
See App Ia (Debussy, Godet).

GODOWSKY, Leopold
See also:

America (music in)	Pianists
Composers–3a	Piano Music

ARONSON, MAURICE
A key to the miniatures of Leopold
Godowsky. vi, 21 p, mus ex. paper.
C. Fischer 1935.   .25
*Analytical essays on the forty-six "Minia-
tures" for piano four-hands.*

GOETHE, Johann Wolfgang von
See also:

Beethoven–2	Opera
History	Poetry
Literature	Song(s)
Mann (essays)	Song Translations

Also: Opera–2 & 3 and Program Notes, for
material on works by Dukas, Gounod,
Liszt, Schubert, etc, on Goethean texts or
subjects.

*Note: Only a sampling is listed of the large
Goethe literature, currently augmented by a
flood of special bicentennial publications.*

FERCHAULT, GUY. See App Ia ("Faust: une légende et ses musiciens").

FISCH, SAMUEL. See App Ib.

MANN, THOMAS (ed)
The permanent Goethe. xliii, 655 p, bds. Dial 1948.　　　　　　　5.00
Anthology of the best-known writings, many in new translations by Stephen Spender, & others. "Permanent Library" series.

NETTL, PAUL. See App Ib ("G. und Mozart").

NOHL, WALTHER. See App Ib ("G. und Beethoven").

ROLLAND, ROMAIN. See App Ib.

SCHÜNEMANN, GEORG (ed). See App Ib.

SCHWEITZER, ALBERT.
Goethe: four studies. Tr & Intro Charles R. Joy. 116 p. Beacon 1949. 2.50
Enlarged edition of "Goethe: 2 addresses" (1948), including the same 2 speeches of 1928 (now newly translated) & 1932; plus another speech and a magazine article of 1932.

Goetschius, Percy. Author. See:
Composers–1. Masters of the symphony (1929).　　　　　　　　2.50
Counterpoint–1. Applied (1902).　　3.50
Counterpoint–2. Exercises in elementary counterpoint (1910).　　3.00
Form. Homophonic (1898).　　　3.00
——. Larger forms (1915).　　　2.50
——. Lessons in (1904).　　　　1.50
Harmony–2. Material used in music composition (1889).　　　　3.00
——. Theory & practice of tone relations (1892/1916).　　　　2.50
Melody Writing. Exercises (1900). 2.25
Theory–1. Structure (1934).　　　2.50

Co-author (with Hamilton, et al). See:
Theory–3. Music theory for piano students (1924/30), 2 v.　　　2.00

Goff, Frederick R. Author.
See Bibliography.
Goffin, Robert. Author.
See Armstrong, Jazz.
Goldbeck, Frederick. Author.
See Appreciation.
Goldman, Edwin Franko. Author.
See Band–1.
Goldman, Morris F. Author.
See Theory–2.
Goldman, Richard Franko. Author.
See American Music, Band–1.

GOLDMARK, Karl
Note: The autobiographical "Notes from the life of a Viennese composer" (1927) apparently is O/P.

Goldsmith, Francis Howard. Author.
See Sound Recording & Reproduction.
Gollomb, Joseph. Author.
See App IIa (Schweitzer juvenile).

GOODMAN, Benny
See: Dance Bands, Jazz, Popular Music.
Note: The Goodman & Kolodin "Kingdom of swing" (1939) apparently is O/P.

Goodrich, Alfred John. Author.
See Interpretation.
Goodrich, Wallace. Author. See Organ.
Gopal, Ram. Author. See Dances–2.
Gordon, Dorothy. Author.
See Children–1.

GORDON, Gavin
See: esp Ballet (ed Haskell, also Posner, "Rake's Progress" ballet).

Gordon, Hamilton Adair. Author.
See Dictionaries of Terms.
Gordon, Louis Morton. Author.
See School Music–3.
Gordon, Philip. Author.
See American Music.
Gosling, Henry F. Author. See Violin.
Goss, Madeline. Author.
See App IIa (Bach, Beethoven, Brahms, & Schubert juveniles).

GOSSEC (Gossé), François-Joseph
See: esp App Ia (Prod'homme biog).
Chamber Music　　　　Opera
Composers–1　　　　　Phonograph Records
French Music　　　　　Symphony
History　　　　　　　Violin Music
Note: Standard works apparently O/P (or not easily available) include those in French by Gregoir, Hédouin, Tonnard, etc.

GOTTSCHALK, Louis Moreau
See:
America (music in)　　　History
American music　　　　Phonograph Records
Composers–3a　　　　　Piano Music
Note: The autobiographical "Notes of a pianist" (1881) and Hensel's "Life & Letters" (1870) both apparently are O/P.

GOUNOD, Charles-Francois
Note: The "Autobiographical reminiscences" (1896) are O/P.

See also:

Appreciation	Phonograph Records
Composers– **1 & 3d**	Program Notes
French Music	Rolland
History	Vocal Music
Opera	

DEMUTH, NORMAN
Introduction to the music of Gounod.
62 p, mus ex. Dobson 1950.   1.00

Gow, George Coleman. Author.
See Theory–2.

Grabbe, Paul. Author.
See Orchestral Music, Program Notes.

Grace, Harvey. Author. See:
Bach–1. Miniature biog. (1939).   .40
Bach–2. Organ works (1922).   (3.50)
Choir/Choral–2. Choral training &
conducting (1932).   (1.25)
Church Music. Music & worship
(1935), with W. Davies.   2.50
Franck. Organ works (1948).   (.90)
Organ Playing. Complete (1920).   2.00
Rheinberger. Organ works (1925). (2.75)
*Note: Several other books, including a collec-
tion of essays, "A musician at large" (1928),
apparently are O/P (or not easily available).*

Gradenwitz, Peter. Author.
See Jewish Music.

Graf, Max. Author. See:
Composers–1. From Beethoven to
Shostakovitch (1947).   4.75
Criticism. Composer & critic (1946).   4.00
Modern Music. Music & composers
of our time (1946).   3.00
Opera–1. Its future (1941).   4.75
*Note: A book about Vienna, "Legend of a
musical city" (1945), apparently is O/P.*

Graham, Alberta Powell. Author.
See Dance Bands.

GRAINGER, Percy Aldridge
See: esp R. L. Taylor ("The running pian-
ist," which includes a profile of Grainger).
Also:

Appreciation	Phonograph Records
American Music	Piano Music
Composers–3a	Program Notes
Interpreters	Pianists

Note: D. C. Parker's study (1918) is O/P.

GRAMMAR (of Conducting)
See: Baton–1.

GRAMMAR (of Music)
See: Musicianship (note only), Theory.

**GRAMOPHONE/GRAMOPHONE REC-
ORDS**
See:

Phonograph	Sound Recording &
Phonograph Records	Reproduction

GRANADOS (y Campina), Enrique
See: esp App Ia (Collet: "Albéniz et Gran-
ados").
Also:

Appreciation	Phonograph Records
Composers–1 & 2	Piano Music
History	Program Notes
Opera	Spanish Music

Granet, Marcel. Author.
See Chinese Music.

Grant, Gail. Author. See Ballet.

Granville, Charles Norman. Author.
See Singing–2.

GRAY, Cecil. Author.
Contingencies and other essays. viii,
199 p, mus ex. Oxford 1947.   4.00
*Outspoken studies & revaluations of Brahms,
Liszt, Bellini, Meyerbeer, Verdi, etc, plus
a revised version of the Gesualdo biography
originally published in "Carlo Gesualdo" by
Gray & Heseltine (1926), but long O/P.*

Musical chairs: or, Between two
stools (life & memoirs). 324 p. Home
& Van Thal, London, 1948.   (3.50)
*The British music critic's autobiography, up
to 1939: an unusual account of dual careers
in music & literature.*

See also:
Bach–2. The "48" (1938).   1.75
Composers–2. Survey of contem-
porary music (1924/7).   4.00
History–2. History (1928/31).   4.50
Sibelius. Biography (1931/8).   3.00
——. The symphonies (1935).   1.00

*Note: Besides the book on Gesualdo, mentioned
above, a study of Peter Warlock (1934) and
a collection of essays, "Predicaments, or
music & the future" (1936) apparently are
O/P.*

Gray, Roland Palmer. Editor.
See Folksongs–2.

GREAT BRITAIN
See: England (Music in), English Music.

**"GREAT LIVES" (series)
"GREAT MUSICIANS" (series)**
*Note: the "Great Lives" series, published by
Duckworth in London, is re-titled "Great
Musicians" in A. A. Wyn's U. S. A.
reprints. For individual books in this group*

of brief biographies (uniform in format, but not in treatment), see:

Bach–1 (Meynell)
Beethoven–2
(Pryce–Jones)
Brahms–1 (Hill)
Chopin–1 (Maine)
Debussy–2 (Myers)
Handel–1 (Dent)

Liszt (Hill)
Mozart–2 (Talbot)
Rimsky-Korsakov
(Abraham)
Tchaikovsky–1
(Abraham)
Wagner–2 (Turner)

See also: Biographies of Great Musicians, for Novello's series of miniature biogs.

GREECE (Music in) /GREEK MUSIC

See:

Ancient Music
Anthologies
Appreciation
Aristotle
Dances–2 (ed Alford:
Crossfield)
Byzantine Music
Church Music

Folklore
History
Instruments
(esp Schlesinger)
Medieval/Renaissance
Mode (esp Perfield)
Phonograph Records
Scales

Note: Reinach's "La musique grecque" (1926) apparently is O/P.

Greenfield, Marjorie E. Author.
See Children–6.
Greenleaf, Elizabeth Bristol. Editor.
See Sea Shanties.
Greenlees, Arthur Edward. Author.
See Sound Recording & Reproduction.
Gregor, Joseph. Author. See App Ib.
Greeff, Paul. Author. See App Ib.
Green, G. P. Author. See Chinese Music.
Green, Harriet C. Co-author (with Potter & Kopp). See Speech.
Greene, Harry Plunkett. Author.
See Singing–1. Co-author (with Bairstow).
See Singing–2.
Greene, Richard Leighton. Editor.
See Carols.
Greene, Theodore Meyer. Author.
See Aesthetics–1.

GREGORIAN (Chant, Music)

General Note: Although there is a fine distinction between Gregorian Chant and Plainsong (the latter term embraces other liturgical chants besides those of the Roman Catholic Church), it is not always observed either in common usage or book titles. For convenience, however, the titling is followed here in listing books under the two subject-headings,— although as a matter of fact, some of the books included under Plainsong deal almost exclusively with Gregorian Chant.

(It might be added that purists object to any of the books dealing with Gregorian or Plainsong accompaniments, for they insist that authentic performances of the chants are— without exception—sung entirely unaccompanied.)

See also: esp Church Music, Plainsong.

Also:

Accompaniment
Ancient Music
Anthologies
Appreciation
Byzantine Music
Children–7 (Field)
Choir/Choral–3
Counterpoint–1 (esp
Soderlund)

History
Hymns/Hymnody
Mass
Medieval/Renaissance
Mode
Monophony
Organ Playing
Palestrina
Phonograph Records

Note: Standard works apparently O/P (or not easily available) include those by Pierik, Schrembs et al, P. Wagner (in English & German); also those in French by Biron, Dupré, Gajard, Gastoué, Gevaert, Suñol, etc.

(BENEDICTINES OF SOLESMES, eds)
The Liber Usualis: with introduction & rubrics in English. xlx, 1912 + 38 p, music (Gregorian notation). Society of St John the Evangelist, Desclée & Cie, Tournai, Belgium, 1934 (1947) via J. Fischer.   6.25

A modern combination of the Graduale & Antiphonale, with the items of the Office & the Mass in their proper order of the day. This is only one of many available liturgical books (music & texts), but it is included here as a representative example and because it contains an introduction dealing with the chants & their proper performance.

BRAGERS, ACHILLE P.
A short treatise on Gregorian accompaniment: according to the principles of the monks of Solesmes. 82 p, mus ex. C. Fischer 1934.   3.00

HÜGLE, (*Very Rev*) P. GREGORY
Catechism of Gregorian chant. 123 p, mus ex, paper. J. Fischer 1928 (3rd pr 1944).   .75
18 concise lessons; pocket-size format.

JOHNER, (*Dom*) P. DOMINICUS
A new school of Gregorian chant. Tr Hermann Erpf & Max Ferrars. xvi, 363 p, mus ex, 2–p bibl. Pustet 3rd Eng ed 1925.   3.00
Based on the 5th German ed, 1920, of a work originally published in German in 1906.

KLARMANN, (*Rev*) ANDREW F.
Gregorian chant: a textbook for seminaries, novitiates, & secondary schools. ix, 148 p + chart, mus ex. Gregorian Institute of America, Toledo, Ohio, 1945.   3.00
Stressing Solesmes principles & including chapters on Latin pronunciation, church music history & legislation.

MERCURE, GEORGES. See App Ia.

MOCQUEREAU, (*Dom*) ANDRÉ
("Le nombre musical grégorien")
A study of Gregorian musical rhy-

thm: **V** 1, pt 1, The origin of rhythm. Tr Aileen Tone. 140 p, illus, mus ex, bibl refs, paper. Society of St John the Evangelist, Desclée & Cie, Tournai, Belgium, 1932, via J. Fischer.   3.00
The first section of a standard study, originally published in French 1908/27. For the complete work, in French, see App Ia.

PEETERS, FLOR
A practical method of plain-chant accompaniment (Methode pratique pour l'accompagnement du chant grégorien). viii, 97 p, mus ex, 1–p bibl, paper. H. Dessain, Mechlin (Malines), Belgium, n d (1949?).   3.50
Text in English & French.

PIERIK, MARIE
The song of the church. xi, 274 p, illus. Longmans 1947.   3.00
Dealing mainly with Gregorian chant. (The author's "Spirit of Gregorian chant", 1939, apparently is O/P.)

POTHIER, (Dom) JOSEPH. See App Ia.

POTIRON, HENRI
Treatise on the accompaniment of Gregorian chant. Pref Jean-Hébert Desrocquettes. Tr Ruth C. Gabain. xxv, 153 p, mus ex, paper. Society of St John the Evangelist, Desclée & Cie, Tournai, Belgium, 1933, via J. Fischer.   3.00
Studies in modal harmony, rhythm, & plainsong tonality. A standard work on Gregorian accompaniment, originally published in French 1925, 2nd edition 1927.

STEVENS, (Mother) GEORGIA
Gregorian chant. 96 p, music, paper. Macmillan 1944.   1.12
The "Gregorian supplements" originally included in books 4/5/6 of the "Tone & rhythm" series of children's songbooks, 1938/41.

SUÑOL, (Dom) GREGORIO M.
Text book of Gregorian chant: according to the Solesmes method. Tr & intro G. M. Durnfold. xviii, 221 p. mus ex, bibl refs. Society of St. John the Evangelist, Desclée & Cie, Tournai, Belgium, 1930, via J. Fischer.   3.00
A standard over-all study, originally published in Spanish, 1905. The present translation is from the 6th French edition.

WAESBERGHE, JOSEF SMITS VAN
Gregorian chant and its place in the Catholic liturgy. Tr W. A. G. Doyle-Davidson. 64 p, illus, mus ex, bds. Continental n d (1947).   2.50

"Symphonia" series. An introduction for non-experts in church music and for non-Catholic readers in particular.

Gregory, Julia. Compiler.
See Bibliography.

Greiner, Albert. Author. See App Ib.

Grenier, Hélène. Author. See App Ia.

GRÉTRY, André-Ernest-Modeste

See: esp App Ia (Clercx).

Appreciation	Phonograph Records
Composers–1 & 3d	Program Notes
French Music	Opera
History	Vocal Music

Grew, Eva Mary & Sydney. Authors.
See Bach–1.

GRIEG, Edvard Hagerup

See also:

Appreciation	Phonograph Records
Chamber Music	Piano Music
Composers–1	Program Notes
Concerto	Song(s)
History	Themes
National Music	Vocal Music

Also: App IIa (Acker, Deucher, Purdy).
Note: Finck's "Grieg & his music" (1909) apparently is O/P (or not easily available), as are works in French by Closson and Rokseth, and in German by Schjelderup & Niemann.

ABRAHAM, GERALD (ed)
Grieg: a symposium. 144 p + 40–p mus ex, 2–p bibl. (1948) Oklahoma 1950.   3.00
Originally published in London by Drummond in "Music of the Masters" series. Articles on various aspects of Grieg's music, by Gerik Schjelderup, Kathleen Dale, Astra Desmond, Hubert Foss, Alan Frank, John Horton, Edmund Rubbra, & the editor.

CHERBULIEZ, A. E. See App Ib.

JOHANSEN, DAVID MONRAD
Edvard Grieg. Tr Madge Robertson. vii, 400 p, illus. (1938) Tudor repr 1945.   1.98
Reprint of the first complete Grieg biography, originally published (in English) by the American-Scandinavian Foundation.

STOECKLIN, PAUL DE. See App Ia.

Grierson, Mary. Author. See Tovey.

GRIFFES, Charles Tomlinson

See also:

American Music	History
Appreciation	Phonograph Records
Composers–3a	Program Notes

MAISEL, EDWARD M.
Charles T. Griffes: the life of an
American composer. xviii, 347, xi
p, illus. Knopf 1943. 3.50

Griffin, Nard. Author. See Jazz.
Griffiths, Vernon. Author.
Grim, Harriet Elizabeth. Author.
See Speech.
Grimm, Wilhelm Karl & Ludwig, Karl.
Authors. See App IIa (Humperdinck).
Grimson, Samuel B. Author.
See Violin Playing.
Gronowicz, Antoni. Author.
See App IIa (Rachmaninoff & Tchai-
kovsky) & App IIb ("Bolek").
Grout, Donald Jay. Author.
See Opera–1.
Grove, (Sir) George. Author, editor.
See Beethoven–3, Composers–1, Diction-
aries of Music.
Grovlez, Gabriel. Author. See App Ia.
Gruenberg, Eugene. Author.
See Violin, Violin Playing.
Grundy, Enid. Author.
See Piano Playing–2.
Grüninger, Fritz. Author. See App Ib.
Gruppe, M. Author.
See Wind Instruments.

GUADAGNINI FAMILY
See also: Violin.

DORING, ERNEST N.
The Guadagnini family of violin
makers. 335 p, 66 pl + 11 label
facs, 2–p bibl. Wm. Lewis & Son, △
Chicago, 1949. 12.50
*The first extensive study in English of a
noted Italian family of 18th-century violin
makers: richly illustrated and including a
genealogical table and correspondence.*

GUARNERIUS FAMILY
See: Violin.
*Note: Books by the Hill brothers and by
Petherick on this even more famous family
of Italian violin makers apparently are O/P
(or not easily available in this country).*

GUATEMALA (Music in)
See: Latin America.

GUILBERT, Yvette
*Note: For two books of memoirs (in French)
see App Ia. "How to sing a song" (1918)
apparently is O/P, at least in English.*

Guggenheim, Louis Kaufman. Author.
See Hearing.

Gullan, Marjorie. Author.
See Choral Speaking.

GUNDRY, Inglis. Composer, author.
Men of the hills: introduction to a
new English opera, "The Partisans."
Forew Rutland Boughton. 48 p,
frontis por, mus ex, paper. Hinrichsen n d (1946). .75
*"Miniature Survey" series M-5. Includes the
libretto of the opera & an article by Gundry,
and essays by Corbett, Lloyd, & Lawson.*
Author. See: Opera–1.

Gurlitt, Willibald. Author. See App Ib.
Guthrie, Tyrone. Author.
See Opera–1. (ed Crozier).

GUTHRIE, Woody
Bound for glory. 428 p, illus
(Guthrie's sketches). Dutton 1943. 3.50
*The autobiography of an American folksong
singer & collector.*

GYPSY MUSIC
See also:

Dances–2	Hungarian Music
Folklore	Liszt
History	National Music

LISZT, FRANZ
The gypsy in music. Tr Edwin
Evans, Sr. 2 v: x 370 p, 7 pors. △
Reeves 1926 (1930). (7.50)
*A standard work, originally published in
French (1859). The present edition, which
includes an essay on Liszt & his work by
Evans, is temporarily O/P, but is definitely
scheduled for early re-issue.*

PARKER, D. C.
Some aspects of gypsy music. 61 △
p, mus ex. Reeves n d (1913) (1.50)
Brief introductory essays.

STARKIE, WALTER
Don Gypsy: adventures with a
fiddle in Barbary, Andalusia, &
La Mancha. xvi, 525 p, 7 illus,
maps, mus ex, 8–p annot bibl.
Dutton 1937. 4.00
Raggle-taggle: adventures with a
fiddle in Hungary & Roumania. 361
p, illus, mus ex, 8–p annot bibl.
(1933) Transatlantic 1949. 2.85
Spanish raggle-taggle: adventures
with a fiddle in northern Spain.
xv, 488 p, illus, map, mus ex, 7–p
annot bibl. Dutton 1934. 4.00
*Autobiographical stories of Gypsy life, music,
& musicians.*

—H—

Haake, Charles J. & Gail Martin. Authors (with McConathy). See Sight-Playing & Reading. Co-authors (with Schelling). See Teaching–2.

Haas, Robert Maria. Author. See App Ib (ed Bücken).

Haberl, Franz Xaver. Co-compiler (with Eitner & others). See App Ib.

Hadamowsky, Franz. Author. See App Ib.

Haddon, William. Author (with Walters). See Theory–3.

HADLEY, Henry

See:

America (music in)	Composers–3a
American Music	Phonograph Records

Hadow, (Sir) William Henry. Author. See Beethoven–3, History–1 (Oxford, note only), History–2, Wagner–2.

Note: Numerous other books by Hadow, including his "Collected essays" (1928) apparently are O/P (or not easily available).

Hagedorn, Hermann. Author. See Schweitzer–2.

Hagedorn, Ivan Henry. Author See Hymns/Hymnody–2.

HAGER, George

BELL, CLAIR HAYDEN
Georg Hager: a Meistersinger of Nürnberg, 1552–1634. 4 v: xix, 431, 1645 p, illus (pors, facs, etc). mus ex, 6–p bibl. California 1947. 20.00
University of California publications in modern philology, volumes 29/32. The last 3 sections are devoted entirely to song-texts & notes, in typescript reproduction.

HAGGIN, Bernard H.

Music in the Nation. ix, 376 p, 6–p bibl. Duell Sloan 1949. 5.00
A collection of the hard-hitting New York critic's articles & book reviews, originally published in the "Nation" magazine from 1929 to 1948.

Author. See also:

Appreciation. Music for the man who enjoys Hamlet (1944). 2.75

History–2. Pratt class notes, rev & aug Haggin (1938). .30

Phonograph Records. Music on records (1938/46). 2.00
Note: Haggin's "A book of the symphony" (1937) is O/P.

HAHN, Reynaldo

See:

Composers–2	Phonograph Records
French Music	Song(s)
History	Song Translations
Operetta	Vocal Music

Author. See App Ia ("Thèmes variés").

HAITI (Music in)/HAITIAN MUSIC

See:

Dances–2 (Leaf)	History
Folklore (esp	Latin America
Courlander)	Negro Music

Hale, Noel V. Author. See Education.

Hale, Philip. Author.
Note: Two collections of Hale's celebrated program notes for the Boston Symphony Orchestra (1935, 1939) apparently are O/P.

Hall, David. Author. See Phonograph Records.

Hall, Gertrude. Author. See Wagner–3.

Hallstrom, John. Author. See Phonograph Records.

Hambourg, Mark. Author. See Piano Playing–1.

Hamel, Fred. Editor (with Hürlimann). See App Ib.

Hamilton, Anna Heuerman. Author. See Children–8, Hymns/Hymnody–1, Keyboard Harmony.

Hamilton, Clarence Grant. Author. See:

Acoustics. Sound and its relation to music (1912). 1.50

Appreciation. Music appr. (1920). 2.50

History–2. Epochs in musical progress (1926). 1.50

——. Outlines of (1908/36). 2.25

Ornamentation. Ornaments in classical & modern music (1930). .75

Piano Music. Its composers & characteristics (1925). 2.00

Piano Playing–1. What every piano student should know (1928). 2.00

Piano Playing–2. Touch & expression in piano playing (1927). .75

Teaching–3. Piano teaching (1910). 1.50

Theory–3. For piano students, by Hamilton, Goetschius, Marshall, & Earhart. 2 v (1924/30). 2.00

Hamilton, Edna Vance. Co-author (with Lynch). See Children–2.

Hamilton, Mary Neal. Author. See Spain (music in).

Hamilton, Wallace F. Author. See Health.

Hamma, Fridolin. Author. See App Ib.

HAMMERSTEIN, Oscar, II

See also:

America (music in)	Popular Music
American Music	Songwriting
Operetta	Vocal Music

Lyrics. Pref Richard Rodgers. xv, 215 p. S & S 1949. 2.50

Notes on lyrics & lyric-writing by a noted American practitioner, plus some 71 texts of songs to music by Rodgers, Kern, Bizet, & Romberg.

HAMMOND ORGAN

See also:

| Church Music | Organ |
| Instruments | Organ Playing |

BARANOSKI, STEPHEN
Stephen Barnoski's ABC's of Hammond organ playing. 24 p, diagrs, music, paper. E. Smith, N. Y., 1949. 1.00

Performance instructions, plus a bit of elementary theory & some simple pieces

(HAMMOND COMPANY)
Playing the Hammond organ: elementary instruction book. 46 p, illus, mus ex, paper, spir. Hammond Co, Chicago, 1936. 1.00

IRWIN, STEVENS
Dictionary of Hammond-organ stops: an introduction to playing the Hammond electric organ & a translation of the pipe-organ stops into Hammond-organ number-arrangements. vi, 89 p, illus, tables. G. Schirmer 1939. 2.00

THORPE, CLARENCE RADFORD
Hammond organ playing: principles & first steps. 46 p, 1 illus, music, paper. G. Schirmer 1948. 2.00

Showing off the Hammond organ. vi, 35 p, music, paper. G. Schirmer 1949. 1.25

The first book is a "method" in 15 lessons; the second contains demonstration & recital pieces, with descriptive notes on the instrument & the various "stops" demonstrated.

HANDBOOK(S) (Musical)

Note: Many instruction and "guide" books on various musical subjects bear this term in their main or sub titles. See especially under the subject-headings Dictionaries of Terms & Theory.

HANDEL, George Frideric
1. Life   2. Works

HANDEL (1. Life)

See also:

Appreciation	England (music in)
Baroque Era	History
Church Music	Opera
Composers–1	Program Notes
Dryden	Rolland

Also: App IIa (juvenile by Wheeler).

Note: Standard works apparently O/P (or not easily available) include an English edition of Handel's "Letters & writings" (ed Mueller, 1935), biographies by Chrysander and Leichtentritt (in German), Mainwaring (in English, but see App Ib for the German version), Rockstro, Rolland (in English, but see App Ib for the German version), Streatfeild, Williams, etc.

CHERBULIEZ, A. E. See App Ib.

DENT, EDWARD J.
Handel. 140 p, frontis por, 1–p bibl. (1934) Wyn 1949. 1.00

"Great Musicians" series; originally published by Duckworth, London. A short biography & condensed list of works.

FLOWER, NEWMAN
George Frideric Handel: his personality & his times. 399 p, illus (4 col pl, 37 b&ws), 20–p bibl (William C. Smith). (1923) Scribner new rev ed 1948. 6.00

A standard work in a new edition embodying the results of Handelian research since the original publication, by Cassell, in 1923.

MAINWARING, JOHN. See App Ib.

MÜLLER VON ASOW, E. H. & HEDWIG (eds). See App Ib

ROLLAND, ROMAIN. See App Ib.

SMITH, WILLIAM C.
Concerning Handel: his life & works, an essay. Forew Newman Flower. 299 p, 15 pl (pors & facs), mus ex. Cassell 1948. 4.75

Discussions of Handel's finances & portraits; early editions of Messiah & the Water Music; also Acis & Galatea, Gustavus Waltz, etc.

WEINSTOCK, HERBERT
Handel. xv, 326, xliii p, 26 pl (pors, facs, etc), 4–p bibl, mus ex. Knopf 1946. 5.00
An extensive recent biography, including Handel's letters & documents.

WESTRUP, J. A.
Handel. 22 p, cover por, paper. Novello n d (1938). .40
Miniature biography ("great musicians").

YOUNG, PERCY M.
(*See also Handel–2.*)
Handel. x, 246 p, 8 pl (pors, etc), 3–p bibl, mus ex. Dent 1947 (1948), via Pellegrini 1949. 2.50
"Master Musicians" series, with usual personalia, calendar, & catalogue of works. (This replaces the 1913/35 biography in this series by C. F. Abdy Williams.)

HANDEL (2. Works)

See also:

Appreciation	Keyboard Music
Baroque Era	Opera
Chamber Music	Orchestral Music
Choir/Choral	Organ Music
(esp Woodgate)	Phonograph Records
Choir/Choral–3	Piano Music
Church Music	Program Notes
Composers–1	Themes
Concerto	Timing
Dryden	Trumpet (Menke)
English Music	Violin Music
History	Vocal Music

Note: Standard works apparently O/P (or not easily available) include those by Abert (in German), Bairstow, Benson, Chorley, Chrysander (in German), Ehrlinger (in German) Volsung (in German), etc.

(HARROW REPLICAS)
No. 8. Selections from the original manuscript of the "Messiah": an oratorio by G. F. Handel. Unp (28–p facs) + 4–p notes (Henry Havergal). Heffer 1945. △ 7.50
Including facsimile reproductions of the MS of 3 arias & the Hallelujah Chorus.

HERBAGE, JULIAN
Messiah. 72 p, illus (7 col pl, 35 b&ws). Chanticleer 1948. 2.50
"World of Music" series No. 1: the story of the oratorio, elaborately illustrated.

MYERS, ROBERT MANSON
Handel's Messiah: a touchstone of taste. xxii, 338 p, 13 illus, 17–p bibl. Macmillan 1948. 5.00

A critical evaluation of the work, its history & social influences. Includes the complete text & list of subscribers to the original full-score edition

SHAW, H. WATKINS
Handel's Messiah: the story of a masterpiece. 32 p, diagr, mus ex, paper. Hinrichsen 1946. .50
"Miniature Survey" series M–2.

YOUNG, PERCY M.
(*See also Handel–1.*)
The oratorios of Handel. 244 p, 10 pl (pors, facs, etc), mus ex. Dobson 1949; Roy 1950. 4.50
Commentary on the works and the contemporary oratorio singers & conditions of performance.

HANDS

See:

Baton	Piano Playing
Conducting	(esp 2, Unschuld)
Organ Playing	Violin Playing

Note: Meier's "Lions' paws: the story of famous hands" (1917) apparently is O/P.

Handschin, Jacques. Author. See App Ib.

HANDWRITING (Musical)
See: Manuscript.

HANDY, William Christopher

See also:

America (music in)	Negro Music
American Music	Popular Music
Jazz	Phonograph Records

Father of the blues: an autobiography. Ed Arna Bontemps; forew Abbé Niles. xiv, 317 p, illus, mus ex. Macmillan 1941 (1947). 4.00
The life-story of the composer of the undying "St. Louis Blues" & "Memphis Blues."

Editor. See also:
Negro Music & Musicians. Unsung American sung (1944/6). 3.50
Negro Spirituals & Songs. A treasury of the blues (1926/49). 5.00
Note: Handy's "Authors & composers in the United States" (1936) and "Book of Negro Spirituals" (1938) apparently are O/P.

Hanks, Howard. Co-author (with Robyn). See Children–8.
Hannikainen, Ilmari. Author. See Sibelius.
Hansen, Jules. Author. See App Ia.

HANSLICK, Eduard

See also:

Aesthetics–2　　　　　　Romantic Era
Criticism (musical)　　　Vienna
History

Note: The English edition of Dr. Hanslick's "The beautiful in music" (1891) is O/P, and his many books in German all apparently are O/P (or not easily available in this country).

DEAS, STEWART
In defence of Hanslick. 114 p, 1–p bibl. Williams & Norgate 1940.　　2.50
A re-evaluation of the noted but often maligned Viennese critic, with biographical sketch, excerpts from his writings, & a discussion of his aesthetic theories.

PLEASANTS, HENRY (*ed & tr*)
Vienna's golden years of music: 1850–1900.　xxvi, 341 p, 31 illus (pors, etc). S & S 1950.　　3.75
A collection of Hanslick's critical writings, with a biographical introduction.

HANSON, Howard

See:

America (music in)　　　Opera
American Music　　　　　Phonograph Records
Composers–3a　　　　　　Program Notes
Education　　　　　　　　Symphony
History

Harap, Louis. Author. See Aesthetics–1.
Haraszti, Émile. Author. See Bartók.
Harding, Harry Alfred. Author.
See Beethoven–3.

HARDING, Rosamond Evelyn Mary

Note: Harding's "Anatomy of inspiration" (1940) & a history of the pianoforte (1933) apparently are O/P (or not easily available in this country).
Origins of musical time and expression.　xi, 115 p, 26 pl, mus ex, bibl refs. Oxford 1938.　　4.25
An unclassifiable book of four unusual musicological studies: The metronome & its precursors; Imitations of musical instruments by other instruments & by voices; The pitchpipe in England; Origins & history of the forte & piano, the crescendo & diminuendo.

Hardy, T. Maskell. Author.
See Children–3 & 7, School Music–4.

HARMONICA (Mouth Organ)

See also: History, Instruments

PLANTA, P. V.
How to make music on the harmonica.　109 p, illus, mus ex, paper. Leisure League of America, N. Y., via Sentinel 1939.　　.60

Including a brief history of the mouth organ & lists of songbook material for playing.

HARMONIC ANALYSIS

See: Harmony–2.

HARMONIUM

See: Instruments, Karg-Elert, Organ.

HARMONY

1. **General & Specialized Studies**
2. **Methods, including Harmonic Analysis**

General Note: The distinction between these two sub-categories should not be taken too seriously: it is used here primarily as a convenience in separating the more general & the specialized "studies" from the "methods" & textbooks—some of which are largely series of exercises to be worked out by the student.

Many books on Appreciation, Composers (& individual composers), Contemporary Music, History, Program Notes, etc, discuss various phases of harmony as used in various eras & in various types of compositions. But for more specific cross-references—

See also:

Arranging–1 & 2　　　　Piano Playing–3
　(esp Warrington)　　　Scales
Bach–2 (esp Gannett)　　Songwriting
Children–3 & 8　　　　　Theory (esp–4)
Composition　　　　　　Tonality/Atonality
Counterpoint　　　　　　Transposition
Ear-Training　　　　　　Twelve-Tone
Improvisation　　　　　　Technique
Keyboard Harmony　　　Violin Playing
Mode/Modality　　　　　　(esp Norden)
Modulation

Note: Standard works apparently O/P (or not easily available) include those by Bullis, Casella, Coussemaker (in French), Hába (in German), Kurth (in German), Macpherson, Oettingen (in German), Schenker (in German), Shirlaw, Weidig, Ziehn, etc.

HARMONY

(1. General & Specialized Studies)

ABBOTT, LAWRENCE
The listener's book on harmony. xvi, 237 p, mus ex. Presser 1941.　　3.50
"Appreciation" treatment; primarily a layman's introduction to harmony & "theory."

BUDGE, HELEN
A study of chord frequencies: based on the music of representative composers of the 18th & 19th centuries. ix, 82 p, tables, mus ex, 2–p bibl. Teachers College 1943.　　1.85
"Contributions to Education" No. 882: a

statistical study indicating a revised order of presenting material to the student of diatonic harmony.

CARNER, MOSCO
A study of twentieth-century harmony: a treatise & guide for the student-composer of today. V 2: Contemporary harmony. vi, 81 p, mus ex, paper. Williams (1942) 2nd ed 1944.   2.50
For volume 1, see Lenormand below.

DOUEL, JEAN. See App Ia.

FINNEY, ROSS LEE
The game of harmony. **167** p, mus ex. Harcourt 1947.   3.00
An introductory primer for laymen.

HULL, A. EAGLEFIELD
Modern harmony: its explanation & application. xiii, 235 p, mus ex, paper. (1914) Kalmus 1934.   3.50

JONES, VINCENT
Essentials in teaching of harmony a book for teachers. ix, 60 p, mus ex. Jones 1931.   1.50

KITSON, C. H.
  (*See also Harmony–2*)
The evolution of harmony: a treatise on the material of musical composition, its gradual growth, & elementary use. xii, 456 p, mus ex. Oxford (1914) 2nd ed 1924 (1945).   5.00
A treatise that discards the figured bass as a method of teaching and deals primarily with part rather than chord progressions. There are special chapters on modern tendencies, word-setting, pedals, etc.

KOECHLIN, CHARLES. See App Ia.

LENORMAND, RENÉ
A study of twentieth-century harmony: a treatise & guide for the student-composer of to-day. V 1: Harmony in France to 1914. Tr Herbert Antcliffe; pref Mosco Carner. xiv, 142 p, mus ex, paper. Williams (1915) new ed 1940.   2.50
Originally published in French (1913). 1st English edition titled "A study in modern harmony." For the companion volume 2, see Carner above.

MCKAY, GEORGE F.
Technique of modern harmony: a laboratory plan for advanced study. xi, 87 p, mus ex, typescript repro, paper. Gamble (1941) 1947.   2.00
An attempt to extend orthodox harmonic studies to cover actual contemporary practices.

MILLER, HORACE ALDEN
New harmonic devices: a treatise on modern harmonic problems. 206 p, mus ex. Ditson 1930.   2.00

NORMAN, PHILIP B.
Quantitative study in harmonic similarities in certain specified works of Bach, Beethoven & Wagner. 35 p, mus ex, tables, paper. C. Fischer 1945.   .60

PFROGNER, HERMANN. See App Ib.

SCHOENBERG, ARNOLD
Theory of harmony (Harmonielehre). Tr. Robert D. W. Adams. xviii, 336 p, mus ex. Philosophical 1948.   7.50
The famous "Harmonielehre" first appeared in German (1911, 3rd ed 1921). The present (first) English version is an abridgment (about one half) of the latter edition, using the text portions indicated in Erwin Stein's "Praktischer Leitfaden zu Schönbergs Harmonielehre." Intended as a student's edition, for practical use, it omits most of the philosophical material that did much to give the original complete work its stature.

SESSIONS, ROGER
Harmonic practice. Harcourt 1951, in prep.

HARMONY
(2. Methods, including Harmonic Analysis)

For general cross-references (to Keyboard Harmony, etc), see under the main subject-heading, Harmony, above.

Note: Long as the following list is, it still omits an approximately equal number of works apparently O/P (or not easily available in this country), as well as a considerable number of works either quite antiquated or comparatively new but published for limited distribution only—i.e., among an author-teacher's pupils or the students of a particular conservatory or college. Also omitted, as a general rule, are separately published "key" or "solution" booklets.

[Without departing too far from our general rule of no critical evaluations, it might be of some interest to the bewildered prospective reader or student (who has not been referred to a specific textbook) for the present compiler to furnish his personal list of what appear to him to be usually considered "standard" works. Among the older authorities, I'd be inclined to think first of Buck, Chadwick, Foote & Spalding, Goetschius, Jadassohn, Prout, Richter, & Rimsky-Korsakov. Among the most promising newer works, I'd

*be inclined to think first of those by Andrews,
Hindemith, Kitson, Morris, Orrey,
Otterström, Piston, Tweedy, & Wedge.*]

ALCHIN, CAROLYN A.
Applied harmony. Rev Vincent Jones.
V 1: Diatonic harmony & simple
modulation. ix, 143 + 19 p, mus ex.
Jones (1917) rev ed 1931 (1935).   2.50
V 2: Modulation & chromatic harm-
ony. vii, 103 + 5 p, mus ex. Jones
(1917) rev ed 1930.   2.25

ANDERSON, ARTHUR OLAF
The first 40 lessons in harmony.
124 p, mus ex. Birchard (1923) rev
ed 1948.   1.60
The second 40 lessons in harmony.
vi, 110 p, mus ex. Birchard (1923)
rev ed 1948.   1.60
Modern resources: third book of
"Lessons in harmony." 106 p, mus
ex. Birchard 1938.   1.75

ANDREWS, H. K.
The Oxford harmony: V 2. vii, 241
p, mus ex. Oxford 1950.   3.00
*Chromatic harmony & modulation, including
sections on string writing, piano accompaniments, setting words, unacc. choral writing,
harmonizing basses, etc. For volume 1,
see Morris below.*

ANGER, J. HUMPHREY
A treatise on harmony: with **exer-**
cises. 3 v. Boston 1906/12.
V 1: xiii, 180, xii p, mus ex, paper.
(1906) rev ed (J. Clough-Leighter)
1919.   2.00
V 2: 174, xxiv p, mus ex, paper.
(1907) rev enl ed n d.   2.00
V 3: xi, 313, xxx p, mus ex, paper.
1912.   O/P

APPENZELLER, ELSE. See App Ib.

BARNES, A. F.
Practice in modern harmony. 40 p,
mus ex, paper. Oxford 1937 (1943).   .75

BUCK, PERCY C.
Unfigured harmony: a short treatise
on modulation, harmonization of
melodies, unfigured basses, inner
melodies, canons, & ground basses.
174 p, mus ex. Oxford (1911) 2nd
ed 1920 (repr 1946).   1.75
*Especially designed as a "follow-up" course
to conventional elementary methods.*

BUSSLER, LUDWIG
Elementary harmony: a practical &
thorough course in 54 exercises,
adapted for public or private teach-

ing & self-instruction. Tr Theodore
Baker. xiii, 227 p, mus ex, flex. G.
Schirmer 1891 (1919).   2.50
From the 2nd German edition of 1885.

CARRILLO, JULIÁN. See App Id.

CESANA, OTTO
Course in modern harmony. Unp
(17 p, mus ex, paper, spir. King
1939.   3.00

CHADWICK, GEORGE W.
Harmony: a course of study. xvi,
260 p, mus ex. Wood (1897) rev ed
1922 (86th pr n d).   5.00
One of the standard older American texts.

CHAPPLE, STANLEY
Language of harmony. viii, 129 p,
mus ex. Boosey 1941 (repr in prep).   △
*A companion to Trotter & Chapple's "Prin-
ciples of musicianship" (see Children–8).*

CLARKE, HUGH A.
A system of harmony founded on key
relationship, by means of which a
thorough knowledge of the rules that
govern the combinations & succes-
sions of sound may be easily acquired
with or without a teacher. xiv, 152
p, mus ex, paper. Presser 1898
(1926).   1.50

CUTTER, BENJAMIN
Harmonic analysis: a course in the
analysis of the chords & of the non-
harmonic tones to be found in music,
classic & modern. xi, 130 p, mus ex.
Ditson 1902 (1930).   1.50
"Music Student Library" series.

DALE, B. J. See Theory–4 (ed Dyson).

DETHIER, J. V.
High school harmony: Part 1. 39 p,
mus ex, paper. Birchard 1934.   .75

DUNSTAN, RALPH
First steps in harmony and the
harmonizing of melodies: a concise
manual for beginners. 76 p, mus ex,
paper. Curwen (1895) 13th rev ed
n d.   (1.35)

EMERY, STEPHEN A.
Elements of harmony. 131 p, mus
ex. Schmidt (1879) rev enl ed 1924.   1.50

FOOTE, ARTHUR & SPALDING, W. R.
Modern harmony in its theory and
practice. vii, 270 p, mus ex. Schmidt
(1905) aug rev ed 1936.   3.00
A standard American textbook.

GARDNER, CARL E.
Music composition: a new method

of harmony. xviii, 161 p, mus ex.
C. Fischer 1918. 1.25
With some material on modulation & form.

GARIEL, EDUARDO
A new system of harmony: based on
four fundamental chords. vii, 56
p, mus ex. G. Schirmer (1915) 2nd
ed 1916. 1.00
For a Spanish edition, see App Id.

GIBBS, GEORGE A., *Jr*
Modern visualized harmony: with
an introduction to instrumentation.
64 p, mus ex, paper. Mills 1938. 2.00
Primarily for arrangers of popular music.

GOETSCHIUS, PERCY
The material used in musical
composition: a system of harmony
designed originally for use in the
English harmony classes of the
Conservatory of Music at Stuttgart.
ix, 265 p, mus ex. G. Schirmer (1889)
rev 14th ed 1913 (1941). 3.00
Based on the teachings of Immanuel Faisst.
First published in German (1882).

The theory and practice of tone-
relations: an elementary course of
harmony with emphasis upon the
element of melody. 187 p, mus ex.
G. Schirmer (1892) rev enl ed 1916
(24th pr 1931). 2.50
Concord harmonies, discord harmonies, modu-
lation, & inharmonic tones; plus a reference-
index & a 10-p appendix of solutions.

HARRIS, CUTHBERT
Lessons in elementary harmony. 39
p, mus ex, paper. Schmidt n d
(1937?) 1.00

HINDEMITH, PAUL
A concentrated course in traditional
harmony: with emphasis on exercises & a minimum of rules. vi,125
p, mus ex. Associated (1943) rev ed
1944. 2.00
An unusual modern approach to the funda-
mentals, based on the composer-teacher's
courses at the Yale School of Music.

JADASSOHN, S.
A manual of harmony. Tr. Theodore
Baker. viii, 292 p, mus ex. G.
Schirmer (1893) 14th pr n d. 3.00
Originally published in German (1883).
The present English version is based on the
3rd augmented & revised German edition.

JOHNSTONE, J. ALFRED
Beginners' guide to harmony. 71
p, mus ex, paper. Boston n d. 1.00

JONES, ROBERT GOMER
Harmony and its contrapuntal treatment. viii, 187 p, mus ex. Harper
1939. 2.75
Workbook for "Harmony and its contrapuntal treatment." 151 p, mus
ex, paper. Harper 1939. 1.75

KASSCHAW, HOWARD
An introduction to harmony. 47
p, mus ex, paper. Schroeder 1941. .75

KITSON, C. H.
(*See also Harmony–1.*)
Elementary harmony. Complete in
1 volume. 309 p, mus ex. Oxford
(1931) 3rd ed 1943. 3.50
Same, in 3 v. (repr 1946). Each: 1.50
Contrapuntal harmony for beginners.
viii, 93 p, mus ex. Oxford (1931) 3rd
ed 1943. 1.50
Two standard British works. The former
covers ear-training, diatonic & chromatic
harmony; the latter is a companion work
carrying on the course through contrapuntal
harmony.

LEHMANN, FRIEDRICH JOHANN
Harmonic analysis. ix, 156 p, mus
ex. Comings 1910. 2.00

LEIGHTON, GEORGE A.
Harmony: analytical and applied:
a practical textbook. xiii, 208 p,
mus ex. Boston 1927. 3.00

LEWIS, LEO RICH
Do and don't in harmony: a sketch-
book of essentials. xvi, 272 p, mus
ex, typescript repro, bds. Tufts
College Press, Medford, Mass., 1943. 2.00
Practical workbook with blanks to be filled.

LIEBERSON, SAMUEL A.
Manual of functional harmony: &
key to 216 exercises. viii, 167 p, mus
ex. Lewis 1946. 3.50

MACPHERSON, STEWART
Melody and harmony: a treatise for
the teacher & student. xv, 304 p,
mus ex, paper. Williams n d (1920). 6.25
Melodic movement, elementary harmonic
progression, & advanced harmony; with an
analytic index by Sylvia Curry. Also avail-
able in 3 separate volumes.

MANSFIELD, ORLANDO A.
The student's harmony. Intro Hugh
A. Clarke. vii, 312 p, mus ex.
Presser 1896. 1.75

McCONATHY, OSBOURNE (& *others*)
An approach to harmony. xii, 179
p, mus ex. Silver 1927 2.00

Co-authors: Anton H. Embs, Maude M. Howes, & Charles Elliott Fouser.

MESSAIEN, OLIVIER. See App Ia.

MITCHELL, WILLIAM J.
Elementary harmony. xix, 290 p, mus ex. Prentice (1939) 2nd ed 1948.   5.35
Revised edition of a college textbook emphasizing contrapuntal treatment.

MOKREJS, JOHN
Lessons in harmony. 128 p, mus ex. Odowan Pub Co (1913) 1924, via Summy.   1.50

MORRIS, R. O.
Foundations of practical harmony and counterpoint. xii, 148 p, mus ex. Macmillan (1925) 2nd ex 1931 (1949).   1.50
Harmony p 1/79; counterpoint p 83/148.
The Oxford harmony. V 1: vi, 139 p, mus ex. Oxford 1946.   3.00
A recent but sure to be standard work, covering diatonic harmony, common methods of ornamentation, 3- & 4-part writing. For v 2 in this series, see Andrews above.

MURPHY & STRINGHAM. See Theory–2.

NORRIS, HOMER A.
Practical harmony: a comprehensive system of musical theory on a French basis. Presser 1894/1924.
V 1: Consonance. vi, 91 p, mus ex, flex. (1894) 1922.   1.25
V 2: Dissonance. 124 p, mus ex, paper. (1895) 1923.   1.25
V 3: Key to harmony. 79 p, mus ex only, paper. 1924.   1.00

OAKEY, GEORGE
Textbook of harmony analysis. 268 p, mus ex. Curwen (n d) 7th ed 1946.   (3.15)

OREM, PRESTON WARE
Harmony book for beginners: a text book & writing book for the first year's work. . . 144 p, mus ex, bds. Presser 1916.   1.25
Students' harmony book. 128 p, mus ex. Summy 1934.   1.50

ORREY, LESLIE
The foundations of harmony and composition. Forew Gordon Jacob. x, 137 p, mus ex, 2–p bibl. Pitman 1948.   3.00
Progressive British approach: 10 general chapters followed by 36 detailed lessons, designed as an introduction to elementary harmony & composition, with emphasis on musical style & shape.

OTTERSTRÖM, THORWALD
A manual of harmony. ix, 118 p, mus ex, paper. Chicago 1941.   2.75
Elementary exercises in various systems.

PISTON, WALTER
Harmony. vi, 344 p, mus ex. Norton (1941) rev ed 1948.   5.25
One of the now standard newer American textbooks, with special emphasis on harmonic rhythm & expressive means.
Principles of harmonic analysis. vii, 90 p, mus ex. E. C. Schirmer 1933.   2.50
Mostly musical examples, by various composers, subjected to complete analysis.

PROUT, EBENEZER
Harmony: its theory and practice. xvii, 342 p, mus ex. Augener (1889) 20th rev ed 1903, via Boston.   4.00
One of the older standard textbooks.

PROUT, LOUIS B.
Harmonic analysis. vii, 84 p, mus ex, paper. Augener 1894 (2nd pr n d).   1.50

REBER, HENRI. See App Ia.

RICHTER, ERNST FRIEDRICH
Manual of harmony: a practical guide to its study, prepared especially for the Conservatory of Music at Leipzig. Ed Alfred Richter; tr Theodore Baker. G. Schirmer 1912 (1940).   2.50
A standard older work, first published in German (1935). The version above was translated from the 25th German edition, that listed below from the 7th German edition ("Music Students Library" series).
Manual of harmony. Tr J. C. D. Parker. 215 p, mus ex. Ditson 1873.   2.00

RIMSKY-KORSAKOV, N. A.
Practical manual of harmony. Tr. J. Achron. 142 p, mus ex. C. Fischer 1930.   3.00
First published in Russian (1888), in German (tr H. Schmidt, 1893). The present translation is from the 12th Russian edition.

ROBERTSON, ANNE
Music is tonal magnetism: elementary harmony. 32 p, mus ex, typescript repro, paper. Coleman 1948.   1.25

SAAR, LOUIS VICTOR
Examples for the first grade of harmony: Part 1. 50 p, mus ex, paper. Willis 1912.   .50

SAFRANEK, V. F.
Safranek's guide to harmony: a self-help course in harmonic theory

& practice. 68 p, mus ex, paper. Jacobs, Boston, 1923. 2.00
With introductory chapters on the fundamentals of notation by Charles H. Leach.

SHEPARD, FRANK H.
Graded lessons in harmony. Rev & prepared by A. Agnes & Florian A. Shepard. xiv, 200 p, mus ex. G. Schirmer 1914. 1.25
Directions for teaching in courses using "Harmony simplified" below.

Harmony simplified: a simple & systematic exposition of the principles of harmony, designed not only to cultivate a thorough knowledge of chord-construction, but also to practically apply that knowledge and to develop the perceptive faculties. viii, 242 p, mus ex. G. Schirmer (1896) 25th issue rev & aug 1924. 2.00
Part 1 of this book is also available separately (see Children–8).

SPENCER, S. REID
Harmony. 117 p, mus ex. Willis 1915. 1.00

SPIELTER, HERMANN
A manual of harmony: with notebook exercises. 65 p, mus ex, paper. G. Schirmer 1919 (1920). 1.00
Workbook with blanks to be filled in.

STAINER, JOHN
Harmony: with an appendix containing 100 graduated exercises. 126 p, mus ex. Ditson n d. 1.50
"Music Students Library" series.

STRUBE, GUSTAV
The theory and use of chords: a textbook of harmony. 175 p, mus ex. Ditson 1928. 2.00

TAPPER, THOMAS
First year harmony. vii, 177 p, mus ex. Schmidt (1908) aug rev ed 1938. 1.50
Second year harmony. 142 p, mus ex. Schmidt (1912) aug rev ed 1940. 1.50

THIMAN, ERIC H.
A guide to elementary harmony. 56 p, mus ex, bds. Curwen 1941. (1.20)

THOMPSON, JOHN WINTER
A course in harmony. 112 p, mus ex, paper. E. H. Morris, N. Y., 1923. 1.50

TWEEDY, DONALD
Manual of harmonic technic: based on the practice of J. S. Bach. xxi, 307 p, mus ex. Ditson 1928. 3.00
Published for the Eastman School of Music.

VOGLER, JULIUS
How to harmonize melodies. 21 p, mus ex, paper. Briegel 1935. .50
A modern course in harmony. 3 v: 79, 75, 75 p, mus ex, paper. Briegel 1929/1940. 3.00
Also separately, $1.00 each.

WARBURTON, ANNIE O.
Harmony for schools and colleges: a textbook for class use on aural foundations. xiii, 314 p, mus ex. Longmans 1938. 3.00

WEDGE, GEORGE
Applied harmony: a text-book. 2 v. G. Schirmer 1930/1.
V 1: Diatonic. viii, 165 p, mus ex. 1930. 2.50
V 2: Chromatic. vi, 117 p, mus ex. 1931. 2.50
Practical treatment of principles, with emphasis on simplification of their presentation to the student.

WOOD, CARL PAIGE
Texture of music: a manual of elementary harmony. 161 p, mus ex. Humphries 1931. 2.00

YORK, FRANCIS L.
Harmony simplified. 142 p, mus ex. Ditson (1897) rev enl ed 1926. 1.50
"Music Students Library" series.

HARP

See also:

Ancient Music	Ireland (music in)
History	Orchestra
Instrumentation	Scotland (music in)
Instruments	Wales (music in)

Note: Standard works apparently O/P (or not easily available) include those by Armstrong, Flood, Salzedo, Zingel (in German), etc.

RENSCH, ROSLYN
The harp: from Tara's halls to the American schools. xv, 198 p, 29 pl, diagrs, mus ex, 9–p bibls. Philosophical 1950. 6.00
A history, with sections on harp music, harpists, harp technique, harp recordings, etc.

THOMAS, JOHN ("*Pencerdd Gwalia*")
History of the harp: from the earliest period down to the present day. 19 p, △ paper. Reeves n d. (1.50)
Brief sketch only, by a noted Welsh harpist.

Harper, Ralph Moore. Author.
See Voice.

HARPSICHORD

See: esp Keyboard Instruments & Music, & App Ia (Dufourcq "Le clavecin").

Also: History, Instruments, Piano.

Note: The harpsichord, instruments of the harpsichord family, & their music are discussed at some length in many of the books listed in the following categories:

Bach	England (Music in)
Baroque Era	Handel
Chamber Music	Medieval/Renaissance

Harris, Clement Antrobus. Author.
See Troubadours/Trouvères.

Harris, Cuthbert. Author. See

Children–3. First steps in ear-training (1926) .75

Form. Student's short course in musical forms (1932/45). 1.00

Harmony–2. Lessons in elementary harmony (1937). 1.00

History–3. Short outline (1931). 1.25

Harris, Cyril M. Co-author (with Knudsen). See Acoustics.

Harris, Elizabeth Fontaine. Author (with Sims). See Children–3.

HARRIS, Roy

See also:

American Music	Contemporary Music
Appreciation	Phonograph Records
Composers–2 & 3a	Program Notes

SLONIMSKY, NICOLAS
Roy Harris.
G. Schirmer in prep. · △

"Schirmer's Contemporary Composers" series: biography, analyses & catalogue of works, bibliography, & discography.

Harrison, Luther A. Author (with McKinney). See Theory–3.

Harrison, Sidney. Author.
See Appreciation.

Harrow Replicas. Facsimile reproductions published by Heffer, London. See Elizabethan Music, Facsimiles, Handel–2.

HART, Lorenz

See: esp Rodgers & Hart.

America (music in)	Popular Music
Operetta	Song(s)

Hart, William John. Author.
See Hymns/Hymnody–2.

Hartshorn, William C. Author (with Leavitt). See Children–2.

HARVARD UNIVERSITY

Note: Spalding's "Music at Harvard" (1935) apparently is O/P.

See:

America (music in)	Criticism (French)
Boston (music in)	Hearing (Miller)
Colleges	Insects (Pierce)

Harvey, Harry B. Author.
See App IIa (Debussy juvenile).

Harwell, Richard Barksdale. Author.
See American Music.

Haskell, Arnold Lionel David. Author, editor. See Ballet, Tchaikovsky–2.

Haslam, W. E. Author. See Singing–2.

Hatherley, Stephen G. Author.
See Byzantine Music.

HAWAII (Music in)

Note: No pertinent publications seem to be easily or generally available (at least outside Hawaii itself), but attention should be called to Helen Heffner Roberts' "Ancient Hawaiian music," pub by the Bishop Museum, Honolulu, 1926.

Haward, Lawrence. Editor.
See Pictures/Portraits.

Hawn, Henry Gaines. Author.
See Diction.

HAYDN, Franz Josef

See also:

Appreciation	Piano Music
Chamber Music	Program Notes
Choir/Choral–3	String Quartet
Classic Era	Symphony
Composers–1	Themes
Concerto	Timing
History	Vienna
Orchestral Music	Vocal Music
Phonograph Records	

Also: App IIa (juvenile by Ewen, and by Wheeler & Deucher).

Note: Standard works apparently O/P (or not easily available) include those by "Brenet," Fox, Hadow, etc, and those in German by Kobald, Pohl, Schnerich, Tenschert, etc.

ANDERSON, W. R.
Haydn. 16 p, cover por, paper.
Novello n d (1939). .40
Miniature biography ("great musicians").

FRÖHLICH, JOSEPH. See App Ib.

GEIRINGER, KARL
Haydn: a creative life in music.
342 p, 17 illus (pors, facs, etc), 6–p
bibl. (1941) Norton 1946. 5.00
A new authoritative biography, apparently a new version of the same author's "Joseph Haydn: his life & work," published by Allen & Unwin, London, 1941.

GEIRINGER, KARL *(comp)*
A thematic catalogue of Haydn's settings of folksongs from the British

Isles. Musurgia 1951, pending. △
*"Musurgia Studies in Musicology," series
A, v 1; on subscription only.*

HUGHES, ROSEMARY
Haydn. xi, 244 p, 9 pl (pors, facs,
etc), mus ex, 4–p bibl.   Dent &
Pellegrini 1950.   2.50
*"Master Musicians" series, with the usual
calendar, personalia, & catalogue of works.
A replacement of the biography by J. Cuthbert
Hadden (1902/36).*

HUSSEY, DYNELEY
Introduction to the music of Haydn.   △
Dobson 1950 in prep.   1.00

JACOB, H. E.
Joseph Haydn: his art, times & glory.
Tr Richard & Clara Winston. xv,
368 p, 9 pl (pors), mus ex, 6–p bibl.
Rinehart 1950.   5.00
*A recent romanticized biography with com-
paratively little material on the music.*

LARSEN, JENS PETER (*ed*). See App Ib.

NOWAK, LEOPOLD. See App Ib.

REICH, WILLI. See App Ib.

Haydon, Glen. Author. See Musicology.

HAYES, Roland
See also:
America (music in)   Negro Spirituals
Interpreters   Phonograph Records
Negro Music   Singers
Editor. See Negro Spirituals.

HELM, MACKINLEY
Angel Mo' and her son, Roland
Hayes. ix, 289 p, col frontis. Little
Brown 1942 (11th pr 1947).   3.50
Quasi-autobiography of the noted tenor.

Haywood, Frederick Howard. Author.
See Singing–2.
Haywood, Charles. Compiler.
See Folklore.
Heacox, Arthur Edward. Author.
See Ear-Training, Instrumentation, Key-
board Harmony.
Headland, Helen. Author.
See App IIa (Bull, Lind, Nilsson juveniles).

HEALTH (and Music)
**(Musical Therapy, Music & Medicine,
etc.)**
See also:
Aesthetics   Industry (music in)
Appreciation   Philosophy
Children–1   Psychology
Community Music   Religion
Hearing   School Music–1

*Note: Pertinent works apparently O/P (or
not easily available) include those by Savill,
Singer ("Diseases of the musical profession,"
1937), Van de Wall, etc. The lists below do
not include journal-paper reprints or variously privately printed booklets by Eisenberg, Fineberg, Freeman, Heline, Seymour,
etc. For information on these and other
related publications, see the bibliographies in
some of the works below, especially those by
Schullian & Schoen, and Soibelman.*

HAMILTON, WALLACE F.
Health hints for music students.
81 p, illus, paper. Ditson 1927.   .75
*Practical advice on health maintenance, in-
cluding setting-up exercises and special exercises for pianists, singers, violinists.*

LANDOWSKI, WANDA. See App Ia.

LICHT, SIDNEY H.
Music in medicine. Forew Alexander
Tansman. xx, 132 p, 4–p bibl. New
England Conservatory of Music,
Boston, 1946.   3.00
*A physician's psychological & physical review
of the uses of music in healing treatment.*

LICHT, SIDNEY H. (*ed*)
Occupational therapy source book.
Intro C. Charles Burlingame. 97 p,
bibl. Williams & Wilkins, Baltimore,
1948.   1.00

MARMELSZADT, WILLARD
Musical sons of Aesculpius. Forew
Victor Robinson. 116 p, illus, 2–p
bibl. Froben Press, N. Y., 1946.   3.00
*European & American physician-musicians
(Berlioz, Borodin, Schweitzer, et al.); musical
life in the medical profession, etc.*

PODOLSKY, EDWARD
Music for your health. 134 p, diagrs,
2–p bibl, bds. Ackerman 1946, via
Beechhurst.   2.50
*Popular approach: "Music as a good tonic
for the heart," "Music drives away pain,"
etc; including some material originally
published in the author's "The doctor pre-
scribes music" (Stokes 1939).*

SCHULLIAN, D. M. & SCHOEN, MAX (*eds*)
Music and medicine. x, 499 p, illus,
65–p bibl. Henry Schuman Inc,
N. Y., 1948.   6.50
*A symposium by 16 authorities (Frances
Densmore, Howard Hanson, R. L. Cardinell,
Alfred Whittaker, etc) covering various aspects
& eras of musical therapy & magic, and the
occupational diseases of musicians.*

SOIBELMAN, DORIS
Therapeutic and industrial uses of

music: a review of the literature. vi, 274 p, 38–p bibl. Columbia 1948. **3.25**
A detailed, extensive survey of published material & experimental work in progress.

VAN DE WALL, WILLEM
Music in hospitals. 86 p, diagr. paper. Russell Sage Foundation, N. Y., 1946 (1948). **2.00**

HEARING

See also:

Acoustics   Speech
(esp Helmholtz)   Stokowski
Heiner   Voice
Psychology   Warfield
Sound Rec & Repro

Note: Only a sampling (of some musical interest) of the large available literature is listed here. One standard work, now unfortunately O/P, deserves special mention, despite its lack of any specifically musical material: the Polyak-McHugh-Judd "Human ear: in anatomical transparencies," published under the auspices of the Sonotone Corporation (1946).

DAVIS, HALLOWELL (*ed*)
Hearing and deafness: A guide for laymen. Forew Louise Tracy; intro C. Stewart Nash. xv, 496 p, illus (photos, diagrs, etc), chap bibls. Murray Hill Books, N. Y., via Rinehart, 1947 (3rd pr n d). **5.00**
Articles by various authorities on audiology, hearing & hearing loss, tests & aids, rehabilitation, education & psychology, social & economic problems.

FLETCHER, HARVEY
Speech and hearing. Intro H. D. Arnold. xv, 331 p, diagrs, tables, bibls refs. Van Nostrand 1929 (3rd) pr 1936). **5.50**
A standard technical work, based on the Bell Telephone Laboratories' studies of speech, music & noise, hearing, and the perception of speech & music.

GUGGENHEIM, LOUIS KAUFMAN
Phylogenesis of the ear. 277 p, diagrs, bibl. Murray & Gee, Culver City, Calif, 1948. **12.50**
A history of the ear in animals & men.

LLOYD, L. S.
The musical ear. ix, 87 p, illus. Oxford 1940. **2.50**
Seven essays on sound vibrations & aural perception, and the conflicts of scientific theory & musical practice. A complementary work to the author's "Music and sound" (1937, currently O/P).

MEYER, MAX F.
How we hear: how tones make music. 117 p, 20 diagrs, brief bibl. Charles T. Branford Co., Boston, 1950. **2.50**
A summary of some 50 years' work in musical acoustics, including material originally published in some 30 periodical articles.

MILLER, GEORGE A. (*& others, comps*)
A bibliography in audition: a project of the Psycho-Acoustic Laboratory, Harvard University. 2 v: viii, 200; vi, 195, p, typescript repro, paper. Via Harvard 1950. **3.00**
A monumental reference work, prepared under a Navy contract, of some 5500 entries arranged alphabetically by author, with cross-references from such classifications as anatomical, physiological, psychological, deafness, & auditory theory. Co-compilers: Walter A. Rosenblith, Robert Galambos, & Ira J. Hirsch; bibliographer: Shirley K. Hirsch.

STEVENS, S. S. & DAVIS, HALLOWELL
Hearing: its psychology & physiology. Forew Edwin G. Boring. xv, 489 p, 167 illus (photos, diagrs, tables, etc), 16–p bibl. Wiley 1938 (3rd pr 1948). **5.00**
A standard, modern technical work: a systematic inventory of recent discoveries.

WEVER, ERNEST GLEN
Theory of hearing. xiv, 484 p, 138 illus, 23–p bibl. Wiley 1949. **6.00**
Wiley "Publications in Psychology" series. A detailed review in the historical origins & modern developments of the "classical" resonance or place theories & the simple frequency theories; and a presentation of the illuminating new "volley" theory, based on recent electro-physical experimental studies.

HEBREW MUSIC
See: Jewish Music.

Hector, Luther Grant. Author.
See Acoustics.
Hedley, Arthur. Author. See Chopin–1.
Heger, Theodore E. Co-author (with Moore). See Symphony.
Heidelberger, Pauline. Author.
See Teaching–3.
Heikel, Yngvar. Author (with Collan).
See Dances–2 (ed Alford).
Heimeran, Ernst. Co-author (with Aulich).
See String Quartet.

HEINE, Heinrich
See also:

History   Schumann–1 & 2
Poetry   Song(s)
Romantic Era   Song Translations

EWEN, FREDERIC (ed)
The poetry and prose of Heinrich
Heine. xxii, 874 p. Citadel 1948.   6.00
*Some 500 selection translated by Untermeyer,
Wolfe, Lazarus, Kramer, & Ewen, plus a
biographical sketch by the editor.*

LAZERUS, EMMA (tr)
Poems and ballads.   279 p, illus
(Fritz Kredel).   (Hartsdale 1947).
Perma Giants repr 1950.   .95

HEINER, Marie Hays
Hearing is believing.   Intro Rupert
Hughes.   126 p. World Pub Co,
Cleveland, 1949.   2.00
*Memoirs of a struggle with deafness, by the
head of the Cleveland Hearing & Speech
Center.*

Heinetz, Wilhelm. Author.
See App Ib (ed Bücken).

HEINRICH, Antony Philip
*Note: William Treat Upton's study (1939)
of the once-famous, now-forgotten early
American composer apparently is O/P.*

HEINSHEIMER, Hans W.
Menagerie in F sharp.   275 p.
Doubleday 1947 (3rd pr 1949).   3.00
*Facts of musical life in Europe, the United
States, and Hollywood—as seen with both
satirical & sympathetic insight by a noted
figure in the publishing world & writer on
musical subjects, who began a new career in
this country.*

Heintz, Albert. Author. See Wagner–3.
Heline, Corinne Dunklee. Author.
See Wagner–2.
Helm, MacKinley. Author. See Hayes.
Helmholtz, Hermann von. Author.
See Acoustics.
Hemery, Haydn. Author. See Singing–1.
Henderson, Charles. Author (with Palmer).
See Singing–3.
Henderson, William. Editor (with Zucker).
See Almanacs.

Henderson, William James. Author.
See Orchestra, Wagner–2.
*Note. Several other books by Henderson,
including "Preludes and studies" (1891),
"What is good music" (1898), and works
on history, opera, singing, etc, apparently are
O/P.*

Henning, Laura. Author. See App Ib.
Henry, Mellinger Edward. Editor.
See Folksongs–2.
Henry, Nelson Bollinger, Jr. Editor.
See Teaching–1.

HENSCHEL, (Sir) George
See: Boston (music in), History.
Author. See Singing–2.
*Note:Henschel's own"Musings and memories
of a musician" (1919) and a biography
by his daughter, "When soft voices die"
(1944) both apparently are O/P (or not
easily available in this country).*

Henschel, Walther. Author. See App Ib.
Hepworth, William. Author.
See String Instruments.
Herbage, Julian. Author. See Handel–2.

HERBERT, Victor
See:

America (music in)	Opera
American Music	Operetta
Appreciation	Phonograph Records
Composers–3a	Program Notes
History	Vocal Music

Also: App IIa (juveniles by Bartlett,
Purdy).

*Note: Kaye's biography (1931) is O/P; a
biography by Edward N. Waters has been in
preparation for some years, but no definite
publication date has yet been announced.*

Herbert-Caesari, Edgar F. Author.
See Singing–1.
Herman, Julius. Author
See Africa (music in).
Herman, Michael. Compiler.
See Dances–2.
Herman, Reinhold Ludwig. Author.
See Singing–2.

HERMANNUS (Contractus)
See: History, Medieval/Renaissance.
*Note: Ellinwood's "Musica Hermanni Con-
tracti" (1936) apparently is O/P.*

Herold, Hugo. Co-author (with Noatzsch).
See App Ib.

HÉROLD, Louis-Joseph-Ferdinand
See: History, French Music, Opera.
Also: App Ia (Pougin biog, in French).

Heron-Allen, Edward. Author.
See Violin.
Herrmann, Virginia Hitchcock. Compiler
(with Waterman & others). See Asiatic
Musics.
Herter-Norton, Mary Dows. Catalogued
under Norton, Mary Dows Herter.

Hertz, Lilly. Translator.
See Song Translations.
Herzel, Catherine & Frank. Authors.
See Hymns/Hymnody-2.

HESELTINE, Philip ("Peter Warlock")
Note: Heseltine's own books and the Cecil Gray biography (1934) all apparently are O/P (or not easily available in this country).

Hévésey, André de. Author. See App Ia.
Hewett-Thayer, Harvey W. Author.
See Hoffmann.
Heynssen, Adda. Author.
See Dance Music.
Heywood, Robert B. Editor.
See Schoenberg.
Hiebner, Armand. Author. See App Ia.
Higgins, Helen Boyd. Author.
See App IIa (Foster).
Higgs, James. Author. See Fugue.
Hill, Alfred. Author. See Composition.

HILL, Edward Burlingame
See:
America (music in)   Boston (music in)
American Music   Composers-3a
Note: Hill's own book, "Modern French music" (1924), apparently is O/P.

Hill, Frank W. Author (with Searight).
See Theory-3.
Hill, Jim. Author.
See Piano Playing-3, Transposition.

Hill, Ralph. Author, editor. See:
Brahms-1. Biography (1941/8).   1.00
Liszt. Biography (1936/50).   1.00
Program Music. In prep.   △
Symphony. The symphony (1949).   .65
Yearbooks. Musical yearbook,
1945/6, ed Hinrichsen & Hill.   5.00
———. Music 1950 (1950).   .35

Hill, Richard Synyer. Editor.
See Libraries.
Hille, Waldemar. Editor.
See Songbooks.

HINDEMITH, Paul
See:
Appreciation   Modern Music
Composers-2   Phonograph Records
Contemporary Music   Program Notes
History
Also: App Ib (Strobel biog in German).
Author. See:
Composition. The craft of musical
composition, 2 v (1937/45).   7.00

Ear-Training. Elementary training
for musicians (1946).   4.00
Harmony-2. Concentrated course in
traditional harmony (1943/4).   2.00

Hindsley, Mark Hubert. Author.
See Band-2, School Music-3.

HINDU MUSIC
See: India (Music in)/Indian Music.

Hinman, Florence Lamont. Author.
See Singing-2.
Hinrichsen, Max. Editor.
See Yearbooks.
Hipscher, Edward Ellsworth. Author.
See Opera-3.
Hirsch, Ira J. Co-compiler (with Miller, & others). See Hearing.
Hirsch, Paul Adolf. Compiler.
See App Ib.
Hirsch, Shirley J. Bibliographer.
See Hearing (Miller & others).
Hissarlian-Lagoutte, Pierrette. Author.
See App Ia.

HISTORICAL COLLECTIONS OF MUSIC

General Note: Since the policy of the present Guide is to exclude collections of music only and since, in any case, most of the standard ones apparently are O/P (or not easily available in this country), we do not list—

The various "Denkmäler" series ("Denkmäler der Tonkunst in Oesterreich," "Denkmäler der Tonkunst in Bayern," "Denkmäler deutscher Tonkunst," etc).

A. Einstein's "Beispielsammlung zur älteren Musikgeschichte" (1917). However, this collection—with revisions & notes—is included in the "Short history of music" (see History-2, Einstein).

H. Expert's "Monuments de la Musique Française au temps de la Renaissance" (1924/29; via Broude Bros. 1950, $75.00).

H. Riemann's "Musikgeschichte in Beispielen" (1912).

In spite of the general policy, however, some historical collections of music are included in the Guide. See, in particular—

Anthologies (Davidson & Apel, Gleason, Schering).
Counterpoint-1 (Soderlund).
Facsimilies
French Music (Apel).
History-2 (Einstein, as noted above)

HISTORY (of Music)

General Note: The category "history" would require very little stretching to embrace the large majority of all books (other than instruction "methods") on music & musicians. The present lists, however, are confined to histories of music in general, or music-histories as that term is commonly understood.

There still remain so many and such varied works to be considered that the following sub-categories are employed for convenience—

1. General & Large Works

(That is, works about music history in addition to the more extensive, multi-volume music-histories themselves.)

2. Over-all Histories

(General music-histories, other than the multi-volume works in 1. above. Most of these, however, are confined to occidental music, and many of them actually concentrate attention primarily on the music of the last few centuries.)

3. Short & Outline Histories

4. Special Periods

(This is a brief list only, confined to books that cannot be assigned conveniently to the specific periods that have individual subject-headings in the present Guide.)

5. Specialized Studies

(Here, again, the list is confined to books that cannot be assigned conveniently to more specific individual subject-headings.)

For general cross-references, see:

Aesthetics	Dictionaries of Music
Anthologies	Documents
Appreciation	Encyclopedias of Music
Burney	Facsimiles
Children–2	Musicology
Composers (& under	Philosophy
individual names)	Program Notes
Criticism	Yearbooks

Also: under the names of individual nations.

For period & specialized cross-references, see under History–4 & History–5 below.

HISTORY (1. General & Large Works)

Note: Standard works apparently O/P (or not easily available) include those by Ambros, Moser, & Riemann (in German), and in French by Combarieu, Fétis, Lavignac, Woollett, etc.

ADLER, GUIDO. See App Ib.

ALLEN, WARREN D.
Philosophies of music history. xxvi, 382 p, frontis fac, 23–p bibl. American 1939.   **3.00**

A history of music-histories and illuminating study of the changing philosophies underlying all writing about music in various ages & countries. It includes summaries of many early, generally unavailable works.

LEICHTENTRITT, HUGO
(*See also History–3.*)
Music, history, and ideas. xxv, 296 p, 10–p bibl, Harvard 1938 (8th pr 1947).   **3.50**
Studies in the integration of music in general culture and the evolution of the art in relation to its social backgrounds.

(NORTON HISTORY OF MUSIC, ed P. H. LANG)

V 1: The rise of music in the ancient world. (See Ancient Music, Sachs.)

V 2: Music in the Middle Ages. (See Medieval/Renaissance, Reese.)

V 3: Music in the Renaissance. (See Medieval/Renaissance, Reese.)

V 4: Music in the baroque era. (See Baroque Era, Bukofzer.)

V 4: Music in the classic era. (See Classic Era, Lang).

V 5: Music in the romantic era. (See Romantic Era, Einstein.)

(OXFORD HISTORY OF MUSIC, NEW SERIES ed J. A. WESTRUP)

Note: An extensive series in 10 volumes now is in preparation, with the first two announced for 1951 publication, to supersede the older series noted below.

(OXFORD HISTORY OF MUSIC, ed W. H. HADOW)

Note: The following brief listing is largely of academic interest, for after many years of useful service, the standard "Oxford History" is being withdrawn to make way for the new series noted above. Although officially O/P, many of the older volumes probably will be available for purchase at some bookstores for some time (the current list price is $6.00 per volume), as well as of course available for reference in music libraries.

Introductory Volume. Ed P. Buck. 1929.

V 1: Polyphonic period I, 330–1400. Ed H. E. Wooldridge. (1901). 2nd rev ed (P. C. Buck) 1929.

V 2: Polyphonic period II, 1400–1600. Ed H. E. Wooldridge (1901). 2nd rev ed (P. C. Buck) 1929.

V 3: The music of the 17th century. Ed. C. H. H. Parry (1902). 2nd rev ed (E. J. Dent) 1938.

V 4: The age of Bach and Handel. Ed J. A. Fuller Maitland (1902). 2nd rev ed 1931.

V 5: The Viennese period. Ed. W. H. Hadow. (1904) 2nd rev ed 1931.

V 6: The romantic period. Ed. E. Dannreuther. (1904) 2nd rev ed 1932.

V 7: Symphony and drama. Ed H. C. Colles 1934.

SALAZAR, ADOLFO. See App Id.

STRUNK, OLIVER (*comp*)
Source readings in music history: from classical antiquity through the romantic era. xxi, 919 p, mus ex, bibl refs. Norton 1950. **8.50**
A monumental anthology of important writings on music by 87 authors, from Plato & Aristotle to Berlioz, Schumann, & Wagner. Some three-fourths of the selections appear here for the first time in English or in new English translations.

SUBIRÓ, JOSÉ. See App Id.

WESTRUP, J. A.
An introduction to musical history. Hutchinson in prep. △
A discussion of sources & backgrounds.
The meaning of musical history. 32 p, paper. Oxford 1946. .50
The Philip Maurice Deneke lecture delivered at Lady Margaret Hall, Oxford, 11 November 1945.

HISTORY (2. Over-all Histories)
Note: Standard works apparently O/P (or not easily available) include, among many others, those by Abbiati (in Italian), Burney, Dickinson, Dommer (in German), Landormy (in English; see App Ia for the French edition), Stanford & Forsyth, etc.

BALTZELL, W. J.
A complete history of music: for schools, clubs, & private reading. 659 p, illus, mus ex. Presser (1905) rev enl ed 1931. **2.25**

BAUER, MARION & PEYSER, ETHEL R.
Music through the ages: a narrative for student & layman. xiii, 632 p, chap bibls. Putnam (1932) 2nd rev ed 1946. **5.00**
Same, Student's edition. **4.00**

BELGODÈRE-JOHANNES, V. See App Ia.

BRUYR, JOSÉ. See App Ia.

COLLES, H. C.
The growth of music: a study in musical history for schools. 3 v in 1: 530 p, map, mus ex, chap bibls. Oxford (1912/6) 2nd ed 1939 (1945). **5.00**
The 3 parts (no longer available separately) are: "From the troubadours to J. S. Bach," 160 p, 1912; "The age of sonata from C. P. E. Bach to Beethoven," 176 p, 1913; "Ideals of the 19th century," 194 p, 1916.

COOKE, JAMES FRANCIS
Standard history of music: 43 lessons in the development of musical art . . . together with a map of musical Europe. 321 p, illus, col map. Presser (1910) rev enl ed 1936. **1.50**

DUFOURCQ, NORBERT. See App Ia.

EINSTEIN, ALFRED
A short history of music. Tr (by various hands) from the German xi, 438, xii p, mus ex. Knopf (1937) 3rd rev enl American ed 1947. **4.00**
A standard concise over-all survey, originally published in German (1934). This 3rd American edition includes 39 complete musical examples (p 257/411), ranging from primitive melody to Mozart, Haydn, & Gluck (a revision, with notes, of the collection originally published as "Beispielsammlung zur älteren Musikgeschichte," 1917).
Note: a 5th (English) edition was issued in 1948 by Cassell in London.

FERGUSON, DONALD N.
A history of musical thought. xii, 647 p, 31 drwgs, some 70 mus ex, 21-p bibl. (Crofts 1935) Appleton rev ed 1948. **6.50**
A standard American college textbook on the history of music in Western culture.
A short history of music. x, 500 p, mus ex, chap bibls. Crofts 1943 (4th pr 1947). **5.50**
A shortened & revised version of the original edition of the work above.

FINNEY, THEODORE M.
A history of music. x, 720 p, illus, mus ex, chap bibls. Harcourt (1935) rev ed 1947. **5.00**
A standard American college textbook.

GRAY, CECIL
History of music. viii, 284 p, 4–p bibl. Knopf (1928) 2nd rev ed 1931 (8th pr 1948). **4.50**
In the "History of Civilization" series. A highly individual survey (not a textbook), with special emphasis on the pre-Bach era, and a concluding "Outline of musical aesthetic"

that summarizes the views of various musical aesthetic schools.

HADOW, W. H.
Music. x, 198 p, 5-p bibl. (1924, rev ed 1925) Oxford. 3rd ed (rev Dyson) 1950.   2.00
"Home University Library" series, originally published in the U. S. A. by Holt.

HAMILTON, CLARENCE G.
Epochs in musical progress. 278 p, illus, mus ex. Ditson 1926.   1.50
Fourth year of a "Study Course in Musical Understanding," adopted by the National Federation of Music Clubs.

Outlines of music history. xxxix, 308 p, illus. Ditson (1908) rev enl ed 1936.   2.25
"Music Students Library" series.

HANDSCHIN, JACQUES. See App Ib.

HIEBNER, ARMAND. See App Ib.

LANDORMY, PAUL. See App Ia.

LANDOWSKI, W. L. See App Ia.

LANG, PAUL HENRY
Music in western civilization. xxii, 1107 p, 25 pl, 3 maps, 21-p bibl. Norton 1941 (10th pr n d).   9.50
The most extensive recent one-volume over-all survey, correlating musical with other contemporary activities in literature, painting, architecture, etc.

LANGHANS, WILHELM
The history of music in 12 lectures. Tr. J. H. Cornell. viii, 184 p, mus ex. G. Schirmer 1886.   1.50
From the 2nd, enl German edition (1879).

MATTHEWS, W. S. B.
A popular history of the art of music: from the earliest times to the present. 585 p, illus. Church (1891) rev ed 1906 (1915).   2.50

McKINNEY, H. D. & ANDERSON, W. R.
Music in history: the evolution of an art. xx, 904 p, illus, 7-p bibl. American 1940 (1949).   5.50
A profusely illustrated over-all survey with emphasis on the correlation of music with the other arts & cultural history.

(NATIONAL FEDERATION OF MUSIC CLUBS)
A study outline in music history: for use with McKinney & Anderson's "Music in history." 28 p, paper. American 1942.   .30

NEF, KARL
  (*See also App Ib*)
An outline of the history of music.

Tr Carl F. Pfatteicher. xviii, 400 p, mus ex, 8-p bibl. Columbia 1935 (6th pr 1947).   4.00
Columbia University "Studies in Musicology" No. 1. Translated & enlarged from the 2nd German ed, 1930 (orig ed 1920).

PAHLEN, KURT
Music of the world: a history. Tr James Galston. 422 p, 216 pl, 143 b&ws. Crown 1949.   5.00
A popular survey in "appreciative" style, notable only for its wealth of illustrations. Originally published in German, 1947, as "Musikgeschichte der Welt."

PRATT, WALDO SELDEN
The history of music: a handbook & guide for students. With an additional chapter on the early 20th century by Arthur Mendel. 713, 34, 4 p, 111 illus, 19 pors, 3 maps. G. Schirmer (1907) rev enl ed 1935 (1942).   6.00
A standard, compactly organized, & comprehensive over-all survey.

Class notes in music history: general course. 41 p, bibl refs, paper. G. Schirmer (1908) 5th issue rev & aug (by B. H. Haggin) 1938.   .30
An outline for textbook use of the author's (or any other similar) history of music.

RIEMANN, HUGO. See App Ib.

SACHS, CURT
Our musical heritage: a short history of music. xiv, 400 p, 16 pl, chap bibls. Prentice 1948.   5.00
A concise survey covering oriental as well as occidental music, and correlated with the "Anthologie Sonore" series of phonograph recordings edited by Dr. Sachs.

Note: Dennis Dobson, London, publishes a British edition (1949) under the title, "A short history of world music."

SCHOLES, PERCY A.
  (*See also History-3 & 5.*)
The listener's history of music: a book for any concert-goer, gramophonist, or radio listener. 3 v in 1 separately paged (see below) + encyclopaedic index. Oxford (1923/9) 1930 (6th pr 1947).   7.00
(also separately)
V 1: To Beethoven. xiv, 175 p, illus, mus ex. (1923) 6th ed 1943.   2.50
V 2: The romantic & nationalist schools of the 19th century. xii, 216 p, illus, mus ex. (1929) 3rd ed 1942 (1944).   1.75

V 3: To the composers of today.
xii, 169 p, illus, mus ex. (1929) 4th
ed 1950. 1.75
(not available separately):
Encyclopaedic index. iv, 52 p.
1930 (6th pr 1947).

TAPPER, THOMAS
First year music history. v, 269 p,
mus ex. Schmidt 1926. 1.75

VUILLERMOZ, ÉMILE. See App Ia.

HISTORY
(3. Short Histories, Outlines, etc.)
See also: Baroque Era (Gleason). History–
2 (Pratt), Medieval/Renaissance (Gleason).

BOYDEN, DAVID D.
The history and literature of music:
1750 to the present, with special
emphasis on analysis of style & form.
187 p, mus ex, 1–p bibl, typescript
repro, paper. California 1948. 2.75
University Extension correspondence course
with chronological chart & lesson assign-
ments for course "Music XB 30B."

BUCK, PERCY C.
A history of music. 96 p. (1920)
Benn new ed 1947. 1.35

CHAMPIGNEULLE, BERNARD. See App Ia.

DAVEY, HENRY
The student's musical history. viii,
148 p, paper. Curwen (1891), 11th
ed 1932. (1.50)

DURAND, JACQUES. See App Ia.

HARRIS, CUTHBERT
A short outline of musical history
from ancient times to the present
day. 60 p, mus ex, bds. Schmidt
(American ed) 1931. 1.25

KAUFMANN, HELEN L.
The little history of music. xii, 307
p, illus (Reise Lonette). Grosset
1949. .75
Pocket-size "Little Music Library" series.

LEICHTENTRITT, HUGO
(*See also History–1.*)
Everybody's little history of music.
Tr Arnold Elston. ii, 61, 6 p, paper.
Associated 1938. .60

MILLER, HUGH MILTON
An outline-history of music. xiii,
254 p, illus, 4–p bibl, charts, paper.
Barnes & Noble 1947. 1.00
"College Outline" series.

OLIVER, BEATRICE
Compact music history: with contemporary events of general history
in chart form. unp (9 p), paper. Composers Press, N. Y., 1937. 1.00

PARRY, C. HUBERT H.
Summary of the history and develop-
ment of mediaeval and modern Euro-
pean music. vii, 143 p, paper.
Novello (1893) rev ed 1905. (2.25)
For a supplementary book, see History–4
(McNaught: "A short account").

REESER, EDUARD
A bird's-eye history of music. Tr
W. A. G. Doyle-Davidson. 87 p, 20
illus, charts, bds. Continential n d
(1946/7?). 2.50
"Symphonia" series of extensively illustrated
monographs.

ROSENWALD, HANS
A new handbook of music history.
221 p. Wilcox Follett 1950. 2.50
A history in catechism style (some 466 groups
of questions & answers) with concise dis-
cussion. Originally published as "Hand-
book of music history" (1940, Leo Stern,
Chicago; 3rd ed 1945, Wilcox & Follett,
Chicago).

SCHOLES, PERCY A.
(*See also History–2 & 5.*)
A miniature history of music: for
the general reader & student. 53 p.
Oxford (1928) 2nd ed 1934 (5th pr
1941). .75

TURNER, W. J.
Music: a short history. 104 p, illus.
Black (1932) 2nd ed 1949, via Trans-
atlantic. 1.50
"How and Why" series No. 8.

WILSON, M. EMETT
Music history at a glance. ii, 94 p,
paper. Rubank 1942. 1.00

HISTORY (4. Special Periods)
See also:

Ancient Music	History–1, 2, 3
Baroque Era	Medieval/Renaissance
Byzantine Music	Modern Music
Classic Era	Plainsong
Contemporary Music	Restoration Era
Dictionaries of Music	Romantic Era
Elizabethan Music	Troubadours/
Encyclopedias of	Trouvères
Music	Yearbooks
Gregorian Chant	

ABRAHAM, GERALD
A hundred years of music history.

320 p, mus ex, 9–p bibl. (1938)
Macmillan 2nd ed 1949. 3.25

"100 Years" series, covering the century from the death of Beethoven. Originally published in England by Duckworth (1938).

BÜCKEN, ERNST. See App Ib.

GÉROLD, THÉODORE. See App Ia.

MCNAUGHT, W.
A short account of modern music and musicians. v, 211 p, paper. Novello 1937. (3.50)

A supplementary book, covering the period 1900–1936, to Parry's "Summary of musical history" (see History–2 above).

PIRRO, ANDRÉ. See App Ia.

PRUNIÈRES, HENRY
A new history of music: the middle ages to Mozart. Intro Romain Rolland; tr & ed Edward Lockspeiser. xv, 413 p, mus ex, 19–p bibl. Macmillan 1943 (3rd pr 1946). 5.00

With special emphasis on 17th-century opera.

HISTORY (5. Specialized Studies)

See also (for some of the more important cross-references only):

Acoustics	Negro Music
Ballad	Notation
Ballet	Opera
Carols	Operetta/Opéra-
Chamber Music	Comique
Church Music	Orchestra
Concerto	Organ
Conducting	Piano
Criticism	Pilgrims
Dance	Plainsong
Form	Popular Music
God Save the King	Psalms/Psalmody
Gregorian Chant	Publishers
Health	Puritans
Hymns/Hymnody	Scales
Instruments	School Music
Jazz	Sheet Music
Jewish Music	Song(s)
Keyboard Instruments	Sound Rec & Repro
Literature	Symphony
Madrigal	Tonality/Atonality
March	Twelve-Tone
Minstrels/	Technique
Minstrelsy	Variation
Mode/Modality	Violin
Monophony	Waltz
National Music	Women

Also:

Africa	Ireland
America	Italy
Bali	Latin America
Belgium	Mexico
Boston	Norway
Brazil	Philadelphia
Covent Garden	Philharmonic
Czechoslovakia	Poland
Dominican Republic	Queen's Hall
England	Russia
French Music	Scotland
India	Wales

Also: App IIb (juveniles by Barbour & Freeman, Buchanan, Cooke, Macy).

Note: Pertinent works apparently O/P (or not easily available) include Kinsky's "History of music in pictures" (1930), Sonneck's "Miscellaneous studies in the history of music" (1921), etc.

DYSON, GEORGE
The progress of music. 238 p. Oxford 1932. 1.50

A series of historical essays on "The Church," "Castle & Chamber," "The Stage," "The Concert-Hall," "Men & Machines."

EWEN, DAVID (ed)
From Bach to Stravinsky: the history of music by its foremost critics. xii, 357 p. Norton 1933. 4.00

A collection of 20 articles, by various writers, mostly on individual composers.

PARRY, C. HUBERT H.
The evolution of the art cf music. x, 342 p, mus ex. Routledge repr Δ (?) 1950. (2.50)

A standard study, but embodying conclusions now widely held to be antiquated: originally published by Kegan Paul in 1893 as "The art of music"; in 1896 in an enlarged edition under the present title: in 1930 in a revised edition with additional chapters & "A survey: 1893–1929" by H. C. Colles.

Note: The present publication has not yet been available for checking, but presumably it is a reprint of the 1930 Colles edition, rather than a new revision.

SCHOLES, PERCY A.
The Columbia history of music through eye and ear. 5 v: each illus, mus ex, paper. Oxford 1930/8.

Period I: To the opening of the 17th century. 44 p. 1930 (7th pr 1948). 1.25

Period II: From the beginning of the opera & oratorio to the death of Bach & Handel. 52 p. 1931 (6th pr, rev, 1948). 1.25

Period III: From Bach's sons to Beethoven. 46 p. 1932 (6th pr, rev, 1948). 1.25

Period IV: Music as romance and as national expression. 43 p. 1934 (4th pr 1948). 1.25

Period V: The 20th century. 72 p. 1938. 1.25

Brief historical surveys & program notes designed to be used in conjunction with the phonograph-record series, "The Columbia history of music through eye and ear."

Hivale, Shamrao. Co-author (with Elwin).
See India (music of).
Hjortsvang, Carl. Author.
See Choir/Choral–2.
Hobbs, Cecil. Compiler (with Waterman
& others). See Asiatic Musics (note only).

HOBBY (Music as a)
See:

Amateur Music	Children
Appreciation	Community Music

Hoeller, Susanne Winternitz. Compiler.
See Toscanini.
Hoelty-Nickel, Theodore. Editor.
See Bach–1, Church Music.
Hoesli, Irma. Author. See App Ib.

HOFFMANN, Ernst Theodore Amadeus
See also:

History	Romantic Era
Literature	Schumann
Program Notes	

*Note: The great 19th-century German romanti-
cist was himself a composer & conductor, but
he is usually remembered nowadays (apart
from his literary influence) via Offenbach's
opera & Schumann's "Kreisleriana."*

GREEF, PAUL. See App Ib.

HEWETT-THAYER, HARVEY W.
Hoffmann: author of the tales. xi,
416 p, 13 pl (pors, etc), 5–p annot
bibl. Princeton 1948.   6.00
*The first comprehensive biography in Eng-
lish, covering Hoffmann's musical as well as
literary career, & including a list of works.*

HOFFMANN, E. T. A. See App Ib

ISTEL, EDGAR. See App Ib.

Hoffmann, Hans. Author. See App Ib.
Hofmann, Josef. Author.
See Piano Playing–1.
Hofmann, Rostislavo. Author. See App Ia.
Hofmannsthal, Hugo von. Author.
See App Ib (also R. Strauss).

HOFMEISTER, Friedrich
*Note: The 19th-century German publisher &
compiler is known by a long series of catalogues, bibliographies, & handbooks bearing
his name: invaluable reference works to German music & music-book publications over
many years. Interrupted by World War II,
publication of some of the Hofmeister series
has been resumed by the Deutsche Bücherei,
but we have no specific availability-informa-
tion on either the old or new series.*

Hoggard, Lara G. Author.
See Choir/Choral–2.

HOLBROOKE, Josef
See: Composers–2 & 3c, English Music.
*Note: Lowe's biography (1920) apparently
is O/P (or not easily available).*

Holcomb, Clifford A. Author.
See Choir/Choral–3.
Holl, Karl. Author. See App Ib.
Holland, Arthur Keith. Author.
See: Puccini (ed Crozier), Purcell.

HOLMES, Sherlock

WARRACK, GUY
Sherlock Holmes and music. 56 p, 1 △
mus ex, bibl refs. Faber n d (1950?). (1.75)
*A mock-serious musicological study of all
aspects of the great detective's musical gifts,
tastes, habits, & attitudes, including a discussion of Holmes' legendary monograph on
the motets of Lassus.*

HOLST, Gustav (Theodore)
See also:

Choir/Choral–3	English Music
(esp Manners)	History
Composers–2 & 3c	Phonograph Records
Contemporary Music	Program Notes

*Note: A biography (1938) by Holst's
daughter, Imogen, apparently is O/P (or not
easily available in this country).*

HOLST, IMOGEN
The music of Gustav Holst. 164 p,
4 facs, mus ex. Oxford 1951.   3.50

RUBBRA, EDMUND
Gustav Holst. 49 p, frontis por, mus
ex, paper. Lyrebird 1947.   2.00

Holt, Hilda. Author.
See Keyboard Harmony.

HOMER, Louise & Sidney
See: America (music in), Opera.
*Note: Sidney Homer's "My wife and I"
1939) apparently is O/P.*

HONEGGER, Arthur
See:

Appreciation	Modern Music
Composers–2	Phonograph Records
Contemporary Music	Program Notes
History	

Also: App Ia (Tappolet: biog in French).
Author (with others). See App Ia.

Hood, Marguerite Vivian. Author (with Schultz). See Children–3.
Hoover, Kathleen O'Donnell. Author. See Opera–1.
Hopkinson, Cecil. Compiler. See Berlioz–2.

HOPKINSON, Francis

See: America (music in), American Music.

Note: Hastings' biography (1926) and Sonneck's "Hopkinson and Lyon" (1905) both apparently are O/P.

HORNE, Lena

See also:

| Negro Music & Musicians | Phonograph Records Popular Music |

In person—Lena Horne. As told to Helen Arnstein & Carlton Moss. 249 p, 16–p photos. Greenberg 1950. 3.00
The life-story of the noted popular songstress & film-star.

Horne, Olive Brown. Co-author (with Scobey). See App IIa.
Horowicz, Bronislaw. Author. See App Ia.
Horrocks, Cyril R. H. Author. See Teaching–3.
Horst, Louis. Author. See (The) Dance.
Horton, John. Author. See Franck, Mendelssohn–3, Program Music.
Hospers, John. Author. See Aesthetics–1.

HOSPITALS (Music in)

See: Health (and music).

Hostetler, Lawrence A. Author. See Dances–3.
House, L. Margueritte. Author. See Children–8.
Houston-Peret, Elsie. Editor. See App Ia.
Howard, Francis Edward. Author. See Children–7.

Howard, John Tasker. Author. See:

American Music. Our American music (1931/46).	6.00
Composers–3a. Our contemporary composers (1941).	4.00
Foster. America's troubadour (1934/45).	1.98
Modern Music. This modern music (1942).	2.50
Opera–3. World's great operas (1948/50).	1.49
Studies of contemporary American composers (booklets, 25c each).	

See under individual names: Burleigh, Crist, Dunn, Kramer, Lane, Russell, Skilton, (Taylor, *O/P*), Whithorne.

Note: Several other books by Howard, including a biography of Ethelbert Nevin (1935), apparently are O/P.

Howe, Alfred. H. Author. See Piano.
Howe, Mark Antony de Wolfe. Author. See Berkshire Festivals.

Note: Howe's "Boston symphony orchestra" (1931) apparently is O/P.

Howerton, George. Author. See School Music–4. Co-author (with Rohner). See Theory–3.

Howes, Frank Stewart. Author. See:

Ballet. Haskell, ed: Job & Rake's Progress (1949).	.50
Beethoven–3. Orchestral works, analyses (1933).	1.00
Byrd. Biography (1928).	2.75
Gluck. Miniature biog (n d).	.40
Orchestra. Full orch. (1942/9).	(2.50)
Philosophy. Man, mind & music (1948).	3.00
Vaughan Williams. Dramatic works & later works (1937). 2 v.	2.00
Walton. Music of Walton (1942/3).	2.00

Note: Several other works by Howes, including his "Borderland of music and psychology" (1926), apparently are O/P (or not easily available in this country).

Howes, Maude M. Co-author (with McConathy, & others). See Harmony–2.
Hubbell, Richard Wittaker. Author. See Television.
Huber, Anna Gertrud. Author. See App Ib.
Huber, Louis Joseph. Author. See Band–2.
Hudson, Arthur Palmer. Author. See Folksongs–2.
Hughbanks, (Rev) Leroy. Author. See Phonograph.

HUGHES, Adella Prentiss

Music is my life. Forew Archie Bell. 319 p, frontis por, 62 photos. World 1947. 4.00
Memoirs of a leading American impresario, with special emphasis on the Cleveland Orchestra & musical activities in Cleveland.

Hughes, Charles William. Author. See Philosophy.

Hughes, Dorothy. Author. See Dances–1.

Hughes, L. E. C. Author.
See Sound Recording & Reproduction.

Hughes, Rosemary. Author. See Haydn.

Hughes, Rupert. Editor.
See Encyclopedias of Music.

Hughes, Russell M. Catalogued under La Meri (pseud).

HUGHES, Spike (Patrick Cairns)

Second movement. △
Pilot 1949. (3.75)
Continuation of the autobiography of a British dance-music composer & conductor, begun in "Opening bars" (1946), which apparently now is O/P.

Co-author (with McFadyean). See Opera–1

Hughey, (Mrs) Fannie Elizabeth. Author.
See Children–3.

Hügle, (Very Rev) P. Gregory. Author.
See Gregorian Chant.

Hull, Arthur Eaglefield. Author, editor.
See Harmony–1.

Note: Numerous other books by Hull apparently are O/P (or not easily available in this country).

HUMOR (Musical)

See also:

Anecdotes	Quizzes
Broekman	Wechsberg
Folklore	Willson
Miscellanies	

Note: Finck's "Musical laughs" (1924) apparently is O/P.

LEVY, NEWMAN
Opera guyed. 87 p, illus (Rea Irvin). Knopf, 1923 (12th pr 1948). 2.00
Satirical verse spoofing some 14 operas.

SIMONT, MARC (*illus*)
Opera soufflé: 60 drawings in bravura. Unp (89 p). Henry Schuman Inc., N. Y., 1950. 2.50
Satirical drawings (some with brief captions) of opera scenes & opera-goers.

HUMPERDINCK, Engelbert

See:

Appreciation	Phonograph Records
Composers–1	Program Notes
History	Vocal Music
Opera	

Also: App IIa (Hänsel & Gretel juvenile).

Humphrey, Martha Burnham. Author, illustrator. See Boston (music in).

Humphreys, Dena. Author. See App IIa (Mendelssohn & Verdi juveniles).

HUNEKER, James Gibbons

See also: America (music in), Criticism.

Note: Except for the single entry below, the many books by one of the most provocative & influential of American writers on music apparently all are (inexplicably & inexcusably) O/P. Among them are his standard biographies of Chopin & Liszt, numerous collections of essays, and his autobiography, "Steeplejack" (1921).

Intimate letters. Col & ed Josephine Huneker; forew Benjamin DeCasseres. 322 p, pors. Liveright (1924) 1936. 2.98
"Black and Gold Library" series.

HUNGARIAN MUSIC/HUNGARY (Music in)

See also:

Appreciation	Folklore
Bartók	Folksong–1
Composers–1 & 2	Gypsy Music
Dances–2	History
(ed Alford:Buday)	Liszt

Note: Standard works apparently O/P (or not easily available) include those by Bartók, Haraszti (in French), Kaldy, Kodály & Bartha (in German), etc.

PALOTAY, IRENE BANYAY
The history of Hungarian music. ? △
p, mus ex, bibl. Wetzel 1951. 6.50
Announced as the first comprehensive history of Hungarian music in any language.

Hunt, Cecil. Author. See Quizzes.

Hunt, Noel A. Bonavia. Catalogued under Bonavia-Hunt, Noel A.

Hunt, Reginald. Author.
See Theory–3.

Hunter, Lewis Guy. Author.
See Theory–3.

Huntington, (Mrs) Harriet E. Author.
See Children–4.

HUNTINGTON LIBRARY
See: Libraries (Backus).

Huntley, John. Author. See Film Music.

Hürlimann, Martin. Editor. See App Ib.

HUROK, Solomon
See: Ballet, (The) Dance, Opera.
Note: "Impresario: a memoir" (1946), by Hurok & Ruth Goode, apparently is O/P.

Hussey, Dyneley. Author. See:
Haydn. Introduction to the music of (1950) in prep. 1.00

Mozart–3. Introduction to the music of (1950) in prep.   1.00

Tchaikovsky–2. Haskell ed: Sleeping beauty (1949), includes an essay by Hussey.   .50

Verdi–1. Biography (1940/8).   2.50

——. Miniature biography (n d).   .40

Verdi–2. Il Trovatore (1947).   .60

Note: Several other books by Hussey apparently are O/P (or not easily available in this country).

Hutcheson, Ernest. Author.
See Piano Music, R. Strauss. Editor. See "World of Music" series.

Hutchings, Arthur J. B. Author.
See Delius, Mozart–3, Schubert–1.

HUTCHINSON FAMILY

See also: America (music in).

BRINK, CAROL
Harps in the wind: the story of the singing Hutchinsons. v, 312 p, illus (pors, facs), 2–p bibl. Macmillan 1947.   3.50

JORDON, PHILIP D.
Singin' Yankees. xi, 305 p, 12 illus. Minnesota 1946.   3.50

Two accounts of the singing family famous for its sentimental & topical ballads in the mid-nineteenth century.

HYMNS/HYMNODY

1. **General, Handbooks, Hymnals, Specialized Studies**
2. **Hymn Stories & Hymn Writers**

General Note: Hymns generally are classified into two main groups: Ancient/Medieval and Modern; or broken down more specifically into such sub-divisions as Greek (& other ancient hymns), Hebrew, Eastern Church, Western Church (medieval, Ambrosian, Gregorian, etc), German (Lutheran chorale), British & American. Out of the enormous literature on this general subject, the books listed below deal mainly with the British & American hymnody of the last two centuries, and although the term "hymn" covers both texts & music of "songs of praise," our primary attention here is to works dealing at least to some extent with the music itself.

As with many other specialized subjects, whose comprehensive bibliography would require whole volumes in themselves, it is im-

possible for the present Guide to provide more than a selection of the available literature, designed to serve as a representative introduction to the subject rather than as a thorough survey. Besides the actual listings below, other pertinent works (especially those dealing at least in part with ancient, medieval & Lutheran hymnody) may be found under some of the subject-headings given as cross-references below. Others are noted in the bibliographies of some of the books listed. The interested reader who wishes to pursue the subject further is also referred to the Hymn Society of America, 279 Fourth Avenue, New York City 10, which publishes numerous papers & addresses on various aspects of hymnody (price list on application to the society) and also a periodical, "The Hymn."

See also: esp Church Music.

Also:

America (music in)	Jewish Music
Ancient Music	Luther
Asiatic Musics	L. Mason
(Note only)	Medieval/Renaissance
Byzantine Music	Organ Music
California	(esp Stellhorn)
Carols	Organ Playing
Community Music	Pilgrims
England (music in)	Plainsong
Greek Music	Psalms/Psalmody
(Note only)	Puritans
Gregorian Chant	Scotland (music in)
History	Vocal Music
Improvisation	Watts

HYMNS/HYMNODY
(1. General, Handbooks, Hymnals, Specialized Studies)

Note: Since it is not the general policy of this Guide to list collections of music only, few hymnals are included in the listings below and these only because of their unusual musical interest or their inclusion of considerable text (historical introductions, etc) in addition to the words & music of the hymns themselves.

Pertinent works apparently O/P or not easily available) include those by Brooke, Fleming, Foote ("Three centuries of American hymnody," 1940), Julian ("Dictionary of hymnology," 1907/15), Moffat & Millar, Ninde, Patrick, etc.

Unfortunately also O/P (but of course available for reference at libraries) is the late Canon Winfred Douglas's "Church music in history & practice," 1937, which devotes three chapters to the pre-Reformation liturgical hymn and Anglican eclectic hymnody.

BRITT, MATTHEW (ed)
The hymns of the breviary and the missal. Pref Hugh T. Henry.

xxxvi 416 p, 3–p bibl. Benziger Bros, N. Y., (1922) rev enl ed 1948. 6.75
A study of the (Roman) Hymns of the Psalter, Proper of the Seasons, Proper of the Saints, & Common of the Saints.

BYRNES, AQUINAS (*ed*)
The hymns of the Dominican missal and breviary. xi, 694 p. Herder 1943. 4.75
Latin & English texts on facing pages. No music, but biographies of the saints & explanation of the Dominican traditions.

COVERT, WILLIAM CHALMERS (*ed*)
Handbook to the hymnal. lxi, 566 p, 1–p bibl. Presbyterian Board of Christian Education, Philadelphia, 1935, via Westminster. 3.50
Associated editor, Calvin Weiss Laufer. Biographical & background notes for the Presbyterian Hymnal (1933).

DEARMER, PERCY (& *others, eds*)
Songs of praise: enlarged music edition. xv, 914 p, music. Oxford (1925) enl ed ed 1932 (10th pr 1947). 3.00
Co-editors: Ralph Vaughan Williams & Martin Shaw. Music only, but included here as a notable modern collection of old & new hymns of exceptional musical interest.

Note: A companion work, "Songs of praise discussed"(1933), apparently is O/P, at least in this country, but a re-issue is to be expected in the near future.

ELLINWOOD, LEONARD (*ed*)
The Hymnal 1940 companion. xxviii, 732 p, 9 pl (pors, facs, etc), mus ex, 1–p bibl. Church Hymnal Corp, N. Y., 1949. 4.50
Prepared by the Joint Commission on the Revision of the Hymnal of the Protestant Episcopal Church. It includes extensive historical & biographical data, including a melodic index, and an index to organ works based on tunes in the Hymnal 1940 (compiled by Berniece Fee Mozingo). The Companion is also available boxed with the Hymnal 1940 ($6.25).

HAMILTON, ANNA HEUERMANN
Art of hymn-tune playing: consisting of preparatory exercises & studies and familiar hymn-tunes, with fingering suggestions. 22 p, mus ex, paper. Church 1898. .25

(HYMNS ANCIENT AND MODERN)
Hymns ancient and modern for use in the service of the church: historical

edition with notes on the origins of both hymns & tunes, and a general historical introduction. cxi, 911 p, illus (pors, facs), music. (1861) Colwes & Sons, London, historical ed 1909, via Oxford. 6.75
Perhaps the most famous of present-day hymnals, with (in this edition) an extensive historical introduction by Bishop Walter Howard Frere.

JEFFERSON, H. A. LEWIS
Hymns in Christian worship. xvi, 282 p, 15 pors, 2 facs, 2½–p bibl. Macmillan 1950. 3.50
A survey, primarily of the development of English hymns of all sects, with brief treatment of the musical aspects from the practical standpoint of congregational singing.

MARKS, HARVEY B.
The rise and growth of English hymnody. Forew James DeW. Perry; intro H. Augustine Smith. 288 p, chap bibls. Revell 1937. 3.00
A standard historical survey.

McCUTCHAN, ROBERT GUY
Hymns in the lives of men: the First Annual Southwestern University Lectures, Georgetown, Texas, 1943. 208 p. Abingdon n d (1945). 1.50
A general survey, with special reference to the Methodist Hymnal.

Our hymnody: a manual of the Methodist hymnal. With an index of scriptural texts by Fitzgerald Sale Parker. 619 p, mus ex, 4–p bibl. (Abingdon 1937) Methodist Book Concern, N. Y., 2nd ed 1942. 3.50

PHILLIPS, C. S.
Hymnody: past and present. x, 301 p. Macmillan 1937 (1948/9?). 3.25
Historical & practical aspects of hymnology. Originally published by the Society for Promoting Christian Knowledge, London.

POLACK, WILLIAM G. (*comp*)
The handbook to the Lutheran hymnal. xiii, 679 p. Concordia 1942. 4.50
Biographical & historical background notes.

RIDDLE, BLANCHE LEE
Gospel song and hymn playing. 116 p, mus ex, music. Broadman 1950. 1.00
"Enlarging" 4-pt vocal scores on the piano or organ. One of a "Church Music Curriculum" series sponsored by the Baptist Sunday School Board.

ZAHN, JOHANNES. See App Ib.

HYMNS/HYMNODY

(2. Hymn Stories & Hymn Writers)

*Note: Corresponding (mutatis mutandis) to
the "appreciation" type of program notes &
"opera stories," books of this type enjoy a
similar popularity. Only a sampling of the
large available literature is listed below, but
others are to be found in the catalogues of
most religious-book publishers, such as
Abingdon-Cokesbury, Augsburg, Broadman,
Wilde, Zondervan, etc.*

BAILEY, ALBERT EDWARD
The Gospel in hymns: background &
interpretation. xx, 600 p, illus, bibl
refs & 5–p bibl. Scribner 1950.　　6.00
*History & stories of some 300 hymns, with
biographical data on noted hymn-writers.*

BONSALL, ELIZABETH HUBBARD
Famous hymns with stories and
pictures. 136 p, illus, music. Union
Press, Philadelphia, (1923) 2nd rev
enl ed 1929 (18th pr 1947).　　1.25

BROCK, EARL E.
A devotional interpretation of familiar hymns. 88 p. Revell 1947.　　1.25

HAGEDORN, IVAN H.
Stories of great hymn writers.　128
p. Zondervan 1948.　　1.50

HART, WILLIAM J.
Hymn stories of the 20th century.
Forew Bishop W. Earl Leden. 139 p,
bibl. Wilde 1948.　　1.75

HERZEL, CATHERINE & FRANK B.
To Thee we sing. 254 p. Muhlenberg
1946.　　2.00
*Quasi-juvenile treatment: a Lutheran clergy-
man talks informally to his children on hymns
& hymn writers.*

PRICE, CARL F.
One hundred and one hymn stories.
112 p. Abingdon 1923.　　1.50

SMITH, H. AUGUSTINE
Lyric religion: the romance of im-
mortal hymns.　xv, 517 p, illus.
Century 1931, via Revell.　　2.95

WELLS, AMOS RUSSEL
A treasury of hymns: brief biogra-
phies of 120 leading hymn-writers
with their best hymns.　Pref H.
Augustine Smith.　392 p.　(1914)
Wilde 1945.　　2.00
*Originally published (1914) by the United
Society of Christian Endeavor.*

WHEELER, OPAL. See App IIb (juvenile).

—I—

Idelsohn, Abraham Z. Author.
See Jewish Music.
Ikonnikov, Alexandrei. Author
See Miaskovsky.

IMITATION
See:
Composition   Fugue
Counterpoint

IMPRESSIONISM (in Music)
See:
Appreciation   History
Composers–2 & 3d   Modern Music
Contemporary Music   Program Notes
Debussy   Ravel
French Music

IMPROVISATION/EXTEMPORIZATION
See also:
Children–3   Modulation
Composition   Organ Playing
Keyboard Harmony   Piano Playing–3
Keyboard Instruments
*Note: Standard works apparently O/P (or
not easily available) include those by Ferand
(in German), Richardson, Thiman, Wehle
(in German), etc.*

ANSON, H. V. See Theory–4, ed Dyson.

DUPRÉ, MARCEL. See App Ia.

MacDOUGALL, HAMILTON C.
First lessons in extemporizing on the
organ. vii, 23 p, mus ex, paper.
G. Schirmer 1922.   .75

SAWYER, FRANK J.
Extemporization.   64 p, mus ex. △
paper. Novello n d (1890?).   (2.50)

SCHLIEDER, FREDERICK W.
Improvisation at the organ: Book
I. xi, 58 p, music, loose-leaf pages
without binder.   Schlieder Book
Foundation, Decatur, Illinois, 1950. 2.00
*Elementary principles: the first of a projected
series in three or four books.*

WHITMER, T. CARL
The art of improvisation: a handbook
of principles & methods . . . based
upon melodic approach. 73 p, mus
ex, paper. Witmark (1934) rev ed
1941.   2.50
Church organist & concert improvisation.

INDIA (Music in)/INDIAN MUSIC
*Note: The following list is unfortunately brief
& unrepresentative, for most books on this
subject apparently are O/P (or not easily
available in this country), among them those
by Clements, Day, Sachs (in German),
Shirali, Tagore, etc.*
See also:
Ancient Music (Sachs)   Folklore
Asiatic Musics (note   Folksongs–1
  only)   History
(The) Dance (esp Go-   Instruments
  pal & Dadachanji)   (esp Sachs)
Dances–2 (Spreen)   Scale (esp Daniélou)
*The 8th installment of the "Bibliography of
Asiatic Musics" (referred to above) was devoted
to India ("Notes" for September 1949).*

DANIÉLOU, ALAIN
Northern Indian Music. 2 v. Christopher Johnson, London, & Visva Bha-
rati, Calcutta.
V 1: Theory and technique. 163 p,
diagrs, tables, mus ex, 18–p bibl.
1949.   (7.00)
V 2: The main ragas of Northern
Indian music. In prep.   △
*A scholarly study, with extensive documenta-
tion from original Sanskrit sources, dealing
with the theory, technique, & definition of
the ragas. The 2nd volume will contain
transcriptions of some 40 ragas, analyzed in
detail.*

ELWIN, VERRIER
Folk songs of Chhattisgarh. With a
comment by W. G. Archer. lxi, 466
p, 17–p bibl. Oxford 1946.   7.50

ELWIN, VERRIER & HIVALE, SHAMRAO
Folk songs of the Maikal hills. xxix,
410 p, mus ex. Oxford 1944.   7.50
*Both books above include "specimens of the
oral literature of Middle India."*

FOX STRANGWAYS, A. H.
The music of Hindustan. xii, 364 p,
15 pl (photos, etc), 2 foldout charts,
mus ex, 7–p bibl. Oxford 1914.   5.50
*A standard work, based on a study-trip made
in 1910/1.*

GANGOLY, ORDHENDRA COOMAR
Ragas & raginis: a pictorial & icon-
ographic study of Indian musical

modes based on original sources.
V 1: text: history of ragas, iconography, ragmala texts & criticism.
xvi, 224, facs, 2–p bibl. Nalanda
Publications, Bombay, India, 1948. △
*Originally pub in a 1935 limited ed, now
reprinted with a supplementary bibliography.
V 2 (illustrations) is not yet reprinted. A
fantastically detailed, elephant-sized, standard study.*

MARCEL-DUBOIS, CLAUDIE. See App Ia.

ROSENTHAL, ETHEL
The story of Indian music & its instruments: a study of the present &
a record of the past, together with
Sir William Jones' celebrated treatise
in full. xxvii, 220 p, 19 pl, mus ex. △
map, 9–p bibl. Reeves n d (1929) (3.75)

INDIANS (American) (Music of)

See also:

America (music in)   Folksongs–2
American Music   History
Dances–1 & 2   Instruments
Folklore   (esp B. S. Mason)

*Note: Standard works apparently O/P (or
not easily available) include those by Burlin,
Burton, Densmore (many titles), Fletcher &
La Flesche, Ricketts, etc.*

BUTTREE, JULIA M.
The rhythm of the redman: in song,
dance, & decoration. Intro, illus,
& art section by Ernest Thompson
Seton.   xv, 280 p, 94 illus (col &
b&w), music (tunes only), 4–p bibl.
Barnes 1930.   5.00

DENSMORE, FRANCES
The American Indians and their music. 150 p, photos, mus ex, 2–p bibl.
Woman's Press, N. Y. (1926), 2nd
rev ed 1936.   1.00
A standard introductory survey by an authoritative & prolific writer on the subject.

FLETCHER, ALICE C.
Indian games & dances: with native
songs arranged from American Indian
ceremonials & sports.   viii, 139 p,
pl, diagrs, music. Birchard 1915.   2.00

GALE, ALBERT & MARTHA BROCKWAY;
KRONE, BEATRICE & MAX
Songs and stories of the American
Indians. 49 p, illus (photos, b&ws &
map by Mary Finley Fry & Albert
Gale), music, 1–p bibl, paper. Kjos
1949.   1.00
*"A World in Tune" series, book 9, directed
primarily to school children. The music is
recorded & harmonized by Albert Gale; the*

explanatory material & glossary are by
Martha Brockway Gale; the accompaniments
& English texts by Beatrice & Max Krone.

JAEGER, ELLSWORTH
Council fires.   253 p, illus, diagrs.
Macmillan 1949.   2.95
*Indian songs & dances for campers: with a
section on musical instruments (p 231/250).*

MASON, BERNARD S.
Dances and stories of the American
Indians. x, 269 p, 26–p photos (Paul
Boris, et al.), 111 b&ws (Frederic H.
Koch). Barnes (1944) repr 1950.   5.00
*Re-issue of a work originally published in a
limited edition only: detailed information
on the dances and their performance, costumes,
etc, including a chapter on bells, drums, &
rattles used.*

WHEELWRIGHT, MARY C.
Hail chant and water chant. 237 p +
24 col pl. Museum of Navajo Ceremonial Art, Sante Fe, New Mexico, △
1946.   20.00
*V 2 of a "Navajo Religious" series: little on
music, but notable for its poetry & handsome
"sand-painting" reproductions.*

INDO-CHINA (Music of)

See: Asiatic Musics (note only).

*Note: The ninth installment of the "Bibliography of Asiatic Musics" ("Notes,"
December 1949) was devoted to Indo-China.*

INDONESIA (Music of)

See:

Asiatic Musics   Bali (music in)
 (note only)   Java (music in)

*Note: Pertinent works apparently O/P (or not
easily available) include those by Hasselt &
Snelleman (in Dutch), Holt (in English),
Hornbostel (in German), Kunst (in English,
German, & Dutch), Martin (in German), etc.
The ninth installment of the "Bibliography of
Asiatic Musics," cited above, also includes
sections on Indonesia.*

INDUSTRY (Music in)

*General Note: A relatively recent development
(although "work" music goes back to the dawn
of history), the use of music in industry became widespread during the war. There have
been many pertinent publications, but of these
only a few are generally available (or not disqualified from present listing by reason of
reprint format or highly specialized nature).
A 4–p bibliography, with notes, by Wheeler
Beckett & Lee Fairley was published in the
Music Library Association's "Notes" for
September 1944.*

See also: England—music in (Nettel), Health.

C. M. Ayars's book on a different aspect of the music & industry relationship, "Contributions to the art of music in America by the music industries of Boston, 1640 to 1936" (1937) apparently is O/P.

BENSON, BARBARA ELNA
Music and sound systems in industry. xi, 124 p, illus (photos & diagrs), 8-p bibl, 41-p discography. McGraw 1945. **1.50**
"Industrial Organization & Management" series. An attempt to coordinate the available material in industrial broadcasting.

CLARK, KENNETH S.
Music in industry: a presentation of the facts as brought forth by a survey made by the National Bureau for the Advancement of Music, on musical activities among industrial & commercial workers... Forew C. M. Tremaine. vii, 383 p, photos. National Bureau for the Advancement of Music 1929, via National Recreation Assn. **3.00**
One of the earliest surveys.

KERR, WILLARD A.
Experiments on the effects of music on factory production. 40, p, illus, bibl, paper. Stanford 1945. **1.10**
Applied Psychology monograph No. 4, for the American Association of Applied Psychology.

LANDOWSKI, WANDA. See App Ia.

SMITH, HENRY CLAY
Music in relation to employee attitudes, piecework production, & industrial accidents. Forew Joseph Tiffin. 59 p, 8 diagrs, tables, 1-p bibl, paper. Stanford 1947. **1.00**
Applied Psychology monograph No. 14.

d'INDY, Vincent.
See: esp App Ia (Vallas biography).
Appreciation   French Music
Composers   Phonograph Records
History   Program Notes
Author. See Beethoven–2.

Inghelbrecht, Désiré-Émile. Author.
See App Ia.

INSECTS (Music of)
See also: Ultrasonics, App II b (Mason).
PIERCE, GEORGE W.
The songs of insects: with related material on the production, propaga-

tion, detection, & measurement of sonic & supersonic vibrations. vii, 329 p, col frontis, 243 illus (photos & diagrs), 26 tables. Harvard 1948. **5.00**
A report on the work, equipment used, & results obtained at the Cruft Memorial Laboratory & the Research Laboratory of Physics.

INSPIRATION
See:
Aesthetics   Psychology
Piano Playing   Tests
  (esp Schmitz)
Note: Books by R. E. M. Harding & Frank Howes apparently are O/P (or not easily available).

INSTRUCTION (Musical)
See:
Appreciation   Education
Children   School Music
Colleges   Teaching
Also: Organ Playing, Piano Playing, Singing, Violin Playing, Theory (& under such specialized branches as Composition, Counterpoint, Harmony, etc.).

INSTRUMENTATION/ ORCHESTRATION
General Note: These two terms are lumped together here, for the distinction between them is seldom observed either in book titles or in common usage. Most of the works listed are— regardless of what the title may say—actually on instrumentation: i.e., individual instruments and how to write for them. True orchestration (writing for groups of instruments in combination) is seldom treated at any great length. It is given some attention, however, in the books by Jacob, Prout (v2), & Rimsky-Korsakov.

See also:
Appreciation   Instruments
Arranging–1 & 2   Orchestra
Band   Score-Reading
Composition   String Instruments
Film Music   Transposition
  (esp Skinner)   Wind Instruments
Standard works apparently O/P (or not easily available) include those by Carse, Coerne, Evans, Guiraud (in French), Hoby, Hofmann, Wellesz (in German), etc.

ANDERSEN, ARTHUR OLAF
Practical orchestration. 249 p, illus, mus ex. Birchard 1929. **3.50**

BERLIOZ, HECTOR (& STRAUSS, RICHARD)
Treatise on instrumentation. Enl & rev Richard Strauss. Tr. Theodore Front. 111, 424 p, mus ex, stiff paper. (1905) Kalmus repr 1948. **7.50**

The best-known standard work, orig pub in French 1843, Strauss ed in German 1905. The present reprint includes Berlioz's essay on conducting (see also Conducting).
An abridged treatise on modern instrumentation & orchestration. 64 p, mus ex, paper. C. Fischer repr (1947?). 1.25
Super-title: "Supplement to Logier's System of Harmony."

BICCHIERI, ROCCO (*comp*)
The Luz Brothers instrumentation chart for band, voice, & orchestra. 3-p chart, paper. Luz Bros, N. Y., 1939. .50

BORCH, GASTON
Practical manual of instrumentation: with numerous musical illustrations & particular references to the reduction of large scores for small orchestra. 56 p, mus ex. paper. Boston 1918. 1.00

BOZZA, E. See App Ia.

CARSE, ADAM
Practical hints on orchestration. 55 p, mus ex, paper. Augener (1919?) 4th pr n d. 1.00

COLLINSON, FRANCIS M.
Orchestration for the theatre. Forew Charles B. Cochrane. 351 p, frontis, mus ex. Lane 1941. 4.00
Scoring for operettas & musical comedies, with quotations from typical scores.

DEUTSCH, MAURY
Instrumentation and voice leading: for composer & arranger. 31 p, mus ex, typescript repro, paper. Author, N. Y., 1949. 1.00
Orchestration for arranger, composer: ensembles, counterpoint, polyharmony, form. 32 p, mus ex, typescript repro, paper. Author, N. Y., 1949. 1.00
Both in a series of practical booklets; see also Arranging–1, Psychology, Theory–4.

FORSYTH, CECIL
Choral orchestration. 84 p 22 p music, mus ex. Novello 1920 2.00
Scoring accompaniments for choral works, with score of W. H. Hall's Festival Te Deum.
Orchestration. xii, 530 p, 12 pl, mus ex. Macmillan (1914) 2nd ed 1935 (1948). 7.50
A standard work on instrumentation.

GARDNER, MAURICE
The orchestrator's handbook. 53 p, mus ex, paper. Staff 1948. 2.00
A concise reference manual.

GEVAERT, F. A.
A new treatise on instrumentation. Tr Edward Suddard. 339 p, mus ex, paper. Henry Lemoine, Paris, n d (1910?), via Elkan. 12.50

GROVLEZ, GABRIEL. See App Ia.

HEACOX, ARTHUR EDWARD
Project lessons in orchestration. 180 p, mus ex, bibl. Ditson. 1.50
Music supplement to project lessons in orchestration. 63 p, music, paper. Ditson 1928. .75

JACOB, GORDON
Orchestral technique: a manual for students. 106 p, mus ex. Oxford (1931) 2nd ed 1940 (3rd pr 1947). 1.75
Particularly notable for its section on orchestral tuttis & its original examples of specific transcription problems.

KLING, H.
Modern orchestration and instrumentation. Tr Gustav Saenger. vi, 346 p, mus ex. C. Fischer 1905 (1929?). 6.00
3rd American ed, rev enl by the author; includes Berlioz's essay on conducting.

LANG, PHILIP J.
Scoring for the band. vii, 215 p, some 314 mus ex. Mills 1950. 5.00
A practical handbook with many "work projects" in devices, techniques, & mechanics of scoring, especially for symphonic band.

LANGE, ARTHUR
Arthur Lange's Spectrotone system of orchestration: book 1. 29 p + col chart, por, mus ex, paper. Co-Art, Hollywood, 1943. 1.50
A "colorgraphic" exposition of tone-color combinations & balance.

PROUT, EBENEZER
Instrumentation. 144 p, mus ex. Ditson repr n d. 1.50
Originally pub as a Novello primer (1876).
The orchestra. 2 v. Augener 1897/9.
V 1: Technique of the instruments. xiv, 287 p, mus ex. 11th pr n d. 4.25
V 2: Orchestral combination. xi, 290 p, mus ex. 9th pr n d. 4.25

RIMSKY-KORSAKOV, NICOLAI
Principles of orchestration: with musical examples drawn from his own works. Tr Edward Agate. Ed Maximilan Steinberg. xii, 152 p (text), 333 p (mus ex), bds. Kalmus n d (1930). 7.00
Same, paper cover 5.00
A standard work, written in 1891 but not pub

(in Russian) until 1913. Special emphasis on instrumental combinations (true orchestration).

Principles of orchestration: Digest, sel & ed Adolf Schmid. 68 p, mus ex + 83-p music in score, paper. Boosey 1950.   2.25

A condensed version of the Agate translation—Steinberg edition listed above.

WIDOR, C. M.
The technique of the modern orchestra: a manual of practical instrumentation. Tr Edward Suddard. Appendix by Gordon Jacob. 216 p, mus ex. Williams (1906) rev ed 1946.   7.50

A standard work, originally pub in French in 1904 as a supplement to Berlioz's treatise.

INSTRUMENTS

See also: esp Children–4, Instrumentation.

Also:

Africa (music in)	Keyboard Instruments
Appreciation	Latin America
Arabia (music in)	(Slonimsky)
Bagpipe	Orchestra
Bali	Organ
Band	Piano
Bassoon	Program Notes
Bugle	Sax/Saxophone
Children–2, 4, 5, 6	School Music–3
Flute	Score-Reading
Harp	String Instruments
History	Trombone
India (music in)	Trumpet
Indians (American)	Violin
Jewish Music	Wind Instruments

Also: App IIb (juveniles by Balet, Commins, Dushkin, Freeman, Gest, McPhee, Posell).

Standard works apparently O/P (or not easily available) include those by Elson, Farmer, Galpin, Hayes, Hopkins, Sachs (in German), Schlesinger, Schwartz, etc.

ANDERSSON, OTTO
The bowed harp: a study showing fresh light on the history of early musical instruments. Tr Mary Stenbäck, ed Kathleen Schlesinger, rev author. xviii, 319 p, 116 illus, col frontis, mus ex, 8-p bibl. Reeves Δ n d (1930)   (10.00)

BAKALEINIKOFF, VLADIMIR & ROSEN, M.
The instruments of the band and orchestra: an encyclopedia. iv, 53 p., illus, paper. Boosey 1940.   1.00

BESSARABOFF, NICHOLAS
Ancient European musical instruments: an organological study of the musical instruments in the Leslie Lindsey Mason collection at the Museum of Fine Arts, Boston. Pref Edwin J. Hipkiss. Forew Francis W. Galpin. xxxiii, 503 p, 16 pl, 73 drwgs, mus ex, 17–p bibl. Harvard 1941.   10.00

A detailed study with extensive notes, pub for the Museum of Fine Arts.

BOZZA, E. See App Ia.

BORLAND, JOHN E.
The instruments of the orchestra. 47 p, illus, paper. Novello n d Δ (1926?)   (1.50)

BRAND, ERICK D.
Band instrument repairing manual. x, 198 p, illus, tables. H. & A. Selmer, Elkhart, Indians (1939) 4th ed 1946.   5.00

A practical, detailed instruction book.

DONINGTON, ROBERT
The instruments of music. xiv, 175 p, 37 pl, 28 b&ws, 4–p annot bibl. Methuen 1949.   3.75

"What is music?," "How musical instruments work," "Musical instruments described," & "Instruments in consort." Notable for its up-to-date illustrations.

DOUGLAS, ALAN
The electronic musical instrument manual: a guide to theory & design. Forew Osborne H. Peasgood. vii, 141 p, 106 illus (photos, b&ws, 2 foldout diagrs), 1½–p bibl. Pitman 1949.   4.50

Survey, description of commercial instruments & experimental methods, and study of detailed electronic circuits.

EDGERLY, BEATRICE
From the hunter's bow: the history & romance of musical instruments. Ed Boris Erich Nelson. xviii, 491 1 p, illus (author), 5–p bibl. Putnam 1942.   3.50

A largely non-technical survey for general readers.

FARMER, HENRY GEORGE
The Glen collection of musical instruments. 7 p, 16 illus. Hinrichsen 1945.   1.00

FARMER, HENRY GEORGE (ed & tr)
Turkish instruments of music in the seventeenth century: as described in the "Siyahat nama" of Ewliya Chelebi. vi, 47 p, illus. (Civic Press, Glasgow, 1937) via Hinrichsen.   5.00

A translation, with notes.

GALPIN, FRANCIS W.
A textbook of European musical instruments: their origin, history, &

character.   256 p, 10 pl, 8 diagrs, 4–p bibl.   Dutton 1937.   3.75
A standard work by a historical specialist.

GEIRINGER, KARL
Musical instruments: their history in western culture from the stone age to the present.   Tr Bernard Miall. xix, 278 p, 27 pl. 14 drwgs, 5-p bibl. (1943) Oxford 1945 (2nd pr 1946).   5.00
A standard work of concise data on acoustics & instruments—studied in historical order rather than in type classifications.

HEINETZ, WILHELM.   See App Ib (ed Bücken).

JOHNSTONE, A. E.
Instruments of the modern symphony orchestra & band: a pictorial & explanatory guide for music lovers.   102 p, photos, paper.   C. Fischer (1917) 2nd rev aug ed 1948.   1.50

KELLEY, EDGAR STILLMAN
Musical instruments. iv, 243 p, illus, mus ex.   Ditson 1925.   1.50
National Federation of Music Clubs study course in music understanding (3rd year).

LEWER, S. K.
Electronic musical instruments.   101 p, diagrs, tables, 4–p bibl, paper. Electronic Engineering Office, London, 1948.   1.40

MACMAHON, DESMOND
Brass, wood-wind, and strings: the instruments of the orchestra.   xvii, 101 p, 19 pl, 30 diagrs. mus ex, 1–p bibl.   Nelson 1949.   3.00
Non-technical description for laymen, with notes on (British) orchestras & conductors.

MASON, BERNARD S.
Drums, tomtoms, and rattles: primitive percussion instruments for modern use.   208 p, illus (Frederic H. Kock).   Barnes 1938.   2.50
Quasi-juvenile: informal history with notes on how to make & play the instruments.

MASON, DANIEL GREGORY
The orchestral instruments and what they do.   104 p, illus, mus ex.   Gray 1908 (16th ed, n d, 1937?).   3.00

MATZKE, HERMANN.   See App Ib.
NEF, KARL.   See App Ib.

SACHS, CURT
The history of musical instruments. 505 p, 24 pl, 167 drwgs, 19–p bibl. Norton 1940.   7.50
A standard work, superseding Sachs' "Real-lexikon der Musikinstrumente" (1913) &

"Handbuch der Musikinstrumentenkunde" (1920, 1930).   Special emphasis on primitive, ancient, & oriental instruments; and a systematic classification scheme for all instruments.

SCHLESINGER, KATHLEEN
The Greek aulos: a study of its mechanism & of its relation to the modal system of ancient Greek music followed by a survey of the harmoniai in survival or rebirth in folk-music.   Intro J. F. Mountford.   l, 577 p + fold-out chart, 18 pl, 109 diagrs & tables, mus ex.   Methuen 1939.   △ (9.50)
A standard, scholarly, technical study.

SMITH, HAROLD D.
Instruments of the orchestra handbook: by sight, sound, & story.   88 p, illus, paper.   RCA Victor (1918) rev ed 1940.   1.00
With a 4–p (RCA Victor) record list.

YOUNG, T. CAMPBELL
The making of musical instruments. xviii, 190 p, illus.   Oxford 1939 (2nd pr 1947).   3.00
The only book available devoted exclusively to instrumental manufacturing details.

INTERNATIONAL SOCIETY FOR CONTEMPORARY MUSIC

See:

Composers–2	Yearbooks
Contemporary Music	(esp Myers)
Modern Music	

INTERPRETATION

Note: General & specific interpretative aspects of musical works frequently are discussed in books on various types of music (Chamber Music, Concerto, etc.) and on the music of various periods & nationalities.   Also, of course, in books dealing with composers collectively (see Composers) & individually (see under the name of individual composers).

See also:

Accompaniment	Organ Playing
Aesthetics–2	Ornamentation
Appreciation	Piano Playing
Conducting	Program Notes
Criticism	Psychology
Expression	Singing
History	String Playing
Keyboard Instruments	Vibrato
(Bach)	Violin Playing

Standard works apparently O/P (or not easily available) include those by Cortot, Fuller-Maitland, etc.

DART, THURSTON
The interpretation of music.   Hutchinson 1950, in prep.   △

DOLMETSCH, ARNOLD
Interpretation of the music of the
17th & 18th centuries: as revealed
in contemporary evidence. Pref Carl
F. Dolmetsch. x, 493 p, mus ex. No-
vello (1916) rev ed 1946; Oxford 1949.   **4.50**
*Revised reissue of a standard work covering
expression, ornamentation, thorough-bass
realization, etc., and a discussion of the
instruments of the time. No formal bibliography, but many 17th & 18th century
books are mentioned & quoted at some length.*

DORIAN, FREDERICK
The history of music in performance:
the art of musical interpretation from
the Renaissance to our day. Intro
Eugene Ormandy. 387 p, 19 illus,
mus ex, 5–p bibl. Norton 1942.   **5.00**
*A detailed study of the relationship between
musical creators & interpreters, based on the
practice & writing of various eras, from "the
birth of modern interpretation" to the objective
present."*

GOODRICH, A. J.
Theory of interpretation: applied to
artistic musical performance. 293
p, mus ex. Presser 1899.   **2.50**

HAAS, ROBERT. See App Ib (ed Bücken).

MATTHAY, TOBIAS
Musical interpretation: its laws &
principles, and their application in
teaching & performing. xiv, 168 p,
mus ex. Boston (1913) new enl ed
n d.   **3.00**
*Primarily from a pianist's point of view, but
applicable to other forms of interpretation.*

POCHON, ALFRED. See App Ia.

SEASHORE, CARL EMIL (ed)
Objective analysis of musical performance. 379 p, diagrs, tables, mus
ex, chap bibls, paper. Iowa 1936.   **2.00**
*University of Iowa "Studies in the Psychology
of Music," v IV: analytical studies, by Seashore & other writers, of vocal, piano, violin,
& speech performances recorded by phono-
photographic techniques.*

WATKINS, JOHN GOODRICH
Objective measurement of instrumental performance. x, 98 p. Teachers College 1942.   **1.60**
*"Contributions to Education" No 860: an
analytical & statistical study.*

WOODHOUSE, GEORGE
Creative technique: for artists in
general & pianists in particular. 54 p,
Augener 1921 (2nd pr n d).   **1.25**

INTERPRETERS
See also:

Dictionaries of Music	Who's Who
Encyclopedias	Yearbooks
of Music	

Also: App IIa (juveniles, esp Burch &
Walcott).

Also:

Composers	Pianists
Conductors	Singers
Pictures/Portraits	Violinists

And under the names of individual musicians.
*Standard works apparently O/P (or not easily
available) include those by Goodworth, Grew,
etc.*

EWEN, DAVID
Living musicians. 390 p, 450 pors.
Wilson 1940 (2nd pr 1946).   **5.00**
*Concise biographical sketches of some 500
virtuosi: 123 conductors, 92 pianists, etc.*

Men and women who make music. x,
233 p, illus. (1939) Merlin rev ed
1949.   **3.00**
*Originally pub by Crowell (1939) & repr by
Readers Press (1945). The new ed includes
16 new photos & studies of Larry Adler,
Anderson, Brailowsky, Casals, Flagstad,
Heifetz, Horowitz, Kreisler, Lehmann, &
others (26 artists in all).*

FINCK, HENRY T.
Success in music and how it is won.
xiv, 471 p. Scribner 1909 (1936).   **3.00**
*Includes a chapter by Paderewski on tempo
rubato, discussions of the "secrets" of many
famous interpreters, and practical advice to
teachers, parents, & pupils.*

INTERVALS
See:

Acoustics	Scales
Harmony	Theory

INTONATION
See:

Acoustics	Singing
Choir/Choral–2	String Playing
Piano	Violin Playing
Psychology	Violoncello Playing

INVECTIVE (Musical)
See: esp Miscellanies (Slonimsky).
Also:

Appreciation	History
Criticism	Program Notes

INVENTION
See: Bach–2, Counterpoint–1 (esp Goetschius).

IRAN/PERSIA (Music in)
See: Arabia (music in), Asiatic Musics (note only).
Note: The 7th installment of the "Bibliography of Asiatic Musics" ("Notes" for June 1949) includes a section on Iran.

IRELAND (Music in)/IRISH MUSIC
See also:

Dances–2	Harp
Folklore	History
Folksongs–1	National Music

Standard works apparently O/P (or not easily available) include those by Fox, Henebry, etc.

FLEISCHMANN, ALOYS (*ed*)
Music in Ireland. ("Survey" series.)
Hinrichsen in prep for 1951.   Δ

FLOOD, W. H. GRATTAN
Irish musical history: an introductory
sketch.   100 p, pors. Reeves n d. Δ
(1922?).   (2.75)

IRELAND, John
See also:

Composers–2 & 3c	Phonograph Records
English Music	Program Notes

RADCLIFFE, PHILIP
John Ireland. Dobson in prep.   Δ

Irwin, Stevens. Author.
See Hammond Organ.

ISAAK (Isaac), Heinrich
See:

Choir/Choral–3	Medieval/Renaissance
Composers–1	Phonograph Records
History	Vocal Music

Note: The recent publication of Isaak's "Choralis Constantinus," Book 3 (transcribed from the 1st edition, Formschneider, 1555, by Louise Cuyler) is not formally entered here, for it consists mainly of music: x, 456 p (52–p commentary), illus, 3–p bibl, music; Michigan 1950, $6.00.

ISRAEL (Music in)
See: Jewish Music.

Istel, Edgar. Author.
See Opera–2, also App Ib.

ITALIAN-AMERICAN MUSICIANS
See: America—music in (Schiavo).

ITALIAN LANGUAGE
See also:

Dictionaries of Terms	Pronunciation (Jones)
(for pronunciations)	Singing

CERMINARA, GINA
Italian for students of singing. 94

p, paper, spir. Author, Milwaukee,
Wisconsin, 1940.   1.50
A concise handbook with study material drawn from operatic & other musical sources.

ITALIAN MUSIC/ITALY (Music in)
See also:

Appreciation	Madrigal
Baroque Era	(esp Einstein)
Composers (& under	Medieval/Renaissance
individual names)	Opera (esp Jones)
History	Program Notes
	Violin

Also: App IIa (Acker: "4 sons of Italy").

Note: Emil Vogel's famous "Bibliothek der gedruckten weltlichen Vokalmusik Italiens aus den Jahren 1500-1700," as revised & edited by Alfred Einstein, has been published serially as "Bibliography of Italian Secular Vocal Music . . . 1500-1700" in the Music Library Association "Notes" (13 installments, running from June 1945 to September 1948), but a separate book publication has not yet been announced.

O'BRIEN, GRACE
The golden age of Italian music. 191
p, 15 illus. Jarrolds n d (1948?);
Philosphical 1950.   4.25
15th to 18th centuries; artistic & social life at Renaissance Courts, Venice, & Rome.

OLSCHKI, LEONARDO
The genius of Italy. ·vii, 481 p, 2–p
bibl note. Oxford 1949.   5.00
Scholarly essays on various aspects of Italian culture, including a chapter on "The triumph of music" (p 401/429).

RUBSAMEN, WALTER H.
Literary sources of secular music in
Italy (ca. 1500). 82 p, frontis facs
(music), 4–p bibl. California 1943. 1.25
Univ. of California pubs in music, V 1, No. 1. Music & verse in the frottola, strambotto, & other precursors of the madrigal.

(TEATRO DI SAN CARLO.) See App Ic.

IVES, Burl
Wayfaring stranger. 253 p. Whittlesey 1948.   3.50
Informal autobiography of a folk singer.

IVES, Charles Edward
See:

American Music	History
Composers–2 & 3a	Modern Music
Contemporary Music	Phonograph Records

Note: Ives's "Essays before a sonata" (1921) apparently is O/P, although excerpts are included in the music ed of the 2nd ("Concord") piano sonata.

—J—

Jackson, George Pullen. Author, editor.
See Folksongs–2, Songbooks.
Jackson, Sheila. Author. See Ballet.
Jacob, Archibald. Author. See Manuscript.

Jacob, Gordon (Percival Septimus).
Author. See:
Instrumentation. Technique (1931-
40).   1.75
Score-Reading. How to (1944).   1.00
Theory–4. Harmony, counterpoint
(by Jacob), improvisation (ed Dyson). 4.25

Jacob, Heinrich Edward. Author.
See Haydn, Strauss Family.
Jacobs, Arthur. Compiler.
See Anthologies.
Jacobs, Dick. Author. See Arranging–2.
Jacobs, Naomi Ellington. Author.
See Opera–1.
Jacobs, Robert L. Author.
See Puccini (ed Crozier), Wagner–2.
Jacobs, Ruth Krehbiel. Author.
See Children–7.
Jacques, Henry. Co-author (with Gilbert).
See App Ia.
Jacques, Reginald. Author.
See School Music–4.
Jadassohn, Salomon. Author.
See Form, Harmony–2.
*Note: None of Jadassohn's many other books
seems to be in print today.*
Jaeger, Ellsworth. Author.
See Indians (American).

JANÁČEK, Leoš
See: esp App Ia (Muller).
Czechoslovakian   Composers–2
Music   History

Janis, Harriet. Co-author (with Blesh).
See Jazz.
Jankélévitch, Vladimir. Author.
See App Ia.

JANNEQUIN (or Janequin), Clément
See: esp App Ia (Levron biog in French).
Also:
Choir/Choral–3   Madrigal
French Music   Medieval/Renaissance
History   Phonograph Records

JAPAN (Music in)/JAPANESE MUSIC
See also:
Ancient Music   Instruments (esp
Asiatic Musics (note   Sachs)
  only)   History
Bibliography   Oriental Music (note)
  (Bartlett)

*Note: Except for the sparse entries below, most
works on this subject, such as Piggott's
"Music & musical instruments of Japan"
(1909), apparently are O/P, or (like a number
of Japanese publications, some of which are
in English) not easily available in this country.
The 10th installment of the "Bibliography
of Asiatic Musics," referred to above, includes
a section on Japan ("Notes" for March
1950).*

PERI, NOEL. See App Ia.

TANABE, HISAO
Music in Japan. Included in "Western influence in modern Japan: a
series of papers on cultural relations,"
by Nitobé & others. xii, 532 p, illus,
mus ex. Chicago 1931.   4.00
*Tanabe's paper, p 469/523, was once issued
separately, but we have no information on
its current availability or price.*

JAQUES-DALCROZE, Émile
See: (for books by & about Jaques-
Dalcroze) Eurhythmics, App Ia (3 books in
French).

Jarnette, Reven E. de. Catalogued under
De Jarnette.
Jarosy, Albert. Author. See App Ia.
Jarecka, Louise Llewellyn. Author.
See Poland (music in).
Jaspert, Werther. Author. See App Ib.

JAVA (Music in)/JAVANESE MUSIC
See also:
Asiatic Musics   Instruments
  (note only)   Oriental Music
Bali (music in)   (note only)
History   Phonograph Records
*Note: Pertinent works apparently O/P (or not
easily available) include those in Dutch by
Buys & Buys-van Zijp, Groneman & Land,
Kunst, etc.*

KUNST, JAAP
Music in Java: its history, theory
and its techniques. Tr Emile van
Loo; intro E. M. von Hornbostel.
2 v: xvi, 640 p, 165 b&ws, col maps,
charts, mus ex, bibl (407 entries).
Martinus Nijoff, The Hague (1934), △
2nd rev enl ed 1949, via Musurgia. (17.75)
*A standard, immensely detailed work, with
complete musical works in score.*

JAZZ

*General Note: This might well be considered
two distinct subjects: the "true," "hot," or
"real" jazz of the aficionados (which may or
may not, according to the individual authority,
include such current manifestations as Be-
Bop), and the commercial "jazz" of popular
usage & practice, which is vehemently dis-
owned by the true jazzman. Fortunately, however, practically all of the available books on
the subject are by purists (although of various
schools); less rigorous studies by Osgood,
Whiteman, & others, apparently are O/P,
like those of more "acceptable" authorities
as Dexter, Goffin (in French), Hobson, Panassié (in English & French), Rosenthal &
Zachary etc. Apparently O/P also are the
series of Esquire Jazzbooks, ed Anderson
(1947) & Miller (1944/5/6).*

*In the list of cross-references below, those that
might well be considered dubious by some
"true" jazz aficionados are given in parentheses, including that to Africa, for the importance of African influences on Jazz is one
that splits even the experts into opposing
camps.*

See also:
(Africa–music in)	Handy
America (music in)	History
American Music	Horne
(Appreciation)	S. Hughes
Armstrong	(Latin America)
Arranging–2	Mezzrow
Baker	Morton
(Carmichael)	Negro Music
Condon	Phonograph Records
Contemporary Music	(Piano Playing–3)
(Crosby)	(Popular Music)
(Cugat)	E. Waters
Dance Bands	(Whiteman)
Ellington	Who's Who
(Gershwin)	Yearbooks

BLESH, RUDI
Shining trumpets. xvi, 365, xvii p,
24–p mus ex, illus. Knopf 1946.   5.00
*History, with special emphasis on African &
Afro-American heritage; record lists.*

BLESH, RUDI & JANIS, HARRIET
They all played ragtime: the true
story of an American music. xviii,
338, xviii p + 16–p illus (pors, facs,
etc), mus ex. Knopf 1950.   4.00

*A lively history, largely based on inter-
views with surviving ragtime composers. The
illustrations include a facsimile score of
"Maple Leaf Rag;" the appendices include a
chronology, lists of published music, disc &
cylinder records, & player-piano rolls.*

DELAUNAY, CHARLES
New hot discography: the standard
directory of recorded jazz. Ed Walter
E. Schaap & George Avakian. xviii,
608 p. Criterion 1948.   7.50
*A standard reference work listing over 20,000
jazz records with personnel data. This ed
supersedes the original "Hot Discography"
pub in France in 1936.*

FEATHER, LEONARD G.
Inside be-bop. 103 p, photos, mus
ex, paper. Robbins 1949.   2.00
*History, detailed musical analysis, & brief
biographies of some 100 practitioners.*

FINKELSTEIN, SIDNEY
Jazz: a people's music. ix, 278 p,
illus (Jules Halfant). Citadel 1948.   3.00
*A history with sociological emphasis on jazz
as an expression of "social protest" & de-
emphasis of African influence. Record lists.*

GOFFIN, ROBERT
Jazz: from the Congo to the Metropolitan. Tr Walter E. Schaap &
Leonard G. Feather. xii, 254 p, 6–p
bibl. Doubleday 1944 (1946).   O/P
*A history by the Belgian author of "Aux
frontières du jazz" (1932, now O/P).*

GRIFFIN, NARD
To be or not to bop. Unp (24 p),
photos, paper. Author, N. Y., 1948.   .50
Discussion of be-bop musicians & recordings.

LANG, IAIN
Jazz in perspective: the background
of the blues. 148 p, 8 photos.
Hutchinson n d (1947).   2.50
Includes an anthology of 60 blues texts.

PANASSIÉ, HUGUES
The real jazz. Tr Anne Sorelle
Williams. Adapted for American
pub by Charles Edward Smith. xiv,
326 p. Smith & Durrell 1942 (5th pr
1946); via Crown 1950.   2.50
*A new study, including a 90-p discography,
by the French specialist, author of "Hot Jazz"
(1936, now O/P).*

RAMSEY, FRED. C. & SMITH, CHAS. E. (eds)
Jazzmen. xv, 360 p, 56 photos. Har-
court 1939.   4.50
*An anthology of articles on various aspects
of hot jazz & jazzmen by the editors, E. Sims
Campbell, Roger Pryor Dodge, Otis Ferguson,*

Wilder Hobson, Edward J. Nichols, William Russell, Stephen W. Smith.

SARGEANT, WINTHROP
Jazz: hot and hybrid. 287 p, mus ex, 8–p bibl. (1938) Dutton new enl ed 1946.   5.00
Originally pub by Arrow Editions: one of the more scholarly & detailed technical analyses of the musical language of jazz.

SMITH, CHARLES EDWARD (& *others*)
The jazz record book. xiv, 515 p, 2–p annot bibl. Durrell 1942 (6th pr 1946); via Crown 1950.   3.50
Co-authors: Frederic Ramsey, Jr, Charles Payne Rogers, & William Russell. A 108–p jazz history, followed by classified record lists with personnel data, etc.

TOLEDANO, RALPH DE (*ed*)
Frontiers of Jazz. Forew Milton Gabler. xiv, 178 p, mus ex. Durrell 1947; via Crown 1950.   1.50
An anthology of 16 critical & biographical articles by Ernest Ansermet, Roger Pryor Dodge, Otis Ferguson, Louis Harap, Wilder Hobson, Abbé Niles, Hugues Panassié, etc.

Jean-Aubry, G. Author.
See App Ia (Debussy).
Jeans, (Sir) James. Author.
See Acoustics.
Jefferson, H. A. Lewis. Author.
See Hymns/Hymnody–1.

JEFFERSON, Thomas
BERMAN, ELEANOR
Thomas Jefferson among the arts: an essay in early American æsthetics. Pref Horace M. Kallen. xviii, 305 p, illus, 9–p bibl. Philosophical 1947.   5.00
Documentary evidence on Jefferson's attitudes towards the arts, including that of music.

Jelagin, Juri. Author.
See Russia (music in).
Jelliffe, Clara Marston. Author.
See Schumann–2.
Jellinek, Auguste. Co-author (with Fröschels). See Speech.
Jenkins, Grant B. Author.
See Trombone.
Jeppesen, Jeppe. Author.
See Dances–2 (ed Alford).

Jeppesen, Knud. Author. See:
Counterpoint–1. Cntpt (1939).   5.00
Organ Music. Italian, in prep.   △
Palestrina. Style of (1927/1946).   6.50
App Ib. Italienische Orgelmusik.   7.50

JERITZA, Maria
See: Opera, Singers.
Note: An autobiography, "Sunlight & song" (1924) apparently is O/P.

Jewett, Albert D. Author. See Teaching–3.

JEWISH MUSIC & MUSICIANS

General Note: With the re-establishment of the state of Israel, possibly Israel (Music in)/ Israeli Music might be a preferable subject-heading. However, except for very recent publications, most of the literature on this subject deals with its wider aspects as music throughout history & the world by Jewish composers or dealing with Jewish subjects or materials. The 3rd & 4th installments of the "Bibliography of Asiatic Musics," referred to below, include material on Jewish Music ("Notes" for June & September 1948).

See also:

Ancient Music	Facsimiles (Harrow
Asiatic Musics (note)	Replica No 6)
Byzantine Music	Folklore (esp Ausubel)
Church Music	History
Dances–2	Wagner–1
(esp Chochum)	

Standard works apparently O/P include those by Ewen, Finesinger, etc.

GRADENWITZ, PETER
The music of Israel: its rise & growth through 5000 years. 334 p, 16 pl, 7 b&ws, mus ex, 9–p bibl. Norton 1949.   6.00
A comprehensive survey by an Israeli musicologist. The appendices include a chronological table, Biblical references to music & instruments, and a discussion of the Jewish National Anthem "Hatiqvah."

IDELSOHN, A. Z.
Jewish music: its historical development. xiv, 535 p, mus ex. (1929) Tudor repr 1944 (1948).   2.98
Detailed surveys of "The song of the synagogue" & Jewish folksong.

SALESKI, GDAL
Famous musicians of Jewish origin. xvi, 716 p, illus (pors). Bloch (1927) 1949.   8.50
Superseding the author's "Famous musicians of a wandering race" (1927): biographical sketches of some 96 composers, 64 conductors, 68 violinists, 14 'cellists, 86 pianists, 42 singers, etc.

SAMINSKY, LAZARE
Music of the ghetto and the Bible. vii, 261 p, mus ex. Bloch 1934.   2.50

SENDREY, ALFRED
Bibliography of Jewish music. Forew
Curt Sachs.   xli, 404 p.   Columbia
1951.   (*See Addenda note, p 399*.)   12.50

STAINER, JOHN
Music of the Bible: with an account
of the development of modern musical instruments from ancient types.
xii, 230 p, illus, mus ex, 1–p bibl.   △
Novello (1879) new ed 1914.   2.25
Revised edition with notes by F. W. Galpin.

WILEY, LULU RUMSEY
Bible music. xv, 218 p. Paebar 1945.   3.00
*Biblical musical references & a study of in-
struments mentioned in the Bible.*

YASSER, JOSEPH
Bibliography of articles & books on
Jewish music.   6 p, paper.   Nat.   △
Jewish Music Council, N. Y., 1947.   .10

JIVE
See: Jazz, Mezzrow.

JOACHIM, Joseph
See:

Brahms	String Playing (esp
History	Bajarnsky)
Schumann	Violinists

*Note: Bickley's edition of the letters (1914)
& Fuller-Maitland's biography (1905) apparently are O/P.*

Johansen, David Monrad. Author.
See Grieg.
Johner, (Rev) O. Dominicus. Author.
See Gregorian Chant.
Johns, Clayton. Author.
See Piano Playing–2.
Johnson, Claude Ellsworth. Author.
See Boy Voices.
Johnson, Edith. Author. See Dances–2.
Johnson, Frederick. Author.
See Ear-Training.
Johnson, Gerald E. Author.
See Amateur.
Johnson, Guy B. Co-author (with Odum).
See Negro Spirituals.
Johnson, Harold Earle. Author.
See Boston (music in).
Johnson, Harold M. Author.
See Manuscript.
Johnson, Harriett. Author. See Career.
Johnson, J. Barham. Author.
See Keyboard Harmony.
Johnson, William Ward. Author.
See Appreciation.
Johnston, Lawrence. Author. See Band–2.
Johnstone, Arthur Edward. Author.
See Instruments.
Johnstone, J. Alfred. Author.
See Beethoven–3, Harmony–2, Piano-Play-
ing–1.

Jones, Archie Neff. Author. See:
Choir/Choral–2. Techniques in choral
conducting (1948).   3.00
Tests. Music recognition (1949).   1.25
Theory–2. Introduction to musical
knowledge, with Barnard (1935).   2.00

Jones, Charles Reed. Editor. See Career.
Jones, Charles T. H. Author (with Wilson).
See Operetta.
Jones, John Paul. Author.
See School Music–1.
Jones, Llewellyn Bruce. Author.
See School Music–3.
Jones, Robert Gomer. Author.
See Harmony–2, Theory–2.
Jones, Ruth Whitney. Author.
See Dances–1.
Jones, Vincent. Author. See:
Colleges. Music education (in prep.)   △
Harmony–1. Essentials (1931).   1.50
Harmony–2. Alchin: Applied har-
mony, rev Jones (1930/1). 2 v.   4.75
Theory–2. Exploring music (1941).   1.68

Jonson, G. C. Ashton. Author.
See Chopin–2.
Jordan, Diana. Author. See Dances–1.
Jordan, Philip D. Author.
See Hutchinson Family.
Jose, Everard. Author. See Elgar.
Jourdan-Morhange, Helen. Author.
See App Ia.
Joussé, John. Author. See Theory–3.
Jouve, Pierre Jean. Author. See App Ia.
Joy, Charles R. Author, editor.
See Schweitzer–1 & 2.

JOYCE, Eileen
See also: Pianists.

ABRAHALL, C. H.
Prelude: the early life of Eileen
Joyce. 240 p, illus (Anna Zinkeison).   △
Oxford 1947.   (2.50)

Jubb, Florence. Author. See Theory–3.
Judson, Clara Ingram. Author.
See App IIa (Dvořák juvenile).

JUILLIARD SCHOOL OF MUSIC
See: esp Erskine ("My life in music").

Jusserand, Jean (Adrian Antoine) Jules.
Author. See Minstrels/Minstrelsy.

JUVENILES
See: Appendix II (selected lists).

Juzek, Robert. Author.
See Violin Playing.

—K—

Kabala, P. Author. See Manuscript.
Kagen, Sergius. Compiler, author.
See Singing–1, Vocal Music.
Kahl, Willi. Editor. See App Ib.
Kahn, Ely Jacques, Jr. Author.
See Sinatra.
Kahn, Marvin. Author.
See Piano Playing–3.
Kaho, Elizabeth E. Author. See Colleges.
Kanitz, Ernest. Author.
See Counterpoint–2.
Kantor, MacKinlay. Author.
See Folklore.
Kantorowicz, Ernst H. Author.
See Medieval/Renaissance.
Kanzell, Maxwell. Author.
See Sight-Playing.
Kappel, Vagn. Author.
See Denmark (music in)/Danish Music.

KARG-ELERT, Sigfrid
See also: Organ Music.
*Note: Karg-Elert's own books (in German)
& a biographical sketch by Schenk apparently are O/P (or not easily available).*

SCEATS, GODFREY
The organ works of Karg-Elert: a
guide to the organ & harmonium
works of Sigfrid Karg-Elert. 50 p
(incl 3–p music), illus (pors, facs),
mus ex, paper. (1940) Hinrichsen
2nd rev ed 1950.   1.50
*Biographical sketch, letters, & analytical
notes by a British admirer of the German composer best known for his organ music.*

Karpeles, Maud. Editor.
See Folksongs–2 (Sharp).

KARSAVINA, Tamara
Theatre street: the reminiscences of
Tamara Karsavina. xi, 301 p, photos.
Dutton (1931), new ed 1950.   4.00
*Memoirs, by a ballet-partner of Nijinsky,
in a new edition, to which has been added an
"intimate portrait" of Diaghileff.*
Author. See also Tchaikovsky–2 (Haskell).

Kasschaw, Howard. Author.
See Harmony–2.

Kastendieck, Miles Merwin. Author.
See Campion.
Kastner, Rudolf. Author.
See Beethoven–3.
Katz, Adele T. Author. See Tonality.

Kaufmann, Helen Loeb. Author.
See:
Anecdotes. Little book of (1948).   .75
Appreciation. Little guide (1947).   .75
Composers–1. Stories of 100 great
composers (1943).   .75
Dictionaries of Terms. Little dic-
tionary (1947).   .75
History–3. Little (1949).   .75

Keith, Alice. Author.
See Children–2, Radio.
Kelberine, Alexander. Author.
See Beethoven–3.
Keller, Hans. Author. See Britten.
Keller, Hermann. Author. See App Ib.
Kelley, Edgar Stillman. (Composer),
Author. See Instruments.
Kellogg. Irwin. Author.
See Breathing.
Kemp, David. Compiler. See Songbooks.
Kempers, K. Ph. Bernet. Author.
See Opera–1.
Kempner, Stanley. Editor.
See Television.
Kendall, Patricia R. Co-author
(with Lazarfeld). See Radio.
Kendrie, Frank Estes. Author.
See Conducting.
Kennedy, Douglas Neil. Author.
See Dances–2.
Kennedy-Fraser, Marjory. Author.
See Folklore, Scotland (music in).
*Note: The autobiographical "A life of song"
(1929) apparently is O/P.*

Kent, Charles. Co-author (with
Lautner). See Counterpoint–2.
Kenyon, C. Fred. Author. See Memory.
Kenyon, Max. Author.
See Keyboard Instruments.
Keppie, Elizabeth E. Author.
See Choral Speaking.
Kerr, Russell. Co-editor (with Taylor).
See Encyclopedias of Music (Hughes).
Kerr, Willard A. Author.
See Industry.

Ketting, Piet. Author.
See Debussy–2.

KETTLE DRUMS

See: Instrumentation, Instruments.

Kettring, Donald D. Author.
See Church Music.

KEY, Francis Scott

See:

America (music in)   Star-Spangled Banner
American Music   App IIb (Bakeless)

*Note: Biographies by Delaplaine (1937),
Holland (1943), & Weybright (1935) apparently are O/P.*

KEYBOARD HARMONY

See also:

Children–7   Modulation
Ear-Training   Transposition
Harmony   (esp Rees-Davies)
Improvisation

ALCHIN, CAROLYN A.
Keyboard harmony. 3 v, mus ex,
paper. Jones 1923.
V 1: Intervals, scales, chord struc-
ture, primary harmony. 32 p.   .50
V 2: Non-chordal tones, secondary
harmony. 50 p.   .50
V 3: Chromatic harmony, modula-
tion. 96 p.   1.00

CHAPPLE, STANLEY
The class way to the keyboard: a
three terms' course of musicianship
... also a short course in extemporisa-
tion at the piano. Pref H. S. Gordon.
94 p, frontis por, mus ex, paper.
Bosworth 1937.   2.00

DILLER, ANGELA
Keyboard harmony course. 4 v,
paper. G. Schirmer 1936–1949.
V 1: Featuring melody making. 65
p, mus ex. 1936.   1.00
V 2: Featuring harmonic develop-
ment & chord vocabulary. 57 p, mus
ex. 1937.   1.00
V 3: Featuring harmonizing melo-
dies with an elementary vocabulary.
96 p, mus ex. 1943.   1.25
V 4: Featuring harmonizing melo-
dies & analyzing illustrative material.
126 p, mus ex. 1949.   1.50
*The first two volumes originally were pub-
lished under the title "Keyboard music study:
creative method based on ear-training."*

FOWLES, ERNEST
Harmony in pianoforte-study: a book
for the individual student. xvi, 87
p, mus ex. G. Schirmer 1918.   1.50

HAMILTON, ANNA HEUERMANN
Keyboard harmony & transposition:
a practical course in keyboard work
for every piano & organ student.
3 v, paper. Summy 1916 (1944).
Preliminary studies for earlier grades.
24 p, mus ex.   .40
V 2: The principal triads & dissonant
chords; the secondary triads; passing
notes. 31 p, mus ex.   .40
V 3: Suspensions, anticipations,
modulation, altered chords, organ-
point. 24 p, mus ex.   .40

HEACOX, ARTHUR E.
Harmony for ear, eye, and keyboard.
x, 185 p, mus ex. Ditson 1922.   1.50
*First-year studies, including ear-training
outlines by Gladys Ferry Moore.*
Keyboard training in harmony: exercises graded & designed to lead from
the easiest 1st-year keyboard harmony up to the difficult sight-playing
tests set for advanced students. 2
v, paper. Schmidt 1917.
V 1: 59 p, mus ex.   1.25
V 2: 63 p, mus ex.   1.25

HOLT, HILDA
Harmony at your keyboard: a practical approach to keyboard harmony.
108 p, mus ex. C. Fischer 1950.   3.00

JOHNSON, J. BARHAM
Keyboard harmony for beginners.
iv, 59 p, mus ex, paper. Oxford 1947.   2.50
*Especially for beginners at the piano who
have not yet studied harmony.*

LOWRY, MARGARET
Keyboard approach to harmony. vi,
87 p, mus ex. Presser 1949.   1.25

McHOSE, ALLEN I. & WHITE, DONALD F.
Keyboard and dictation manual. xii,
169 p, mus ex. Crofts 1949.   3.25
*"Eastman School of Music" series. Correla-
ting keyboard & dictation drills with written
work; designed to supplement McHose's
"Contrapuntal harmonic technique of the 18th
century" (see Counterpoint–1).*

MORRIS, R. O.
Figured harmony at the keyboard,
Part 1. vi, 57 p, mus ex, paper.
Oxford 1932.   1.50
*For beginners as a supplement to paper work
with a harmony textbook. Part 2, largely de-
voted to Bach chorales (music only), is $1.25.*

NEVINS, WILLARD I. & LANG, VIOLA
Harmony at the keyboard. 48 p, mus
ex.   Gray 1946.   2.50

ROEDER, CARL M.
A practical keyboard harmony: presenting the subject of keys & chord
drills in a simple & comprehensive
course. Forew George Wedge. 32
p, mus ex, paper. Schroeder 1939.   .75
Exercises only, except for brief foreword.

SCOVILL, MODENA
Keyboard harmony. vi, 150 p, mus
ex, paper, spir. C. Fischer 1939.   1.25

SMITH, USELMA CLARKE;
Keyboard harmony: a practical
course for use in class or self-instruction. xi, 87 p, mus ex, paper. Boston
1916.   1.25

TAPPER, THOMAS
The ABC of keyboard harmony. 27
p, mus ex, paper. Schmidt n d.   1.25

WEDGE, GEORGE
Keyboard harmony: a practical application of music theory, including
the study of melody harmonization,
broken chords & arpeggios, modulation, & improvisation. vi, 194 p, mus
ex. G. Schirmer 1924.   3.00
*A companion work to the author's other
manuals. See Ear-Training, Harmony-2,
Rhythm, & Theory-2.*

KEYBOARD INSTRUMENTS & MUSIC

See also:
Accompaniment   Medieval/Renaissance
Appreciation   Organ
Elizabethan Music   Organ Music
England-music in (esp   Organ Playing
  Van den Borren)   Piano
History   Piano Music
Instruments   Piano Playing
Interpretation
Also: Composers (& under individual
names).
Note: James's *"Early keyboard instruments"*
(1930) apparently is O/P.

BACH, CARL PHILIPP EMANUEL
Essay on the true art of playing keyboard instruments. Tr & ed William
J. Mitchell. xiii, 449 p, 4 illus (pors
& facs), mus ex, 4–p bibl. Norton
1949.   6.00
*The famous "Versuch über die wahre Art das
Clavier zu spielen" (1753 & 1762) in its first
complete English translation, including Bach's
revisions for later German editions. An
authoritative work on 18th-century music in
general, it includes detailed studies on finger-*

*ing, ornamentation, thoroughbass realization,
accompaniment, & improvisation.*

BEDBROOK, GERALD STARES
Keyboard music from the middle ages
to the beginnings of the baroque.
xvi, 170 p, col frontis, 12 pl (pors,
facs, etc), mus ex, 10–p bibl. Mac-
millan 1949.   4.50
*A critical study of early music for keyboard
instruments up to the North European schools
and the first examples of baroque.*

DUFOURCQ, NORBERT. See App Ia.

KENYON, MAX
Harpsichord music: a survey of the
virginals, spinet, harpsichord, & their
Continental equivalents; the people
who played upon them; the composers for them; & the music they
wrote. 256 p, 9–p illus, mus ex, chap
bibls. Cassell 1949.   4.25
*A survey for the general reader, inspired by
performances of relatively unfamiliar music
on the BBC's "Third Programme."*

SACHS, CURT (ed)
The evolution of piano music, 1350-
1700. 39 p, 3 pl, music, paper. Marks
1944.   1.00
*An anthology of some 20 keyboard composi-
tions with historical notes, pub to accompany
harpsichord recordings of the same works by
Sylvia Marlowe (Bost Records).*

Keynes, Geoffrey. Author.
See Ballet (ed Haskell).
Kidd, J. R. Co-author (with Strauss).
See Teaching-1.
Kidson, Frank. Author.
See Beggar's Opera.
Killough, Gibbon Chambers. Author.
See Theory-3.

KINDERGARTEN

See:
Children   School Music
Education   Teaching

King, A. Hyatt. Author.
See Chamber Music.
King, George S. Author.
See Beethoven-2.

KING'S MUSIC

See:
England-music in   Medieval/Renaissance
  (esp Lafontaine)   (esp Kantorowicz)

Kinscella, Hazel Gertrude. Author.
See:
Children-2. History sings (1948).   2.00

School Music–1. Music in the small school (1939). New ed in prep. △

School Music–2. Music & romance (1930/41). 2.25

App IIb. Stories, 6 v (1939/51). △

Kirkell, Miriam H. Author.
See Dances–2.

Kirkpatrick, Ralph. Editor.
Bach–2, Scarlatti, App Ib (Forkel).

Kirstein, Lincoln. Author.
See Ballet (ed Haskell).
Note: Other books by Kirstein, including "Dance" (1935), apparently are O/P.

Kisch-Arndt, Ruth. Author.
See Singing–2.

Kitson, Charles Herbert. Author.
See:
Composition. Elements of (1936). 1.50
——. Unacc. vocal (1930). 1.25
Counterpoint–1. Art of (1924). 4.00
——. Applied strict (1916/49). 1.75
Counterpoint–2. Beginners (1927). 1.50
—. Invertible & canon (1928). 2.00
Fugue. Elements (1929). 2.50
Harmony–1. Evolution of (1924). 5.00
Harmony–2. Elementary (1920). 3.50
——. Contrapuntal (1931/43). 1.50
Theory–3. Rudiments (1927). 1.00

Klarmann, (Rev) Andrew Francis.
Author. See Gregorian Chant.

Klauwell, Otto. Author.
See Piano Playing–2.

Klein, Adrian Bernard Leopold. Author.
See Color (& music).

Klein, Hermann. Author.
Note: All of Klein's books (on Bel Canto Opera, Patti, etc.) apparently are O/P.

Klein, John. Editor. See Organ Music.

Klein, Walter Conrad. Author.
See Beissel.

Kling, H. Author.
See Instrumentation, Transposition.

Klotz, Hans. Author. See App Ib.

Knapp, Ida C. Author. See Children–1.

Kneisel, Franz. Author.
See Violin Playing.

Kneisel, Jessie Haskam. Author.
See Mörike.

Knight, W. F. Jackson. Editor.
See Augustine.

Knight, George Moran, Jr. Author.
See Copyright.

Knorr, Frederick. Arranger.
See Cowboy (Shaw).

Knott, Thomas B. Author.
See Piano Playing–2.

KNOWLEDGE (Musical)
See:

Appreciation	History
Dictionaries of Music	Musicianship
Dictionaries of Terms	(note only)
Encyclopedias of	Musicology
Music	Theory

Note: Most books whose titles include this term deal with Theory.

Knox, William Morgan. Author.
See Violin Playing.

Knudsen, Vern Oliver. Author.
See Acoustics.

Kobald, Karl. Author. See App Ib.

Kobbé, Gustav. Author. See Opera–3.
Note: Various other books by Kobbé apparently are O/P.

Koch, Casper P. Author.
See Organ Playing.

Köchel, Ludwig Ritter von. Editor.
See Mozart–3, App Ib.

Kochnitzky, Leon. Author.
See Sax/Saxophone.

KODÁLY, Zoltán
See:

Appreciation	Hungarian Music
Composers–2	National Music
Contemporary Music	Phonograph Records
Folklore	Program Notes
History	

Note: Kodály's own books on folksong (written in Hungarian) apparently are O/P or not easily available in this country.

Koechlin, Charles Louise Eugène.
Author. See Counterpoint–2, Fauré, App Ia.

Kolb, Annette. Author. See App Ib.

Kolb, John Harrison & Sylvia. Editors.
See Folksongs–2.

Kolodin, Irving. Author.
See Opera–4, Phonograph Records.
Note: "The critical composer" (1940) ed by Kolodin & "The kingdom of swing" (1939) by Goodman & Kolodin apparently are O/P.

Komorzynski, Egon. Author. See App Ib.

Kopp, George A. Co-author (with Potter & Green). See Speech.

Kopp, Tilly. Editor. See App Ib.

Korb, Arthur. Author.
See Song-writing.

KOREA (Music in)/KOREAN MUSIC
See: Asiatic Musics (note only).
Note: The 10th installment of the "Bibliography of Asiatic Musics" ("Notes" for March 1950) contains a section on Korea.

Korn, Ralph Herman. Author.
See Amateur Music.

Korson, George. Editor. See Folklore.
Co-editor (with Emrich). See Children–7.

Kothe, Bernhard. Compiler.
See App Ib (Weigl).

KOUSSEVITZKY, Serge

See also:

America (music in)	Conductors
American Music	Interpreters
Berkshire Festivals	Phonograph Records
Boston (music in)	

Note: Koussevitzky's own paper, "Poetry and music" (1938), & a biography by Lourié (1938) apparently are O/P.

LEICHTENTRITT, HUGO
Serge Koussevitzky: the Boston
Symphony Orchestra & the new
American music. vi, 199 p, frontis.
Harvard 1946.   3.00

Except for 2 chapters ("The Artist Koussevitzky" & "Koussevitzky as an educator"), this book deals mainly with the American composers sponsored by the conductor.

SMITH, MOSES
Koussevitzky. 400 p, photos. Allen
Towne 1947, via Crown.   4.00

A full-length, unauthorized (& protested), but far from unsympathetic biography. The appendices include lists of recordings, world premières, American composers, & commissioned compositions.

KRAMER, A. Walter.

See also: America (music in), Composers–3a.

HOWARD, JOHN TASKER
A. Walter Kramer. 30 p, frontis por,
mus ex, paper. J. Fischer 1926.   .25
List of works & brief analyses.

Krasno, Hecky. Co-author (with Eisenberg). See Children–2.

Kraus, Oscar. Author.
See Schweitzer–2.

Kraus, Richard G. Author. See Dances–2.

Kreckel, Philip. Author.
See Modulation.

Krehbiel, Henry Edward. Author.
See Appreciation, Opera–3.

Note: Various other books by Krehbiel apparently are O/P.

KREISLER, Fritz

See also:

America (music in)	Violin Playing
Phonograph Records	Violinists

Note: Roy's biography apparently is O/P.

LOCHNER, LOUIS P.
Fritz Kreisler. xx, 455 p + 9 pl
(pors, etc), 1 fac, 9–p bibl, 6–p
thematic catalogue. Macmillan
1950.   5.00

Announced as the "first & only biography," with chapters on Kreisler's "hoaxes," accompanists, colleagues, violins, rare-book collection, etc, plus 12-p discography.

KŘENEK, Ernst. Composer, author.

See:

Composers–2	History
Contemporary Music	Modern Music

For books by Křenek, See Counterpoint–1,
App Ib.

Note: Křenek's book on modern music (in German 1936, in English, "Music here and now" 1939) apparently is O/P, while 2 collections of Hamline Studies in Musicology, ed Křenek, either are O/P or not easily available.

Kretzschmar, Florence. Editor.
See Bibliography.

KREUTZER, Rodolphe

See also:

History	Violin Playing
Violin Music	

CUTTER, BENJAMIN
How to study Kreutzer: a handbook
for the daily use of violin teachers &
violin students. . . iv, 56 p, mus ex.
Ditson 1903.   1.25
"Music Students Library" series.

WINN, EDITH L.
How to prepare for Kreutzer: a book
for teachers. . . . iv, 265 p, mus ex.
C. Fischer 1910 (1930).   1.50

How to study Kreutzer: a detailed
descriptive analysis of how to practice these studies . . . viii, 61 p, por,
mus ex. C. Fischer (1910?) 1926.   1.00

Krevit, William. Author.
See Children–1.

Krinke, Harry. Author. See Theory–3.

Krone, (Mrs.) Beatrice Perham.
Author. Catalogued under Perham, Beatrice.

Krone, Max Thomas. Author. See:

Choir/Choral–2. Expressive conducting (1945).   1.50

Indians (American). Songs & Stories, by Gales & Krones (1949).   1.00

School Music–4. Chorus & its conductor (1945).   2.00

Theory–2. Fundamentals of musicianship, by Smith & Krone (1937/-40). 2 v, each   3.00

Same, abridged ed. 2 v, each   2.00

Krug, James I. Co-translator (with Spaeth). See Opera–3.
Kruseman, Philip. Editor. See Beethoven–1.
Kull, Hans. Author. See App Ib.
Kunel, Maurice. Author. See App Ia.

Kunst, Jaap. Author. See Java (music in)/Javanese Music.
Kurth, Ernst. Author. See App Ib.
Kurtz, Marion. Co-author (with Reever). See Children–8.
Kvet, J. M. Author.
Note: Kvet's studies of Dvořák & Smetana, once announced by Hinrichsen as "in preparation," have been indefinitely postponed.

Kwalwasser, Jacob. Author. See School Music–1. (With Dykema). Tests.
Kwartin, Bernard. Author. See Singing–1.
Kwasnik, Walter. Author. See App Ib.

—L—

Lacey, Marion. Author. See Children–4.
Lacroix, Jean. Editor. See App Ib.
Lachmann, Robert. Author.
See App Ib (ed Bücken).
Ladd, Valeria Gibson. Author.
See Dances–1.
Lafontaine, Henry Cart de. Author.
See England (music in).
Lagerberg, A. Co-compiler (with Eitner, et al.). See App Ib (Eitner).

Lahee, Henry Charles. Author.
See Pianists, Singers.
Note: Numerous other books by Lahee, especially on opera, apparently are O/P.

Lake, M. L. Author. See Arranging–1.
Lakond, Wladimir. Editor.
See Tchaikovsky–1.
La Laurencie, Lionel de. Author.
See App Ia.
Lalo, Pierre. Author. See App Ia.

LAMBERT, Constant
See also:

Ballet	Contemporary Music
Choir/Choral–3	English Music
(esp Manners)	History
Composers–2 & 3d	Phonograph Records
Conductors	Program Notes

Author. See also Purcell (Mandinian).

Music ho!: a study of music in de-
cline. 295 p. (1934) Scribner 1935.   **3.75**
Same, cheap ed. 240 p. Faber 2nd
rev ed 1937 (repr 1947).   **(2.75)**
Same, Penguin repr 1949.   Δ
A controversial, extremely lively study of modern music & its composers, including discussions of "Nationalism and the exotic," "The mechanical stimulus," etc. The British Penguin reprint apparently is restricted from sale in the United States.

LAMOND, Frederic
See also: Phonograph Records, Pianists.
The memoirs of Frederic Lamond.
Forew Ernest Newman; intro Irene
Triesch Lamond. 130 p, 11 pl (pors,
etc). William Maclellan, Glasgow,
1949.   **(3.00)**
The noted Scottish pianist's reminiscences; introduction & postscript by his widow.

Note: Lamond's own booklet, "Beethoven: notes on the sonatas," apparently is O/P (or not easily available in this country).

Lambotte, Lucien. Author. See App Ia.
La Meri (pseud of Russell Meriwether Hughes). Author. See Dances–2.
Lamperti, Francesco. Author.
See Singing–2.

LANDINO (Landini), Francesco
See: History, Medieval/Renaissance.
Note: Ellinwood's edition of Landino's works (1939) apparently is O/P.

Landormy, Paul. Author. See App Ia.
Landowski, Wanda Alice. Author.
See App Ia.

LANE, Eastwood
See also: American Music, Composers–3a.

HOWARD, JOHN TASKER
Eastwood Lane. 29 p, frontis por,
mus ex, paper. J. Fischer 1925.   .25
List of works & brief analyses.

Lang, Iain. Author. See Jazz.
Lang, Paul Henry. Author.
See Classic Era, History–2.
Lang, Philip J. Author.
See Instrumentation/Orchestration.
Lang, Viola. Co-author (with Nevins).
See Keyboard Harmony.
Lange, Arthur. Author.
See Instrumentation.
Langer, Susanne K. Author.
See Philosophy.
Langhans, Wilhelm. Author.
See History–2.

LANGUAGE(S)
See: German, French, Italian, Latin.
Also:

Choral Speaking	Pronunciation
Diction	Speech

LANGUAGE (TONE)
See: Speech (Pike).

Langwill, Lyndsay G. Author.
See Bassoon.

LANIER, Sidney

See also: Literature, Poetry.

Note: Lanier's own "Music and poetry" (1898) *apparently is O/P.*

STARKE, AUBREY
Sidney Lanier: a biographical &
critical study. xvi, 525 p, 30 illus
(pors, facs, etc), mus ex, 19–p bibl.
North Carolina 1933.   5.00
A study of the famous American poet, musician, & writer on music. Chapter 8 is on "Music" (p 160/74), chapter 17 on "Music & poetry" (p 346/61).

LaPrade, Ernest. Author.
See Children–4, Radio Music.

Larsen, Jens Peter. Author. See App Ib.

Larson, Glen. Author.
See Wind Instruments.

Larson, William S. Editor.
See Education.

La Salle, Dorothy. Compiler.
See Dances–1.

LASSUS, Orlande de

See: App Ia (Van den Borren).

Also: History, Medieval/Renaissance.

Latham, Peter. Author. See Brahms–1.

LATIN LANGUAGE

See also:

Church Music	Plainsong
Diction	Pronunciation
Gregorian (esp	Singing
Klarmann)	

Also (for books in Latin): App Ie.

Note: Scarre's "Introduction to liturgical Latin" (1933) apparently is O/P.

DE ANGELIS, MICHAEL
The correct pronunciation of Latin
according to Roman usage: with a
phonetic arrangement of the texts of
the Ordinary of the Mass, Requiem
Mass, Responses at Mass, Benediction Hymns, & Hymns in honor of
the Blessed Virgin Mary. Ed Nicola
A. Montani. 47 p, mus ex, paper.
St Gregory Guild, Philadelphia (1937)
2nd rev ed n d.)   1.00

LATIN AMERICA (Music in)/LATIN-AMERICAN MUSIC

General Note: Out of the large literature on this subject, comparatively few books appear to be in print or at least easily & generally available. Readers anxious to obtain more detailed information are advised to consult the bibliographies of some of the books listed below

& also the Music Division of the Pan American Union, Washington 6, D. C., which has published a long series of pamphlets, many of which are now O/P.

For convenience, we itemize herewith the twenty Latin-American republics, whose musical activities are discussed in Slonimsky's "Music of Latin America" (see below). In *the present Guide only those countries indicated with an asterisk (*) have major subject-heading entries; the others are merely cross-referenced to the present subject-heading.*

Argentina	Haiti
Bolivia	Honduras
*Brazil	*Mexico
Chile	Nicaragua
Colombia	Panama
Costa Rica	Paraguay
Cuba	*Peru
*Dominican Republic	(El) Salvador
Ecuador	Uruguay
Guatemala	Venezuela

See also:

Chávez	Dances–2 (esp
Composers–2 & 3a	Leaf, Sedillo)
Contemporary Music	Folklore
	Songbooks

(An 8-page mimeographed list, "Our Neighbors to the South," MP-310, periodically revised, available for 15¢ from the National Recreation Association, includes references to works on Latin-American music, dances, games, costumes, etc.)

AGUILERA, FRANCISCO & SHELBY, C. *(eds)*
Handbook of Latin American studies,
1946, No 12. x, 364 p. Harvard 1950.   8.50
Music section by Charles Seeger, p 308/317. For earlier works in this series, see Burgin (ed) below.

BOGGS, RALPH STEELE *(comp)*
A bibliography of Latin American
folklore. x, 109 p. Wilson 1940.   1.50
Inter-American Bibliographical & Library Association publications, Series I, v 5.

BURGIN, MIRON *(ed)*
Handbook of Latin American studies,
1945, No 11: a selective guide . . .
x, 404 p. Harvard 1948.   7.00
Music section by Charles Seeger, p 343/351. Also includes material on Anthropology, Archives, Art, Folklore, Philosophy, etc. Companion volumes for 1943, No. 9 & 1944, No. 10 are still available ($7.00 each), but the 8 earlier volumes in this series are O/P.

CHASE, GILBERT
A guide to Latin American music.
Pan American Union.   In prep.   △
A revision of a book pub by the Musical Division of the Library of Congress (1945, now O/P), including a general bibliography, individual country bibliographies, & a key to periodicals.

MAYER-SERRA, OTTO. See App Id.

PEREIRA SALAS, EUGENIO. See App Id.

SLONIMSKY, NICOLAS
Music of Latin America. viii, 374 p,
illus (pors, facs, etc), mus ex. Crowell 1945 (2nd pr 1946). 3.75
*An extensive survey in "panorama" and by
20 individual republics, plus a dictionary of
musicians, songs, dances, & instruments.*

THOMPSON, LEILA FERN (*comp*)
A partial list of Latin American
music obtainable in the United
States. ii, 57, iii p, paper. Pan
American Union 3rd rev enl ed 1948. .25
*Including a supplementary list of books & a
selective list of phonograph records. The
1941/2 eds were compiled by Gilbert Chase.*

Selected list of Latin American song
books & references for guidance in
planning programs of music & dance.
12 p, paper. Pan American Union
(1942) 6th rev ed 1947. △
*Apply to the Pan American Union, Music
Division, Washington 6, D. C.*

Selected references in English on
Latin American music: a reading
list. 20 p, mim, paper. Pan American Union 1944. .10

LAUDER, Harry
See: App IIa (Malvern juvenile).
*Note: Lauder's own "A minstrel in France"
(1918) apparently is O/P.*

LAUDES
See: Medieval/Renaissance (esp Kantorowicz).

Laufer, Calvin Weiss. Co-author (with
Covert). See Hymns/Hymnody–1.
Lautner, Lois. Author. See Counterpoint–2.
Laver, James. Author.
See Ballet (ed Haskell).
Laux, Karl. Author. See App Ib.

LAWES, Henry
See also:
Church Music   History
Elizabethan Music   Poetry
English Music   Restoration

EVANS, WILLA MCCLUNG
Henry Lawes: musician and friend
of poets. xvi, 250 p, illus (pors, facs),
3–p bibl note. Modern Language
Association of America, N. Y., 1941. 2.50
*Biography with analyses of Lawes's songs
in relation to contemporary poetry.*

Lawrence, Lucile. Author (with Salzedo).
See Modulation.

LAWRENCE, Marjorie
See also: Opera, Singers, Phonograph
Records.
Interrupted melody: the story of my
life. ix, 307 p, 16 photos. Appleton
1949. 3.50
*Life-story of the Australian soprano & her
heroic recovery from polio.*

Lawrence, Robert. Co-author (with Peltz).
See Opera–4. Author. See Ballet.
Lawrence, Sidney J. Author.
See Children–1.
Lawson, Franklin D. Author.
See Voice.
Lawson, Joan. Author.
See Ballet (ed Haskell), Gundry.
Lawton, Mary. Co-author (with Pade-
rewski). See Paderewski.
Lazarsfeld, Paul Felix. Author.
See Radio.
Lazarus, Emma. Translator. See Heine.
Leach, May A. Co-editor (with Parker &
Lichtenwanger). See Church Music.
Leaf, Earl. Author. See Dances–2.
Leavitt, Helen S. Author & co-author (with
Hartshorn). See Children–2.
Co-author (with Freeman). See School
Music–2.
Lederman, Minna. Editor.
See Stravinsky.
Lee, Ernest Markham. Author.
See Brahms–2.
*Note: Numerous other books by Lee apparently
are O/P (or not easily available).*

Lee, Roger L. Author. See Baton–2.
Lee, Rupert. Author. See Mozart–3.
Leeder, Joseph A. Co-author
(with Thomas). See Folksongs–2.
Leeming, Joseph & Avery. Authors.
See Amateur Music.

LEHÁR, Franz (Ferenc)
See: App Ib (Czech).

Lehmann, Friedrich Johann. Author.
See Form, Harmony–2.

LEHMANN, Lilli. Author. See Singing–1.
Note: An autobiography (1919) is O/P.

LEHMANN, Lotte. Soprano, author.
For Mme Lehmann's "More than
singing" see Song.
See also: Opera, Singers.

Note: An autobiography, "Midway in my song"—or "Wings of song" in the English ed —(1938), & a novel, "Eternal flight" (1937) apparently are O/P.

My many lives. Tr. Frances Holden. 262 p, 16-p photos. Boosey 1948. **3.75**
A sequel to "More than singing": operatic memoirs & studies of role-projection.

Leibowitz, René. Author.
See Schoenberg, App Ia.

Leichtentritt, Hugo. Author. See:
Form. Musical (1951, in prep). **6.00**
History–1. Music, history, & ideas (1938). **3.50**
History–3. Everybody's (1938). **.60**
Koussevitzky. Title (1946). **3.00**
Motet. History (tr in prep). △
App Ib. Formenlehre (1907/48). **6.00**

Leidzén, Erik. Author.
See Arranging–1.

Leighton, George A. Author.
See Harmony–2.

Leimer, Karl. Author (with Gieseking).
See Piano Playing–2.

Lein, Herbert S. Co-author (with Hector & Scouten). See Acoustics.

Leirens, Charles. Author.
See Belgian Music.

Leland, Valborg. Author.
See Violin Playing.

Lemaître, Georges Edouard. Author.
See Beaumarchais.

LEMARE, Edwin Henry
Organs I have met: autobiography & reminiscences. Wetzel, in prep. △
Memoirs of the popular organist & composer.

Le Massena, C. E. Author.
See Galli-Curci, Schubert–2.

Léner, Jenö. Author. See String Quartet.

Lénom, Clément. Author.
See Solfège/Solfeggio.

Lenormand, René. Composer, Author.
See Harmony–1.
Note: Wollett's biography (in French, 1930) apparently is O/P.

Lentz, Donald A. Author.
See Transposition.

Leonard, Richard Anthony. Author.
See Composers–1.

Leonardo. Catalogued under Vinci, Leonardo da.

Le Roux, Maurice. Author. See App Ia.

Le Roy, Perry J. Author.
See Piano Playing–4.

LESCHETIZKY, Theodor
See:
Piano Playing–1   Teachers
  (esp Brée)   Teaching–3
Piano Playing–2
  (esp Unschuld, Wells)
Note: Books about Leschetizky and his piano method, which apparently are O/P, include those by Hullah, Newcomb, Potocka, etc.

LETTERS (of Musicians)
See also: Documents.
See also under the names of individual musicians. Nearly all autobiographies & biographies include at least some examples; in some cases collections of letters are published separately. For some of the more important collections, see esp:

Beethoven–1   Mussorgsky (Leyda &
Busoni   Bertensson)
Debussy–1   Schubert–1 (Deutsch)
Foster (Morneweck)   Tchaikovsky–1 (Bo-
Huneker   wen & Von Meck)
Mahler   Verdi–1 (Werfel &
Mendelssohn–1   Stefan)
Mozart–1

Note: Many standard collections of letters (by Joachim, Wagner, etc) apparently are O/P.

NORMAN, GERTRUDE & SHRIFTE, M. L. (eds)
Letters of composers: an anthology, 1603–1945. xviii, 422, xx p, 5-p bibl. Knopf 1946. **5.00**
Some 224 letters by 99 composers, from Sweelinck & Monteverdi to Schuman & Diamond.

PINCHERLE, MARC. See App Ia.

Letz, Hans. Compiler. See Violin Music.

LEVANT, Oscar
See: American Music, Composers–3a.
Note: Levant's own "A smattering of ignorance" (1940) apparently is O/P.

Levron, Jacques. Author. See App Ia.

Levy, Louis (b. 1893). Author.
See Film Music.

Levy, Louis (b. 1911). Author (with Mammen & Sonkin). See Speech.

Levy, Newman. Author. See Humor.

Lewer, S. K. Author. See Instruments.

Lewis, Al. Author. See Songwriting.

Lewis, Henry. Editor. See Facsimiles.

Lewis, Joseph. Author.
See Conducting, Singing–2.

Lewis, Leo Rich. Author. See:
Appreciation. The ambitious listener (1929). **.75**
Harmony–2. Do & don't (1943). **2.00**
Sight-Singing. Gist of (1931). **.75**

Leyda, Jay. Editor, translator.
See Films (Eisenstein), Mussorgsky, **Rach-**
maninoff.

LEXICONS
See: Dictionaries of Music, **Encyclopedias**
of Music, Miscellanies.

Lhévinne, Josef. Author.
See Piano Playing–2.

LIBRARIES (of Music)
See also: Bibliography.
Note: Ruth Wallace's "Care & treatment of
music in a library" (1927) is O/P

BACKUS, EDYTHE N.
Catalogue of music in the Huntington Library printed before 1801. ix,
773 p. Huntington Library, San
Marino, Calif., 1949.   10.50
Arranged by author & title, with chronologi-
cal, composer, & first-line indices.

BOHMAN, ESTHER L. & DILLON, J. K.
The librarian and the teacher of
music: experimenting together. 55 p,
paper. American Library Association, Chicago, 1942.   .75
Elementary school level; includes book lists
useful in music-library activities.

HILL, RICHARD S. (*ed*)
Music and libraries: selected papers
of the Music Library Association
presented at its 1942 meetings. 69
p, paper. Music Library Association,
Washington, D. C., 1943.   1.00
8 papers by various authors, including Chase,
Reese, Upton, & others.

HIRSCH, PAUL. See App Ib.

McCOLVIN, LIONEL R. & REEVES, H.
Music libraries: their organization
& contents, with a bibliography of
music & musical literature. 2 v: vii,
239 p; 318 p. Grafton 1937/8.   △
A standard work, outgrowth of a thesis,
"Music in public libraries" (1924) by
McColvin. Temporarily O/P (1949) but ex-
pected back in print shortly. The former price
was $10.50.

MOORE, ARTHUR PRICHARD
The library-museum of music and
dance: a study of needs & resources,
leading to suggestions for an educational program. xi, 186 p, 9–p bibl.
Teachers College, Columbia, 1938.   2.25
Contributions to education, No. 750. The
appendix includes chronological tables.

MYERS, KURTZ (*comp*)
The library and audio-visual materi-
als: a bibliography. 24 p, paper.
Audio-Visual Materials Consultation
Bureau, College of Education, Wayne
University, Detroit, rev ed 1949.   .50
Includes lists of books & articles on phono-
graph records, radio, & television.

(U. S.) LIBRARY OF CONGRESS
See:

America (music in)	Foster (Sonneck)
American Music (Son-	Libraries
neck & Upton)	MacDowell (Sonneck)
Bibliography (Bart-	Opera–2 (Sonneck)
lett, Goff, Gregory,	Orchestral Music
Library of Con-	(Sonneck)
gress)	Star-Spangled Banner
Copyright (Library of	(note only)
Congress)	

LIBRETTOS (Operatic)
See: Opera–2.

Licht, Sidney H. Author. See Health.
Lichtenberger, Henri. Author. See App Ia.
Lichtenwanger, William. Editor (with
Parker & Leach). See Church Music.
Lieber, Leslie. Co-author (with Whiteman).
See Dance Bands.
Lieberson, Samuel A. Author.
See Harmony–2.
Liebling, Emil. Co-author (with Matthews).
See Dictionaries of Terms.
Liebling, Estelle. Co-author (with Pierce).
See School Music–4.

LIEDER
See: Song(s)

Liess, Andreas. Author. See App Ib.

LIFAR, Serge
See: Ballet, (The) Dance.
Note: Lifar's biography of Diaghilev (1940)
apparently is O/P, as are several books in
French by and about Lifar.

LIND, Jennie
See also: App Ia (Benét & Headland).
Note: Standard works apparently O/P in-
clude those by Holland & Rockstro, etc.

ROCKSTRO, W. S.
Jenny Lind: a record and analysis of
the "method" of the late Madame
Jenny Lind-Goldschmidt. 20 p +
xxvii p mus ex, frontis por. Novello   △
1894.   (2.00)
Includes illustrative "cadenze, solfeggi, abelli-
menti, etc," ed Otto Goldschmidt.

Lindfors, Eula Ashworth. Author.
See Scales.

Lindgren, Ernest. Author. See Films.

Lindsay, George L. Co-author (with Shaw). See Voice.

Lingg, Ann M. Author. See App IIa (Mozart juvenile). '

Linscott, Eloise Hubbard. Editor. See Folksongs–2.

Lissfelt, J. Fred. Author. See Singing–2.

LISTENING

See:

Appreciation	Hearing
Ear-Training	Program Notes

LISZT, Franz

See also (for Liszt's own writings): Chopin–1, Gypsy.

Note: Several collections of letters (in French & German) apparently are O/P.

See also:

Appreciation	Phonograph Records
Composers–1	Piano Music
History	Program Notes
Hungarian Music	Vocal Music
National Music	Wagner–1 & 2

Standard works apparently O/P (or not easily available) include those by Harsányi, Huneker, Newman, de Pourtalès, Siloti, Stiwell, Wallace, etc; in German by Raabe, etc.

Brockway, Wallace (Biography. S & S. In prep.)   △

Chantavoine, Jean. See App Ia.

Hill, Ralph
Liszt. 144 p, frontis, 2–p bibl. Wyn 1950.   1.00
"Great Musicians" series; originally pub by Duckworth, London, 1936.

Reboux, Paul. See App Ia.

Searle, Humphrey   △
Liszt. Dent, in prep.   2.50
"Master Musicians" series.

Westerby, Herbert
Liszt, composer, and his piano works: descriptive guide & critical analysis . . . xxii, 336 p, 5 pors, 24 mus ex,   △
13–p bibl. Reeves n d (1936).   3.75
A short biography, detailed study of the piano works, notes on the preparation of concert repertory & teaching courses, chronological table, and catalogue of compositions.

Westrup, J. A.
Liszt. 16 p, cover por, paper. Novello n d (1939).   .40
Miniature biography ("Great Musicians").

LITERATURE (of Music)

Please see the general note (there are no book entries) under Historical Collections.

Also:

Anthologies	History
Bibliography	Libraries
Dictionaries of **Music**	Musicology
Encyclopedias of	Repertory
Music	

LITERATURE (& Music)

See also:

Aesthetics	Madrigal
Appreciation	Philosophy
Italy—music in	Poetry
(esp Rubsamen)	Program Notes

Note: Lightwood's "Music and literature" (1931) apparently is O/P.

Brown, Calvin S.
Music and literature: a comparison of the arts. xi, 287 p, mus ex, 7–p bibl notes. Georgia 1948.   4.50
The first extensive study in English of the relationship between literature & music, the reciprocal influence of their techniques & forms, and their comparative aesthetics. Includes material on program music.

LITTLE MUSIC LIBRARY

Note: This is a series of miniature handbooks, mostly of an "appreciative" nature, directed toward the general listener & published by Grosset & Dunlap. Eight books are now available, either individually (75c each) or in two groups of four books, boxed, at $2.95.

Group 1: Mendelsohn: The story of 100 operas (Opera–3); Grabbe: The story of orchestral music and its times (Orchestral Music), & The story of 100 symphonic favorites (Program Notes); Kaufmann: The story of 100 great composers (Composers –1).

Group 2: Kaufmann: The little dictionary of music terms (Dictionaries of Terms), The little guide to music appreciation (Appreciation), The little book of music anecdotes (Anecdotes), The little history of music (History–3).

(All eight books are entered individually under the subject-headings in parentheses above.)

Littlehales, Lillian. Author. See Casals.

LITURGY/LITURGICAL MUSIC

See: esp Church Music

Also:

Byzantine Music	Luther
Gregorian Chant	Mass
History	Medieval/Renaissance
Jewish Music	Plainsong

Lloyd, A. L. Author. See Gundry.

Lloyd, Llewelyn Southworth. Author. See Decibel, Hearing, Scales.
Note: Lloyd's book on acoustics, especially

for musicians, "*Music & sound*" (*1937*), is O/P but announced for 1951 re-issue.

Lloyd, Margaret. Author. See Dance.
Lobe, Johann Christian. Author.
See Theory–3.
Locard, Paul. Author. See App Ia.
Lochner, Louis P. Author. See Kreisler.
Locke, Arthur Ware. Compiler.
See Choir/Choral–3.
Lockspeiser, Edward. Author.
See Berlioz–2, Debussy–2.

LOEWE, (Johann) Carl (Gottfried)
See: esp App Ib (Seitz).
Also:

Appreciation	Phonograph Records
Composers—1	Song(s)
History	Vocal Music

Logier, Johann Bernhard. Author.
See Theory–1.
Lomax, Alan. Author. See Morton.
Compiler. Catalogued under Lomax, John Avery & Alan.

LOMAX, John Avery
Adventures of a ballad hunter. xi, 302 p, illus (Ken Chamberlain).
Macmillan 1947.   5.00
The autobiography of a pioneer in American folklore & folksong collection.
Author. See also:
Cowboy Music. Songs of the cattle trail (1919/50).   3.00
Lomax, John Avery & Alan. Compilers. See:
Cowboy. Cowboy songs (1910/38).   5.00
Folksongs–2. American ballads (1934).   6.00
—. Folk song U. S. A. (1948).   6.00
—. Our singing country (1941).   6.50
Note: The Lomaxes' "Negro folk songs as sung by Lead Belly" (1936) apparently is O/P.

LONDON (Music in)
See:

Berlioz–2 (Ganz)	Queen's Hall
Burney	Philharmonic
Convent Garden	Shaw
England (music in)	

London, Kurt. Author. See Film Music.
Longo, Teodosio. Author. See Voice.
Longy-Miquelle, Renée. Author.
See Theory–3.
Loofbourow, Reginaldus. Author.
See App IIb (juvenile).
Lord, Albert B. Co-editor (with Bartók).
See Folklore.
Lorenz, Ellen Jane. Author.
See Choir/Choral–, Organ Playing.
Lossing, Laverna L. Co-author (with Wright). See School Music–4.

Louÿs, Pierre. Author.
See App Ia (Debussy: Correspondence).
Lovelock, William. Author.
See Counterpoint–2, Teaching–2.
Lovett, Benjamin B. Compiler.
See Dances–2.
Lowery, H. Author. See Psychology.
Lowinsky, Edward Elias. Author.
See Medieval/Renaissance.
Lowry, Margaret. Author.
See Keyboard Harmony.
Lubinová, Mila. Author.
See Dances–2 (ed Alford).

LUDWIG, II (of Bavaria)
See: History, Wagner–1 & 2.
Note: The English translations of books by Mayr-Offen and Zarek apparently are O/P. We have no availability information on a book by Annette Kolb (1947) in German.

Ludwig, Charles. Author. See Sankey.
Ludwig, Emil. Author.
See Beethoven–2.
Lumpkin, Ben Gray. Editor.
See Folksongs–1.
Luper, Albert T. Co-compiler (with Gleason). See Bibliographies.

LUTE/LUTENISTS
See: esp App Ia (Cabos).
Also:

Children–4	Instruments
Elizabethan Music	Madrigal
English Music	(esp Fellowes)
History	Medieval/Renaissance

Luther, Frank. Author. See Song-books.

LUTHER, Martin/LUTHERAN MUSIC
See also: esp App Ib (Bücken ed: Blume).

Bach	History
Church Music	Hymns/Hymnody

BAINTON, ROLAND H.
Here I stand: a life of Martin Luther.
422 p, illus, 8–p bibl. Abingdon 1950.   4.75
The 1950 Abingdon award-winning biography, illustrated with over 100 woodcuts, contemporary engravings, & satirical drawings.
NETTL, PAUL
Luther and music. Tr. Frida Best & Ralph Wood.   vii, 174 p, 3–p bibl. Muhlenberg 1948.   2.25
Includes an outline of evangelical church music as well as a discussion of Luther's own contributions to the liturgy.

Lyle, Watson. Author. See Rachmaninoff.
Lynch, Virginia. Author. See Children–2.
Lyons, John Henry. Author. See App IIb.
Lytle, Victor Vaughn. Author.
See Counterpoint–2.

—M—

Mac... /Mc...
General Note: Names beginning with Mac (which follow immediately below) are not grouped together with names beginning with Mc (which follow later, after Mayo, in proper alphabetical order).

MacArdle, Donald W. Editor.
See Beethoven–2 (Thayer, note only).
MacDougall, Hamilton Crawford.
Author.
See Improvisation, Psalms/Psalmody.

MacDOWELL, Edward Alexander
See:

America (music in)	Phonograph Records
American Music	Piano Music
Appreciation	Program Notes
Composers–3a	Song(s)
Concerto	Themes
History	Vocal Music

Also: App IIa (Wheeler & Deucher juvenile).

Note: Standard works apparently O/P (or not easily available) include those by Gilman, Porte, etc.

(MACDOWELL, EDWARD A.)
Critical and historical essays: lectures delivered at Columbia University.
Ed W. J. Baltzell. vii, 282 p, mus ex.
Schmidt 1912.   2.50
Essays on the origins of music, music of the Greeks & Romans, notation, folksong, instruments, opera, declamation, etc.

MACDOWELL, MARIAN
Random notes on Edward Mac-Dowell and his music. Intro Una L. Allen. v, 37 p, 10 photos (pors, etc), paper. Schmidt 1950.   1.25
Informal comments on the piano works, with a biographical sketch by Una L. Allen.

SONNECK, OSCAR G. *(comp)*
Catalog of first editions of Edward MacDowell (1861–1908). 89 p.
Library of Congress, via GPO, 1917.   .40
Detailed catalogue of compositions, classified by those with & without opus numbers, published under pseudonyms, and editions of other composers' works.

MacDowell, Marian (Mrs Edward Mac-Dowell).
Author. See Edward MacDowell.
MacDowell, Tremaine. Author.
See America (music in).
Machabey, Armand. Author. See App Ia.
Mackinnon, Lilas. Author.
See Memory, Piano Playing–2.
Macklin, Charles E. Author.
See Piano Playing–2.
MacMahon, Desmond. Author.
See Appreciation, Instruments. Co-author (with Chamberlain). See School Music–4.
MacPhail, Ian Shaw. Author.
See Orchestra.

Macpherson, (Charles) Stewart. Author.
See:
Bach–2. "48" commentary (1934).   (3.50)
Form. Form in music (1908/30).   3.50
——. Studies in phrasing & form (1911/32).   2.00
Harmony–2. Melody & harmony (1920).   6.25
Theory–3. Rudiments (1908/39).   .75
——. Questions & exercises.   .60

Note: Several other books by Macpherson apparently are O/P (or not easily available in this country).

Macy, James C. Author.
See App IIb (juveniles)
Maddocks, Durward. Author.
See Dances–2.
Maddy, Joseph E. Author (with Giddings).
See School Music–3.

MADRIGAL
See also:

Appreciation	Fellowes
Byrd	Form
Choir/Choral–3	History
Composers–1 & 3c	Italy (music in)
Counterpoint–1	Medieval/Renaissance
(esp Kitson, Morris)	Milton
Elizabethan Music	Phonograph Records
English Music	Poetry & Music

EINSTEIN, ALFRED
The Italian madrigal. Tr Alexander H. Krappe, Roger Sessions, & Oliver Strunk.   3 v, boxed; v 1 & 2: xvi,

890 p; v 3: xxx, 333 p; 24 illus, mus
ex, music, bibl refs. Princeton 1949.   30.00
A monumental study, actually a literary &
musical history of the 16th century, acclaimed
as the first truly comprehensive history of a
musical form. The 324-p music section
(v 3) includes some 97 complete madrigals.
mostly hitherto unpublished.

The golden age of the madrigal: 12
Italian madrigals for 5-part chorus of
mixed voices never before published
in a modern edition.   With English
versions by Gustave Reese.   95 p,
music, paper.   G. Schirmer 1942.   1.25
Madrigals by Arcadelt, A. & G. Gabrieli, da
Gagliano, Luzzaschi, Marenzo, Monte,
Merulo, Porta, Rore, Vecchi, Wert; with
3 pages of annotations.

FELLOWES, E. H.
The English madrigal,   111 p, 11
illus (pors, facs, etc), mus ex.
Oxford 1925.   2.00
A standard, concise, over-all survey, dealing
with music in the Elizabethan home, the music
& words of the madrigals, and including brief
sketches of 37 composers.

The English madrigal composers. 364
p, mus ex, tables.   Oxford (1921)
2nd rev ed 1949.   5.00
A standard detailed study of the music & its
composers, with biographical synopses of the
madrigalists & lutenists, index to first lines,
& references to original editions.

The English madrigal school: a guide
to its practical use.   91 p, mus ex,
paper.   Stainer n d.   1.25
A reprint of the preface (1913) to the first
four volumes of the standard edition of English
madrigals, "The English Madrigal School";
with advice on madrigal singing.

English madrigal verse, 1588–1632:
edited from the original song books.
xxiv, 644 p.   Oxford (1920) 2nd ed
1929.   4.00
Texts only of the best-known madrigals &
lutenists' ayres.

SCOTT, CHARLES KENNEDY
Madrigal singing: a few remarks on
the study of madrigal music with an
explanation of the modes and a note
on their relation to polyphony.
114 p, mus ex.   Oxford (1907) 2nd
ed 1931.   2.00
Practical advice on madrigal performance.

Magnat, G. E.   Author.   See App Ia.

Magriel, Paul.   Editor, compiler.   See:
(The) Dance.   Bibliography of danc-
ing (1936).   4.75
——. 4th supplement (1941)   1.85
——. Chronicles of the American
dance (1948).   5.00
Duncan.   Isadora Duncan (1947).   3.50
Nijinsky.   Essays & photos (1946).   3.50
Pavlova.   Essays & photos (1947).   3.50

Mahler, Alma Maria Schindler.   Author.
See Gustav Mahler.

MAHLER, Gustav
See also:
Appreciation   Song(s)
Composers–2 & 3b   Symphony
   (esp Newlin)   Themes
Conductors   Timing
History   Vienna
Phonograph Records   Vocal Music
Program Notes   Walter

Note: Pertinent works apparently O/P (or
not easily available) include those by Adler
(in German), Engel, Schiedermann (in
German), Specht (in German), Stefan (in
English & German), Walter (in English
& German), etc.

MAHLER, ALMA MARIA SCHINDLER
Gustav Mahler: memories & letters.
Tr Basil Creighton.   vi, 277 p, 8 illus
(por, fac).   Viking 1946.   5.00
An English version of "Erinnerungen und
Briefe" (Amsterdam 1940) by the composer's
widow.   89 pages of Mahler letters are
included.

Mahrenholz, Christhard.   Author.
See App Ib.

Maine, Basil (Stephen).   Author.
See Chopin–1.
Note: Several other books by Maine, includ-
ing an autobiography (1937), apparently
are O/P (or not easily available).

Mainwaring, John.   Author.   See App Ib.
Maisel, Edward F.   Author.   See Griffes.

MALAYA (Music in)/MALAYAN MUSIC
See:
Asiatic Musics   History
   (note only)   Instruments
Bali (music in)   Java (music in)

Note: The bibliography of Asiatic Musics,
referred to above, includes a section on Malaya
& the Malay Archipelago (East Indies)
in its 9th installment (Music Library Assn
"Notes" for December 1949).

Malherbe, Henry. Author. See App Ia.

MALIPIERO, G. Francesco
See:

Appreciation	Italy (music in)
Composers-2	Modern Music
Contemporary Music	Phonograph Records
History	Program Notes

Author. See App Ic ("Strawinsky").

Note: A booklet on the orchestra apparently is O/P (or not easily available), at least in the English edition (1921). We have no information on the availability of several recent books in Italian by & about Malipiero.

Malvern, Gladys. Author.
See App IIa (Lauder, Pavlova juveniles).
Mammen, Edward W. Co-author (with Levy & Sonkin). See Speech.
Manchester, Arthur Livingston. Author.
See Singing–2.
Manchester, P. W. Author (with Morley).
See Ballet.
Mandinian, Edward. Photographer.
See Purcell.
Mann, Klaus. Author.
See Tchaikovsky–1.

MANN, Thomas
Doctor Faustus: the life of the German composer Adrian Leverkühn, as told by a friend. Tr H. T. Lowe-Porter. vi, 510 p. Knopf 1948.   3.50
A fictional biography, which is both a modern version of the Faust legend and a study of musical genius. "Leverkühn" has no actual counterpart as a composer, but his life & disease are based in part on those of Nietzsche.
Essays of three decades. Tr H. T. Lowe-Porter. vii, 472 p, frontis por. Knopf 1947.   4.00
A collection of essays (1910-1939), including four dealing with Goethe, and two with Richard Wagner and his "Ring."
Author. See also Anthologies (ed Fabricant & Werner).
Editor. See:
Goethe.   The permanent Goethe (1948).   5.00

Mann, William. Author. See Bach–2.
Manners, Zeke. Author. See Dances–2.

MANNES, David
See also:

America (music in)	Education
Conductors	Teaching–2
Damrosch Family	

Music is my faith: an autobiography. Forew Franklin P. Adams; pref Maria Mannes. 270 p, 8 photos. (1938) Dover Press, N. Y., 2nd ed 1949.   2.75
Re-issue ("by his friends") of the noted conductor-&-teacher's memoirs, originally published by Norton in 1938.

Manning, Rosemary. Author.
See Choir/Choral–3.

MANONE, Wingy
See: Jazz, Popular Music.
Note: The New Orleans jazzman's memoirs, "Trumpet on the wing" (1948), written in collaboration with Paul Vandervoort II, apparently are O/P.

Manser, Ruth Baldock. Author (with Finlan). See Speech.
Mansfield, Grace Yarrow. Recorder (with Greenleaf). See Sea Shanties.
Mansfield, Orlando Augustine. Author.
See Harmony–2.
Manuel, Roland (Lévy, Roland Alexis Manuel). Author. See Ravel (also App Ia.)

MANUSCRIPT (Musical)
General Note: Entries under this subject-heading are confined to books dealing with the preparation of musical manuscript and do not include those on more general aspects of notation.
See also:

Autographs	Notation
Facsimiles	Theory

Note: Pertinent works apparently O/P (or not easily available) include those by Breslaur, Harris, Manhire, Stackpole, Taylor, etc.

HANSEN, JULES. See App Ia.

JACOB, ARCHIBALD
Music handwriting: or how to put music on paper; a handbook. Pref Henry Wood. vii, 108 p, illus, mus ex. Oxford (1937) 2nd rev ed 1947.   1.50
Practical advice on materials, writing, notation, spacing, orch. parts, scores, etc.

JOHNSON, HAROLD M.
How to write musical manuscript: an exercise-method handbook. 29 p, illus, mus ex, paper. C. Fischer 1946.   .75
Concise advice, with exercises.

KABALA, P.
Musical shorthand: a system of rapid musical notation. 28 p, mus ex, paper. Musical Shorthand, Wheeling, West Va., 1940.   .50

Devices for simplifying & speeding the writing of ordinary musical notation.

MAGNAT, G. E. See App Ia.

MARBECK (or Merbecke), John
See: Church Music (esp Fellowes).

Marcel-Dubois, Claude. Author.
See App Ia. Co-author (with Andral). See Dances–2. (ed Alford)

MARCH
See also:

Appreciation	Military Music
Band	Phonograph Records
Gilmore	Program Notes
History	Sousa

ALLEN, WARREN D.
Our marching civilization: an introduction to the study of music & society. xii, 112 p, diagr, mus ex, 2–bibl. Stanford 1943.   2.50

The first study in English of the march and its sociological significance, a "by-product" of the author's work-in-progress on music and society.

Marchesi (de Castrone), Salvatore.
Author. See Singing–2.
Marcouiller, S. M. de S. M. Author.
See Theory–3.

Marek, George Richard. Author. See:
Appreciation. Good Housekeeping guide to musical enjoyment (1949).   3.50
Opera–1. A front seat at the opera (1948).   4.00
Puccini. Biography (1951).   5.00

Marie-Jeanne (*pseud* of Marie-Jeanne Pelus). Author. See App IIb (juveniles).

MARIMBA
See:

Bali (music in)	Latin America
Children–4 (Coleman)	(esp Slonimsky)
Instruments	Mexico (music in)

MARKS, Edward Bennet
Note: Two books of the music-publisher's memoirs, "They all had glamour" (1944) & "They all sang" (1934), apparently are O/P.

Marks, F. Helena. Author.
See Mozart–3.
Marks, Harvey Blair. Author.
See Hymns/Hymnody–1.

Marmelszadt, Willard. Author.
See Health.
Marsh, Agnes Lewis & Lucile. Authors.
See Dances–3.
Marshall, John Patton. Co-author (with Hamilton & others). See Theory–3.

Martens, Frederick Herman. Author.
Note: Several books by Martens, on opera & ballet, singing, & violin playing, apparently are O/P.

Martens, Vi. Author. See Singing–2.
Marti, Samuel. Author.
See String Playing.
Martin, "Deac" (Charles Trimble).
Author. See Barbershop.
Martin, John. Author.
See (The) Dance.

MARTINU, Bohuslav
See also:

Composers–2	History
Contemporary Music	Modern Music
Czechoslovakia (music	Phonograph Records
in)	Program Notes

ŠAFRÁNEK, MILOŠ
Bohuslav Martinu: the man & his music. xviii, 127, vi p, 14 illus (pors, facs, etc), mus ex, 1–p bibl. Knopf 1944.   3.00

A compatriot's biography of the contemporary Czech composer now resident in this country. Includes a catalogue of works to 1943.

Martynov, Ivan. Author.
See Shostakovitch.
Mason, Bernard Sterling. Author.
See Indians (American), Instruments.

MASON, Daniel Gregory
Note: For material about Mason as a composer, see America (music in), American Music, & Composers–3a.

Apart from the works listed below, several others by Mason apparently are O/P (or not easily available): "Artistic ideals" (1925), "Contemporary composers (1918/29)," "From Grieg to Brahms" (1921/36), "The romantic composers (1906/30), & "Tune in, America" (1931).

The dilemma of American music: and other essays. xii, 306 p, mus ex. Macmillan 1928.   3.00
Besides the title piece, there are essays on "Our orchestras," rhythm, Beethoven, etc.

Music as a humanity: and other essays. v, 125 p, frontis por (De Coppet). Gray 1921 (1926).   2.00

*V 4 of a series, of which v 1 is Surette &
Mason's "Appreciation of music" (see Appreciation). The 17 essays here are grouped
under the headings "Of universities & the
public taste," "Of festivals & patrons," "Of
aesthetics & psychology."*

Music in my time: and other reminiscences. 409 p, 42 illus. Macmillan
1938.   5.00
*A book of memoirs: the experiences of an
American composer & teacher, with anecdotes
about many friends & contemporaries.*

See also:

Appreciation.   From song to sym-
phony (1924).   1.50
——. Guide to music (1909).   2.00
——. The appreciation of music
(1907), by Surette & Mason.   2.00
Beethoven–3. The quartets (1947).   5.00
Brahms–2. Chamber music (1933)   3.50
Composers–1. Beethoven & his fore-
runners (1904/30).   3.00
——. Great modern composers (1916).   2.00
Instruments. Orchestral (1908).   3.00
Program Notes.   Short studies in
great masterpieces (1918).   2.00

Mason, George Frederick.   Author.
See App IIb.
Mason, Henry Lowell.   Compiler, author.
See Lowell Mason, Opera–3.

MASON, Lowell

See also:

America (music in)	Education
American Music	Hymns/Hymnody
Church Music	School Music–1

MASON, HENRY L. *(comp)*
Hymn-tunes of Lowell Mason: a
bibliography. ix, 118 p, frontis por.
Harvard 1944.   O/P
*A complete catalogue and detailed study of
Lowell Mason's 1697 hymn-tunes.   (O/P
1950.)*

RICH, ARTHUR LOWNDES
Lowell Mason: "The father of singing among the children." vii, 224 p,
frontis por, bibls. North Carolina
1946.   3.00
*A biography, including a 35-p bibl of
Mason's writings & a 22-p bibl of other
sources.*

MASONIC MUSIC

See also: England (music in), Mozart.

ELLINGFORD, HERBERT F.
Masonic music in England: a historical survey. 24 p, frontis por, mus ex,
paper. Hinrichsen n d (1947?).   .50
"Miniature Survey" series M-14.

MASQUES

See: esp Poetry (ed Boas).
Also:

Campion	Lawes
Elizabethan Music	Minstrels/Minstrelsy
England (music in)	Opera–1 (esp Dent)
English Music	Purcell
History	Restoration Era

MASS

See also: esp Church Music.
Also:

Ancient Music	History
Appreciation	Latin Language
California (music in)	Medieval/Renaissance
Choir/Choral–3	Phonograph Records
Elizabethan Music	Plainsong
Baroque Era	Program Notes
Gregorian Chant	Psalms/Psalmody

Also: Composers–1, and under the names of
individual Mass composers, esp Bach,
Beethoven, Bruckner, Byrd, Palestrina,
etc.

*Note: Standard works apparently O/P (or not
easily available) include those by Cabrol,
O'Brien, Schnerich (in German), P. Wagner
(in German), etc. In addition, of course,
there are many other books, in & out of print,
which deal with the Mass, but with little
attention to its musical aspects.*

GASSNER, JEROME
The canon of the Mass: its history,
theology, & art. Forew Mark Braun.
x, 404 p, bibl refs. Herder 1949.   5.00
*Historical information & scriptural back-
grounds; little on the music of the Mass.*

PIERIK, MARIE
When the people sang.   Forew
Richard J. Cushing. 32 p, bibl refs,
paper. McLaughlin & Reilly 1949.   .50
*Includes a 5-p introduction on Gregorian
Chant, with a condensed story-history of the
entire Mass—Proper and Ordinary.*

SALLAWAY, FRANCIS X.
The music of the Mass: radio commentaries upon 44 texts of the Mass
& their various musical expressions.
59 p, paper. Rumble & Carty,
St Paul, Minn., 1946.   .25
*A general description followed by detailed
commentaries (a broadcast series in the Essex
County, Mass., Catholic Radio Program).*

Massell, James. Author. See Singing–2.

MASSENET, Jules
See also:

Appreciation	Phonograph Records
Composers–1	Program Notes
French Music	Song(s)
History	Vocal Music
Opera	

Note: The composer's "My recollections" (English ed 1919) apparently is O/P (or not easily available), as are studies by Brancour (in French), Finck, etc.

COLSON, PERCY
Massenet: Manon. 31 p + 6 pl, mus ex, brief bibl, paper. Boosey 1947.   .60
"Covent Garden Operas" series.

Masson, Paul-Marie. Author. See App Ia.

"MASTER MUSICIANS" (Series)
Note: This is an extensive & widely circulated series of composers' biographies, written by various authors, but published in uniform format & general style under the editorship of Eric Blom. Each book includes appendices providing a calendar of the composer's life, a catalogue of his works, "personalia" (on contemporaries mentioned), and a bibliography. Published by Dent in England, these books long were issued in this country by Dutton, but American rights in the series were taken over in 1949 by Pellegrini & Cudahy. Currently (Fall, 1950), some 15 books appear under the combined Dent & Pellegrini imprint, but most of the others are still available from London and presumably will be issued here later. See:

Bach–2 (Grew)	Mendelssohn–2 (Radcliffe, in prep)
Beethoven–2 (Scott)	
Berlioz–2 (Elliot)	Mozart–2 (Blom)
Bizet (Dean)	Mussorgsky
Brahms–1 (Latham)	(Calvocoressi)
Chopin–1 (Hedley)	Palestrina (Coates)
Debussy–2	Purcell (Westrup)
(Lockspeiser)	Ravel (Demuth)
Dvořák (Robertson)	Schubert–1
Elgar (Reed)	(Hutchings)
Fauré (Suckling)	Schubert–2 (Chissell)
Gluck (Einstein,	Tchaikovsky–1
temp O/P)	(Evans)
Handel–1 (Young)	Verdi–1 (Hussey)
Haydn (Hughes)	Wagner–2 (Jacobs)
Liszt (Searle, in prep)	Weber (Saunders, temp O/P)

MATHEMATICS (of Music)
See: esp App Ia (Huygens).
Also:

Acoustics	Scales
Aesthetics–1 (esp	Sound Recording &
Schillinger) & 2	Reproduction
Monophony (Partch)	Theory

Mathews, Ferdinand Schuyler. Author. See Birds.
Mathews, Ruth Vendley. Author. See Miscellanies.
Mathews, William Smythe Babcock. Author. See Composers–1, Dictionaries of Terms, History–2.
Note: Several other books by W. S. B. Mathews apparently are O/P (or not easily available).

Mattfeld, Julius. Compiler (with Davis). See Song(s).
Matthewson, Royal C. Author. See Theory–3.
Matthaei, Karl. Author. See App Ib.
Matthay, Jessie Henderson. Author. See Tobias Matthay.

MATTHAY, Tobias
See also:

Interpreters	Teachers
Pianists	Teaching–2
Piano Playing	

COVIELLO, AMBROSE
What Matthay meant: his musical & technical teachings clearly explained & self-indexed. 72 p, paper. Bosworth n d.   1.75
Notes on the "Matthay method," with a dictionary list of details, and 164 questions & answers.

MATTHAY, JESSIE HENDERSON
The life and works of Tobias Matthay. Pref Forbes Dennis. xiii, 114 p, 22 illus. Boosey 1945 (1946).   5.00
An intimate biography of the great pedagogue.

Author (Matthay's own books). See:
Children–5. Child's 1st steps in piano playing (1912).   .75
Interpretation. Musical (1913).   3.00
Memory. On memorizing (1926).   .75
Piano Playing–1. The visible & invisible in piano technique (1932/47).   3.00
Piano Playing–2. Fore-arm rotation principle (1912).   .75
———. Relaxation studies (1908).   5.00
Note: Many other works by Matthay, particularly on piano playing, apparently are O/P (or not easily available in this country).

MATTHESON, Johann
See also: Baroque Era, History.

CANNON, BEEKMAN C.
Johann Mattheson: spectator in

music. xv, 244 p, 2 pl, 5–p bibl. Yale
1947. **3.00**
*First of a series of "Yale Studies in the
History of Music," edited by Leo Schrade.
A scholarly attempt to clarify the effect of
the Enlightenment upon the musical life &
thought of Germany in the first part of the
18th century. It includes an evaluation of
Mattheson's place in music and a 72-p
critical bibliography of his works.*

Matzke, Hermann. Author. See App Ib.
Maurice-Jacquet, H. Author.
See Singing–2.
Maus, Cynthia Pearl. Editor.
See Carols.

May, Florence. Author. See Brahms–1.
*Note: May's "Girlhood of Clara Schumann"
(1911) apparently is O/P.*

Mayer-Serra, Otto. Author.
See Mexico (music in), App Id.
Mayo, Margot. Author. See Dances–2.

Mc . . .
*Note: For entries beginning with "Mac",
please see above in proper alphabetical order.
Those beginning with "Mc" follow in order
below.*

McClintock, Lorene. Author.
See Piano Playing–4.
McColvin, Lionel Roy. Author (with
Reeves). See Libraries.
McConathy, Osbourne. Author (with
Embs & others). See Harmony–2. (With
Miessner & others). See School Music–1.
Co-author (with Haake & Haake). See
Sight-Playing & Reading. (With Schelling
& others). See Teaching–3.
McCord, David Thompson Watson.
Author. See H. T. Parker.

McCORMACK, John
See also:
Interpreters   Phonograph Records
Opera   Singers
*Note: Pierre Key's biography (1919) appar-
ently is O/P.*

McCORMACK, LILY
I hear you calling me. 210 p, 27 pl
(pors, facs, etc). Bruce 1949. **2.75**
*The story of the great tenor's life, by his
widow. The 12-p discography of McCormack's recordings is compiled by Philip F.
Roden.*

STRONG, L. A. G.
John McCormack: the story of a
singer. ix, 309 p, 20 pl (pors). (1941)
Peter Nevill, London, 1949. **3.75**
*Reprint of a biography first published by
Methuen, London, in 1941.*

McCormack, Lily. Author.
See John McCormack.
McCoy, Guy. Compiler.
See Pictures/Portraits.
McCray, Walter. Author (with Busch).
See Conducting.
McCutchan, Robert Guy. Author.
See Hymns/Hymnody.

McEwen, (Sir) John Blackwood. Author.
See Aesthetics–2.
*Note: Several other works, mostly textbooks,
by McEwen apparently are O/P (or not easily
available in this country).*

McFadyean, Barbara. Author (with
Hughes). See Opera–3.
McGehee, Thomasine C. Author.
See Children–2.

McHose, Allen Irvine. Author. See:
Composition. Basic principles of
18th-century technique (in prep). **3.50**
Counterpoint–1. Contrapuntal har-
monic technique of the 18th-century
(1947). **7.00**
Dictation. Teachers' dictation manual
(1948). **3.00**
Keyboard Harmony. Keyboard
& dictation manual (1949), by
McHose & White. **3.25**
Sight-Singing. Manual (1944/45), by
McHose & Tibbs. **2.50**

McKay, George Frederick. Author.
See Harmony–1.
McKinney, B. B. Co-author (with Harri-
son). See Theory–3.

McKinney, Howard Decker. Author. See:
Appreciation. Discovering music
(1935/43), by McKinney & Anderson. **4.75**
——. How to listen to good music
(1943/7), by McKinney & Anderson. **1.00**
——. Music & man (1948). **3.00**
History–2. Music in history (1940),
by McKinney & Anderson. **5.50**

McKinney, Lawrence. Author.
See Orchestra.

McLachlan, Norman William. Author.
See Acoustics.
McMillan, Fiona. Author.
See Piano Playing–2.
McNally, William James. Author.
See Wagner–2.
McNamara, Daniel Ignatius. Editor.
See Composers–3a
McNaught, William. Author, editor.
See Beethoven–2, Elgar, History–4.
McNeil, Norman L. Co-editor (with
Lumkin). See Folksongs–1.
McPhee, Colin. Author. See Bali, App IIb.
McProud, C. G. Editor.
See Sound Recording & Reproduction.
McSpadden, Joseph Walker. Author.
See Opera–3.

MEANING OF MUSIC
See: Aesthetics–1 & 2, Philosophy.

"MECHANICAL" MUSIC
See:

Film Music	Radio Music
Phonograph Records	Sound Rec & Repro

Meck, Barbara von. Co-author (with
Bowen). See Tchaikovsky–1.

MEDIEVAL/RENAISSANCE ERAS
*General Note: Long and musically significant
as each of these eras is, it is more convenient
as a rule to consider them together rather
than separately, especially since there is no
generally accepted solution to the problem of
where one ends and the other begins. For our
present purposes, we consider the time-span
to be that between the period of Ancient Music and the Baroque Era—roughly from 500
A.D. to 1500 (for the Medieval Era) and
from 1500 to 1600 (for the Renaissance Era).
Actually, of course, there is considerable
over-lapping.*

See also: esp History.

Also:

Acoustics	Keyboard Instruments
Ancient Music	& Music
Anthologies	Luther
(Davison & Apel)	Madrigal
Appreciation	Mass
Augustine	Minstrels/Minstrelsy
Baroque Era	Mode/Modality
Byzantine Music	Notation (esp Apel)
Carols	Opera
Chamber Music	Organ Music
Choir/Choral–3	Phonograph Records
Church Music	Plainsong
Composers–1	Psalms/Psalmody
Counterpoint–1	Religion & Music
Elizabethan Music	Rounds (esp Bukofzer)
Gregorian Chant	Troubadours/
Hymns/Hymnody	Trouvères
Instruments	Variation
	Vocal Music

*Note: Standard works apparently O/P (or not
easily available) include those by Ficker (in
German), Gérold (in French), Landowska,
Petrucci ("Harmonice musices odhecaton,"
ed Hewitt, 1942), etc.*

BESSELER, HEINRICH. **See App Ib** (ed
Bücken).

BUKOFZER, MANFRED F.
(*See also Kantorowicz below.*)
Studies in medieval and Renaissance
music. 324 p + 7 pl (facs), mus
ex, bibl refs. Norton 1950.   6.00
*Scholarly discussions of specialized topics
in early English & Renaissance music:
The Old Hall MS., The beginnings of choral
polyphony, "Caput: a Liturgico-Musical
Study," etc.*

COUSSEMAKER, EDMOND DE (*ed*). See
App Ie.

GERBERT, MARTIN (*ed*). See App Ie.

GLEASON, HAROLD (*comp*)
Music literature outlines. Series I:
Music in the Middle Ages & Renaissance. viii, 128 p, mus ex, chap bibls,
typescript repro, paper. Levis Music
Stores, Rochester, N. Y., 1949.   2.50
*A guide to the study of music from the earliest
times through the Renaissance in concise
factual outline, with special reading lists, book
& periodical bibliographies, lists of representative music & recordings. Of the 15 outlines,
4 are devoted to medieval monophony, 5 to
medieval polyphony, and 6 to music of the
Renaissance. (For No. 2 in this series,
see Baroque Era.)*

KANTOROWICZ, ERNST H.
Laudes Regiae: a study in liturgical
acclamations & medieval ruler wor-
ship, with a study of the music of the
Laudes & musical transcriptions by
Manfred F. Bukofzer. xxii, 292 p, 15
pl, mus ex, paper. California 1946.   3.00
*University of California Publications in
History, Vol XXXIII.*

LOWINSKY, EDWARD E.
Secret chromatic art in the Netherlands motet. Tr Carl Buchman. xix,
191 p + 23–p mus ex, 8–p bibl.
Columbia 1946.   4.50
*Columbia University Studies in Musicology
No 6. A detailed analysis & proposed solution of the long-debated problems of "musica
ficta" & "musica reservata," especially in
the works of Clemens non Papa & Waelrant.
Also a novel study of "double meaning" in
16th-century arts & sciences.*

REESE, GUSTAVE
Music in the middle ages: with an
introduction on music of ancient
times. xvii, 502 p, 9 pl, 39-p bibl.
Norton 1940 (6th pr n d).   7.50
*An extensive standard work, covering the
period up to 1453, with special emphasis on
the stylistic analysis of the music itself and
on the discoveries of recent researchers. The
two main sections are: Western European
monody to about 1300 & Polyphony based on
the perfect consonances and its displacement
by polyphony based on the third. Also included is a 16-p list of phonograph recordings.*

Music in the Renaissance.
Norton in prep.   Δ
*An eagerly awaited companion work to the
author's "Music in the middle ages."*

WOLF, JOHANNES
Music of the earlier times: vocal &
instrumental examples. 158 p, music, paper. Broude 1946 (?).   2.50
*Music only, in representative examples of the
period from the 13th century to Bach.*

MEDICINE (Music and; Music as)
See: Health.

MEDTNER, Nikolai
See:

Composers–2 & 3e	Phonograph Records
Contemporary Music	Russian Music
History	Song(s)

*Note: Pertinent works apparently not gener-
ally available include Drinker's song translations (but see the note under the author-entry
for Henry S. Drinker), a booklet by Holt, and
a biography (in Russian & German) by
Jakovlev.*

Meers, Ernest George. Co-author (with
Ellingford). See Organ Playing.
Meierhoffer, Virginia. Co-author (with
Burk & Phillips). See School Music–2.

MELBA, Nellie
See:

History	Phonograph Records
Interpreters	Singers
Opera	Singing

*Note: Melba's memoirs (1925) apparently are
O/P (or not easily available), as are studies
by Colson (1933), and Murphy (1909).*

Mellalieu, William Norman. Author.
See Boy Voices.

Mellers, Wilfrid. Author.
See Composers–2, Couperin, England.
Mellichamp, Nell V. Author.
See Children–5.
Mellor, Hugh. Author. See Dances–2.
Mellquist, Jerome. Editor (with Wiese).
See Rosenfeld.
Melnik, Henry. Author. See Theory–2.

MELODIES (Harmonizing of)
See:

Composition	Melody-Writing
Harmony	Piano Playing–3
Improvisation	Songwriting

MELODRAMA
See: esp App Ic (Subirá: "Iriarte").

*Note: Standard works apparently O/P (or not
easily available) include those by Augsten
(in French), Capri (in Italian), Istel (in
German), J. F. Mason, Steinitzer (in German), Van Bellen (in French), etc.*

MELODY
*General Note: While melody is discussed at
length in many books (especially those listed
under the cross-reference subject-headings
below), it is curious indeed that there seems
to be no available book devoted primarily to
the general aspects of what is probably the
most significant element in all music.*

See:

Aesthetics–1 & 2	Harmony (esp 2,
Appreciation	Macpherson)
Composition	History
Dictionaries of Music	Melody Writing
Encyclopedias of Mu-	Monophony
sic	Songwriting
Form (esp Bigelow)	Theory
	Variation

*Note: Pertinent works apparently O/P (or not
easily available) include Danckert's "Ursym-
bole und melodische Gestaltung" (1932),
Gibbon's "Melody and the lyric" (1930), etc.*

MELODY-WRITING
See also:

Children–3 & 8	Scales
Composition	(esp Slonimsky)
Harmony (esp 2,	Songwriting
Macpherson)	Theory
Ornamentation	

GOETSCHIUS, PERCY
Exercises in melody-writing: a systematic course of melodic composition,
designed for the use of young music
students, chiefly as a course of exercises collateral with the study
of harmony. viii, 99 p, mus ex.
G. Schirmer (1900) rev ed 1923.   2.25

In two parts, respectively "Essential tones" & "Unessential or embellishing tones."

PATTERSON, FRANK
How to write a good tune: a treatise.
vii, 122 p, mus ex. G. Schirmer 1925.   1.50
Practical advice on the various factors that help to ensure tunefulness.

TAPPER, THOMAS
First year melody writing. iv, 138 p.
mus ex. Schmidt (1911) rev & aug
ed 1946.   1.50

VOGLER, JULIUS
Musical speech: classification of progressions employed in composition.
20 p, mus ex, paper. Briegel 1934.   .50
An attempt to classify the material employed in the making of a melody.

WOLFAHRT, HEINRICH
Guide to musical composition: in the invention of melodies, their transformation, development, & suitable accompaniment. Tr John S. Dwight.
vi, 96 p, mus ex. Ditson n d.   1.50
"Music Students Library" series. A sequel to the author's "Introduction to the theory of harmony" (apparently O/P).

MEMORIZATION/MEMORY (Musical)

See also:

Conducting	Psychology
Interpretation	Sight-Playing & Reading (esp Rubinstein)
Piano Playing	

Note: Pertinent works apparently O/P (or not easily available) include those by Cumberland, Goodrich, Hoffzimmer, Kinne, Rubin-Rabson, Shinn, etc.

COOKE, JAMES FRANCIS
How to memorize music. 138 p, mus
ex, 2-p bibl. Presser 1948.   1.50
Practical advice by the author, plus a symposium (p 76/135) of helpful hints by noted conductors, pianists, & other musicians.

KENYON, C. FRED
How to memorize music: with numerous musical examples. 56 p, mus ex.
Reeves n d (1904?) 6th ed n d (1950?).   1.50

LAMBOTTE, LUCIEN. See App Ia.

MACKINNON, LILIAS
Music by heart. vi, 141 p. Oxford
1938.   2.50
The primary subject is memory-training, but the book also includes informal discussions of musicians' "nerves," fatigue, the subconscious, relaxation, etc.

MATTHAY, TOBIAS
On memorizing: and on the laws of practice generally. 20 p, mus ex, paper. Oxford 1926 (5th pr 1948).   .75
The fifth of six lectures on practical psychology for music teachers.

Mendel, Arthur. Co-author (with David).
See Bach-1. (With Howard). See Composers-3a. (With Pratt). See History-2.
Translator. See Composition (Hindemith, v 1). (With Broder). See Mozart-2 (Einstein).

Mendelsohn, Felix (1876–1938). Author.
See Opera-3.

MENDELSSOHN (-BARTHOLDY), Felix

1. Letters, Own Writings
2. Life.   3. Works

MENDELSSOHN (1. Letters, Own Writings)

Note: In addition to the works listed below, many volumes of correspondence (in English & German) apparently are O/P (or not easily available).

Note: Standard works apparently O/P (or not easily available) include those by Benedict, Hensel, Hiller, Kaufman, Lampadius (in German), Rockstro, Stratton, etc.

SCHNEIDER, MAX & REICH, WILLI (eds).
See App Ib ("Denkmal im Wort und Bild").

SELDEN-GOTH, G. (ed)
Mendelssohn's letters. 373 p, 33 illus (pors, facs, etc), mus ex, 2-p bibl.
Pantheon 1945.   4.50
Selections from the Wallace translations of the "Letters" (now O/P), plus excerpts from the correspondence with Moscheles, Klingemann, et al.

SIETZ, RHEINGOLD (ed). See App Ib ("Sein Leben in Briefen").

MENDELSSOHN (2. Life)

See also:

Appreciation	History
Church Music	Program Notes
Composers-1	Romantic Era

Also: App IIa (Erskine, Humphreys juveniles).

PETITPIERRE, JACQUES
The romance of the Mendelssohns.
Tr G. Micholet-Coté. 251 p, col
frontis, 95 pl (pors, facs, etc), 3-p
bibl. Dobson 1947; Roy 1950.　　4.00
*An English edition of "Le mariage de Men-
delssohn, 1837-1937," originally published
in France (1937) by Payot et Cie.*

RADCLIFFE, PHILIP
Mendelssohn.
Dent, via Pellegrini, in prep.　　△
"Master Musicians" series.

SCOTT, MARION M.
Mendelssohn. 14 p, cover por, paper.
Novello n d (1938).　　.40
Miniature biography ("great musicians").

WERNER, JACK
(*See also Mendelssohn-3.*)
Felix Mendelssohn.
Hinrichsen in prep.　　△
"Miniature Survey" series M-17.

MENDELSSOHN (3. Works)

See also:

Appreciation	Piano Music
Chamber Music	Program Notes
Choir/Choral-3	Song(s)
Church Music	Symphony
Composers-1	Themes
Concerto	Timing
Orchestral Music	Violin Music
Phonograph Records	Vocal Music

*Note: Standard works apparently O/P (or not
easily available) include those by Armstrong,
Buick, Clerjot & Marchet (in French),
Edwards, Hathaway, Mansfield, Pearce, etc.*

HORTON, JOHN
The chamber music of Mendelssohn.
65 p, mus ex, paper. Oxford 1946.　　1.00
"Musical Pilgrim" series of analyses.

WERNER, JACK
(*See also Mendelssohn-2.*)
Elijah: an illustrated guide to
Mendelssohn's oratorio. Hinrichsen △
in prep.　　1.50
"Miniature Survey" series M-6.

WINN, CYRIL
Mendelssohn. 41 p, mus ex, paper.
Oxford 1927.　　1.00
*"Musical Pilgrim" series of analyses, cover-
ing the Midsummer Night's Dream music,
Violin Concerto, Hebrides (Fingal's Cave)
Overture, Prelude & Fugue in E minor.*

YOUNG, PERCY
Introduction to the music of Mendels-
sohn. 93 p, mus ex, 1-p bibl.
Dobson 1949.　　(1.00)
A concise over-all analytical survey.

MENGELBERG, Willem

See:

Conductors	Interpreters
History	Phonograph Records

*Note: Sollitt's "Mengelberg & the symphonic
epoch" (1929) apparently is O/P.*

Menke, Werner. Author.
See Trumpet (also App Ib.)
Mercure, (Dom) Georges. Author.
See App Ia.

MERIMÉE, Prosper

See: Bizet, Opera.

*Note: Sylvia Lyon's "Life & times of Prosper
Merimée" (Dial 1948) apparently is O/P.*

Merrill, Kathleen Gruppe.　　Co-author
(with Fox). See Dances-2.
Merritt, Arthur Tillman. Author.
See Counterpoint-1.
Mersmann, Hans. Author.
See App Ib (ed Bücken, Mersmann).

MESSAGER, André (-Charles-Prosper)

See: esp App Ia (Février).

Ballet	Operetta
French Music	Phonograph Records
History	Program Notes

MESSIAEN, Olivier

See:

Composers-2	Modern Music
Contemporary Music	Phonograph Records

Author. See App Ia.

Metfessel, Milton. Author.
See Folklore.

METRONOME

See also: Harding, Piano Playing.
*Note: Zwintscher's "The metronome," Baker
translation of 1904, apparently is O/P.*

FRANZ, FREDERICK
Metronome techniques: being a brief
account of the history & use of the
metronome, with many practical
applications for the musician. Forew
Howard Hanson. 52 p, mus ex, 1-p
bibl, paper.　　Author, New Haven,
Conn, 1947.　　1.00

METROPOLITAN OPERA COMPANY

See: esp Opera-4.

Also:

American (music in)	History
Gatti-Casazza	Opera–1 & 3

MEXICAN MUSIC/MEXICO (Music in)

See also:

Dances–2	Folklore (esp Toor)
Chávez	History
Composers–2 & 3a	Latin America

Note: Standard works apparently O/P (or not easily available in this country) include those in Spanish by Galindo, Salvidar, etc.

COVARRUBIAS, MIGUEL
Mexico south: the isthmus of Tehuantepec. xxviii, 427, viii p, illus (paintings, drgs, photos by Miguel & Rose Covarrubias). Knopf 1946.   7.50

MAYER-SERRA, OTTO
(See also App Id.)
The present state of music in Mexico (El estado presente de la musica en Mexico). Forew Charles Seeger; English tr Frank Jellinek. xiii, 47 p, paper. Pan American Union 1946.   .50
Music series No 14, with text in English & Spanish. An over-all survey of the folk music, art music (importation & imitation), and the development of musical nationalism.

Meyer, Kathi. Editor (with Hirsch).
See App Ib.
Meyer, Max Friedrich. Author.
See Hearing, Theory–1.
Meyer, Marie Antoine. Author.
See App Ia.

MEYERBEER, Giacomo

See:

Appreciation	Phonograph Records
Composers–1	Program Notes
History	Vocal Music
Opera (esp 1, Crosten)	

Note: Standard works apparently O/P (or not easily available) include those by Hervey (in English), Curzon, Dauriac, & de Lasalle (in French), Kapp & Mendel (in German), etc.

Meynell, Esther. Author.
See Bach–1 (also App Ib.)

MEZZROW, Milton "Mezz"

See also: Jazz, Popular Music.

MEZZROW, MILTON & WOLFE, BERNARD
Really the blues. 388 p. Random House 1946.   3.00
Outspoken confessions & memoirs of a jazz musician; with appendices on "Chicago style," jive language, the Panassié-Mezzrow recordings, & a 10-p glossary of jive terms.

MIASKOVSKY, Nikolai Yakovlevitch

See also:

Composers–2 & 3e	Phonograph Records
Contemporary Music	Program Notes
History	Russian Music

IKONNIKOV, ALEXANDREI A.
Myaskovsky: his life & work. 162 p, illus (por & facs). Philosophical 1946.   2.75
The only biography in English; includes a catalogue of Miaskovsky's works.

Michaut, Pierre. Author. See App Ia.
Michelman, Joseph. Author. See Violin.

MICKIEWICZ, Adam

See: Chopin, Poland (music in).

Note: A work by Arthur P. & Marion M. Coleman ("Mickiewicz in music: a study of the musical uses to which the poems of Adam Mickiewicz have been put, together with 25 of the many songs written to the poet's words from 1827 to 1947"), was published by the New York Klub Polski in 1947 (161 p, $3.00), but apparently it is not available for general distribution.

MIDDLE AGES (Music of)

See: Medieval/Renaissance Eras.

Middleton, M. H. Author.
See Ballet (ed Haskell).
Mies, Paul. Author. See App Ib.
Miessner, William Otto. Co-author (with McConathy & others). See School Music–1.
Migot, Georges. Author. See App Ia.

MILÁN, Luis

See:

History	Medieval/Renaissance
Keyboard Instruments	Spain (music in)

Note: J. B. Trend's "Luis Milán and the vihuelistas" (1925) apparently is O/P.

MILHAUD, Darius

Note: Augsbourg's "La vie de Darius Milhaud en images" (1938) apparently is O/P (or not easily available in this country).

See: esp App Ia (Beck, annotated catalogue; Collaer, biography; both in French).

Also:

Appreciation	Modern Music
Chamber Music	Phonograph Records
Composers–2	Piano Music
Contemporary Music	Program Notes
French Music	Song(s)
History	Vocal Music

Author. See App Ia (memoirs in French).

Milinowski, Marta. Author. See Carreño.

MILITARY MUSIC

See also:

Ancient Music	Medieval/Renaissance
Appreciation	Phonograph Records
Band–1	Program Notes
Bugle	Psychology
Community Music	Romantic Era
Gilmore	Sousa
History	Trombone
Industry	Trumpet
Instruments	Wind Instruments
March	

Note: Standard works apparently O/P (or not easily available) include Brenet's "La musique militaire" (1921), Panoff's "Militärmusik in Geschichte und Gegenwart" (1921), etc.

FARMER, H. G.
The rise and development of military music.   Pref Lt. A. Williams.   xxi, 156 p, illus, mus ex.   Reeves n d △ (1912).   (3.75)
Super-title: "Military music & its story."

Military music.   72 p, 4 col pl, 37 b&ws.   Chanticleer 1950.   2.50
"World of Music" series No 12: an extensively illustrated monograph.

WHITE, WILLIAM CARTER
A history of military music in America.   272 p, 93 illus (pors, facs, etc), mus ex, bibl refs.   Exposition 1944.   3.00
An informal account, stressing the story of Army bands and including biographical sketches of many bandmasters.

Miliukov, Paul. Author.
See Russia (music in).

Miller, Dayton Clarence. Author.

Note: Several books by Miller, on acoustics & the flute, apparently are O/P. For a list of books in the Dayton C. Miller collection, Library of Congress, see Bibliography (Bartlett).

Miller, George Armitage. Compiler.
See Hearing.

Miller, Glenn. Author.   See Arranging–2.
Miller, Horace Alden. Author.
See Harmony–1.
Miller, Hugh Milton. Author.
See History–3.
Miller, Philip Lieson. Translator.
See Song Translations.
Milligan, Harold Vincent. Author.
See Opera–3.
Mills, John. Author.
See Sound Recording & Reproduction.
Milne, A. Forbes. Author.
See Beethoven–3.

MILTON, John (the elder)

See also:

Elizabethan Music	History
England (music in)	Madrigal
English Music	Poetry

BRENNECKE, ERNEST, Jr.
John Milton the elder and his music. xiv, 224 p, 13 illus (facs), 47-p mus ex, 8–p bibl.   Columbia 1938.   3.50
Columbia "Studies in Musicology" No 2; includes a list of Milton's musical works.

MILTON, John (the poet)

Note: Sigmund Spaeth's thesis, "Milton's knowledge of music" (1913) apparently is not generally available.

Mingotti, Antonio. Author. See App Ib.

MINIATURE BIOGRAPHIES (Series)

See: Biographies ("Great Musicians" series), for a list of the miniature-biography pamphlets published by Novello.

MINIATURE SCORES

See: esp Score-Reading.
Also: Instrumentation, Orchestra.

Note: Miniature scores themselves are not listed in the present Guide.

Mininberg, Ian. Author.
See Piano Playing–2.
Minneapolis Public Library, Music Dept. Compilers. See Dances–2.

MINNESINGERS (Minnesänger)

See:

Appreciation	Song(s)
Hager	Troubadours/
History	Trouvères
Medieval/Renaissance	Vocal Music
Minstrels/Minstrelsy	Wagner–3

Note: Standard works apparently O/P (or not easily available) include those by Gennrich (in German), etc.

MINSTRELS/MINSTRELSY

General Note: While these terms usually are associated today with music-hall (especially "black-face") entertainment,—their original and more exact use was to designate the professional musical entertainers (mimes, jongleurs, gleemen, etc) of the Middle Ages, and their music.

See also:

America (music in)	Medieval/Renaissance
Appreciation	Negro Music &
California (Gagey)	Musicians
England (music in)	Popular Music
Foster	Song(s)
Folklore	Troubadours/
Foster	Trouvères
History	Vocal Music

Note: Standard works apparently O/P (or not easily available) include those by Edgar, Grossmann (in German), etc.

DUNCAN, WILLIAM EDMONSTOUNE
The story of minstrelsy. xv, 337 p, col frontis, illus, mus ex, 2-p bibl. Scott 1907, via Reeves.   (3.00)
"Music Story" series, (now O/P in the Scribner American edition), including a glossary & a chronological table.

JUSSERAND, JEAN JULES
English wayfaring life in the middle ages (14th century).   Tr Lucy Toulmin Smith. 315 p, illus. (1888) Putnam 4th ed 1950.   6.00
A standard study, with a chapter devoted to the minstrels of the period.

WINTER, MARION H.
Juba and American minstrelsy.   ? p, illus, paper. Auvergne 1949/50, in prep.   1.00

MINUET

See:

Appreciation	Dances-1, 2, & 3
Baroque Era	Form
Classical Era	French Music
(The) Dance	Program Notes
Dance Music	Symphony

MISCELLANIES

See also:

Anecdotes	Humor
Anthologies	Quizzes

HAMEL, FRED & HÜRLIMANN, M. (eds).   See App Ib.

MATHEWS, RUTH VENDLEY
You need music: the power of music to make you healthy, happy, & wise. 95 p, illus (Corl D. La Ross). Kjos 1942.   1.50
A collection of inspirational quotations.

SCHMID, GOTTFRIED (ed).   See App Ib.

SIEGMEISTER, ELIE (ed)
The music lover's handbook. xiii, 817 p, mus ex. Morrow 1943 (1946).   5.00
A collection of some 150 pieces on various aspects of music, by some 52 composers, critics, & other writers.

SLONIMSKY, NICOLAS (comp)
A lexicon of musical invective. Coleman in prep.   3.50
An anthology of critical assaults on composers since the time of Beethoven.

A thing or two about music.   305 p, illus (Maggi Fiedler).   Allen Towne 1948, via Crown 1949.   3.00
A singular grab-bag of musical limericks, paradoxes, oddities, & hitherto unpublished anecdotes about music & musicians.

Mitchell, William John. Author, editor. See Harmony-2 Keyboard Instruments (Bach).

Mittag, Erwin. Author. See Philharmonic-2.

Mize, John Townsend Hinton. Author, editor. See Crosby, Who's Who.

Mizwa, Stephen Paul. Editor. See Chopin-1, Poland (music in).

Mocquereau, (Dom) André. Author. See Gregorian Chant, (also App Ia.)

MODE/MODALITY

See also:

Acoustics	Instruments
Ancient Music	(esp Schlesinger)
Baroque Era	Madrigal (esp Scott)
Byzantine Music	Medieval/Renaissance
Composition	Monophony
Counterpoint-1	Plainsong
(esp Morris)	Scales
Form	Theory
Gregorian Chant	Tonality/Atonality
Harmony	Twelve-Tone
History	Technique

Note: Standard works apparently O/P (or not easily available) include those by Miller, Monroe, Werner, Winnington-Ingram, etc.

PERFIELD, EFFA ELLIS
Greek modes and church modes: modal & secular harmonizations. 15 p, mus ex, paper. Author, N. Y., 1938 (1940).   1.50

A brief outline of the various modes, with hints on proper harmonizations.

RICHARDSON, A. MADELEY
Mediaeval modes: their melody & harmony for the use of the modern composer. Forew Rubin Goldmark. 88 p, frontis, mus ex, paper. Gray 1933. 2.00
A standard work, with representative examples by various composers.

MODERN MUSIC

General Note: No attempt has been made here to observe proper distinction between "modern" and "contemporary" music. Many older publications (not listed here), which include the term "modern" in their titles, of course actually deal with music considered modern (e.g., that of Wagner) at the time of writing.

See also: esp Contemporary Music.

Also:

Appreciation	Program Notes
Composers-2 (& under individual names)	Tonality/Atonality
	Twelve-Tone
History	Technique
Phonograph Records	

Note: Standard works apparently O/P (or not easily available) include those by Gilman, Heyman ("Relation of ultramodern to archaic music," 1921), Křenek ("Music here & now", English ed 1939, German ed 1936), Myers, Swan, Weissmann, etc.

ABRAHAM, GERALD
This modern stuff: an introduction to contemporary music. Forew Sir Walford Davies. 104 p, mus ex. (1933, 2nd ed 1939) Citadel repr 1947. 1.40
A discussion of the modern idiom, including the quarter-tone & twelve-tone systems; originally published by Duckworth, London.

ESCHMAN, KARL
Changing forms in modern music. xii, 180 p, mus ex. E. C. Schirmer 1945. 3.00
An analytical study of modern extensions & variants of traditional musical forms.

GRAF, MAX
Modern music: composers and music of our time. Tr Beatrice R. Maier. 320 p. Philosophical 1946. 3.00
Including R. Strauss, Debussy, Mahler, Puccini, Stravinsky, etc, but with special emphasis on the Viennese school.

HOWARD, JOHN TASKER
This modern music: a guide for the bewildered listener, which explains why he may not like modern music & how he can enjoy it more. 234 p, mus ex, 2–p bibl. Crowell 1942 (3rd pr 1946). 2.50
The "appreciative" approach to musical modernism, including a selected record list.

LANDOWSKI, W. L. See App Ia.

MERSMANN, HANS. See App Ib (ed Bücken).

MIES, PAUL. See App Ib.

PARROTT, IAN
Pathways to modern music. 55 p, △ mus ex, paper. Unwin 1947. (1.00)

MODULATION

General Note: The books listed below are confined to the practical aspects only of modulation; many of them are little more than lists or charts of convenient modulations from one key to another.

See also:

Composition	Mode/Modality
Harmony	Scales
Improvisation	Theory
Keyboard Harmony	Transposition

Note: Riemann's "Systematische Modulationslehre" (1887) apparently is O/P (or not easily available in this country), while numerous chart, table, & dial publications either are not generally available or do not seem important enough for listing here.

ANCIS, S.
Scheme modulations. vii, 95 p, mus ex. C. Fischer 1929. 1.50

BARNES, EDWARD SHIPPEN
Modulation in theory and practice: and interludes for the church organist. 153 p, music. J. Fischer 1949. 4.00
Mainly music. Part 1 outlines modulation by the use of common chords; part 2 is a set of modulations between all keys; part 3 is a set of short interludes in all keys.

BAUER, HAROLD
A primer for practical keyboard modulation. 15 p, music, paper. G. Schirmer 1949. .75
Mostly musical exercises in keyboard modulations, with notes & a 1-p introduction.

FOOTE, ARTHUR
Modulation and related harmonic questions. 99 p, mus ex. Schmidt 1919. 1.25
A standard, practical work.

KRECKEL, PHILIP G.
Modulations: for organists, pianists,
& students. 17 p, music, paper. J.
Fisher 1946.   1.00
Exercises, especially for organists.

LAWRENCE, LUCILE & SALZEDO, CARLOS
The art of modulating: for harpists,
pianists, organists; including modulations, extensions, cadenzas, & a
complete illustration of harmonic
fluxes (formerly called "glissandi");
followed by 10 fragments of dances &
5 easy characteristic pieces for harp
by Salzedo. Forew Leopold Stokowski.
v, 61 p, 2 photos, music, paper.
G. Schirmer 1950.   3.50
*With tables of intervals & formulas, rules
governing modulation, examples, etc.*

OREM, PRESTON WARE
Manual of modulation. 44 p, mus
ex, paper. Presser 1930.   .40

OTTERSTRÖM, THORWALD
A theory of modulation (Eine Modu-
lation-Theorie). viii, 162 p, mus ex.
Chicago 1935.   2.50
*A standard work of mathematical interpreta-
tion, with text in English & German.*

PEERY, ROB ROY
Practical keyboard modulation. iv,
68 p, mus ex, bds. Presser 1944.   1.00
*A series of some 132 4-bar study-models, with
a supplement of modulating interludes.*

REGER, MAX
On the theory of modulation. Tr
John Bernhoff. 50 p, mus ex, paper.
(1904) Kalmus repr n d (1948).   1.00
*A standard work: the translation of "Beiträge
zur Modulationslehre" (1930), originally
published by Kahnt, Leipzig, as "Supplement
to the theory of modulation."*

VOGLER, JULIUS
526 "ready-to-use" modulations: to
& from all keys. 62 p, mus ex, paper.
Briegel 1936.   1.00
A modern method of modulation. 22
p, mus ex, paper. Briegel 1933.   .50

ZOELLER, CARLI (ed)
The art of modulation: a handbook
showing at a glance the modulations
from one key to any other in the
octave, consisting of 1008 modulations. iii, 48 p, mus ex. Reeves 5th
ed n d. (*Tables.*)   3.00

Mohler, Louis. Author. See Teaching–2.

Moisenko, Rena. Author.
See Composers–3e.
Mokrejs, John. Author.
See Counterpoint–2, Harmony–2. Sight-
Playing & Reading.
Moncur-Sime, A. H. Author.
See Shakespeare & Music.

MONODY/MONOPHONY

*General Note: Although these two terms are
used more or less synonymously, Monody is
literally music for a single singer—especially
the accompanied solo song of the Italian
"Nuove musiche" around 1600, whereas
Monophony strictly is music for a single
melodic line, sung or played without accompaniment.*

See also:

Acoustics	Instruments
Ancient Music	Intonation
Anthologies (esp Davi-	Italy (music in)
son & Apel, Gleason)	Medieval/Renaissance
Appreciation	Minstrels/Minstrelsy
Byzantine Music	Plainsong
Church Music	Scales
Folklore	Song(s)
Folksongs	Troubadours/
Gregorian Chant	Trouvères
History	Vocal Music

PARTCH, HARRY
Genesis of a music: monophony, the
relation of its music to history & contemporary trends; its philosophy,
concepts, & principles; its relation
to historic & proposed intonations;
and its applications to musical
instruments. Forew Otto Luening.
xx, 362 p, 17 pl, 30 diagrs, 4–p bibl.
Wisconsin 1949.   10.00

*An extraordinary work, the first part of which
is a plea for "corporeal" (growing from the
spoken word, like minstrelsy) as opposed to
"abstract" music. The rest is devoted to a
study of intonation, the author's system of
monophony using a 43-tone scale, and the
instruments & notation he has devised for it.*

Monrad-Johansen, David.   Catalogued
under Johansen, David Monrad.
Montagu-Nathan, Montagu. Author.
See Russian Music.
Montani, Nicola Aloysius. Author.
See Solfège/Solfeggio.

MONTEVERDI, Claudio

See also:

Appreciation	Medieval/Renaissance
Composers–1	Opera
History	Phonograph Records
Italy (music in)	Program Notes
Madrigal	Vocal Music

Note: Standard works apparently O/P (or not easily available) include those by Leichtentritt (in German); Prunières (in English & French), Schneider (in French); and those in Italian by Malipiero, Picenardi, etc.

POLI, DOMENICO DE'. See App Ic.

REDLICH, HANS FERDINAND. See App Ib.

SCHRADE, LEO
Monteverdi: creator of modern music. 384 p, 11 pl (pors, fac, etc), 100 mus ex, 7–p bibl. Norton 1950. 6.00

The most recent extensive biography, but also an illuminating interpretation of Monteverdi's style as a foundation of 17th century music and—in basic conceptions, at least—of the music of our own day.

Moody, Charles Henry. Author.
See Boy Voices.
Moor, Arthur Prichard. Author.
See Libraries.
Moore, Earl Vincent. Author (with Heger).
See Symphony.
Moore, Douglas Stuart. Author.
See Appreciation
Moore, Elizabeth Conover. Author.
See Almanacs & Calendars.
Moore, Gerald. Author.
See Accompaniment.

MOORE, Grace
See: Opera, Singers, Phonograph Records.

Note: An autobiography, "You're only human once" (1944), apparently is O/P.

Moore, Stephen Sidney. Author.
See School Music–1.

MOORE, Thomas
See:

History	Poetry
Ireland (music in)	Song(s)
Minstrels/Minstrelsy	Vocal Music

Note: Biographies by Jones (1937) & Strong (1937) apparently are O/P.

Mooser, R. Aloys. Author. See App Ia.
Moresby, Emily Isabelle. Author.
See Australia (music in).
Moreux, Serge. Author. See App Ia.
Morgan, Hazel Beckwith Nohavec.
Author. See Education. Co-author (with Ranks). See Children–8.

Morgan, Russell Van Dyke. Co-author (with Skeat & Clarke). See Arranging–1.
Morgan, Vincent. Author.
See School Music–1.
Morgenstern, Sam. Co-compiler (with Barlow). See Themes.

MÖRIKE, Eduard Friedrich
See also:

History	Romantic Era
Literature	Song(s)
Poetry	Song Translations

Author. See Mozart–2 (also App Ib).

KNEISEL, JESSIE HOSKAM
Mörike and music. xiii, 236 p, mus ex, 10–p bibl, typescript repro, paper. Author, N. Y., 1949. △

A study of the romantic German author (whose texts were set by Wolf, Brahms, & many other Lieder composers), including a list of musical works based on his poems.

Morin, Raymond. Author.
See Worcester Music Festival.
Morley, Iris. Co-author (with Manchester), photographer. See Ballet.

MORLEY, Thomas
See:

Appreciation	History
Choir/Choral–3	Madrigal
Church Music	(esp Fellowes)
Composers–1 & 3c	Medieval/Renaissance
Elizabethan Music	Phonograph Records
English Music	Vocal Music

Note: Morley's own "Plaine and easie introduction to practicall musike" (1597/1608) apparently is O/P in the facsimile edition of 1937 (Oxford, for the Shakespeare Assn).

Morneweck, Evelyn Foster. Author.
See Foster.

MORRIS (DANCE)
See:

(The) Dance	England (music in)
Dance Music	Folklore
Dances–1 & 2	History

Note: Numerous collections of Morris-Dance music, ed by Sharp & others, are not listed in the present Guide.

Morris, Alton Chester. Editor.
See Folksongs–2.

Morris, Reginald Owen. Author. See:
Counterpoint–1. Contrapuntal technique in the 16th century (1922). 3.00

Counterpoint–2. Introduction to
counterpoint (1944). **1.00**
Form. Structure of music (1935). **1.25**
Harmony–2. Oxford harmony, v 1
(1946). **3.00**
——. Foundations of practical harmony & counterpoint (1925/49). **1.50**
Keyboard Harmony. Figured harmony at the keyboard (1932). **1.50**
Sight-Playing & Reading. Preparatory exercises in score reading (1931),
by Morris & Ferguson. **2.00**

Morse, Philip McCord. Author.
See Acoustics.

MORTON, Jelly Roll
(Ferdinand Joseph LaMenthe)
See also: Jazz, Phonograph Records.

LOMAX, ALAN
Mister Jelly Roll: the fortunes of
Jelly Roll Morton, New Orleans
Creole & "Inventor of Jazz." xvii,
318 p, illus (drwgs by David Stone
Martin), mus ex, music. Duell Sloan
1950. **3.50**

*The extraordinary story of a pianist-composer
(and of the early days of jazz), related
largely in his own words, as recorded at the
Library of Congress. The book includes end-
paper maps of New Orleans jazz locales,
several Morton tunes & scores, and detailed
lists of his works & recordings.*

Moser, Hans Albrecht. Author.
See App Ib.

Moser, Hans Joachim. Author.

*Note: Numerous works in German by H. J.
Moser apparently are O/P (or not easily
available in this country).*

Moses, Julian Morton. Compiler.
See Phonograph Records.
Moskowitz, Harry. Co-compiler (with
Broderick). See Radio.
Mosoriak, Roy. Author. See Boxes.
Moss, Carlton. Co-author (with Horne &
Arnstein). See Horne.
Motchane-Morhange, Marthe. Author.
See Sight-Playing & Reading.

MOTET
*Note: Standard works apparently O/P (or not
easily available in this country) include those*

*in German by Balmer (Lassus's motets),
Leichtentritt, Lowinsky (Lassus's motets),
Meyer, Neyses, Stephan, etc.*

See also:
Appreciation　　　　　　Elizabethan Music
Baroque Era　　　　　　History
Choir/Choral–3　　　　　Italian Music
Church Music　　　　　　Medieval/Renaissance
Composers–1 (& under　　　(esp Lowinsky)
　individual names)　　　Phonograph Records
Counterpoint–1　　　　　Program Notes
　(esp Kitson, Morris,　　Vocal Music
　Porter)

LEICHTENTRITT, HUGO
History of the motet.
Musurgia 1951, pending. △
*"Musurgia Studies in Musicology," Series
A, v 3/4/5 (on subscription only). The long-
awaited English version of a standard work,
"Geschichte der Motette" (1908).*

MOTION-PICTURE MUSIC
See: Film Music, Films.

Mottinger, Alvina H. Editor.
See Carols.

MOUSSORGSKY
Catalogued under Mussorgsky.

Moy, Edgar. Compiler. See Children–8.

MOZART, (Johann Georg) Leopold
See:
Baroque Era　　　　　　Mozart–1 & 2
Classic Era　　　　　　Phonograph Records
History　　　　　　　　Violin Playing
Author. See Violin Playing.

MOZART, Wolfgang Amadeus
1. Letters　2. Life　3. Works

MOZART (1. Letters)
*Note: Mersmann's edition of the letters (tr
Bozman, 1928) apparently is O/P (or not
easily available), as is a book of documentary
excerpts by Kerst (1905).*

ANDERSON, EMILY (ed & tr)
The letters of Mozart and his family:
chronologically arranged . . . with an
introduction, notes, & indices. With
extracts from the letters of Constanze
Mozart to Johann Anton André, tr
& ed C. B. Oldman. 3 v: xxxix,
xxix, xxvii, 1560 p, 3 facs, 40 illus
(pors, etc). Macmillan 1938. **10.50**

*All the authenticated Mozart letters, based
on the standard Schiedermair ed (in German),
but with many additions & much new
material, extensive notes & references, indices
of Mozart's works, etc.*

*(Special Note: Every rule deserves to be broken
at least once and this is the ideal occasion to
shatter ours covering strictly non-critical annotations. Surely the present compiler is only
one of many who believe that the Mozart letters
not only contain some of the most illuminating
passages ever written about music, but also
comprise a psychological & historical document of truly incomparable significance!)*

HOESLI, IRMA. See App Ib.

MÜLLER VON ASOW, HEDWIG & E. H. (eds)
See App Ib.

REICH, WILLI (ed). See App Ib.

MOZART (2. Life)

See also:

Appreciation	Goethe
Autographs	Letters
Casanova	Opera
Classic Era	Program Notes
Composers–1	Vienna

Also: App IIa (juveniles by Lingg, Wheeler
& Deucher, Wheeler & Purdy).

*Note: Standard works apparently O/P (or not
easily available) include those in English by
Breakspeare, Deiters (also in German),
Ghéon (but see App Ia for French ed),
Holmes, Hussey, Jahn (also in German),
Kolb (but see App Ib for German ed),
Sitwell, etc; in French by Buenzod, Curzon,
Pitrou, etc; in German by Deiters, Farga,
Haas, Jahn & Abert, Komorzinski, Lert,
Mersmann, Nettl, Niemtschek, Schaeffner,
Schiedermair, Schurig, etc.*

BLOM, ERIC
Mozart. xi, 388 p, 8 pl (pors, facs,
etc), mus ex, 3–p bibl.   Dent 1935
(1936); Pellegrini 1949.   2.50
*"Master Musicians" series, with the usual
calendar, personalia, catalogue of works, etc.
This replaces the earlier Master Musicians
biography by Breakspeare, 1902.*

BONAVIA, FERRUCCIO
Mozart. 22 p, cover por, paper.
Novello n d (1939).   .40
Miniature biography ("great musicians").

BORY, ROBERT. See App Ia.

BOSCHOT, ADOLPHE. See App Ia.

BÜCKEN, ERNST. See App Ib.

CHANTAVOINE, JEAN. See App Ia.

DAVENPORT, MARCIA
Mozart. xi, 400 p, 16 pl (pors, facs),
4–p bibl. Scribner 1932 (1947).   3.75
*A popular, but unromanticized, life-story by
the daughter of Alma Gluck.*

EINSTEIN, ALFRED
   (*See also Mozart–3, Köchel & Einstein.*)
Mozart: his character, his work. Tr
Arthur Mendel & Nathan Broder.
x, 492 p, 6 pl (pors), mus ex. Oxford
1945.   5.00
*Less an orthodox biography than a detailed
analysis of the personality & technique of
the man—and genius, by the present-day
Mozart authority. The book includes a
condensed catalogue of works by "K" numbers.*

GHÉON, HENRI. See App Ia.

GINZKEY, FRANZ K. (ed). See App Ib.

KOLB, ANNETTE. See App Ib.

MÖRIKE, EDUARD
Mozart on the way to Prague. Tr &
intro by Walter & Catherine Alison
Phillips.   127 p, 13 drwgs (Eliane
Bonabel). Pantheon 1947.   2.75
*Originally published in German in 1855 (see
App Ib), this is a romantic poet's fictional
(but based on facts) narrative of an episode
in Mozart's life just before the first perform-
ance of "Don Giovanni."*

NETTL, PAUL. See App Ib ("Goethe und
Mozart"), also Mozart–3.

PARROT, LOUIS. See App Ia.

PAUMGARTNER, BERNHARD. See App Ib.

REICH, WILLI (comp). See App Ib.

TALBOT, J. E.
Mozart.   125 p, frontis por, 1–p
bibl. (1934) Wyn 1949.   1.00
*"Great Musicians" series, originally pub-
lished by Duckworth, London, in 1934.*

SAINT-FOIX, GEORGES DE. See App Ia.
   (*See also Mozart–3.*)

TURNER, W. J.
Mozart: the man and his works. xiv,
458, vi p, 17 illus, 3–p bibl. Knopf
1938.   4.00
Same. Tudor repr n d.   1.98
*A highly individual approach, which en-
deavors to depict a Mozart of far greater*

stature than realized by most earlier biographers.

VALENTIN, ERICH. See App Ib.

WYZEWA, TÉODOR DE & SAINT-FOIX. See App Ia

MOZART (3. Works)

See also:

Appreciation	Opera
Beaumarchais	Orchestral Music
Berlioz–1 (essays)	Organ Music
Chamber Music	Phonograph Records
Choir/Choral–3	Piano Music
Church Music	Program Notes
Classic Era	Song(s)
Composers–1	String Quartet
Concerto	Symphony
Haydn	Themes
History	Timing
Masonic Music	Violin Music
Mozart–1 & 2	Vocal Music

Note: Standard works apparently O/P (or not easily available) include those in English by Coviello, Pole, Tobin, etc; in German by Ballin, Conrad, Heinrich, Komorzynski, Lert, Nagel, Reineke, Schultz, Schünemann, Weltner, etc.

BENN, CHRISTOPHER
Mozart on the stage. Intro Richard Capell. 178 p, 10 col illus (Kenneth Green), 1–p bibl. Coward 1946.   5.00
A study of staging & producing the Mozart operas, based largely on the Glyndebourne Festival practices. The appendix includes brief biographies of Lorenzo da Ponte & Emanuel Schikaneder.

CHANTAVOINE, JEAN. See App Ia.

CROZIER, ERIC (ed)
Così fan tutte. 48 p, 12 photos, mus ex, paper. Lane 1945 (1946).   .50
"Sadler's Wells Opera Books" No 2: essays by Eric Blom (history of the opera), Clemence Dane (the playgoer at the opera), & Edward J. Dent (music of the opera).
The marriage of Figaro. 48 p, 13 illus, mus ex, paper. Lane 1948.   .50
"Sadler's Wells Opera Books" No 5: essays by Eric Blom (music of the opera), Scott Goddard (history of the opera), & Thomas Walton (Beaumarchais, da Ponte, & Figaro).

DENT, EDWARD J.
Mozart's operas: a critical study. xi, 276 p, 9 illus (pors & fac), mus ex. (1913) Oxford 2nd ed 1947.   4.75
A standard work (originally published by Chatto & Windus in 1913) in a completely revised edition, embodying the results of recent research.

DENT, EDWARD J. (tr)
Don Giovanni: a comic opera in two acts, words by Lorenzo da Ponte; English version. xix, 72 p, paper. Oxford 1938.   .80
The magic flute (Die Zauberflöte): an opera in two acts, words by Carl Ludwig Gieseke & Emanuel Schikaneder; English version. xv, 49 p, paper. Oxford 1937 (1943).   .80
The marriage of Figaro (Le Nozze di Figaro): a comic opera in four acts, Italian words adapted from the comedy of Beaumarchais . . . by Lorenzo da Ponte; English version. xiii, 96 p, paper. Oxford 1937 (3rd pr 1946).   .80
The three Mozart items in Professor Dent's series of librettos in English, with notes.

DICKINSON, A. E. F.
A study of Mozart's last three symphonies. 58 p, mus ex, paper. Oxford (1927) 2nd ed 1940 (1947).   1.00
"Musical Pilgrim" series of analyses.

DUNHILL, THOMAS F.
Mozart's string quartets. 2 v: 49, 44 p, mus ex, paper. Oxford 1927.   2.00
"Musical Pilgrim" series of analyses: v 1: early quartets through K. 428; v 2: later quartets, including Adagio & Fugue, K. 546.

GIRDLESTONE, C. M.
Mozart's piano concertos. 511 p, mus ex. Cassell 1948.   6.00
The author's own translation of a study that appeared originally in French in 1939 (see App Ia). The concertos are analyzed in detail and there is a list of recordings, also a thematic-index detachable book-mark.

HUSSEY, DYNELEY
Introduction to the music of Mozart. Dobson in prep.   (1.00)

HUTCHINGS, ARTHUR
A companion to Mozart's piano concertos. xiv, 211 p, mus ex, 1–p bibl. Oxford (1948) 2nd ed 1950.   4.00
Detailed analyses of 24 concertos with a brief survey of the evolution of the concerto in general, and a list of recordings. The new edition adds an index and a list of Mozart's own concerto cadenzas.

JOUVE, PIERRE JEAN. See App Ia.

KÖCHEL, LUDWIG VON (comp) & EINSTEIN, ALFRED (ed)
Chronologisch-thematischesVerzeichnis sämtlicher Tonwerke Wolfgang Amade Mozarts. xlix, 1052 p,

mus ex. Edwards repr of 3rd ed 1937 △
+ supplement 1947.   12.50

As an exception to our general rule, this standard reference work in German is listed here as well as in App Ib (German books), since it is so vitally useful (& useable) as a thematic index even by non-German readers. Köchel's original edition appeared in 1862; Einstein's 3rd edition in 1937; the present version includes marginal notes & a supplement—"Berichtigungen und Zusätze" (p 982/1052)—by Einstein.

LEE, RUPERT
Mozart: The magic flute. 35 p + 7
pl, mus ex, brief bibl, paper. Boosey
1947.   .60
"Covent Garden Operas" series.

MARKS, F. HELENA
The sonata: its form & meaning as exemplified in the piano sonatas by Mozart; a descriptive analysis. xl, 167 p, frontis, mus ex, 3-p bibl, paper. Reeves n d (1921).   (4.25)
Detailed analyses of 20 sonatas, prefaced by a chapter (p xvii/xl) on sonata form

NETTL, PAUL (ed)
(See also App Ib.)
Mozart-Goethe: Das Veilchen—The Violet; the history of a song. Unp (12-p text + 8-p facs), illus, mus ex. Storm 1949.   7.50
A handsome gift edition of Mozart's 1785 manuscript & the Edition Princips of 1789 in facsimile reproductions, plus the song-text in German & English, and an editorial commentary.

SAINT-FOIX, GEORGES DE
(See also App Ia.)
The symphonies of Mozart. Tr Leslie Orrey. xii, 217 p, illus, mus ex, 2-p bibl. (1947) Knopf 1949.   3.00
The first English edition (published in 1947 by Dobson, London) of a standard work originally published in French by Mellottée, Paris, 1932. About half the book is devoted to the earlier symphonies; the other half to a more detailed study of the last three, and to a comparison of these works with Haydn's last symphonies.

TOBIN, J. R.
Mozart and the sonata form: a companion book to any volume of the sonatas for piano, including an analysis of the form of each movement, with notes upon treatment &   △
tonality. 156 p. Reeves 1916.   (2.25)
Listed O/P above, but just re-issued.

UNESCO DISCOGRAPHY
The works of Wolfgang Amadeus Mozart: general discography. Archives of Recorded Music UNESCO 1951, in prep.   △
In preparation for 1951 publication, first in French, later in English.

Mueller, Grover W. Co-author (with Stecher). See Dances–1.
Muller, Daniel. Author. See App Ia.
Müller, Ernst. Author. See App Ib.
Müller von Asow, Hedwig & Erich H. Editors. See App Ib (Bach, Mainwaring).
Müller-Blattau, Joseph. Author. See App Ib.
Murphy, Howard Ansley. Author. See Form, Teaching–2. (With Stringham). See Theory–2.
Murphy, Lyle Spud. Author. See Twelve-Tone Technique.
Murray, Arthur. Author. See Dances–2.
Murray, Josephine. Author (with Bathurst). See School Music–1.

Mursell, James Lockhart. Author. See:
Education. Musical growth (1948).   3.75
——. Human values in (1934).   3.00
Psychology. Of school music teaching (1938), Mursell & Glenn.   3.20
School Music–1. Music in American schools (1943).   3.10
Teaching–1. Developmental (1949).   3.50
——. Successful teaching (1946).   3.75
Tests. Psychological (1947).   4.00
Note: Several other books by Mursell, including his "Psychology of music" (1937), apparently are O/P.

MUSIC . . .

General Note: For titles such as "Music and ...," "Music in ...," "Music of ...," "Musical ...," etc, see under the key word.

In general it may be assumed that nearly all subject-headings in the present Guide are qualified by a preceding "Musical" or a following parenthesis, ("Music in"), ("Music of"), etc. For example, the entry Form should be read (Musical) Form; the entry Appreciation as Appreciation (Musical) or Appreciation (of Music).

MUSIC (Nature of)
See: Aesthetics–1 & 2, Philosophy.

MUSIC BOXES

See: Boxes—musical (Mosoriak).

Music Educators National Conference.

Publishers, sponsors.　See:

Community Music (MENC)　　MENC & note)
Education (Larson, Morgan)　　School Music–3 (NSBOVA entry, Sur)
School Music–1 (Best,

Note: For information about the MENC and its publications (both those already available & those in preparation), please address the Music Educators National Conference, 64 East Jackson Boulevard, Chicago.

MUSIC HALLS

See:
America (music in)　　Operetta/Opéra-
England (music in)　　　Comique
History　　　　　　　Popular Music
Minstrels/Minstrelsy

MUSIC-LOVER(S)

General Note: Most books incorporating this awkward (but apparently indispensable) phrase in their titles turn out to deal with Appreciation, or so closely related a subject as Program Notes.

MUSIC ROOMS & EQUIPMENT

See: School Music–1 (Best).

Also:
Appreciation　　　　Phonograph Records
Colleges　　　　　　School Music
Community Music　　Teaching
Education

"MUSIC STUDENTS LIBRARY" (Series)

Note: This is an extensive catalogue of books more or less uniform in format, but not in style or organization of material, which are devoted mainly to various aspects of applied or practical musicianship (Conducting, Counterpoint, Form, Instrumentation/Orchestration, Piano Playing, Singing, etc). There is also a companion "Pocket Music Student" series. Both are published under the Oliver Ditson imprint by Presser.

Music Supervisors National Conference, Research Council.

Sponsors (in cooperation with the National Bureau for the Advancement of Music).　See Colleges.

MUSICA FICTA (Musica Falsa)
MUSICA RESERVATA

See: History, Medieval/Renaissance (esp Lowinsky).

MUSICAL COMEDY

See: Operetta, Popular Music.

"MUSICAL PILGRIM" (Series)

Note: This is a series (in uniform paper-cover, pocket-size format, and more or less uniform style & organization of material) of detailed musical analyses of various composers' works, written by various authors under the general editorship of Dr Arthur Somervell. For works currently in-print, see:

Bach–2　　　　　　　Schubert–2
Beethoven–3　　　　Sibelius
Berlioz–3　　　　　　R.Strauss
Brahms–2　　　　　　Stravinsky–2
Composers–3d　　　　Tchaikovsky–2
　(Debussy & Ravel)　Vaughan Williams
Franck　　　　　　　Wagner–3
Mendelssohn–3　　　　Walton
Mozart–3

MUSICAL TIMES (London)

See: England (music in) (esp Scholes).

MUSICIANS

See: under the names of individuals.

Also:
Composers　　　　　　Organists
Conductors　　　　　　Pianists
Dictionaries of Music　　Singers
Encyclopedias of Music　Teachers
History　　　　　　　Violinists
Interpreters　　　　　　Who's Who
　　　　　　　　　　　Yearbooks

MUSICIANSHIP— APPLIED & "THEORETICAL"

General Note: Altogether apart from books dealing with composers & their works; apart from music-histories and detailed studies of the music of particular periods, regions, & nationalities; apart too from such "listeners'-aids" as books on "appreciation," collections of program notes, opera "stories," etc;—a great many publications listed in the present Guide are directed primarily to actual & potential practitioners of music: the amateurs, students, & executants of various kinds who are endeavoring to learn, or to extend their knowledge of, the craft of musicianship itself.

The present entry, intended for the convenience & guidance of such practitioners, lists the specific subject-headings under which most of these books are listed.

There are no actual book-entries here, for—curiously enough and despite the plethora of "methods," textbooks, handbooks, & study-courses in various aspects of practical musi-

cianship—there seems to be no appropriate available general *publication. Indeed one will look in vain in most bibliographies, dictionaries, & encyclopedias of music for any entry under the subject-heading of Musicianship!*

Of course, the requirements demanded for the adequate training of any practising musician are well enough known to all professional musicians & educators; most of them are discussed in many books on music education, school music, teaching, etc; numerous books outline the specific requirements for graduation, qualifications, or degrees at various conservatories & university courses. But what seems to be lacking is a comprehensive over-all survey: a book or syllabus for the information of the prospective music student (or the interested layman), which systematically outlines & defines the basic requirements of practical musicianship in general, and the further, specialized requirements of such individual fields of application as conducting, singing, solo & ensemble playing, etc.

[A new book, published after the above words were written, appears at first glance as an answer to my prayers, for it seems to fill many of the needs I've outlined, except that it is directed primarily to teachers—rather than to students & interested laymen—of music. See, under Teaching-2, Howard A. Murphy's "Teaching musicianship: a manual of methods & materials" (1950).]

The various subjects involved under the general heading of Musicianship customarily are divided into two main groups: those dealing with the "applied," "practical," "aural," or "sounded" aspects of music-making itself; and those concerned with the "theoretical," "paper-work," or "background-study" aspects.

Obviously, such a division is largely artificial and fortunately it is not taken very seriously, at least nowadays, in actual practice. A "theoretical" subject like Harmony, for example, can be studied & practised, like mathematics, solely on paper; but such procedure is abstract & sterile indeed unless it is augmented in the "applied" field by translating the harmony exercises into actual sound by singing or playing & listening to them. In the final instance, music *of any kind, even in the form of a harmony exercise, is not merely marks on a sheet of paper, but an organized pattern of sound waves and a corresponding pattern of auditory sensations in the mind of a listener.*

Since, however (as pointed out in the general note under the subject-heading "Theory"),

"theory" is a term firmly embedded in common use and certain related subjects generally are considered "theoretical," the fictional division between the latter and other closely related subjects generally considered "applied" will be observed for convenience in the following references. But one always should remember that, regardless of general classification, no subject can be considered or practised in complete isolation, and that most books (or at least the best ones) on any specific "theoretical" subject also deal with its "applied" aspects, and vice versa.

MUSICIANSHIP—APPLIED

See:

Accompaniment	Keyboard Harmony
Amateur Music &	Memorization/
Music-Making	Memory
Baton–1	Organ Playing
Breathing	Piano Playing
Children–3, 4, 6, 7	Pronunciation
Choir/Choral–1 & 2	School Music–3 & 4
Community Music	Score-Reading
Conducting	Sight-Playing & **Read**-
Diction (Enunciation)	ing
Ear-Training	Sight-Singing
Eurythmics	Solfège/Solfeggio
Expression	String Playing
Hearing	Teaching
Improvisation/	Tests
Extemporization	Violin Playing
Interpretation	Violoncello Playin

In addition, many books on individual & collective instruments contain some "applied" material dealing with actual performance on the instruments. See:

Bagpipes	Orchestra
Band	Organ
Bassoon	Piano
Bugle	Recorder
Clarinet	String Instruments
Flute	String Quartet
French Horn	Trombone
Hammond Organ	Trumpet
Harmonica	Violin
Instruments	Wind Instruments

MUSICIANSHIP—"THEORETICAL"

See:

Acoustics	Manuscript
Aesthetics–2	Melody-Writing
Arranging	Mode/Modality
Children–8	Modulation
Composition	Musicology
Counterpoint	Notation
Criticism	Ornamentation
Dictionaries of Music	Philosophy
Dictionaries of Terms	Psychology
Education	Rhythm
Encyclopedias of Mu-	Scales
sic	Songwriting
Form	Tempo
Fugue	"Theory"
Harmony	Tonality/Atonality
History	Transposition
Instrumentation/Orch-	Twelve-Tone Tech-
estration	nique

MUSICOLOGY

General Note: While systematic investigations & scholarly studies of various musical fields, both central & peripheral, have been practised to a greater or less extent throughout recorded history, the general term for such activities is a comparatively new one and it has not come into common use without considerable debate & confusion. Many musicians still consider it synonymous with musical "science," which is at once too loose & too tight a meaning, as well as one tending to place undue emphasis on such "natural science" elements in musicology as acoustics, the physiology & psychology of hearing, etc. Others, including most laymen as well as still too many musicians, fearfully persist in regarding "musicology" as denoting the exceptionally dry, boring, or "intellectual" aspects of music—a kind of archeology exclusively (abhorrent dealings with music's fossils & mummies), or else a species of equally abhorrent mathematics.

Some at least of the confusion & prejudice can be removed by a rational consideration of two acceptable definitions of musicology: Harap's "the sum of those collective disciplines—relating to music—that employ a rigorous technique;" and Haydon's "that branch of learning which concerns the discovery and systematization of knowledge concerning music."

In other words, then, musicology embraces almost every musical study that is not concerned with the mechanics of composition & performance, and whose procedures do not dispense with scholarly rigor.

As Haydon points out (in the work listed below), there are two main branches of musicology: systematic & historical. They should be considered as complementary approaches, of course, and not as distinct divisions, but for convenience the former may be said to include (true) music-theory and the sciences auxiliary to music—acoustics, aesthetics, pedagogy, psycho-physiology, and anthropology (the last, involving the study of folk music & non-European musical systems, often is called "comparative" musicology). Historical musicology, on the other hand, covers not only the actual history of music in general, but all historical research on musical subjects, including individual composers & their works.

In one sense, then, most of the books listed in the present Guide (except "methods" & other examples of applied musicianship) might be considered musicological in nature; unfortunately, however, a lack of rigorous scholarship, or the substitution of a willingness to "popularize" & "romanticize" rather than to dig up & stick to authentic facts, rules many of them out. For primarily it is the method or range of treatment, rather than the subject itself, that determines a book's claim to musicological worth.

And in view of the popular awe of—if not distaste for—musicology & musicologists, it might be well to add that musicological worth doesn't necessarily imply either dryness or the recondite: a few very lively and many extremely practical & useful books on music & musicians have been written by the finest musicologists. Then, too, there are at least some notable examples of first-rate musicology by authors who hold no formal academic degree.

Accordingly, the customary series of pertinent cross-references is impracticable to include here: it would be excessively long, for one thing, and for another it necessarily would involve the critical evaluations of individual books that our general editorial rules forbid.

Note: Standard works (dealing with the general subject of musicology) apparently O/P (or not easily available) include those by Logan, Schiedermair (in German), Riemann (in German), etc. Also not listed are many collections (ed Křenek, & others) and many individual reprints of papers from musicological journals, published for limited distribution only.

BÜCKEN, ERNST (*ed*). See App Ib ("Handbuch der Musikwissenschaft" reprint).

HAYDON, GLEN
Introduction to musicology: a survey of the fields, systematic & historical, of musical knowledge & research. xiii, 329 p, chap bibls & 13-p general bibl. Prentice 1941 (3rd pr 1947).   **4.65**

The only available general survey: one especially designed to introduce the non-specialist reader to the scope, philosophy, & methods of musicology.

(MUSURGIA STUDIES). See "Musurgia Studies in Musicology" (series).

MUSSORGSKY, Modest Petrovitch
(*Variant spellings:* Moussorgsky, Musorgsky)

See also:

Appreciation	Program Notes
Composers–1 & 3e	Rimsky-Korsakov–
History	Russian Musi
Opera	Son (s)
Orchestral Music	Themes
Phonograph Records	Timing
Piano Music	Vocal Music

Note: Standard works apparently O/P (or not easily available) include the letters & documents (1931, in Russian), and books by Belaiev, Montagu-Nathan, Riesemann (in English & German), Schindler, etc.

ABRAHAM GERALD
Boris Godounov: Rimsky-Korsakov version. 31 p + 8 pl, mus ex, brief bibl, paper. Boosey n d (1948). .60
"Covent Garden Operas" series: history, story, & musical analysis of the opera.

CALVOCORESSI, M. D. (& ABRAHAM, G.)
Mussorgsky. viii, 216 p, 8 pl (pors, facs, etc), mus ex, 2-p bibl. Dent 1946. 2.50
"Master Musicians" series (eventually to be issued in this country by Pellegrini), with the usual calendar, personalia, & catalogue of works. Completed & edited by Gerald Abraham, this work supersedes Calvocoressi's earlier biography, published in French in 1911, and in Hull's English translation in 1919.

GODET, ROBERT. See App Ia.

LEYDA, JAY & BERTENSSON, S. (eds & trs)
The Musorgsky reader: a life of Modeste Petrovich Musorgsky in letters & documents. xviii, 474 p, 13 pl (pors, facs, etc), mus ex, 4-p bibl. Norton 1947. 6.00
All the known documentary material, much of it published in English for the first time. The appendix includes lists of phonograph records (Philip L. Miller), letters, & works, plus a chronology.

"MUSURGIA STUDIES IN MUSICO-LOGY" (Series)
Note: This is a currently announced series to be devoted to hitherto-unpublished mono-graphs & translations of works hitherto unavailable in English. Publication (beginning in 1951) is pending, dependent on the receipt of a sufficient number of subscriptions. The subscription rate for all six works in Series A is announced as $80.00. For the individual titles, see:

American Music (Britton)
Haydn (Geiringer)
Motet (Leichtentritt)
Organ Music (Jeppesen)
Piano (Parrish)
Romantic Era/Romanticism (Frank)

MYASKOVSKY
Catalogued under Miaskovsky.

Myer, Edmund John. Author.
See Singing–2.
Myers, Kurtz. Compiler. See Libraries. Co-editor (with Kretzschmar & Tilly). See Bibliography.
Myers, Louise Kifer. Author.
See School Music–1.

MYERS, Rollo H.
Music in the modern world. 211 p, mus ex. Longmans_(1939) 2nd rev ed 1948. 1.50

Informal essays on the function of music; music and: society, humanity, the interpreter, listener, theatre, future, etc.

Author, editor. See also:
Debussy–2. Biography (1948/9). 1.00
English Music. Since 1939 (1947). .50
Satie. Biography (1948). 2.50
Stravinsky–2. Introduction to the music of (in prep). (1.00)
Yearbooks. Music today (1949). 2.50

Myers, Robert Manson. Author.
See Handel–2.

—N—

NABOKOV, Nicholas
Old friends and new music. 294 p.
Little Brown 1951.   3.50
*Reminiscences (by the Russian-American
composer) of Stravinsky, Diaghilev, et al.*

Napier-Tauber, Diana. Author.
See Tauber.
Nardi, Piero. Author. See App Ic.

NATIONAL ANTHEMS
See: National Music (esp Nettl).

National Association of Schools of Music.
Publishers. See Bibliography.
**National Bureau for the Advancement of
Music.** (Publications now distributed by
the National Recreation Assn.)
National Federation of Music Clubs.
Sponsors. See History–2 (McKinney &
Anderson study outline); also, for references
only, to Understanding.

NATIONAL MUSIC/NATIONALISM
*General Note: Not many years ago this was
one of the most controversial & spiritedly
discussed of all musical subjects. Today it
still preoccupies many of the "appreciation"
writers & propagandists of American music,
but elsewhere it no longer seems a burning
issue in itself, although naturally it plays a
considerable part in "comparative" musicology & studies of "national-school" composers (such as the Russian "Five").*

See also:

Africa	Hungary
America	India
Appreciation	Indians (American)
Arabia	Ireland
Bali	Italy
Brazil	Jewish Music
China	Lambert
Composers (esp 3, &	Latin America
under individual	Mexico
names)	Musicology
Contemporary Music	Negro Music
Czechoslovakia	Negro Spirituals
Dances–2	Poland
England	Program Notes
Folklore	Romantic Era
Folksongs	Russia
France	Scotland
Germany (note only)	Songbooks
Gypsy Music	Spain
History	Wales

*Standard works apparently O/P include those
by Engel, Forsyth, Vaughan Williams, etc.*

CHORLEY, HENRY FOTHERGILL
The national music of the world.
Ed H. G. Hewlett. viii, 225 p, mus △
ex. Reeves (1880) 2nd ed 1882.   (3.15)
*One of the earliest standard works, but largely
devoted to folk music.*

NETTL, PAUL
National anthems past and present.
Storm 1950, in prep.   3.00
*Note: A set of official versions of National
Anthems of the American Republics is issued
by the Pan American Union (1949, $2.00).*

National Recreation Association. Pub-
lishers. See esp Community Music (note
& Frieswyk, NRA, Zanzig entries), also
notes under Nature & Negro Music below.
**National School Band, Orchestra, and
Vocal Association.** Publishers. See
School Music–3.

NATURE (& Music)
See:

Aesthetics	Insects
Appreciation	Philosophy
Birds	Ultrasonics

*Note: Standard works apparently O/P in-
clude those by Fils (in French), Gilman, etc.
(A 5-sheet mimeographed list of "Nature
music," MP–211, periodically revised, is
available for 15¢ from the National Recreation
Association.)*

NEEL, Boyd
See also:

Conductors	Orchestra
England (music in)	Phonograph Records

The story of an orchestra. Intro
Benjamin Britten. ix, 133 p, frontis
por. Vox Mundi, London; Irving
Ravin, N. Y., 1950.   2.50
*The account of a medical practitioner who
formed a string ensemble in 1932, and of the
development of this group into the noted,
world-touring, prolifically recording Boyd
Neel Orchestra of today.*

Nef, Karl. Author. See History–2, App Ib.

NEGRO MUSIC & MUSICIANS

See also: esp Negro Spirituals.

Also:

Africa	Folksongs
America (music in)	Handy
American Music	Hayes
Anderson	History
Armstrong	Horne
Bland	Jazz
Composers–3a	Latin America
Ellington	Popular Music
Folklore (esp	Robeson
Metfessel)	Songbooks
	E. Waters

Note: Hare's "Negro musicians & their music" (1936) apparently is O/P. (A 3-sheet mimeographed list of "Negro Spirituals and music composed by Negroes," MP–214, periodically revised, is available for 15¢ from the National Recreation Association.)

HANDY, W. C.
Unsung Americans sung. 236 p, illus (photos & drwgs, Beauford De Laney), music, 2–p bibl. Handy Bros. Music Co., N. Y., (1944) 2nd ed 1946.   5.00
Songs celebrating various famous Negroes.

NEGRO SPIRITUALS (& Folksongs)

See also:

Anderson	Folksongs–2
America (music in)	Hayes
American Music	Robeson
Folklore (esp	Songbooks
Metfessel)	

Note: Standard works apparently O/P include those by Johnson, Krehbiel, the Lomaxes, Odum & Johnson, Scarborough & Gulledge, etc.

CRITE, ALLAN ROHAN (*illus*)
Three spirituals from earth to heaven. Forew Roland Hayes. unp (165 p), illus. Harvard 1948.   3.95
Black-&-white illustrations for "Nobody Knows," "Swing Low," & "Heaven,"— designed as "translations" from musical into visual rhythms.

CURTIS, (BURLIN) NATALIE
Negro folk-songs (Hampton Series). 4 v, music, bibl refs, paper. G. Schirmer 1918/9.   Complete: 2.00
V 1: Spirituals. 42 p. 1918.   .60
V 2: Spirituals. 44 p. 1918.   .60
V 3: Work- & play-songs. 40 p. 1918.   .60
V 4: Work- & play-songs. 50 p. 1919.   .60
A standard collection of words & part-music arrangements for 17 songs, plus brief introductions & notes (esp 8-p text in v 2).

HANDY, W. C. (*ed*)
A treasury of the blues: complete words & music of 67 great songs from "Memphis Blues" to the present day. Intro Abbé Niles.   258 p, illus (Miguel Covarrubias), 2-p bibl, music. Boni (1926) rev ed 1949, via S & S.   5.00
Revised version, including 24 new selections, of a standard collection (originally titled "Blues: an anthology"), particularly notable for the accompanying historical & critical study by Niles.

HAYES, ROLAND
My songs: Aframerican religious folk songs, arr & interpreted.   x, 128 p, music.   Little Brown 1948.   3.00
30 of the tenor's concert favorites, with notes; prefaced by a discussion of African influences, problems of dialect pronunciation, etc.

JOHNSON, JAMES WELDON & J. ROSAMOND
The books of American Negro spirituals: including "The book of American Negro spirituals" & "The second book of Negro spirituals." 2 v in 1: 187, 189 p, music.   Viking 1940 (4th pr 1947).   4.95
Except for the prefaces (p 11/50 & 11/24), these are collections of the words & music of some 120 songs, originally published in separate volumes, 1925 & 1926.

ODUM, HOWARD W. & JOHNSON, GUY B.
The Negro workaday songs.   xiii, 278 p, charts, mus ex, 6–p annot bibl.   North Carolina 1926.   3.00
Mostly verses only, but with some musical examples & phono-photographic charts. Companion work (in "Social Studies" series) to "The Negro & his songs" (1925), now O/P.

PARISH, LYDIA
Slave songs of the Georgia sea islands. Intro Olin Downes.   xxxi, 256 p, illus (map, photos), 4–p bibl, music (trans Creighton Churchill & Robert Mac-Gimsey).   Creative Age 1942.   3.50

THURMAN, HOWARD
The Negro spiritual speaks of life and death: being the Ingersoll lecture on the immortality of man.   56 p, Harper 1947.   1.00

WHITE, NEWMAN IVEY
American Negro folk-songs.   xii, 501 p, 12–p bibl.   Harvard 1928.   5.00

WORK, JOHN WESLEY (*comp & arr*)
American Negro songs: a comprehensive collection of religious & secular folk songs, for mixed voices. 259 p. music, 5–p bibl, paper.   (1940) Presser 1948.   1.50

A 46-p foreword discusses origins & various types of Negro songs. Words & music are given for some 200 songs (mostly arr for 4-part choir), but words & tunes only are given for some of the blues & other secular songs.

Nelson, Robert U. Author, compiler.
See Film Music, Variation.
Nemmers, Erwin Esser. Author.
See Church Music.
Nern, Allan. Author. See Sight-Singing.
Nestyev, Israel Vladimirovich. Author.
See Prokofiev.

NETHERLANDS
See:

Baroque Era	History
Dances–2 (esp ed	Medieval/Renaissance
Alford: Van der	(esp Lowinsky)
Ven-ten Bensel)	

Nettel, Reginald. Author, editor.
Anthologies. To soothe a savage breast (1950). (3.50)
Brian. Ordeal by music (1945). 3.25
England (music in). Music in Five Towns, 1940–1915 (1944) 3.50
—. Orchestra in England (1946). 3.00
Orchestra. While the orcnestra assembles (1949). 2.25

Nettl, Paul. Author, editor. See:
Dance Music. Story of (1947). 4.75
Documents. Book of (1948). 5.00
Luther. Luther & music (1948). 2.25
Mozart–3. Veilchen (1949). 7.50
National Music. National Anthems (1950 in prep). 3.00
Waltz. Birth of (1950 in prep). .75
App Ib. Goethe & Mozart (1949). 1.00

Neumann, Angelo. Author.
See Wagner–2.
Neumann, Werner. Compiler.
See Bach–2, also App Ib.
Neupert, Hanns. Author. See App Ib.

NEVIN, Ethelbert Woodbridge
See:

America (music in)	Composers–3a
American Music	History
Appreciation	

Note: Biographies by Howard (1935) & Vance (1913) apparently are O/P.

Nevin, Gordon Balch. Author.
See Organ Playing.
Nevins, Willard Irving. Author (with Lang). See Keyboard Harmony.

Newitt, John H. Author.
See Sound Recording & Reproduction.
Newlin, Dika. Author. See Composers–3b.
Newman, Elizabeth. Author.
See Children–1.

NEWMAN, Ernest
A musical motley: "The weary willies of music" & other studies. xi, 362 p. Knopf (1919) rev ed 1934. 2.00

Author. See also:
Berlioz–1. Memoirs, ed Newman (1932). 2.98
Opera–3. Stories (1928/30). 1–v repr. 2.95
—More stories (1934). 4.00
Wagner–2. Life (1933/46). 4 v. 25.00
—. As man & artist (1924). 5.00
—. Same, reprint ed. 1.98
—. Miniature biography (1940). .60
Wagner–3. Wagner operas (1949). 7.50

Note: Many other books by Newman, including his studies of Beethoven, Gluck, Liszt, Strauss, Wolf, etc., apparently are O/P (or not easily available in this country).

Newman, William S. Author.
See Piano Playing–1.
Newmarch, Rosa Harriet. Author.
See:
Czechoslovakia. Music of (1942). 3.00
Program Notes. Concert-goer's library (1928/38). 6 v, each: 1.75
App Ia. L'Opéra russe (1922). 1.00
Newton, Joy. Author.
See Tchaikovsky–2 (ed Haskell).
Newton, Leonard G. Author.
See School Music–3.
New York Singing Teachers' Association.
See Singing–1 (N.Y.S.T.A.).
New York State School Music Association. Publishers. See School Music–1.

NICARAGUA (Music in)
See: Latin America.

Nicholson, Margaret. Author.
See Copyright.
Nicholson, Sydney Hugo
Author. See Boy Voices. Co-author (with Harter). See Church Music.
Nicoll, Irene Howland. Author (with Dennis). See Singing–2.
Niecks, Friedrich. Author.
Note: Lives of Chopin & Schumann, and other books, all apparently are O/P today.
Niemann, Walter. Author. See Brahms–1.
Niessen, Carl. Author. See App Ib.

NIETZSCHE, Friedrich Wilhelm
See:
History   Wagner
Romantic Era

Note: Nietzsche's own writings on music, especially the famous attack on Wagner, apparently are O/P (or not easily available), except for the "Randglossen zu Carmen," just reprinted in German (See App Ib).

See also Mann, for the novel "Doctor Faustus," whose protoganist's genius, as affected by disease, is based in part on Nietzsche's.

Nievergelt, Edwin. Author. See App Ib.
Nijinsky, Romola. Author.
See Nijinsky.

NIJINSKY, Vaslav
See also: Ballet, (The) Dance.
Note: Nijinsky's "Diary" (1936) & the Bourman "Tragedy of Nijinsky" (1936) apparently are O/P.

MAGRIEL, PAUL (ed)
Nijinsky: an illustrated monograph.
ix, 81 p, 65 photos, 2-p bibl. Holt
1946 (2nd pr 1947).   3.50
Articles by Edward Denby, Robert Edmond Jones, & Carl Van Vechten; shorter pieces by Marsden Hartley, H. T. Parker, & Stark Young.

NIJINSKY, ROMOLA
Nijinsky: by his wife. Forew Paul
Claudel. xvii, 447 p, 17 pl. S & S
1934 (1947).   3.75

Niles, (Edward) Abbé. Author.
See Negro Spirituals (Handy, intro).
Niles, John Jacob. Editor (collector & arranger). See Carols, Folksongs-2.

NILSSON, Christine
See:
Opera   Singers
History   Singing
Also: App IIa (juvenile by Headlead).

Nininger, Ruth. Author.
See Church Music.
Nitobé, Inazo Ota. Author.
See Japan (music in).
Nitze, William Albert. Author.
See Poetry.
Noatzsch, Richard. Co-author (with Herold). See App Ib.
Noble, Peter. Editor. See Ballet.
Noble, Thomas Tertius. Author.
See Boy Voices. Co-author (with Wright).
See Ear-Training.

Nohavec, Hazel. Catalogued under Morgan, Hazel N.
Nohl, Walther. Author. See App Ib.

NOISE
General Note: There are listeners, of course, who might call for an extension of the cross-references below to include Contemporary & Modern Music, to say nothing of Jazz. However, there is a genuine relationship between noise & music: particularly in the existence of non-musical sounds generally emitted (along with musical tones) by most instruments outside as well as in the percussion family, but also in the effect of noise in general in raising the threshold of hearing & "masking" other sounds, both in concert & recorded performance of music.

See:
Acoustics (esp Red-   Instruments
field)   Phonograph Records
Decibel   Radio Music
Hearing   Sound Rec & Repro
Instrumentation

McLachlan's "Noise, a comprehensive survey" (1935) apparently is O/P.

Noli, (Bishop) Fan Stylian. Author.
See Beethoven-2.
Norden, Hugo. Author.
See Composition, Violin Playing.
Nordholm, Harriet. Co-author (with Thompson). See School Music-1.
Nordin, Dayton W. Editor.
See Choir/Choral-2.
Norman, Gertrude. Editor.
See Letters.
Norman, Philip B. Author.
See Harmony-1.
Normann, Theodore Frederick. Author.
See School Music-3.
Norris, Homer Albert. Author.
See Counterpoint-2, Harmony-2.
Northcote, Sydney. Author.
See Ballad, Duparc.
Norton, Edward Quincy. Author.
See Piano.
Norton, Mary Dows Herter. Author.
See String Quartet.

NORWAY (Music in)/NORWEGIAN MUSIC
See also:
Appreciation   Grieg
Dances-2   History
Folklore   Phonograph Records
Folksongs-1   Program Notes

Also: App IIa (Acker: "4 sons of Norway").

QVAMME, BÖRRE
Norwegian music and composers.
64 p, frontis fac, 9 pors.   Bond Pub.
Co., London, 1949.   1.50
*The first separate survey in English, covering
folk music, the national revival, the generation
of Grieg & Svendsen, the turn of the century,
& modern music.*

NOTATION

*General Note: This is one of the primary sub-
jects of most books on elementary musicianship ("Theory", etc.), where of course it is
studied from a practical rather than a historical point of view.   In addition to conventional
"staff" notation, there is a "Tonic Sol-Fa"
notation that is used almost exclusively in
England & the British Empire for elementary
teaching purposes.   Since it is seldom if
ever used in this country, however, none of the
considerable British literature is included here.*

*Standard works apparently O/P (or not easily
available) include those by Button, David &
Lussy (in French), Williams, Wolf (in German), etc.*

See also: esp Children–8, Theory–2 & 3.
Also:

Dictionaries of Terms	Rhythm
Ear-Training	Score-Reading
Gregorian Chant	Sight-Playing & Read-
History	ing
Instrumentation	Sight-Singing
Manuscript	Solfège/Solfeggio

APEL, WILLI
The notation of polyphonic music,
900–1600. xxv, 462 p + 28 p mus ex
(88 facs), bibl refs. Mediaeval (1942),
4th rev ed 1949.   8.00
*An extensive study of early systems (white &
black mensural, square, tablature, etc.).*

SIVIC, STANLEY A.
Visual slide rule system.   Unp (7),
mus ex. Mode Harmony, Bloomfield,
N. J., 1947.   1.00
*A substitute for staff notation in elementary
theory teaching.*

TAPPOLET, WILLY.   See App Ia.

Nowak, Leopold.   Author. See App Ib.

-O-

Oakey, George. Author. See Harmony–2.
Oberndorfer, (Mrs) Ann Shaw Faulkner.
Author. Catalogued under Faulkner.

OBOE
See:

Band–1	Orchestra
Instrumentation	School Music–3
Instruments	Wind Instruments

O'Brien, Grace. Author.
See Italian Music.
O'Connell, Charles. Author.
See Phonograph Records, Program Notes,
Symphony.

OCCUPATIONS (Musical)
See: Career.

Odermatt, Hermann. Author. See App Ib.
Odum, Howard W. Author.
See Negro Spirituals.

OFFENBACH, Jacques
See: App Ia (Brindejont-Offenbach).
Also:

Appreciation	Operetta
History	Phonograph Records
Opera	Program Notes

*Note: Studies by Kracauer (in Eng, 1938)
& Sitwell (1938) apparently are O/P.
Offenbach's own "Offenbach in America"
(1877) has been O/P for years.*

Ogden, Charles Kay. Co-author (with
Richards & Woods). See Aesthetics–1.
Ogden, Robert Morris. Author.
See Aesthetics–1.
Ohl, John F. Co-editor (with Parrish).
See Anthologies.
Oldroyd, George. Author.
See Fugue.
Oliver, Alfred Richard. Author.
See Criticism.
Oliver, Beatrice. Author. See History–3.
Oliver, Sy. Author. See Arranging–2.
Olivévoff, André. Author. See Pavlova.
Ollén, Olof. Editor.
See Sweden (music in).
Olschki, Leonardo. Author.
See Italian Music/Italy (music in).
Olson, Harry Ferdinand. Author.
See Acoustics.
Onnen, Frank. Author.
See Ravel, Stravinsky–2.

OPERA
1. **General, History, National Schools**
2. **Librettos**
3. **"Appreciation," Plots, Stories, Quizzes, etc.**
4. **Metropolitan Opera Company & House**

OPERA (1. General, History, National Schools)
See also:

Acting	Humor (Levy,
Appreciation	Simont)
Bel Canto	Lehmann
California (Gagey)	Operetta/Opéra-
Composers (& under	Comique
individual names)	Phonograph Records
Covent Garden	Program Notes
I. Cook	Singing
Galli-Curci	Television (esp Royal)
Gatti-Casazza	Theatre (esp Scholz)
History	Vocal Music

Also: App IIb (Marie-Jeanne juvenile).

*Standard works apparently O/P (or not easily
available) include those by Apthorp, Bekker,
Bie (in German), Elson, Gilman, Goldschmidt
(in German), Henderson, Klein, Kobbé,
Krehbiel, Lahee, Lowenberg, Newmarch (in
English, but see App Ia for French ed),
Scholes, Sonneck, Taubman, etc.*

BARKER, FRANK GRANVILLE
Stars of the opera. Forew Geoffrey
Handley-Taylor. 51 p, 10 pors,
paper. Lotus Press, for British △
Poetry-Drama Guild, London, 1949. (1.00)
*Studies of Gigli, Dal Monte, Melchior,
Welitsch, & other contemporary singers.*

BOUCHER, JEAN. See App Ia.

BRANDL, WILLY. See App Ib.

BROCKWAY, WALLACE & WEINSTOCK, H.
The opera: a history of its creation
& performance, 1600–1941. viii,
525 p, 28 illus. S & S 1941.   3.75
*Includes a list of recommended recordings
prepared by George Clark Leslie.*

CAPELL, RICHARD
Opera. 132 p. Benn (1930), 2nd
rev ed 1948.   (1.50)
Concise survey: Peri to Britten

COOPER, MARTIN
Russian Opera.
Chanticleer in prep.   △
"World of Music" series No 14.

CROSTEN, WILLIAM L.
French grand opera: an art and a
business. ix, 162 p, 9–p bibl. King's
Crown Press, Columbia Univ, 1948.   2.75
*A detailed study of "bourgeois" opera, whose
pattern was established in the years 1828/
1836. With special emphasis on works by
Auber, Meyerbeer, Rossini, & the librettist
Scribe.*

CROZIER, ERIC (*ed*)
Opera in English. 45 p, 14 photos,
paper. Lane 1945 (1946).   .50
*"Sadler's Wells Opera Book" No. 1: articles
by Tyrone Guthrie, Edwin Evans Jr, Joan
Cross, Edward J. Dent, & Ninette de Valois.*

DENT, EDWARD J.
Foundations of English opera: a
study of musical drama in England
during the 17th century. xi, 242 p,
mus ex. Cambridge 1928.   3.50
A standard work.

Opera. 192 p, 16 pl, 20 b&ws (Kay
Ambrose), 2–p bibl, paper. Penguin   △
1940.   (.35)
*An "introduction, for those who are just
beginning to take an interest in opera"; outline history, stressing English opera.*

DOISY, MARCEL. See App Ia.

DUMESNIL, RENÉ. See App Ia.

FARGA, FRANZ. See App Ib.

GRAF, HERBERT
The opera and its future in America.
305 p, 105 pl, 14 b&ws, mus ex, 6–p
bibl. Norton 1941.   4.75
*A study of operatic history, stressing the
continual struggle to find new means of expression. With production suggestions for
the "new" opera & estimates of the potentialities of the movies, radio, & television.*

GROUT, DONALD JAY
A short history of opera. 2 v: xiv,
711 p, 25 illus, mus ex, 122–p bibl.
Columbia 1947.   Boxed: 10.00
Same, text edition, 1 v.   6.00
*The most extensive study yet published in
English, tracing its subject through 5 eras:
Renaissance, Baroque, 18th century, Roman-
ticism to modernism, & Between 2 wars.*

GUNDRY, INGLIS
Opera in a nutshell. Pref Edward J.
Dent. 32 p, 3–p bibl, paper. Hin-
richsen 1945.   .50

*Concise "miniature survey", including a list
of (British) opera recordings.*

HOFMANN, R. See App Ia.

HOOVER, KATHLEEN O'DONNELL
Makers of opera. Intro Carleton
Sprague Smith. xiii, 209 p+50-p
illus, bibl notes. Bittner 1948   7.50
Studies of 18 composers: Peri to R. Strauss.

HOROWICZ, BRONISLAW. See App Ia.

JACOBS, NAOMI & ROBERTSON, JAMES C.
Opera in Italy. Forew W. J. Smith.
234 p, 19 photos, mus ex. Hutchinson 1948.   5.25
*Studies of 19 opera houses, Italian opera in
general, 16 individual operas, 10 composers.*

KEMPERS, K. P. B. & BAKKER, M. G.
Italian opera. Tr M. M. Kessler-
Button. 58 p, illus, mus ex, bds.
Continental n d (1948/9?).   2.50
"Symphonia" series of monographs.

LA LAURENCIE, LIONEL DE. See App Ia.

MAREK, GEORGE R.
A front seat at the opera. 307 p.
Allen Towne 1948, via Crown.   4.00
*Miscellany of informal essays originally
written for the Metropolitan's program-books.*

MOOSER, R.-ALOYS. See App Ia.

NEWMARCH, ROSA. See App Ia.

NIESSEN, CARL. See App Ib.

ROLLAND, ROMAIN. See App Ia.

SCHOLES, PERCY A.
A miniature history of opera: for
the general reader & the student.
69 p, mus ex. Oxford 1931 (1949).   .50

SHEA, GEORGE E.
Acting in opera: its A-B-C, with
descriptive examples, practical hints,
& numerous illustrations. xiii, 90 p,
illus. G. Schirmer 1915 (2nd ed n d).   1.50
With posed photographs of the author.

TEASDALE, MAY SILVA
20th century opera at home and
abroad: 1900 through season 1937–
1938. 240 p. Dutton 1938.   2.25
*Nationality & character, time & place of
premières, arranged chronologically, with
principals of casts in U. S. productions.*

WELLESZ, EGON
Essays on opera. Some tr Patricia
Kean. 158 p, 6 pl (facs, etc), mus
ex. (Dobson 1950), Roy 1950.   3.75
A selection of scholarly articles & lectures.

OPERA (2. Librettos)

Note: The librettos of nearly all standard operas are of course available in published form, but only a few of the better-known collections are included here.

See also: Gilbert & Sullivan for G & S librettos, and Opera-3 for "stories" & "plots" of the operas.

For the individual publications of Edward J. Dent's English versions, see: Auber, Beethoven-3, Donizetti, Flotow, Gluck, Mozart-3, Rossini, Tchaikovsky-2, Verdi-2, Weber.

(THE OPERA LIBRETTO LIBRARY)
The authentic librettos of the Wagner operas: complete with English & German texts & music of the principal airs. vi, 470 p, music. Crown 1938 (11th pr, n d). 2.50
The authentic librettos of the Italian operas: complete with English & Italian texts & music of the principal airs. vii, 481 p, music. Crown 1939. 2.50
The authentic librettos of the French & German operas: complete with English & French or German texts & music of the principal airs. v, 504 p, music. Crown 1939. 2.50
All 3 volumes, boxed: 7.50
The librettos of 10 Wagner operas, 11 Italian operas, 12 French & German operas.

DENT, EDWARD J. (*tr*)
The pocket libretto library. 4 v, boxed. Allen Towne 1948, via Crown. 2.50
Includes Rossini's "The Barber of Seville," Verdi's "Rigoletto," "La Traviata," & "Il Trovatore." See under Rossini & Verdi-2 for individual listings of these English versions.

ISTEL, EDGAR
The art of writing opera librettos: practical suggestions. Tr Theodore Baker. vi, 157 p. G. Schirmer 1922. O/P
The only available manual on this subject, including, as a practical example, an analysis of Scribe's "Le Part du Diable." (O/P 1950.)

SONNECK, OSCAR G. (*comp.*)
Catalogue of opera librettos printed before 1800. 2 v: 1674 p, frontis por, fac. Library of Congress 1914, via GPO. 2.00
Includes some 6,000 entries, based mainly on the Albert Schatz collection purchased by the Library of Congress in 1908. V 1 is the title catalogue; v 2 contains author & composer lists, & aria index.

OPERA (3. "Appreciation," Plots, Quizzes, Stories, etc.)

See also:

Appreciation	Opera-2 & 3
Humor (esp Levy, Simont)	Program Notes
	Quizzes

Standard works apparently O/P (or not easily available) include those by Annesley, Davidson, England, Fullerton, Funk, Martens, Melitz, Young, etc.

BIANCOLLI, LOUIS & BAGAR, ROBERT (*eds*)
The Victor book of operas. xxiv, 596 p, illus. S&S 1949. 3.95
Covers 119 operas & includes lists of (RCA Victor) phonograph records. This supersedes earlier editions (some titled "Victrola book of the opera") begun in 1912. Earlier editors included Samuel Holland Rous (9th ed, 1936) & Charles O'Connell (10th ed, 1939).

BROOK, DONALD
Companion to opera. 222 p, 64 pl, mus ex, 1-p bibl. Rockliff 1947. 4.25
Historical survey in narrative style with libretto outlines, performance data, etc.

CHANTAVOINE, JEAN. See App Ia.

CROSS, MILTON
Milton Cross' complete stories of the great operas. xii, 627 p, illus (Dolores Ramos), 2-p annot bibl. Doubleday 1947 (1948). 3.75
72 opera stories recounted by the Met's radio announcer-commentator, with comments on "How to enjoy an opera," "A brief history," & "The ballet in opera."

HIPSHER, EDWARD ELLSWORTH
American opera and its composers: a complete history of serious opera with a summary of the lighter forms which led up to its birth. 478 p, illus, 3-p bibl. Presser 1927 (1934). 3.50
Primarily stories of American operas with brief composer biographies.

HOWARD, JOHN TASKER
The world's great operas. xxvii, 488 p. Random 1948. 2.95
Same, Grosset repr 1950. 1.49
Plots of some 205 operas by 95 composers; includes brief biographies, lists of librettists & plot sources, & an index of operatic characters.

KOBBÉ, GUSTAV
The complete opera book: the stories of the operas, together with 400 of the leading airs & motives in musical notation. xxii, 1009 p, 63-p photos, mus ex. Putnam (1919) rev ed 1938, 20th (aug) pr 1950. 6.00

Long a standard work, completed after the author's death by Kathleen Wright, with additions by F. Bonavia & Ethel Peyser. The 1950 edition has a new index and added material on Britten, "Turandot," etc.

KREHBIEL, HENRY EDWARD
A book of operas: their histories, their plots & their music. 2 v in 1: xvii, 345 p; xiii, 243 p, 16 illus, mus ex. Macmillan 1919 (1936). 3.00
Reprint ed combining "A book of operas" (1909) & "A second book of operas" (1917).

MASON, HENRY L. (ed)
Opera stories. v, 177 p, illus. Willis (1920) enl ed 1923. 2.00
Stories of some 300 operas & ballets.

McFADYEAN, BARBARA & HUGHES, SPIKE
Nights at the opera. 410 p, mus △ ex. Pilot 1948. (5.00)
Analyses with musical quotations of 15 standard operas; includes record lists.

McSPADDEN, J. WALKER
Operas and musical comedies. Intro John Tasker Howard. 607 p, mus ex. Crowell 1946 (1947). 3.50
A reference book covering some 350 operas & operettas, etc. superseding the author's earlier standard works: "Opera synopses" (1911), "Light opera & musical comedy" (1936).

MENDELSOHN, FELIX
The story of 100 operas. xi, 332 p. (1913) Grosset 1940. .75
"Little Music Library" series, pocket size.

MILLIGAN, HAROLD VINCENT
Stories of the famous operas. ix, 274 p, bds. Permabooks 1950. .35
Brief summaries of some 70 popular operas.

MILLIGAN, H. V. & SOUVAINE, G. (eds)
The opera quiz book: questions & answers from the opera quiz. Forew Edward Johnson. 192 p. Wyn 1948. 2.00
From the Met intermission broadcasts, with additional discussions by Olin Downes, Deems Taylor, Sigmund Spaeth, & others.

NEWMAN, ERNEST
Stories of the great operas and their composers. 3 v in 1: 889 p, mus ex. (1928/30) Garden City repr 1935 (1951). 2.95
V 1: Wagner (1928); v 2: Mozart to Thomas (1920); v 3: Verdi to Puccini (1930). This reprint was O/P in 1950, while the original Knopf edition in 3 separate volumes has been O/P for some time. However, see Wagner–3 for a revised edition of v 1.

More stories of famous operas. xvi, 585, vii p, mus ex. Knopf 1943. 4.00
Same, Blakiston repr 1946. 1.98
A companion volume to "Stories of the great operas," covering 29 works not included there.

PELTZ, MARY ELLIS (ed)
(See also: Opera–4)
Opera lover's companion. xi, 385 p, 33 photos. Ziff-Davis 1948. 5.00
Sponsored by the Metropolitan Opera Guild. Studies by various authors (originally pub in "Opera News") of 38 of the most frequently produced Met operas.

SÉNÉCHAUD, MARCEL. See App Ia.

SIMON, HENRY W. (ed)
A treasury of grand opera. x, 403 p, illus (Rafaello Busoni), music (arr Albert Sirmay). S & S 1946. 7.50
Same, paper-bound. 5.00
Pictures, stories, analyses, words (tr George Mead) & music (arr voice & piano) of some 66 excerpts from 7 standard operas.

SIMON, HENRY & VEINUS, ABRAHAM
The pocket book of great operas. 373 p + 66–p mus ex, illus (Louis Glanzman). Pocket Books 1949. .25
Same, "Collectors'" ed. 1.25
22 favorites: "Aida" to "Il Trovatore."

SPAETH, SIGMUND (ed)
Fifty favorite operatic arias. 51 p, paper. Ricordi 1947. .50
Texts only in original language & new translations by Spaeth & James I. Krug.

STREATFEILD, R. A.
The opera: a sketch of the development of the opera, with full descriptions of all works in the modern repertory. Intro J. A. Fuller-Maitland. xx, 402 p. Routledge & Curwen (1896), 5th rev, enl ed (E. J. Dent) 1925 (1948). (3.25)
A standard collection of opera plots combined with an outline of opera history, in E. J. Dent's revised edition.

THOMPSON, OSCAR (ed)
Plots of the operas: 266 stories of the operas as compiled for the International Cyclopedia of Music & Musicians. xvii, 517 p. (1938) World repr 1943 (1950). 1.59
Same, Dodd Mead pocket ed 1950. 2.50

UPTON, GEORGE P. & BOROWSKI, FELIX
The standard opera guide. xvii, 474 p. Halcyon rev enl ed 1936 (1947). 1.98
Plots of some 152 operas by 64 composers & Borowski's article "The Evolution of Opera."

Based on Upton's "The Standard Operas"
(1885), rev & enl by Borowski 1933.

WILLIAMS, STEPHEN
Come to the opera! Forew Sir Thomas
Beecham. 302 p, mus ex. Beechhurst
1948.   3.00
Some 57 operas with an index of characters.

OPERA (4. Metropolitan Opera Company & House)

See also:

America (music in)	Lehmann
I. Cook	Opera-1 (esp Marek)
Galli-Curci	Opera-3 (esp Cross,
Gatti-Casazza	Milligan, Peltz)
History	App IIb (Dike)

*Standard works apparently O/P include those
by Knight, Peltz, Sanborn, etc.*

KOLODIN, IRVING
The Metropolitan opera, 1883–1939.
Intro W. J. Henderson. xxi, 646 p,
illus. Oxford (1936) 2nd rev enl ed
1940; Knopf new ed 1951, in prep.   △
*A detailed record including much original
research, with repertory table, record of casts
of premières, noted débuts, etc.*

PELTZ, MARY ELLIS
Behind the gold curtain: the story
of the Metropolitan Opera, 1883–
1950. Forew Mrs August Belmont.
96 p, illus. Farrar Straus 1950.   2.50
*A history of the Met. illustrated with some
100 photographs.*

Metropolitan opera milestones.
Forew Mrs August Belmont. v, 74 p,
illus, bibl, bds. Metropolitan Opera
Guild Inc., N. Y., 1944.   1.00
A brief summary of the Met's history.

PELTZ, MARY ELLIS & LAWRENCE, ROBERT
The Metropolitan opera guide: the
standard repertory of the Metro-
politan Opera Association, Inc. as
selected by Edward Johnson, general
manager. Forew Mrs August
Belmont. 497 p, illus (Alexandre
Serebriakoff), mus ex, 6–p bibl.
Modern Library 1939 (7th pr 1947). 2.45
Includes synopses of the plots.

SELTSAM, WILLIAM H. (*compiler*)
Metropolitan opera annals: a chronicle of artists & performances. Intro
Edward Johnson. xvi, 751 p, 127
photos. Wilson 1947, 2nd cor pr
1949.   7.00
*Published in association with the Metropoli-
tan Opera Guild. Tabulated data, season by
season, 1883–1947, of personnel, programs,
casts, etc., with excerpts from press reviews.*

(Same), Index to composers; lists of
errata. 6 p, paper. Wilson 1949.   △
*Supplementary material to "Metropolitan
opera annals"; bound in the 2nd printing,
supplied gratis by the publishers (on application) to purchasers of the 1st edition.*

OPERETTA/OPÉRA-COMIQUE

See also:

Amateur Music	History
(Korn)	Opera-1
America (music in)	Opera-3
Appreciation	(esp McSpadden)
California (Gagey)	Poetry (ed Boas)
Community Music	Popular Music
Composers (& under	Program Music
names of individuals)	Rodgers & Hart
Gershwin	School Music
Gilbert & Sullivan	Theater
Hammerstein	

*Standard works apparently O/P include those
by Beach, Mackinlay, McSpadden (but see
Opera–3), etc.*

BEACH, FRANK A.
Preparation and presentation of the
operetta. Forew Wm. Allen White.
204 p, illus, 2–p bibl. Ditson 1930. 2.00
Practical manual, primarily for school use.

COOPER, MARTIN
Opéra comique. 72 p, 4 col pl, 30
b&ws, mus ex. Chanticleer 1949.   2.50
*"World of Music" series No 7. A survey-
history, stressing the "golden age" of opéra-
comique in France in the 18th century.*

GENEST, EMILE. See App Ia.

HADAMOWSKY, FRANZ & OTTE, HEINZ.
See App Ib.

JONES, CHARLES T. H. & WILSON, DON
Musico-dramatic producing: a man-
ual for the stage & musical director.
140 p, photos, drwgs (Clark Fiers &
Karl Bradley, facs, mus ex, paper.
Gamble (1930), 2nd rev enl ed 1939. 1.50
*Practical advice, especially for producing
school & amateur operettas.*

SMITH, CECIL
Musical comedy in America. x, 374
p + 64 pl (pors, facs, etc). Theatre
Arts 1950.   5.00
*An informal historical survey of the popular
musical stage on Broadway from "The Black
Crook" to "South Pacific."*

UMFLEET, KENNETH R.
School operettas and their production. 128 p, illus, 2–p bibl. Birchard
1929.   2.00
*Practical manual, including classified lists
of recommended operettas.*

Opienski, Henryk. Author. See App Ia.

ORATORIO

See: App Ia (Raugel: "L'Oratorio") & App Ic (Alaleona: "Storia dell' oratorio musicale in Italia").

Also:

Appreciation	History
Choir/Choral-3	Phonograph Records
Church Music	Program Music
Handel-2 (Young)	Vocal Music

Also: Composers (& under names of individual oratorio composers, esp Bach-2 & 3, Handel-1 & 2, Haydn, Mendelssohn-2 & 3, etc).

Standard works apparently O/P (or not easily available in this country) include those by Patterson, Schering (in German), Upton, etc.

ORCHESTRA

See also:

America (music in)	Koussevitzky
Appreciation	B. Neel
Arranging	Orchestral Music
Berlioz	Philadelphia
Boston-music in	Philharmonic
(Humphrey)	Queen's Hall
Children-2 & 4	School Music-3
(esp LaPrade)	Score-Reading
Community Music	Stokowski
Conducting	Symphony
Conductors	Toscanini
(esp Brook)	Walter
England (music in)	Weingartner
History	Wind Instruments
Instrumentation	Wood
Instruments	App Ia (Pincherle)

Also: App IIb (juveniles by Balet, Commins, Gest, McPhee, Posell).

Standard works apparently O/P (or not easily available) include those by Bekker, Grant & Hettinger, Howes, Malipiero, Montague-Nathan, etc.

BARNE, KITTY
Listening to the orchestra. 299 p, illus. (1941) Bobbs-Merrill 1946.   **2.75**
Appreciative approach, largely in terms of principal composers & national schools.

CARSE, ADAM
Orchestra. Intro Sir Adrian Boult. 72 p, 4 col pl, 40 b&ws. Chanticleer 1949.   **2.50**
"World of Music" series No 8. A story-history including chapters on famous conductors & instrumentalists of the past.

The orchestra in the 18th century. viii, 176 p, illus, mus ex, tables, 4–p bibl. Heffer 1940 (1950); Broude 1950.   **3.75**
A standard, detailed study of orchestral con-

stitutions & strengths, personnel, directors, scores, standards, etc.
The orchestra from Beethoven to Berlioz: a history of the orchestra in the first half of the 19th century, & of the development of orchestral baton-conducting. xiii, 514 p, 3 col pl, 23 pl, 51 b&ws, 5–p bibl, tables. Heffer 1948; Broude 1950.   **(7.50)**
Companion to "The orchestra in the 18th century"; an extensive & detailed study that undoubtedly will rank as the standard work.

DALY, WILLIAM H.
The orchestra: a guide for the amateur to orchestral instruments & orchestral music. 83 p, frontis pl, mus ex, paper. Paterson (1905), new ed 1923, via C. Fischer.   **1.00**

HENDERSON, W. J.
The orchestra and orchestral music. xi, 238 p, 8 pors, mus ex. Scribner (1899) 1927.   **2.00**
How the orchestra is made up, used, & directed; how it & orchestral music have grown.

HOWES, FRANK
Full orchestra. viii, 176 p, illus, mus ex. Secker (1942) 2nd rev ed 1943 (9th pr, 1947).   **(2.50)**
Historical survey, with sections on conductors' styles, acoustics, instruments, etc.

MACPHAIL, IAN SHAW
You and the orchestra: a pocket guide. Overture by John Barbirolli, coda by Scott Goddard. xv, 114 p, illus (col & b&w), 8–p bibl. Macdonald & Evans, London, 1947.   **1.50**
Concise survey of the orchestra & its music, with a list of selected works & a glossary of musical terms.

McKINNEY, LAURENCE
People of note: a score of symphony faces. 63 p, illus (Gluyas Williams). Dutton 1940 (15th pr 1947).   **1.25**
Light verse with Williams's caricatures.

NETTEL, REGINALD
While the orchestra assembles: a simple introduction. 144 p, 9 photos, 6 b&ws, mus ex, table. Cape 1949.   **2.25**
An introduction to the orchestra, its instruments, & conductors.

TOBIN, J. RAYMOND
A seat at the Proms: for lovers of the orchestra. 143 p, illus (B. Gordon Smith). Evans Bros., London, 1948; Transatlantic 1949.   **2.75**
Interpretation & appreciation.

ORCHESTRAL MUSIC

See also:

Appreciation	Phonograph Records
Baroque Era	Program Notes
Classic Era	Repertory
Composers (& under	Romantic Era
individual names)	School Music-3
Contemporary Music	Symphony
History	Themes
Modern Music	Timing
Orchestra	Vienna

Note: For information about the celebrated descriptive catalogues of the Edwin A. Fleischer collection of orchestral music, please consult the Philadelphia Free Library.

ALTMANN, WILHELM (*comp.*)
Orchester-Literatur-Katalog. vii, 197 p, mus ex, bds. (Leuckart, Leipzig, 1919) via E. C. Schirmer.   2.00
Although written in German, this standard work is included here, for it can be used for reference purposes without difficulty by non-German readers. It includes all types of orchestral works published since 1850. A 2nd ed (1926) & a supplementary volume (1936) apparently are O/P, or not easily available in this country.

GRABBE, PAUL
The story of orchestral music and its times. viii, 216 p, illus (J. C. Wonsetler). Grosset 1942.   .75
"Little Music Library" series; many program notes with references to contemporary events.

SALTONSTALL, CECILIA D. & SMITH, H. C. (*comps*)
Catalogue of music for small orchestra. Ed Otto E. Albrecht. 267 p. Music Library Association, Music Div, Library of Congress, 1947.   3.00
Same, paper covers.   2.00
998 works arranged by composers, with notes on instrumentation, playing time, publishers, location of manuscripts, etc.

SEREDY, JULIUS S. (*comp*)
Carl Fischer analytical orchestra guide: a practical handbook for the profession. 224 p. C. Fischer 1929. 1.50
A catalogue of Carl Fischer publications with mood & form classification, indications of time, key, tempo, & duration.

SONNECK, OSCAR G. (*ed*)
Orchestral music (class M 1000–1268): catalogue, scores. 663 p. Library of Congress 1912, via GPO. 2.00
A catalogue of orchestral music in the Library of Congress.

ORCHESTRATION
See: Instrumentation/Orchestration.

Orcutt, William Dana. Author.
See Stradivari.

Orel, Alfred. Author. See App Ib.

Orem, Preston Ware. Author. See:

Counterpoint–2. Art of interweaving melodies (1937).	1.25
Fugue. Manual of (1939).	.75
Harmony–2. For beginners (1916).	1.25
—. Student's book (1934).	1.50
Modulation. Manual of (1930).	.40
Theory–1. Theory & composition of music (1924).	1.25

ORGAN

General Note: Out of the enormous published literature on various aspects of the organ, comparatively few books appear to be in print or easily available in this country.

For convenience, the listings of the available works are grouped in four categories:

Organ (General, Building, Repair, Tuning)

Organ Music

Organ Playing (Registration, Stops, etc)

Organists

ORGAN (General, Building, Repair, Tuning)

See also:

Acoustics	Lemare
Hammond Organ	Organ Music
History	Organ Playing
Instruments	Organists
Keyboard Instruments	Schweitzer-1

Standard works apparently O/P (or not easily available) include those by Audsley, Bonavia-Hunt, de Brisay, Clarke, Freeman, Hinton, Leet, Matthews, Milne, Pearce, Smith, Statham, Whitworth, Williams, etc.

APEL, WILLI
Early history of the organ. 25 p, illus, mus ex, paper. Mediæval 1946.   1.00
Offprint from "Speculum, a Journal of Mediæval Studies," Vol. 23, No 2, April 1948.

AUDSLEY, GEORGE ASHDOWN
The temple of tone: a disquisition on the scientific & artistic tonal appointment & control of concert-room, church, & theatre organs, according to the advanced system of compound tonal flexibility, & expression, with complete specifications. 260 p 2-p Audsley bibl, illus, tables. J. Fischer 1925.   3.50

A detailed technical & philosophical study, plus an "Appreciation of George Ashdown Audsley" by T. Scott Buhrman.

BARNES, WILLIAM H.
The contemporary American organ: its evolution, design, & construction. 355 p, 31 pl, 115 b&ws, 3–p bibl. J. Fischer (1930) 4th ed 1948.   4.75
Latest revision of a standard work, which includes a section on electronic "organs."

BONAVIA-HUNT, NOEL A.
The modern British organ: a theoretical & practical treatise on the tone & mechanism of the king of instruments. xii, 267 p, illus (8 photos, 18 pl, 46 b&ws), tables. Weeks 1947.   7.50
Summing up the views & experience of a British authority; includes complete specifications of 4 famous British organs.

BROADHOUSE, JOHN
The organ as viewed from within: a practical handbook on the mechanism of the organ, with a chapter on tuning.   viii, 133 p, illus mus ex. △ Reeves n d (2nd ed 1926).   (3.00)

CELLIER, ALEXANDRE & BACHELIN, HENRI. See App Ia.

DUFOURCQ, NORBERT. See App Ia.

FARMER, HENRY GEORGE
The organ of the ancients: from eastern sources (Hebrew, Syriac, & Arabic).   Forew F. W. Galpin. xxiii, 185 p, col frontis, pl, tables, 8–p △ bibl.   Reeves n d (1931).   (10.00)

FLINT, EDWARD N.
The Newberry memorial organ at Yale University: a study in the history of American organ building. 82 p, frontis, tables. Yale 1930.   2.00

GOODRICH, WALLACE
The organ in France: a study of its mechanical construction, tonal characteristics, & literature, with suggestions for the registration of French organ music upon American instruments. xv, 168 p, 20 illus, mus ex, 2–p bibl.   Boston 1917.   3.00
A standard work on its specialized subject.

KLOTZ, HANS. See App Ib.

KWASNIK, WALTER. See App Ib.

MAHRENHOLZ, CHRISTHARD. See App Ib.

PERKINS, JOCELYN
The organs and bells of Westminster Abbey. 109 p, illus (pors, facs), bibl △ notes. Novello 1937.   (4.50)

SKINNER, ERNEST M.
The modern organ: with illustrations, drawings, specifications. 48 p, illus, tables, bds. Gray (1917) 6th ed 1945.   2.00

SMITH, HERMANN
Modern organ tuning: the how & why, clearly explaining the nature of the organ pipe & the system of equal temperament, together with an historical record of the evolution of the diatonic scale from the Greek tetrachord.   x, 120 p, mus ex, tables. Reeves n d (1902).   (2.25)

SUMNER, W. L.
A history & account of the organs of St Paul's Cathedral.   47 p, illus, tables, stiff paper.   Musical Opinion 1931.   1.50
Includes lists of the organists & studies of Stanley Marchant & Henry Willis.

WHITWORTH, REGINALD
The electric organ: historical introduction & a comprehensive description of modern usage of electricity in organ building. 257 p, illus. Musical Opinion (1935) 3rd enl ed 1948.   7.50
A student's guide to the organ: a non-technical description of the pipe organ. 91 p, 9 illus, tables. Musical opinion (1935) new ed n d (1947?).   3.00
Outline history, how the organ "works," descriptions of concert-hall & theater organs.

ORGAN MUSIC

See also: esp Church Music, Organ Playing.
Also:

Appreciation	Keyboard Instrs &
Baroque Era	Music (esp Bed-
Choir/Choral	brook)
English Music	Medieval/Renaissance
History	

Also: Composers (& under names of individual organ-music composers, esp Bach, Franck, Handel, Karg-Elert, Mendelssohn, Rheinberger, etc).

Standard works apparently O/P (or not easily available in this country) include those by Frotscher (in German, rev from Ritter), Rokseth (in French), Williams, etc. Grace's "French organ music" (1919), however, is scheduled to appear again shortly in a revised edition.

DIETRICH, FRITZ. See App Ib.

DUFOURCQ, NORBERT. See App Ia.

JEPPESEN, KNUD (ed)
Italian organ music of the early sixteenth century. Tr Conrad H. Rawski. Musurgia 1951, pending. △

First English translation of a new, enlarged edition of a standard work (see also App Ib for the original German ed of 1943). "Musurgia Studies in Musicology", series A, v 7 (on subscription only).

KLEIN, JOHN (ed)
The first four centuries of music for the organ: from Dunstable to Bach (1370–1749). Forew E. Power Biggs. 2 v: xxx, 477 p, 33 pl, chart, music, 3–p bibl. Associated 1948. Boxed: 20.00
An anthology of 71 organ works by different composers, with elaborate notes on the composers, the registration & interpretation of their works, etc.

SCHWEIGER, HERTHA (ed)
A brief compendium of early organ music (ca. 1600/ca. 1850). Compiled & provided with biographical, analytical, & technical comments. xv, 86 p, 4 illus, music, paper.   G. Schirmer 1943.   2.50
Introductory notes on organ building, pedals, dynamics, & registration; anthology of 15 works from Frescobaldi & Sweelinck to Bach's sons & Schumann.

STELLHORN, MARTIN H. (comp)
Index to hymn preludes: including also postludes, voluntaries, paraphrases, variations, & other organ compositions based on hymns, chorales, & carols.   151 p, paper. Concordia 1948.   2.00
Alphabetical listing of some 2200 compositions based on tunes in use in the Lutheran church; notes on key, difficulty, length.

WATERS, CHARLES F.
Growth of organ music: an historical survey. 62 p, paper. Musical Opinion 1931.   1.00
Surveyed by national schools of composers.

WEIGL, BRUNO (ed). See App Ib ("Handbuch der Orgelliteratur").
Note: A 1931 revision of eds by Kothe & Fochhammer (1890) and Burkert (1909), this is an indispensable reference work to all types of organ music, even for non-German readers.

WESTERBY, HERBERT
International repertoire-guide: (historical, educational, & descriptive) to foreign, British, & American works. xii, 117 p + 36–p pl, 2–p bibl. (1927) Reeves n d.   5.00
Super-title: "The complete organ recitalist." Foreign works grouped by national schools; British & American by type of composition. Includes brief notes on famous organs & many illustrations of organs & organists.

ORGAN PLAYING (Registration, Stops, etc.)

See also:

Accompaniment	Interpretation
Choir/Choral	Organ
Church Music	Organ Music
Hammond Organ	Organists
Improvisation	

Standard works apparently O/P (or not easily available in this country) include those by Boyd, Bonavia-Hunt, Goss-Custard, Hull, Lochner, Pearce, Ramin (in German), Richards, Wedgewood, etc.

(AGO EXAMINATION COMMITTEE)
Examination booklet 1946.   46 p, mus ex, paper. American Guild of Organists 1946.   1.00
Analysis of the AGO examination requirements, with suggestions for preparatory study by Norman Coke-Jephcott, H. W. Friedell, et al.

AUDSLEY, GEORGE ASHDOWN
Organ stops: and their artistic registration; names, forms, construction, & offices in scientific combination. 294 p, 5 pl, tables. Gray 1921.   2.50
Alphabetical list with detailed notes.

CONWAY, MARMADUKE P.
Playing a church organ.   Forew E. S. Roper.   144 p, frontis photo. Latimer House, London, 1949; Macmillan 1950.   1.50
Not a method, but a handbook, including a study of the evolution of the organ, lists of anthems & voluntaries, etc.

DEMAREST, CLIFFORD
Hints on organ accompaniment. 43 p, mus ex. Gray 1910.   1.00

DICKINSON, CLARENCE
The technique and art of organ playing. With the collaboration of H. A. Dickinson, 203 p, music, bds. Gray 1922.   5.00
Same, paper cover.   4.00
Introductory instructions (54 p), followed by exercises for practice purposes.

DUNHAM, ROWLAND W.
Pedal master. Presser in prep.   △

ELLINGFORD, HERBERT F.
The art of transcribing for the organ: a complete text book for the organist in arranging choral & instrumental music. lx, 158 p, mus ex. Gray 1922   6.00
Same, boards.   5.00
Notes on transcribing orchestral accompaniment of choral works, works for various orchestral, chamber, & piano combinations.

ELLINGFORD, H. F. & MEERS, ERNEST G.
The science of organ pedalling.
Forew Henry Willis. xii, 64 p, mus
ex, diagrs. Musical Opinion (1928?)
rev repr 1932 & 1942.   5.00
*Title essay & a note on Bach pedalling by
Ellingford; "Organ pedalling & its system-
atisation" by Meers; with appendices on
scales, arpeggios, & footing movements.*

EVANS, EDWIN, Sr
Technics of the organ: an illuminating treatise on many points & difficulties connected therewith; special
treatment of rhythm, minimisation of
the use of accessories, extemporisa-
tion, expressive regulation of organ
tone & accompaniment. xv, 140 p, mus
ex. (Reeves 1937) Scribner repr 1938.   4.00

GLEASON, HAROLD
Method of organ playing. xiii, 250
p, music, 2–p bibl, typescript repro.
Crofts (1937) 4th ed 1949.   5.50
*Revised edition of a work in the "Eastman
School of Music" series. Includes outlines
of graded courses in piano & organ playing,
specifications of various organs, surveys of
early organ music & Bach organ editions.*

GRACE, HARVEY
The complete organist. Intro P. C.
Buck.   240 p, mus ex, 4–p annot
bibl. Richards Press, London, 1920
(4th pr 1950).   2.50
*Informal practical advice, originally pub-
lished in the "Musical Times", 1913/15*

KOCH, CASPER
The organ student's gradus ad parnassum: Book 1, the elements of
interpretation.   xvi, 80 p, mus ex,
bibl refs.   J. Fischer 1945.   2.00
*Chapters on tempo, rhythmic conventions,
dynamics, ornamentation, registration, practice, etc. (Book 2: progressive organ studies,
135 p, 1950, $2.50, consists of music only.)*

LORENZ, ELLEN JANE
The amateur organist's manual: a
booklet for acquainting the beginner
with the organ, the manipulation of
its stops, & the technique of playing,
with suggestions for the church service. 32 p, mus ex, paper. Lorenz
1941.   .60

MATTHAEI, KARL. See App Ib

NEVIN, GORDON BALCH
Primer of organ registration: with
numerous illustrations & a dictionary
of organ stops. xi, 103 p 12 pl, 29
b&ws, tables, mus ex. Ditson 1920.   1.50
"Music Students Library" series

SCEATS, GODFREY
The liturgical use of the organ. 47 p,
music. Musical Opinion 1922.   2.00
*Includes 26 original interludes & postludes
for use with plainsong in the 8 modes.*

TOURNEMIRE, CHARLES. See App Ia.

TRUETTE, EVERETT E.
Organ registration: a comprehensive
treatise on the distinctive qualities of
tone of organ stops . . . 257 p, illus
ex. C. W. Thompson & Co., Boston
(1919), 4th ed n d, via Boston.   4.00
*A standard work, whose full sub-title goes on:
"The acoustical & musical effect of combining individual stops, & the selection of stops
& combinations for the various phrases of
organ compositions; together with a suggested
registration for 100 organ compositions,
hymn & anthems intended to be played on
specific organs."*

ORGANISTS

See also:

Choir/Choral–2	Organ
Church Music	Organ Music
Interpreters	Organ Playing
Lemare	Schweitzer

Also: Composers (& under names of individual organ composers, esp Bach, Franck,
Handel, Karg-Elert, Mendelssohn, etc.).

(AMERICAN GUILD OF ORGANISTS)
50th anniversary year book and
directory. 250 p, paper.   American
Guild of Organists 1946.   1.00

BALDWIN, SAMUEL ATKINSON
The story of the American Guild of
Organists. 80 p, frontis, bds. Gray
1946.   2.00
Documentary record of 50 years' activity.

DUFOURCQ, NORBERT. See App Ia.

STOCKS, H. C. L.
British cathedral organists: with an
appendix giving some other relevant
information. 32 p, paper. Hinrichsen 1949.   1.25
*"Miniature Survey" series M-25: mainly
lists of names & dates.*

WEST, JOHN E.
Cathedral organists, past and present: a record of the succession of
organists of the cathedrals, chapels
royal, & principal collegiate churches
of the United Kingdom, from about
the period of the Reformation to the
present day. xii, 141 p, 3–p bibl. △
Novello 1899.   (4.50)

ORGANUM

See:

Anthologies (esp	Medieval/Renaissance
Davison & Apel)	Organ Music
History	Plainsong

ORIENTAL MUSIC

General Note: "Music" to most of us means Occidental or western music so exclusively that we tend to ignore or minimize the ancient, extensive musical cultures & traditions of the Orient. And unfortunately this tendency is not counteracted by any easy or widespread dissemination of authentic information. No books at all are available for listing under this general subject-heading, since an appropriate few all apparently are either O/P or not easily available in this country: e.g., Cousins' "Music of the Orient & Occident" (1935), Searson-Kiwi's "Music of the Orient" (1949, in Hebrew), Hirosi's bibliography (1929 Tokyo), Lachmann's "Musik des Orients" (1929), etc.

However some pertinent material (if by no means as much as could be desired) is available in some of the specialized cross-references below:

See: esp Asiatic Musics (note only).

Ancient Music	History–1 & 2
(esp Sachs)	(esp Sachs)
Anthologies (esp	India (music in)
Davison & Apel)	Instruments
Appreciation	(esp Sachs)
Arabia (music in)	Japan (music in)
Bali (music in)	Java (music in)
Byzantine Music	Jewish Music
China (music in)	

ORNAMENTATION

See also:

Accompaniment	Interpretation
(esp Arnold)	(esp Dolmetsch)
Bach–2 (esp Aldrich,	Keyboard Instruments
David)	& Music
Composition	Organ Playing
Counterpoint	Piano Playing
England–music in	Singing
(esp Van den Borren)	Violin Playing (esp
Harmony	Mozart)

Standard works apparently O/P (or not easily available) include those by Arger (in French), Brunold (in French), Dannreuther, Dunn, Ehrlich (in German), Fowles, Goldschmidt (in German), Kuhn (in German), Schenker (in German), etc.

ALDRICH, PUTNAM
Ornamentation in the 17th and 18th △
centuries. Coleman, in prep.   17.50

FAY, HARRY F. (*comp*)
Ornaments in music: described & illustrated. 86 p, mus ex. Boston 1893.   1.25
Originally pub by Miles & Thompson, Boston.

HAMILTON, CLARENCE G.
Ornaments in classical and modern music. 76 p, mus ex, stuff paper. Boston 1930.   .75
"Pocket Music Student" series. Historical survey & analyses of classes of ornaments.

RUSSELL, LOUIS ARTHUR
The embellishments of music: a study of the entire range of musical ornaments from the time of J. S. Bach. 66 p, mus ex.   Presser 1894.   1.25

ORNSTEIN, Leo

See:

American Music	History
Composers–2 & 3a	Modern Music
Contemporary Music	

Note: Martens' biography (1918) is O/P.

Orrey, Leslie. Author.
See Harmony–2.

Ortmann, Otto Rudolph. Author.
See Dictation. Translator. See Composition (Hindemith).

Note: Ortmann's standard studies of the physical & physiological bases of piano playing apparently are O/P.

Osborn, Loraine. Author.
See Speech.

Osburn, (Mrs) Mary Hubbell.
Author. See Composers–3a.

O'Toole, William. Author.
See Teaching–3.

Ottani, Giancarlo. Author. See App Ic.

Otte, Heinz. Co-author (with Hadamowsky). See App Ib.

Otterstein, Adolph W.   Author
See Baton–1.

Otterström, Thorwald. Author.
See Harmony–2, Modulation

Overhoff, Kurt. Author. See App Ib.

Overmyer, Grace. Author.
See App IIa (juvenile biographies).

OVERTURE

See:

Appreciation	Opera
Composers (& under	Orchestral Music
individual names)	Phonograph Records
History	Program Notes

Note: Botstiber's *"Geschichte der Ouvertüre"* (1913) apparently is O/P (or not easily available in this country).

Owens, Lee. Author. See Dances–2.
Owens, William A. Editor.
See Folksongs–2.

—P—

Paap, Wouter. Author.
See Beethoven–2.

PADEREWSKI, Ignace Jan

See also:

America (music in)	Opera
Appreciation	Phonograph Records
Composers–1 & 2	Pianists
Concerto	Piano Music
History	Poland (music in)
Interpreters	Program Notes

Note: Biographies apparently O/P (or not easily available) include those by Baughan, Landau, and Phillips.

OPIENSKI, HENRYK. See App Ia.

PADEREWSKI, I. J. & LAWTON, MARY
The Paderewski memoirs. x, 404 p, 41 illus (pors & programs).
Scribner 1938.   5.00

STRAKACZ, ANIELA
Paderewski as I knew him. Tr. Halina Chybowska. 338 p + 15-p photos (pors, etc). Rutgers 1949.   5.00
Reminiscences from a diary (1917/41) by the wife of Paderewski's secretary.

PAGANINI, Nicolò

See:

Appreciation	Phonograph Records
Berlioz–1 & 2	Program Notes
Composers–1	Romantic Era
Concerto	Violin Music
History	Violin Playing

Also: App IIa (Acker, Wheeler).
Note: Standard works apparently O/P (or not easily available) include those by Day, Fétis, Jarosy, Komroff, Pulver, Salzedo, Stratton, etc. (But see App Ia for Jarosy, in French.)

Page, Kate Stearns. Co-author (with Diller). See Children–3 & 6.
Page, Nathaniel Clifford. Editor.
See Sight-Singing (Panseron).
Page, Ralph. Co-author (with Tolman).
See Dances–2.
Pahissa, Jaime. Author. See App Id.
Pahlen, Kurt. Author. See History–2.
Painter, Paul. Co-author (with Benner).
See Baton–2.

PAINTING (& Music)
See: Pictures/Portraits.

PALESTRINA, Giovanni Pierluigi da

See also:

Appreciation	History
Choir/Choral–3	Italian Music
Church Music	Madrigal
Composers–1	Mass
Counterpoint–1 (esp	Medieval/Renaissance
Bush, Merritt,	Phonograph Records
Soderlund)	Program Notes

Note: Standard works apparently O/P (or not easily available) include those by Pyne; in Italian by Baini, Cametti, Casimiri, etc; in French by Brenet, Raugel, etc.

COATES, HENRY
Palestrina. ix, 243 p, 8 pl, mus ex, 2-p bibl.   Dent 1938 (1948), via Pellegrini 1949.   2.50
"Master Musicians" series, with usual calendar, personalia, & catalogue of works.

JEPPESEN, KNUD
The style of Palestrina and the dissonance. Intro E. J. Dent. Tr Margaret Hamerik & Annie I. Fausboll. 306 p, mus ex, bibl refs, paper. Munksgaard & Oxford (1927) 2nd rev enl ed 1946.   6.50
A standard work, originally published in German in 1922, which not only analyzes Palestrina's music in great detail, but delves deeply into the larger problems of polyphonic style in general.

Palmer, Charles. Co-author (with Henderson). See Singing–3.
Palmer, Edgar A. (*pseud* of Posselt, Erich). Editor. See Songbooks.
Palmer, Russell. Compiler.
See England (music in).
Palmer, Winthrop Russell. Author.
See Ballet.
Palotay, Irene Banyay. Author.
See Hungarian Music.

PANAMA (Music in)
See: Latin America.

PAN-AMERICAN MUSIC
See: esp Latin America.

America (music in)	Folklore
American Music	App Id (Pereira)

Note: For information about the activities & publications of the Pan American Union, address the Pan American Union, Division of Music & Visual Arts, Washington 6, D. C.

Panassié, Hugues. Author.
See Jazz, App Ia.
Panigel, Armand. Editor.
See Chopin–2, also App Ia.
Panòff, Petr Assèn. Author.
See App Ib (ed Bücken).
Panseron, Auguste-Mathieu. Author.
See Sight-Singing.

PANTOMIME

See:

Acting	Films
Ballet	History
(The) Dance	Medieval/Renaissance
Dances–1 & 2	Minstrels/Minstrelsy
England (music in)	Opera

Note: Standard works apparently O/P (or not easily available) include those by Avery, Broadbent, Disher, etc.

Panum, Hortense. Author.
See String Instruments.
Panzéra, Charles. Author. See App Ia.
Paoli, Domenico de'. Author. See App Ic.

PARAGUAY (Music in).

See: Latin America.

Parker, (Mrs.) Alvin A. Editor (with Lichtenwanger & Leach). See Church Music.
Parker, Douglas Charles. Author.
See Gypsy Music.

PARKER, Henry Taylor (H. T. P.)

See also:

America (music in)	Criticism
Boston	Koussevitzky

Note: H. T. P.'s own sole book publication, "Eighth notes" (1922), is O/P.

McCORD, DAVID
H. T. P.: portrait of a critic, viii, 25 p, frontis por, 4-p facs. Coward 1935.   1.00
Tribute to a great American music critic, in a reprint of an original limited edition.

PARKER, Horatio William

See also:

America (music in)	Education
American Music	History
Composers–3a	Phonograph Records

Note: A memoir (1942) by the composer's daughter, Isabel Parker Semler, apparently is O/P.

CHADWICK, GEORGE W.
Horatio Parker: 1863–1920. 26 p, bds. Yale 1921.   .60
A tribute delivered as an address before the American Academy of Arts & Letters in 1920.

Parkhurst, Howard Elmore. Author.
See Ancient Music.

PARRATT, (Sir) Walter

See: England (music in), Organists.
Note: The biography by Tovey & Geoffrey Parratt (1941) apparently is O/P (or not easily available in this country).

Parrish, Carl. Editor (with Ohl).
See Anthologies. Author. See Piano.
Parrish, Lydia. Author.
See Negro Spirituals.
Parrot, Louis. Author. See App Ia.
Parrott, Ian. Author. See Modern Music

PARRY, (Sir) Charles Hubert Hastings

See:

Church Music	English Music
Composers–3c	History
England (music in)	Program Notes

Author. See Composers–1, History–1 (Oxford v 3, note only), History–3 & 5.
Note: The Graves biography (1926) & a study by Fuller-Maitland (1934) apparently are O/P (or not easily available in this country), as are several of Parry's own books.

Parry, W. H. Author. See Church Music.
Partch, Harry. Author. See Monophony.

PARTHENIA

See: Elizabethan Music (Harrow Replica).

Pastene, Jerome. Author.
See Strauss Family.
Patrick, Millar. Author.
See Psalms/Psalmody.
Patterson, Floyd. Author.
See Church Music.
Patterson, Frank (Franklin P.) Author.
See Melody Writing.

PATTI, Adelina

See: Opera–1, Singers.
Note: Hermann Klein's "The reign of Patti" (1920) apparently is O/P.

Pattison, Bruce. Author. See Poetry.
Pauer, Ernst. Author. See Form.
Paumgartner, Bernard. Author.
See App Ib.

PAVLOVA, Anna

See also: Ballet, Dance.

MAGRIEL, PAUL (ed)
Pavlova: an illustrated monograph.
ix, 78 p, 60 photos, 4-p bibl. Holt 1947.   3.50
With chronology and essays by Pavlova, Van Vechten, Moore, & Stuart.

MALVERN, GLADYS. See App IIa (juvenile)

OLIVÉVOFF, ANDRÉ
Flight of the swan: a memory of
Pavlova, as told to John Gill. xii,
258 p, 16 photos. Dutton 1932 (4th
pr 1935). 4.50
Anecdotal biography by Pavlova's manager.

PAYNE, John Howard
See: America (music in), American Music.
*Note: Trinka's biography (1922) of the author
of "Home, sweet home" apparently is O/P.*

Payne, May de Forest. Compiler.
See Bach–2.

Pearce, Charles William. Author. See:
Counterpoint–2. Student's (1926). 1.75
Theory–3. Rudiments (1920) 1.00
*Note: Many other books by Pearce apparently
are O/P (or not easily available in this
country).*

Pearson, Hesketh. Author.
See Gilbert & Sullivan.

PEDAGOGY
See:
Children   School Music
Education   Teaching

Also:
Organ Playing   Singing
Piano Playing   Etc.

PEDAL/PEDALLING
See:
Organ   Meers)
Organ Playing   Piano Playing
  (esp Ellingwood-   (esp 2, Bowen)

Peery, Paul Denver. Author.
See Carillon.
Peery, Rob Roy. Author.
See Modulation
Peeters, Flor. Author. See Gregorian.
Pei, Mario Andrew. Author.
See Troubadours/Trouvères.
Pelterson, Bertha K. Author.
See Children–8.
Peltz, Mary Ellis Opdycke. Author.
See Opera–3 & 4.

PENMANSHIP (Musical)
See: Manuscript.

Pennington, Jo. Author.
See Eurhythmics.

PENNSYLVANIA (Music in)
See:
America (music in)   Folklore (esp Korson)
Beissel   Philadelphia
Church Music (esp ed   Yearbooks
  Parker)

PEPUSCH, John Christopher
See:
Beggar's Opera   English Music
England (music in)   History

PEPYS, Samuel
*Note: Studies of Pepys, as a lover of music,
by Bennett and by Bridge, apparently are O/P
(or not easily available in this country).*

PERCUSSION INSTRUMENTS
See:
Band–1   Instruments
Children–4 & 6   Military Music
Instrumentation   Orchestra

Pereira Salas, Eugenio. Author.
See App Id.
Perfield, Effa Ellis. Author.
See Mode/Modality.

PERFORMANCE
See: esp Interpretation.

Also:
Conducting   Psychology
Memory   Singing
Organ Playing   Stage Fright
Piano Playing   Violin Playing
Also: App Ib (ed Bücken: v 8, Haas).

Perham, Beatrice (Krone). Author.
See School Music–1.
Peri, Noël. Author. See App Ia.

PERIODICALS (Musical)
See: Bibliography (esp Kretzschmar "Music
Index"), App Ib (Arginteanu).
*Note: Periodical articles (& reprints for
limited distribution) are not listed in the
present Guide. References to such material
may be found in "The Readers' Guide to
Periodical Literature" series, published by the
H. W. Wilson Company, 950 University
Avenue, New York City 52, and—for material
from 1949 on—to the Kretzschmar "Music
Index" referred to above.*

Perkins, Clella Lester. Author.
See Children–1.
Perkins, Jocelyn Henry Temple. Author.
See Organ.
Perry, Adelaide Trowbridge. Compiler.
See Piano Music.
Perry, Edward Baxter. Author.
See Piano Music.
Persichetti, Vincent. Author (with Schrei-
ber). See W. Schuman.

PERU (Music in)
See also: Latin America.

TOOR, FRANCES
Three words of Peru.   ix, 239 p,
illus, map, bibl. Crown 1949.   3.50
*Includes material on Peruvian dancing &
music, and photographs of musical instruments.*

Peters Edition Music Calendar.
See Almanacs & Calendars.
Peterson, Franklin Sivewright.   Author.
See Theory–3 & 4.
Peterson, Houston.   Editor.
See Teachers.
Peterson, Phebe Lewis.   Author.
See Choir/Choral–2.
Petitpierre, Jacques.   Author.
See Mendelssohn–2.

PETRUCCI, Ottaviano dei.   Printer.
*Note: Hewitt's 1942 annotated edition of
Petrucci's "Harmonice musices odhecaton"
(1501) has just gone O/P.*

Peyser, Ethel Rose.   Co-author (with
(Bauer). See Children–2, History–2.
Peyser, Herbert F.   Author.
See America—music in (ed Eaton: includes
a contribution by Peyser), Bach–1, Schu-
bert–1.
Pfister, Kurt.   Author. See App Ib.

PFITZNER, Hans Erich
See: App Ib (Rutz: biog in German).

Pfrogner, Hermann.   Author. See App Ib.

PHILADELPHIA (Music in)
See also: America (music in), History.
*Note: Works by Madeira on music in Phila-
delphia (1896) & by Wister on the Philadelphia Orchestra (1925) apparently are O/P.
A 50th anniversary brochure on the Philadelphia Orchestra by Donald L. Engle (1950)
apparently is not available generally.*
GERSON, ROBERT A.
Music in Philadelphia: a history
of Philadelphia music, a summary of
its current state, & a comprehensive
index dictionary. viii, 422 p, illus,
chart, 4–p bibl. Presser 1940.   3.50
Survey from Colonial times to the present.

**PHILHARMONIC (London, Royal, Phil-
harmonic-Symphony of New York,
Vienna, etc).**
See also:
America (music in)   Program Notes (esp
Conductors   Bagar & Biancolli)
England (music in)   Toscanini
History   Vienna
Orchestra   Walter
Phonograph Records   Yearbooks

*Note: Histories of the Philharmonic-Sym-
phony Society of New York by Krehbiel
(1892), Huneker (1917), & Erskine (1943)
apparently all are O/P, as is Russell's "Philharmonic" (London, 1942).*

ELKIN, ROBERT
Royal Philharmonic: the annals of
the Royal Philharmonic Society.
Forew Pau Casals.   192 p, 22 illus,
bibl refs. Rider 1946.   5.00
*With lists of first performances, gold medals,
officers, & programs 1912/1945.*

MITTAG, ERWIN
The Vienna Philharmonic: published
for the Vienna Philharmonic Orchestra. Tr J. R. L. Orange & G. Morice.
125 p, 28 illus (pors, facs, etc), brief
bibl, paper.   Gerlach & Wiedling,
Vienna, 1950.   (1.75)
*An informal historical survey of the famous
orchestra & its conductors.*

RUSSELL, THOMAS
Philharmonic decade.   171 p. Hut-
chinson 1945.   (4.25)
*The story of the London Philharmonic
Orchestra, told by its secretary-manager.*

PHILIPPINE ISLANDS (Music in)
See: Asiatic Musics (note only), Dances–2
(Reyes-Tolentino).
*Note: The 9th installment of the Asiatic
Musics bibliography (December 1949
"Notes") includes a Philippine section.*

Phillips, Charles Stanley.   Author.
See Hymns/Hymnody–1.
Phillips, Charles Henry.   Author.
See Church Music.
Phillips, Claude Anderson.   Co-author
(with Burke & Meierhoffer). See School
Music–2.

PHILOSOPHY (& Music/of Music)
*General Note: Although this subject-heading
is not recognized as yet by most dictionaries
& encyclopedias of music, we include it here
if only for the pragmatic reason that it figures
implicitly, if not explicitly, in the titles of a
number of books. Few of them, to be sure,
currently are "in print," and of these few
some could be classified under other headings
(such as Aesthetics); nevertheless, a genuine
need exists for the present category, even if
it is less than adequately met at present.*

*Actually, of course, many books on varied
subjects exhibit a true philosophical approach
to at least specialized aspects of music &
musical experience. (See for notable example*

Allen's "*Philosophies of music history.*") *A similar approach to the larger or "wholistic" aspects is likely to become increasingly evident in the future.*

See also:

Aesthetics-1 & 2	Musicology
Appreciation	Psychology
History-1 (esp Allen)	Religion

Note: Standard works apparently O/P (or not easily available) include those by Britan, Howes, Pole, Scott, etc.

CUVELIER, ANDRÉ. See App Ia.

HOWES, FRANK
Man, mind, and music. viii, 184 p, mus ex. Secker 1948.   3.00
The relations of music to anthropology, philosophy, psychology, & sociology.

HUGHES, CHARLES W.
The human side of music. xviii, 341 p. Philosophical 1948.   3.75
Music as an expression of human needs; how music is organized from sounds.

LANGER, SUSANNE K.
Philosophy in a new key: a study in the symbolism of reason, rite, & art. 248 p, bibl refs, paper. (1942) Mentor 1948.   .35
Originally published by Harvard University Press, 1942. Includes two chapters, p 165/216, "On significance in music" and on "artistic import."

SMITH, CHARLES T.
Music and reason: the art of listening, appreciating, & composing. ix, 158 p, 4 pl. Social Sciences 1948.   3.25
A British educator's "defense of reason," with emphasis on the relationship between music & religion.

PHON

See:

Acoustics	Sound Recording
Decibel (Lloyd)	& Reproduction

PHONETICS/PHONOLOGY

See: esp Voice.

Diction	Singing
Pronunciation	Speech

PHONOGRAPH/GRAMOPHONE

*General Note: The distinction between these two terms of course is one of national usage only: both "phonograph" & "gramophone" refer to same general type of record-reproducing instrument. Curiously enough, especially considering the popularity & usefulness of the "radio" or "electronic" phonograph today (and despite the existence of a mush-*rooming literature on phonograph recordings), there is no available publication that deals adequately with the history & development of the instrument, or for that matter, none that explains its principles & proper use in terms the average musician or general reader can understand.*

See also: esp Phonograph Records.

Acoustics (esp Olson)	School Music-1
Appreciation (esp	(esp Best)
Spaeth "At home")	Sound Rec & Repro
	Stokowski

Note: Pertinent books apparently O/P (or not easily available in this country) include those in English by Buick, Gaydon, Rogers, Wilson & Webb, etc; and in French by Gautier, Hurm, Weiss, etc.

HUGHBANKS, LEROY
Talking wax: the story of the phonograph simply told for general readers. ix, 142 p, 8–p bibl, typescript repro. Hobson Book Press, N. Y., 1945.   2.50
Anecdotal historical sketches in folksy style; little or no data on recent developments.

PHONOGRAPH (GRAMOPHONE) RECORDS

General Note: The widespread recording of music (that is, as it actually sounds, rather than in printed notation) is a contemporary phenomenon whose significance seems to have been better understood by the general listening public than by musicologists. Eventually, of course, it will be the latter who may best realise and articulate the full import of this revolution in the methods of disseminating music, but meanwhile the cataloguing & evaluation of record releases is being carried out on a largely pragmatic basis. The available literature (listed below, except for books dealing with such specialized subjects as Children's & Jazz Records) includes two general types of publications: 1) more or less complete surveys of the entire available repertory of "serious" music on discs; 2) critical evaluations of, or "appreciative" introductions to, selected segments of that repertory.

See also: Children-2 (esp Barbour & Freeman, Eisenberg & Krasno), Jazz (esp Delauny, Smith).

Also:

Acoustics	Opera-3 (Biancolli &
Appreciation	Bagar)
Chopin-2 (Panigel,	Phonograph
also App Ia)	Program Notes
Concerto (Veinus)	School Music-2 (esp
Folklore	Leavitt) & 4 (esp
Folksongs-1	Howerton)
(esp Lumpkin)	Sound Rec & Repro
History-5 (Scholes)	Stokowski
Libraries (esp Moor,	Symphony
Myers)	(O'Connell)

Most recent books on individual or collective musicians & their works, and many recent books on specialized subjects, include "discographies"—i.e., lists of pertinent phonograph recordings.

Note: Pertinent works apparently O/P (or not easily available) include those by Bryson, Coeuroy & Clarence (in French), Freer, Gómez (in Spanish), Hines et al, Hurst, Scholes, etc.

AFFELDER, PAUL
How to build a record library: a guide to planned collecting of recorded music. Forew Sigmund Spaeth. 256 p. Dutton 1947. **3.50**
Inspirational approach for novices, with recommended records of some 700 compositions.

BALL, JOHN, *Jr.*
Records for pleasure. ix, 214 p, 2-p bibl. Rutgers 1947. **2.50**
Practical advice for the collector, with a recommended basic library of some 200 works & a glossary of phonographic terms.

BAUER, ROBERT (*comp*)
The new catalogue of historical records, 1898–1908/09. 494 p. (1937) Sidgwick 2nd ed 1947. **7.50**
A standard reference work: acoustical vocal records listed alphabetically by singers.

CLOUGH, F. F. & CUMING, G. J. (*comps*)
The world's encyclopedia of recorded music. Sidgwick in prep. Δ
A monumental reference work (many years in preparation, but now scheduled for 1951) that promises to be the most detailed & authoritative of any over-all, non-critical compilation yet attempted.

GAISBERG, FREDERICK W.
Music on record. Forew Compton Mackenzie. 269 p, illus. (1942) Δ Robert Hale Ltd, London, 1946. (4.50)
Memoirs of some 50 years of British recording & recording artists, originally published in 1942 by Macmillan as "The music goes round."

GILBERT, J. M. & JACQUES, HENRY.
See App Ia.

HAGGIN, B. H.
Music on records: a new guide to the music, the performances, the recordings. vi, 279, iii p. (1941) Knopf 4th rev ed 1946. **2.00**
Superseding an earlier work with the same title (Oxford 1938), this is an outspoken critical evaluation of selected music & record-

ings, plus informative material on starting a library, jazz records, the phonograph itself, & phonographic accessories.

HALL, DAVID
The record book: a guide to the world of the phonograph. viii, 1395 p. Durrell (1940) new International ed 1948, via Citadel 1949. **3.95**
Extensive discographies of some 774 composers, including European & deleted releases, with "appreciative" evaluations; plus an introductory survey, with notes on record collecting, the choice & care of phonograph & records, etc.

Records: 1950 edition. ix, 524, xx p. Knopf 1950. **5.00**
The most recent & extensive compilation of releases (domestic & European, LP's & 45's as well as 78's) through 1948, 1949, and early 1950. With a discussion of the new types of records, "appreciative" annotations to many works, indices of composers & principal performers, etc.

HALLSTROM, JOHN
Relax and listen: how to enjoy music through records. iv, 272 p. Rinehart 1947. **2.50**
The informal, "lowbrow" approach to music appreciation via records for novices, with recommended (RCA Victor only) recordings.

KOLODIN, IRVING
The new guide to recorded music: international edition. xvii, 524 p. Doubleday (1941) 3rd rev enl ed 1950. **4.00**
Extensive discographies of some 246 compositions, with concise evaluations, plus an index of performing artists. The 1st edition ("guide to recorded music") appeared in 1941; the 2nd ("New guide to recorded music") in 1947; the present 3rd includes over 700 new entries, among them "LP" & foreign releases.

MOSES, JULIAN MORTON (*comp*)
Collectors' guide to American recordings, 1895–1925. Forew Giuseppe De Luca. 200 p, paper. American Record Collectors' Exchange, N. Y., 1949. **3.75**
Superseding a booklet, "The record collector's guide" of 1936, this includes acoustical discographies of some 339 artists (from Abott to Zimbalist), a numerical guide (including 5500 Red Seal records), index of operas represented, & instrumental index.

O'CONNELL, CHARLES
The other side of the record. xi, 332, xi p. Knopf 1947. **3.50**

The outspoken memoirs of a recording director, with candid, "debunking" portraits of many famous recording artists.

REID, ROBERT H. *(supervising ed)*
The Gramophone Shop encyclopedia of recorded music. xii, 639 p. (1936)
Crown 3rd rev enl ed 1948.   **5.00**
Latest version of the first catalogue raissonné of all serious music on discs, listing (without evaluations) some 75,000 recordings in some 800 composer-discographies, plus a performers' index. This supersedes earlier editions published by the Gramophone Shop (1936, ed R. D. Darrell) & Simon & Schuster (1942, ed George Clark Leslie).

SEMEONOFF, BORIS
Record collecting: a guide for beginners; with a chapter on collecting jazz records by Alexander Ross. 101 p, frontis & 6 pl (label facs), map. Oakwood Press, London, 1949.   (2.50)
Practical advice from the British point of view; including a chapter on record catalogues, books, & magazines, and a map of London shops.

SMITH, MOSES
Selective record guide. 300 p. Macmillan 1950.   **4.50**
Directed primarily at beginners with emphasis on music rather than recorded performances, this includes a Basic List (costing around $100) with program notes, a Selected Record Library of broader range, & a 3rd list of more specialized works. Works available in "LP" & "45's" are indicated by asterisks.

UNESCO DISCOGRAPHIES
Note: An extensive series of detailed composer & subject discographies is now in preparation under the auspices of the Archives de la musique enregistrée UNESCO. The first of these is devoted to Chopin (see App Ia: Panigel, and for an English version in preparation: Chopin-2). Later works will be devoted to Bach, Mozart, Indian Music, Chinese Music, Museum Collections, etc.

WHITEMAN, PAUL
Records for the millions. Ed David A. Stein. Forew Deems Taylor. xiv, 331 p. Hermitage 1948.   **3.50**
The dance-band conductor's phonographic reminiscences, plus lists of his favorite "classical" & popular recordings.

PHONOPHOTOGRAPHY

See: Folklore (Metfessel), Negro Spirituals (Odum & Johnson), Interpretation (Seashore).

PHRASING

See: esp Interpretation.

Also:

Conducting	Piano Playing
Form	Singing
(esp Macpherson)	Violin Playing
Organ Playing	

PHYSICS (Physical Aspects of Music)

See: Acoustics, Sound Rec & Repro.

PIANISTS

See also:

Bauer	Joyce
Composers (& under	Lamond
names of individual	Matthay
composer-pianists)	Paderewski
Busoni	Phonograph Records
Carreño	Piano
Ellington	Piano Music
Foldes	Piano Playing
Gershwin	Popular Music
Godowsky	Rachmaninoff
History	Who's Who
Interpreters	Yearbooks
Jazz	

Note: Brower's "Modern masters of the keyboard" (1926) apparently is O/P.

BROOK, DONALD
Masters of the keyboard. 184 p, 35 pl, 1–p bibl. Rockliff 1946 (1950).   **3.50**
Biographical sketches of virtuosi of the past & prominent British pianists today.

BURCH, GLADYS & WOLCOTT, JOHN.   See App IIa.

COOKE, JAMES FRANCIS
Great pianists on piano playing: study talks with foremost virtuosos; a series of personal educational conferences . . . presenting the most modern ideas upon the subjects of technic, interpretation, style, & expression. 418 p, pors. Presser 1913 (1917).   **3.00**
Biographical sketches & interviews.

LAHEE, HENRY C.
Famous pianists of today and yesterday. vi, 345 p, 10 pors. Page 1901.   **2.00**
"Music Lovers" Series.

PIANO

Note: The available literature on various aspects of this instrument is divided here into the following categories (in addition to the Pianists entry above):

Piano
Piano Music
Piano Playing
   1. **General, Larger Aspects & Methods.**

2. **Short Methods, Specialized Studies.**
3. **Popular & Jazz Styles.**
4. **Self-Instruction Guides**

PIANO (General, History, Repairs, Tuning)

See also:

History	Keyboard Instruments
Instruments	& Music

Note: Standard works apparently O/P (or not easily available) include those by Bie, Blom, Brinstead, Fischer, Harding, Hipkins, Krehbiel, Nalder, Smith, Wier, etc.

CLOSSON, ERNEST
History of the piano. Tr Delano Ames. 168 p, photos, b&ws (Jacques Closson), 11-p bibl. Paul Elek, London, 1947.   (3.50)
Originally pub in French, 1944 (now O/P); includes a discussion of the clavichord, spinet, & harpsichord, as well as the piano.

HOWE, ALFRED H.
Scientific piano tuning and servicing. xvi, 267 p, 54 illus, mus ex, 2-p bibl. Author (1941) rev enl ed 1947.   6.00
An individual approach, emphasizing the use of musical notation in teaching tuning.

LOCARD, PAUL. See App Ia.

NORTON, EDWARD QUINCY
The construction, tuning, & care of piano-forte. 117 p, 3 illus, paper. Ditson 1915.   1.25
With an appendix listing all material used in piano construction.

PARRISH, CARL
The early piano and its influence on keyboard technique and compositions in the 18th century. Musurgia 1951, pending.   △
"Musurgia Studies in Musicology," Series A, v 6 (on subscription only).

SMITH, HERMANN
The art of tuning the piano: a new & comprehensive treatise, to enable the musician to tune his pianoforte upon the system founded on the theory of equal temperament. xvi, 90 p, diagrs. mus ex, flex. Reeves rev enl ed n d.   (2.00)
Old, but scholarly.

WHITE, WILLIAM BRAID
Piano tuning and allied arts. vii, 295 p, 34 illus, tables, 2-p bibl. Tuners Supply Co., Boston, (1917) 5th rev enl ed 1946 (1948).   3.00

Latest edition of a standard American work, which covers all aspects of tuning & repairing, plus a glossary, & notes on the Conn chromatic stroboscope & mean-tone temperament.

PIANO MUSIC

See also:

Appreciation	Keyboard Ints & Music (esp Bedbrook)
Chamber Music	
Children–5	Pianists (esp Cooke)
Composers (& under individual names)	Piano Playing
	Program Notes
Concerto	School Music–3
History	Teaching–2

Note: Standard works apparently O/P (or not easily available) include those by Cortot (in English), Fillmore, Holmes & Karn, Lockwood, Pannain (in Italian), Prosniz (in German), Schünemann (in German) Sieffert (in German), Westerby, etc.

APEL, WILLI
Masters of the keyboard: a brief survey of pianoforte music. 323 p, illus, facs, mus ex, music, 7-p bibl. Harvard 1947.   5.00
Historical sketches of keyboard instruments & their literature, with analyses of some 140 compositions (some 70 given here in their entirety) from the late Middle Ages to Impressionism & the New Music.

BROWER, HARRIETTE
What to play—what to teach: an annotated outline of the pianoforte material arranged in programme form from the first beginnings to the works of the great pianists. 281 p. Presser 1925.   2.00

CORTOT, ALFRED. See App Ia.
Note: V 1 of Cortot's "La musique française de piano" (listed in App Ia) apparently is O/P in the English edition (Oxford 1932). As yet, the other volumes in this series have not been translated into English.

FERGUSON, DONALD N.
Piano music of six great composers. xi, 370 p, mus ex. Prentice 1947.   5.00
Detailed analyses of some 47 compositions by Beethoven, Brahms, Chopin, Debussy, Schubert, & Schumann.

GEORGII, WALTER See App Ib.

HAMILTON, CLARENCE G.
Piano music: its composers & characteristics. 235 p, illus, mus ex, chap bibls. Ditson 1925.   2.00
"Music Students Library" series, with introductory "evolution of the piano," & recommended compositions for study.

HUTCHESON, ERNEST
The literature of the piano: a guide
for amateur & student.   viii, 374,
xxxv p, pors,   mus ex, 11–p bibl.
Knopf 1948 (1949).   6.00
*Extensive survey with analyses, background
material, graded lists, information on various
editions & publishers.*

PERRY, ADELAIDE TROWBRIDGE (*comp*)
Compendium of piano material: a
book of reference . . . 187 p, 18–p
classified bibl.   Trowbridge-Perry
Publications, Los Angeles, (1929) 3rd
rev aug ed 1948.   5.00
Lists of publications & publishers.

PERRY, EDWARD BAXTER
Descriptive analyses of piano works:
for the use of teachers, players, &
music clubs. 290 p. Presser 1902.   2.00
Stories of standard teaching pieces:
containing educational notes & legends pertaining to the best known &
most useful pianoforte compositions
in general use. 236 p. Presser 1910.   2.00
The "appreciative" approach.

ROSTAND, CLAUDE. See App Ia.

ROWLEY, ALEC
Four hands—one piano: a list of
works for duet players. 38 p, paper.
Oxford 1940.   .75
*A unique guide to original literature for piano
duet, with some annotations.*

WESTERBY, HERBERT
How to study the pianoforte works
of the great composers.   ix, 302 p, 8
pors, 1 fac, mus ex, chap bibls. △
Reeves n d (1913).   (3.00)
Bach, Clementi, Handel, Haydn, Mozart, etc.

WILKINSON, CHARLES W.
Well-known piano solos and how to
play them.   294 p. Presser (1915)
rev ed (E. E. Hipsher) 1924.   2.00
"Appreciative" analyses of some 155 works.

PIANO PLAYING

*General Note: The published literature in
this main category is enormous—almost un-
believably so, except perhaps to well-informed
piano teachers. However, a large proportion
of it is either out-of-print or excluded from the
present lists as not generally available, of
ephemeral or localized interest, etc. Also excluded, of course, are "methods" or "schools"
that consist principally of exercises with little
or no accompanying text. What remains,
even after such pruning, is still large enough*

*to demand some kind of sub-division—a task
that might best be done by some rigorous scheme
of detailed classifications, but that we have
attempted here only roughly, and primarily
for convenience, in the following four sub-
categories:*

1. **General, Larger Aspects & Methods**
2. **Short Methods, Specialized
Studies**
3. **Popular & Jazz Styles**
4. **Self-Instruction Guides**

See also: esp Children–5 (Piano Playing) &
Teaching–3 (Piano Teaching).

Also:

Accompaniment	Lamond
Amateur Music	Liszt
Bauer	Matthay
Busoni	Memory
Carreño	Metronome
Chamber Music	Paderewski
Chopin	Pianists
Expression	Piano
Godowsky	Piano Music
Improvisation	Psychology
Interpretation	Rachmaninoff
Interpreters	School Music–1 & 3
Jazz	Sight-Playing & Read-
Keyboard Harmony	ing
Keyboard Instruments	Stage-Fright
(esp C. P. E. Bach)	

PIANO PLAYING
(1. General, Larger Aspects & Meth-
ods)

*Note: Standard works apparently O/P (or
not easily available) include those by Breithaupt (in English & German), Brower, Chase,
Christiani, Germer, Kullak, Levinskaya,
Ortmann, Sternberg, etc.*

BRÉE, MALWINE
The groundwork of the Leschetizky
method: issued with his approval . . .
with 47 illustrative cuts of Leschetizky's hand.   Tr Theodore Baker.
v, 100 p + 21 p additional exercises,
illus, mus ex, paper.   G. Schirmer
1902.   3.50
By an assistant of the pianist-teacher.

CHING, JAMES
Piano playing—a practical method:
a rationale of the psychological &
practical problems of pianoforte playing & teaching in the form of 25
lectures . . . xv, 356 p, illus, mus ex.
Bosworth (1946) 3rd ed 1947.   4.00
*Freudian approach to pianistic problems,
originally presented as lectures, 1944/5, and
supplementing an earlier, purely theoretical
book, "Piano technique: foundation prin-*

ciples" *(1934, now apparently O/P, or not easily available in this country).*

COHEN, HARRIET
Music's handmaid. 173 p, mus ex. Faber (1936) rev ed 1950.   3.00
Enlarged edition of a study dealing with the composer, the performer, & the pianist's approach to the music of Bach, Mozart, Chopin, Brahms, Falla, Vaughan Williams, Bartók, & Bax.

CORTOT, ALFRED
The rational principles of piano technique. Tr R. LeRoy-Métaxas. 102 p, mus ex, paper. Salabert 1930.   4.50
A standard work, also available with the original French text.

COVIELLO, AMBROSE
Foundations of pianoforte technique: co-ordination exercises. 99 p, mus ex. Oxford 1934.   1.25

FIELDEN, THOMAS
(See also Piano Playing–2.)
The science of pianoforte technique. xii, 194 p, 16 illus, mus ex, 1–p bibl. Macmillan (1927) 2nd ed 1934 (1949).   2.50

FOLDES, ANDOR
Keys to the keyboard: a book for pianists. 117 p, mus ex. Dutton 1948.   2.00
Introducing young people to the piano & discussing specific pianistic problems, plus a list of contemporary music for study.

GARROWAY, WILL
Pianism. Forew Merle Armitage. iii, 206 p, illus, mus ex. C. Fischer 1939.   3.00
A résumé of the pyschological & physical exigencies encountered in the various phases of piano playing, with emphasis on strengthening memory & overcoming fears.

HAMBOURG, MARK
How to play the piano: with practical illustrations & diagrams, & an abridged compendium of 5–finger exercises, scales, thirds, arpeggi, octaves, as practised by him. viii, 122 p, illus, mus ex. Presser 1922.   1.50

HAMILTON, CLARENCE G.
(See also Piano Playing–2.)
What every piano pupil should know: a manual for piano students. 160 p, illus, mus ex. Presser 1928.   2.00
A textbook with study-questions.

HISSARLIAN-LAGOUETTE, P. See App Ia.

HOFMANN, JOSEF
Piano playing and piano questions answered. 2 v in 1: xiii, 89 p; xviii, 183 p, 12 photos, mus ex. Presser 1920.   2.00
"A little book of simple suggestions" combined with the answers to some 200 pianistic questions, originally published in "The Ladies Home Journal."

JOHNSTONE, J. ALFRED
Essentials in piano playing: and other musical studies. viii, 243 p, △ frontis por. Reeves n d (1913).   (2.50)

MATTHAY, TOBIAS
(See also Piano Playing–2.)
The visible and invisible in piano technique: being a digest of the author's technical teaching up to date (together with epitome). xiii, 176 + 59 p, photos, mus ex. Oxford (1932) cor 2nd pr 1947.   3.00
The 59–p "epitome" apparently is O/P as a separate publication.

MOSER, HANS ALBRECHT. See App Ib.

NEWMAN, WILLIAM S.
The pianist's problems: a modern approach to efficient practice & musicianly performance. Pref Arthur Loesser. xiv, 134 p, illus (John V. Allcott), mus ex, 2–p annot bibl. Harper 1950.   2.50
Practical, informal, generalized discussions of fundamental problems in musicianship, technique, practice, & performance.

PIRON, CONSTANTIN. See App Ia.

SCHAUFFLER, LAWRENCE
Piano technic: myth or science. 123 p, illus, mus ex, 3–p bibl. Gamble 1937.   1.75
Individual, rational approach to physical laws governing pianists' performances.

SCHMITZ, E. ROBERT
The capture of inspiration. Ed José Rodriguez. Forew Merle Armitage. iv, 134 p, frontis, diagrs, mus ex, 1–p bibl. C. Fischer 1935 (1944).   4.00
The fundamentals of the highly individual, "scientifically-based" Schmiz system.

SCHULTZ, ARNOLD
The riddle of the pianist's finger: and its relationship to a touch-scheme. xii, 317 p, 9 diagrs, 1 table, mus ex, bibl refs (1936) C. Fischer repr 1949.   5.00
A method of touch-mechanics based on new theories opposed to those of standard "relax-

ation" systems, with detailed critical analyses of the teachings of Leschetizky, Matthay, Breithaupt, & Ortmann. Originally published by the University of Chicago Press (1936).

VENABLE, MARY
The interpretation of piano music. vii, 252 p, mus ex. Ditson 1913.   2.00
"Music Students Library" series. Not a method, but studies in the meaning & interpretation of the notation of piano music.

PIANO PLAYING
(2. Short Methods, Specialized Studies)

Note: Standard works apparently O/P (or not easily available) include those by Carreño, Dunn, Ehrenfechter, Eisenberg, Farjeon, Johnstone, Lindo, Mason, Matthay, Pauer, Riemann, Rubinstein, Simpson, Ward-Jackson, Woodhouse, etc.

AMEY, ELLEN
Conscious control in piano study. ix, 99 p, illus, mus ex. Flammer 1921. **1.75**

BOWEN, YORK
Pedalling the modern pianoforte. 28 p, mus ex, paper. Oxford 1936.   **2.25**
A standard work on its specialized subject.

BURROWES, J. F.
Pianoforte primer: containing the rudiments of music & a method of study. Rev & ed S. Austen Pearce. 77 p, mus ex, paper. G. Schirmer 1909.   .50
Modern ed of a popular 19–century primer.
Same, rev & ed Frederic Field Bullard, & including a pronouncing dictionary. 86 p, paper. Ditson 1905.   .75
"Music Students Library" series.

CAMPBELL, LEROY B.
Velocity plus: an intensive study of the problems of musical velocity in piano playing & teaching. 60 p, mus ex, paper. Creative 1940.   2.00

FAELTON, REINHOLD (comp)
A catechism of the Faelton system. 24 p, illus, mus ex, paper. Schmidt 1908.   .60

FIELDEN, THOMAS
(See also Piano Playing-1.)
A new approach to scales and arpeggios: combining them with technical exercises together with some notes on fingering. 20 p, mus ex, paper. Williams 1949.   Δ (.50)

FOOTE, ARTHUR
Some practical things in piano playing. 34 p, paper. Schmidt 1909   .60

FRISKIN, JAMES
The principles of pianoforte practice. 36 p, paper. Gray 1921.   1.00
Essays from the "Music Review."

GRUNDY, ENID
The happy pianist. viii, 80 p, mus ex, 4–p annot bibl, paper. Oxford 1927 (3rd pr 1947).   .75

HAMILTON, CLARENCE G.
(See also Piano Playing-1.)
Touch and expression in piano playing. 72 p, photos, mus ex, paper. Ditson 1927.   .75
"Pocket Music Student" series.

JOHNS, CLAYTON
The essentials of pianoforte playing: a practical system of mind & finger training. ix, 86 p, photos, mus ex, paper. Ditson 1909 (1927)   1.00

KLAUWELL, OTTO
On musical execution: an attempt at a systematic exposition of the same, primarily with reference to piano playing. Tr Theodore Baker. vii, 135 p, mus ex, flex. G. Schirmer 1890.   .75

KNOTT, THOMAS B.
Pianoforte fingering: its principles & applications. 23 p, mus ex, paper. Oxford 1928.   .75

LEIMER, KARL & GIESEKING, WALTER
Rhythmics, dynamics, pedal: and other problems of piano playing. Tr Frederick C. Rauser. 64 p, mus ex, paper. Presser 1938 (1949).   1.50
Detailed technical advice; originally published by Schott's Söhne, in German, 1938.
The shortest way to pianistic perfection. Intro James Francis Cooke. 75 p, pors, mus ex, paper. Presser 1932.   1.50
Foundations of the Gieseking method; originally published in German, 1930.

LHÉVINNE, JOSEF
Basic principles in pianoforte playing. 48 p, illus, mus ex, paper. Presser 1942.   .60

MACKINNON, LILAS
Musical secrets. 95 p. Oxford 1936 (4th pr 1946).   2.00
Pocket-size collection of essays on the various "secrets" of technique: concentration, sign-reading, phrasing, practising, etc.

MACKLIN, CHARLES B.
The pianist's daily dozen: a set of finger gymnastics to be done away from the piano. 31 p, illus, paper. Presser 1927.   .75

MATTHAY, TOBIAS
(*See also Piano Playing-1.*)
The fore-arm rotation principle in pianoforte playing: its application & mastery. 12 p, illus, mus ex, paper. Boston 1912.   .75

Relaxation studies in the muscular discrimination required for touch, agility, & expression in pianoforte playing. xii, 142 p, illus, mus ex, paper. Bosworth 1908.   5.00
Cover title: "Muscular relaxation studies for students, artists, & teachers."

McMILLAN, FIONA
The fingering of scales and arpeggi. 8 p, mus ex, paper. Oxford 1934.   .25

MININBERG, IAN
A visual approach to piano technique. 33 p, illus, paper. G. Schirmer (1935) 1937.   1.00
A concise survey of technical explanations, including those of Matthay, Deppe, Townsend, Breithaupt, Leschetizky, etc.

REEDER, BETAH
The singing touch. 64 p, illus, paper. Galaxy 1943.   1.25
Characteristics of piano tone-qualities & the various types of "touch."

ROEDER, CARL M.
Liberation and deliberation in piano technique: how to develop ease & mastery through understanding correct processes & drill. 50 p, photos, mus ex, paper. Schroeder 1941.   1.50

SMITH, MACDONALD
From brain to keyboard: a system of hand & finger control for pianists & students. vi, 63 p, photos, mus ex, paper. Ditson 1917.   .60

UNSCHULD, MARIE VON
The pianist's hand. xii, 103 p, photos, facs, mus ex, paper. C. Fischer 1909.   1.25
Based on Leschetizky teaching methods; originally published in German, 1901.

VOGT, HANS. See App Ib.

WELLS, HOWARD
Ear, brain, and fingers: a text book for piano teachers & pupils. 97 p, illus, mus ex. Ditson 1914.   1.25
"Music Student Library" series; based on Leschetizky ideas & exercises.

The pianist's thumb: a text book for teachers & pupils. 73 p, mus ex. Ditson 1926.   1.25
"Music Students Library" series.

WHITESIDE, ABBY
The pianist's mechanism: a guide to the production & transmission of power in playing. viii, 57 p, illus (Martha Eaton), bds. G. Schirmer 1929.   1.50
Clues to simplicity in motor patterns, especially for women pianists.

PIANO PLAYING
(3. Popular & Jazz Styles)
Note: Only a sampling of the large available literature (most of which has little or no text) is included here.

See also:

Carmichael	Jazz
Dance Bands	Morton
Ellington	Piano Playing-4
Improvisation	Popular Music

GIBBS, GEORGE A., Jr
Harmonizing melodies at sight. 24 p, mus ex, paper. Clef 1941 (1934).   1.00
Mostly chord diagrams, including those for guitar, ukulele, & tenor banjo.

Modern chord construction and analysis for all instruments: an aid to the art of improvising. 36 p, mus ex, paper. Mills 1937.   1.25
Emphasizing the quick use & variation of chords essential in "swing" or "hot" playing.

HILL, JIM
The art of improvising: how to play popular songs in a modern swing style. Book 1. 64 p, illus, mus ex, paper. Cole 1937 (1943?).   1.00

KAHN, MARVIN
Chord construction and hints for popular piano playing. 44 p, mus ex, paper. Mills 1943.   1.00

Modern styles and harmonic constructions for popular piano playing. 43 p, mus ex, paper. Mills 1947.   1.00

SPENCER, BERNARD
Popular piano playing: an elementary course in popular music. vi, 48 p, illus, music paper. Ditson 1947.   1.00

PIANO PLAYING
(4. Self-Instruction Guides)
See also:

Amateur Music	Sight-Playing & Reading
Children-5	
Piano Playing-1, 2, 3	

BAILEY, DOROTHY SEYL
Popular piano playing simplified: pocket edition of simplified chords arranged alphabetically & a quick method for playing designed to help you help yourself. 32 p, illus, mus ex, paper, spir. Garden City 1950.   .50
Vest-pocket size: chord tables & pointers in sight-reading, playing by ear, etc.

COOKE, CHARLES
Playing the piano for pleasure. xv, 247 p, mus ex, 3–p bibl. S & S 1941 (6th pr n d).   3.00
An infectiously enthusiastic amateur discusses piano playing as a hobby & the means by which amateur playing can be improved.

FRAY, JACQUES & SAPERTON, DAVID
How to play the piano by the Jacques Fray speed method. vi, 121 p, chart, illus, diagrs, music, paper. Doubleday 1949.   2.95
With 40 arrangements of well-known songs & a 2½-foot cardboard note chart.

McCLINTOCK, LORENE
Everyone can play the piano: McClintock method: an interval approach to sight reading. viii, 117 p, diagrs, mus ex, music, chart, paper. Crowell (1947) repr n d.   2.95
Originally titled "Teach yourself to play the piano." Includes a cut-out cardboard "keyboard concealer" & 23 easy pieces.

LE ROY, P. J.
Learn to play the piano by ear: the quick, easy, simple way. 72 p, illus, chart, paper. (1941?) Blue Ribbon repr 1944.   1.00
Includes a fold-out keyboard chart.

RICHTER, ADA
You can play the piano: a book for the older beginner. 3 v: each 48 p, illus (Dorothea J. Byerly), music, paper. Presser 1947/8.   2.25

Piazza, H. Printer. See Beethoven-3.

PICTURES/PORTRAITS

General Note: Nearly all biographies, or collective studies, of musicians and most books on specialized subjects include reproductions of portraits or other pertinent pictures. Special mention for the number & range of illustrations included might well go to Scholes's "Oxford Companion to Music" (see Dictionaries of Music).

See also:

Bach-1 (Geiringer)	Instruments
Ballet (esp Amberg)	Orchestra (esp
Boston—music in	McKinney)
(Humphrey)	"Symphonia" series
Children-4 (esp Hunt-	Who's Who
ington, Lacey)	"World of Music"
Facsimiles (esp Har-	series
row Replica No. 6)	App II (juveniles)

Note: Kinsky's "History of Music in pictures" (1930) apparently is O/P.

BORY, ROBERT (ed). See App Ia.

COOKE, JAMES FRANCIS. See App IIb.

HAWARD, LAWRENCE (ed)
Music in painting. 24 p, 10 col pl, paper. Pitman 1948.   1.95
Color reproductions, with notes, of noted paintings dealing with musical subjects.

McCOY, GUY (comp)
Portraits of the world's best-known musicians: an alphabetical collection of notable musical personalities of the world, covering the entire history of music. 251 p, illus. Presser 1946.   3.50
Nearly 5000 thumbnail reproductions, originally published serially in "The Etude."

RAUPACH, HANS (ed). See App Ib.

SCHNEIDER, MAX F. (ed). See App Ib.

Pierce, Anne Elsie. Author (with Liebling). See School Music-4.   Co-author (with Barrows). See Voice.
Pierce, George Washington. Author. See Insects.
Pierik, Marie. Author. See Gregorian Chant, Mass.
Piersig, Johannes. Author. See App Ib.
Piguet, J.-Claude. Author. See App Ia.
Pike, Kenneth Lee. Author. See Speech.

PILGRIMS (Music of the)

See also:

America (music in)	Hymns/Hymnody
Church Music	Psalms/Psalmody
History	Puritans

PRATT, WALDO SELDEN
The music of the pilgrims: a description of the psalm-book brought to Plymouth in 1620. 80 p, 2 facs, music, paper. Ditson 1921.   1.25
A study, with melodies & first verses, of Ainsworth's psalter (Amsterdam, 1612).

Pincherle, Marc. Author. See App Ia.
Pine, Leslie G. Editor. See Who's Who.
Piper, John. Author. See Britten (Britten & others)

PIPES (Shepherd's)
See:

Bagpipes
Children–4 (esp Zan-
  zig) & 6

Community Music
  (Bergmann)
Instruments
Recorder

Piron, Constantin. Author. See App Ia.
Pirro, André. Author. See App Ia.

PISTON, Walter
See:

American Music
Composers–2 & 3a
Contemporary Music

Koussevitzky
Phonograph Records
Program Notes

Author. See Counterpoint–1, Harmony–2.

PITCH
See:

Acoustics
History
Instruments
Monophony

Psychology
Scale
Speech (esp Pike)
Tests

Note: Standard works apparently O/P (or not easily available) include those by Bailey, Ellis, Weddell, etc.

Pitrou, Robert. Author. See App Ia.
Pitts, Carol Marhoff. Author.
  See Singing–2.
Pitts, Lilla Belle. Author.
  See School Music–1 & 2.

PIZZETTI, Ildebrando
See also:

Composers–2
Contemporary Music

Italian Music
Program Notes

Note: Studies in Italian apparently O/P (or not easily available in this country) include those by Fondi (1919) & Gavazzeni (1937).
Author. See App Ic ("Musica italiana dell' ottocento").

Gatti, Guido M.
Ildebrando Pizzetti. 124 p + 8 pl
(pors, fac, etc), mus ex, 1-p bibl.
Dobson 1951.   (3.00)

PLAINSONG (Plain Chant)
General Note: While the term Plainsong properly embraces other liturgical chants besides those of the Roman Catholic Church (Gregorian Chant), the distinction between the two terms often is ignored in common usage and in book titles. The actual titling, however, is followed in the present listings, although some of the books entered below deal almost exclusively with Gregorian Chant.
And again it might be noted, too, that purists object to any of these books listed below (or under Gregorian Chant) that deal with plain-song accompaniments, for they insist that

authentic performances of the chants are always, without exception, sung unaccompanied.
See also: esp Gregorian Chant

Accompaniment
Ancient Music
Anthologies
Appreciation
Byzantine Music
Children–7 (Field)
Choir/Choral–3
Counterpoint–1 (esp
  Merritt, Soderlund)

History
Hymns/Hymnody
Mass
Medieval/Renaissance
Mode
Organ Playing
Phonograph Records

Note: Standard works apparently O/P (or not easily available) include those by Arnold, Briggs, Burgess, Oldroyd & Pearce, etc.

Arnold, J. H.
Plainsong accompaniment.   Pref
Geoffrey Shaw.   xv, 175 p, mus ex,
bibl refs.   Oxford 1927.   4.50
Includes a tone-table with suggested harmonies for accompaniment in the psalm-tones common to the "Manual of plainsong" & the "Sarum psalter."

(A Benedictine of Stanbrook)
A grammar of plainsong. 106 p +
chart, mus ex, paper.   Rushworth
(1905) 3rd ed 1934.   1.50

Burgess, Francis
The rudiments of plainchant. 41 p,
mus ex, bibl, paper.   Musical Opinion
1923 (3rd pr 1938).   .75
"Handbooks of Church Music" series.

Clokey, Joseph W.
Plainsong: interpretation, notation,
with examples in modern notation.
12 p, music, paper. Birchard 1934.   .35
Mostly music, except 1–p foreword.

Evans, Edwin (Sr)
The modal accompaniment of plain
chant: a practical treatise. 145 p, △
mus ex.   Reeves 1911.   (2.25)
Part 1, theoretical; part 2, practical school, 240 exercises with notes.

Gajard, (Dom) Joseph
The rhythm of plainsong: according
to the Solesmes school.   Tr Dom
Aldhelm Dean. 67 p, mus ex, paper.
J. Fischer 1945.   1.00
Fundamental Gregorian principles.

Robertson, Alec
The interpretation of plainchant: a
preliminary study.   xi, 116 p, mus
ex, 4–p annot bibl.   Oxford 1937
(1949).   1.75
Especially for Catholic choirmasters.

(Society of St John the Evangelist)
Plainsong for schools: masses &

occasional chants. 2 v: xiii, 90 p; x, 96
p, music, paper.　Rushworth 1934
(1946/7).　Complete:　　　　　　.60

SPRINGER, MAX
The art of accompanying plain chant.
Tr Benedictine Fathers, Conception,
Missouri.　xiii, 238 p, mus ex, bds.
J. Fischer 1908.　　　　　　　3.00

Planta, P. V.　Author.　See Harmonica.

PLAYER-PIANO

See: Piano.

*Note: Apparently the literature on this sub-
ject went obsolete even more quickly than the
once-popular (and still unfairly maligned)
instrument itself. O/P works include those by
Grew, Kobbé, Newman, White, etc.*

**Playground & Recreation Association of
America** (Book prepared by).　See Com-
munity Music.　See also note under
National Association.

Pleasants, Henry, 3rd.　Editor, translator.
See Hanslick.

Pochon, Alfred.　Author.　See App Ia.

Podolsky, Alfred.　Author.　See Health.

POE, Edgar Allan

See also: Poetry.

EVANS, MAY GARRETTSON
Music and Edgar Allan Poe: a bibliographical study.　97 p, frontis fac,
1-p bibl.　Johns Hopkins 1939.　　1.75
*A detailed study of Poe's influence on music,
plus lists of some 252 compositions—by
some 134 composers—based on his works.*

POETRY (& Music)

See also:

Aesthetics	Poe
Appreciation	Program Notes
Aristotle	Restoration Era
Ballad	Shakespeare
Campion	Song(s)
Dryden	Song Translations
Duparc	Songwriting (esp
Elizabethan Music	Wood)
Folklore	Troubadours/
Lanier	Trouvères
Literature	d'Urfey
Madrigal (esp	
Fellowes)	

Also: Composers, and under the names of
individual song composers.

*Note: Standard works apparently O/P (or not
easily available) include those by Campbell-
Innes, Colles, Hadow, Koussevitzky, Lanier,
Naylor, Raymond, etc.*

BOAS, FREDERICK S. (*ed*)
Songs and lyrics from the English
masques and light operas.　176 p, 2
facs.　Harrap 1949.　　　　　2.25
*An anthology (poetry only) of Jacobean,
Gregorian, Victorian, etc, lyrics, including
those from the light operas of Gay & W. S.
Gilbert.*

CLINTON-BADDELEY, V. C.
Words for music.　xi, 168 p.　Cam-
bridge 1941.　　　　　　　　2.25
*Word/Music problems discussed largely from
the poet's point of view, with a chapter on
W. B. Yeats & the art of song.*

NITZE, WILLIAM A.
Arthurian romance and modern
poetry and music.　xi, 101 p, illus.
Chicago 1940.　　　　　　　1.00

PATTISON, BRUCE
Music and poetry of the English
renaissance.　ix, 220 p, mus ex, 9-p
bibl.　Methuen 1948.　　　　O/P
*Points of contact and the reciprocal influences
of the English lyric & music. O/P 1950.*

RILEY, ALICE C. D.
Elements of English verse correlated
to music: a manual for teachers.　viii,
144 p, mus ex.　(Weekes 1906) via
Summy.　　　　　　　　　1.80
*Clarifying the various elements of music &
verse so that teachers may be able to present
their basic unity to children in the 1st to 8th
grades.*

STAIGER, EMIL.　See App Ib.

Pohl, Karl Ferdinand.　Co-compiler (with
Eitner & others).　See App Ib (Eitner).

Polack, William Gustave.　Compiler.
See Hymns/Hymnody-1.

POLAND (Music in)/POLISH MUSIC

See also:

Appreciation	Folklore
Chopin-1 & 2	History
Composers-1 & 2	Paderewski
Dances-2	Program Notes

*Note: Standard works apparently O/P (or not
easily available) include those by Opienski
(in French), Simon, Sulikowsky, Wieniawski
(in French), etc.*

GRONOWICZ, ANTONI.　See App IIb
("Bolek").

JARECKA, LOUISE
Made in Poland: living traditions of
the land.　xii, 289, vii p, illus (M. S.

Nowicki), 3-p bibl, mus ex. Knopf
1949.   3.50

*Cultural history, primarily for young people,
but not "written-down," & including chapters
on folksongs, folk dances, musical instruments, & Chopin.*

MIZWA, STEPHEN PAUL (*ed*)
Great men and women of Poland.
xxviii, 397 p, illus. Macmillan 1941. 5.00
With chapters on Chopin & Paderewski.

RAYSON, ETHEL
Polish music and Chopin, its laure-
ate: a historical account from 995
to the present time. vii, 64 p, 4 pors. △
Reeves n d (1916).   (1.50)

Poleman, Horace I. Compiler (with Waterman & others). See Asiatic Musics (note
only).

POLYPHONY
See: esp Counterpoint
Also:

Anthologies (esp Gleason, Davidson & Apel)	Church Music
Baroque Era	Form
Choir/Choral	Fugue
Composers (& under individual names, esp Bach, Palestrina)	History
	Madrigal
	Medieval/Renaissance
	Monophony
	Organ Music

POLYTONALITY
See: Tonality/Atonality.

PONCHIELLI, Amilcare
See:

Appreciation	Opera
Composers–1	Phonograph Records
History	Themes
Italian Music	Vocal Music

*Note: Standard works apparently O/P (or
not easily available) include those in Italian
by Cesari, de Napoli, Mandelli, etc.*

Pope, Isabel. Author.
See Spain (music in).
Poppen, Hermann Meinhard. Author.
See App Ib.

POPULAR MUSIC
*General Note: The term "popular" is used
here in its common, contemporary sense—
i.e., to cover both jazz (in various degrees of
heat) and all types of musical comedy, "light"
music, & ersatz ballads.*

*Note: Standard works apparently O/P (or not
easily available) include those by Gilbert,
Goldberg, Spaeth, etc.*

See also:

Amateur Music	Instrumentation
America (music in)	Jazz
American Music	Latin America
Armstrong	Melody Writing
Arranging–2	Mezzrow
Ballad	Minstrel/Ministrelsy
Barbershop	Morton
Berlin	Opera–3 (esp McSpadden)
Broekman	Operetta
Carmichael	Phonograph Records
Chevalier	Piano Playing–3
Community Music	Radio Music
Composers–2 & 3a	Rodgers & Hart
Composition	Romberg
Condon	Sheet Music
Crosby	Sinatra
Cugat	Singing–3
Dance Band	Song(s) (Mattfeld & Davis)
Ellington	Songbooks
Film Music	Songwriting
Folklore	Troubadours/
Folksongs	Trouvères
Foster	Waters
Gershwin	Who's Who
Hammerstein	Willson
Handy	Yearbooks
History	
Spike Hughes	

BURTON, JACK (*comp*)
The blue book of tin pan alley:
a human interest anthology of
American popular music. 520 p,
illus (pors, facs, etc). Century
House, Watkins Glen, N. Y., 1950. 7.50
*Brief biographies of popular songwriters &
lyricists from 1776 to the present, with lists
of titles & recordings.*

EWEN, DAVID
Men of popular music. 213 p, illus
(pors), 1–p bibl. Ziff-Davis (1944)
2nd rev ed 1949, via Prentice 1950. 3.00
*Studies of Armstrong, Berlin, Ellington,
Gershwin, Goodman, Grofé, Handy, Kern,
Porter, Rodgers, Whiteman, & others.*

FREEMAN, LARRY
The melodies linger on: 50 years of
popular songs. 212 p, illus (some col).
Century House, Watkins Glen, N. Y.,
1950.   5.00
*Mementos of popular songs, with reproduced
covers & advertisements, and a discussion of
trends in popular taste.*

SPAETH, SIGMUND
A history of popular music in
America. xv, 729 p, 5–p bibl. Random 1948.   5.00
*An extensive survey (but almost exclusively
of popular songs) from colonial times to the
present; with biographical sketches of the
more important composers & lists of works.*

Porte, John Fielden. Author.
See Chopin–2.
*Note: Several other works by Porte, on Elgar,
MacDowell, Stanford, etc, apparently are
O/P (or not easily available).*

Porter, Quincy. Author.
See Counterpoint–2

PORTRAITS
See: Pictures/Portraits.

PORTUGAL (Music in)/PORTUGUESE MUSIC
See: esp Dances–2 (ed Alford: Armstrong).
Also:

Folklore	Medieval/Renaissance
History	Spain–music in

Posell, Elsa Z. Author. See App IIb.
Posner, Sandy. Author. See Ballet.
Also individual Posner books in the "Ballet Pocket Library" series under Adam, Delibes, Stravinsky–2, Tchaikovsky–2.
Potamkin, Frank J. Author.
See Teaching–3.
Pothier, (Dom) Joseph. Author.
See App Ia.
Potiron, Henri. Author.
See Gregorian Chant
Potter, Louis, Jr. Author.
See Violoncello Playing.
Potter, Ralph K. Author (with Kopp & Green). See Speech.
Pougin, Arthur. Author. See App Ia.
Pourtalès, Guy de. Author. See App Ia.
Powell, (Mrs) Richard. Author.
See Elgar.

PRACTICE/PRACTICING
See:

Amateur Music	Singing
Organ Playing	Violin Playing
Piano Playing	Teaching

PRAETORIUS, Michael
See:

Baroque Era	Madrigal
Choir/Choral–3	Medieval/Renaissance
Church Music	Organ
Composers–1	Organ Music
History	Phonograph Records

Note: Standard works apparently O¹P (or not easily available) include those in German by Blume and Gurlitt, as well as the 1929 facsimile edition of Praetorius's own great work, "Syntagma Musicum" (3 v, 1615/20). However, v 2 ("De Organographia"), parts 1 & 2, of the latter has been privately published in an English translation by Harold Blumenfeld, 6643 Kingsbury Blvd.; St. Louis, Missouri (vi, 80 p, illus; 1949; $2.50).

Pratt, Waldo Selden. Author. See:
Church music. Musical ministries in the church (1902/23).   1.50
Dictionaries of Music. Grove's sup, ed Pratt & Boyd (1928/40).   7.50

Encyclopedias. New (1924/29).   6.00
History–2. (1907/35).   6.00
——. Class notes in (1908/38).   .30
Pilgrims. Music of (1921).   1.25
Note: Pratt's "American music & musicians" & "Music of the French psalter" (1939) apparently are O/P.

Prescott, Gerald R. Author (with Chidester). See School Music–3.
Preussner, Eberhard. Author. See App Ib.
Price, Carl F. Author.
See Hymns/Hymnody–2.
Price, (Frank) Percival. Author.
See Carillon.

PRIMERS OF MUSIC
See: Children–8, Theory–2 & 3.
Note: This term generally is used for books on the elementary "theory" of music, but often appears also, of course, in the titles of elementary methods or elementary books on various specialized subjects.

PRIMITIVE MUSIC
See: esp Ancient Music.
Also:

Arabia (music in)	Indians (American)
Asiatic Musics	Instruments
(note only)	Java (music in)
Folklore	Oriental Music
History	(note only)

PRINTERS/PRINTING (of Music)
See: esp Publishers/Publishing.
Also:

America (music in)	History
Beethoven–3 (Piazza)	Philadelphia
Bibliography	(music in)
Boston (music in)	Popular Music
Composers–3a (esp	Sheet Music
McNamara)	Who's Who
England (music in)	Yearbooks

Prod'homme, Jacques-Gabriel. Author.
See App Ia.

PROFESSION (of Music)
See: esp Career.
Also:

Colleges	School Music
Education	Teaching
Radio	Yearbooks

PROGRAM MUSIC
See also: esp Program Notes.

Appreciation	Literature (esp
Children–2	Brown)
Composers (& under	Poetry
individual names)	Romantic Era
History	School Music–1

Note: Standard works apparently O/P (or not easily available) include those by Niecks, Spaeth, etc.

ELKIN, ROBERT
The stories behind music: a handbook of orchestral programme music.
Forew Sir Adrian Boult. 152 p, 20
illus (Beryl Thornborough). Rider
1949.   (2.25)

*Notes on some 128 program-music works by
some 38 composers, Balakirev to Weber.*

HILL, RALPH
Programme Music.
Chanticleer, in prep.   △
"World of Music" series No 13.

HORTON, JOHN
Legends in music. vi, 66 p, 14 illus
(W. Payne), mus ex, bibl refs. Nelson
1948 (1949).   1.00

*Notes on some 14 popular orchestral works
(mostly overtures or suites) based on pictorial
or story programs. Apparently directed
toward juvenile readers, but far more adult
in approach than most "juveniles."*

PROGRAM NOTES

*General Note: Oddly enough, this is not a sub-
ject-heading customarily encountered in musical bibliographies, but if its justification here
is not self-evident, we might point out two good
reasons for its use. First, it is precise: program notes describe exactly the material included in the books listed below; most of it was
written originally for publication in actual
concert "program books" or to accompany
phonograph-record albums, and the rest is
written in much the same vein. Second, the
use of this category is convenient, especially
in that it shortens to some extent the excessive
length of the listings under the subject-heading
Appreciation, where collections of program
notes usually are located—properly enough
in some cases, but certainly not in all.*

*"Analysis" & "Annotations" are other pos-
sible subject-headings for the present listings,
but we have avoided the former for its looseness
(program notes usually include biographical
& descriptive material as well as true musical
analyses), and the latter was discarded more
or less arbitrarily.*

*It should be noted in addition that the books
listed below deal with musical compositions in
several mediums or for orchestra alone. For
collections of similar program notes dealing
exclusively with chamber music, concertos,
operas, piano music, symphonies, etc, see
under those subject-headings; for notes on and
analyses of the works of individual composers,
see under the composers' names.*

Note: Standard works apparently O/P (or not

*easily available) include those by E. Downes,
O. Downes, Gilman, Goepp, Hale, Upton, etc.*

See also:

Appreciation   Organ Music
Chamber Music   Phonograph Records
Children-2   Piano Music
Composers (& under   School Music-2
  individual names)   Song(s)
Concerto   Symphony
Opera-3 & 4   Violin Music

Also: App IIa (juveniles)

BAGAR, ROBERT & BIANCOLLI, LOUIS
The concert companion: a compre-
hensive guide to symphonic music.
Intro Deems Taylor. xi, 868 p.
Whittlesey 1947.   4.95

*Notes on some 475 compositions by some 163
composers, written originally for the N. Y.
Philharmonic-Symphony program books and
relying heavily on quotations from various
authorities.*

BALDWIN, LILLIAN
A listener's anthology of music. 2 v.
Silver 1948.

V 1: The master builders of music.
xiii, 400 p, mus ex.   4.80
V 2: The musician as poet, painter,
& dramatist. xvii, 528 p, mus ex.   5.80
*Not an anthology, but "appreciative" notes
on standard works classified by period or by
national schools.*

CHANTAVOINE, JEAN. See App Ia.

DOWNES, EDWARD
Adventures in symphonic music. xii,
323 p, illus (John O'Hara Cosgrave
II). Farrar 1944 (4th pr n d).   2.75
*Originally broadcast "appreciative" notes on
some 200 works by some 58 composers.*

EWEN, DAVID
Music for the millions: the encyclopedia of musical master-pieces. viii,
692 p, 14 pors, 7-p bibl. Arco 1944
(5th pr, enl, 1946), Grosset repr 1950. 2.98
*Notes on works in various mediums by some
259 composers from Albéniz to Wolf, with
biographical sketches & record lists.*
Same, Mentor repr, 288 p, paper
1950.   .35
*Pocket-size abridged edition, covering some
40 composers only (Bach to Wolf), with brief
record lists.*

GRABBE, PAUL
The story of 100 symphonic favorites.
xx, 300 p, 3-p bibl. Grosset 1940.   .75
Pocket-size, in "Little Library" series.

MASON, DANIEL GREGORY
Short studies in great master-pieces.
iv, 152 p, mus ex. Gray 1918.   2.00

V 3 of a series, the first of which is by Surette & Mason (see Appreciation). Notes on some 12 works by Bizet, Brahms, Dvořák, Elgar, Franck, d'Indy, Rimsky-Korsakov, Saint-Saëns, Stanford, R. Strauss, Tchaikovsky.

NEWMARCH, ROSA
The concert-goer's library of descriptive notes. 6 v. Oxford 1928/48.

V 1: viii, 127 p. 1928 (1943).	1.75
V 2: viii, 106 p. 1929.	1.75
V 3: xi, 145 p. 1930.	1.75
V 4: viii, 134 p. 1932 (1946).	1.75
V 5: viii, 98 p. 1938.	1.75
V 6: Choral works. 124 p. 1948.	1.75

Except for v 6, these are notes on symphonic works, mostly written for Queen's Hall programs between 1908 & 1927. A combined edition of the first four volumes (1937) now apparently is O/P.

O'CONNELL, CHARLES
Victor book of overtures, tone poems, and other orchestral works. xix, 614 p, mus ex.   S & S 1950.   **3.95**
A companion work to the same author's "Victor book of symphonies" (see Symphony) and to Veinus's "Victor book of concertos" (see Concerto) & Biancolli's & Bagar's "Victor book of operas" (see Opera–3). The present notes were written originally to accompany (RCA Victor) record-albums.

SCHMID, WILLY.   See App Ia.

SEAMAN, JULIAN *(comp)*
Great orchestral music: a treasury of program notes.   Intro Deems Taylor. xxii, 476 p, 5 pors. Rinehart 1950.   **5.00**
"Field of Music" series No 5: an anthology of program notes by various American authors dealing with standard works by some 70 composers, from Arensky to Vaughan Williams.

SÉNÉCHAUD, MARCEL.   See App Ia.

SKOLSKY, SYD.   See App IIb (juveniles).

SPAETH, SIGMUND
A guide to great orchestral music. xii, 532 p, mus ex, 1–p bibl.   Modern Library 1943.   2.45
Modern Library "Giants" G–61: notes arranged by classified groups of composers, & accompanied by Columbia & RCA Victor record lists.

Stories behind the world's great music. xiv, 373 p, mus ex, 4–p bibl. McGraw 1937.   O/P
A Garden City reprint (1940) apparently is also O/P.

TOVEY, DONALD F.
Essays in musical analysis. **6 v.** Oxford 1935/9.

V 1: Symphonies (1).   viii, 223 p, mus ex. 1935 (7th pr 1946).   2.75
V 2: Symphonies (2).   xiv, 212 p, mus ex. 1935 (7th pr 1948).   2.75
V 3: Concertos. ix, 226 p, mus ex. 1936 (7th pr 1948).   2.75
V 4: Illustrative music. viii, 176 p, mus ex. 1937 (5th pr 1946).   2.75
V 5: Vocal music. vi, 256 p, mus ex. 1937 (5th pr 1946).   2.75
V 6: Miscellaneous notes, index, & glossary. vii, 188 p, mus ex. 1939 (5th pr 1948).   2.75

A (if not the) standard collection of program notes, originally written for Tovey's own Reid Concerts at Edinburgh and notable in particular for their detailed, strictly musical analyses.

Note: See Chamber Music for an additional volume of "Essays in musical analysis," ed Foss & published posthumously (1944).

UPTON, GEORGE P. & BOROWSKI, FELIX
The standard concert guide. xxiii, 486 p, mus ex. (1908, 1930) Halcyon repr, 4th rev ed 1947.   **1.98**
Notes on some 450 works by composers from d'Albert to Wolf-Ferrari; originally written by Upton alone (1908), in 1917 combined with his "standard concert repertory" of 1909, and in 1930 revised by Borowski.

PROGRAMS (of Music)
See: esp Repertory.
Also:

Appreciation	Philharmonic
Conducting	Program Notes
Conductors	School Music
Opera	Yearbooks

PROKOFIEV, Sergei Sergeievitch
See also:

Appreciation	Opera
Ballet	Phonograph Records
Chamber Music	Piano Music
Composers–2 & 3e	Program Notes
Concerto	Russian Music
Contemporary Music	Symphony
Film Music (esp	Themes
Eisenstein)	Timing
History	Violin Music
Modern Music	Vocal Music

Also: App IIa (Deakin, Prokofiev juveniles —"Peter & the Wolf").

NESTYEV, ISRAEL V.
Sergei Prokofiev: his musical life. Tr Rose Prokofieva. Intro Sergei Eisenstein. xxvii, 193, xiv p, frontis por, mus ex. Knopf 1946.   3.00

The first substantial biography & critical appraisal (in English) of the Soviet composer. Includes a catalogue of works.

PROMS (Promenade Concerts)

See:

England–music in   Queen's Hall
(esp Russell)   H. Wood

PRONUNCIATION

See also:

Acting	Gregorian Chant
Appreciation	(esp Klarmann)
Church Music	Italian Language
Dictionaries of Terms	Latin Language
(esp Baker)	Scotland (music in)
Diction	Singing
French Language	Speech
German Language	Voice

Note: Only a sampling of the large available literature (especially on English pronunciation) is listed below. Alexander J. Ellis's "Pronunciation for singers" (1877) apparently is O/P (or not easily available).

BENDER, JAMES F. (*comp*)
NBC handbook of pronunciation.
Forew James Rowland Angell. 372 p.
Crowell (1943) 2nd enl ed 1951.   4.50
Dictionary word list (some 15,000 entries) with pronunciations in broad international phonetic alphabet & respelled versions.

JONES, ARCHIE N. (& *others*)
Pronouncing guide to French, German, Italian, Spanish. 203 p, paper.
C. Fischer 1945.   1.50
Co-authors: Irving Smith & Robert B. Walls. Pronouncing vocabularies with phonetic symbols & tables of common terminations.

Proschowski, Frantz. Author.
See Singing–1.
Protestant Episcopal Church, U. S. A., Joint Commission on Church Music.
Authors. See Church Music.

PROUST, Marcel

Note: Florence Hier's "La musique dans l'oeuvre de Marcel Proust" (New York, 1933), apparently is O/P (or not easily available).

Prout, Ebenezer. Author. See:

Counterpoint–2. Strict & free (1890).	4.25
——. Additional exercises (1890)	2.30
——. Double, & canon (1891).	4.25
Form. Applied (1895).	4.25
——. Musical form (1893).	4.25
Fugue. Fugue (1891).	4.25
——. Fugal analysis (1892).	4.25

Harmony–2. Theory & practice (1889).	4.00
——. Analytical key (1903).	3.50
Instrumentation. Primer (1876).	1.50
——. Orchestra, 2 v (1898/9).	8.50

Note: A few other works by Prout, on Bach's fugues & cantatas, apparently are O/P.

Prout, Louis Beethoven. Author.
See Harmony–2.
Prunières, Henry. Author.
See History–4, App Ia.
Prüwer, Julius. Co-author (with Röse).
See R. Strauss.
Pryce-Jones, Alan. Author.
See Beethoven–2, R. Strauss.

PSALMS/PSALMODY

See also: esp Church Music.

Also:

America (music in)	Jewish Music
Ancient Music	Mass
Anthologies	Medieval/Renaissance
Asiatic Musics	Mode
(note only)	Monophony
Choir/Choral–3	Pilgrims
England (music in)	Plainsong
Gregorian Chant	Puritans
History	Scotland (music in)
Hymns/Hymnody	Vocal Music

Note: Standard works apparently O/P (or not easily available) include those by Cross, Foote, Harris & Mingana, Keet, Pratt, Richardson, Terry, Warington (bibl, 1898), Welch, etc.

BROWN, RAY F. (*ed*)
The Oxford American psalter: the psalms & canticles according to the use of the Protestant Episcopal Church in the United States of America. Pointed & set to Anglican chants. xiv, 242 p, music. Oxford 1949.   3.50
Mainly music, except for the introduction & an appendix on the characteristics of Anglican chant, speech-rhythm, etc.

MACDOUGALL, HAMILTON C.
Early New England psalmody: an historical appreciation, 1620–1820.
x, 179 p, illus (facs), mus ex. Stephen Daye Press, Brattleboro, Vermont, 1940.   3.50
Includes a discussion of Billings & a full account of the famous Bay Psalm Book, 1640.

PATRICK, MILLAR
Four centuries of Scottish psalmody.
xxiii, 234 p, 12 pl (facs, etc), mus ex, bibl refs. Oxford 1950.   3.00
An authoritative history of the Scottish Psalter, the metrical versions of which date from 1650: with studies of metrical psalmody

in general & the "insufficiencies" of the Scottish Psalter.

PSALTERY

See:

Ancient Music	History
Children–4 (esp	Instruments
Coleman)	Jewish Music
Harp	Medieval/Renaissance
Music	

PSYCHOLOGY (& Music/of Music)

General Note: Like "Philosophy," this term often is loosely if not badly used by writers on music, and generally it is ignored as a subject-heading in musical dictionaries & encyclopedias. Here, however, there is a much larger body of literature (again with a considerable portion O/P), although it is dominated to such an extent by the works of Seashore & his school that many readers must have come to associate "Musical Psychology" almost exclusively with the behaviorist school in general and with "musical talent tests" in particular.

Other psychological schools and musical applications are represented less extensively, for example by Mursell, in his applications of "Gestalt" theory to teaching & to musical experience in general, and by Ching, in his use of Freudian theory in analyses of piano performance & of stage fright. And of course many writers have applied, or mis-applied, Freudian & other psychological theories in their studies of various composers' lives & works.

Psycho-physiological aspects of musical perception & experience are touched upon to some extent in various books on acoustics, aesthetics, & hearing, but much remains to be done here, as in the whole general field, both in compiling further data and in reconciling the currently widely divergent views.

See also:

Acoustics	Piano-Playing–1
Aesthetics	(esp Ching)
Appreciation	Philosophy
Children–1	(esp Howes)
Color	Religion
Health	School Music–1
Hearing	Teaching–1 & 2
Industry	(esp Mursell)
Interpretation	Tests
Memory	Tonality/Atonality
Musicology	Vibrato

Note: Standard works apparently O/P (or not easily available) include Mursell's "Psychology of music" (1937) & Schoen's "The effects of music" (1940); also other works by Diserens & Fine, Farnsworth, Howes, Matthay, Mursell, Pratt, Seashore, Wallace, etc.

BARTHOLOMEW, E. F.
Relation of psychology to music.

286 p, diagrs. New Era Pub Co, via Augustana (1899) 2nd rev ed 1902.   1.75

BUCK, PERCY C.
Psychology for musicians. viii, 115 p, diagrs, mus ex, 1–p bibl. Oxford 1944 (5th pr 1949).   1.50

A study of learning & teaching processes.

DEUTSCH, MAURY
Musical psychology: the art of expression for composer, arranger; colorful effects with music & moods. 32 p, mus ex, typescript repro, paper. Author, N. Y., 1948.   1.00

Theory of psychological associations: for arranger & composer. 32 p, mus ex, typescript repro, paper. Author, N. Y., 1949.   **1.00**

Two in a series of practical composer's & arranger's handbooks (see also under Arranging–1, Instrumentation, Theory–4). The present booklets deal primarily with "mood" effects & the means of obtaining them.

HANDSCHIN, JACQUES. See App Ib.

KURTH, ERNST. See App Ib.

LOWERY, H.
The background of music. Hutchinson 1950 in prep.   △

Psychological introduction to musicology, musical talent, memorization, taste, performance, applause, criticism, etc.

MURSELL, JAMES L. & GLENN, MAYBELLE
The psychology of school music teaching. v, 386 p, mus ex, chap bibls. Silver (1931) 1938.   3.20

A standard work, covering factors in music-mindedness, executant factors in education, measurements, materials, & aims.

RÉVÉSZ, GÉZA (*See also App Ib.*)
The psychology of a musical prodigy. ix, 180 p, frontis por, 4 b&ws, mus ex, 24-p music, bibl refs. Kegan Paul △ & Curwen 1925.   (3.75)

A standard, scholarly study of a child genius, Erwin Nyiregyházi, and his development.

SCHOEN, MAX
The psychology of music: a survey for teacher & musician. vii, 258 p, diagrs, tables, mus ex, 17–p bibls. Ronald 1940 (1950).   3.25

A standard work, recently reprinted, intended primarily for the musician interested in the findings of experimental psychology.

SEASHORE, CARL E.
Pioneering in psychology. Pref George D. Stoddard. vii, 232 **p**, 8 illus, 8–p bibl. Iowa 1942.   2.50

The story of the University of Iowa's notable work in musical pyschology.

The psychology of music. xix, 408 p, illus, diagrs, tables, 11–p bibl. McGraw 1938 (5th pr n d).   5.00

A standard work, summing up the views of the Seashore-Iowa school.

Why we love music. vi, 82 p. Ditson 1941.   1.50

Musical experience at various ages & the backgrounds of "feeling for music."

SWISHER, WALTER SAMUEL
Psychology for the music teacher. 78 p, mus ex, chap bibls, paper. Ditson 1927.   .75

"Pocket Music Student" series.

PUBLISHERS/PUBLISHING of (Music)

See: also:

America (music in)	Medieval/Renaissance
Bibliography	Philadelphia
Boston (music in)	(music in)
Composers–3a (esp	Popular Music
McNamara)	Sheet Music
England (music in)	Who's Who
History	Yearbooks

Note: Standard works apparently O/P (or not easily available) include those by Dunn, Gamble, Kidson, Marks, Squire, Steele, Witmark & Goldberg, etc.

DURAND, JACQUES. See App Ia.

FISHER, WILLIAM ARMS
One hundred and fifty years of music publishing in the United States: an historical sketch, with special reference to the pioneer publishers Oliver Ditson Co, Inc, 1783–1933. xvi, 146 p, illus. Ditson 1933 (1934).   2.00

A revision of "Notes on music in old Boston" (1918). The illustrations show some 28 buildings, views, & maps; plus 9 musical facsimiles & 24 portraits.

PUCCINI, Giacomo

See also:

Appreciation	Opera
Composers–1	Phonograph Records
History	Themes
Italian Music	Vocal Music

Note: Standard works apparently O/P (or not easily available) include the Puccini letters (ed Adami, in English 1931, but see App Ib for a German edition); books by Dry, Seligman, Specht (in English & German), Weissmann (in German); and those in Italian by Bonaventure, Brüggemann, Marotti & Pagni, Merlin, Salerno, Torrefranco, etc.

ADAMI, GIUSEPPE. See App Ia & Ib.

CROZIER, ERIC (ed)
La Bohème. 48 p, 12 photos, mus ex, paper. Lane 1948.   .50
"Sadler's Wells Opera Books" No. 6, with essays by Mosco Carner (Puccini's Capriccio sinfonica), Robert L. Jacobs (history & music of the opera), & Gladys Scott Thomson (England & "The Bohemians" 1897).

Madame Butterfly. 39 p, 12-photos, paper. Lane 1945 (1946).   .50
"Sadler's Wells Opera Books" No. 4, with essays by Mosco Carner ("In defence of Puccini"), A. K. Holland (Puccini as a craftsman), Robert L. Jacobs (history of the opera), & the story of the opera.

MAREK, GEORGE
Puccini: a biography. xviii, 412 p + 17-p illus (pors, facs, etc), 3-p bibl. S & S 1951.   5.00

Pudovkin, Vsevolod Illarionvich. Author.
See Films.

Pulver, Jeffrey. (Author), editor.
See String Instruments (Panum).

Note: Several books by Pulver, including a biography of Paganini (1936), apparently are O/P (or not easily available).

PURCELL, Henry

See also:

Appreciation	Phonograph Records
Baroque Era	Piano Music
Chamber M uic	Poetry (esp Boas)
Choir/Choral–3	Program Notes
Church Music	Restoration Era
Composers–1 & 3c	Song(s)
Dryden	String Quartet
English Music	Themes
History	d'Urfey
Opera–1 (esp Dent)	Vocal Music

Note: Standard works apparently O/P (or not easily available) include those by Arundell, Azulay, H. Dupré (in French & English), Runciman, etc.

CUMMINGS, WILLIAM H.
Purcell. 124 p. (1881, 3rd ed 1911, △ pop ed 1923) Reeves n d.   (1.80)

FAVRE-LINGOROW, STELLA. See App Ib.

HOLLAND, A. K.
Henry Purcell: the English musical tradition. 191 p, mus ex, 1–p bibl, paper. (1932) Penguin repr 1948.   .35
Not a biography, but an illuminating study of the composer's times & musical accomplishments.

Purcell. 14 p, cover por, paper. Novello n d (1939).   .40
Miniature biography ("great musicians").

MANDINIAN, EDWARD (*photographer*)
Purcell's "The Fairy Queen," as
presented at the Royal Opera House,
Covent Garden: a photographic
record, with articles . . 36 p, 53 pl. △
Lehmann 1947.   (6.30)
*The articles are by Michael Ayrton (study of
the "design & device"), E. J. Dent (preface),
& Constant Lambert (the music).*

WESTRUP, J. A.
Purcell. xi, 323 p, 7 pl (pors & facs),
mus ex, 4–p bibl. Dent 1937 (1947),
via Pellegrini 1949.   2.50
*"Master Musicians" series, embodying the
latest research and including genealogical
data as well as the usual calendar, personalia,
& catalogue of works.*

Purdy, Claire Lee. Author.
See App IIa (juveniles):

Dvořák   Herbert
Foster   Mozart (with Benson)
Gilbert & Sullivan   Tchaikovsky
Grieg

PURITANS (& Music)
See also:
America (music in)   History
Boston (music in)   Hymns/Hymnody
Church Music   Pilgrims
England (music in)   Psalms/Psalmody

SCHOLES, PERCY A.
The puritans and music in England
& New England: a contribution to
the cultural history of two nations.
xxii, 428 p, 26 pl (pors, facs, etc),
16–p bibl. Oxford 1934.   7.50
*An inquiry into the alleged Puritan antipathy
to music & dancing, with incidental illumination on various aspects of 16th- & 17th-
century musical life.*

Pushee, Ruth. Author. See Church Music.

—Q—

Qvamme, Børre. Author.
See Norway (music in).

QUARTER-TONES
See:
Acoustics   Monophony
Composition   Scales
Contemporary Music   Tonality/Atonality
Harmony–1   Twelve-Tone
History   Technique

QUARTET
See:
Amateur Music   Choir/Choral
Appreciation   Church Music
Barbershop   School Music
Chamber Music   String Quartet

QUEEN'S HALL (London)
See also:
England (music in)   Program Notes
History   (esp Newmarch)
Philharmonic   H. Wood

ELKIN, ROBERT
Queen's hall, 1893-1941.   Forew
Malcolm Sargent.   160 p, photos,
4 plans. Rider 1944.   5.50
*Moving account of the life & death (by bomb-
ing) of the famous concert hall, home of the*

*"Proms." With a note on the hall organ
& a BBC memorial broadcast script.*

QUIZZES
See also: Miscellanies, Opera-3 (Milligan
& Souvaine).
*Note: Musical quiz-books apparently O/P
include those by Burch & Ripperger (but for
their "Junior Quiz," see App IIb), Ranson
& Pack, Wier, etc.*

BAUER, MARION
Musical questions and quizzes: a
digest of information about music.
xiii, 286 p, 16-p bibl. Putnam 1941. 2.75
*More serious than most quizzes & covers a
wide range of musical information.*

COTT, TED
The Victor book of musical fun:
a brand new collection of musical
quiz games, anecdotes, & cartoons.
vi, 170 p, illus (Leo Garel), mus ex.
S & S 1945 (4th pr).   1.50

HUNT, CECIL
Music lovers' quiz: more than
2000 testing & informative questions, with answers from the realms
of music & musicians. 100 p, paper.
Bosworth 1947.   1.00

—R—

Rabaud, Henri. Co-author & editor (with Danhauser). See App Ia.

Rabineau, Lauretta Byrnes. Author. See Children–5.

RACHMANINOFF, Sergei Vassilievitch

See also:

Appreciation	Piano Music
Composers–2 & 3e	Program Notes
Concerto	Russian Music
History	Song(s)
Interpreters	Symphony
Phonograph Records	Themes
Pianists	Vocal Music

Also: App IIa (Gronowicz juvenile).

Note: Riesemann's "Rachmaninoff's recollections" (1934) apparently is O/P.

ANDERSON, W. R.
Rachmaninov and his concerti. 24 p, mus ex, paper.   Hinrichsen n d (1946).   .50
"Miniature Survey" series No 7, including a brief bibl & list of phonograph records. Covers other works besides the concertos

BERTENSSON, SERGE & LEYDA, JAY
Sergei Rachmaninoff: his life & music. Hutchinson 1950, in prep.   △ (3.75)
A full-scale biography, written in collaboration with Sophia Satina.

CULSHAW, JOHN
Rachmaninov: the man & his music. 174 p, illus (pors, facs), mus ex. Dobson 1949, Oxford 1950.   3.00
Originally in Dobson's "Contemporary Composers" series. Includes a catalogue of works, brief bibliography, & 4-p list of (British) phonograph records.

LYLE, WATSON
Rachmaninoff: a biography.   Pref Leff Pouishnoff. xii, 247 p, 2 pors. Reeves 1938 (1950).   (3.75)
Reprint (not brought up to date) of a British study, including a critical survey of Rachmaninoff's gramophone records by Wilson G. Lyle, & a catalogue of works.

SEROFF, VICTOR I.
Rachmaninoff. Forew Virgil Thomson. xiv, 269 p + 12-p illus (21 photos), 12-p bibl. S & S 1950.   3.50
A new, full-scale biography, devoted primarily

to Rachmaninoff's character & career rather than to his compositions.

Radcliffe, Philip. Author. See J. Ireland, Mendelssohn–2.

Rader, Melvin. Editor. See Aesthetics–1.

RADIO/BROADCASTING (General)

General Note: Only a small sampling of the large available literature is listed below. For further exploration, consult the bibliographies by Broderick or Rose, or those included in some of the other books listed.

See also: esp Radio Music

Also:

Acoustics	School Music
Acting	(esp–1, Best)
Career	Sound Rec & Repro
Education	Stokowski
Libraries (Myers)	Teaching
Pronunciation	Television
Quizzes	Yearbooks

ABBOT, WALDO
Handbook of broadcasting. 494 p, 61 illus. McGraw (1937) 3rd ed 1950. 5.00
Latest edition of a popular over-all survey in non-technical language.

BRODERICK, GERTRUDE G. (*comp*)
Radio & television bibliography. Forew E. I. Grigsby. Harry Moskowitz, assistant comp. iv, 33 p, paper. GPO 1949.   .15
An U.S. Education Office bulletin. Classified under such headings as General, Careers in Radio, Broadcast Technique & Scriptwriting, FM, Equipment, Periodicals, etc.

COOPER, ISABELLA M. (*comp*)
Bibliography on educational broadcasting. ix, 576 p, typescript repro, paper. Chicago 1942.   5.00
Annotated bibliographies, including a section (p 371/9) on "Music—instructional, cultural."

COTT, TED
How to audition for radio: a handbook for actors, a workbook for students. Forew Arch Oboler, xiii, 142 p, illus, 1-p bibl. Greenberg 1946.   2.50
Includes a sample script, radio actors' dictionary, & list of hand signals.

CREWS, ALBERT R.
Professional radio writing. xii, 473
p. Houghton 1946. **5.50**
Radio production directing. x,
550 p, 30 pl. Houghton 1944. **5.50**
*Handbooks in a "Radio Broadcasting" series.
The former includes a chapter (p 133/54) on
"Writing music program continuity," illus-
trated by sample scripts.*

KEITH, ALICE
How to speak & write for radio: a
manual of broadcasting technique.
xiv, 236 p. Harper 1944. **3.00**
*Includes specimen scripts & a chapter on
"music continuity," pp 120/145.*

LAZARSFELD, PAUL F. & KENDALL, P. L.
Radio listening in America: the
people look at radio again. Report on
a survey conducted by the National
Opinion Research Center, analyzed
& interpreted. v, 178 p, charts,
diagrs. Prentice 1949. **2.50**
*A scholarly report on public opinion: favorite
types of programs, reaction to advertising
"commercials," etc.*

ROSE, OSCAR (comp)
Radio broadcasting & television:
an annotated bibliography. 120 p.
Wilson 1947. **1.50**
Mainly radio bibliography, p 10/89.

SIEPMANN, CHARLES A.
Radio's second chance. xiv, 282 p,
tables. Little Brown 1946. **2.50**
*The sins of omission & commission of com-
mercial broadcasting, with special emphasis
on the potentialities for good of FM.*

Radio, television, and society. vii,
410 p, tables, diagrs, map, 9–p bibl.
Oxford 1950. **4.75**
*A detailed review of broadcasting systems,
here & abroad (including a study of the BBC
"3rd Programme"), plus a discussion of the
social implications of radio & television.*

WALLER, JUDITH C.
Radio, the fifth estate. Forew James
Rowland Angell. xiv, 483 p, 6 pl,
charts, 18–p bibl. Houghton 1946. **5.00**
*An extensive over-all survey, in the "Radio
Broadcasting" series.*

WHITE, LLEWELLYN
The American radio: a report on the
broadcasting industry in the U. S.
from the Commission on Freedom
of the Press. xxi, 260 p. Chicago
1947. **3.25**
*Background material on the technology,
finances, & politics of broadcasting.*

WILLIAMS, ALBERT N.
Listening. 152 p. Denver 1948. **2.75**
*Some 25 critical articles, mostly from the
"Saturday Review of Literature," on net-
works, programs, advertising, the bookshelf,
etc.*

RADIO (BROADCAST) MUSIC

See also:
Appreciation	History
Career	Phonograph Records
Children–1	Program Notes
(esp Gordon) & 2	Radio
Composers–2 & 3a	School Music
Contemporary Music	Sound Rec & Repro
Copyright	Stokowski
Film Music (esp	D. Taylor
Nelson&Rubsamen)	Yearbooks

*Note: Kinscella's "Music on the air" (1937),
& Scholes' "Everybody's guide to radio music"
(1926) apparently are O/P.*

CHASE, GILBERT (ed)
Music in radio broadcasting. xi,
152 p. McGraw 1946. **2.50**
*Development of an NBC-Columbia University
lecture series, with articles by Chotzinoff,
Belviso, Bennett, Black, Dunham, Graf, Hall,
LaPrade, Mamorsky, & Chase.*

DAVIS, GEORGE
Music-cueing for radio-drama: a
practical treatise on the application
of music to the radio-script. 39 p,
mus ex, paper. Boosey 1947. **1.25**

LAPRADE, ERNEST
Broadcasting music. xii, 236 p, 27
illus (incl mus facs), 5–p bibl.
Rinehart 1947, text ed. **2.50**
*An over-all survey, with special emphasis on
vocational requirements, by the NBC director
of music research.*

Radir, Ruth Anderson. Author.
See Dances–1.
Rael, Juan B. Co-compiler (with Tully).
See Folklore.

RAGTIME
See: Jazz (esp Blesh & Janis), Popular
Music.

Ramani, R. Co-author (with Spreen).
See Dances–2.

RAMEAU, Jean-Philippe
See: esp App Ia (La Laurencie biog in
French, Masson "L'Opéra de Rameau",
Meyer).
Also:
Appreciation	& Music
Composers–1	Opera–1
Baroque Era	Phonograph Records
French Music	Program Notes
History	Rolland
Keyboard Instruments	Vocal Music

Ramuz, Charles Ferdinand. Author.
See App Ia.
Ramsey, Frederic, Jr. Author.
See Jazz
Randolph, Vance. Editor.
See Folksongs–2.
Ranks, Harry W. Author (with Nohavec).
See Children–8.
Rao, V. V. Lakshamana. Author.
See Decibel.
Rasmussen, Carrie E. Author.
See Speech.
Ratcliffe, Bertram. Co-author (with A.
Ysaye). See Ysaye.
Ratter, Magnus C. Author.
See Schweitzer–2

RATTLES

See: Instruments (esp Mason)

Rau, Heribert. Author.
See Beethoven–2.
Raugel, Félix. Author. See App Ia.
Raupach, Hans. Editor. See App Ib.
Rauterkus, Joseph A. Author.
See Theory–3.

RAVEL, Maurice

See also:

Appreciation	Modern Music
Ballet	Opera 1 & 3
Chamber Music	Orchestral Music
Composers–2 & 3d	Phonograph Records
Concerto	Piano Music
Contemporary Music	Program Notes
Dance Music	Song
French Music	Vocal Music
History	Waltz

*Note: Goss's "Boléro—the life of Maurice
Ravel" (1940) apparently is O/P.*

BRUYR, JOSE. See App Ia.

DEMUTH, NORMAN
Ravel. ix, 214 p, 8 pl (pors & fac),
1–p bibl. Dent 1947.   2.50
*"Master Musicians" series, with usual calen-
dar, personalia, & catalogue of works.*

JOURDAN-MORHANGE, HELEN. See App Ia.

LANDOWSKI, W. L. See App Ia.

MANUEL, ROLAND
Maurice Ravel. Tr Cynthia Jolly.
Intro Scott Goddard. 152 p, 21 pl
(pors, fac), mus ex, 4–p bibl. Dobson 1947.   2.50
*"Contemporary Composers" series: a study of
the man & his music, by one of Ravel's pupils;
published in French, 1938 (see App Ia).*

ONNEN, FRANK
Maurice Ravel. Tr W. A. Doyle-
Davidson. 64 p, 16 pl + fac, mus ex,

1–p bibl, bds. Continental n d
(1946?).   2.50
*"Symphonia" series of illustrated mono-
graphs.*

Ray, John M. Author. See Theory–3.
Rayleigh, Lord (John William Strutt).
Author. See Acoustics.
Raymond, William F. Author.
See Trombone.
Rayner, Robert Macey. Author.
See Wagner–3.
Rayson, Ethel. Author
See Poland (music in).
Read, Oliver. Author.
See Sound Recording & Reproduction.

READING (Musical)

See:

Amateur Music	Sight-Playing &
Appreciation	Reading
Children–3 & 8	Sight-Singing
Ear-Training	Solfège/Solfeggio
Notation	Psychology
Rhythm	Teaching
School Music	Theory
Score-Reading	

READING ROTA

See: Rounds (esp Bukofzer).

Reber, Napoléon-Henri. Author.
See App Ia.
Reboux, Paul (pseud of Paul Amillet).
Author. See App Ia.

RECITATIVE

See:

History	Singing
Opera	Vocal Music

RECORDED MUSIC

See: Phonograph Records.

RECORDER

See also:

Children–4 & 6	Flute
Community Music	History
(Bergmann)	Instruments

*Note: Welch's "Six lectures on the recorder"
(1911) apparently is O/P.*

TWITTENHOFF, WILHELM
How to play the recorder. Tr Edgar
H. Hunt. 16 + chart, mus ex, paper.
Nagel & Associated n d.   .35

Reddick, William J. Author. See Timing.
Redfield, John. Author. See Acoustics.
Redlich, Hans Ferdinand. Author.
See Wagner–3, App Ib.

Redmond, Bessie Carroll.　Co-author (with Burrows).　See Themes.
Reed, J. Owen.　Author.　See Theory–3.
Reed, William Henry.　Author.　See Elgar.
Reeder, Betah.　Author.
See Piano Playing–2.

REEDS
See: Wind Instruments (esp **Larson** & **Baxter**).

Rees-Davies, Ieuan.　Author.
See Transposition.
Reese, Gustave.　Author.
See Medieval/Renaissance.
Reeser, Eduard.　Author.　See:
　Bach Family.　Sons of Bach (1947).　2.50
　History–3.　Bird's-eye (1946/7).　2.50
　Waltz.　History of (1947)　2.50

Reever, Grace.　Author (with Kurtz).
See Children–8.
Reeves, Aubrey.　Compiler.
See Sight-Singing.
Reeves, Harold.　Co-author (with McColvin).
See Libraries.
Refardt, Edgar.　Author, editor.　See App Ib.

REFERENCE WORKS
See:

Bibliographies	History
Dictionaries of Music	Who's Who
Encyclopedias of	Yearbooks
Music	

REGER, Max
See: esp App Ib (Poppen).

Appreciation	Organ Music
Composers–1	Phonograph Records
History	Program Notes

Note: Pertinent works apparently O/P (or not easily available) include those in German by Hasse, Huesgen, Lindner, Stein, Unger, etc.

Author.　See Modulation.

REGISTRATION
See: Organ Playing.

Rehberg, Paula & Walter.　Authors.
See App Ib.
Reich, Willi.　Author, editor.
See Berg, also App Ib.
Reid, Cornelius L.　Author.　See Bel Canto.
Reid, Joseph V.　Author.　See Violin.
Reid, Robert H.　Editor.
See Phonograph Records.
Reinecke, Karl (Heinrich Carsten).　Author.
See Beethoven–3.
Reis, Claire (Raphael).　Author.
See Composers–3a.

RELIGION (& Music)
See also:

Aesthetics	Mass
Church Music	Philosophy
History	Psalms/Psalmody
Hymns/Hymnody	Schweitzer

Note: Works apparently O/P (or not easily available) include those by Camdo, Hunter, Longford, Wibberly, etc.

VOGT, VON OGDEN
Art and religion.　xvii, 280 p, col frontis, 13 photos, mus ex. (1921, 1929) Beacon rev ed 1948.　　　　4.50
Originally published by Yale Univ. Press (& by Oxford in England).　Chapter 18 (p 174/9) deals with music.

RENAISSANCE
See: esp Medieval/Renaissance.

History	Troubadours/
Keyboard Instruments	Trouvères

Rensch, Roslyn.　Author.　See Harp.

REPERTORY
See also:

Chamber Music	Piano Music
Choir/Choral–3	Program Notes
Church Music	Songs
Concerto	Symphony
Opera	Themes
Orchestral Music	Timing
Organ Music	Violin Music

BOLL, ANDRÉ & DAMAIS, EMILE.
See App Ia.

SWAN, ALFRED JULIUS
The music director's guide to musical literature (for voices & instruments).　xii, 164 p, charts, mus ex.　Prentice 1941.　　　　　　　3.00
Historical survey with lists of some 3000 works by some 150 composers.

REPLICAS
See: Autographs, Facsimiles.

RESPIGHI, Ottorino
See also:

Appreciation	History
Ballet	Italian Music
Composers–2	Phonograph Records
Contemporary Music	Program Notes

ROBERTSON, MARION
La boutique fantasque: the story of the ballet.　96 p, illus, incl 4 col pl (Joyce Millen).　Wolsey, London, 1947, via Transatlantic.　　　　.75
"Ballet Pocket Library" series.

RESTORATION ERA

See also:

Dryden	History
England (music in)	Purcell
English Music	d'Urfey

STEAD, PHILIP JOHN (*ed*)
Songs of the restoration theatre:
edited from the printed books of the
time with an introduction. xvii, 91 p,
frontis. Methuen 1948.   2.00
The poetry only, with notes on the authors.

THORP, WILLARD (*ed*)
Songs from the restoration theater.
138 p, frontis, music facs. Princeton
1934 (1949).   2.50
27 songs in facsimile, with notes.

Reszke. Catalogued under De Reszke.
Reuter, Evelyn. Author. See App Ia.
Révész, Géza. Author.
See Psychology, also App Ib.
Reyes-Tolentino, Francisca S. Editor.
See Dances–2.
Rhea, Lois & Raymond. Authors.
See Choir/Choral–3.

RHEINBERGER, Josef (Gabriel)

See also:

History	Organists
Organ Music	

Note: Molitor's book (in German) on Rheinberger's organ works apparently is O/P.

GRACE, HARVEY
The organ works of Rheinberger.
xi, 130 p, mus ex. Novello (1925)
2nd ed 1932.   (2.75)

RHYMING DICTIONARIES

See: Songwriting (esp Lewis, Wood).

RHYTHM

See also:

Children–3, 6, & 8	Notation
Dances–1	Sight-Playing &
Ear-Training	Reading
Eurhythmics	Sight-Singing
Form (Macpherson)	Solfège/Solfeggio
Ballet (esp Robertson)	Tempo
Interpretation	Theory

Also: Conducting, Piano Playing, Singing, etc.

Standard works apparently O/P (or not easily available in this country) include those by Fogerty, Glyn, Lussy, Morris, Prout, Riemann (in German), etc.

DUMESNIL, RENÉ. See App Ia.

VANASEK, BENEDICT
Student's manual of music rhythms:
including a modern music vocabulary; questions & answers for vocal &
instrumental students. 20 p, mus
ex, paper. Mills 1938.   .75

WEDGE, GEORGE A.
Rhythm in music: a textbook. vii,
54 p, mus ex. G. Schirmer 1927.   2.00
A standard exposition of the theory of rhythm, supplemented by 37 practical drills.

Rice, Eustace B. Author.
See Transposition.
Rice, Arthur Lowndes. Author.
See L. Mason.
Richards, G. Darlington. Author.
See Church Music.
Richardson, Alfred Madeley. Author.
See Fugue, Mode.
Note: Numerous other books by Richardson apparently are O/P.
Richardson, Edward Gick. Author.
See Acoustics.
Richter, Ada. Author.
See Piano Playing–4.
Richter, Ernst Friedrich. Author.
See Harmony–2.
Rickaby, Franz. Editor. See Sea Songs.
Rickert, Edith. Editor. See Carols.
Riddle, Blanche Lee. Author.
See Hymns/Hymnody–1.

Riemann, Hugo. Author.
See: Bach–2, Score-Reading, App Ib.
Note: Numerous other books by Riemann (in English editions as well as in the original German versions) apparently are O/P (or not easily available in this country).

Rigby, Charles. Author. See Barbirolli.
Righter, Charles Boardman. Author.
See Band–2, School Music–3.
Riley, Alice Cushing Donaldson. Author.
See Poetry.

RIMSKY-KORSAKOV, Nikolai Andreyevitch

1. Own writings
2. Life & Works

RIMSKY-KORSAKOV (1. Own Writings)
My musical life. Tr. Judah A. Joffe.
Ed. & intro by Carl Van Vechten.
xliv, 480, xxii p, 15 pors, 1 fac, mus
ex. Knopf (1923) 3rd rev ed 1942.   6.00
One of the best-known musical autobiographies

& *personal panoramas of musical life in Russia. The present version is translated from the 4th & 5th Russian editions (original publication, in Russian, 1908).*
See also:
Harmony–2. Practical Manual of Harmony (1888/1930).   3.00
Instrumentation. Principles of Orchestration (1912/1930).   7.00
——. Same, Schmid digest (1950).   2.25

RIMSKY-KORSAKOV (2. Life & Works)

See also:

Appreciation	Orchestral Music
Ballet (esp Robertson)	Phonograph Records
Composers–1 & 3e	Program Notes
History	Russian Music
Opera	Vocal Music

Note: Montagu-Nathan's biography (1916) apparently is O/P.

ABRAHAM, GERALD
Rimsky-Korsakov: a short biography. 142 p, 2–p bibl. (1945) Wyn 1949.   1.00
Originally included in Calvocoressi's & Abraham's "Masters of Russian Music" (1936). (See Composers 3e.) Pub separately first by Duckworth, London, in 1945.

Ripperger, Helmut Lothar. Co-author (with Burch). See App IIb.
Ritter, Fanny Raymond. Author, editor. See Schumann–1, Women.
Roback, Abraham. Editor. See Schweitzer–2.
Robert, Grace. Author. See Ballet.
Roberts, Helen V. S. Author. See School Music–1.
Robertson, Alec. Author. See Brahms–1, Church Music, Dvořák, Plainsong.
Robertson, Anne. Author. See Harmony–2.
Robertson, James. Co-author (with Jacobs). See Opera–1.
Robertson, Marion Eva. Author See Ballet. Also (for individual books in the Ballet Pocket Library) under Respighi, Tchaikovsky–2.

ROBESON, Paul
See: Negro Music & Musicians.
Note: Eslanda Goode Robeson's biography (1930) and a juvenile biography by Shirley Graham (1946) apparently are O/P.

Robinson, Emmett. Co-author (with Fracht). See Singing–2.
Robinson-Duff, Sarah. Author. See Singers.

Robjohns, Sydney. Author. See Violin Playing.
Robson, James. Editor. See Arabia (music in).
Robyn, Louise. Author. See Children– 8.
Rockstro, Richard Shepherd. Author. See Flute.
Rockstro, William Smith. Author. See Lind.
Note: Numerous other books by Rockstro apparently are O/P (or not easily available).

ROCOCO (Era & Music)
See: esp App Ib (Bücken).

Anthologies (Davison & Apel, v 2)	French Music
	History
Baroque Era	Italian Music

RODGERS & HART
See also:

America (music in)	Phonograph Records
American Music	Popular Music
Hammerstein	Song(s)
Operetta	Songbooks

RODGERS, RICHARD (*ed*)
The Rodgers & Hart songbook. Pref Oscar Hammerstein II. Illus H. Lawrence Hoffman. S & S 1951, in prep.   7.50
Words & music of some 47 hit tunes.

RODGERS, Richard
See: Rodgers & Hart.

Roeder, Carl M. Author. See Keyboard Harmony, Piano Playing–2.
Rogers, Clara Kathleen. Author. See Diction, Singing–2.
Note: Rogers's "Memories of a musical career" (1919) apparently is O/P.
Rogers, Frederick Rand. Editor. See Dances–1.
Rohner, Traugott. Author. See Theory–3.
Rohrbough, Lynn. Editor. See Dances–2.
Roland-Manuel. Catalogued under Manuel.

ROLLAND, Romain. Author.
Romain Rolland's essays on music. xi, 371 p, frontis por. Allen Towne 1948, via Crown.   5.00
A "distillation" of 5 books O/P in English: "Beethoven the creator," "Handel," "A musical tour," "Musicians of today," & "Some musicians of former days."

Jean-Christophe. Tr Gilbert Cannon. 3 in 1: vi, 600, 473, 504 p. Modern Library repr n d. 2.45
One of the best-known works of fiction dealing with music & musicians. Originally pub in French 1905/1912, in English 1910/1913.
Journey within. Tr Elsie Pell. xi, 171 p, frontis. Philosophical 1947. 3.00
Rolland's autobiography.
Note: Rolland's other books apparently are O/P in English translations, but see App Ia ("L'Histoire de l'opéra") & App Ib ("Handel", in German). Stefan Zweig's biography of Rolland (1921) apparently is O/P.

STARR, WILLIAM THOMAS (*comp*)
A critical bibliography of the published writings of Romain Rolland. xxiii, 138 p. Northwestern University Press, Evanston, Illinois, 1950. 3.50
"Northwestern Univ. Studies in the Humanities" No 21: annotated bibliographies of Rolland's works & of books & articles about him, with an introductory study of Rolland's character & the nature of his writings.

ROMAN CATHOLIC CHURCH MUSIC
See:

Ancient Music	History
Choir/Choral–3	Mass
Church Music	Medieval/Renaissance
(esp Nemmers)	Phonograph Records
Gregorian	Plainsong

Also: under names of individual composers (esp Palestrina).

ROMANTIC ERA/ROMANTICISM
See also:

Aesthetics	Piano Music
Appreciation	Poetry (& music)
Chamber Music	Program Music
Composers (& under	Program Notes
individual names)	Song
Concerto	Theatre (Scholz)
History	Violin Music
Literature (& music)	(esp Swalin)
National Music	Vocal Music
Orchestral Music	App Ia (Dumesnil)

BARZUN, JACQUES
Romanticism and the modern ego. viii, 359 p. Little Brown 1943. 3.50
A re-valuation of the romantic movement in music, literature, & other arts.

EINSTEIN, ALFRED
Music in the romantic era: a history of musical thought in the 19th century. xii, 371 p, 15 pors. Norton 1947. 6.75
Norton History of Music series. The history & philosophy of musical romanticism, in-

cluding chapters on nationalism, musical aesthetics, & musicology.

FRANK, PAUL L.
The concept of musical romanticism in the light of a comparative criticism of style. Musurgia 1951, pending. △
"Musurgia Studies in Musicology," Series A, v 2 (on subscription only).

REICH, WILLI. See App Ib.

TIERSOT, JULIEN. See App Ia.

ROMBERG, SIGMUND
See also:

America (music in)	Operetta
American Music	Phonograph Records
Appreciation	Popular Music
Composers–3a	Vocal Music

ARNOLD, ELLIOTT
Deep in my heart: a story based on the life of Sigmund Romberg. ix, 511p. Duell Sloan 1949. 4.50
A romanticized biography, including lists of shows & musical numbers, an alphabetical list of songs, and a chronology.

RONALD, (Sir) Landon
See: Conductors, England (music in).
Note: Two books of memoirs & a biography of Schumann, by Sir Landon Ronald, apparently are O/P (or not easily available).

Roncaglia, Gino. Author. See App Ic.
Rood, Louise. Author
See Score-Reading.
Rorke, Genevieve A. Author.
See School Music–4.

RORKE, J. D. M. Author.
A musical pilgrim's progress. 155 p. Oxford (1921) 3rd ed 1933. 2.00
The personal adventures & discoveries of a British musical amateur.
See also:
Appreciation. Latch-key (1942) .70

Rose, Oscar. Compiler. See Radio.
Röse, Otto. Co-author (with Prüwer). See R. Strauss.
Rosen, Milton. Co-author (with Bakaleinikoff). See Instruments.
Rosenblith, Walter A. Co-compiler (with Miller & others). See Hearing.

ROSENBURG, Robert Kemper
Music and its environment. Intro Ruth Ray. 80 p. Island 1949. 2.00

Quasi-"appreciative" & generalized essays on Bach, Mozart, Beethoven, Romanticism, Opera, Nationalism, American music, etc.

ROSENFELD, Paul

Author. See:
American Music. Hour with (1929). 1.00
Note: Rosenfeld's other books ("Musical chronicles," 1923; "Discoveries of a music critic," 1936; etc.) apparently all are O/P.

MELLQUIST, JEROME & WIESE, L. (*eds*)
Paul Rosenfeld: voyager in the arts.
xxv, 284 p, frontis por, 18–p bibl.
Creative Age 1948. 3.50
A garland of tributes to one of the most influential American writers on music, by some 49 friends, including Edmund Wilson, Lewis Mumford, Sherwood Anderson, & others.

Rosenthal, Ethel. Author.
See India (music in).
Rosenwald, Hans Hermann. Author.
See History–3.
Ross, William Ernest. Author.
See Singing–2.

ROSSINI, Gioacchino

See also:

Appreciation	Opera
Beaumarchais	Phonograph Records
Composers–1	Program Notes
History	Themes
Italian Music	Vocal Music

Note: Standard works apparently O/P (or not easily available) include those by Azevedo (in French), Bonaventura, Derwent, Edwards, Stendhal (in English & French), etc; also correspondence & works in Italian by Corradi, Radiciotti, Silvestri, etc.

BACCHELLI, RICARDO. See App Ic.

BONAVIA, FERRUCCIO
Rossini. 16 p, cover por, paper.
Novello n d (1941). .40
Miniature biography ("great musicians").

DENT, EDWARD J. (*tr*)
The barber of Seville (Il barbiere di Siviglia): a comic opera in 2 acts; Italian words adapted from the comedy of Beaumarchais by Cesare Sterbini. English version. 57 p, paper. Oxford 1940 (1949). .80
Dent series of libretto translations.

PFISTER, KURT. See App Ib.

RONCAGLIA, GINO. See App Ic.

TOYE, FRANCIS
Rossini: a study in tragi-comedy.

xiii, 220, xiii p, 8 pl (pors, fac). Knopf 1934 (1947). 3.50
The standard biography in English.

Rossman, Floy Adele. Author.
See Children–1.
Rostand, Claude. Author. See App Ia.
Rostron, Richard. Author.
See App IIa (Dukas juvenile).
Roth, Ernst. Author. See App Ib.
Roth, Muriel. Co-author (with Cochem).
See Dancing–2.

ROUNDS

See also: Counterpoint, Songbooks.

BUKOFZER, MANFRED F.
"Sumer is icumen in": a revision.
vi, 79/113 p, 3 facs, mus ex, bibl refs, paper. California 1944. .75
A scholarly re-examination of the evidence bearing on the famous "Reading Rota's" date of composition, long accepted as c. 1240, now suggested as c. 1310.

TAYLOR, MARY CATHERINE (*comp*)
Rounds and rounds. 144 p, illus (Richard Erodes), music (designed by Joseph Zizza). Sloane 1946. 1.00
Originally priced at $3.00; now remaindered & probably soon going out-of-print.

ROUSSEAU, Jean-Jacques

See:

Composers–1	History
Criticism (Oliver)	Opera
French Music	Phonograph Records

Note: Pertinent works apparently O/P (or not easily available) include those in English by Mowat and Sells; in German by Istel and Schütte; in French by Gérin, Jansen, Moffat, Pougin, Sénelier, etc. Rousseau's own writings on music probably are available in French (in his collected works), but not in English.

ROUSSEL, Albert

See also:

Composers–2	Orchestral Music
Contemporary Music	Phonograph Records
French Music	Program Notes
History	Vocal Music

Note: The Hoerée biography (in French, 1938) apparently is O/P (or not easily available in this country).

BERNARD, R. See App Ia.

DEMUTH, NORMAN
Albert Roussel: a study. 151 p, por, fac, mus ex. United Music Publishers, London, 1947. (3.75)
The only study in English. A catalogue of Roussel's works is included.

Routley, Erik. Author. See Church Music.
Rowen, Ruth Halle. Author.
See Chamber Music.
Rowley, Alec. Author
See Piano Music.
Royal, John Francis. Editor.
See Television.

RUBATO
See: esp Interpretation.
Also:

Chopin	Rhythm
Conducting	Singing
Piano Playing	Violin Playing

Rubbra (Duncan-Rubbra), Edmund.
Author. See Counterpoint–1, Holst.
Rubel, Edith. Author. See App IIb.
Rubin, Ruth. Editor. See Folksongs–1.

RUBINSTEIN, Anton Gregoryevitch
See:

Appreciation	Piano Music
Composers–1 & 3e	Piano Playing
History	Program Notes
Opera	Russian Music
Phonograph Records	Vocal Music

*Note: An autobiography (1890) & other books
by Rubinstein apparently are O/P (or not
easily available), as is a biography by Hervey.
Also O/P is Catherine Drinker Bowen's
"Free artist: the story of Anton and Nicholas
Rubinstein" (1939).*

Rubinstein, Beryl. Author.
See Sight-Playing & Reading, Teaching–3.
Rubsamen, Walter Howard. Author.
See Italy (music in). Co-author (with
Nelson). See Film Music.
Rudge, Olga. Editor. See App Ic.

RUDIMENTS (of Music)
See: esp Theory.
Also:

Children	Rhythm
Dictation	Sight-Playing &
Dictionaries of Terms	Reading
Ear-Training	Sight-Singing
Notation	Solfège/Solfeggio

Rudolf, Max. Author. See Baton–1.
Ruff, Albert E. Author. See Voice.

RUGGLES, Carl
See: American Music, Composers–3a.

Rusette, Louie E. de Author.
See Children–6, also App IIb.

RUSSELL, (George) Alexander
See also: American Music, Composers–3a.

HOWARD, JOHN TASKER
Alexander Russell. 15 p, frontis por,
mus ex, paper. J. Fischer 1925.   .25
List of works & brief analyses.

Russell, Louis Arthur. Author. See:
Diction. English diction for singers
& speakers (1905).   1.25
Ornamentation. Embellishments
of music (1894).   1.25
Voice. Commonplaces of vocal art
(1907).   1.50
Russell, Thomas. Author.
See England (music in), Philharmonic.

RUSSIA (Music in)
See also:

Ballet	Opera
Encyclopedias	Rimsky-Korsakov
History	Russian Music

*Note: Standard works apparently O/P (or
not easily available) include those by Boelza,
Newmarch, etc.*

JELAGIN, JURI
Taming of the arts. Tr Nicholas
Wreden. 333 p. Dutton 1951.   3.50
*What has happened to Russian composers,
musicians, writers, & theatrical prouders
under totalitarian state control.*

MILIUKOV, PAUL
Outlines of Russian culture. Ed
Michael Karpovich. Tr Valentine
Ughet & Eleanor Davis. V 3: archi-
tecture, painting, & music. v, 159 p,
illus, 4–p bibl. Pennsylvania 1942
2nd pr 1943).   2.00
Music section, p 101/145.

MOOSER, R. A. See App Ia.

VODARSKY-SHIRAEFF, ALEXANDRIA (*comp*)
Russian composers and musicians:
a biographical dictionary. 158 p.
Wilson 1940.   1.75
*Composers, performers, teachers, writers,
arranged chronologically from Volkov (b.
1729) to Yurovski (b. 1915).*

WERTH, ALEXANDER
Musical uproar in Moscow. 103 p. △
Turnstile Press, London, 1949.   (1.80)
*An objective report on the fantastic case of
Soviet composers vs their State, based prim-
arily on the verbatim report of the Conference
of Musicians, January, 1948.*

RUSSIAN MUSIC
*Note: Standard works apparently O/P (or not
easily available) include those by Abraham,*

Montagu-Nathan, Newmarch (in English, but see App Ia for a French edition), Pougin, Sabaneyeff (in English & German), etc.

See also:

Appreciation	Film Music
Ballet	History
Chamber Music	Opera
Choir/Choral–3	Piano Music
Church Music	Phonograph Records
Composers, esp 3e	Program Notes
(& under individual	Romantic Era
names)	Russia (music in)
Concertos	Songs
Contemporary Music	Symphony
Dance	Vocal Music

ABRAHAM, GERALD
On Russian music: critical and historical studies. 279 p, frontis, mus ex. Reeves 1939, also Scribner 1939. **3.75**
Glinka's operas; works by Balakirev, Borodin, Glazounov, Mussorgsky, Rimsky-Korsakov, Tchaikovsky, etc.

Studies in Russian music: Rimsky-Korsakov & his contemporaries. ix, 335 p, pors, mus ex. Reeves n d △ (1935). (5.00)
Essays on Glinka, "The Five," Rimsky's operas, Tchaikovsky, etc. (The Scribner American edition of 1935 apparently is O/P).

CALVOCORESSI, M. D.
A survey of Russian music. 142 p, △ illus, bibl refs, paper. Penguin 1944. (.35)
A pocket-sized outline-history.

MONTAGU-NATHAN, M.
A history of Russian music: being an account of the rise & progress of the Russian school of composers, with a survey of their lives & a description of their works. 346 p, frontis por. Reeves (1914), 2nd rev ed 1918 (1950). (4.50)
A standard, but somewhat out-dated work, O/P for some years in Scribner's American edition, but recently reprinted by Reeves.

PANÒFF, PETR A. See App Ib (ed Bücken).

Rutledge, Abbie. Co-author (with Duggan & Schlottmann). See Dances–2.
Rutters, Herman. Authors. See Verdi–1.
Rutz, Hans. Author. See App Ib.
Ruud, Martin Brown. Translator (with Blegen, ed). See Folksongs–1.
Ryan, Grace Laura. Compiler See Dances–2.
Ryan, Willie. Author. See Singing–2.

—S—

Saar, Louis Victor. Author.
See Harmony–2.

Sachs, Curt. Author. See:

Aesthetics–1. Commonwealth of Art (1946).	6.00
Ancient Music. Rise of music in the ancient world (1943).	6.75
——. See App Ib (Bücken, ed: Handbuch der Musikwissenschaft v 1).	△
Dance. World history (1937).	7.50
History–2. Our heritage (1948).	5.00
Instruments. History of (1940).	7.50
Keyboard Instruments & Music. Evolution of piano music (1944).	1.00

Sackville-West, Edward. Author.
See Britten (ed Crozier).

SADLER'S WELLS
See:

Ballet (esp Beaumont)	History
Covent Garden	Opera
England (music in)	Yearbooks

Also (for Sadler's Wells Opera Book series): see Crozier, ed; and individually under Britten, Mozart–3, Opera–1, Puccini.

Šafránek, Miloš. Author
See Martinu.
Safranek, V. F. Author.
See Bugle, Harmony–2.
Saint-Foix, Georges de. Author.
See Mozart–3, App Ia.
Saint Gregory (Society of). Editors.
See Church Music.

SAINT-SAËNS, Camille
See: esp App Ia (Chantavoine biography in French).
Also:

Appreciation	Opera
Chamber Music	Organ Music
Composers–1 & 3d	Phonograph Records
Concerto	Piano Music
French Music	Program Notes
History	Vocal Music

Note: Saint-Saëns's own books of memoirs

(1919) & essays (1912), in English, apparently are O/P, as are biographies by Harvey, Lyle, etc.

Salazar, Adolfo. Author.
See Contemporary Music, App Id.
Saleski, Gdal. Author.
See Jewish Music.
Sallaway, Francis X. Author.
See Mass.
Saltonsall, Cecilia Drinker. Compiler (with Smith). See Orchestral Music.

(EL) SALVADOR (Music in).
See: Latin America.

Salvén, Erik. Author.
See Dances–2 (ed Alford).

SALZBURG/SALZBURG FESTIVAL
See: App Ib (Tenschert "Salzburg und seine Festspiele").

Salzedo, Carlos. Co-author (with Lawrence).
See Modulation.

Samaroff (-Stokowski), Olga. Author.
See Appreciation.
Note: The autobiographical "An American musician's story" (1939) apparently is O/P.

Saminsky, Lazare. Author.
See Composers–3a, Jewish Music.
Samoiloff, Lazar S. Author.
See Singing–2.
Sampson, Brook. Author. See Bach–2.

SAMPSON, George
Seven essays. vii, 232 p. Cambridge
1947.   3.00
Studies of "Bach & Shakespeare," "The operas of Mozart," etc.
Author. See also Bach–2.

Samson, Joseph. Author. See App Ia.

SAND, George
(*pseud* of Aurore Dudevant)

See also:

Chopin　　　　　　　　Liszt
History　　　　　　　　Romantic Era

WINWAR, FRANCES
The life of the heart: George Sand
& her times. 312 p, 8 pors, 6-p bibl.
Harper 1945 (4th ed n d). 　　　　**3.00**
A romantic biography of the French author.

Sandburg, Carl. Compiler.
See Folksongs–2.
Sandys, W. Author (with Forster).
See Violin.

SANKEY, Ira David

See also:

America (music in)　　　　History
Church Music　　　　　　Hymns/Hymnody

*Note: Sankey's own "My life and sacred
songs" (1900) apparently is O/P (or not
easily available in this country).*

LUDWIG, CHARLES
Sankey still sings. 164 p, 2-p bibl.
Warner Press, Anderson, Indiana
1947. 　　　　　　　　　　　　**1.25**
A biography of the singer & hymn composer.

Sansom, Clive. Editor. See Speech.
Santayana, George. Author.
See Aesthetics–1.
Saperton, David. Co-author (with Fray).
See Piano Playing–4.

SARGEANT, Winthrop
Geniuses, goddesses, and people.
317 p. Dutton 1949. 　　　　　**3.50**
*Memoirs of a music & art critic; sketches of
life among orchestral musicians; and pro-
files of celebrities (some originally published
in "Life"): including Sibelius, Beecham,
Pinza, Rubinstein, Toscanini, & Robert
Kiesow—Met. Opera cymbalist.*
Author. See also:
Jazz. Hot & hybrid (1938/46). 　　**5.00**

Sarnette, Eric. Editor. See App Ia.

SATIE, Erik

See also:

Appreciation　　　　　　History
Ballet　　　　　　　　　Phonograph Records
Composers–1 & 2　　　　Piano Music
Contemporary Music　　　Program Notes
French Music　　　　　　Vocal Music

MYERS, ROLLO H.
Erik Satie. Intro Scott Goddard.
150 p, 13 pl (pors, facs, etc), mus ex.
Dobson 1948. 　　　　　　　　　**2.50**
*The first extended study in English, including
lists of works & recordings.*

TEMPLIER, P. D. See App Ia.

Satina, Sophia. Co-author (with Bertensson
& Leydal). See Rachmaninoff.
Saunders, Richard Drake. Editor.
See California (music in). Co-editor (with
Whitlock). See America (music in).
Saunders, William. Author.
See Weber (O/P note only).

SAUVEUR, Joseph
See: Acoustics, also App Ib (Scherchen).

Sawyer, Frank Joseph. Author.
See Improvisation.

SAX, Adolphe/SAXOPHONE

See also:

Band　　　　　　　　　Instrumentation
Berlioz　　　　　　　　Instruments
History　　　　　　　　Wind Instruments

*Note: Kool's "Das Saxophon" (1931) appar-
ently is O/P (or not easily available).*

KOCHNITZKY, LÉON
Adolph Sax and his saxophone. 50
p, 14 illus (pors, facs, caricatures,
etc), 2-p bibl refs, paper. Belgian
Government Information Center,
N. Y., 1949. 　　　　　　　　　△

*Apply to the Belgian Information Center, 630
Fifth Avenue, New York City. A sprightly,
informal, but detailed story of the man, his
Frankenstein's creation, & some of his
other inventions; plus a list of articles by
Berlioz referring to Sax, and a selected list of
compositions featuring the saxophone.*

SCALES

See also:

Acoustics　　　　　　　Notation
Children–3 & 8　　　　　Piano Playing
Dictation　　　　　　　Sight-Reading
Ear Training　　　　　　Sight-Singing
Harmony　　　　　　　Singing
History　　　　　　　　Solfège/Solfeggio
Mode/Modality　　　　　Theory
Monophony　　　　　　Violin Playing

AUDA, ANTOINE. See App Ia.

CREEDY, E. J.
The major scale simply explained.
viii, 72 p, diagrs, mus ex. Oxford
1950. 　　　　　　　　　　　　**1.25**

DANIÉLOU, ALAIN
Introduction to the study of musical
scales. iv, 279 p, tables, diagrs, mus
ex, 7–p bibl, bds. India Society, △
London, 1943 (1947).   (9.00)
*A scholarly study of the physical possibilities
in sound relations and their application to
the main musical systems of the world, with
excursions into numerical symbolism &
metaphysics.*

DUNK, JOHN L.
The structure of the musical scale.
144 p, illus, tables, mus ex. Lane
1940 (repr n d).   3.50
A scholarly study.

LINDFORS, EULA ASHWORTH
The majors and their relatives: complete scale family in one-octave form
& principal triads in all keys. 31 p,
music, paper. J. Fischer n d (1930?).   1.00

LLOYD, L. S.
A musical slide-rule. 25 p, tables,
mus ex, paper + 2 paper rulers.
Oxford 1938.   .50
*An introduction to the study of musical scales,
with separate slide-rules for mean-tone temperament & equal temperament.*

SLONIMSKY, NICOLAS
Thesaurus of scales and melodic
patterns. xiii, 243 p, music. Coleman 1947.   12.00
*A functional musical equivalent of language
phrase-books & dictionaries of idiomatic expressions, this is a source book of tonal vocabularies in all possible idioms. Essential to
composers, it is fascinating—if not directly
useful—to all musicians.*

Scarborough, Dorothy. Author.
See Folksongs–2.

SCARLATTI, Alessandro
See:
Appreciation   Italian Music
Baroque Era   Opera
Composers–1   D. Scarlatti
History   Vocal Music
*Note: Standard works apparently O/P (or not
easily available) include those by Dent,
Lorenz (in German), Van den Borren (in
French), etc.*

SCARLATTI, Domenico
*Note: Standard works apparently O/P (or not
easily available) include those by Gerstenberg
(in German), Longo (in Italian), Sitwell, etc.*

See also:
Appreciation   Keyboard Instruments
Ballet   & Music
Baroque Era   Opera
Composers–1   Phonograph Records
History   Piano Music
Italian Music   Program Notes

KIRKPATRICK, RALPH
Biography. Knopf in prep.   △

VALABREGA, CESARE. See App Ic.

Sceats, Godfrey. Author.
See Karg-Elert, Organ Playing.
Schaffner, Georg. Author. See App Ib.
Schaffnit, Irma K. Co-author (with
Kirkwell). See Dances–2.
Schallenberg, Evert William. Author.
See Bach–1, Chopin–1.
Schattmann, Alfred. Author.
See R. Strauss.
Schauffler, Lawrence. Author.
See Piano Playing–1.

Schauffler, Robert Haven. Author. See:
Amateur Music. Fiddler's folly
(1942).   2.00
——. Fiddler's luck (1920/41).   2.00
Beethoven–2. The man who freed
music (1929).   2.49
Schubert–1. Ariel (1949).   5.00
Schumann–2. Florestan (1945).   3.75
App IIa. Brahms (1943), by Goss &
Schauffler.   3.00
App IIb. Magic of music (1935).   2.75
*Note: Schauffler's "The unknown Brahms"
(1933) apparently is O/P.*

Schelling, Ernest. Author (with Haake &
McConathy). See Teaching–3.
*Note: Schelling's collection of anecdotes,
"Tromboners" (1932), apparently is O/P.*

Schenk, Erich. Author. See App Ib.

SCHENKER, Heinrich
See: Tonality (Katz), Church (Routley).
*Note: Schenker's own books (in German) on
harmony, counterpoint, etc, all apparently
are O/P (or not easily available).*

Scherchen, Hermann. Author.
See Aesthetics–1, Conducting, App Ib.

Schering, Arnold. Editor.
See Anthologies.
*Note: Several other books by, or edited by,
Schering apparently are O/P (or not easily
available in this country).*

Schiavo, Giovanni Ermenegildo. Author.
See America (music in).

Schiedermair, Ludwig. Author.
See App Ib.

SCHIKANEDER, Emanuel (Johann)
See: esp App Ib (Komorzynsky: biography
in German).
Also: Mozart–3 (Benn, Dent).

Schillinger, Frances. Author.
See J. Schillinger.

SCHILLINGER, Joseph
SCHILLINGER, FRANCES
Joseph Schillinger: a memoir by his
wife.　　xi, 224 p, 9 pl (pors, etc).　△
Greenberg 1949.　　　　　　　　5.00
*Limited, autographed edition of an informal
biography of the composer-theorist.*
Author. See:
Aesthetics–1.　　Mathematical basis
of the arts (1948).　　　　　　　15.00
Composition.　　The Schillinger sys-
tem, 2 v (1946).　　　　　　　　30.00
Theory–4. Kaleidophone (1940).　　3.00

Schindler, Kurt. Author. See Folklore.

**SCHIRMER'S CONTEMPORARY COM-
POSERS SERIES**
See (for works in preparation):
Barber (Broder)　　　W. Schuman (Persi-
Copland (Berger)　　　chetti & Schreiber)
Harris (Slonimsky)
*Note: This is a series of biographical &
analytical studies edited by Nathan Broder.*

Schlesinger, Kathleen. Author.
See Instruments.

SCHLIEDER, Frederick William
Beyond the tonal horizon of music.
43 p.　　Schlieder Book Foundation,
Decatur, Illinois, 1948.　　　　　3.50
Inspirational aphorisms & epigrams.
Author. See also:
Composition.　　Lyric composition
through improvisation (1927).　　3.00
——. Same, 2nd year (1946).　　4.50
Improvisation. At the organ, Book I
(1950).　　　　　　　　　　　　2.00

Schlottmann, Jeanette. Co-author (with
Duggan & Rutledge). See Dances–2.

Schluer, Carl G. Author.
See Score–Reading.

Schmid, Adolf. Author. See Baton–1.
Editor.　See Instrumentation (Rimsky).

Schmid, Gottfried. Editor. See App Ib.

Schmid, Willy. Author. See App Ia.

Schmieder, Wolfgang. Editor.
See App Ib (Spitta), also Bach–2.

Schmitz, Elie Robert. Author.
See Debussy–2, Piano Playing–1.

Schmitz, Mary M. Author.
See App IIa (juveniles).

SCHNABEL, Artur
See: esp Beethoven–3 (Kastner).
Also:
History　　　　　Phonograph Records
Interpreters　　　Pianists
*Note: Schnabel's own books of commentaries,
"Music and the line of most resistance"
(1942) & "Reflections on music" (1934),
apparently are O/P.*

Schneider, Max. Co-editor (with Springer
& Wolffheim). See App Ib.

Schneider, Max Ferdinand. Editor (with
Reich). See App Ib (Mendelssohn).

SCHOECK, Othmar
See: App Ib (Corrodi: monograph in Ger.).

Schoen, Max. Author.
See Psychology. Co-author (with Schullian.)
See Health.
*Note: Numerous other books written or edited
by Schoen, and dealing mostly with aesthetics
& psychology, apparently are O/P (or not
easily available).*

SCHOENBERG, Arnold
1. Own Writings　　1. Life & Works

SCHOENBERG (1. Own Writings)
*General Note: Since coming to live in the
United States, the composer has abandoned
the original use of an umlaut in his name
(Schönberg), but it still appears in this form
in many reference works.*
Style and idea.　　Ed (& some tr)
Dika Newlin.　　vii, 224 p, mus ex.
Philosophical 1950.　　　　　　4.75
*Fifteen essays & sketches ("the summation of
the thought of Arnold Schoenberg"), dating
from 1912 to the present, and dealing with*

Mahler, Brahms, 12-tone technique, ear-training, etc. One of them, "Heart and brain in music" is reprinted from "The works of the mind", edited for the Committee on Social Thought by Robert B. Heywood (University of Chicago Press, 1947, $4.00).

See also:

Composition. Models for beginners
in composition (1942).   2.00
Harmony–1. Theory of (1948).   7.50

SCHOENBERG (2. Life & Works)

See also:

Appreciation	History
Berg	Modern Music
California	Phonograph Records
(ed Saunders)	Program Notes
Composers–2 & 3b (esp	Tonality/Atonality
Newlin)	Twelve-Tone
Contemporary Music	Technique

Note: Standard works apparently O/P (or not easily available) include those by Armitage, Schindler, Stefan (in German), Wellesz, etc.

LEIBOWITZ, RENÉ
Schoenberg and his school: the contemporary stage of the language of music. Tr Dika Newlin. xxvi, 305 p, 1-p bibl. Philosophical 1949.   4.75

The first extended study in English, translated from the French edition of 1947 (which is listed in App Ia). Analytical studies of Berg & Webern also are included, together with lists of works & recordings of all three composers.

Schoen-René, Anna Eugénie. Author.

Note: A book of memoirs, "America's musical heritage" (1941), apparently is O/P.

Scholes, Percy Alfred. Author. See:

Appreciation. Listener's guide to
music (1919/42).   2.00
——. History & technics (1936).   4.00
Bibliography. List of books about
music (1940).   .75
Burney. Great Dr Burney (1949).   19.00
Children–2. Complete book of the
great musicians (1931).   3.50
Dictionaries of Music. Oxford companion (1938/47).   14.50
Dictionaries of Terms. Scholes music
handbook (1936).   1.50
Ear-Training. Beginner's guide to
harmony (1922/4).   1.25
England—music in. Mirror of music
(1947).   25.00

God Save the King. (1942).   .85
History–2. Listener's (1923/43).   7.00
History–3. Miniature (1928/34).   .75
History–5. Columbia (5 booklets,
1930/8).   6.25
Opera–1. Miniature hist. (1931).   .50
Puritans. And music (1934).   7.50

Note: A book of essays, "Crochets" (1924), & several other appreciation books apparently are O/P (or not easily available).

SCHÖNBERG, Arnold

Catalogued under Schoenberg (in conformity with the composer's current practice).

SCHOOL MUSIC

1. **General, Historical**
2. **Appreciation, Phonograph Records, etc.**
3. **Instrumental**
4. **Choirs & Singing**

General Note: The distinction between this main category and such related subject-headings as Children, Education, Teaching, etc (see cross-references below) is drawn often for convenience only and should not be taken too seriously. Insofar as possible, however, the books listed below deal specifically with music in schools and they are of primary interest to school-music teachers, supervisors, & students—although of course many of them also are useful to private teachers, parents, & independent students.

General textbooks & "methods" of various kinds, which are used in many schools but which are not written primarily for school use, are not included here, but are listed under the specialized subjects (Counterpoint, History, etc).

SCHOOL MUSIC
(1. General, Historical)

See also:

America (music in)	Libraries (Bohman &
Children	Dillon)
Colleges	Operetta (Jones &
Composition (Hill)	Wilson)
Community Music	Psychology (esp Mursell & Glenn)
Dances–1	School Music–2, 3, 4
Education	Teaching
Examinations	Tests
History	

Note: Standard works apparently O/P (or not easily available) include those by Beattie et al, Cady, Danington, Dykema, Farnsworth, Fox

& Hopkins, Giddings & Baker, Griffiths, Heffernan & Ireland, Hubbard, Mayne, McKenzie, Norton, Tapper, Van Peursem, etc.

ANNETTE, THOMAS
Music in the rural schools: a simple & direct guide ... viii, 123 p, diagrs, mus ex, 11–p bibl (& music & record list). Boston 1938.   1.50

BEST, CLARENCE J.
Music rooms and equipment. Pref William R. Sur. 111 p, illus (photos, diagrs, floor plans, etc), 3–p bibl, paper. Music Educators National Conference 1949.   1.50
Music Education Research Council Bulletin No 17: a comprehensive study, covering all pertinent practical problems.

BIRGE, EDWARD BAILEY
History of public school music in the United States. 323 p, illus, 2–p bibl, mus ex. Ditson (1928) rev aug ed 1939.   2.10
A standard over-all survey.

BORLAND, J. E.
Musical foundations: a record of musical work in schools & training colleges; and a comprehensive guide for teachers of school music. viii, 87 p, mus ex. Oxford 1927.   1.00
From the British point of view.

BROOKS, B. MARIAN & BROWN, HARRY A.
Music education in the elementary school. viii, 376 p, 8 photos, 20-p annot bibl. American 1946.   4.25
Music education in transition in America, foundations for a new music education, curriculum & teaching, substance of a world program for music education in the elementary school.

COLE, NATALIE ROBINSON
The arts in the classroom. 137 p, 16–p photos (C. K. Eaton). Day 1940 (4th pr n d).   2.75
Including sections on creative painting & clay work, free rhythmic dancing, etc

DYKEMA, PETER W. & CUNDIFF, H. M.
New school music handbook: a guide for teaching school music ... xiv, 382 p, illus mus ex, 18–p bibl. Birchard (1923) rev ed 1939.   3.50
A general introduction, especially for teachers in the grades & junior high schools.

DYKEMA, PETER W. & GEHRKENS, K. W.
The teaching and administration of high school music. xxiv, 614 p, illus, mus ex, chap bibls. Birchard 1941.   4.40

A comprehensive, detailed survey, including specimen courses of study.

EARHART, WILL
The meaning and teaching of music. xii, 250 p, mus ex, 4–p bibl. Witmark 1935.   4.00
Aesthetic, philosophical, & psychological considerations in teaching.

FLAGG, MARION
Musical learning: a guide to child growth. xi, 195 p, diagrs, mus ex. Birchard 1949.   2.75
Includes notes on discipline—old & new— & classroom management techniques.

GEHRKENS, KARL W.
(See also Dykema & Gehrkens above.)
An introduction to school music teaching. vii, 174 p, charts, 8-p annot bibl. Birchard 1919.   2.00
Music in the grade schools: grades 1 to 6. 236 p, mus ex. Birchard 1934 (1948).   2.50
Music in the junior high school: grades 7 to 9. xvii, 228 p. Birchard 1936 (6th pr 1947).   2.75
Three standard works by a noted authority.

GIDDINGS, T. P.
Grade school music teaching for superintendents, music supervisors, & grade teachers. viii, 257 p, 2 illus. Congdon 1919.   1.80
With emphasis on sight-singing, & a chapter on music appreciation by A. M. Fryberger.

GRIFFITHS, VERNON
An experiment in school music-making. xii, 103 p, fold-out table, mus ex, 3–p bibl. Oxford 1941.   2.00
New Zealand Education Research Series 15.

JONES, JOHN PAUL
The director of school music. vii, 134 p, diagrs, 2–p bibl. Jenkins Music Co, Kansas City, Missouri, 1949.   2.00
Practical notes on the requirements, demands, & techniques.

KINSCELLA, HAZEL G. & TIERNEY, E. M.
Music in the small school. x, 176 p, photos, charts, mus ex, 5–p bibl. Nebraska 1939 (1941).   Δ
A new (1951) edition is in preparation.

KWALWASSER, JACOB
Problems in public school music. vii, 159 p. Witmark (1932) rev ed 1941.   2.50
Highly individual views on "false objectives," "sciences vs art," etc.

McConathy, Osbourne (& others)
Music in rural education: based on
"The music hour" courses. vii, 310
p, tables, 1–p bibl. Silver 1933 (1937). 2.00
Co-authors: W. Otto Miessner, Edward Bailey
Birge, & Mabel E. Bray, in collaboration
with Fannie W. Dunn, Frank A. Beach, &
Josephine Murray.

Moore, Stephen S.
The golden string: the story of the
origin, rise, & development of non-
competitive school music festivals.
xiv, 97 p, 7 photos (pors, etc). △
Nelson, London, 1949. (1.80)

Morgan, Vincent
Music in the secondary school: a
study of music education in private
boys' schools in New England. 71 p.
Worcester Art Museum, Worcester,
Mass., 1940. 2.25
Reports on visits to some 27 schools.

Murray, Josephine & Bathurst, E. G.
Creative ways for children's programs. xiv, 396 p, photos, mus ex,
9–p annot bibl. Silver 1938. 3.10

Mursell, James L.
Music in American schools. v, 312
p, photos. Silver 1943. 3.10
A comprehensive, authoritative survey.

(Music Educators National Confer-
ence). (*See also Best above.*)
Music supervision and administra-
tion in the schools. 32 p, paper.
MENC 1949. .50
Prepared by Charles M. Dennis, Peter W.
Dykema, & others. Music Education
Research Council Bulletin No 18.

Note: In addition to various yearly reports
& program-outlines, already published, the
MENC is preparing a booklet on "School
Music in action," an implementation of the
"Music education source book" (see Educa-
tion, ed Morgan).

Myers, Louise Kifer
Teaching music: in the elementary
school. xvi, 327 p, mus ex, 20–p annot
bibl. Prentice 1950. 5.00
A suggested program & its implementation;
with sources of materials, chapter subjects
for discussion & teacher's suggestions.

(N. Y. State School Music Assn)
The NYSSMA manual, 1949: the
classification plan, graded music for
band, orchestra, choirs, & vocal &
instrumental solos. 180 p, paper.

N. Y. State School Music Association (1940) rev ed 1948, via MENC. 1.50
A state classification plan for music com-
petition festivals.

Perham (Krone), Beatrice
Music in the new school. x, 188 p,
illus, mus ex, 1–p bibl & chap bibls.
Kjos (1937) rev ed 1951 (1947). 3.00
"Progressive" educators' points of view.

Pitts, Lilla Belle
The music curriculum in a changing
world. v, 165 p, 7 charts. Silver
1944. 2.65
The effect of school changes on the study of
music in the schools.

Roberts, Helen V. S.
Music-work in the school: a handbook for class-teachers. Forew
Ernest Read, viii, 154 p, mus ex, chap
bibls. Heffer n d (1937). 2.75
Bird's-eye (British) survey, with a summary
of teaching devices & material lists.

(School Music Section, ISM)
An outline of musical education: pro-
gressive schemes of work from nursery
school to university. 30 p, paper.
Curwen 1948. .75
Prepared by the school music section of the
(British) Incorporated Society of Musicians.

Smith, W. J.
Music in education. 160 p, 2–p bibl.
Faber 1947. (2.50)
An account of the progressive, experimental
work at Alleyn's School, Dulwich, England,
where musical peformance is made an integral
part of boys' education.

Taylor, Frederick A.
Course of study in music. 90 p,
mus ex. Humphries 1946. 2.00
For elementary grades & jr high school.

Thompson, Carl O. & Nordholm, H.
Keys to teaching elementary school
music. xii, 271 p + 3–p index, illus,
mus ex, chap bibls. Schmitt 1949. 4.00
With supplementary materials & record lists,
glossary of musical terms, etc.

Ward, Arthur E.
Music education for high schools.
xii, 330 p, illus, tables, mus ex, chap
bibls. American 1941. 2.75
With practical music-course outlines.

Wilson, Harry Robert
Music in the high school. vii, 440 p,
photos, diagrs. Silver 1941. 3.50
Modern trends in secondary education,

musical experience, & administration. Lists of materials are included.

WRIGHT, FRANCES
Elementary music education: theory & practice. 238 p, tables, mus ex, 13–p bibl. (1939) C. Fischer rev ed 1941.   3.50

SCHOOL MUSIC
(2. Appreciation, Phonograph Records, etc)

See also:

Appreciation   Program Notes
Children–2   School Music–1
Phonograph Records   Teaching–1

Note: Standard works apparently O/P (or not easily available) include those by Giddings & others, Glenn & Lowry, etc.

BURKE, CASSIE (& *others*)
America's musical heritage. 368 p, illus (Milo Winter), music, 2–p bibl. Laidlaw 1942.   2.00
Co-authors: Virginia Meierhoffer & Claude Anderson Phillips. A junior high-school text stressing the importance of music in the development of American culture.

FAULKNER (OBERNDORFER), ANNE SHAW
What we hear in music: a course of study in music appreciation & history for use in high schools, normal schools, colleges, & universities. 704 p, illus. RCA Victor (1913) 12th rev ed 1943 (1948).   2.50
A standard textbook for school (& home) use. Includes detailed analyses (p 379/643) of RCA Victor record illustrations. (For a companion work, see Kinscella below.)

FAVILLE, MILDRED
Brief history and appreciation of music. 78 p, paper. Kenyon Press, Wisconsin (1926) 2nd rev ed 1931.   .75
Concise textbook for secondary schools.

FRYBERGER, AGNES MOORE
Listening lessons in music: graded for schools. Intro Osbourne Mc-Conathy. xvi, 255 p, 2–p bibl. Silver (1916) rev ed 1925.   2.40
Descriptive notes with record references.

KINSCELLA, HAZEL GERTRUDE
Music and romance: a course of study in music appreciation. Forew Frances Elliott Clark. 572 p, illus, mus ex. RCA Victor (1930) new ed 1941.   2.25
For junior high-school use with recommended (RCA Victor) records. Preparatory work to that by Faulkner above.

LEAVITT, HELEN S. & FREEMAN, W. S.
Recordings for the elementary school. viii, 127 p, mus ex, 3–p bibl. Durrell 1949, via Crown 1950.   2.40
Up-to-date classified record lists; a companion work to Barbour & Freeman's "Children's record book" (see Children–2).

PITTS, LILLA BELLE
Music integration in the junior high school. Intro Peter W. Dykema. xiii, 218 p, mus ex. Birchard 1935.   2.75
The correlation of music with other activities. Includes lists of picture sources & a 12-p bibl of collateral reading.

SCHOOL MUSIC
(3. Bands, & Orchestras, Conducting, Instrumental)

See also:

Arranging–1   Instruments
Band–1 & 2   Orchestra
Children–4 & 6   School Music–1 & 4
Community Music   Teaching–2 & 3
Conducting

Note: Standard works apparently O/P (or not easily available) include those by Abbot, Clifford, King, Van Bodegraven, Vandercook, Victor, etc.

ALLEN, J. WORTH
The orchestra director's manual: practical suggestion & useful information for orchestra directors. iv, 59 p. C. Fischer n d (1927?).   1.00

BAKALEINIKOFF, VLADIMIR
Elementary rules of conducting: for orchestra, band, & chorus. 52 p, mus ex, diagrs, paper. Belwin 1938.   1.25
A practical manual, intended especially for high-school band & orch. leaders.

CARR, RAYMOND NORMAN
Building the school orchestra: a guide for leaders. 111 p, illus, mus ex. Conn 1923.   2.00

CARSE, ADAM
On conducting school orchestras. 16 p, paper. Augener n d (1924?).   .50

CHURCH, NORVAL L. & DYKEMA, P. W.
Manual for the use of the Church & Dykema "Modern Band Training Series" (Book I, parts 1 & 2, complete): graded material for simultaneous performance by players of various degrees of advancement; adapted for instruction in full band & in class groups. vi, 107 p, mus ex, paper. Birchard 1939.   1.00

Instructor's manual for the Church
and Dykema "Modern Orchestra
Training Series," Books I & II. 69
1934. .60

GORDON, LOUIS MORTON
The modern school orchestra and its
development: the string choir, the
brass choir, the wood-wind choir,
instruments of percussion. 108 p,
illus, mus ex. Willis 1919. 1.25
*For conductors of school or community
orchestras.*

HINDSLEY, MARK H.
School band and orchestra administration. 107 p, diagrs, tables,
paper. Boosey 1940. 2.00
*A detailed, practical manual on administra-
tive procedures.*

JONES, LLEWELLYN BRUCE
Building the instrumental music
department. vi, 143 p, charts, chap
bibls. C. Fischer 1949. **3.50**
*Notes on organizing & directing the musical
activities program, administering the physical
plant & equipment, and establishing favorable
teacher-pupil relations.*

MADDY, J. E. & GIDDINGS, T. P.
Instrumental class teaching: a prac-
tical teachers guide in instrumental
music classes . . . 99 p, illus, mus ex.
Willis 1928. 1.50
For use with "The Universal Teacher."

Instrumental technique for orchestra
and band: an exhaustive & practical
textbook for teachers, conductors, &
students. viii, 267 p, illus, mus ex.
Willis (1926) 7th enl rev ed n d. 3.00
*A practical manual with appendices on the
dance orch. & instrument repairing.*

(NATIONAL SCHOOL BAND, ORCHESTRA, AND
VOCAL ASSOCIATION)
Instrumental ensembles: woodwind,
brass, string, & mixed; graded lists
of recommended materials. 39 p,
paper. NSBOVA 1948, via MENC. 1.00
Music lists for band, orchestra, string
orchestra, & chorus. 23 p, paper.
NSBOVA 1949, via MENC. .50
*Obtainable from the National School Band,
Orchestra, & Vocal Association, 64 East
Jackson Blvd, Chicago, Illinois.*

NEWTON, L. G. & YOUNG, T. CAMPBELL
The book of the school orchestra.
xii, 159 p, frontis, diagrs, mus ex.
Oxford 1936. 1.50
From the British point of view.

NORMANN, THEODORE F.
Instrumental music in the public
schools. vii, 349 p, charts, mus ex,
chap bibls. (1939) Ditson 1941. 3.00

PRESCOTT, G. R. & CHIDESTER, L. W.
Getting results with school bands.
xiii, 273 p, 16 pl, 69 charts & b&ws,
5-p bibl & chap bibls. C. Fischer &
P. A. Schmitt 1938 (6th pr 1947). 5.00
*A practical, detailed textbook for school band
& orchestra leaders.*

RIGHTER, CHARLES BOARDMAN
Success in teaching school orchestras
and bands. ix, 211 p, mus ex, 2-p
bibl. Schmitt 1945. 3.50
*A conductor's handbook on technical &
administrative problems.*

SUR, WILLIAM R. (*ed*)
Piano instruction in the schools: a
report & interpretation of a national
survey. vii, 63 p, photos, tables, 1-p
bibl, paper. MENC 1949. 1.00
*Based on a survey by the research department
of Foote, Cone, & Belding, with an educational analysis by the editor.*

VAN BODEGRAVEN, PAUL, & WILSON, H. R.
The school music conductor: problems & practices in choral & instrumental conducting. vi, 168 p, illus,
mus ex, chap bibls. Hall McCreary
1942. 2.00

WARD, SYLVAN DONALD
The instrumental director's handbook. 93 p, illus, bds. Rubank 1940. 1.25

WOODS, GLENN H.
Public school orchestras and bands.
204 p, 18 illus, diagrs, mus ex, 2-p
bibl. Ditson 1920. 2.00

SCHOOL MUSIC
(4. Choirs & Singing)
See also:

Amateur Music	Folksongs
Children–7	Operetta
Choir/Choral	School Music–1 & 3
Christiansen	(Van Bodegraven &
Community Music	Wilson)
Dann	Song(s)
Finn	Songbooks

*Note: Standard works apparently O/P (or not
easily available) include those by Callinan,
Quigley, Taylor, Venables, etc.*

*The list below does not include numerous
series of song & chorus collections (largely
words & music only) especially designed for
school use: "The American Singer," Dann's*

"Year" series, "The Music Hour," "Singing School," "Universal Song," "World of Music," etc.

BURNS, SAMUEL T.
Harmonic skills used by selected high-school choral leaders. viii, 115 p, tables, bibl refs. Teachers College 1945. 1.85
Teachers College "Contributions to Education" No 905: a thesis based on data supplied by some 624 selected choral leaders.

DANN, HOLLIS
Conductor's book: a guide to choral song interpretation. 172 p, mus ex. American 1936. 2.00
For use with the Dann "Song" series; includes record lists, biographical sketches, & correlation units.

HARDY, T. MASKELL
Practical suggestions for the teaching of vocal music in schools. 3 v. Diagrs, mus ex, paper. Curwen.
V 1: The infants' school. xvi, 114 p. N d. (1.50)
V 2: The junior school. xxiii, 185 p. 1937. (1.80)
V 3: The senior or secondary school. xxvii, 235 p. 1937. (2.25)
From the British point of view.

HOWERTON, GEORGE
The use of Victor records in the high school choral training program. v, 58 p, paper. RCA Victor 1944. .50

JACQUES, REGINALD
Voice training in schools. viii, 108 p, mus ex. Oxford 1934. 1.25
An elementary British approach, involving use of the "tonic sol-fa" notation.

KRONE, MAX T.
The chorus and its conductor: from organization to performance. x, 134 p, illus, mus ex, paper. Kjos 1945 (1948). 2.00
Primarily for school choir-leaders.

MACMAHON, D. & CHAMBERLAIN, M.
A school music course: new approach to music in schools; complete guide for the teacher on method & syllabus. iv, 72 p, mus ex, paper. Novello 1939. (1.80)

PIERCE, ANNE ELSIE
Class lessons in singing: with added suggestions by Estelle Liebling. xi, 212 p, illus, music, ½-p bibl. Silver 1937. 3.25

RORKE, GENEVIEVE A.
Choral teaching at the junior high school level. Intro Louis Woodson Curtis. xii, 114 p, illus, mus ex, ½-p bibl. Hall McCreary 1947. 2.00

VENABLES, LEONARD C.
The school teacher's music guide. xvi, 333 p, diagrs, mus ex. Curwen (1911) 2nd ed n d. (3.50)
Preparation in ordinary & tonic sol-fa notations for the British School Teachers' Music Certificate in voice production.
Voice training for schools. v, 80 p, mus ex, paper. Curwen 4th ed n d (1932?). (.80)

WELCH, LUCY M.
Song teaching: a general handbook. 196 p, mus ex. Curwen n d (1932?). (2.25)
Practical advice on children's classes.

WRIGHT, FRANCES & LOSSING, LAVERNA
Song source material for social study units. xv, 47 p, paper. Teachers College (1932) 4th rev enl ed 1946. .90
Classified song lists (some 5000 references from some 200 collections), arranged by national sources & subjects.

School Music Section of the Incorporated Society of Musicians. Publishers. See School Music–1.

Scholz, János. Editor. See Theatre.

SCHOPENHAUER, Arthur
See: App Ib (Schopenhauer: "Schriften über Musik")

Schrade, Leo. Author.
See Beethoven–2, Monteverdi.
Schreiber, Flora Rheta. Co-author (with Persichetti). See W. Schuman.

SCHUBERT, Franz
1. Life　　2. Works

SCHUBERT (1. Life)
See also:

Appreciation	History
Autographs	Letters
Classic Era	Program Notes
Composers–1	Romantic Era
Facsimiles	Vienna

Also: App IIa (juveniles by Goss, Wheeler & Deucher).

Note: Standard works apparently O/P (or not

easily available) include the letters ed Deutsch (but see App Ib for a German edition by Reich); also biographies by Bates, Bie, Bruyr (in French), Cluisam, Dahms (in German), Duncan, Ewen, Janetschek (in German), Kreissle von Hellborn, Landormy (in French), Stefan (in German), etc.

BLOM, ERIC
Schubert. 14 p, cover por, paper.
Novello n d (1938).   .40
Miniature biography ("great musicians").

BUENZOD, EMMANUEL.   See App Ia.

DEUTSCH, OTTO ERICH
The Schubert reader: a life of Franz Schubert in letters & documents.
Tr Eric Blom. xxxii, 1040 p, 37 pl, 42 b&ws, 4-p bibl. Norton 1947.   10.00
A monumental documentary work, revised & enlarged from the author's "Franz Schubert: die Dokumente seines Lebens und Schaffens," published in 1913. It includes letters & a catalogue of Schubert's works, as well as every known document bearing on his life.

EINSTEIN, ALFRED
Schubert: a musical portrait. Tr. David Ascoli. ix, 343 p, mus ex, bibl refs. Oxford 1951.   5.00
A companion work to "Mozart: his character, his work" (see Mozart-2).

FLOWER, NEWMAN
Franz Schubert: the man and his circle. x, 262 p, 28 pl, 33-p bibl incl Schubert editions).   Cassell (1928) rev ed 1949.   5.50
A standard work, O/P for some years in this country (including reprint editions).

HUTCHINGS, ARTHUR
Schubert. vi, 233 p, 8 pl (pors facs, etc), mus ex, 3-p bibl. Dent 1945; Pellegrini 1949.   2.50
"Master Musicians" series, including the usual calendar, personalia, catalogue of works, etc. This work supersedes an earlier biography in the same series by Edmonstoune Duncan (1905, 1934).

KOBALD, KARL.   See App Ib.

Note: Marshall's English translation of Kobald's biography (1928) is O/P.

KOLB, ANNETTE.   See App Ib.

MALHERBE, HENRY.   See App Ia.

PAUMGARTNER, BERNHARD.   See App Ib.

PEYSER, HERBERT F.
Schubert and his work. v, 58 p, 11 illus (pors, facs, etc), bds.   Grosset 1950.   .50

"N. Y. Philharmonic-Symphony Society Musical Biographies" series. Originally published, for society members only, in 1946.

REHBERG, WALTER & PAULA.   See App Ib.

REICH, WILLI (ed).   See App Ib.

SCHAUFFLER, ROBERT HAVEN
Franz Schubert: the Ariel of music.
xiv, 427 p, 25 pl (pors, facs, etc), mus ex, 3-p bibl. Putnam 1949.   5.00
A new romantic biography (including a psychoanalysis of Schubert's love-life) & "appreciative" study of the more important works; plus a glossary, index of compositions, & 6-p representative list of recordings.

WEINGARTNER, FELIX & STUDER, CARMEN.
See App Ib.

WHITAKER-WILSON, C.
Franz Schubert: man & composer, the story of a man who never wasted time. xi, 266 p, illus (Ruby Margaret Whittemore), mus ex. Reeves 1928 (repr n d).   (4.50)
A Schubert centenary publication.

SCHUBERT (2. Works)

See also:

Appreciation	Program Notes
Chamber Music	Song(s)
Choir/Choral-3	Songbooks
Church Music	Song Translations
Composers-1	String Quartet
Concerto	Symphony
Goethe	Themes
Orchestral Music	Timing
Phonograph Records	Violin Music
Piano Music	Vocal Music

Note: Standard works apparently O/P (or not easily available) include those by Brent-Smith, Capell, Fox Strangways, Garren, Porter, etc; those in French by de Curzon, Gallet, etc; those in German by Bauer, Günther, Lafite, von der Pfordten, Rissé, Wissig, etc.

ABRAHAM, GERALD (ed)
The music of Schubert. 342 p, mus ex, 8-p bibl (A. Hyatt King).
Norton 1947.   3.00
An anthology of critical studies by Carner, Dale, Deutsch, King, Pritchard, Robertson, Rosenthal & Loft, and Westrup; plus a chronology & catalogue of works.

BRENT-SMITH, ALEXANDER
Schubert quartet in D minor & octet.
60 p, mus ex, paper.   Oxford 1927 (1948).   1.00
"Musical Pilgrim" series of analyses.

COEUROY, ANDRÉ.   See App Ia.

CRABSHAW, CYRIL M.
Schubert's Unfinished Symphony:
a study of the immortal favorite.
Hinrichsen in prep.   **1.00**
"Miniature Survey" M–8.

LE MASSENA, C. F.
The songs of Schubert: a guide for
singers, teachers, students, & accompanists, with interpretative suggestions by Hans Merx. vii, 184 p, mus
ex. G. Schirmer 1928.   **2.50**
*Descriptive summaries and analyses of individual songs, plus indices by English titles,
poets, & vocal compasses.*

SCHÜNEMANN, GEORG (*ed*). See App Ib.

WESTRUP. J. A.
Introduction to the music of Schu- △
bert. Dobson in prep.   **1.00**

Schuh, Willi. Author, editor. See App Ib.
Schullian, Dorothy May. Author (with
Schoen). See Health.
Schultz, Arnold. Author.
See Piano Playing–1.
Schultz, Ernest John. Co-author (with
Hood). See Children–3.

SCHUMAN, William Howard
See also:

American Music	Contemporary Music
Appreciation	Phonograph Records
Composers–2 & 3a	Program Notes

PERSICHETTI, V. & SCHREIBER, F. R.
William Schuman.
G. Schirmer in prep.   △
*"Schirmer's Contemporary Composers" series; biography, list & analyses of works,
bibliography, & discography.*

SCHUMANN, Clara (*née* Wieck)
See: esp App Ib (Henning: "Die Freundschaft Clara Schumanns mit Johannes
Brahms"), App IIa (Spaeth juvenile).
Also:

Appreciation	Pianists
Brahms–1	Romantic Era
History	R. Schumann–1 & 2
Mendelssohn–1 & 2	Song(s)

*Note: Standard works apparently O/P (or not
easily available) include those by Burk, Kleefe'd (in German), Litzmann, May, Eugenie
Schumann, etc.*

Schumann, Elisabeth. Author.
See Song(s).

SCHUMANN, Robert
1. Own Writings   2. Life & Works

SCHUMANN (1. Own Writings)
*Note: Various editions of the letters (in English & German) apparently are O/P (or not
easily available in this country).*

(REICH, WILLI, *ed*). See App Ib.

(RITTER, FANNY RAYMOND, *ed & tr*)
Music and musicians: essays & criticisms. 2 v. Reeves 1877-1880 (repr
n d).   **8.50**
V 1: xii, 418 p, frontis, mus ex. 8th
ed (n d).
V 2: xiii, 540, mus ex. 4th ed.
*Still perhaps the most notable examples of
music criticism by a composer.*

*Note: Another edition (ed Konrad Wolff, tr
Paul Rosenfeld), pub by Pantheon in 1947,
apparently is O/P.*

SCHUMANN (2. Life & Works)
See also:

Appreciation	Piano Music
Ballet (ed Haskell)	Program Notes
Brahms–1	Romantic Era
Chamber Music	C. Schumann
Composers–1	(refs only)
Concerto	Song(s)
Criticism	Song Translations
History	Symphony
Hoffmann	Themes
Letters	Timing
Literature	Vocal Music
Phonograph Records	

Also: App IIa (Spaeth, Wheeler juveniles).

*Note: Standard works apparently O/P (or not
easily available) include those by Abert (in
German), Basch, Bedford, Dahms (in German), Drinker (but see note under author
entry), Fox Strangways & Wilson, Fuller
Maitland, Garren, Herbert, Niecks, Painter,
Patterson, Pitrou (in French) Reissmann,
Eugenie Schumann, Wasielewski, etc.*

CHISSELL, JOAN
Schumann. xi, 275 p, 8 pl (pors, facs,
etc), mus ex, 2–p bibl. Dent 1948.   **2.50**
*"Master Musicians" series, with the usual
calendar, personalia, catalogue of works, etc.
Not yet announced for American issue by
Pellegrini & Cudahy*

EVANS, EDWIN, *Jr*
Schumann. 14 p, cover por, paper.
Novello n d (c. 1940?).   **.40**
Miniature biography ("great musicians").

JELLIFF, CLARA MARSTON
The courtship of Robert Schumann:
a play in 3 acts. 93 p. Wetzel Pub
Co, Los Angeles, 1947.   2.50

MÜLLER, ERNST. See App Ib.

SCHAUFFLER, ROBERT HAVEN
Florestan: the life & work of Robert
Schumann. xiv, 574 p, 19 illus (pors
& fac), mus ex, 3–p bibl. Holt 1945
(5th pr 1946).   3.75
*A romantic biography, with genealogical
chart, lists of works & recordings, etc.*

WÖRNER, KARL H. See App Ib.

SCHUMANN-HEINK, Ernestine
See:
America (music in)   Phonograph Records
History   Singers
Opera   Singing
Note: M. Lawton's biography (1928) is O/P.

Schünemann, Georg. Editor. See App Ib.

SCHÜTZ, Heinrich
See: App Ia (Pirro biography in
French), App Ib (Piersig study in German,
Schütz letters in German).

Also:
Appreciation   History
Baroque Era   Madrigal
Choir/Choral-3   Phonograph Records
Church Music   Program Notes
Composers-1   Vocal Music
Concerto

*Note: Standard works apparently O/P (or not
easily available) include those in German by
Einstein, Gerber, Moser, Müller, Schäfer,
Schuh, Spitta, etc.*

Schweiger, Hertha. Editor.
See Organ Music.

SCHWEITZER, Albert

1. Own Writings   2. Life & Work

*Note: Although most of Schweitzer's books
listed below do not deal with music, they are
included here owing to the general interest
in all activities of this remarkable man, whose
later fame may have eclipsed—but never
obliterated—his distinction as a musician.*

See also:
Bach–1. Biography (1911).   8.00
Goethe. Four studies (1949).   2.50
App. Ib. Bach (in German).   14.00

—. Bergel, ed: Albert Schweitzers
Leben und Denken, autobiographical
selections in German.   1.90

*Note: Except for the last two works im-
mediately above, Schweitzer's books in German are not included in the present Guide.
One of special musical interest, "Deutsche und
französische Orgelbaukunst und Orgelkunst"
(Breitkopf & Härtel 1927), has not been translated, as far as we know, and the German edition apparently is O/P (or not easily available
in this country).*

African notebook. Tr Mrs C. E. B.
Russell. 144 p, photos, map. Holt
1939.   2.00

Christianity and the religions of the
world. Tr Johanna Powers; forew
Nathaniel Micklem. xix, 86 p.
(1923) Holt 1939.   1.25

Indian thought and its development.
Tr Mrs C. E. B. Russell. xii, 272 p.
Holt 1936 (1947?).   2.50
*Discusses poems & hymns, but not Indian
music itself. Originally in German, 1934.*

Memoirs of childhood and youth.
Tr C. T. Campion. 78 p. (1924)
Macmillan 1949.   1.75
*First American edition of a companion work
to "Out of my life and thought" (see below).
Includes considerable material on Schweitzer's
early musical experiences & training.*

The mystery of the kingdom of God:
the secret of Jesus' messiahship &
passion. Tr & intro Walter Lowrie.
xv, 174 p. (1914) Macmillan new ed
1950.   3.00

The mysticism of Paul the Apostle.
Tr William Montgomery; pref F. C.
Burkitt. xv, 411 p. Holt 1931.   3.00

On the edge of the primeval forest;
and More from the primeval forest.
2 v in 1. Tr C. T. Campion. vii,
222 p, 35 photos. Macmillan 1948.   4.50
*The first work was originally published in
German in 1921, in English in 1922; the latter
(titled in some editions "The forest hospital
at Lambaréné") was originally published in
German in 1925/6/8, in English in 1931.
In its combined form, the book covers the
"experiences & observations of a doctor in
equatorial Africa," 1913/7 & 1924/7.*

Out of my life and thought: an autobiography. Tr C. T. Campion; postscript Everett Skillings. 274 p. (1933)
Holt rev ed 1949.   3.50
*The famous autobiography (a companion
work to the "Memoirs of childhood & youth".*

above), originally published in German in 1931, in English in 1933; now brought up to date by Skillings's "postscript", which deals with the period 1932/49. Chapter 7 is on "The Bach book," chapter 8 "On organs & organ building.

Paul and his interpreters: a critical history. Tr W. Montgomery. xiii, 253 p, bibl refs. Macmillan 1912 (1951). **3.50**

The philosophy of civilization. Tr C. T. Campion; rev Mrs C. E. B. Russell. 2 v in 1: xvii, 347 p, bibl refs. (1923) Macmillan 1949. **5.00**

Schweitzer's major philosophical work, originally published in 2 volumes: "The decay & restoration of civilization" (1923, 2nd ed 1932) & "Civilization & ethics" (1923, tr J. Naish; 3rd ed tr Campion, rev Russell, 1946). A 3rd volume is in preparation.

The psychiatric study of Jesus: exposition & criticism. Tr & ed Charles R. Joy; forew Winfred Overholser. xii, 81 p. Beacon 1948. **2.00**
The first English version of a work originally written in German in 1913.

The quest of the historical Jesus: a critical study of its progress from Reimarus to Wrede. Tr M. Montgomery; pref F. C. Burkitt. x, 410 p. (1910) Macmillan 2nd ed 1922 (1948). **5.00**

JOY, CHARLES R., (*ed*)
Albert Schweitzer: an anthology. xxviii, 323 p, 3–p bibl. Beacon presentation ed 1947. **5.00**
Same, Harper trade ed 1947. **3.75**
Representative selections from Schweitzer's writings, including "The search for beauty" from the Bach biography (see Bach–1). The editor contributes a biographical introduction.

The animal world of Albert Schweitzer: jungle insights into reverence for life. 207 p, photos (Joy), illus (Richard Bartlett). Beacon 1950. **3.00**
An anthology of Schweitzer's writings about animals, translated by the editor.

Music in the life of Albert Schweitzer: with selections from his writings. Intro Charles Münch. xvii, 300 p, 10 pl (pors, etc), bibl refs. Beacon, also Harper, 1951. **4.00**
An anthology of Schweitzer's writings on music, many of which have been unavailable hitherto in English.

The wit and wisdom of Albert Schweitzer. vii, 104 p, bibl refs. Beacon 1949. **2.00**
An anthology of aphorisms, maxims, etc,

translated & with an introduction by the editor.

SCHWEITZER (2. Life & Work)

See also:
Bach	Organ Playing
History	Organists
Interpreters	Phonograph Records

Also: App IIa (Gollomb juvenile).

Note: Regester's "Albert Schweitzer: the man & his work" (1931) apparently is O/P.

CAMPION, C. T. (*comp*)
Albert Schweitzer: philosopher, theologian, musician, doctor; some biographical notes. 30 p, illus, bds. Macmillan 1928. **1.00**
A booklet by the translator of many of Schweitzer's works.

HAGEDORN, HERMANN
Prophet in the wilderness: the story of Albert Schweitzer. 221 p, frontis por, 6–p bibl. Macmillan 1947. **3.00**

JOY, CHARLES R. & ARNOLD, MELVIN
The Africa of Albert Schweitzer. Unp (159 p,) photos (Charles R. (Joy). Beacon 1948. **3.75**
Mainly pictures, with colored end-paper maps, and a concluding essay by Schweitzer: "Our task in equatorial Africa."

KRAUS, OSCAR
Albert Schweitzer: his work & his philosophy. Tr E. G. McCalman; intro A. D. Lindsay. x, 75 p, frontis por, 2–bibl. Macmillan 1944 (1947). **2.00**

RATTER, MAGNUS C.
Albert Schweitzer: life & message. 215 p, frontis por, bibl refs. (1935) Beacon rev enl ed 1950. **2.75**

Revised version of a book originally published in England in 1935, including late entries dealing with Schweitzer's recent American visit, and a chapter on "Music & the organ" (p 83/105).

ROBACK, A. A. (*ed*)
The Albert Schweitzer jubilee book. 508 p, illus (photos & facs), 14–p bibl. Sci-Art n d (1946). **7.50**
An anthology (edited with the coöperation of J. S. Bixler & George Sarton) of tributes by many writers, including such musicians as Archibald T. Davison, Alice Ehlers, Leo Schrade, & Carl Weinrich.

SEAVER, GEORGE
Albert Schweitzer: Christian revolutionary. 130 p, 3–p bibl. Harper 1944 (repr 1949?). **2.00**

Albert Schweitzer: the man and his mind. xiii, 346 p, 30 photos. Harper 1947.   3.75

A standard biography, but one that stresses Schweitzer's philosophy rather than the events of his life. Two of the chapters are "On organs & organ building" and "Music & the music of Bach".

Schwimmer, Franciska. Author. See App IIa (juvenile biographies).

SCIENCE (& Music)

See:

Acoustics	Musicology
History	Sound Recording
Hearing	& Reproduction

Scobey, Katherine Lois. Author (with Horne). See App IIa (juveniles).

SCORE-READING

General Note: The term is restricted here to apply only to books dealing with orchestral score-reading. For books dealing principally with instrumental & vocal music to be read from open score, please see Sight-Playing & Reading, and Sight-Singing.

See also:

Accompaniment	Notation
Arranging	Orchestra
Instrumentation	Organ Playing
Instruments	Piano Playing
Keyboard Instruments	Solfège/Solfeggio
(esp Bach)	Transposition

BERNSTEIN, MARTIN (*ed*)
Score reading: a series of graded excerpts. iv, 106 p, music, paper. Witmark (1932) rev ed 1947.   3.00

Mainly music (seventy-one excerpts) for study & sight-performance at the piano.

GÁL, HANS
Directions for score-reading. 50 p + chart, illus, mus ex, paper. Universal 1924 (1948).   1.35

A concise standard work, uniform in format with the Philharmonia editions of miniature orchestral scores.

JACOB, GORDON
How to read a score. 63 p, mus ex, brief bibl, paper. Boosey 1944 (1946).   1.00

A concise manual, including notes on "aural imagination" & playing from score.

RIEMANN, HUGO
Introduction to playing from score. Tr anon. 120 p, mus ex, paper. Augener n d (1902).   1.50

A standard older work, with notes on simple forms of arrangement & substitutes for orchestral effects.

ROOD, LOUISE
An introduction to the orchestra score. 37 p, illus (Janice Rood), mus ex, 1–p bibl, paper. Kalmus 1948.   1.00

Mainly an instrumental chart showing names in various languages, written & sounding ranges, and notes on transposition; plus a brief historical sketch.

SCHULER, CARL G.
An introduction to score reading. ix, 103 p, mus ex. Presser 1950.   1.50

Mostly musical examples of vocal, instrumental, & orchestral scores in various clefs, plus notes on playing full orchestral scores at the piano.

SCOTLAND (Music in)/SCOTTISH MUSIC

See also:

Appreciation	Harp
Bagpipes	History
Church Music	Hymns/Hymnody
Dances–2	Minstrels/Minstrelsy
England (music in)	Psalms/Psalmody
Folklore	(esp Patrick)
Folksongs–1	Songbooks

FARMER, HENRY GEORGE
A history of music in Scotland. 557 p, 15 pl. Hinrichsen n d (1947).   5.00

Hinrichsen "Survey" series: a comprehensive survey from Celtic era to the present.

Music in 18th century Scotland. 16 p, paper. Hinrichsen n d (1946).   1.00

Reprint of an article from "Scottish Arts & Letters," for Spring 1946.

Music in mediaeval Scotland. Intro Richard R. Terry. 23 p, illus, paper. Reeves n d (1930).   △ (1.50)

Music making in the olden days: the story of the Aberdeen concerts, 1748-1801. x, 122 p, 6 pl (pors, etc), bibl refs, bds. Hinrichsen 1950.   5.00

The story of a famous musical society, with many sidelights on old musical customs.

KENNEDY-FRASER, MARJORY
Hebridean song: and the laws of interpretation. 21 p, paper. Paterson 1922, via C. Fischer.   .40

Lowland Scots pronunciation. 14 p, paper. Paterson 1922, via C. Fischer.   .40
"Festival Booklets" Nos 6 & 8.

Scott, Charles Kennedy. Author. See Madrigal.

SCOTT, Cyril Meir

See:

Composers-2 & 3c	History
Contemporary Music	Phonograph Records
English Music	Piano Music

Note: Scott's own books and a biography by Hull apparently all are O/P (or not easily available in this country). [As we go to press, Rider, London, announces a 5th new & extended edition of Scott's metaphysical study, "Music: its secret influence through-out the ages," originally published in 1933.]

Scott, Marion Margaret. Author.
See Beethoven-2, Mendelssohn-2.
Scott, Mary Margareta. Author.
See Children-4.
Scouten, Clifford E. Co-author (with Hector & Lein). See Acoustics.
Scoville, Modena. Author.
See Keyboard Harmony.

SCRIABIN, Alexander Nikolaievitch

See:

Appreciation	Modern Music
Color (& music)	Phonograph Record
Composers-2 & 3e	Piano Music
Contemporary Music	Program Notes
History	Russian Music
Koussevitzky	Themes

Note: Pertinent works apparently O/P (or not easily available) include those by Hull, Montagu-Nathan, and Swan.

SEA SHANTIES & SONGS

See also:

Folklore	Songbooks
Folksongs-1 & 2	Vocal Music

Note: Standard works apparently O/P (or not easily available) include those by Colcord ("Songs of American Sailormen," 1938, originally "Roll and Go," 1924), Crosley, Terry, Whall, etc.

DOERFLINGER, WILLIAM MAIN (*comp*)
Shantymen and shantyboys: songs of the sailor & lumberman. xxiii, 374 p, 20 illus, mus (tunes only), 9-p bibl. Macmillan 1951. 8.00
Words & music for over 150 sailors' and lumbermen's songs, with detailed notes on the songs & their singers, in what is sure to be a standard collection. The music editors are Samuel P. Bayard, Hally Wood, & Joseph Wood.

GREENLEAF, ELIZABETH B. (*ed*)
Ballads and sea songs of Newfound-land. Pref H. N. MacCracken. xliv,

395 p, 8 photos, music (tunes only), bibl refs. Harvard 1933. 5.00
Some 184 songs based on field recordings by Grace Yarrow Mansfield & the editor.

RICKABY, FRANZ
Ballads and songs of the shanty-boy. xlii, 244 p, 9 photos, music (tunes only). Harvard 1926. 3.50

SHAY, FRANK
American sea songs and chanteys: from the days of iron men & wooden ships. 217 p, illus (col & b&w, by Edward A. Wilson), music (tunes only), arr Christopher Thomas. (1924) Norton 1948. 5.00
Some 76 songs in a revision of the collection originally published in 1924 by Doubleday as "Iron men and wooden ships."

Seaman, Julian. Compiler.
See Program Notes.
Seabright, Roland. Co-author (with Hill).
See Theory-3.
Searle, Humphrey. Author. See Liszt.
Sears, Minnie Earl. Compiler.
See Song (s).

Seashore, Carl Emil. Author, editor.
See:
Aesthetics-2. In search of beauty in music (1947). 4.50
Interpretation. Objective analysis of musical performance (1936). 2.50
Psychology. Pioneering in (1942). 2.50
———. Psychology of music (1938). 5.00
———. Why we love music (1941). 1.50
Vibrato. The vibrato (1932). 2.50
———. Psychology of (1936). 2.50

Seaver, George. Author. See Schweitzer-2.
Sedgwick, Russell. Photographer.
See Tchaikovsky-2.
Sedillo, Mela. Catalogued under Brewster, Mela Sedillo.
Seeger, Charles Louis. Compiler.
See Latin America (ed Burgin).
Seeger, Ruth Crawford. Author.
See Children-7.
Seiber, Mátyás. Author. See Bartók.
Selden-Goth, Gisella. Editor.
See Mendelssohn-1.
Seltsam, William Henry. Compiler.
See Opera-4.
Semeonoff, Boris. Author.
See Phonograph Records.

Sendrey, Alfred. Compiler.
See Jewish Music.
Sénéchaux, Marcel. Author. See App Ia.
Seredy, Julius S. Compiler.
See Orchestral Music.
Sérieyx, Auguste. Editor.
See App Ia (d'Indy).

Seroff, Victor Ilyich. Author. See:
Composers–3e. Mighty five (1948). 4.00
(Same, in French, 1949). 2.75
Rachmaninoff. Biography (1950). 3.50
Shostakovitch. Biography (1943). 3.50

SESSIONS, Roger
See also:
American Music
Appreciation
Composers–2 & 3a
Contemporary Music

Modern Music
Phonograph Records
Program Notes
Symphony

The musical experience: of composer,
performer, listener. 127 p, mus ex.
Princeton 1950. 2.50
*6 lectures, originally delivered at the Juilliard
School of Music, Summer 1949, on music as
a unified whole & shared experience.*

Author. See also:
Harmony–1. Harmonic practice
(1951 in prep). Δ

Severn, Merlyn. Photographer.
See Ballet.
Seymour, Harriet Ayer. Author.
See Children–2.
Seymour, Maurice. Photographer.
See Ballet.
Shafter, Alfred Martin. Author.
See Copyright.

SHAKESPEARE (& Music)
See also:
Appreciation
Elizabethan Music
English (music in)
English Music

History
Literature
Poetry
Program Notes

*Note: Standard works apparently O/P (or not
easily available) include those by Bridge,
Cowling, Elson, Greenhill, et al, Naylor,
Noble, etc.*

DENT, EDWARD J.
Shakespeare and music. An essay in
"A companion to Shakespeare stud-
ies," ed Harley Granville-Barker & G.
B. Harrison. x, 408 p, 4 pl (facs), 6
b&ws, 22–p annot bibl. Cambridge
1934. 3.75
Dent's essay is on p 137/161. The bibliog-

*raphies include one page (p 355) devoted to
"Shakespeare & Music."*

MONCUR-SIME, A. H.
Shakespeare: his music and song.
vii, 196 p, illus, music. Kegan Paul
1917, 4th pr n d (1948?). 2.00
*"Music Lovers' Library" series: includes
seven traditional melodies.*

Shakespeare, William (1849–1931).
Author. See Singing–1.
Shapiro, Elliott. Co-author (with Dichter).
See Sheet Music.

Sharp, Cecil. Author. See Folklore. Compiler. See Folksongs–1 & 2.
*Note: A biography of the great folklorist (by
Fox Strangways & Karpeles, 1933) apparently is O/P.*

SHAW, George Bernard
*Note: "The perfect Wagnerite" (1899 & later
eds) apparently is O/P (or not easily available,
at least in this country), as is the collection
of Shaw's music criticisms: "London music
in 1888-89 as heard by Corno di Bassetto
(later known as Bernard Shaw), with some
further autobiographical particulars" (1931,
1937).*

Music in London: 1890–94. 3 v:
302, 325, 320 p. Constable standard
ed 1932 (repr 1950). 6.00
Single volumes, each: 2.50
*Shaw's critical contributions to "The World,"
from 1890 to 1894—his last years as a practising (newspaper) music critic.*

Shaw, Harold Watkins. Author, editor.
See:
Beethoven–3. 5th concerto (1946). .50
Blow. Dr John Blow (1946). 1.25
Education. Symposium (1947). 2.50
Handel–2. Messiah (1946). .50

Shaw, Lloyd. Author.
See Cowboy Music, Dances–2.

Shaw, Martin. Author. See Church Music.
Co-editor (with Dearmer & Vaughan Williams). See Carols, Hymns/Hymnody–1.
*Note: An autobiography, "Up to now"
(1929), apparently is O/P.*

Shaw, William Warren. Author (with Lindsay). See Voice.
Shawe-Taylor, Desmond. Author.
See Covent Garden.
Shay, Frank. Author.
See Sea Shanties & Songs.
Shea, George Edward. Author.
See Opera–1.
Shedlock, John South. Author.
See Beethoven–3.
Sheehy, Emma Dickson. Author.
See Children–1.

SHEET MUSIC

See also:

America (music in)	Songs (Mattfeld &
American Music	Davis)
(esp Harwell)	Yearbooks
Popular Music	

DICHTER, HARRY (*comp*)
Handbook of American sheet music:
a catalogue of sheet music for sale by
the compiler & publisher. Intro John
Tasker Howard. 100 p, illus (facs),
paper. Author, Philadelphia, 1947.   2.00
Classified catalogue with detailed notes.

DICHTER, HARRY & SHAPIRO, ELLIOTT
Early American sheet music: its lure
& its lore; including a directory of
early American music publishers.
xxvii, 287 p, 32 pl (facs), 1–p bibl.
Bowker 1941.   O/P
*A standard work: classified & annotated list
of over 600 songs, plus a list of lithographers
& artists before 1870 comp by Edith A.
Wright & Josephine A. McDevitt. (O/P 1950.)*

Shelby, Charmion. Co-editor (with Aguilera). See Latin America.
Shepard, Frank Hartson. Author.
See Children–8, Harmony–2.
Shepherd, Arthur. Author.
See Beethoven–3. Co-author (with Keith).
See Children–2.
Shera, Frank Henry. Author.
See Amateur Music, Composers–3d.
Shields, Elizabeth McEwen. Author.
See Children–1.
Shinn, Frederick G. Author.
See Ear-Training.
Shirley, Paul. Author.
See String Playing.
Shore, Bernard. Author.
See Conductors, Symphony. Editor (with Tours). See Viola/Viola Playing.

SHORTHAND (Musical)
See: Manuscript.

SHOSTAKOVITCH, Dmitri
See also:

Appreciation	Modern Music
Chamber Music	Opera
Composers–2 & 3e	Phonograph Records
Concerto	Program Notes
Contemporary Music	Russian Music
History	Symphony

Also (for a book by Shostakovitch & others):
Tchaikovsky–1.

MARTYNOV, IVAN
Shostakovich: the man and his work.
Tr T. Guralsky. 197 p, frontis por.
Philosophical 1947.   3.75
*From the Soviet point of view; includes a
complete catalogue of compositions.*

SEROFF, VICTOR ILYICH
Dmitri Shostakovich: the life &
background of a Soviet composer.
In collaboration with Nadejda Galli-
Shohat, aunt of the composer. x, 260,
vii p, 13 photos. Knopf 1943 (3rd pr
1947).   3.50

*A full-length biography based largely on in-
formation from the aunt of the composer;
includes a catalogue of works.*

Shrifte, Miriam Lubell. Co-editor (with Norman). See Letters.
Shurr, Gertrude. Author (with Yocum).
See Dances–1.

SIAM (Music in)/SIAMESE MUSIC
See:

Asiatic Musics	Instruments
(note only)	Oriental Music
History	(note only)

*Note: The bibliography of Asiatic Musics
referred to above includes a section on Siam
in its 9th installment (Music Library Association "Notes," December 1949).*

SIBELIUS, Jean
See also:

Appreciation	Piano Music
Composers–2	Program Notes
Concerto	Song(s)
Contemporary Music	Symphony
History	Themes
Phonograph Records	Vocal Music

Also: App IIa (juvenile by Arnold)

*Note: Standard works apparently O/P (or not
easily available) include those by Newmarch
and Törne, plus several studies in Finnish,
Swedish & German.*

ABRAHAM, GERALD (*ed*)
The music of Sibelius. 218 p, 27–p
mus ex, 2–p bibl. Norton 1947.   3.00

A symposium with articles on various aspects of Sibelius's work by the editor, Blom, Cherniavsky, Desmond, Goddard, Hill, & Wood. Includes a chronology (to 1925) & a catalogue of compositions.

EKMAN, KARL
Jean Sibelius.   Tr Edward Birse; forew Ernest Newman.   xxiv, 298, x p, illus, 2–p bibl. (1936) Tudor 1945.   1.98
Reprint (from the Knopf ed of 1938, now O/P) of a biography originally pub in Finnish 1935 and in English 1936.

GRAY, CECIL
Sibelius.   224 p. Oxford (1931) 2nd ed 1934 (4th pr 1945).   3.00
Sibelius: the symphonies.   77 p, mus ex, paper.   Oxford 1935 (5th pr 1947).   1.00
A study of the man & his music by a British admirer, and a booklet of symphonic analyses in the "Musical Pilgrim" series.

HANNIKAINEN, ILMARI
Sibelius and the development of Finnish music. Tr Aulis Nopsanen; pref Toivo Haapanen. 47 p, photos, facs, map, 1–p bibl, bds. Hinrichsen n d (1948).   2.50
Hinrichsen "Miniature Surveys" S-21.

Sickels, Vera Abigail.   Co-author (with Avery & Dorsey). See Speech.
Siegmeister, Elie.   Editor.
See Miscellanies, Songbooks. Co-author. (with Downes). See Folksongs–2.
Siepmann, Charles Arthur.   Author. See Radio.
Sietz, Rheinhold.   Author, editor. See App Ib.

SIGHT-PLAYING/READING/SINGING

General Note: Although the meanings of sight-playing & sight-singing are distinct enough, sight-reading is ambiguously synonymous with both—for it implies the whole process of interpreting musical notation (one of the principal subjects of so-called musical "theory") and even the too-rare ability to "read" music to oneself (i.e., so that it "sounds" only in the imagination).

Here, for convenience, we restrict the Sight-Singing category to books dealing exclusively with vocal reading-performance, while we group those dealing with instrumental sight-playing and those dealing with both instrumental & vocal "reading" under Sight-Playing & Reading.

SIGHT-PLAYING & READING
(Instrumental sight-playing; instrumental & vocal sight-reading)

See also:

Accompaniment	Organ Playing
Amateur Music	Piano Playing
Choir/Choral–2	Rhythm
(Hoggard)	Score-Reading
Children–5	String Playing
Conducting	Teaching–2
Ear-Training	Theory
Improvisation	Transposition
Interpretation	Violin Playing
Notation	

BAUMAN, ALVIN
Elementary musicianship. x, 246 p, music. Prentice 1947.   5.00
Rhythms, sight-singing, melodic & harmonic dictation, practice, theory, & analysis, with exercises & drills, including an appendix (some 40 p) of canons, rounds, etc.

BRADLEY, VINCENT
Playing at sight: for violinists & other instrumentalists; some practical hints.   35 p, music, paper. Oxford 1948.   .85
With special emphasis on preliminary observation before beginning to play.

DEUTSCH, LEONHARD
Guided sight-reading: a new approach to piano study.   xiii, 107 p, diagrs, mus ex. Crown 1950.   2.00
An approach to sight-reading based on Adlerian psychology, with chapters on repertory, self-instruction, teaching suggestions, etc.

ELKAN, IDA
Piano sight-reading can be taught. 63 p, frontis por, illus (caricatures), paper.   Music Sight-reading Pubs, via C. Fischer 1948.   1.00
Inspirational pep talks and advice.

HAAKE, CHARLES J. (& others)
Teaching music reading with the Oxford piano course.   43 p, mus ex, paper.   Oxford & C. Fischer 1941.   .50
Co-authors: Gail Martin Haake & Osbourne McConathy.   A supplement to the Oxford Piano Course (see Teaching–3, Schelling).

KANZELL, MAXWELL
How to read music: a new & simplified approach to reading music at sight, for home or classroom study. 76 p, mus ex, spir. C. Fischer 2nd rev ed 1944.   1.75
Same, paper cover.   1.25
Including considerable elementary "theory."

MOKREJS, JOHN
Lessons in sight reading at the piano.

38 p, mus ex, paper. Summy 1909.
(*Mostly exercises.*) .75

MORRIS, R. O. & FERGUSON, HOWARD
Preparatory exercises in score-reading. 110 p, music, paper. Oxford
1931. 2.00
*Except for a prefatory note, this is devoted
exclusively to musical exercises in 2 to 5 parts,
in all C clefs.*

MOTCHANE-MORHANGE, MARTHE
A quick way to learn how to read
music in a few lessons. Forew Darius
Milhaud. 39 p, mus ex, paper. Salabert n d. .85
*Elementary sight-reading, rhythm, reading
and rhythm combined in songs.*

RUBINSTEIN, BERYL
The pianist's approach to sight-reading and memorizing. 67 p, mus ex,
paper. C. Fischer 1950. 1.00
*The value of fluency in sight-reading & the
value of memorization, with analyses of the
mental & manual processes involved, and
graded lists of suitable piano material.*

TAPPER, THOMAS
Sight-reading and memory lessons for
the pianoforte. 48 p, music, paper.
Schmidt (1905) aug ed 1906. (*Mostly
music.*) 1.00

TAYLOR, COLIN
Commonsense on instrumental sight-
reading: and kindred subjects. Pref
George Dyson. 25 p, mus ex, paper.
Curwen n d. (.60)
*Concise notes & specific details, with a list
of music for study, p 22/5.*

VANDRE, CARL
Sing or play: sight-reading fun in the
book with a plan. 56 p, illus (Lorain
Acker), mus ex, paper. Handi-Folio
Milwaukee, Wisconsin, 1942. .50
*Mainly exercises for voice alone, "sym-
phonet," straight flute, or combinations.*

SIGHT-SINGING

*General Note: Although most solfège (or
solfeggio) books are largely devoted to sight-
singing, they have been listed separately under
their own subject-heading, since "solfège"
has come to imply a French system of basic
music training, which makes primary use of
sight-singing, but also includes ear-training,
rhythmic drill, & other elementary "theory"
subjects.*

Another related, but separate, subject-heading

*might well have been Tonic Sol-Fa, but since
this British system (employing a special sol-fa
notation) is used so little in this country, none
of the considerable literature available in
England is listed here. Those interested in
such material should consult the catalogues of
Curwen, Novello, Williams, etc, for the many
works by Curwen, Field-Hyde, & others.*

*The actual entries below are a sampling of the
large available literature on sight-singing,—
a good part of which is devoted to musical
exercises only, with little or no text.*

See also: esp Solfège/Solfeggio.

Also:

Amateur Music	School Music–4
Children–3, 7, & 8	Score-Reading
Choir/Choral	Sight-Playing &
Community Music	Reading
Dictation	Singing
Ear-Training	Songbooks
Notation	Theory
Rhythm	Vocal Music

ANDERSON, W. R. & DOORLEY, C. C.
Rhythmic sight-singing. 2 v, paper.
J. Fischer 1922/33.

V 1 (by Doorley): Diatonic. 79 p,
music. 1922. .50

V 2 (by Anderson): Chromatics,
minor mode, compound time. 34 p,
music. 1933. .50

CLIPPINGER, D. A.
Sight-singing: based on rhythmic-
melodic-harmonic ear training. 64
p, music. FitzSimons 1931. 1.25

DAMROSCH, FRANK
Popular method of sight-singing. 164
p, music. G. Schirmer (1894) 1923. 1.00

DAMROSCH, FRANK; GARTLAN, GEORGE H.;
& GEHRKENS, KARL W.
Supplementary sight-singing exercises. 281 p, music only. Hinds 1925
(1948); Barnes & Noble 1950. 3.75

GLASSON, T. BATH
Practical studies in reading vocal
music: for use in academies, normal
& grammar schools, & singing classes.
164 p, music, flex. J. Fischer 1908. 1.00

LEWIS, LEO RICH
The gist of sight-singing. xi, 96 p,
music paper. Ditson 1921. .75
*"Pocket Music Student" series, including
"Rudimentary facts of music," p 80/96.*

McHOSE, ALLEN I. & TIBBS, RUTH N.
Sight-singing manual. v, 105 p,
music. Crofts (1944) 2nd ed 1945
(5th pr 1947). 2.50

"Eastman School of Music" series, with melodies chosen from 18th to 20th century literature for first-year-work.

NERN, ALLAN
Simplified sight-singing: a course in music reading based upon the study of intervals. vii, 50 p, music, paper. Elkan 1940.   .75

PANSERON, A. M.
ABC of music: a primer of vocalization containing the elements of music & solfeggi. vi, 148 p, music. (1846) Ditson rev enl (N. Clifford Page) 1908.   1.50
"Music Students Library" series.

REEVES, AUBREY (comp)
Studies in vocal score-reading. Pref Sir Walter Alcock. 2 v: vii, 55; vii, 55 p, music, paper. Hammond & Co, London, 1938.   6.00
Mainly exercises (by British composers), suitable for examination purposes.

TKACH, PETER
Vocal technic: a fundamental course in voice & sight-singing; teacher's manual with piano accs. 64 p, illus, music, paper. Kjos 1948.   1.00
Primarily individual & class sight-singing.

Silbermann, Alphons. Author.
See Aesthetics–2.
Simon, Eric. Co-author (with Edwards).
See Children–8.
Simont, Marc. Illustrator. See Humor.
Simon, George Thomas. Author.
See App IIb (juveniles).
Simon, Henry William. Editor.
See Opera–3.
Sims, Hines. Author.
See Church Music.
Sims, Mary Louise. Co-author (with Harris). See Children–3.

SINATRA, Frank (Francis Albert)
See also: Popular Music, Singing–3.

Note: Sinatra's "Tips on popular singing" (1942) apparently is O/P. However, he is the author of a chapter, "Start singing" in "Your career in motion pictures, television, & radio" (see Career, ed Jones).

KAHN, E. J., Jr
The voice: the story of an American phenomenon. xvii, 125 p + 16–p photos. Harper 1947.   2.00
An expanded "New Yorker" profile of the popular singer's fantastic career.

SINGERS
See also:

America (music in)	Lind
(esp Schiavo)	McCormack
Anderson	Negro Music & Musi-
Caruso	cians
Cook	Opera (esp Barker)
Crosby	Phonograph Records
Ffrangcon-Davies	(esp Bauer)
Galli-Curci	Sankey
Gatti-Casazza	Sinatra
Hayes	Singing
History	Slezak
Hutchinson Family	Swarthout
Interpreters	Tauber
B. Ives	Thursby
Jewish Music & Musi-	Trapp Family
cians (Saleski)	Waters
Lawrence	Yearbooks
Lehmann	Who's Who

Note: Standard works apparently O/P (or not easily available) include those by Klein, Martens, etc.

BROOK, DONALD
Singers of today. xv, 226 p, 41 pl (pors). Rockliff 1949.   (3.75)
Mostly British singers, from Norman Allin to Tom Williams, but including Flagstad, Gigli, Elisabeth Schumann, et al.

COOKE, JAMES FRANCIS
Great singers on the art of singing: educational conferences with foremost artists, a series of personal study-talks with the most renowned opera, concert, & oratorio singers of the time. 304 p, pors mus ex. Presser 1921.   2.25

LAHEE, HENRY C.
Famous singers of to-day and yesterday. ix, 421 p, illus. Page (1898) rev ed 1936.   2.50

ROBINSON-DUFF, SARAH
Simple truths used by great singers. 113 p, frontis por, bds. Ditson 1919. 1.00

SINGING

1. General, Larger Methods, etc.

2. Shorter Methods, Specialized Studies, etc.

3. Popular

General Note: Books dealing with the vocal mechanism only, or with both singing & speaking, are entered under the subject-heading Voice.

For an extensive, annotated bibliography of singing, see especially Singing–1: Field's "Training the singing voice."

See also: cross-references under Singers.

Also:

Accompaniment	Interpretation
Amateur Music	Opera
Barbershop	Pronunciation
Bel Canto	School Music (esp 4)
Boy Voices	Sight-Singing
Breathing	Singers
Children (esp 7)	Solfège/Solfeggio
Choir/Choral–1 & 2	Song(s)
Church Music	Teaching–2
Community Music	Vibrato
Diction	Vocal Music
History	Voice

SINGING

(1. General, Larger Methods, etc)

Note: Standard works apparently O/P (or not easily available) include those by Barbereux-Parry, Drew, Behnke, Henderson ("Art of singing", 1906/38, & "Early history of singing", 1921), Mackinlay, Marchesi, Miller, Santley, Scott, Smith, Taylor, Thompson, Wood ("Gentle art of singing," 4 v, 1927/8), etc.

BACHNER, LOUIS
Dynamic singing: a new approach to free voice production. Intro Marjorie Lawrence. ix, 144 p. Wyn 1944 (3rd pr n d).   2.75

BROWN, RALPH MORSE
The singing voice. 167 p, frontis por (Garcia), mus ex. Macmillan 1946 (3rd pr 1947).   2.50
A practical over-all survey of requirements and techniques.

CONGER, KATHERINE (comp)
Helps to the singer: a list of books on singing technique prepared by the Fine Arts Department, Enoch Pratt Free Library. 16 p, illus (Gluyas Williams), paper, mim. Enoch Pratt Free Library, Baltimore, 1950.   .07
Voice lifting: a list of books on singing technique prepared by the Fine Arts Department, Enoch Pratt Free Library. 7 p, illus, paper. Enoch Pratt Free Library, Baltimore, 1950.   .05
The latter (printed) booklet contains a selection from the larger mimeographed list.

EVETTS, E. T. & WORTHINGTON, R. A.
The mechanics of singing. xvi, 133 p, illus, mus ex. Dent 1928.   3.00
A correlation of the physiology of the voice with an actual method of singing; includes 3 radiographs (X-ray photographs).

FIELD-HYDE, F. C.
   (*See also Singing–2.*)
The art and science of voice training.

xii, 223 p, illus, charts, mus ex, brief bibl. Oxford 1950.   3.25
A method based on "manipulative potentialities of all the chief vowels," & on the "secrets" of the old masters.

FIELDS, VICTOR ALEXANDER
Training the singing voice: an analysis of the working concepts contained in recent contributions to vocal pedagogy. xii, 337 p, 11 tables, 62-p annot bibl. Columbia 1947.   4.25
A survey of the literature from 1928 through 1942, plus reports on conferences with noted singers. The annotated bibliography includes some 700 entries.

GREENE, HARRY PLUNKET
   (*See also Singing–2, Bairstow & Greene.*)
Interpretation in song. xii, 323 p, mus ex. Macmillan (1912) 1926 (1948).   3.75
A standard work by a noted British singer.

GREINER, ALBERT. See App Ib.

HEMERY, HAYDN
The physiological basis of the art of singing. xviii, 139 p, 59 illus. H. K. Lewis & Co, London, 1939.   3.25

HERBERT-CAESARI, EDGAR F.
The science and sensations of vocal tone: a school of natural vocal mechanics. Forew Noel Bonavia-Hunt; pref Dinn Gilly. xxiv, 199 p, 42 diagr. Dent 1936.   3.00
A standard, detailed study of vocal technique, endorsed by Tetrazzini & others.

KAGEN, SERGIUS
On studying singing. 119 p. Rinehart 1950.   2.00
"Field of Music" series No 4: a commonsense survey of the general problems involved, the natural equipment required, the scope & purpose of related studies, basic procedures, etc.

KWARTIN, BERNARD
Fundamentals of vocal art: including the theory of tone focus & organization of vocal instruction. 178 p, 31 pl, mus ex, 4–p bibl. (1941) via Omega Music Corp, N. Y.   3.50
The illustrations are repeated on a separate large chart for studio use.

LEHMANN, LILLI
How to sing. Tr Richard Aldrich. xi, 303 p, illus (frontis por & drwgs). Macmillan (1902) 3rd rev & supplemented ed (tr Clara Willenbücher) 1924 (1949).   4.00

A standard work, originally published in German, 1900, as "Meine Gesangkunst."

(N. Y. SINGING TEACHERS' ASSN)
Twenty years of the New York Singing Teachers' Association, Inc: a record of agreement on essentials.
193 p. Presser 1928.   2.50
Statements, resolutions, and noteworthy papers by various authors.

PROSCHOWSKI, FRANTZ
The singing school of Frantz Proschowski. V 1: the beginner's voice book. 206 p, illus, music, paper. Presser 1927.   2.00
Mainly exercises, illustrated with anatomical drawings by the author.

SHAKESPEARE, WILLIAM
The art of singing: based on the principals of the old Italian singing masters & dealing with breath-control & production of the voice, together with exercises . . . 201 p, 10 illus, music, paper. Ditson (1905) rev ed 1921.   2.50
Plain words on singing: in the absence of a master. xiv, 119 p, 2 pl, mus ex. Putnam (1924) new rev ed 1938.   2.00
Respectively a detailed method with many musical exercises and a more generalized discussion of techniques, with special emphasis on the teachings of the old Italian masters.

WATERS, CRYSTAL
Song: the substance of vocal study. 135 p + 13-p blank staves, mus ex, bds. G. Schirmer 1930.   2.50
The "case method" applied to vocal instruction, with lists of song material.

WHITE, ERNEST G.
Science and singing: a consideration of the capabilities of the vocal cords & their work in the art of tone production. Forew Reginald F. Price. xiv, 186 p, 33 illus, mus ex. Dent (1909) 5th rev ed 1938.   (3.75)
Light on the voice beautiful: presenting the science & art of sinus tone production as it has appeared in various forms to many minds. 210 p, 3 pl, James Clarke & Co, London, n d (1930), via Rogers.   (2.50)
Sinus tone production. Intro Oliver C. de C. Ellis. xix, 145 p, 21 illus. Dent 1938 (1948).   (2.25)
The three books above form a trilogy advancing in great detail the unorthodox theory that the center of voice production is in the sinuses,

rather than in the larynx. *The 1st book, "Science & singing," was entitled "The voice beautiful" in its 2nd, 3rd, & 4th editions The 2nd book is largely devoted to discussions of the author's theories, reprinted from the correspondence columns of various British periodicals.*

WITHERSPOON, HERBERT
(See also Singing-2.)
Singing: a treatise for teachers & students. 126 p, diagrs, mus ex. G. Schirmer 1925 (6th pr n d).   2.50
A treatise on "natural" laws and an exposition of the system of teaching developed by the noted basso for his own pupils.

SINGING

(2. Shorter Methods, Specialized Studies, etc.)

Note: Standard works apparently O/P (or not easily available) include those by Austin-Bell, Behnke, Brown, Croker, Greer, Greene, Guilbert, Hemery, Key, Lamperti, McNeilly, Myer, Nordica, Palmer, Proschowski, Reeves, Rogers, Shaw, Stockhausen, Taylor, Weer, etc.

In addition, there undoubtedly are many other books, mostly of comparatively limited circulation & importance, which have been omitted either arbitrarily or by oversight from the lengthy list below.

ANGELL, WARREN M.
Vocal approach. ix, 76 p, music, brief annot bibl. Broadman 1950.   1.00
"Baptist Sunday School Board Church Music Curriculum" series, with 13 hymns.

BAIRSTOW, EDWARD C. & GREENE, H. P.
Singing learned from speech: a primer for teachers & students. 83 p, music, paper. Macmillan & Stainer 1945 (1946).   2.50

BROWN, WILLIAM EARL
Vocal wisdom: maxims of Giovanni Battista Lamperti, recorded & explained by his pupil & assistant. 127 p. Author, N.Y., 1931.   2.50

BURRITT, WILLIAM NELSON
A process of vocal study. 46 p, illus, mus ex, bds. Summy rev ed 1922.   .50

BUZZI-PECCIA, A.
How to succeed in singing: a practical guide for singers desiring to enter the profession. 156 p, frontis por, diagrs, mus ex. Presser 1925.   **2.00**

CLIPPINGER, D. A.
Collective voice training: a manual
of the principles of voice training
designed for use in classes, choirs,
choruses, high schools, etc. 55 p,
music, paper. Fearis 1924.   1.00

Fundamentals of voice training. 111
p, mus ex, paper. Ditson 1929.   .75

The head voice and other problems:
practical talks on singing. vi, 102 p,
mus ex, 2–p bibl. Ditson 1917.   1.25

*The latter two works are in the "Pocket Music
Student" & "Music Students Library" series.*

Systematic voice training.   63 p,
music, brief bibl, paper.   Gamble
1910 (1937).   1.25

CONKLIN, MAURICE
Fundamental vocal technique.   110
p, diagrs, mus ex. Dorrance 1936.   2.00

DENGLER, CLYDE R.
Read this and sing!: for voice and students, chorus & choir singers. iv, 47
p, diagrs, mus ex, paper. Presser
1944.   .35

Same, Teacher's manual.   52 p,
diagrs, mus ex, paper. Presser 1945.   1.50

DOSSERT, DEANE
Sound sense for singers. Intro Adrian
C. Boult.   56 p, mus ex. J. Fischer
1932.   .80

DOUTY, NICHOLAS
What the vocal student should know:
an introduction to the art of singing,
with daily exercises for all voices ...
64 p, mus ex, bds.   Presser 1924.   1.00

DOWNING, WILLIAM B.
Vocal pedagogy: for student, singer,
& teacher.   76 p, diagrs, mus ex. C.
Fischer 1927.   1.25

DREW, WILLIAM SYDNEY
Notes on the technique of song-inter-
pretation.   55 p, mus ex.   Oxford
1926.   .75

*A sequel to the author's "Voice training"
(1924), which apparently is O/P.*

FIELD-HYDE, F. C.
(*See also Singing-1.*)
Vocal vibrato, tremolo, and judder:
their nature, causes, & treatment.
vii, 43 p, 2 illus, mus ex, bibl refs,
paper.   Oxford 1946.   1.25

FRACHT, J. ALBERT & ROBINSON, E.
Sing well—speak well. vii, 178, illus
(Emmett   Robinson).   Chemical
1948.   3.75

*Primarily on singing: breezy, "inspirational"
approach, enlivened by cartoons.*

FREEMANTEL, FREDERIC
High tones and how to sing them.
96 p, frontis por, illus, mus ex. Freemantel Voice Institute, N. Y., 1946.   3.00

Includes a brief autobiography.

GAMBLER, EUGENE
Your guide to successful singing.
Forew & editorial coöperation by
Allan Carpenter.   160 p, 29 photos,
3 charts (1 foldout), 1–p bibl. Wind-
sor Press, Chicago, 1950.   3.00

*Self-help, popularized advice on "getting
the right start," "some fundamentals," &
"refining your technique."*

GESCHEIDT, ADELAIDE
Make singing a joy: a system that
develops the natural function of the
voice & the ideal quality of pure tone
without voice placement or breathing
method. . . . Forew Sigmund Spaeth.
88 p, frontis por.   Huntzinger 1930,
via Willis.   1.50

GRANVILLE, CHARLES NORMAN
The voco study plan: for voice
classes or individual instruction.   80
p, diagrs, mus ex, paper.   Gamble
(1931) new ed 1934.   1.25

HASLAM, W. E.
Style in singing. ix, 104 p, mus ex.
G. Schirmer 1911.   1.50

*Laws governing the effective interpretation of
vocal music.*

HAYWOOD, FREDERICK H.
Universal song: a voice-culture course
in 3 volumes, for the studio & the
class room.   Paper.   (1917/21) G.
Schirmer 1933/42.

V 1: 20 lessons in the fundamental
principles of automatic breathing &
breath control . . . iii, 44 p, mus ex.
(1917) rev ed 1933 (1944).   .75

V 2: 20 lessons in the fundamental
principles of voice control . . . 32 p,
mus ex. (1919) new rev ed 1936.   .75

V 3: 20 lessons embracing the study
of tone extension, the dramatic forte
tone, agility, embellishments, & the
bravura style. 32 p, music.   (1921)
rev ed 1942.   .75

*The various volumes include separate treat-
ments of each vowel; also vocal exercises by
Sieber, Bonoldi, & Lamperti.*

HENSCHEL, GEORGE
Articulation in singing: a manual
for student & teacher. 53 p, frontis.
mus ex. Church 1926.   1.25

HERMAN, REINHOLD L.
An open door for singers: hints to
vocalists. xi, 321 p, mus ex. G.
Schirmer 1912 (5th pr n d). 1.50
Explanatory and practical "hints."

HINMAN, FLORENCE LAMONT
Slogans for singers. x, 76 p, mus ex.
G. Schirmer (1934) 2nd rev ed 1936. 2.50
*Maxims and notes on technical problems, plus
several "model" programs.*

KISCH-ARNDT, RUTH
A primer of style-singing: a guide to
the singing of early music. 12 p, mus
ex, 1–p bibl, paper. Art & Science,
Inc, N. Y., 1948. 2.00
Notes on clefs & ornaments, and a glossary.

LAMPERTI, FRANCESCO
The art of singing. Tr J. C. Griffith.
62 p, music, paper. G. Schirmer rev
ed n d. 1.00
*A method by a noted 19th-century teacher.
See also Brown above for Lamperti maxims.*

LEWIS, JOSEPH
Singing without tears: a handbook
for beginners of all ages. Forew
Leslie Woodgate. 58 p, paper.
Ascherberg 1939 (1948). 1.00
*Breathing; tone, vowel, & word production;
interpretation; for novices.*

LISSFELT, J. FRED
Basic principles of artistic singing.
xi, 54 p, frontis, mus ex, paper. E. C.
Schirmer 1938. 1.50
Based on Lilli Lehmann principles.

MANCHESTER, ARTHUR L.
Twelve lessons in fundamentals of
voice production. 92 p, mus ex.
Ditson 1908 (1936). 1.25
*"Music Students Library" series: particu-
larly for use in choir-training.*

MARCHESI, SALVATORE
A vademecum for singing-teachers
and pupils. 49 p, mus ex, bds.
G. Schirmer 1902. 1.00
*Concise notes and advice on fundamentals,
posture, practice, analysis, style, etc.*

MARTENS, VI
How's your voice? 18 p, bds. C.
Fischer 1939. .75

MASSELL, JAMES
To sing or not to sing: practical suggestions & exercises for voice culture.
36 p + 8–p mus ex. Author, N. Y.,
(1926) 2nd ed n d. 1.65

MAURICE-JACQUET, H.
The road to successful singing.
Forew Charles Henry Meltzer. xv,
81 p. Ditson 1947. 2.00
*An attempt to correlate "scientific" &
"spiritual" approaches to singing.*

MYER, EDMUND J.
The renaissance of the vocal art: a
practical study of vitality, vitalized
energy, of the physical, mental, &
emotional powers of the singer,
through flexible, elastic bodily movements. 136 p, mus ex. Boston 1902. 1.50
The vocal instructor. 62 p, diagrs,
mus ex, flex. Presser 1913 (1918). 1.25
*Note: a number of other books or booklets by
Myer apparently are O/P.*

NICOLL, IRENE H. & DENNIS, C. M.
Simplified vocal training. 70 p, mus
ex, 1–p bibl, paper. C. Fischer 1940. 1.00
Lessons in catechism form.

PANZÉRA, CHARLES. See App Ia.

PITTS, CAROL MARHOFF
Pitts voice class method for class and
studio. 2 v, paper. Kjos 1936/39.
V 1: Elementary. 64 p, illus, music.
1936. 1.00
V 2: Intermediate. 64 p, illus, music. 1939. 1.00

ROGERS, CLARA KATHLEEN
Your voice and you: what the singer
should do, a practical application of
psychology to singing. 125 p, mus
ex. Ditson 1925. 1.75

ROSS, WILLIAM ERNEST
Sing high, sing low: a general Ameri-
can school of singing. 135 p, 21 illus,
1–p bibl, paper. C. Fischer 1948. 2.00
*With an appendix on phonetics compiled by
Gardiner H. London.*

RYAN, MILLIE
What every singer should know:
heart to heart talks with vocal students & those contemplating voice
culture. x, 105 p, 17 illus, mus ex.
C. Fischer 1937. 1.25

SAMOILOFF, LAZAR S.
The singer's handbook. x, 138 p, mus
ex. Presser 1942. 3.00
*With program suggestions & a teacher's mem-
oirs; originally published in conjunction with
a set of recordings by the author.*

TAYLOR, BERNARD U.
Group voice: a systematic course in

singing for use in group instruction. 44 p, mus ex (by Victor Young), paper. G. Schirmer (1936) rev ed 1950.   1.00

Twenty lessons on specific details.

TAYLOR, DAVID CLARK
New light on the old Italian method: an outline of the historical system of voice culture, with a plea for its revival. xii, 143 p. Gray 1916.   1.50

A plea for retracing recent steps in voice culture & a reliance on "natural processes"; with comments on the old "methods" by Tosi, Mancini, & Mengozzi.

TETRAZZINI, LUISA
How to sing.   136 p, frontis por, diagrs, mus ex.   Presser 1923.   2.00

Informal practical advice (not a comprehensive "method") by the noted coloratura.

TEYTE, MAGGIE
Letter from Maggie Teyte: vocal exercises by Jean de Reszke, with commentary. 33 p, music, paper. Austin Wilder, N. Y., 1947.   1.00

Pocket-size MS repro on music paper.

TOMLINS, WILLIAM L.
Song and life. Ed Peter W. Dykema. 105 p, frontis por, paper.   Birchard 1945.   1.25

Inspirational essays & technical points plus excerpts from the author's lectures.

WESTERMAN, KENNETH N.
Modern phonetization: V 1, modern phonetization applied to singing. 42 p, illus, mus ex, paper.   Modern Phonetization, Adrian, Michigan, (1934) 2nd ed 1936.   1.00

WITHERSPOON, HERBERT
   (*See also Singing–1.*)
Thirty-six lessons in singing for teacher and student. 51 p, frontis por, diagrs, mus ex, paper. Meissner Institute, Chicago, 1930, via Fitz-Simons.   1.25

WITHROW, MARIE
Some staccato notes for singers. xiv, 111 p.   Ditson 1915.   1.00

Practical advice in the form of maxims.

WOODSIDE, JAMES
Style in singing and song interpretation. Pref Frederick A. Haywood. 29 p, diagrs, paper.   Haywood Institute & G. Schirmer 1931.   .75

Sub-title (on cover only): An outline of study in which the essentials of effective song rendition are presented step by step.

SINGING (3. Popular)

See also:

Career	Radio
Carmichael	Sinatra
Crosby	Songwriting
Popular Music	

Note: Works apparently O/P (or not easily available) include those by Bowlly, the Landt Trio, Sinatra, etc.

HENDERSON, CHARLES & PALMER, CHARLES
How to sing for money: the art & business of singing popular songs professionally.   369 p, mus ex. (1939) Nelson-Hall 1945 (1949).   1.98

Detailed, highly practical information.

SPIER, MIRIAM
The why and how of popular singing: a modern guide for vocalists. Intro Peggy Lee. ix, 53 p, illus (Bud Handelsman), mus ex.   Marks 1950.   1.75

Inspirational & practical advice.

SINGING GAMES

See: Dances–1 & esp 2.

Also: Folklore, Songbooks (esp WPA).

Sitwell, Sacheverell.   Editor, author.
See Ballet, Tchaikovsky–2 (ed Haskell).

Note: Other books by Sitwell, including biographies of Liszt, Mozart, Offenbach, & Domenico Scarlatti, apparently are O/P (or not easily available in this country).

Sivic, Stanley A.   Author.
See Notation.

Skeat, William James.   Author (with Clarke & Morgan).   See Arranging–1.

SKILTON,   Charles Sanford

See also:

American Music	Composers–2 & 3a
Appreciation	History

HOWARD, JOHN TASKER
Charles Sanford Skilton.   28 p, frontis por, mus ex, paper.   C. Fischer 1929.   .25

List of works & brief analyses.

Skinner, Ernest M.   Author.
See Organ.

Skinner, Frank.   Author. See Film Music.

Skinner, Oliver R.   Author.
See Theory–3.

Skolsky, Syd. Author.
See Appreciation, App IIb (juvenile).
Slater, Montagu. Author.
See Britten (ed Crozier).

SLEZAK, Leo
See also: History, Opera, Singers.

Songs of motley: being the remini-
cences of a hungry tenor. 302 p, 13
illus. Wm. Hodge & Co, London,
1938.   4.50

*Informal, amusing memoirs, including traves-
ties on opera "stories." Originally pub in
German in 2 volumes: "Meine sämtliche
Werke," 1922 (see also App Ib for a German
ed), & "Der Wortbuch," 1927; later combined in one volume, 1935.*

Slonimsky, Juri. Author.
See Ballet.

Slonimsky, Nicolas. Author, editor, com-
piler. See:
Children–8. Road to music (1947).   2.75
Contemporary Music. Music since
1900 (1938/49).   7.50
Dictionary of Music. Baker's supple-
ment (1949).   .75
Encyclopedias of Music. Thompson,
ed Slonimsky (1949).   16.00
Harris, Roy. In preparation.   △
Latin America. Music of (1945).   3.75
Miscellanies. Lexicon of musical
invective (in prep).   3.50
——. Thing or two (1948).   3.00
Scales. Thesaurus of scales & melo-
dic patterns (1947).   12.00

Smallman, John. Author (with Wilcox).
See Choir/Choral–1.
Smend, Friedrich. Author. See App Ib.

SMETANA, Bedřich
See:

Appreciation	History
Composers–1 & 3b	Opera
(esp Suermondt)	Phonograph Records
Czechoslovakia	Program Notes

*Note: Except for Suermondt's study of
Smetana & Dvořák (listed under Composers
—3b), the only other study in English (by Ne-
jedly, 1924) apparently is O/P, and a Hinrichsen "miniature survey" of Smetana—
announced as "in preparation" in 1949—
apparently has been indefinitely postponed.*

Smith, Cecil. Author. See Operetta.
Smith, Charles Edward. Author &
co-author (with Ramsey). See Jazz.
Smith, Charles Thomas. Author.
See Philosophy.
Smith, David Stanley. Author.
See Stoeckel.
Smith, Hannah. Author. See App IIa.
Smith, Hannah Coffin. Co-author (with
Saltonstall). See Orchestral Music.
Smith, Harold Davis. Author.
See Instruments.
Smith, Henry Augustine. Author.
See Hymns/Hymondy–2.
Smith, Henry Clay. Author. See Industry.
Smith, Hermann. Author.
See Ancient Music, Organ, Piano.
Smith, Irving. Co-author (with Jones &
Walls). See Pronunciation.
Smith, Julia. Author. See Copland.
Smith, Leo. Author.
See Counterpoint–2. Theory–3.
Smith, Macdonald. Author.
Smith, Melville. Author (with Krone).
See Theory–2.
Smith, Mona. Compiler. See Children–5.
Smith, Mortimer. Author. See Bull.
Smith, Moses. Author.
See Koussevitzky, Phonograph Records.
Smith, Ralph Fischer. Author.
See Theory–2.
Smith, Reed. Editor. See Folksongs–2.
Smith, Roger. Co-editor (with Goldman).
See American Music.
Smith, Uselma Clarke. Author.
See Keyboard Harmony.
Smith, William Charles. Author.
See Handel–1.
Smith, William James. Author.
See School Music–1.

SMYTH (Dame) Ethel Mary
See also:

Composers–2 & 3c	History
Contemporary Music	Program Notes
English Music	Women & Music

*Note: Smyth's "Beecham & Pharoah" (1935)
& several volumes of reminiscences apparently are O/P, at least in this country.*

Impressions that remained: memoirs.
Intro Ernest Newman. xxxv, 509,
xi p, illus, mus ex. (1919) Knopf repr
1946.   5.00

*Originally pub 1919 by Longmans in 2
volumes. Reminiscences & letters of a noted
woman composer, giving an intimate picture
of musical life in Germany & England*

Smolle, Kurt. Author. See App Ib.

SOCIETY/SOCIOLOGY (& Music)

See:

Aesthetics	England (Music in)
Appreciation	(esp Mellers)
Community Music	History
Education	Philosophy
	(esp Howes)

Note: Works apparently O/P include a book & booklet by Siegmeister. A large work on this subject is in preparation by Warren D. Allen, at least one portion of which is available in outline form from the Stanford Bookstore, presumably principally for use in the author's course at Stanford University, California.

Society of Saint John the Evangelist.
Sponsors. See Plainsong.
Soderlund, Gustave Frederic. Author, compiler. See Counterpoint–1.
Soibelman, Doris. Author. See Health.

SOL-FA

See: Sight-Singing (note), **Tonic Sol-Fa** (note only).

SOLFÈGE/SOLFEGGIO

General Note: As noted under Sight-Singing, Solfège (in its larger sense) implies not only sight-singing, but a comprehensive French system of basic musical training, including also ear-training, rhythmic drill, & other elementary "theory" subjects.

See also:

Children–3, 7, 8	Rhythm
Dictation	Sight-Playing &
Ear-Training	Reading
Eurhythmics	Sight-Singing
Notation	Theory

BUCHANAN, WALTER
Solfège. vi, 115 p, mus ex, typescript repro. Author 1947, via Santa Barbara College Bookstores, California.   2.50
Outline for 2 semesters' work in musicianship, with supplement. Despite the connotations of the title, the "movable do" system is employed.

LENOM, CLÉMENT
Rhythm by solfeggio: a practical method for the development of the sense of time & of rhythm. 137 p, mus ex, paper. Coleman 1944.   2.50

Thirty lessons in solfeggio: in the form of questions & answers, comprising instruction in the elements of music, including notation, rhythm, intervals, scales, triads, etc. VIII, 78

p, mus ex, paper. (1925) Coleman rev ed 1947.   1.50
Authentic French principles are used here.

MONTANI, NICOLA A.
Essentials in sight-singing: a modern method of solfeggio (solfège or solfa). Forew J. Lewis Browne. 2 v. Birchard 1931 (1945).
V 1: Fundamentals (rudiments & solfeggi based upon the diatonic scale). 170 p, illus, music.   2.60
V 2: The art of ensemble or a cappella singing. 204 p, music   2.60
Largely musical exercises, with special emphasis on group & choral singing.

SONATA

See:

Appreciation	History
Chamber Music	Organ Music
Composers (& under	Phonograph Records
individual names,	Piano Music
esp Beethoven–3,	Program Notes
Mozart–3)	Themes
Composition	Violin Music
Form	

Note: Standard works apparently O/P (or not easily available) include those by Hadow, Hull, Klauwell (in German), Mayer (in German), Selva (in French), Shedlock, etc.

SONG(S)

See also:

Accompaniment	Minstrel/Minstrelsy
American Music	Mörike
Ancient Music	Negro Spirituals
Appreciation	Phonograph Records
Ballad	Poetry (ed Boas)
Baroque Era	Popular Music
Beggar's Opera	Restoration Era
Campion	Romantic Era
Children–7 (esp	School Music–4 (esp
Wilkins)	Wright & Lossing)
Classic Era	Sea Shanties & Songs
Composers (& under	Sheet Music
individual names)	Singers
Composition	Singing
Contemporary Music	Songbooks
Duparc	Song Translations
Elizabethan Music	Song Writing
English Music	Troubadours/
Folklore	Trouvères
Folksongs	d'Urfey
Lehmann	Vocal Music
Medieval/Renaissance	

Also: App IIb (Lyons juvenile).

Note: Standard works apparently O/P (or not easily available) include those by Bedford, Finck, Kobbé, Sonneck, etc.

LEHMANN, LOTTE
More than singing: the interpretation of songs. Tr Frances Holden; forew

Bruno Walter. 192 p, mus ex.
Boosey 1945 (3rd 1946).   3.50
*Discussions of the noted soprano's inter-
pretations of some 87 songs, mostly German
Lieder; a companion work to her "My many
lives" (see under Lehmann).*

MATTFELD, JULIUS & DAVIS, ELLEN L.
(comps)
Variety song cavalcade: a musical-
historical review, 1800-1948. Forew
Abel Green. 256 p. Prentice 1951, in   △
prep.   4.95
*Year-by-year lists, with data on lyricists,
publishers, 1st performances, etc; with yearly
synopses of outstanding contemporary events.*

REUTER, EVELYN. See App Ia.

SCHUMANN, ELISABETH
German song. Tr D. Millar Craig.
72 p, 4 col pl, 41 b&ws. Chanticleer
1948.   2.50
*"World of Music" series No 7. The noted
Lieder singer writes a brief history of German
song from medieval to modern times (illustrated with portraits & facsimiles), and concludes with a chapter on song interpretation.*

SEARS, MINNIE EARL (comp)
Song index. xxxiv, 650 p, Wilson
1926.   △

SEARS, M. E. & CRAWFORD, PHYLLIS (comp)
Song index supplement. xi, 367 p.
Wilson 1934.   △
*H. W. Wilson Company "Standard Cata-
logue" series. These standard reference
works for some 12,000 songs (main index) &
7,000 songs (supplement) are sold to libraries
on a "service" basis—that is, the fees are
adjusted to the size & resources of the libraries
themselves. For information, apply to the
H. W. Wilson Company, New York City.*

UPTON, WILLIAM TREAT
Art-song in America: a study in the
development of American music. xi,
279 p, mus ex. Ditson 1930.   3.00
*A standard survey, currently supplied with
the following supplement included.*
A supplement to "Art-song in
America": 1930-1938. 41 p, mus ex,
paper. Ditson 1938.   △

WILLIAMS, CHARLES FRANCIS ABDY
The rhythm of song. 151 p, mus   △
ex. Methuen 1925.   1.75

SONGBOOKS

*General Note: Although collections of music
only are excluded as a matter of policy from*

*this Guide, here is one of several instances
where the theoretical rule is honored only in
the breach. Of course, no attempt is made to
give even a "representative sampling" of the
vast songbook literature: the works listed below are merely a few that for one reason or
another (or for no reason at all) frequently are
merchandized and popularly are considered
as "books" rather than as song-collections
only.*

*Others that might have been entered here,
except that they apparently are O/P (or not
easily available), include those by Dolph,
Durham, Jordan & Kessler, Kalmer & Ruby,
Kidson, Kobbé, Loesser, Niles, Posselt,
Spaeth, Van Loon & Castagnetta, etc.*

See also:

Carols	Gershwin
Children—7 (esp	Gilbert & Sullivan
Seeger, WPA)	Hymns/Hymnody
Chinese Music	Negro Spirituals
Cowboy Music	Rodgers & Hart
Folklore	Sea Shanties & Songs
Folksongs—1 & 2	

ADLER, KURT (ed & arr)
Songs of many wars: from the sixteenth to the twentieth century. 221
p, music. Howell 1943.   3.00
Some 65 songs with descriptive notes.

HILLE, WALDEMAR (ed)
The people's song book. Forew
Allan Lomax; pref B. A. Botkin. 128
p, music. Gaer Associates, N. Y.,
1948.   2.50
*100 songs composed or adapted for "leftist"
entertainment or propaganda, but including
many fine tunes unavailable elsewhere.*

JACKSON, GEORGE PULLEN
The story of the Sacred Harp, 1844-
1944: a book of religious folk song as
an American institution. 46 p,
frontis fac, pors. Vanderbilt 1944.   1.00
*Origin & history of a famous sacred songbook
of the South, 1st published in 1844.*

KEMP, DAVID (comp)
The skiers' song book. 79 p, 14 illus,
music (tunes only, ed Norman
Mealy). Pacific 1950.   2.50
75 songs, 50 of them with music.

LUTHER, FRANK
Americans and their songs. xiv,
323 p, music. Harper 1942.   2.20
*Words & music for 75 songs, tunes for 50
others; plus an annotated list of some 400
titles, with background commentaries.*

PALMER, EDGAR A. (ed)
G. I. Songs: written, composed, and/

or collected by the men in the service. 253 p, illus (Richard Loederer & Kurt Werth), music (arr Paul Eisler). Sheridan 1944.   2.00

A preliminary attempt to collect the new & old song hits of World War II. Needless to say, many original texts are bowdlerized.

SIEGMEISTER, ELIE (*ed*)
Work and sing: a collection of the songs that built America . . . 96 p, illus (Julian Brazelton), music, 1-p annot bibl. William R. Scott, New York, n d (1944).   2.50

31 American songs with commentary.

SPAETH, SIGMUND (*ed*)
Read 'em and weep: a treasury of American songs—the songs you forgot to remember—some sad, more merry, some sentimental; with a wealth of amiable anecdote, comment, & fascinating folk-lore—a flavorful feast of melodious music; with an album of elegant art. Forew Richard Rodgers. viii, 248 + 16 p, illus, music (tunes only). (1926, 1935) Arco repr, new rev ed 1945.   3.50

A popular collection, originally published by Doubleday Doran.

WALKER, WILLIAM (*ed*)
The southern harmony: songbook. American guide series. Reproduced, with an intro, by the Federal Writers' Project of Kentucky, W. P. A. xxxii, 335 p, illus, music, bds. Hastings 1939.   2.00

Facsimile reproduction of the 1854 edition of the famous "Southern Harmony & Musical Companion" (1835), sponsored by the Young Men's Progress Club of Benton, Kentucky.

ZANZIG, AUGUSTUS D. (*ed*)
Singing America: song & chorus book. Edition with piano accompaniments. Unp (192 p), music, paper. Birchard 1946.   2.00

Some 128 folk & traditional songs of various nationalities, with notes; compiled for the National Recreation Association. Also available in a "vocal edition" (without accompaniments), for 35c.

SONG TRANSLATIONS

See also:

Appreciation	Program Notes
Composers (& under	Singing
individual names)	Song(s)

Note: Several collections of translations (especially of Schubert & Schumann Lieder

texts), by Fox Strangways & Wildon, Porter, & others, apparently are O/P (*or not easily available*).

For information on the Drinker translations of Brahms, Medtner, Schumann, & Wolf song texts, please see the note under Henry S. Drinker's author-entry in this Guide.

HERTZ, LILLY
Song translations.   47 p, paper.   **C.** Fischer 1945.   .75

Text translations of 10 songs each by Brahms & Wolf, plus some 18 others by Debussy, Grieg, Hahn, Reger, Schubert, R. Strauss, Wagner, & Erich Wolff.

Song translations: volume 2.   28 p, paper.   C. Fischer 1946.   .75

Text translations of 16 Wolf songs, plus 14 others by Brahms, Ferrari, Franz, Paladilhe, Schubert, Schumann, & R. Strauss. There is also a list of Alfred Hertz song orchestrations.

MILLER, PHILIP L.
Note: An extensive collection of song translations is in preparation.

SONGWRITERS

See:

America (music in)	Popular Music
American Music	(esp Burton)
Composers–3a (esp	Songwriting
McNamara; & under	Who's Who
individual names)	Yearbooks
Jazz	

SONGWRITING

General Note: Only the more important of the available books on this subject are listed below. Most of them deal primarily with "popular" songs only.

Others that might have been listed, but which apparently are O/P (or not easily available), include those by Adams, Bruce, Kenny, Newton, Nicholls, Shefter, Silver & Bruce, Spaeth & Bruce, Wickes, etc.

See also:

Career	Hammerstein
Composition	Melody Writing
Copyright	Popular Music
Film Music	Song(s)

BRUCE, ROBERT
How to write a hit song and sell it. xii, 208 p, illus, mus ex. Paragon Music Pubs, N. Y., 1945 (1949).   2.00

CHAFFIN, LUCIEN G.
Song-writing and song-making: a book of advice for the amateur com-

poser. 140 p, frontis por. G. Schirmer
1923. 2.00

A discussion of realities & buncombe in composing & marketing songs.

CRIST, BAINBRIDGE
The art of setting words to music.
95 p, mus ex. C. Fischer 1944. 2.00

One of the few books that deals with art-songs, including analyses of many songs by the author & various other composers.

DUBIN, AL
The art of song writing. 53 p, paper.
Majestic Music Co, N. Y., 1928,
via Mills. 1.00

GARLAND, WALLACE GRAYDON
Popular songwriting methods: the unit system of composing melody, harmony, rhythms, & lyrics. Forew Sigmund Spaeth. 324 p, illus, charts, mus ex. America Music Guild, N. Y., 1942. 2.75

KORB, ARTHUR
How to write songs that sell. Forew Irving Caesar. xii, 179 p, charts, mus ex. Greenberg 1949. 2.95

Practical advice, including a directory of song publishers & recording companies.

LEWIS, AL
From rhymes to riches: a complete guide to successful song writing. Pref Rudy Vallee. 94 p, 2 pors. Donaldson Douglas & Gumble, N. Y., 1935. 1.00

Songwriters' rhyming dictionary. 59 p, 2 pors, paper. Donaldson Douglas & Gumble, N. Y., 1936. 1.00

WOOD, CLEMENT (*ed*)
The complete rhyming dictionary & poet's craft book. xi, 607 p. Garden City 1936. 1.98

The "craft book" (practical advice to verse writers) occupies the first 105 pages.

Poets' and songwriters' guide: the complete book of scansion for writers of poetry, verse, song lyrics, & prose. 240 p, 2-p bibl. Valiant House, N. Y., 1948. 3.50

Sonkin, Robert. Co-author (with Levy & Mamen). See Speech.

Sonneck, Oscar George (Theodore).
Author, compiler, editor. See:
America (music in). Early concert life in America (1907). 10.40

American Music. Bibliography, with Upton (1905/45). 2.00

Beethoven–1. Letters (1927). 10.00

Beethoven–2. Impressions of contemporaries (1926). 3.00

Bibliography. Early books, comp. Gregory, ed Sonneck (1913). .60

Foster. Catalogue of 1st editions, Whittlesey & Sonneck (1915). .40

MacDowell. Catalogue of 1st editions (1917). .40

Opera–2. Catalogue of opera librettos (2 v, 1914). 2.00

Orchestral Music. Catalogue of scores, Lib. of Congress (1912). 2.00

Note: A collection of essays, "Suum cuique" (1916), is O/P, as are "The riddle of the immortal beloved" (1927), & various other books by Sonneck.

SORABJI, Kaikhosru Shapurji

See also: Composers–2, Contemporary Music.

Mi contra fa: the immoralisings of a Machiavellian musician. 247 p. Porcupine 1947. 5.00

Biting, anti-romantic essays on a variety of the musical dislikes (& a few likes) of an extraordinary British composer & writer.

Note: Another collection of essays, "Around music" (1932), apparently is O/P (or not easily available in this country).

Sorantin, Erich. Author.
See Expression.

SOUND RECORDING & REPRODUCTION

General Note: This is not a familiar or conventional subject-heading, especially in musical literature, but it is chosen here as most appropriate for a considerable (and rapidly growing) literature for which Acoustics is too general a heading, and Film, Phonograph, Radio, etc, are too specific. Books in this category deal as a rule with various recording & reproducing means & specific instruments.

Only a sampling of the highly technical literature is included here, but most of the best semi-technical works are listed, with special emphasis on those most likely to prove of interest & usefulness to professional musicians, home radio & phonograph listeners, and amateur tape or disc recorders.

294

For the layman (in electronics, that is, if not music), the best general introduction to this whole subject is probably the Mills work below.

See also:

Acoustics (esp Olson, Redman)	Phonograph Records
Decibel	Radio
Film Music (esp Skinner)	Radio Music
	Stokowski
Films	Television
Phonograph	Theatre (esp Burris-Meyer & Cole)

ALDOUS, DONALD W. (ed)
Sound recording year book: v 1.
Hinrichsen 1951, in prep.   △
Hinrichsen "Survey" series S-11.

(AUDIO DEVICES)
How to make good recordings. 144
p, illus (photos, diagrs), paper.
Audio Devices, N. Y., (1940) 9th
pr, rev & enl, 1948.   2.00
A handbook of practical (disc) techniques, including a 14-p glossary of common terms.

BEGUN, S. J.
Magnetic recording. x, 242 p, illus,
bibl. Murray Hill 1949, via Rinehart. 5.00
One of the first full-length studies of what seems likely to become the most important of all recording media.

BRIGGS, G. A.
Loudspeakers: the why and how of
good reproduction. 88 p, photos,
diagrs, table, paper.   Wharfdale
Wireless Works, Bradford, England,   △
(1948), 3rd ed 1949.   (1.25)

Sound reproduction. 248 p, photos,
diagrs, tables, 1–p bibl. Wharfdale
Wireless Works, Bradford, England,   △
(1949) 2nd rev ed 1950.   (2.25)
Two popular, semi-technical booklets directed primarily to builders & users of wide-range radio-phonograph systems.

DORF, RICHARD H.
Practical disc recording. 96 p, illus,
paper. Radcraft Publications, N.Y.,
1948.   .75

FRAYNE, JOHN G. & WOLFE, H.
Elements of sound recording. vii,
686 p, some 480 illus (photos, diagrs,
tables), chap bibls. Wiley 1949.   8.50
The most recent extensive technical study, including 12 chapters on electronic & mechanical fundamentals, 12 on film recording, 2 on disc, & 1 on magnetic recording.

GOLDSMITH, F. H. & GEISEL, V. G.
Techniques of recording. 43 p, 16
illus, paper. Gamble 1939.   1.50

A simplified, semi-technical survey, stressing disc-recording methods.

GREENLEES, A. E.
The amplification and distribution
of sound. x, 302 p, some 108 diagrs,
tables, 2–p bibl. Chapman, London,
(1938) 2nd rev ed 1948, via Sherwood
Press, Pacoima, Calif., 1949.   6.00
Non-mathematical treatment, emphasizing the installation & operation of sound systems.

HUGHES, L. E. C.
Sound reproduction and recording.
Hutchinson 1950, in prep.   △

MILLS, JOHN
A fugue in cycles and bels. vi, 269 p,
diagrs. Van Nostrand 1935.   3.00
A noted Bell Labs engineer describes in non-technical language what science is doing and what it can do for music. Although this work does not embody the latest developments (i.e., magnetic-tape recording), it remains one of the layman's most effective introductions to sound-reproduction principles & techniques, as well as to the decibel notation, & hearing itself.

McPROUD, C. G. (ed)
Audio anthology: compiled from
Audio Engineering from May 1947
to December 1949. 124 p, photos,
diagrs, tables, bibl refs bds. Radio
Magazines, N. Y., 1950.   3.00
Same, paper covers.   2.00
A collection of articles from the leading periodical in this field, "Audio Engineering," written by the editor, Drisko, Goodell, Pickering, Sarser, & Sprinkle, and others, and dealing mainly with the design & construction of home sound-reproducing equipment.

NEWITT, JOHN H.
High-fidelity techniques: how to improve sound quality in radio re-
ceivers. Some 375 p, some 175 illus.
Murray Hill, via Rinehart, 1950, in
prep.   △

READ, OLIVER
The recording and reproduction of
sound. x, 364 p, photos, diagrs,
tables. Howard Sams & Co, Indianapolis, 1949.   5.00
Episodic studies (some technical, mostly semi-technical) of various techniques & instruments, based on a series originally published in "Radio & Television News," and including a reprint of the proposed American standard acoustical terminology (see also Acoustics).

SOUSA, John Philip

See also:

America (music in)	History
American Music	March
Appreciation	Military Music
Band–1	Phonograph Records
Composers–3a	Program Notes

Note: A book of memoirs by the bandmaster's grandson, "My family right or wrong" (1943) apparently is O/P, as is a juvenile biography by Lewiton (1944).

Marching along: recollections of men, women, & music.   xiii, 384 p, 21 pl. Hale Cushman & Flint, Boston, 1928 (pop repr 1941).   2.00

The bandmaster's autobiography, including a catalogue of his compositions.

SOUTHWEST (U. S. A.)

See: America—music in (Whitlock & Saunders).

Souvaine, Geraldine.   Co-author (with Milligan).   See Opera–3.

Spaeth, Sigmund Gottfried.   Author, editor. See:

Amateur Music.   Music for fun 1939/45).   1.00

Appreciation.   Art of enjoying music. (1939/49).   .35

——. At home with music (1946).   3.95

——. Common sense of music (1924).   2.00

——. Music for everybody (1934/45).   .60

Barbershop.   Ballads (1924/40).   1.96

Opera–3.   Favorite arias (1947).   .50

Popular Music.   History (1948).   5.00

Program Notes.   Guide to great orchestral music (1943).   2.45

Songbooks.   Read 'em & weep (1926).   3.50

Symphony.   Great symphonies. (1936).   .95

App IIa.   Schumann juvenile (1950).   3.00

Note: Numerous other books by this perhaps most prolific of all American writers on music apparently are O/P.

SPAIN (Music in)/SPANISH MUSIC

Note: It is extremely curious that only a couple of pertinent books actually are available for listing here, for most of the considerable literature apparently is O/P (or not easily available in this country), including

standard works by Aubry (in French), Chase, Trend, Salazar (in Spanish), Van Vechten, etc.

See also:

Ancient Music	Gypsy Music
Appreciation	History
Ballet	Latin America
Baroque Era	Medieval/Renaissance
Composers (& under	Opera
individual names,	Orchestra Music
esp Falla)	Phonograph Records
Contemporary Music	Piano Music
Dances–2 (esp ed Al-	Program Notes
ford: Armstrong)	Song(s)
Folklore	Songbooks
Folksongs	Violin Music

Also: Appendix Id, for a selected list of books (on music & musicians) in Spanish.

HAMILTON, MARY NEAL
Music in eighteenth century Spain. 283 p, music, 4–p bibls. Illinois 1937.   3.50

Same, paper covers.   3.00

University of Illinois Studies in Language & Literature, v XXII, Nos 1/2. A scholarly study of both the secular & sacred music, with lists of instruments, music books & methods, etc.

POPE, ISABEL
Spanish secular vocal music of the early Renaissance in relation to the form & style of contemporary musical developments in western Europe. In prep.   Δ

SUBIRÁ, JOSÉ.   See App Ic.

SPALDING, Albert

See also:

| America (music in) | Interpreters |
| History | Violinists |

Rise to follow: an autobiography. 328 p, frontis por (Violet Oakley). Holt 1943 (5th pr 1946).   3.50

The memoirs of the noted American violinist, including his experiences as an aviator in in the first World War, as well as his long career as a concert artist.

Spalding, Walter Raymond.   Author. See:

Appreciation.   Music, an art & a language (1920/39), complete with music supplements.   7.50

Counterpoint–1. Tonal (1904/32).   2.50

Harmony–2.   Modern (1905/36), by Foote & Spalding.   3.00

——. Key to modern harmony.   2.00

SPANISH LANGUAGE
See: Dictionaries of Terms, Pronunciation (esp Jones), App Id.

SPANISH MUSIC
See: Spain (music in)/Spanish Music.

Speck, Jay. Co-author (with Blanké).
See Theory–2

SPEECH
General Note: Only a sampling of the large available literature is listed below.

Other pertinent works, excluded only because they are apparently O/P (or not easily available), include those by Behnke, Kempton, Paget, Russell, Stinchfield, etc.

See also:

Acting	Hearing
Children–7 (esp Wood)	Italian Language
	Pronunciation
Choral Speaking	Radio
Diction	Singing
French Language	Voice
German Language	

ANDERSON, VIRGIL A.
Training the speaking voice. xx, 387, p, illus (Walter B. Schwartz), 3½–p bibl. Oxford 1942 (12 pr 1950).   3.25

AVERY, ELIZABETH (*& others*)
First principles of speech training. xxxviii, 518 p, 30 illus, 2–p bibl. Appleton 1928.   3.25
Co-authors: Jane Dorsey & Vera A. Sickels.

BARNES, GRACE
General American speech sounds. vi, 129 p, illus. Heath 1946.   1.96
The 43 sounds of general American speech and drills for perfecting them.

BEHNKE, KATE EMIL–
The technique of good speech. xiii, 256 p, illus, mus ex, bds.   Curwen △ 1937.   (4.50)
Superseding an earlier work, "The speaking voice," by the author's mother, Mrs Emil-Behnke, but retaining many exercises.

BENDER, JAMES F.
(*See also Fields & Bender below.*)
How to talk well. xii, 262 p. Whittlesey 1949.   3.50
With exercises for cultivating an "improved speech personality."

DESFOSSÉS, BEATRICE
Your voice and your speech: self-training for better speaking.   xiii,

224 p, illus.   Cattell & Co, N. Y., 1946, via Wyn 1949.   2.50

FIELDS, VICTOR & BENDER, JAMES F.
Voice and diction. viii, 368 p. Macmillan 1949.   4.00
Basic vocal theory and drill material for correcting speech faults.

FREEMANTEL, FREDERIC
How to improve your speaking voice. 194 p. Freemantel Voice Institute, N. Y., 1946.   3.00

FRÖSCHELS, EMIL, & JELLINEK, AUGUSTE
Practice of voice and speech therapy: new contributions to voice & speech pathology. 255 p, illus. Expression 1941.   4.00

GRIM, HARRIETT ELIZABETH
Practical voice training: a manual for developing the voice.   xi, 197 p, diagrs, 1½–p bibl. Appleton 1948.   2.25
Primarily speech training, with many selections for practice.

LEVY, LOUIS (*& others*)
Voice and diction handbook.   Intro Gustav F. Schulz. viii, 112 p, diagr, paper.   Prentice 1950.   1.65
Co-authors: Edward W. Mammen & Robert Sonkin.

MANSER, RUTH B. & FINLAN, LEONARD
The speaking voice. xii, 404 p, 23 illus, 4–p bibl. Longmans 1950.   4.00
A study of the voice itself and the correction of vocal faults, with graded reading selections & a 4-p list of voice recordings.

OSBORN, LORAINE
Your voice personality. xiv, 190 p, diagrs.   Putnam (1938) 3rd ed, 2nd pr 1945.   2.50

PIKE, KENNETH L.
Tone languages: a technique for determining the number & type of pitch contrasts in a language, with studies in tonemic substitution & fusion. xii, 187 p, tables, 8–p bibl, typescript repro. Michigan 1948.   3.00
University of Michigan Publications in Linguistics, v 4.

POTTER, RALPH K. (*& others*)
Visible speech. xvi, 441 p, col frontis, illus. Van Nostrand 1947.   4.75
Co-authors: George A. Kopp & Harriet C. Green.   The story of the remarkable Bell Labs electronic device for making speech visible, and some suggested musical applications.   The work includes some 500 specto-

grams showing all sounds & important sound-combinations in American speech.

RASMUSSEN, CARRIE E.
Speech methods in tne elementary
school. ix, 340 p, illus, bibl. Ronald
1949.   3.50

SANSOM, CLIVE (*ed*)
Speech of our time.   228 p, frontis,
chap bibls. Hinrichsen n d (1948).   3.00

Hinrichsen "Survey" S-7: a British sym-posium with specialized articles by some 37 authorities discussing such subjects as Theatre, Radio, Film, Phonograph Records, Speech Education, Speech Therapy, etc.

WALSH, GERTRUDE
Sing your way to speech: a jingle
sequence for the improvement of
articulation & rhythm in speaking.
213 p, illus (Lena Rue), music (arr
Roger Boardman).   Dutton (1939)
rev enl ed 1947. (4th pr 1948).   2.85

Verses, many with musical settings, for consonant & vowel drill exercises.

Spence, Lewis. Author. See (The) Dance.
Spencer, Bernard. Author
See Piano Playing–3.
Spencer, Stanhope Reid. Author.
See Harmony–2.
Spielter, Hermann. Author.
See Harmomy–2.
Spier, Miriam.   Author
See Singing–3.

SPINET
See: Instruments, Keyboard Instruments &
Music (esp Kenyon).

SPIRITUALS
See: Negro Spirituals & Songs.

Spitta, (Johann August) Philipp. Author.
See Bach–1 (note only), App Ib.
Note: Spitta's famous Bach biography is currently O/P in the English edition (al-though there are rumors of a reprint "in preparation") and it is available in German only in a severely abridged "popular" edition.

Spitteler, Carl. Author. See App Ib.

SPONTINI, Gasparo
See: App Ia (Bouvet biog in French).

Also: History, Italian Music, Opera.

Sposa, Louis A. Author.
See Television.

Spreen, Hildegard L. Author.
See Dances–2.

Springer, Max. Author. See Plainsong.
Editor. See App Ib.

Squier, Victor Carroll. Author.
See Stradivari.

Stabenow, Karl. Editor. See App Ib.

STAFF
See:

Children–3 & 8	Score-Reading
Dictation	Sight-Playing &
Ear-Training	Reading
History	Sight-Singirg
Notation	Solfège/Solfeggio
Scale	Theory

STAGE
See:

Acting	Operetta
Conducting	Singing
Drama	Stage-Fright
Opera	Theatre

STAGE-FRIGHT
See also:

Acting	Piano Playing
Interpretation	Psychology
Memory	Singing

Note: A study by Mary Louise Goodhue (1927, 1935) apparently is O/P.

CHING, JAMES
Performer and audience: an investigation into the psychological causes
of anxiety & nervousness in playing,
singing, or speaking before an audience. ix, 96 p. Hall 1947.   2.50
A serious study, by a British pianist & teacher, based on Freudian principles of psychoanalysis & on personal observation.

Staiger, Emil. Author. See App Ib.

STAINER, (Sir) John
See:

Church Music	English Music
Composers	History

Author. See:

Composition. Guide (1880?).   1.00
Dictionaries of Terms.   Abridged,
with W. A. Barrett (1876).   1.75
Harmony–2. Textbook (n d).   1.50
Jewish Music.   Music of the Bible
(1879/1914).   2.25
Note: Several other books by Stainer appar-ently are O/P, at least in this country.

STANFORD, (Sir) Charles Villiers

See:

| Composers | History |
| English Music | Program Notes |

Note: Biographies & studies apparently O/P (or not easily available) include those by Fuller Maitland, Greene, Porte, etc.

Author (with Forsyth).　See Addenda.

Note: Other books by Stanford, including 3 volumes of reminiscences, apparently are O/P, at least in this country.

STANISLAVSKI, Constantin.　Author.

(*Pseud* of Konstantin Sergieevich Aleksieev.)

See also: Acting.

My life in art.　**J. J.** Robbins.　xi, 586 p. (1924) Theatre Arts repr 1948.　　　　　　　　　　3.75

The actor-director's autobiography & reminiscences of the Moscow Art Theatre. Includes chapters on The Conservatory, A. Rubinstein, Attempts in Operetta, The Opera, The Opera Studio, etc.

Stanley, Douglas.　Author.　See Voice.
Stanton, Hazel Martha.　Author.
See Tests.
Staples, H. J.　Author.
See Choir/Choral–2.
Starke, Aubrey Harrison.　Author.
See Lanier.
Starkie, Walter.　Author.
See Gypsy Music.
Starr, William Thomas.　Compiler.
See Rolland.

(THE) STAR-SPANGLED BANNER

See: esp App IIb (Lyons juvenile).

Also:

America (music in)	National Music
American Music	Sheet Music
History	Song(s)
Key (note only)	Songbooks

Note: Muller's bibliographical list of editions (1935) apparently is O/P, as is Sonneck's "Report on 'The Star Spangled Banner,' 'Hail Columbia,' etc" (1909). Sonneck's "The Star Spangled Banner" (1914, rev & enlarged from his earlier report) is on the point of going out-of-print at the Government Printing Office, 1950—hence it is not entered here in detail.

Stead, John Philip.　Editor.
See Restoration Era.

Stebbins, Lucy Poate & Richard Poate.
Authors.　See Weber.
Stecher, William Albin.　Author (with Mueller).　See Dances–1.

Stefan (-Gruenfeldt), Paul.　Author, co-editor (with Werfel).　See Verdi–1.
Note: Numerous other books by Stefan apparently are O/P (or not easily available in this country).

Steglich, Rudolf.　Author.　See App Ib.

STEIN, Gertrude

See also:

| American Music | Opera |
| Contemporary Music | Poetry |

Last operas and plays.　Ed & intro Carl Van Vechten.　xix, 480 p, frontis por.　Reinhart 1949.　　　　5.00
19 works (1917/45), including unabridged versions of "The Mother of Us All" & "Four Saints in Three Acts" (for which musical settings were written by Virgil Thomson).

Stein, Leo.　Author.　See Wagner–2.
Stellhorn, Martin Henry.　Compiler.
See Organ Music.
Stevens, (Mother) Georgia.　Author.
See Gregorian Chant.
Stevens, Halsey.　Author.　See Bartók.
Stevens, Stanley Smith.　Author (with Davis).　See Hearing.
Stickle, Mary L.　Author
See Children–6.

STILL, William Grant

See also:

| American Music | Contemporary Music |
| Composers–2 & 3a | Negro Music |

ARVEY, VERNA
William Grant Still.　Intro John Tasker Howard.　48 p, frontis por, mus ex, paper.　J. Fischer 1939.　　.25
Catalogue of works & brief analyses.

Stillman Kelley, Edgar.
Catalogued under Kelley, Edgar Stillman.

STOCK, Frederick August
See: America (music in), Conductors.
Co-author (with Thomas).　See Beethoven –3.

Stocks, H. C. L.　Author.
See Boy Voices.　Organists.

STOECKEL, Gustav Jakob

SMITH, DAVID STANLEY
Gustave J. Stoeckel: Yale pioneer
in music. 31 p, paper. Yale 1939. 1.00

Stoecklin, Paul de. Author. See App Ia.
Stoessel, Albert. Author.
See Baton–1. Choir/Choral–1.
Stoeving, Paul. Author. See Violin.
Stokes, Adrian. Author. See Ballet.

STOKOWSKI, Leopold

See also:

America (music in)   Interpreters
Conductors   Philadelphia
History   Phonograph Records

Music for all of us. vii, 340 p, frontis,
mus ex. S & S 1943. 2.50

*An unclassifiable book: partly "apprecia-
tion," elementary "theory," & musical philosophy; but perhaps most useful for its illuminating chapters on orchestral training,
acoustics, instruments, phonograph & film
recording, and radio broadcasting.*

Stokowski, Olga Samaroff. Catalogued
under Samaroff (-Stokowski), Olga.
Storr, Muriel. Author. See Children–2.

STRADIVARI (Stradivarius), Antonio

See also:

History   Italy (music in)
Instruments   Violin

Also: App IIa (juvenile by Tinyanova).

*Note: Standard works apparently O/P (or not
easily available) include those by Fétis,
Hill & Sons, Petherick, etc.*

BALFOORT, DIRK J.
Antonius Stradivarius. Tr W. A. G.
Doyle-Davidson. 60 p, illus, brief
bibl, bds. Continental n d (1947). 2.50
*"Symphonia" series. The many illustrations
include 2 pages of Strad labels.*

DORING, ERNEST N. *(comp)*
How many Strads?: our heritage
from the master; a tribute to the
memory of a great genius, compiled
in the year marking the ter-centenary
of his birth; being a tabulation of
works believed to survive produced
in Cremona by Antonio Stradivari
between 1666 & 1737, including relevant data & mention of his two sons,
Francesco & Omobono, 379 p, some
100 illus, 2–p bibl, leather. Wm.
Lewis & Son, Chicago, 1945. 20.00

*History & present location of some 500
Strads, based on extensive research.*

ORCUTT, WILLIAM DANA
The Stradivari memorial at Washington, the national capital. 49 p, 17
pl, paper. Library of Congress,
Gertrude Clarke Whittall Foundation, 1938. .50
*A booklet on sale at the Library's souvenir
stand; postage 10c additional.*

OTTANI, GIANCARLO. See App Ic.

SQUIER, VICTOR CARROLL
Antonio Stradivari: his life & work
(1644–1737). 99 p, 35 illus. Author,
Battle Creek, Michigan, 1944 (1945). 3.50
*A highly individual violin-craftsman's per-
sonal story & tribute, with fictional portraits
of Stradivari's home & workshop.*

Strakacz, Aniela. Author.
See Paderewski.
Strangways, A. H. Fox. Catalogued under
Fox Strangways, Arthur Henry.

STRAUSS FAMILY (The "Waltz Kings")

See also:

Appreciation   Phonograph Records
Ballet   Program Notes
(The) Dance   J. Strauss, Jr
Dance Music   Themes
History   Timing
March   Vienna
Operetta   Vocal Music
Orchestral Music   Waltz

Also: App IIa (Ewen juvenile).

*Note: Pertinent works apparently O/P (or not
easily available) include Teetgen's "The
waltz kings of old Vienna" (1939), and works
in German by Kleinecke, Lange, Scheyrer,
Witeschnik, etc.*

JACOB, H. E.
Johann Strauss, father and son: a
century of light music. Tr Marguerite Wolff; intro Pitts Sanborn. xiii,
385 p, illus, mus ex. (1939) Halcyon
repr 1948. O/P
*First published in English by William Sal-
loch & Greystone, 1939. (O/P 1950.)*

PASTENE, JEROME
Three-quarter time: the life & music
of the Strauss family of Vienna.
Abelard 1951, in prep. 3.50
*A combined family biography & waltz
history, with record lists, etc.*

STRAUSS, Johann, Sr.

See: Strauss Family.

STRAUSS, Johann, Jr. ("The Waltz King")

See also: Strauss Family (& references).

Note: Pertinent works apparently O/P (or not easily available) include those in German by Eisenberg, Kobald, von Prochazka, Schnitzer, Sündermann, etc.

DECSEY, ERNST. See App Ib.

JASPERT, WERNER. See App Ib.

ROBERTSON, MARION E. See Ballet ("Le beau Danube" & "Le tricorne").

Strauss, L. Harry. Author (with Kidd). See Teaching–1.

STRAUSS, Richard

See also:

Appreciation	Phonograph Records
Composers–1 & 2	Program Notes
Conductors	Romantic Era
Contemporary Music	Song(s)
History	Song Translations
Instrumentation	Themes
Modern Music	Timing
Opera	Vocal Music
Orchestral Music	Zweig

Author, editor. For Strauss's own "Betrachtungen und Erinnerungen" (1949), see App Ib. For his revision of Berlioz's "Treatise on instrumentation," see Instrumentation.

Note: Standard works apparently O/P (or not easily available) include the Strauss-Hofmannsthal correspondence; and books about Strauss & his music by Archer, Blom, Finck, Gilman, Newman, etc; in German by Bie, Gregor, Seidl, Specht, Steinitzer, von Waltershausen, etc.

ARMSTRONG, THOMAS
Strauss's tone poems: Don Juan, Tod und Verklärung, Till Eulenspiegels lustige Streiche, Don Quixote, Ein Heldenleben. 56 p, mus ex, paper. Oxford 1931 (1948).   1.00

BRANDL, WILLY. See App Ib.

HUTCHESON, ERNEST
Elektra, by Richard Strauss: a guide to the opera, with musical examples from the score. 61 p, mus ex. G. Schirmer 1910.   1.00

PFISTER, KURT. See App Ib.

PRYCE-JONES, ALAN
Richard Strauss: Der Rosenkavalier. 32 p, mus ex, paper. Boosey 1947.   .60
"*Covent Garden Operas*" series.

RÖSE, OTTO & PRÜWER, JULIUS
Richard Strauss' Elektra: a guide to the music. Tr Alfred Kalisch. v, 42 p + fac & chart of themes, mus ex, paper. Fürstner & G. Schirmer 1910.   .40
A step-by-step analysis of the opera, with a MS score-page in facsimile.

ROSTAND, CLAUDE. See App Ia.

SCHATTMANN, ALFRED
Richard Strauss' Der Rosenkavalier: a guide to the work. Tr Alfred Kalisch. x, 88 p + fac & chart of themes, mus ex, paper. Fürstner & G. Schirmer 1911.   .60
A step-by-step analysis of the opera, with a MS score-page in facsimile.

SCHUH, WILLI. See App Ib.

TENSCHERT, ROLAND. See App Ib.

STRAVINSKY, Igor
1. Own Writings   2. Life & Works

STRAVINSKY (1. Own Writings)

Note: An autobiography, "Chronicle of my life" (1936) is O/P in the English version, and apparently O/P (or not easily available) in the French & German editions.

Poetics of music: in the form of six lessons. Pref Darius Milhaud; tr Arthur Knodel & Ingolf Dahl. xi, 142 p. Harvard 1947.   2.50

The Charles Eliot Norton lectures at Harvard University, 1939/40, first published in the original French (also by the Harvard Press, 1942, now O/P). An outline of the composer's frequently unorthodox ideas on musical aesthetics and a philosophical apologia for his own stylistic development.

STRAVINSKY (2. Life & Works)

See also:

Appreciation	Opera
Ballet	Orchestral Music
Chamber Music	Phonograph Records
Choir/Choral–3	Piano Music
Composers–2 & 3e	Program Notes
Concerto	Russian Music
Contemporary Music	Themes
(The) Dance	Timing
Dance Music	Violin Music
History	Vocal Music
Modern Music	

Note: Standard works apparently O/P (or not easily available) include a symposium ed

Armitage (*but see Corle below*), *and books by Belaiev, Casella* (*in Italian*), *Collaer* (*in French*), *Fleischer* (*in German*), *Handschin* (*in German*), *Schaeffner* (*in French*), *White*, *etc. For an extensive bibliography, see the Lederman entry below.*

CORLE, EDWIN (*ed*)
Stravinsky. 245 p, illus (some col).
Duell Sloan 1949. **6.00**

A symposium (*a "Merle Armitage book"*), *superseding that edited by Armitage & published by G. Schirmer in 1936. In addition to the earlier material* (*by Boys, Cocteau, Goossens, Satie, & de Schloezer*), *there is a new introduction by the editor and 10 new articles by various authors. The illustrations include portraits, photographs, & paintings by Chagall, Klee, Picasso, Weston, & others. There is also a catalogue of works & a 13-p discography* (*by David Hall*) *of Stravinsky recordings.*

DOBRZYNSKI, BORIS
Fabulous Igor. Cosmos in prep. Δ

EVANS, EDWIN, *Jr*
Stravinsky: the Fire-bird and Petrushka. 44 p, mus ex, paper.
Oxford 1933. **1.00**
"Musical Pilgrim" series of analyses.

LEDERMAN, MINNA (*ed & intro*)
Stravinsky in the theatre: a many-sided portrait. 228 p, some 75 pl, mus ex, 38-p bibl (Paul Magriel).
Pellegrini 1949. **3.75**
A symposium, originally published (*1948*) *in shorter form as V 6, Nos 10/12 of "Dance Index."* *The contributors include Ansermet, Balanchine, Berger, Bernstein, Chávez, Copland, Craft, Kirstein, Milhaud, Monteux, Nabokov, Piston, Schuman, Stravinsky, & others. In addition to the definitive bibliography to date* (*by Magriel*), *there is a 5-p discography and a detailed list of world-wide productions of Stravinsky's works in various forms.*

MALIPIERO, G. FRANCESCO. See App Ic.

MYERS, ROLLO H.
Introduction to the music of Stravinsky. 64 p, mus ex. Dobson 1950. **1.00**

ONNEN, FRANK
Stravinsky. Tr M. M. Kessler-Button. 58 p, 18 pl (pors, fac, etc), mus ex, brief bibl, bds. Continental n d (1948); Macmillan 1950. **1.50**
"Symphonia" series of illustrated monographs, with lists of works & recordings.

POSNER, SANDY
Petrouchka: the story of the ballet. 96 p, 4 col pl & some 19 b&ws (Joyce Millen). Newman Wolsey, London, (1945) 4th ed 1947, via Transatlantic. **.75**
"Ballet Pocket Library" series.

RAMUZ, C. F. See App Ia.

ROBERTSON, MARION. See Ballet ("L'Oiseau de feu" & "Schéhérazade").

STRAVINSKY, THÉODORE. See App Ia.

TANSMAN, ALEXANDRE
Igor Stravinsky: the man & his music. Tr Therese & Charles Bleefield. xv, 295 p, frontis por, mus ex. Putnam 1949. **3.75**
A study, originally published in French (*1948, see App Ia*), *by a composer-pianist, who stresses the central unity underlying the apparent jumps & shifts in the development of Stravinsky's art.*

WHITE, ERIC WALTER
Stravinsky: a critical survey. 192 p, 14 pl (pors, facs, etc), 2-p bibl. Philosophical 1948. **3.75**
Originally published in 1947 by Lehmann in England, and superseding the author's "Stravinsky's sacrifice to Apollo" (*1930*). *A catalogue of works & a 5-p discography are included.*

Strawinsky, Théodore. Author.
See App Ia.
Streatfeild, Noel. Author.
See App IIb (juveniles).

Streatfeild, Richard Alexander. Author.
See Opera–3.
Note: Several other works by R. A. Streatfeild apparently are O/P (*or not easily available in this country*).

STRING(S)/STRING INSTRUMENTS

General Note: For convenience this heading is restricted to books dealing with string instruments played with a bow (*i.e., excluding the harp, piano, etc*), *and the actual listings are divided into the following sub-categories—*

String Instruments
String Playing
String Quartet

See also: Harp, Keyboard Instrs, Piano.

STRING INSTRUMENTS

See also:

Acoustics	Medieval/Renaissance
Ancient Music	Neel
Appreciation	Orchestra
Baroque Era	Romantic Era
Chamber Music	Stradivari
Classic Era	String Playing
Concerto	String Quartet
Guadagnini Family	Vibrato
History	Viola/Viola Playing
Instrumentation	Violin
Instruments	

Note: Standard works apparently O/P (or not easily available) include those by Rühlmann (in German), Stoeving, etc.

GILTAY, J. W.
Bow instruments: their form & construction; practical & detailed investigation & experiments regarding vibration, sound results, & construction; including the examination of the views of authors in various languages on the physical & mechanical side of the instruments . . . x, 129 p, illus, paper. Reeves n d (1923). △ (3.00)

With extracts from foreign authors translated by Giltay & E. Van Der Straeten. A cloth-bound edition is temporarily out of stock.

HEPWORTH, WILLIAM
Information for players, owners, dealers, & makers of bow instruments; also for string manufacturers: taken from personal experience, studies, & observations, with illustrations of a Stainer & a Guarnerius violin, etc. 89 p + 3-p pl. Reeves n d (1899?). △ (2.25)

PANUM, HORTENSE
The stringed instruments of the middle ages: their evolution & development; a detailed & comprehensive history, with illustrations, of the evolution of the mediaeval stringed musical instruments from the first appearance in the records of earliest civilizations, through their gradual development in the Greek, Roman, & Christian eras down to more recent times. English ed, rev & ed Jeffrey Pulver. ix, 511 p, some 400 illus. △ Reeves n d (1941). (9.00)

A standard, comprehensive work, originally published in Danish, 1915.

STRING PLAYING

Note: The books listed here deal with bowed string-instrument playing only; for others see Keyboard Instruments, Piano Playing, etc.

See also:

Interpretation	Viola/Viola Playing
Orchestra	Violin Playing
String Quartet	Violoncello Playing

Note: Standard works apparently O/P (or not easily available) include Martens's "String mastery" (1923), etc. Numerous "methods" (devoted primarily to musical exercises) for various types of string instruments are not listed.

BARJANSKY, SERGE
The physical basis of tone production for string instrument players. Intro Gaylord Yost. 32 p, 4 photos, paper. (1939) Volkwein 1941. 1.00

Super-title: "Back to Joachim." Cover only: "After 300 years the basic problem of bow technic finally solved."

MARTI, SAMUEL
Basic violin-viola technique (Technica basica para violin y viola). 74 p, illus, mus ex. Orquesta Sinfonica de Yucatan, Mexico, 1937. 1.00

A practical study, with text in both English & Spanish.

SHIRLEY, PAUL
Right-hand culture: for violin, viola, & 'cello players. 30 p, explanatory drwgs (Florence L. Spaulding), paper. C. Fischer 1917 (6th ed n d). .50

TERTIS, LIONEL
Beauty of tone in string playing. Forew Fritz Kreisler. 22 p, paper. Oxford 1938 (1946). .75

Notes on tonal purity & tone-coloring.

STRING QUARTET

See also:

Amateur Music	Instruments
Appreciation	Phonograph Records
Chamber Music	Program Notes
Instrumentation	String Playing

Also: Composers, and under the individual names of string-quartet composers, esp Bartók, Beethoven, Brahms, Haydn, Mozart, Schubert, etc.

Note: Standard works apparently O/P (or not easily available) include those by Altmann (catalogue in German), etc.

AULICH, BRUNO & HEIMERAN, ERNST
The well-tempered string quartet: a book of counsel & entertainment for all lovers of music in the home. Tr D. Millar Craig. 135 p, 1½-p annot bibl, paper. Gray 1938. 1.75

Originally published in German (1936) as "Das stillvergnügte Streichquartett." Notes on quartet playing, with analyses of many chamber works, including quintets.

Note: A revised, augmented edition (Novello 1949) apparently is not for sale in the United States.

LÉNER, JENÖ
The technique of string quartet playing. English, French, & German text. 42 p + 4 separate parts (25, 25, 26, 26 p), paper. Chester 1935.   **5.00**
Except for the introduction & occasional notes, this is mainly music, with separate books of parts for the four players.

NORTON, M. D. HERTER
String quartet playing: a treatise on chamber music, its technique & interpretation, illustrated with numerous examples in score. 144 p, frontis, 132 mus ex. C. Fischer 1925.   **3.00**
Detailed, practical advice on interpretative & executant techniques.

PINCHERLE, MARC. See App Ia.

Stringham, Edwin John. Author. See Appreciation. Co-author (with Murphy). See Theory–2.
Strobel, Heinrich. Author. See App Ib.
Strong, Leonard Alfred George. Author. See McCormack.
Strube, Gustav. Author. See Harmony–2.

STRUCTURE (Musical)
See:

Composition	History
Form	Theory

Strunk, Oliver. Author. See History–1.
Stuart, Charles. Author. See Britten.
Stubbings, G. W. Author. See Church Music.
Stubbins, William Harold. Author. See Clarinet.
Studer, Carmen. Co-author (with Weingartner). See App Ib.

STUDY (Music)
See: esp Musicianship (note only).

Also:

Appreciation	Education
Children	School Music
Colleges	Theory

Also: the various specialized branches of music-study, such as Composition, Piano Playing, Singing, etc.

STYLE
See:

Aesthetics–1 (esp Sachs) & 2	England (music in) (esp Mellers)
Appreciation	Form
Composers (& under individual names)	History
	Musicology
Composition	Program Notes
	Psychology

Also: American Music & the musics of other national schools; Chamber Music & other types of works; Baroque Era & other historical periods, etc.

Note: Guido Adler's "Der Stil in der Musik" (1911, 1929) apparently is O/P.

Subirá, José. Author. See App Id.
Suckling, Norman. Author. See Fauré.
Suermondt, R. P. Author. See Composers–3b.
Sugrue, Charles. Co-author (with Condon). See Condon.

SULLIVAN, (Sir) Arthur Seymour
See: esp Gilbert & Sullivan.
Also:

Appreciation	Hymns/Hymnody
Composers–1	Operetta
England (music in)	Phonograph Records
English Music	Program Notes
History	Vocal Music

Note: Standard works—dealing primarily with Sullivan alone, rather than with Gilbert & Sullivan—apparently O/P (or not easily available) include those by Findon, Sullivan & Flower, Wyndham, etc.

Sullivan, John William Navin. Author. See Beethoven–2.

SUMER IS ICUMEN IN
See: Rounds (esp Bukofzer).
Also:

England (music in)	Medieval/Renaissance
History	Songbooks

Summerfield, Hattie. Author. See Children–6.
Sumner, William Leslie. Author. See Organ.
Suñol y Baulenas, (Dom) Gregorio Maria. Author. See Gregorian Chant.

SUPERSONICS
See: Ultrasonics.

Note: After some early confusion, it now is generally agreed among physicists that Supersonics be confined to the field of study of aircraft & missiles moving at speeds faster than that of sound; while Ultrasonics be confined to that branch of acoustics dealing with audio waves of higher frequency than those normally audible to the human ear.

SUPERVISORS (Music)
See: Education, School Music, Teaching.

Sur, William Raymond. Editor.
See School Music–3.

SURETTE, Thomas Whitney
Music and life: a study of the relations between ourselves & music.
xvi, 251 p. Houghton 1917.   2.00

Essays in "appreciation" and the correlation of music with other social & artistic activities of everyday life.

Co-author (with Mason). See Appreciation.

Swalin, Benjamin Franklin. Author.
See Violin Music.

Swan, Alfred Julius. Author.
See Repertory.

Note: Swan's books on modern music & Scriabin apparently are O/P.

Swarm, Paul. Editor. See Church Music.

SWARTHOUT, Gladys
See also:

| Interpreters | Phonograph Records |
| Opera | Singers |

Come soon, tomorrow!: the story of a young singer. vii, 278 p. Dodd Mead 1943 (3rd pr 1945).   2.50

Not an autobiography, but a quasi-juvenile novel, in Dodd Mead's "career books" series.

SWEDEN (Music in)/SWEDISH MUSIC
See also:

Dances– 2 (esp ed Alford: Salvén)	Folksongs–1
Folklore	History
	Lind

OLLÉN, OLAF (*ed*)
Sweden in music. 71 p, illus, bds.
American Scandinavian Foundation,   △
N. Y., 1949.   1.50

Originally prepared as a program book for a concert, "Sweden in Music," held in Carnegie Hall, New York City, 11 April 1949.

SWEELINCK, Jan Pieters
See:

Appreciation	Keyboard Instru-
Baroque Era	ments & Music
Choir/Choral–3	Organ Music
Church Music	Phonograph Records
Composers–1	Psalms/Psalmody
History	

Note: Sollitt's "Dufay to Sweelinck" (1933) is O/P and we have not traced any English, French, or German book devoted exclusively to Sweelinck. The standard work is in Dutch, by B. van den Sigtenhorst Meyer: v 1 (instrumental music, 1934), v 2 (vocal music, 1948).

Swert, Jules de.
Catalogued under Deswert, Jules.
Swift, Frederick Fay. Author.
See Theory–3.
Swisher, Walter Samuel. Author.
See Church Music, Psychology.

SWISS MUSIC/SWITZERLAND (Music in)
See: esp App Ib (Cherbuliez, Schmid, Schuh).

Also: Dances–2 (ed Alford: Witzig).

Switten, Henry N. Author.
See Theory–1.

"SYMPHONIA" (Series)
Note: This is a series of extensively illustrated musical monographs, published by the Continental Book Company, Stockholm, Sweden, and distributed in the United States by Albert Bonnier. The books are uniform in format and in general treatment, usually providing a concise survey of their subjects, augmented by many portraits, facsimiles, musical examples, etc.

See:

Bach Family (Reeser)	Gregorian
Bach–1 (Schallenberg)	(Waesbergh)
Beethoven–2 (Paap)	History–3 (Reeser)
Berlioz–2 (Daniskas)	Opera–1 (Kempers &
Chopin– 1 (Schallen-	Bakken)
berg)	Ravel (Onnen)
Composers–3b (Suer-	Stradivari (Balfoort)
mondt: Smetana &	Stravinsky–2 (Onnen)
Dvořák)	Verdi–1 (Rutters)
Debussy–2 (Ketting)	Waltz (Reeser)
Franck (Andriessen)	

SYMPHONIC POEM
See:

Appreciation	Phonograph Records
Composers (& under	Poetry & Music
individual names,	Program Music
esp Liszt, R. Strauss)	Program Notes
History	Romantic Era
Literature & Music	Themes
Orchestral Music	

SYMPHONY

See also:

Appreciation	Orchestral
Composers (& under	Orchestral Music
individual names)	Phonograph Records
Composition	Program Notes
Form	Themes
History	Timing

Also: American music & the musics of other national schools; Classic Era & other historical periods.

Note: Standard works apparently O/P (or not easily available) include those by Berg, Haggin, Lee, Mahling (in German), Nef (in German), Upton, etc.

GRENIER, HÉLÈNE. See App Ia.

HILL, RALPH (*ed*)
The symphony. 458 p, mus ex, paper.
Pelican 1949. .65

Hill on the symphony & its development, followed by 20 articles on symphonic composers from Haydn to Bax by various authors, including Blom, Bonavia, Foss, Gray, Holland, Hussey, McNaught, Robertson, et al.

MOORE, EARL V. & HEGER, T. E.
The symphony and the symphonic poem: analytical & descriptive charts of the standard symphonic repertory. iv, 259 p, charts, mus ex, paper. Authors, via Educational Music Service, N. Y., 1949. 4.00

Form-analyses of some 79 works.

O'CONNELL, CHARLES
The Victor book of symphonies.
xiii, 556 p, mus ex. S & S (1935) 3rd
enl ed 1948. 3.95

A book of program notes, but unlike the earlier editions, this is devoted exclusively to symphonies: some 138 works by 48 composers from Bax to Walton, with a note on the modern orchestra & lists of (RCA Victor) recordings. This is a companion work to the "Victor books" of ballets (see Ballet, Lawrence), concertos (see Concerto, Veinus), operas (see Opera–3, Biancolli & Bagar), and miscellaneous orchestral works (see Program Notes, O'Connell).

SHORE, BERNARD
Sixteen symphonies. Forew Adrian
Boult. xii, 387 p, 16 pors, mus ex.
Longmans 1949 (U. S. A. 1950). 4.00

Analyses of works by & brief essays on Haydn, Mozart, Beethoven, Schubert, Schumann, Brahms, Dvořák, Sibelius, Elgar, Franck, Tchaikovsky, Berlioz, Vaughan Williams, Bax, Walton, & Holst. This is one of the few works of its kind written from the point of view of an orchestral player.

SPAETH, SIGMUND
Great symphonies: how to recognize and remember them. xiv, 361 p, mus ex, bds. (1936) Perma-Giants repr 1949. .95

Works by Beethoven, Brahms, Franck, Haydn, Mozart, etc, discussed in "appreciative" style and illustrated by principal themes to which doggerel texts are attached; plus a glossary of symphonic terms, list of records, & biographical sketches.

WEINGARTNER, FELIX
The symphony since Beethoven. Tr
Maude Barrows Dutton. 98 p, frontis por, fac letter. Ditson 1904. 1.25

The symphony writers since Beethoven: with notice of the author's own No 5 Symphony, by D. C. Parker. Tr Arthur Bles. viii, 168 p, 12 pors. Reeves n d xx (1904) 2nd pr (1925?). (3.75)

Despite the difference in title, both books are from the same German text: "Die Symphonie nach Beethoven," originally published in 1897. The Ditson edition is in the "Music Students Library" series; the Reeves edition includes a note on Weingartner's 5th Symphony, by Parker, p 165/8.

SYMPOSIA

General Note: Many books on specialized subjects & individual composers are collections of articles by various authors. For some of the more important of these, and especially those properly called symposia (in that the articles included usually were written for the specific purpose), see:

America–music in	Schubert–2 (Abraham)
(Eaton)	Schweitzer–2
Britten (Britten et al)	(Roback)
Church Music	Sibelius (Abraham)
(Hoelty-Nickel)	Sound Rec & Repro
Community Music	(Aldous)
(Bergmann)	Speech (Sansom)
Criticism (French)	Stravinsky–2 (Corle,
Education (Shaw)	Lederman)
Films (Elliott)	Tchaikovsky–2 (Abra-
Grieg (Abraham)	ham, Shostakovitch)
Health (Schullian &	Vibrato (Seashore)
Schoen)	Wales–music in
Memory (Cooke)	(Crossley-Holland)

SZIGETI, Joseph

See also:

Bartók	Stravinsky–1 & 2
Interpreters	Violin Playing
Phonograph Records	Violinists

With strings attached: reminiscences & reflections. xiii, 341, xvii p, 15 pl (pors, facs, etc). Knopf 1947. 4.00

Personal experiences in concert life, recording & broadcasting; discussions of violin playing, violinists, & composers; plus a 7-p list of Szigeti's own recordings.

—T—

Tabouret, Jean. Catalogued under Arbeau.
Tagrine, Nadia. Co-author (with Manuel).
See App Ia.
Talbot, John Edward. Author.
See Mozart–3.

TALENT (Musical)
See:

Examinations　　　　Teaching
Psychology　　　　　Tests

Tanabe, Hisao. Author. See Japan.

TANGLEWOOD
See: Berkshire Festivals.

Tansman, Alexandre. Author.
See Stravinsky–2.

Tapper, Thomas. Author. See:

Counterpoint–2. 1st year (1913).	1.50
Form. 1st year analysis (1914).	1.50
Harmony–2. 1st year (1908/38).	1.50
—. 2nd year (1912/40).	1.50
History–2. 1st year (1926).	1.75
Keyboard Harmony. ABC of (n d).	1.25
Melody Writing. 1st year (1911).	1.50
Sight-Playing & Reading. Sight reading & memory lessons (1906)	1.00
Teachers. Education of (1914).	1.75
Theory–3. 1st year (1912/40)	1.25

See also: App IIa (juvenile biographies).

Tappolet, Willy. Author. See App Ia.
Tarnowski, Count. Author. See Chopin–1.

TARTINI, Giuseppe
See: esp App Ic (Capri biography).

Appreciation　　　　Phonograph Records
Concerto　　　　　　Program Notes
History　　　　　　　Violin Music
Italian Music　　　　Violinists

TASTE (Musical)
See also:

Aesthetics–1 & 2　　History
Appreciation　　　　Philosophy
Criticism　　　　　　Psychology

*Note: Calvocoressi's "Musical taste" (1925)
and the Mueller-Hevner "Trends in musical
taste" (1924) apparently are O/P.*

FARNSWORTH, PAUL RANDOLPH
Musical taste: its measurement &
cultural nature. 94 p, 34 tables, bibl
refs, paper. Stanford 1950.　　　　1.50
*A scholarly study of musical taste as a
phenomenon of the social sciences rather than
a conglomeration of chance responses or a set
of absolutes.*

TAUBER, Richard

See also: Phonograph Records, Singers.

NAPIER-TAUBER, DIANA
Richard Tauber. Forew Sir Charles
B. Cochran. 237 p, 36 illus (pors,
etc). Art & Educational Publishers,
London, 1949.　　　　　　　　　　(3.50)
*The life of the noted tenor, conductor, &
film-star, as told by his widow.*

TAUBMAN, Howard. Author.
Music on my beat: an intimate
volume of shop-talk. 267 p. S &
S 1943.　　　　　　　　　　　　　2.50
*Behind-the-scenes notes & sketches of cele-
brities, by a "N. Y. Times" music critic.*
See also: Toscanini.
*Note: Taubman's "Music as a profession"
(1939) & "Opera front & back" (1938)
apparently are O/P.*

Taylor, Bernard U. Author.
See Singing–2.
Taylor, Colin. Author.
See Sight-Playing & Reading.
Taylor, David Clark. Author.
See Singing–2.

TAYLOR, Deems
See also:

American Music　　　Opera
Composers–2 & 3a　　Phonograph Records
History　　　　　　　Program Notes

*Note: A booklet on Taylor & his works by
John Tasker Howard (1927) apparently is
O/P.*

Author:
Of men and music. xviii, 318 p.
S & S 1937 (12th pr 1945).　　　　3.00

The well-tempered listener. xvi, 333 p. S & S 1940 (6th pr 1945).   **3.00**

Music to my ears. xvi, 288 p. S & S 1949.   **3.00**

Collections of essays (on varied musical subjects), based on Taylor's long series of CBS broadcast intermission commentaries.

Moments mousical.   46 p, illus (Walter Kumme). Ziff Davis 1949.   **2.50**

Satirical take-offs on music-history, opera, ballet, etc, in a world of mice, not men.

Editor. See also:

Encylopedias of Music. Hughes (ed. Taylor & Kerr): Music lovers' cyclopedia (1939).   **2.49**

Gilbert & Sullivan: a treasury of G & S (1941).   **6.00**

Taylor, Frederick A. Author.
See Children–1, Scnool Music–1, App IIb.
Taylor, Mary Catherine. Compiler
See Rounds.

TAYLOR, Robert Lewis. Author.
The running pianist. 340 p. Doubleday 1950.   **3.50**

"New Yorker" profiles, including those of Percy Grainger (the title piece), Bobby Clark, Robert Flaherty, etc, & four short stories.

Taylor, Stainton de Bouffles. Author.
See Bach–2.

TCHAIKOVSKY, Peter Ilyitch
1. Own Writings & Life.   2. Works.

See also:

Appreciation	Program Notes
Ballet	Romantic Era
Chamber Music	Russian Music
Composers–1 & 32	Song(s)
Concerto	Symphony
History	Themes
Opera	Timing
Orchestral Music	Violin Music
Phonograph Records	Vocal Music
Piano Music	

TCHAIKOVSKY (1. Own writings, Life)
See also: App IIa (juveniles by Gronowicz, Purdy).
Note: The Jurgenson correspondence apparently is O/P, as are standard biographies by Lee, Newmarch, M. Tchaikovsky, etc.

ABRAHAM, GERALD
  (*See also Tchaikovsky–2.*)
Tchaikovsky. 144 p, frontis por, 1–p bibl. (1944) Wyn 1949.   **1.00**

American ed of "Tchaikovsky, a short biography," pub London 1944; revised from material originally pub in "Masters of Russian music" (1936) by Calvocoressi & Abraham (see Composers–3e).

Tchaikovsky. 14 p, cover por, paper. Novello n d (1938)   **.40**
Miniature biography ("great musicians").

BERBEROVA, NINA. See App Ia.

BOWEN, CATHERINE D. & MECK, B. VON
"Beloved friend": the story of Tchaikovsky & Nadejda von Meck. 484 p, 5 pors. (1937) Dover repr 1946.   **1.98**
Based on the Tchaikovsky-von Meck correspondence, originally pub in Russian 1933/6.

CHERBULIEZ, A. E. See App Ib.

EVANS, EDWIN (*Jr*)
Tchaikovsky. ix, 234 p, 8 pl (pors, facs), 1–p bibl, mus ex. Dent (1906) rev ed 1935 (1948). Pellegrini 1949.   **2.50**
"Master Musicians" series, with usual calendar, personalia, catalogue of works, etc.

LAKOND, WLADIMIR (*ed & tr*)
The diaries of Tchaikovsky. Intro Grigory Bernard. 365 p, 9 pl (pors & facs). Norton 1945.   **5.00**
The famous jottings, irregularly written from 1873 to 1891, pub in Russian 1923.

MANN, KLAUS
Pathetic symphony: a novel about Tchaikovsky. 346 p, Allen Towne 1948, via Crown?   **3.00**
A fictional, romantic biography, originally pub in German 1935.

SHOSTAKOVICH, DMITRI (*& others*)
Russian symphony: thoughts about Tchaikovsky. 271 p, frontis por, 3–p bibl. Philosophical 1947.   **3.75**
A symposium, with articles by Soviet composers & musicologists, plus a catalogue of works.

WEINSTOCK, HERBERT
Tchaikovsky. xii, 386, xxx p, **14** pl, 4–p bibl. Knopf 1943 (1946).   **5.00**
The most extensive biography in English including recent Soviet research material & a chronological catalogue of works.

ZAGIBA, FRANZ. See App Ib.

TCHAIKOVSKY (2. Works)
See also: esp Ballet (ed Haskell: Hamlet etc; Posner: Hamlet, etc).

ABRAHAM, GERALD (*ed*)
(*See also Tchaikovsky–1.*)
The music of Tchaikovsky: a symposium. 277 p, frontis fac, 23–p mus ex, 5–p bibl. Norton 1946.   3.00
Lockspeiser on "the man"; Abraham, Alshvang, Blom, Cooper, Dickinson, Mason, & Wood on works in various mediums; plus a chronology & a catalogue of works.

BIANCOLLI, LOUIS
Tschaikovsky and his orchestral music. 56 p, 6 illus (pors, fac, etc), bds. Grosset 1950.   .50
"N. Y. Philharmonic-Symphony Society Musical Biographies" series, originally published (1944) for subscribers only. Brief biographical sketch & notes on the best-known orchestral works.

BLOM, ERIC
Tchaikovsky: orchestral works. 51 p, mus ex, paper. Oxford 1927.   1.00
"Musical Pilgrim" series of analyses: piano concerto, Nutcracker suite, Romeo & Juliet overture, and the 4th symphony.

DENT, EDWARD J. (*tr*)
Eugene Onegin: an opera in 3 acts; words adapted from the poem of Alexander Pushkin by P. Tchaikovsky & C. S. Shilovsky. English version. 67 p, paper. Oxford 1946.   .80
English translation of the libretto, with an introduction & the story of the opera.

HASKELL, ARNOLD L. (*ed*)
The sleeping beauty. 56 p + 13-p photos, mus ex, paper. Lane 1949.   .50
"Sadler's Wells Ballet Books" No. 1 : essays by Dyneley Hussey, Tamara Karsavina, Joy Newton, & Sacheverell Sitwell.

POSNER, SANDY
The sleeping princess. 96 p, illus incl 4 col pl (Joyce Millen). (Newman Wolsey, London, 1945) 2nd ed Black 1949, via Transatlantic.   .75
"Ballet Pocket Library" series.

ROBERTSON, MARION
Le lac des cygnes. 96 p, illus incl 4 col pl (Joyce Millen). Newman Wolsey, London, 1947, via Transatlantic.   .75
"Ballet Pocket Library" series.

SEDGWICK, RUSSELL (*photographer*)
The Swan Lake as presented by The Sadler's Wells Ballet: a photographic record. The story of the ballet by Cyril W. Beaumont. 8 p text, 30 pl, △ Beaumont, London, 1948.   (6.30)

TEACHERS

See also:
Children	Franck
Christiansen	History
Colleges	Mannes
Dann	Mason
Education	Matthay
Erskine	School Music
Finn	Teaching

Also: Organ Playing, Piano Playing, Singing, Violin Playing.

PETERSON, HOUSTON (*ed*)
Great teachers: as portrayed by those who studied under them. xxi, 351 p. Rutgers 1946.   3.50
Includes Vincent d'Indy on Franck & Ethel Newcombe on Leschetizky.

TAPPER, THOMAS
The education of the music teacher. 223 p, mus ex. Presser 1914.   1.75
A survey of the requirements.

TEACHING

1. **General, Audio-Visual Methods**
2. **Music Teaching in General**
3. **Piano Teaching**

General Note: No hard-&-fast distinctions can be drawn within the large literature in the general area that includes such subjects as Children, Education, School Music, & Teaching. However, we have tried to confine this last-named subject-heading to works primarily concerned with teaching methods & principles, or those that are principally of interest to teachers.

TEACHING
(1. Pedagogy, Audio-Visual Methods)
See also: esp Libraries (Myers), Psychology, School Music–1 (Best).
Note: Only a sampling of the large available literature is listed here.

CHANDLER, ANNA C. & CYPHER, IRENE F.
Audio-visual technique for enrichment of the curriculum. vii, 252 p, illus, 1–p bibl. Noble & Noble, N. Y., 1948.   3.50

EXTON, WILLIAM *Jr*
Audio-visual aids to instruction. xiii, 344 p, illus. McGraw 1947.   4.50

HENRY, NELSON B. *Jr* (*ed*)
The 48th yearbook of the National Society for the Study of Education. Pt 1 : Audio-visual methods materials of instruction. 330 p, bibl. Chicago 1949.   3.75

Various papers on the present status & practical problems of audio-visual aids.

MURSELL, JAMES L.
Developmental teaching. vii, 374 p, 15–p bibl. McGraw 1949.　　3.50
Successful teaching: its psychological principles. xi, 338 p, chap bibls. McGraw 1946.　　3.75
Both in McGraw-Hill "Series in Education."

STRAUSS, L. HARRY & KIDD, J. R.
Look, listen, & learn: a manual on the use of audio-visual materials in informal education. x, 234 p, 11 photos, diagrs, 21–p annot bibl, bds. Association 1948.　　3.50

TEACHING
(2. Music Teaching in General)
See also:

America (music in)	Education
Children	Examinations
Choir/Choral	Psychology
Colleges	School Music
Community Music	Teachers
Dann	Tests

Also: Organ Playing, Piano Playing, Singing, Violin Playing.

Note: Standard works apparently O/P (or not easily available) include those by Curwen, Nohavec, Tovey, Trotter, Turnbull, Weis, White, etc.

BARNETT, DAVID
Music manual for teachers: grade one. 78 p, music, paper, spir. Stewart 1947.　　2.00

BULBER, FRANCIS GERARD
Teacher activities of the vocal school music program. ix, 156 p, 6 tables, 2–p bibl. George Peabody College for Teachers, Nashville, Tenn., 1949.　　2.50
"Contribution to Education" No. 406.

CASE, EDMUND W.
Teacher, parent, and pupil: an integrated approach to success with instrumental music. Intro J. Maynard Wettlaufer. 116 p, 1 illus, mus ex. Author, Miami, Florida, 1949.　　2.50
Informal information on aids to practising, memorization, piano-playing, etc.

CURWEN, MRS. J. SPENCER
Psychology applied to music teaching. xii, 332 p, 1 illus. Curwen n d (1920).　　(4.80)
With 431 examination questions.

DAMROSCH, FRANK
Some essentials in the teaching of

music: for the consideration of music-teachers, music-students, & parents. 101 p. G. Schirmer 1916 (4th pr, n d).　　1.25
Stressing the development of self-expression in music study.

GIBBON, L. D.
How to build a music-teaching connexion. x, 68 p. Oxford 1939.　　1.25
Practical advice (British viewpoint) on the "business" aspects in particular.

LOVELOCK, WILLIAM
Handbook on the art of teaching as applied to music. 159 p, mus ex, paper. Gray 1937.　　1.25

MOHLER, LOUIS
Teaching music from an appreciative basis: the fundamentals of musical development. Forew Peter W. Dykema. 159 p, mus ex. Birchard (1927) rev ed 1950.　　2.50

MURPHY, HOWARD A.
Teaching musicianship: a manual of methods & materials. 275 p, tables, mus ex, 14–p bibl. Coleman 1950.　　4.50
An illuminating clarification of the premises & procedures of "theoretical" studies in musical writing, reading, listening, playing, analyzing, & creating. (See General Note under the Guide entry for Musicianship.) The appendices include notes on basic "theory" & free counterpoint courses, and on surveys of college harmony courses.

ZANZIG, AUGUSTUS D.
The Concord teachers' guide: a manual for all grades. iii, 59 p, paper. E. C. Schirmer 1929.　　.50
A syllabus used in the Brookline, Massachusetts, public schools & as a guide for teachers in the Concord Summer School.

TEACHING (3. Piano Teaching)
See also: esp Children–5, Piano Playing
Note: Standard works apparently O/P (or not easily available) include those by Matthay, Pearce, Tremaine, etc.

BOSWORTH, HARRIETTE DEXTER
Ideas for young piano teachers. 67 p, paper. Ditson 1931.　　.75
"Pocket Music Student" series; informal advisory essays.

CARRÉ, JOHN F.
The psychology of piano music teaching: a text book for teachers, students, & parents. 95 p, illus,

mus ex.   Conservatory Pub Co,
Racine, Wisconsin, 1946.   1.50
Includes graded teaching-material lists.

HAMILTON, CLARENCE G.
Piano teaching: its principles &
problems. v, 171 p, illus, mus ex,
3–p bibl. Ditson 1910.   1.50
*"Music Students Library" series; includes
a chapter on the selection of music.*

HEIDELBERGER, PAULINE
Master method piano normal and
teacher's manual.   55 p, paper.
Willis 1947.   1.00

HORROCKS, CYRIL R. H.
The student's guide to the art of
teaching the pianoforte. xi, 245 p,
nus ex. Reeves (1915) 2nd rev ed Δ
n d.   (3.00)
*Super-title: "How to teach." Includes graded
lists of teaching material.*

JEWETT, ALBERT D.
Idiomatic course of piano instruction
for classwork. 43 p, frontis, tables,
paper. Birchard 1940.   1.00
*Education, theory, ear-training, notation, &
technique of piano playing.*

O'TOOLE, WILLIAM
A five year guide to piano teaching.
96 p, 8–p annot bibl, paper. Creative
Music Pubs, N. Y., (1939) rev ed
1949.   2.50
Graded lists, partly in typescript repro.

POTAMKIN, FRANK J.
Modern piano pedagogy: its scope.
221 p, mus ex. Elkan 1936.   2.50
*Musical memory, tone production, pedalling,
related essays, modern material, etc.*

RUBINSTEIN, BERYL
Outline of piano pedagogy: a series
of papers setting forth the aims &
objectives of piano instruction with
suggestions for solving manifold
problems confronting the serious
teacher. 70 p, paper. C. Fischer
(1929) rev ed 1947.   1.00

SCHELLING, ERNEST (& others)
Oxford piano course: teacher's manuals. Oxford 1921/1932.

1st manual: Guide to "Singing &
Playing" & 1st book. xviii, 197 p.
1921 (1932).   2.50

2nd manual: Guide to 2nd through
5th books & "Beginner's book for
older pupils." xxiv, 239 p. (1932)
rev ed 1946.   2.50
*Co-authors: Charles J. Haake, Gail Martin
Haake, & Osbourne McConathy.*

Teasdale, May Silva. Author. See Opera–1.
Teatro di San Carlo. See App Ic.
Teetgen, Alexander. Author.
See Beethoven–3.

TELEMANN, Georg Philipp
See: esp App Ib (Valentin biography).

Appreciation	Composers–1
Baroque Era	History
Chamber Music	Opera
Choir/Choral–3	Phonograph Records
Church Music	Program Notes

*Note: Standard works apparently O/P (or not
easily available) include those in German by
Büttner, Gräser, Hörner, Ottzenn, Schäfer-
Schmuck, etc.*

TELEVISION
See also:

Acting	Radio (esp Broderick,
Libraries (Myers)	Rose, Siepmann)
Opera	Radio Music

*Note: Only a sampling of the rapidly growing
literature is listed below.*

DUNLAP, ORRIN E., *Jr*
The future of television. xi, 194 p,
illus. Harper (1924) rev ed 1947.   3.00

Understanding television: what it is
and how it works. 128 p, illus, 2–p
bibl. Greenberg 1948.   2.50

HUBBELL, RICHARD W.
4000 years of television: the story
of seeing at a distance. xvi, 256 p,
illus, 2–p bibl. Putnam 1942.   2.75

KEMPNER, STANLEY (*ed*)
Television encyclopedia. xiii, 415 p,
illus, 15–p bibl. Fairchild 1948.   6.50
*Historical survey, biographies, glossary,
merchandising analysis, etc.*

ROYAL, JOHN F. (*ed*)
Television production problems. xi,
179 p, illus. McGraw 1948.   2.50
*NBC-Columbia University broadcasting
series. Includes a chapter (p 105/12) by
Herbert Graf on "Opera in television."*

SPOSA, LOUIS A.
Television primer or production and
direction. viii, 237 p, illus, 1–p bibl.
McGraw 1947.   3.50

TEMPERAMENT
See:

Acoustics	Organ (esp Smith)
Intervals	Piano (esp Smith,
Monophony	White)
Scales	

Templier, P. D. Author. See App Ia.

311

TEMPO
See also:

Harding	Rhythm
Interpretation	Timing
Metronome	

Also: Conducting, Piano Playing, etc.

WERNER, MILT
The new science of tempo: based on the count-vibrato; a presentation, in detail of . . . a simple arithmetical system. 17 p, mus ex, charts, paper. Halmiles Pub Co, N. Y., 1947. .60
Not a study of tempo as such, but a system for marking tempos by a new method.

Tenschert, Roland. Author. See App Ib.

Terry, Charles Sanford. Author. See:

Bach–1.	Biography (1928/33).	5.00
Bach–2.	B minor Mass (1924).	1.00
——.	Cantatas & oratorios (1925), 2 v, complete.	2.00
——.	Passions (1926), 2 v, comp.	2 00
——.	Bach's orchestra (1932).	7.00

Note: Several other books on J. S. Bach, J. C. Bach, & the Bach family apparently are O/P (or not easily available).

Terry, Edward M. Author.
See Wagner–3.

TERRY, (Sir) Richard Runciman
See also:

Church Music	English Music
England (music in)	History

ANDREWS, HILDA
Westminster retrospect: a memoir of Sir Richard Terry. xvi, 186 p, illus. Oxford 1948. 3.50
The story of Terry's career at the cathedral (1901–1924) & his editorial work with Tudor church music. A 4-p bibliography of Terry's publications is included.
Note: Terry's own books, including standard works on church music & two volumes of essays, apparently are O/P (or not easily available in this country).

Tertis, Lionel. Author.
See String Playing.

TESTS (Musical)
See also:

Ear-Training	Organ Playing (AGO)
Education	Psychology
Examinations	School Music
Interpretation (Sea-	Teaching
shore)	

Note: Standard works apparently O/P (or not easily available) include those by Kwalwasser, Rowley & Tobin, Saetveit & Lewis & Seashore, Tobin, etc.

GILDERSLEEVE, GLENN
Music achievement test: for grades 4 to 8. Teachers College, Columbia 1921. Specimen set .15
Also, package of 100 tests, $4.50.

JONES, ARCHIE N.
Music recognition test: piano edition (for teachers). 27 p, music, paper. C. Fischer 1949. 1.25
Individual test-blanks also are available in two packages, $1.50 each.

KWALWASSER, JACOB & DYKEMA, P. W.
K-D music tests: manual of directions. 31 p, paper. C. Fischer 1930. Complete with 100 test blanks & 4 matrix keys. 2.25
For use with RCA Victor records 302/6.

MURSELL, JAMES L.
Psychological testing. xiv, 449 p, charts, 33–p bibl. Longmans 1947 (1948). 4.00
Lists & comments on some 100 types of tests for mental measurements, including a few pages (p 231/5) on music tests.

STANTON, HAZEL M.
Measurement of musical talent: the Eastman experiment. Ed Carl E. Seashore. 140 p, charts, 2–p bibl, Iowa 1935. 1.00
"Studies in the Psychology of Music," v 2.

WING, HERBERT
Tests of musical ability and appreciation. 88 p, illus. Cambridge 1948, via Chicago 1949. 2.00
"British Journal of Psychology" Monograph Supplement XXVII.

Tetrazzini, Luisa. Author.
See Singing–2.
Note: The noted coloratura's autobiography (1921) apparently is O/P.

TEXAS (Music in)
See: America–music in (esp Whitlock & Saunders), Folksongs–2 (esp Owens).

TEXTURE (Musical)
See:

Composers (& under	Harmony
individual names)	Program Notes
Composition	Theory
Contemporary Music	"Tovey ("Musician
(esp Dyson)	talks" v 2)
Counterpoint	

Teyte, Maggie. Author. See Singing–2.
Thatcher, Gladys Knesel. Author.
See Tonality.
Thayer, Alexander Wheelock. Author.
See Beethoven–2 (note only).

THEATRE

See also:

Acoustics
Acting
Ballet
California (Gagey)
Career
Covent Garden
Drama
Films
History

Instrumentation
  (esp Collinson)
Opera
Operetta
Popular Music
Radio
Restoration
Stanislavski
Television

Also: America (music in), England (music in), Italy (music in), etc.

Note: The listings below include only a sampling (of some musical interest) of the large available literature.

BURRIS-MEYER, H. & COLE, EDWARD C.
Theaters and auditoriums: the derivation of plan from analysis of function. viii, 228 p, illus (photos & b&ws), tables. Reinhold 1949.   8.00
An extensive study of construction, production, & maintenance details for buildings housing all types of entertainment.

DENT, EDWARD J.
A theatre for everybody: the story of Old Vic & Sadler's Wells. 151 p, illus (Kay Ambrose). T. V. Boardman & Co, London, 1945.   △ (4.50)
An extensively illustrated history, with chapters on opera in England, ballet, etc.

SCHOLZ, JANOS (ed)
Baroque and romantic stage design. Intro A. Hyatt Mayor. 24 p, 121 pl, bibl. Bittner 1950.   10.00
One of the members of the Roth Quartet edits this handsome collection of stage sets, including some for opera productions.

THEMES

See also: Bach–2 (Payne, Schmieder), Mozart–3 (Köchel-Einstein).

General Note: Various music publishers issue thematic catalogues of the works of individual or grouped composers, but with the exception of the works referred to above & the three listed below, none of them is included here.

However, many of the books listed in the present Guide, particularly those on individual composers & their works, or on specialized subjects such as Chamber Music, Concerto, etc, embody brief thematic illustrations.

BARLOW, HAROLD & MORGENSTERN, SAM (*comps*)
A dictionary of musical themes. Intro John Erskine. xiii, 565 p, mus ex. Crown 1948.   5.00
Some 10,000 themes of standard instrumental compositions, arranged alphabetically by composer & title. There is also a special "notation index," designed to facilitate the location of themes to be identified.
A dictionary of vocal themes. via, 547 p, mus ex. Crown 1950.   5.00
A companion volume, in similar style, devoted to operatic & other vocal works.

BURROWS, R. & REDMOND, B. C. (*comps*)
Symphony themes. Ed assistant George Szell. Intro Deems Taylor. 295 p, mus ex, 5–p bibl. S & S 1942 (4th pr n d).   3.50
Some 1200 principal themes from 100 standard symphonies, plus lists of recordings, available editions, timings, etc.
Concerto themes. xxxviii, 296 p, mus ex, 1–p bibl. S & S 1951.   4.00
Some 1200 themes from 144 concertos.

THEORETICAL MUSICIANSHIP
For a general note on the respective scopes & referenced subject-headings of the fields of applied & theoretical musicianship, please see under Musicianship.

"THEORY" (Musical)
General Note: The quotation marks around this subject-heading do yeoman service: they indicate that we'd like to omit it entirely (as indeed many dictionaries & encyclopedias of music actually do), but the term itself is so firmly implanted in common usage & in book titles, that its omission would cause considerable inconvenience to the users of this Guide.

More than that, the "quotes" signalize the anomalous status of the term itself: most books devoted to musical "theory" actually are practical rather than theoretical in nature. Strictly speaking, they deal primarily with the Rudiments of Musicianship and especially the "paper-work" aspects, although some of them, at least, wisely include or suggest the necessity of simultaneous work in the applied aspects (ear-training, sight-playing & singing, etc.).

For convenience, the books listed are divided into four rather loose sub-categories:

1. General & Over-all Surveys
(*These usually combine the ordinary elementary "theory" subjects with more advanced*

studies in composition or what Toch aptly calls the "shaping forces" in music.)

2. Rudiments: Larger Works

3. Rudiments: Smaller Works

(These are the orthodox "theory" books, differing only in size & scope. They deal with the elementary, paper-work aspects of musicianship: terminology & notation; keys, scales, intervals, & melody; time, meter, & rhythm; form; etc. Usually they lead up to, and sometimes include, beginning work in harmony, counterpoint, composition, instrumentation & orchestration.)

4. Specialized Studies & Miscellanies

(These are mostly combinations of theoretical subjects or studies of chord relationships, etc, that cannot conveniently be located elsewhere.)

See also: Children–8

(These are "theory" books especially designed for use with children, although some of them —especially Slonimsky's "The road to music" —are admirably adapted for adult beginners as well.)

For other books devoted to, or touching on, some of the subjects included in most "theory" works, see also:

Appreciation	Instrumentation
Composition	Melody
Counterpoint	Melody-Writing
Dictionaries of Terms	Notation
Form	Rhythm
Fugue	Scales
Harmony	Score-Reading

For true musical theory, see some of the advanced studies included under the subject-headings above, and others under:

Acoustics	Psychology
Aesthetics	Tonality
Arabia (Farmer)	Twelve-Tone Technique
Aristotle	nique
Philosophy	

For books on allied subjects in applied elementary musicianship, see also:

Children-3	Sight-Playing &
Dictation	Reading
Ear-Training	Sight-Singing
Keyboard Harmony	Solfège/Solfeggio

THEORY (1. General & Over-all Surveys)

Note: Standard works apparently O/P (or not easily available) include those by Cortot & Vaultier (in French), etc.

See also: esp Teaching–2 (Murphy).

GOETSCHIUS, PERCY
The structure of music: a series of articles demonstrating in an accurate though popular manner the origin & employment of the fundamental factors of music structure &

composition for the student & general music lover. 170 p, frontis, mus ex, 4–p bibl. Presser 1934. 2.50

LOGIER, J. B.
Comprehensive course in music harmony, & practical composition. Ed Carl Stein. xi, 316 p, mus ex. C. Fischer (1888) rev Am ed n d. 6.00

Includes a bird's-eye view of the rudiments of music & an explanation of musical characteristics, by John Green; also an abridgment of Berlioz's "Instrumentation, with hints on conducting."

MEYER, MAX F.
The musician's arithmetic: drill problems for an introduction into the scientific study of musical composition. 149 p, illus. Ditson 1929. 2.00

A textbook discussion of music systems & music-theory problems.

OREM, PRESTON WARE
Theory and composition of music: a manual of advanced harmony, melody writing, practical composition, & musical form, for class, private, & self-instruction. 146 p, mus ex. Presser 1924. 1.25

A continuation of the author's "Harmony book for beginners" (see Harmony–2).

SWITTEN, HENRY N.
Living musical theory: a comprehensive course. 3 v, typescript repro, paper. Author, Princeton, N. J., 1940/1946.

V 1: Fundamentals. xv, 221 p, diagrs, mus ex, 6–p bibl. (1940) 2nd rev ed 1942 (1946). 5.00

Note: This volume includes scales, solfège, dictation, analysis, & creative work. We do not have complete details on V 2 & 3.

V 2: Harmony. xiv, 151 p. Δ

V 3: Counterpoint of the 16th century; 2–pt counterpoint. vi, 56 p. Δ

TOCH, ERNST
The shaping forces in music: an inquiry into harmony, melody, counterpoint, form. iv, 245 p, mus ex. Criterion 1948. 5.00

A contemporary composer's "reconciliation" of old & new principles & practices.

THEORY (2. Rudiments: Larger Works)

Note: The only distinction between books in this sub-category and the one following (2. Rudiments: Smaller Works) lies in their size & scope.

Standard works apparently O/P (or not easily available) include those by Curwen, Marx, Palmer, Parkhurst, Samaroff-Stokowski, etc.
See also: esp Teaching-2 (Murphy).

BAUER, MARION
Music is a language: a guide to
fundamentals. Putnam 1951, in prep.   △
*An introduction to music theory for laymen
and for high schools & junior colleges.*

BLANKE, WILTON W. & SPECK, JAY
Gateway to music. iv, 178 p, illus,
ex. Heath 1931.   1.76
*Notation, scales, intervals, instruments, &
music terminology.*

BOYD, CHARLES N. & EARHART, WILL
Elements of musical theory. V 1:
Text & briefer examples. 156 p, mus
ex, bds. G. Schirmer 1938.   2.00
Same. V 2: Supplement containing
the longer examples. 73 p, music
only, bds. G. Schirmer 1938.   1.25
V 1 & 2, complete.   3.00
*An introduction to sound, notation, scales,
intervals, chords, harmony, form, etc.*

COOKSON, FRANK B. (*ed in chief*)
Creative-analytical theory of music.
Bk 1: Building a basic vocabulary.
xiii, 162 p, mus ex, paper, spir.
FitzSimons 1948.   2.70
*With 7 co-authors from the School of Music,
Northwestern University. For book 2, see
under Form (Bigelow, & others).*

DILLER, ANGELA
First theory book. vi, 176, iii p, mus,
bds. G. Schirmer 1921   3.00
Preparatory studies for form, harmony, etc.

ELSON, LOUIS C.
The theory of music: as applied to
the teaching & practice of voice &
instruments. 211 p, mus ex, paper.
N. E. Conservatory (1890) rev ed
(Frederick S. Converse) 1935.   2.70
*An extensive, "systematized" course used at
the New England Conservatory of Music.*

GEHRKENS, KARL W.
The fundamentals of music. 212 p,
illus, mus ex. Ditson 1924.   1.50
*General survey. 1st-year study-course in
musical understanding, adopted by the
National Federation of Music Clubs.*
Music notation & terminology. vii,
168 p, illus, mus ex. (1914) Laidlaw
(1920) rev ed 1930 (1942).   2.20

GOLDMAN, MORRIS F.
Classroom workbook: for use with

"The fundamentals of music" by
Karl W. Gehrkens. 93 p, illus, mus
ex, paper. Ditson 1943.   .60
Questions, vocabulary, blanks to be filled.

GOW, GEORGE COLEMAN
The structure of music: an elementary text-book on notation & harmony... 200 p, mus ex. G. Schirmer
(1895) 1923.   1.25
*Materials of music from a grammatical point
of view.*

JONES, ARCHIE N. & BARNARD, FLOYD P.
Introduction to musical knowledge.
x, 150 p, illus, mus ex. 3-p bibl.
Schmidt 1935 (10th pr 1947).   2.00
*The "tool subjects", plus material on instru-
ments, brief biographies, glossary, etc.*

JONES, ROBERT GOMER
Theory of music: fundamentals of
music & music notation, elementary
harmony & form, the instruments of
the orchestra. vii, 131 p, mus ex.
Harper 1936.   2.25
Pre-harmony textbook for high schools.
Workbook for "Theory of music."
92 p, paper. Harper 1937.   1.25

JONES, VINCENT & BAILEY, BERTHA
Exploring music: a coordinated
course of study for high schools &
junior colleges integrating fundamental music techniques. xvi, 152 p,
illus, mus ex. Birchard 1941.   1.68

MELNIK, HENRY
Developing practical musicianship:
a handbook ... 204 p, illus, mus ex,
5-p bibl. William-Frederick Press.
N. Y., 1949.   5.50
*Textbook for a one-year course, covering
notation, scales, form, instruments, etc.*

MURPHY, H. A. & STRINGHAM, E. J.
Creative harmony and musicianship.
476 p, illus, mus ex. Prentice 1951.   6.00
*Learning to understand music through ex-
periencing it, with studies illustrating the
principles of instruments, keyboard harmony,
analysis, ear-training, reading, etc.*

SMITH, MELVILLE & KRONE, MAX T.
Fundamentals of musicianship. 2
v. Mus ex. Witmark 1934/40.   3.00
V 1: xiv, 196 p. (1934) 1937.   3.00
Same, abridged ed. 143 p.   2.00
V 2: ix, 203 p. 1937 (1939).   3.00
Same, abridged ed. xi, 133 p.   2.00

SMITH, RALPH FISHER
Elementary music theory. 134 p,
mus ex. Ditson 1930. 1.50

TROTIN, CHRISTINE
Key to musicianship: a clear & in-
teresting explanation of all the
fundamental rules of music. 130,
x p, mus ex. Marks 1927. 2.50

WEDGE, GEORGE A.
The gist of music: a ready key to
musical understanding & enjoyment.
ix, 123 p, mus ex. G. Schirmer 1936. 3.00
*Elementary musical concepts & notation: ex-
periments in using the materials of music;
types & forms of compositions, & analyses.*

WEITZMANN, CARL FRIEDRICH
Manual of musical theory: a concise,
comprehensive, & practical textbook on the science of music. Ed
E. W. Bowman. vi, 288 p, mus ex,
paper. Wm. A. Pond & Co, N. Y.,
(1876) 1905. 2.00
*Elements, harmony, simple counterpoint, &
the beginnings of composition.*

THEORY (3. Rudiments: Shorter Works)
*Note: The only distinction between books in
this sub-category and the one preceding (2.
Rudiments: Larger Works) lies in their size
& scope.*
*Standard works apparently O/P (or not easily
available) include those by Barrett-Watson &
others, Bertenshaw, Carse, Crowest, Dimuro,
Lee, Niecks, Oakey, Pearce, de Reszke, Schlieder, Seymour, Wilson, etc.*

BAMPTON, RUTH
Applied theory for musician & lay-
man. Book 1. vi, 74 p, mus ex.
Elkan 1937. 1.50

BLEEKER, JAMES W.
The 1st 15 lessons in music: for
acquiring a fundamentally correct
knowledge & conception of music.
52 p, mus ex, paper. Gray 1931. 1.35

BUSSLER, LUDWIG
Elements of notation and harmony:
with 58 exercises, for use in public
institutions of learning & for self-
instruction. Tr Theodore Baker
(from 5th rev German ed). viii, 131
p, mus ex, flex. G. Schirmer 1890. 2.00

CHAILLEY, J. & CHALLAN, H. See App Ia.

CUMMINGS, WILLIAM H.
Rudiments of music. 72 p, mus ex,
paper. Novello rev ed, n d. 1.25
Novello's "Music Primer" No. 2.

DANHAUSER, A. See App Id.

DANHAUSER, A. & RABAUD, H. See App Ia.

DUSTAN, RALPH
The ABC of musical theory: with
numerous original & selected questions & exercises. 101 p, mus ex,
paper. Curwen 26th rev & enl ed,
n d. 1.50
A manual of music. vi, 303 p, mus
ex. Curwen (1906?) 30th rev, enl
ed n d. 2.50

EVANS, M. G.
Primer of facts about music: questions & answers on the elements of
music. . . 2 p, illus, mus ex, paper.
Presser 1908 (1909). 1.00
*A catechism covering rudiments, instruments,
foreign terms, & music history.*

GARDNER, CARL E.
Essentials of music theory. 65 p,
mus ex, paper. C. Fischer 1912. 1.00

HADDON, WILLIAM & VALTERS, EDWARD
Student's workbook of music theory.
31 p, mus ex, typescript repro,
paper. Birchard 1946. .50
Teaching outline; blanks to be filled.

HAMILTON, CLARENCE G. (& others)
Music theory for piano students:
a manual of fundamentals & key-
board harmony. 2 v, mus ex, paper.
Ditson 1924/30.
V 1: Years 1 & 2. 56 p. 1924. .50
V 2: Years 3 & 4. 65 p. 1930. 1.50

HARRISON, LUTHER A. & McKINNEY, B. B.
Practical music lessons: parts 1 & 2.
vi, 184 p, mus ex. Broadman 1950. 1.00
*Baptist Sunday School Board "Church
Music Curriculum" series.*

HILL, FRANK W. & SEARIGHT, ROLAND
A study outline & work-book in the
elements of music. 66 p + keyboard
chart, paper, spir. Iowa State
Teachers College 1939 (1946). 1.25
*Text material, test questions, & exercises,
with blank worksheets to be filled.*

HUNT, REGINALD
Rudiments of music: Part 1 of the
class teacher's musical theory, a
course for students in training
colleges. viii, 65 p, mus ex, paper.
Rogers n d (1937). 1.50
*"Incorporating the study of tonic sol-fa nota-
tion in so far as it is of assistance in learning
the staff notation."*

HUNTER, LEWIS G.
The musician's hand book: lessons
in applied musical essentials. 79 p,
mus ex, paper. Rubank 1931.　　.85

JOUSSE, J.
A catechism of music. Newly rev
& ed Theodore Baker. With an addendum containing a concise treatise
on natural, abrupt, & enharmonic
modulation into all the major and
minor keys, by J. A. Hamilton; &
Albrechtsberger's 46 modulations.
108 p, mus ex, paper. G. Schirmer
1891.　　.60

JUBB, FLORENCE
The rudiments of music: for piano
students. 39 p, mus ex, paper.
G. Schirmer 1928.　　.75
*Reference book for daily practice problems,
with a set of examination questions.*

KILLOUGH, GIBBON CHAMBERS
Gibbon's catechism of music: a test
book. 76 p, mus ex, paper. Presser
1902.　　.60

KITSON, C. H.
Rudiments of music. 94 p, mus ex.
Oxford 1927 (6th pr 1947).　　1.00
*Concise coverage of pitch, notes, rests, modes,
intervals, time, phrasing, signs, ornaments,
common terms, etc.*

KOECHLIN, CHARLES. See App Ia.

KRINKE, HARRY
An outline of musical knowledge:
a guide for the student's research
to promote musicianship & to afford
a background of musical information
for the music-student. v, 85 p,
paper. G. Schirmer 1930.　　1.50
Lesson assignments with blank forms.

LOBE, J. C.
A new catechism of music on the
plan of J. C. Lobe. Ed Oscar Coon.
vi, 137 p, mus ex, paper. C. Fischer
1905.　　.50

LONGY-MIQUELLE, RENÉE
Music fundamentals. iv, 46, iv p,
paper. Elkan 1936 (1947).　　1.50
Principles of musical theory. Pref
Archibald T. Davison. vii, 101 p,
mus ex. E. C. Schirmer 1925 (8th
pr 1947).　　2.00
*The fundamentals systematically tabulated &
explained; based on French methods, but
adapted to those of American public-school
systems.*

MACPHERSON, STEWART;
Rudiments of music. 84 p, mus ex,
paper. Williams (1908) new ed
1939.　　.75
Questions & exercises upon "Rudiments of music." 64 p, paper.　　.60

MARCOUILLER, S. M. DE S. M.
Musical theory: dedicated to instru-
mentalists-vocalists. vii, 109 p, mus
ex, paper. E. J. Marcouiller, N. Y.
(1913) 6th ed 1942.　　.75
Exercises based on "Musical theory."
64 p, paper, 6th ed 1942.　　.50
Abridgment of the "Musical theory."
viii, 36 p, mus ex, paper. E. J.
Marcouiller 1913 (1941).　　.35

MATHEWSON, ROYAL C.
The wheel of musical knowledge.
Willis 1940.　　.30
*Circular card-chart with key & time signa-
tures, expression terms, etc.*

PEARCE, CHARLES WILLIAM
Rudiments of musical knowledge.
iv, 108 p, mus ex, paper. Rogers
(1920) rev enl ed n d.　　1.00

PETERSON, FRANKLIN
Elements of music. ix, 57 p, mus ex,
paper. Augener 1896 (15th pr n d).　　1.00

RAUTERKUS, JOSEPH A.
Elements of theory. 92, ii p, mus ex.
Volkwein (1934) 1941.　　1.50

RAY, JOHN M.
Elementary theory and harmony: for
the violinist. Forew Gaylord Yost.
36 p, mus ex, paper. Volkwein 1949.　　1.25
*With musical examples treated (contrary to
the practice of most textbooks in theory) from
the aspect of stringed, rather than keyboard,
instruments.*

REED, J. OWEN
Workbook in the fundamentals of
music: with correlated ear-training
& keyboard exercises. viii, 90 p,
mus ex, typescript repro, paper.
Mills (1946) rev ed 1947.　　1.50

ROHNER, TRAUGOTT, & HOWERTON, G.
Fundamentals of music theory: a
concise text with optional objective
tests available. 48 p, mus ex, paper.
Gamble 1943.　　.75
Workbook at junior high-school level.

SCHERCHEN, HERMANN. See App Ib.

SKINNER, OLIVER R.
The first year in theory: a technical

& musical drill in the foundation principles of musical thinking. 58 p, mus ex, flex. Presser 1901.   1.00

SMITH, LEO
Musical rudiments. 153 p, mus ex, paper. Boston 1920.   .85
Toronto Conservatory textbook series No. 1.

SWIFT, FREDERICK FAY
Fundamentals of music. 56 p, mus ex, paper. Belwin 1943.   1.00

TAPPER, THOMAS
First year musical theory: rudiments of music. iii, 115 p. Schmidt 1912 (1940).   1.25

WRIGHTSON, HERBERT J.
Elements of the theory of music. iii, 51 p, mus ex, paper. (1921) Linden Press, Wilmette, Illinois, new rev ed 1937.   .60

THEORY
(4. Specialized Studies & Miscellanies)

See also:

Counterpoint   Improvisation
Harmony   Scales (esp Slonimsky)
  (esp Budge)

Note: Standard works apparently O/P (or not easily available) include those by Haydon, Vanasek, Vogler, etc.

DEUTSCH, MAURY
Dictionary of chords: 7 parts. 30 p, mus ex, typescript repro, paper. Author, N. Y., 1948.;   1.00
Voicing by acoustics: for composer, arranger. 31 p, mus ex, typescript repro, paper. Author, N. Y., 1949.   1.00
Two volumes in a series of practical handbooks: the former is a thesaurus of chords in the modern idiom; the latter deals with the acoustical placement of chord tones.

DYSON, GEORGE (ed)
Musicianship for students series, Bk 2: harmony, counterpoint, & improvisation. 2 v. Mus ex, paper. Novello 1940.

V 1: 106 p. (Primer No. 120,)   2.00
V 2: 154 p. (Primer No. 121.)   2.25
Harmony by B. J. Dale; Counterpoint by Gordon Jacob; Improvisation by H. V. Anson.

GIBBS, GEORGE A., Jr
Modern musical problems analyzed: a study in arranging, instrumentation, & counterpoint. 48 p, mus ex, paper. Mills 1946.   1.50

A sequel to "Modern visualized harmony" (see Harmony–2). Mainly for popular music.

GIVLER, ROBERT CHENAULT (comp)
Chord sequence finder: with keys to unlock chords . . . 30 p, 2 charts, mus ex, paper. (1948) E. C. Schirmer 1950.   2.00
Some 600 progressions to neighboring & remote keys from the plain & "chromatized" chords of any one key.

PETERSON, FRANKLIN
A handbook of musical form: being part II of "The pianist's handbook, a theoretic companion to practice." Paged 71/182, mus ex, paper. Augener 8th pr n d.   1.50
Composition, counterpoint, fugue, form, & music-history.

SCHILLINGER, JOSEPH
Kaleidophone: new resources of melody and harmony; pitch scales in relation to chord structures . . . 95 p, mus ex. Witmark (1940) rev ed n d.   3.00
Aiding the instantaneous location of scales corresponding to any given chord.

THOMPSON, IRENE FOWLER
Chord relation simplified. Ed David Gornston. 24 p, charts, tables, paper. David Gornston, N. Y., 1944.   .75
Classifications of chords in all keys.

TOLMAN, CARL JEAN
Chordmanual: a guide to intervals, scales, triads. 23 p, mus ex, paper. Author, Winthrop, Maine, (1936) 1940.   1.00
Tabulations of chords in all keys.

VOGLER, JULIUS
Rules of chords: taken from "A complete course in harmony" & intended as a means for reference in matters pertaining to chords . . . 29 p, mus ex, paper. Briegel 1936.   .50
Concise definitions and examples.

WILSON, MORTIMER
Basic formulas of chord progression: cadences & contrasts (major & minor modes). 17 p, mus ex, paper. J. Fischer 1921.   .60
Tonal, harmonic, & modulatory relationship. 18 p, mus ex, charts, paper. J. Fischer 1921.   .60
Super-title for both books: "A series of work tables prepared for students of harmony."

THERAPEUTICS/THERAPY (Musical)
See: Health.

THIBAUD, Anton Friedrich Justus
Purity in music. Tr John Broad-
house. vi, 103 p. (1877) Reeves △
1882. (1.50)
*A book of essays (originally published in
German in 1825, and admired by Robert
Schumann) on the chorale, church music,
popular melodies, etc.*

Thibaud, Jacques-Dorian. Author.
See App Ia.
See also: Violinists.

Thiele, Eugen. Author. See App Ib.

Thiman, Eric Harding. Author.
See Counterpoint-2, Harmony-2.

Thomas, Dana Lee (*pseud* of Dana Arnold
Schnittkind). Co-author (with Henry
Thomas). See Composers-1.

Thomas, Henry (*pseud* of Henry Thomas
Schnittkind). Author (with Dana Lee
Thomas). See Composers-1.

Thomas, Jean. Author (with Leeder).
See Folksongs-2.

Thomas, John ("*PencrddGwalia*"). Author.
See Harp.

Thomas, Kurt. Author. See App Ib.

THOMAS, Theodore
See:

America (music in) History
Conductors Orchestra

Author (with Stock). See Beethoven-3.
*Note: Works about Thomas that apparently
are O/P (or not easily available) include those
by Russell, Mrs. Thomas, & Upton.*

Thompson, Carl O. Author (with Nordholm). See School Music-1.

Thompson, Irene Fowler. Author.
See Theory-4.

Thompson, John Winter. Author.
See Harmony-2.

Thompson, Leila Fern. Compiler.
See Latin America.

Thompson, Oscar. Author, editor. See:

Composers-2. Great modern composers (1941). 3.00
Criticism. Practical (1934). 2.50
Encyclopedias of music. International cyclopedia (1938/49). 16.00
Opera-3. Plots (1940/43). 1.00
*Note: Other books by Thompson (on music
appreciation, Debussy, history, & singing)
apparently are O/P.*

Thompson, Randall. Author.
See Colleges.

Thomson, Gladys Scott. Author.
See Puccini (ed Crozier).

THOMSON, Virgil
See:

American Music History
Appreciation Opera
Composers-2 & 3a Phonograph Records
Criticism (esp ed Program Notes
  French) Stein

Author:
The art of judging music: music &
musical life in America & Europe,
1944–1949. x, 318, xviii p. Knopf
1948. 4.25
*The Harvard music-criticism symposium
speech (see also Criticism, ed French), plus
columns & reviews originally published in
the N. Y. "Herald-Tribune" 1944/1947.*

The musical scene. xiv, 301, xv
p. Knopf 1945. 3.50
*Columns & reviews from Thomson's first
years on the "Herald-Tribune," 1940/1944.
Note: "The state of music" (1939) is O/P.
For "Music right & left," see Addenda.*

THOROUGH-BASS
See:

Accompaniment Keyboard Harmony
  (esp Arnold) Keyboard Instruments
Baroque Era   (esp Bach)
Harmony Theory
History

Thorp, Willard. Editor. See Restoration.

Thorpe, Clarence Radford. Author.
See Hammond Organ.

Thurman, Howard. Author.
See Negro Spiritual.

THURSBY, Emma
See also: America (music in), Opera.

GIPSON, RICHARD MCCANDLESS
The life of Emma Thursby, 1845–
1931. xxii, 470 p, 74 pl. N. Y.
Historical Society 1940. 2.00
*A biography, with chronology, of one of the
first world-renowned American singers.*

Thurwanger, Camille. Author.
See French Language.

Tibbs, Ruth N. Co-author (with McHose).
See Sight-Singing.

Tiénot, Yvonne. Co-author (with Arma).
See App Ia.

Tierney, Elizabeth Margaret. Co-author
(with Kinscella). See School Music-1.

Tiersot, Julièn. Author, editor.
See Folksongs-1, also App Ia.

Tilly, H. Dorothy. Co-editor (with Kretzschmar). See Bibliography.

Tilson, Lowell Mason. Author.
See Theory–2.

TIME

See:

Harding	Tempo
Metronome	Theory
Rhythm	Timing

TIMING

See also:

Composers 3-a (Reis)	Radio Music
Conducting	Themes (esp Burrows
Orchestral Music	& Redman)
Program Notes	

*Note: York's "How long does it play?"
(1929) apparently is O/P.*

REDDICK, WILLIAM J.
The standard musical repertoire:
with accurate timings. 192 p.
Doubleday 1947, Blue Ribbon repr. O/P
*Timings for some 2000 works: overtures,
orchestral, piano, violin, songs, choral.*

TIN-PAN ALLEY

See: Jazz, Popular Music.

Tinyanova, Helen. Author.
See App IIa (Stradivari juvenile).
Tkach, Peter. Author. See Sight-Singing.
Tobel, Rudolf von. Author. See App Ib.
Tobin, J. Raymond. Author.
See Form, Mozart–3, Orchestra, Transposition.

TOCH, Ernst

See: Composers–2 & 3a, Contemporary
Music.

Author. See Theory–1.

Toledano, Ralph de. Editor. See Jazz.
Tolentino, Francisca Reyes. Catalogued
under Reyes-Tolentino, Francisca.
Tolman, Beth. Author. See Dances–2.
Tolman, Carl Jean. Author.
See Theory–4.
Tomlins, William L. Author.
See Singing–2.

TOM-TOM

See: Instruments (esp Mason), Indians.

TONALITY/ATONALITY

*General Note: In its larger aspects, Tonality
embraces all systems of tonal relationships,
including both those involving church modes
(as well as the various keys of the major &
minor modes) and that involving the Twelve-
Tone Technique or other systems, in some of
which there apparently is no "tonic" in the
familiar sense of tone-center. For this reason
alone, Atonality (i.e., the absence of tonality)*

*is an extremely loose if not entirely incorrect
term. But it is made even more ambiguous by
the tendency—in common usage—to apply it
to almost any type of modern music that seems
incomprehensible to ears schooled in orthodox
19th-century idioms. In recent years, musicians at least are dropping "atonal" in favor
of "quarter-tone," "duodecuple," or "twelve-
tone" (when, of course, these are applicable).*

See also:

Acoustics	Modulation
Aesthetics	Monophony
Appreciation	Scales
Composition	Theory
Form	Twelve-Tone
Harmony	Technique
Mode	

Also:

Composers (& indi-	Contemporary Music
viduals, esp Schoen-	History
berg)	Modern Music

*Note: Standard works apparently O/P (or not
easily available) include those by Bawden,
Dunk, Karg-Elert (in German), etc.*

KATZ, ADELE T.
Challenge to musical tradition: a
new concept of tonality. xxviii, 408
p, mus ex, 11–p bibl. Knopf 1945.   7.50
*Governing concepts of tonality, elaborated
from original formulations by Heinrich
Schenker, and illustrated by studies of Bach,
Beethoven, Wagner, Debussy, Stravinsky,
Schoenberg, & others.*

MIES, PAUL. See App Ib.

THATCHER, GLADYS KNESEL
Evolving tonality: the new sound in
music. 23 p, mus ex, paper. Author,
La Crescenta, Calif, 1948.   1.00
*Presentations of a single musical theme in
various tonalities.*

YASSER, JOSEPH
A theory of evolving tonality. x,
381 p, illus, mus ex.   American
Library of Musicology (contemporary series, V 1) 1932.   6.50
*A scholarly study, including a glossary of
technical terms, and tables of centitones &
vibration-ratios.*

TONE-POEMS

See:

Appreciation	Literature
Composers (& under	Poetry
individual names)	Program Music
Composition	Program Notes
History	Romantic Era

TONE QUALITY

See:

Aesthetics–2	Singing
Interpretation	String Playing
Piano Playing	Vibrato
Psychology	Violin Playing

TONIC SOL-FA

Conductors   History
England (Music in)   Opera

Note: As also noted under Sight-Singing, use of the tonic sol-fa notation is confined so exclusively to England (& perhaps some of the British Dominions) that none of the extensive British literature is included here.

Toop, Augustus. Author.
See Choir/Choral–2.

Toor, Frances. Author.
See Folklore, Peru.

TORELLI, Giuseppe

See: esp App Ib (Giegling biog in German).

TOSCANINI, Arturo

See also:
America (music in)   History
Conductors   Opera

Note: Standard works apparently O/P include those by Gilman, Nicotra, Stefan, etc.

CORTE, ANDREA DELLA. See App Ia & Ic.

EWEN, DAVID
The story of Arturo Toscanini. xviii, 142 p, frontis por, 1–p bibl. Holt 1951.   2.50
Quasi-juvenile, with complete record list.

HOELLER, SUSANNE WINTERNITZ (*comp*) Arturo Toscanini: a photobiography. Intro Dorothy Thompson. Note by Friderika Maria Zweig. 56 p, 55   △ photos. Island 1943 (limited).   5.00

TAUBMAN, HOWARD
The maestro: the life of Arturo Toscanini. viii, 342 p + 15-p illus (pors, etc). S & S 1951.   5.00
A full-length, illuminating portrait.

Tosi, Guy. Editor. See App Ia.

TOUCH

See: Piano Playing, Psychology.

Tournemire, Charles. Author. See App Ia.
Tours, Berthold. Author.
See Viola, Violin Playing.

TOVEY, (Sir) Donald Francis

A musician talks. Ed note Hubert J. Foss. Pref Ernest Walker. 2 v. Oxford 1941.
V 1: The integrity of music. xv, 161 p. 1941 (3rd pr 1946).   2.00
V 2: Musical textures. xiv, 89 p. 1941 (3rd pr 1946).   2.00
Ten Cramb lectures, delivered at the university of Glasgow, 1936, & four Alsop lectures, at the University of Liverpool, 1938.

The mainstream of music: & other essays. Ed H. J. Foss. ix, 404 p, mus ex. Oxford 1950.   4.00
Published in England as "Essays & lectures on music." Collected with an introduction by Hubert J. Foss. The title lecture was once published separately in 1938; several of the other pieces appeared first in Cobbett's Chamber Music Encyclopedia, "The Heritage of Music," "Music and Letters," "The Listener," etc.

Musical articles from the "Encylopedia Britannica." Pref Hubert J. Foss. vii, 251 p, mus ex. Oxford 1944 (1947).   3.75
A reprinting, with revisions, of the long series of articles on musical subjects (Aria to Variations) originally published in the 11th through 14th editions of the Encyclopedia Britannica.

See also:
Bach–2. Companion to the Art of Fugue (1931).   2.00
Beethoven–3. Beethoven (1945).   3.00
——. Companion to Beethoven's piano sonatas (1931).   5.00
Chamber Music. Essays in musical analysis, added volume (1944).   2.75
Composers–3c. Some English symphonists (1941).   1.75
Program Notes. Essays in musical analysis, 6 v (1935/39). Complete: 16.50
Note: Other books by Tovey, on Form, Parratt, etc, apparently are O/P.

GRIERSON, MAY
Tovey biography, in prep.   △

TOYE, (John) Francis

For what we have received: an autobiography. xi, 311, xiii p, 12 pl. Knopf 1948.   4.00
Travel notes & reminiscences of a noted British biographer of Rossini & Verdi.
See also: Rossini, Verdi–1.
Note: "The well-tempered musician" (1926) apparently is O/P.

Tracey, Hugh. Author.
See Africa (music in)

TRANSLATIONS

See: Opera–2 (librettos), Song Translations.

TRANSCRIPTION

See:
Arranging   Organ Playing (esp
Instruments   Ellingford)
Instrumentation   Score-Reading

TRANSPOSITION

See also:

Accompaniment	Piano Playing (esp 3)
Arranging	Score-Reading
Harmony	Sight-Playing &
Improvisation	Reading
Instrumentation	Sight-Singing
Instruments	Theory
Keyboard Harmony	

Note: Pertinent works apparently O/P include those by Warringer, etc.

HILL, JIM
The art of transposing at the piano at sight: how to play the piano in any key. . . 64 p, music, paper. Cole 1936 (1943?). 1.00
Primarily for light & popular music.

KLING, H.
Transposition: a practical & authoritative guide for all instruments. . . Tr, ed, & aug Gustave Saenger. 44 p, mus ex, paper. C. Fischer 1910 (1938?). 1.00

LENTZ, DONALD A.
Transposition by clef. iii, 27 p, mus ex, paper. Schmitt 1949. 1.00

REES-DAVIES, IEUAN
Transposition at the keyboard. 67 p, mus ex, paper. Curwen n d. 1.80

RICE, EUSTACE B. (*ed*)
Transposition by clef. 84 p, music, paper. N. E. Conservatory of Music, Boston, 1900. 1.25
A New England Conservatory of Music course, primarily for sight-reading & singing.

TOBIN, J. RAYMOND
Transposing at the piano: in 3 stages. 3 v: 22, 23, 23 p, mus ex, paper. Williams (1936), rev eds n d. 1.50

UGGEN, ELMER G.
Transposing tunes: transposition simplified for all instruments & voices. 56 p, mus ex, paper. Schmitt 1947. 1.00

TRAPP FAMILY

See also: Carols (ed Wasner).

TRAPP, MARIA AUGUSTA (*Baroness von*)
The story of the Trapp Family singers. 309 p, 8 photos, Lippincott 1949. 3.50
An informal, folksy account of the family's career abroad & in this country.

TREMOLO

See: Singing, Vibrato, Voice.

Trend, John Brande. Author. See Falla.

TRISTAN & ISOLDE

See: Wagner-3 (esp Bedier).

TROMBONE

See also:

Band	Instrumentation
Bugle (esp Safranek)	Instruments
History	Wind Instruments

JENKINS, GRANT B. (*comp*)
Bibliography of music for the B-flat tenor trombone. 87 p. The Instrumentalist, Glen Ellyn, Illinois, 1949. 1.25
A graded, classified list of some 1800 titles.

RAYMOND, WILLIAM F.
The trombone and its player: a theoretical & practical treatise on both. 26 p, illus, mus ex, paper. Fillmore Pub Co., Cincinnati, 1937. .50
A brief explanatory booklet by a United States Army first trombonist.

Trotin, Christine. Author. See Theory-2.

Trotter, Thomas Henry Yorke. Author. See Children-8.
Note: Numerous other books by Trotter apparently are O/P (or not easily available).

TROUBADOURS/TROUVÈRES

See also: esp Medieval/Renaissance.

Also:

Appreciation	History
French Music	Minstrels

Note: Standard works apparently O/P (or not easily available) include those by Aubry, Beck (in French), Gennrich (in German), Hueffer, Rowbotham, etc. Also a collection of troubadour songs compiled & arranged by Clarence Dickinson.

In addition to the Pei work below, there are, of course, many others that deal primarily with the troubadour texts, rather than the music: Hill & Bergin's "Anthology of the Provençal Troubadours" (Yale, 1941, $5.00), etc.

BECK, JEAN & LOUISE. See App Ia.
Note: Of the series "Les chansonniers des troubadours et des trouvères," V 1, "Le chansonnier Cangé" (1927), is O/P, but V 2, "Le manuscrit du Roi" (1938) is still available.

HARRIS, CLEMENT A.
The troubadour as musician: past & present. 26 p, frontis, bibl refs. △ Reeves n d (192?). (1.50)
An informal introductory essay.

PEI, MARIO A.
French precursors of the chanson
de Roland. xiv, 105 p, 3½–p bibl.
Columbia 1949.   3.00

Truette, Everett Ellsworth. Author.
See Organ Playing

TRUMPET

See also:

Band	Instrumentation
Bugle (esp Safranek)	Instruments
History	Wind Instruments

COLIN, CHARLES
Trumpet: vital brass notes, a text.
27 p, illus, paper. Author, N. Y.,
1948.   1.50
*Practical tips on muscle development, breath
control, etc, for trumpeters.*

MENKE, WERNER
History of the trumpet of Bach and
Handel: a new point of view & new
instruments; forming a history of the
trumpet & its music from its earliest
use as an artistic instrument to the
middle of the 18th century.   Tr
Gerald Abraham. xiii, 233 p, 5 pl, 4
b&ws, 6–p mus ex, paper. Reeves
n d (1934?).   3.75
With facing English & German texts.

Tucker, Archibald Norman. Author.
See Africa (music in).
Tully, Marjorie F. Compiler (with Rael).
See Folklore.

TUNING

See:

Acoustics	Monophony
Organ (esp Smith)	Psychology
Piano (esp Smith,	Scales
White)	

TURKEY (Music in) /TURKISH MUSIC
See:

Arabia (music in)	History
Asiatic Musics (note)	Instruments (Farmer)

*Note: In the bibliography of Asiatic Musics
referred to above, the 7th installment (Music
Library Association "Notes" for June 1949)
includes many listings devoted to this subject.*

*Standard works apparently O/P (or not easily
available) include these by Borrel (in French),
Giese (in German), Kowalski (in Polish),
Ritter (in German), Suphi & others (in
Turkish), etc.*

Turner, Walter James.   Author. See:

Beethoven–2. Search for reality	
(1927/45).	2.00
History–3. Short (1932/49).	1.50
Mozart–2. Man & work (1938).	1.98
Wagner–2. Biography (1933/48).	1.00

*Note: Several other books by Turner, includ-
ing a biography of Berlioz & collections of
essays, apparently are O/P (or not easily
available in this country).*

Tweedy, Donald. Author.
See Harmony–2.

TWELVE-TONE TECHNIQUE
*General Note: As remarked under the subject-
heading Tonality/Atonality, "Twelve-Tone
Technique" is a more exact term for the
musical idiom (developed largely by Schoenberg, Berg, Krenek, & Webern) that often is
called, loosely if not erroneously, "atonal."
This system of composition takes its name
from the fact that it is based on a "tone-row"
or arbitrary sequence embodying all twelve
tones of the chromatic scale.*

See also:

Appreciation	Harmony
Berg	History
Composers–2	Monophony
Contemporary Music	Scales
Counterpoint–1	Schoenberg
(esp Krenek)	Theory
Film Music (Eisler)	Tonality/Atonality

*Of the books listed below, only those by
Leibowitz (in French) are serious technical
studies.*

LEIBOWITZ, RENÉ. See App Ia ("Introduction à la musique de douze sons," 1949,
& "Qu'est-ce que la musique de douze
sons?" 1948).

MURPHY, LYLE SPUD
The new music of a 12-tone system:
for arrangers, composers, pianists,
& all students of ultra-modern music.
63 p, diagrs, mus ex, music, paper.
Crystal Music Pubs., Hollywood,
1949.   3.50
*Title (on cover only): composing & arranging
from chord patterns.*

TWENTIETH-CENTURY MUSIC
See:

Composers–2 (under	Modern Music
individual names)	History
Contemporary Music	

Twittenhoff, Wilhelm. Author.
See Recorder.

—U—

UFFENBACH, Johann Friedrich A. von.
See: App Ib (Preussner).

Uggen, Elmer G. Author.
See Transposition.

Ulanov, Barry. Author.
See Crosby, Ellington.

Ulrich, Homer. Author.
See Appreciation, Chamber Music.

ULTRASONICS

General Note: As noted under Supersonics, it now is generally agreed among physicists that an earlier confusion between these two terms be resolved by confining Supersonics to the field of study of aircraft, rockets, etc., that move at speeds faster than that of sound. Ultrasonics, on the other hand, is that branch of acoustics dealing with audio waves of higher frequencies than those normally audible to human ears. This latter field of study, in which exploration only recently has begun to make significant advances, is of course only remotely (if at all) associated with music, but it is an important extension of acoustics, and for that reason alone a sampling of the growing literature is listed below.

See also:

Acoustics	Sound Recording &
Insects (Pierce)	Reproduction

BERGMANN, LUDWIG
Ultrasonics: and their scientific & technical applications. Tr. H. Stafford Hatfield. ix, 264 p, 148 illus, 32–p bibl. (1938) Wiley 1939.   4.50
One of the first extensive studies, by a University of Breslau physics professor.

CARLIN, BENSON
Ultrasonics: xi, 270 p, illus.
McGraw 1949.   5.00
Current engineering aspects.

WHITE, S. YOUNG
Ultrasonic fundamentals. 36 p, 40 illus, paper. Radio Magazines, N. Y., 1949.   1.75
Reprint compilation of semi-technical articles from "Audio Engineering" magazine.

Umfleet, Kenneth Reynold. Author
See Operetta.

UNDERSTANDING (Music)

See:

Appreciation	School Music
Children	Theory

Note: A series, "Study course in music understanding," adopted by the National Federation of Music Clubs, published by Ditson, includes: Gehrkens's "Fundamentals of music" (see Theory–2), Mason's "From song to symphony" (see Appreciation), Kelley's "Musical instruments" (see Instruments), Hamilton's "Epochs in musical progress" (see History–2), & Goetschius's "Masters of the symphony" (see Composers–1).

UNESCO Publications

See Chopin–2, also App Ia (Panigel).

Note: The Panigel work is the first to appear of a series of discographies in preparation under the auspices of the Archives de la musique enregistrée UNESCO. Later works will be devoted to Bach, Mozart, Indian Music, Chinese Music, Museum Collections, etc.

UNFIGURED   BASSES/UNFIGURED HARMONY
See: Harmony.

UNITED STATES OF AMERICA
See: America (music in), American Music.

Unschuld, Maria von (Marie Unschuld Edle von Melasfeld). Author.
See Piano Playing–2.

Upton, George Putnam. Author.
See Opera–3, Program Notes.

Note: Numerous other books by Upton apparently are O/P.

Upton, William Treat. Author. See Song. Compiler (with Sonneck). See American Music.

Note: Upton's books on Fry and Heinrich apparently are O/P.

d'URFEY, Thomas

See also:

Dryden	Purcell
England (music in)	Poetry
English music	Restoration Era
History	Song(s)

DAY, CYRUS LAWRENCE (*ed*)
The songs of Thomas d'Urfey. x,
168 p, frontis por, 26 facs, bibl notes.
Harvard 1933.   2.50
*Harvard Studies in English No 9, with
reproductions of 26 songs.*

Ursprung, Otto. Author.
See App Ib (ed Bücken).

URUGUAY (Music in)
See: Latin America.

—V—

Vaganova, Agrippina Iakovlevna. Author.
See Dance.
Vaillat, Léandre. Author. See App Ia.
Valabrega, Cesare. Author. See App Ic.
Valensi, Théodore. Author. See App Ia.
Valentin, Erich. Author. See App Ib.
Vallas, Léon. Author.
See Debussy-2, App Ia.
Valois, Ninette de. Author.
See Opera–1 (ed Crozier).

VAMPING
See: Improvisation, Piano Playing–3.

Vanasek, Benedict. Author. See Rhythm.
Van Bodegraven, Paul. Author.
(with Wilson). See School Music–3.
Van de Wall, Willem. Author.
See Health.
Van den Borren, Charles. Author.
See England (music in), App Ia.
*Note: Other books in French & Flemish
apparently are O/P (or not easily available).*
Van der Linden, Albert. Co-editor (with
Clercx). See App Ia.
Van der Ven-Ten Bensel, Elise. Author.
See Dances–2 (ed Alford).
Vandevere, J. Lilian. Author.
See Children–6.

VAN DIEREN, Bernard
See:
Composers–2 & 3c   English Music
Contemporary Music   History
*Note: Van Dieren's provocative essays,
"Down among the dead men" (1935) is O/P.*

Vandre, Carl W. Author.
See Sight Playing.
Van Hoesen, Karl. Author. See Conducting.
Van Loon, Hendrik Willem. Author (with
Castagnetta). See Carols.
*Note: Several other books by Van Loon &
Castagnetta apparently are O/P.*
Vannes, René. Compiler. See App Ia.
Van Straaten, Jan (*pseud* of Bernard Fles).
Author. See App IIa (Dvořák juvenile).

Van Vechten, Carl. Editor (author).
See Stein.
*Note: Van Vechten's "Music of Spain"
(1918) and various books of essays on musical
subjects apparently are O/P.*

VARIATION
See also:

Appreciation	Form
Baroque Era	History
Composers (& under	Improvisation
individual names)	Ornamentation
Composition	Program Notes

*Note: Fischer's "Der Variction" (1930)
apparently is O/P (or not easily available).*

NELSON, ROBERT U.
The technique of variation: a study
of the instrumental variation from
Antonio de Cabezón to Max Reger.
vii, 197 p, mus ex, 6-p bibl. California 1948.   3.50
Same, paper covers.   2.50
*A scholarly study of 7 distinct types of varia-
tion from 1500 to the 20th century.*

VARNISH
See: Violin (esp Fry, Michelman).

Vassenhove, Léon van. Author.
See App Ia.

VAUGHAN WILLIAMS, Ralph
See also:

Appreciation	England (music in)
Ballet (ed Haskell)	English Music
Chamber Music	Opera
Choir/Choral–3	Phonograph Records
(esp Manners)	Program Notes
Contemporary Music	Song(s)
Composers–2 & 3c	Symphony
Concerto	Vocal Music

Co-editor (with Dearmer & Shaw). See
Carols, Hymns–1.

*Note: Vaughan Williams's "National music"
(1934) apparently is O/P.*

DICKINSON, A. E. F.
An introduction to the music of
Vaughan Williams. 84 p, mus ex,
paper. Oxford.   1.00
"Musical Pilgrim" series of analyses.

FOSS, HUBERT J.
Ralph Vaughan Williams: a study.
219 p, frontis por, brief bibl. (Harrap
1950), Oxford 1950.   3.50
*A detailed study of the man & his music,
including a reprint of Vaughan Williams's
1912 article, "Who wants the English composer" (p197/201), chronology, list of works,
& bibliography of the composer's writings.*

HOWES, FRANK
The dramatic works of Ralph
Vaughan Williams. 108 p, mus ex,
paper. Oxford 1937.   1.00
The later works of Ralph Vaughan
Williams. 85 p, mus ex, paper.
Oxford 1937 (1945).   1.00
*Both booklets above are in the "Musical
Pilgrim" series of analyses.*

YOUNG, PERCY M.
Vaughan Williams.
Dobson 1949/50 in prep.   △

Vehanen, Kosti. Author. See Anderson.
Veinus, Abraham. Author. See Concerto.
Co-author (with Simon). See Opera–3.
Venable, Mary. Author.
See Piano Playing–1.
Venables, Leonard C. Author.
See School Music–4.

VENEZUELA (Music in)
See: Latin America.

VERDI, Giuseppe
1. Life   2. Works

See also:

Appreciation	Opera
Composers–1	Phonograph Records
History	Program Notes
Italy (music in)	Themes
Italian Music	Vocal Music

Also: App IIa (Acker, Humphreys).

VERDI (1. Life)
*Note: Standard works apparently O/P (or
not easily available) include those by Bellaigue
(in French), Crowest, etc, and by various
Italian authors.*

BONAVIA, FERRUCCIO
Verdi. 120 p, illus. (1930). Dobson △
1947.   (2.50)

*British re-issue of a standard biography now
O/P in the 1930 Oxford edition.*

CHERBULIEZ, A. E. See App Ib.

HOLL, KARL. See App Ib.

HUSSEY, DYNELEY
Verdi. xii, 355 p, 8 pl (pors, fac,
caricatures, etc), mus ex, 1–p bibl.
Dent (1940) rev repr 1948, via Pelle-
grini 1949.   2.50
*"Master Musicians" series, with usual calen-
dar, personalia, catalogue of works, etc.*
Verdi. 14 p, cover por paper. Novello
n d (194?).   .40
Miniature biography ("great musicians").

RUTTERS, HERMAN
Giuseppe Verdi. Tr. D. Kuenen-
Wicksteed. 59 p, illus, mus ex, bds.
Continental n d (1947?).   2.50
*"Symphonia" series of illustrated mono-
graphs.*

TOYE, FRANCIS
Giuseppe Verdi: his life & works.
Intro Herbert Weinstock. xxi, 414,
xiv p, 15 pl (pors, fac, etc), mus ex,
1–p bibl. (1931) Knopf 1946.   5.00
*A standard biography, originally published
by Heineman in 1931.*

WERFEL, FRANZ
Verdi: a novel of the opera. Tr Helen
Jessiman. vii, 438 p. (1925) Allen
Towne 1947, via Crown.   2.95
*Originally in German, 1924. First published
in the present English translation by Viking
in 1925.*

WERFEL, FRANZ & STEFAN, PAUL (eds)
Verdi: the man in his letters. Tr
Barrows Mussey (preface) & Edward
Downes (letters). 469 p, 13 illus
(pors, facs, etc). (1942) Wyn 1948.   3.50
*The most comprehensive collection of Verdi
letters in English, originally published by L.
B. Fischer, New York, in 1942. Werfel's
preface is a "portrait" of Verdi and the work
also includes an autobiographical sketch,
Verdi's last will, & catalogue of his works.*

VERDI (2. Works)
See also: App IIa (Diller juvenile).

BONAVIA, FERRUCCIO
Verdi: Rigoletto. 27 p + 8 pl, mus
ex, brief bibl, paper. Boosey 1947.   .60
"Covent Garden Operas" series.

DENT, EDWARD J. (tr)
Rigoletto: an opera in three acts.

Words by Salvatore Cammarano; music by Verdi. English version. 46 p, paper. Oxford 1939.   .80

La Traviata (The lady of the camelias): opera in four acts. Words by Francesco Maria Piave; music by Verdi. English version. 46 p, paper. Oxford 1944.   .80

Il Trovatore (The troubadour): opera in four acts. Words by Salvatore Cammarano; music by Verdi. English version. 48 p, paper. Oxford 1944.   .80

All three translations above also are available in the "Pocket Libretto Library" series, Allen Towne, later Crown (see Opera–2).

FISHER, TREVOR
Verdi: La Traviata. 31 p + 8 pl, mus ex, paper. Boosey 1948.   .60

HUSSEY, DYNELEY
Verdi: Il Trovatore (The troubadour). 32 p + 8 pl, mus ex, brief bibl, paper. Boosey 1947.   .60
Both the Fisher & Hussey booklets above are in the "Covent Garden Operas" series.

WILLIAMS, STEPHEN
Verdi's last operas.
Hinrichsen in prep.   △
"Miniature Survey" series M-18.

VIBRATO

See also:

Folklore (Metfessel)	String Playing
Psychology	Violin Playing
Singing (esp 2, Field-Hyde)	Voice (esp Westerman)

SEASHORE, CARL E. *(ed)*
Psychology of the vibrato in voice and instrument. 159 p, illus, charts, 3–p bibl. Iowa 1936.   1.75
V 3 in the University of Iowa studies in the psychology of music; an abridgment with new data) of the book below.

The vibrato. 382 p, illus, diagrs, tables, 6–p bibl. Iowa n d (1932).   2.50
V 1 in the University of Iowa studies in the psychology of music; a collection of papers by various authors.

VIENNA

See also: esp Philharmonic (Mittag).

Appreciation	Romantic Era
Classic Era	Strauss Family
Composers (& under individual names)	J. Strauss, jr.
	Walter
Hanslick	Waltz
History	Weingartner

Note: Pertinent works apparently O/P (or not easily available) include those by D. & F. Ewen, Graf, etc.

FARGA, FRANZ.   See App Ib.

GÁL, HANS
The golden age of Vienna. 72 p, 7 col pl, 32 b&ws, bds. Chanticleer 1948.   2.50
"World of Music" series No 2, lavishly illustrated, and devoted largely to the giants of Vienna's "golden age": Gluck, Haydn, Mozart, Beethoven, & Schubert.

HADAMOWSKY, FRANZ & OTTE, HEINZ.
See App Ib.

KOBALD, KARL.   See App Ib.

LIESS, ANDREAS.   See App Ib.

SCHENK, ERICH.   See App Ib.

VIERNE, Louis

See also:

French Music	Organists
History	Organ Music

GAVOTY, BERNARD.   See App Ia (biography in French).

VILLA-LOBOS, Heitor

See:

Appreciation	Latin America
Composers–2 & 3a	Phonograph Records
Contemporary Music	Program Notes

Ville, Mara.   Author. See Children–8.

Vinci, Leonardo da.   Author.
See Aesthetics–1.
Also: App IIa (Acker juvenile biog).

VIOL

See:

Chamber Music	Instruments
Elizabethan Music	Medieval/Renaissance
History	Violin

VIOLA/VIOLA PLAYING

See also:

Chamber Music	String Playing
History	String Quartet
Instrumentation	Violin
Instruments	Violin Music
Orchestra	(esp Letz)
String Instruments	Violin Playing

Note: Standard works apparently O/P (or not easily available) include those by Altmann & Borissowski (catalogue in German), etc.

DOLEJŠÍ, ROBERT
Modern viola technique. viii, 134 p, illus, mus ex. Chicago 1939.   3.00
A standard modern work.

TOURS, BERTHOLD & SHORE, BERNARD
The viola. v, 121 p, 6 photos, 3
diagrs, Novello (18??) new ed n d △
(1913). (2.25)

*Novello Primer No 61: modern revision of a
standard 19th-century work, superseding the
1902 revision ed by Alfred Gibson.*

VIOLIN

*For convenience, the pertinent literature is
listed below in four categories:*

**Violin (The Instrument, History, Manu-
facture, Repair, Varnish, etc)**
Violin Music
Violin Playing
Violinists

VIOLIN (The Instrument, History, Manufacture, Repair, Varnish, etc)

See also:

Ole Bull	Spalding
Children–2	Stradivari
Guadagnini Family	String Instruments
Instrumentation	String Playing
Instruments	String Quartet
Kreisler	Szigeti
Orchestra	Violin Music
Paganini	Violin Playing
School Music–3	Violinists

*Note: Standard works apparently O/P (or not
easily available) include those by Abele &
Niederheitmann, Bachmann, Ballard, Clarke,
Common, Davidson, Dubourg, Gilbert, Grillet
(in French), Hart, Haubensack (in German),
Haweis, Heron-Allen (bibl, 1890), Lütgen-
dorff (in German), Morris, Moya & Piper,
Otto, Petherick, Poidras, Racster, Schlesinger,
Stainer, Stoeving, Van der Straeten, etc.*

ALTON, ROBERT
Violin and 'cello building and repairing. 182 p, 3 pl, 82 b&ws Cassell
1946. 2.00

Amplification of a work handbook, 1923.

BERR, ALBERT. See App Ib.

BROADHOUSE, JOHN
The violin: its construction, viii,
137 p, 47 illus & folding pl. Reeves △
rev enl ed n d (1892?). (3.00)
*Super-title: "How to make a violin." In-
cludes practical construction details, notes by
Ole Bull, & list of sale prices of old violins.*

CABOS, FRANCINE. See App Ia.

EMERY, F. B.
Violinist's encyclopedia dictionary.
viii, 233 p, illus, mus ex. Reeves △
(1913) new enl ed n d (1925). (3.95)
*Also once published in a 3rd ed (1928) by
the Violin Literature Pub. Co., Chicago.*

FAIRFIELD, JOHN H.
Known violin makers. xiv, 192 p.
Author (via R. Wurlitzer Co, N. Y.)
1942. 2.75
*Dictionaries of European & American manu-
facturers, with reminiscences of the violin
business in America by Jay C. Freeman.*

FARGA, FRANZ
Violins and violinists. Tr Egon
Larsen. xvi, 223 p + 130 pl, 10
b&ws. (Rockliff 1950) Macmillan
1950. 4.50

*An extremely detailed, illustrated study of the
instrument's history & development, its
makers & players, with detailed consideration of Paganini, the Viennese School & the
Romantics. With an additional chapter on
English violin makers by E. W. Lavender.
See App Ib for the 2nd German edition (the
1st German edition was dated 1940).*

FRY, GEORGE
The varnishes of the Italian violin-
makers of the 16th, 17th, & 18th
centuries, and their influence on tone.
xi, 128 p, bibl. Stevens & Sons,
London, n d (1904). 6.00

GOSLING, HENRY F.
The violinist's manual: a treatise on
the construction, choice, care, adjustment, study & technique of the violin
... xv, 270 p, 40 pl, mus ex. Reeves △
1935. (3.75)

*Origin, construction, & adjustment of violin
& bow; study & care; technique, etc.*

GRUENBERG, EUGENE
The violin student's vocabulary. 84
p, mus ex, paper. Ditson 1931. .75

*"Pocket Music Student" series. Actually a
book of elementary musical "theory," with
a historical sketch of violin & bow, lists of
famous violinists, violin & bow makers.*

HAMMA, FRIDOLIN. See App Ib.

HERON-ALLEN, EDWARD
Violin making: as it was and is;
being a historical, theoretical, & practical treatise on the science & art of
violin making...; preceded by an
essay on the violin & its position as a
musical instrument. xxii, 366 p, 6 pl,
196 b&ws, fold-out chart, 15–p bibl.
(1884, 2nd ed 1885) C. Fischer repr
n d. 6.00

*A standard 19th-century work, originally
published by Ward Lock & Co, London.*

MICHELMAN, JOSEPH
Violin varnish: a plausible recreation
of the varnish used by the Italian
violin makers between the years 1550
& 1750. xi, 185 p. Author, Cincinnati, 1946.   3.75
*Includes a discussion of previous publications
on the subject of violin varnishes.*

REID, JOSEPH V.
You can make a "Stradivarius" vio-
lin. 48 p + 8 scale plans. Popular
Mechanics Press, Chicago, 1950.   3.50
Home workshop guidebook.

SANDYS, W. & FORSTER, S. A.
The history of the violin: and other
instruments played on with the bow.
390 p, col frontis, illus. Reeves n d   △
(1864).   (6.30)

STOEVING, PAUL
The violin: its famous makers &
players. 100 p, paper. Ditson 1928.   .75

("Pocket Music Student.")

VANNES, RENÉ *(comp)*. See App Ia.

WHITE, A. W.
The violin: how to construct from
beginning to completion . . how to
keep the violin in order . . . 44 p, 2
fold-out diagrs, paper. Author,
Boston, 1892.   .50

VIOLIN MUSIC

See also:

Appreciation	Program Notes
Chamber Music	Spalding
Composers (& under	String Playing
individual names)	String Quartet
Concerto	Szigeti
History	Violin
Paganini	Violin Playing
Phonograph Records	Violinists

*Note: Standard works apparently O/P (or not
easily available) include those by De Reszke,
Emery, Feinland, Wasielewski (in German),
etc; also catalogues (in German) by Grünberg
& Tottmann.*

LETZ, HANS *(comp)*
Music for the violin and viola. viii,
107 p, bds. Rinehart 1949.   2.50
*V 2 in the "Field of Music" series ed Ernest
Hutcheson; graded listings with remarks.*

SWALIN, BENJAMIN F.
The violin concerto: a study in German romanticism. viii, 172 p, mus
ex, 5-p bibl. North Carolina 1941.   3.50
*Detailed technical & stylistic analyses, plus
a list of phonograph recordings.*

VIOLIN PLAYING

See also:

Ole Bull	Rode
Chamber Music	School Music-3
Children-4 (esp Winn)	Spalding
Concerto	String Instruments
Fiorillo	String Playing
Gaviniés	String Quartet
History	Szigeti
Instruments	Theory-3 (esp Ray)
Interpretation	Vibrato
Kreisler	Violin
Kreutzer	Violin Music
Paganini	Violinists

Also: App Ia (Pochon, Thibaud).

*Note: The books listed do not include violin
"methods" (e.g., those by Dounis, Gardner,
Stoessel, Wilhelmj & Brown, etc), which consist primarily of technical exercises with little
or no text.*

*Standard works apparently O/P (or not easily
available) include those by Althaus, Auer,
Gosling, Grünberg (in German), Hahn,
Hodgson, Kneisel, Knocker, Martens,
Schroeder, Stoeving, Thistleton, Winn, etc.*

BERKLEY, HAROLD
The modern technique of violin bowing: an analysis of the principles of
modern bowing & how to apply them
to musical interpretation. Forew
Louis Persinger. 47 p, 6 illus, mus
ex, paper. G. Schirmer 1941.   1.25
*A supplementary work: "12 studies in modern
violin bowing in the first position" (1943,
75c) is mostly musical exercises.*

BOSTELMANN, LOUIS J.
An analysis of violin practice. 78 p,
illus, mus ex. Ditson 1947.   1.25
*"Music Students Library" series; identifica-
tion & correction of common faults in bowing,
intonation, phrasing, etc.*

BYTOVETZKI, PAVEL L.
How to master the violin: a practical
guide to students & teachers. 108 p,
38 illus, mus ex. Ditson 1917.   1.25
"Music Students Library"; with music lists.

COURVOISIER, KARL
The technics of violin playing. Ed
& tr H. E. Krehbiel. 51 p, illus, mus
ex, flex. (1880). G. Schirmer rev ed
1908.   .75
Originally in German, 1873/1878.

CRAMER, EDWARD E.
The basis of artistry in violin playing.
87 p, illus, mus ex, paper, spir. Southwest 1936.   1.50

FLESCH, KARL
The art of violin playing.   **Tr**

Frederick H. Martens. 2 v, paper. **C** Fischer 1924/1930.

V 1: Technique in general; applied technique. 180 p + 8-p photos. (1924) rev ed 1939.   6.00

V 2: Artistic realization & instruction. iv, 237 p, mus ex. 1930.   6.00
A standard work, originally published in German, 1923/8.

Problems of tone production in violin playing. Tr Gustav Saenger. 24 p, mus ex, paper. C. Fischer 1934.   1.25
Supplementary study to the larger work above; originally pub in German, 1931.

GRIMSON, SAMUEL B. & FORSYTH, CECIL
Modern violin-playing. iii, 98 p, 34 pl & b&ws. Gray 1920.   2.00

GRUENBERG, EUGENE
Violin teaching and violin study: rules and hints for teachers & students. Pref Fritz Kreisler. xii, 150 p, 36 illus, mus ex. C. Fischer rev ed 1919.   2.00
Includes a list of recommended works.

JAROSY, ALBERT. See App Ia.

JUZEK, ROBERT
The simplicity of violin playing: v 1. 114 p, illus, mus ex, typescript repro, spir. Metropolitan Music Co, N. Y., 1948.   7.50
A detailed discussion of fundamental principles. Two additional volumes are also announced for publication (1949/50), at $7.50 each, but other information is lacking.

KNEISEL, FRANZ
Principles of violin bowing and phrasing: hints to serious violin students. 31 p, illus, mus ex, paper. C. Fischer 1925.   .50

KNOX, WILLIAM MORGAN
The violinist's manual: a theoretical textbook . . . 91 p, mus ex, paper. Willis (1921) 2nd ed 1923.   .75
Mainly musical rudiments ("theory").

LELAND, VALBORG
The Dounis principles of violin playing: their meaning & practical application. 62 p, mus ex, paper. Strad 1949.   4.00
Fundamental techniques, particularly of the bow arm & left hand; includes a bibliography of the Dounis methods & editions.

MOZART, LEOPOLD
A treatise on the fundamental principles of violin playing. Tr Edith

Knocker. Pref Alfred Einstein. xxxv, 231 p + fold-out table, facs, mus ex, 1-p bibl. Oxford 1948.   9.00
The famous "Versuch einer gründlichen Violinschule," by Mozart's father; originally published in 1756 and one of the standard pedagogical music books of all time. The present English edition was completed in 1937 & announced for publication in 1940, but was delayed until 1948 by war-time exigencies.

NORDEN, HUGO
Harmony and its application in violin playing. Forew Felix Winternitz. ix, 141 p, mus ex. E. C. Schirmer (1933) 1937.   3.50

ROBJOHNS, SYDNEY
Violin technique: some difficulties & their solution. 107 p, mus ex. Oxford 1930 (1946).   1.50

TOURS, BERTHOLD
The violin. Ed & rev W. H. Reed. 106 p, iv-p photos, 3 b&ws, music, paper. Novello 1934.   (2.00)
Same, ed Ariberto di Butera. 107 p, illus music, paper. G. Schirmer 1923.   1.50
A standard 19th-century work, mostly musical exercises for practice. The G. Schirmer edition has texts in English & Spanish.

WINN, EDITH L.
(*See also Children–4.*)
Representative violin solos and how to play them: 22 representative violin solos analyzed, with practical suggestions as to their technical demands & artistic interpretation. v, 89 p, mus ex. C. Fischer (1911) 6th ed 1936.   1.00

WOOD, BENJAMIN. See App Ia.

YOST, GAYLORD
Basic principles of violin playing. 55 p, illus, mus ex, paper. Volkwein 1940.   1.50

VIOLINISTS

Note: Standard works apparently O/P (or not easily available) include those by Ehrlich, Lahee, Phipson, etc.

BROOK, DONALD
Violinists of today. xiii, 192 p, 28
pors. (1948) Macmillan 1949.   3.00
*Studies of 28 players from Paul Beard to
Zimbalist, originally pub by Rockliff.*

CLARKE, A. MASON
A biographical dictionary of fiddlers:
including performers on the violoncello & double bass, past & present,
containing a sketch of their artistic
career, together with notes of their
compositions, etc. viii, 360 p, 9 pors. Δ
Reeves n d (1895).   (3.00)
An antiquated, but standard work.

VIOLONCELLISTS

See:

Casals	Interpreters
	Violinists (Clarke)

VIOLONCELLO

See:

Casals	Stradivari
History	String Instruments
Instrumentation	String Quartet
Instruments	Violin (esp Alton)
Orchestra	Violoncello Playing

*Note: Standard works apparently O/P (or not
easily available) include those by Broadley,
Van der Straeten, Wasielewski, etc.*

VIOLONCELLO MUSIC

See:

Appreciation	Concerto
Chamber Music	History
Composers (& under	Program Notes
individual names)	String Quartet

*Note: Weigl's "Handbuch der Violoncell
Literatur" (1911) apparently is O/P (or not
easily available in this country).*

VIOLONCELLO PLAYING

See also:

Casals	String Playing
Chamber Music	String Quartet
Concerto	Vibrato
Interpretation	

*Note: Standard works apparenly O/P (or not
easily available) include those by Broadley,
Krall, Schroeder, Van der Straeten, etc.*

ALEXANIAN, DIRAN
Theoretical and practical treatise of
of the violoncello: compiled in com-
plete accord with Pablo Casals. Tr
Frederick Fairbanks. Pref Pablo
Casals. 215 p, photos, mus ex, paper.
A. Z. Mathod, Paris (1910/14) 1922. 10.00
*Super-title (cover only): "The technique of
violoncello playing." Includes a description
of the 'cello by Caressa & Français.*

DESWERT (DE SWERT), JULES
The violoncello. 100 p, 2 illus, mus
ex, paper. Novello n d.   (2.50)
*A standard 19th-century work, mostly musical
exercises, in the Novello "primer" series.*

POTTER, LOUIS Jr.
'Cello handbook: fundamentals of
'cello playing for teachers & students.
39, v p, 17 photos, mus ex, paper.
Author, via Illini Bookstore, Cham-
paign, Illinois, 1948.   2.50

VIRGINALS

See also:

Elizabethan Music	Keyboard Instruments
History	(esp Bach, Kenyon)
Instruments	Medieval/Renaissance

VIRTUOSITY

See:

Piano Playing	Violin Playing
Singing	Etc.

Also: under the name of individual virtuosi.

Viu Salas, Vicente. Author. See App Id.

VIVALDI, Antonio

See also:

Appreciation	Italian Music
Bach	Italy (music in)
Baroque Era	Phonograph Records
Composers-1	Program Notes
Concerto	Violin Music
History	

PINCHERLE, MARC. See App Ia.

RUDGE, OLGA (*ed*). See App Ic.

VOCAL MUSIC

See also:

Appreciation	Italian Music (esp
Ballad	Vogel note)
Children-7	Negro Spirituals
Choir/Choral-3	Opera
Church Music	Operetta
Community Music	Phonograph Records
Composers (& under	Program Notes
individual names)	Rodgers & Hart
Cowboy Music	School Music-4
Folklore	Sea Shanties
Folksongs	Singing
Gershwin	Song(s)
History	Songbooks

KAGEN, SERGIUS (*comp*)
Music for the voice: a descriptive
list of concert & teaching material.
xvi, 507 p. Rinehart 1949.   5.00
*V 3 in the "Field of Music" series, ed Ernest
Hutcheson. Classified & annotated lists of
songs & airs before the 19th century, 19th-
& 20th-century songs, folksongs, & arias.*

WHITE, HERBERT D.
The singing stream: an informal story

of the evolution of vocal music. x, 258 p, illus (H. Weissenborn), mus ex, 4–p bibl. Ginn (London) 1950. (2.25)
Historical survey for laymen, with a 5-p list of recommended recordings.

Vodarsky-Shiraeff, Alexandria. Compiler.
See Russia (music in)
Vogel, Emil. Compiler.
See Italian Music (note only).

Vogler, Julius. Author. See:
Counterpoint–2. Modern (1935). .50
Harmony–2. How to harmonize melodies (1935). .50
——. Modern course (1929/40). 3 v. 3.00
Melody Writing. Musical speech (1934). .50
Modulation. 526 mods. (1936). 1.00
——. Modern method (1933). .50
Theory–4. Rules of chords (1936). .50

Vogt, Hans. Author.
See Piano Playing–2.
Vogt, Van Ogden. Author.
See Religion & Music.

VOICE

General Note: Many books in the general field of voice-culture, singing, speech, etc, are difficult to classify rigorously, but in general the present category is confined to works dealing with both singing & speaking, plus a sampling of the extensive literature on the vocal mechanism itself & its disorders.

See also: esp Singing, Speech.

Also:

Acting	Pronunciation
Bel Canto	Radio
Boy Voices	School Music–4
Breathing	Singers
Children–7	Teaching
Choir/Choral	Vibrato
Diction	Vocal Music
Opera	

Note: Standard works apparently O/P (or not easily available) include those by Aikin, Behnke & Brown, Curry, Felderman, Gib, Grigg-Smith, Guttmann, Heller, Henderson, Krasnoff, Mackenzie, McLellan, Miller, Mills, Palmer, Raubichek, Voorhees, etc.

BANKS, LOUIS
Voice culture: a new approach. 86 p, frontis por, diagrs. Elkan 1948. 2.50
A system of training for tone-quality, pitch range, correct pronunciation, etc.

BARROWS, SARAH T. & PIERCE, A. E.
The voice: how to use it, with exercises for tone & articulation. 181 p,

diagrs, mus ex, 4–p bibl. Expression (1933) rev ed 1938 (3rd pr 1942). 3.00
Exercises for consonants, vowels, intonation, & general control of vocal mechanisms.

BEHNKE, EMIL
The mechanism of the human voice. With a new chapter on Voice Failure by Mrs Emil Behnke. xi, 146 p, 16 illus, mus ex, paper. Curwen (1880) 21st ed n d (1950?). 1.50
A standard 19th-century work.

DUNKLEY, FERDINAND
The buoyant voice, acquired by correct pitch-control: a new, scientific method of training. viii, 106 p, mus ex. Birchard 1942. 1.60

EVETTS, EDGAR T.
Vocal disorders: their cause & cure. viii, 85 p, 5 illus, mus ex. Dent 1933. 1.00
Remedial treatments.

FILLEBROWN, THOMAS
Resonance in singing & speaking viii, 93 p, illus, mus ex, 3–p bibl. Ditson 1911. 1.50
"Music Students Library" series.

HARPER, RALPH M.
The voice governor: give it a chance, correct bodily mechanics does it. 152 p, 40 illus. E. C. Schirmer (1940) 2nd ed 1945. 3.00

LAWSON, FRANKLIN D.
The human voice: a concise manual on training the speaking & singing voice. ix, 94 p, illus, mus ex, forms. Harper 1944 (3rd ed n d). 2.50
A physician on the proper use of the voice.

LONGO, TEODOSIO
Fundamentals of singing & speaking. 112 p, diagrs, mus ex. S. F. Vanni, N. Y., 1945. 3.50

RUFF, ALBERT E.
Vocal fundamentals for speech and song: a brief treatise on the vocal muscular system. 103 p, illus, mus ex. Author, Los Angeles, 1926 (distributed by G. Schirmer). 2.00
Exercises for voice restoration.

RUSSELL, LOUIS ARTHUR
The commonplaces of vocal art: a plain statement of the philosophy of singing in a series of informal chats with vocalists, teachers, students, platform-speakers, & all those who wish to use their voices correctly. viii, 74 p. Ditson 1907. 1.50

"Music Students Library" series; essays on practical problems of singing & speaking.

SHAW, W. WARREN & LINDSAY, GEORGE L.
Educational vocal technique: in song & speech. 2 v: 67/83 p, diagrs, music, paper. Presser 1936   2.00

STANLEY, DOUGLAS
The science of voice: an application of the laws of acoustics, anatomy, physiology & psychology to the problems of vocal technic . . . xii, 384 p, 61 illus, 31 mus ex, 2-p bibl. C. Fischer (1929) 4th rev enl ed 1948.   5.00

With a section on interpretation & musicianship by Alma Stanley, a section on physical principles by S. S. S. Watkins, & appendices outlining recent developments.

Your voice: applied science of vocal art, singing, & speaking. xvi, 366 p, 39 illus. Pitman (1945) 2nd rev ed 1950.   6.00

Includes considerable material from an earlier book by Stanley & J. P. Maxfield, "The voice: its production & reproduction," 1933.

WEER, ROBERT LAWRENCE
Your voice. 115 p, 7 illus. Author, Los Angeles, 1948   3.00

WESTERMAN, KENNETH N.
Emergent voice. xii, 156 p, illus, mus ex, 2-p bibl. Author, Ann Arbor, Michigan, 1947.   5.00

Includes an appendix on the vibrato & 5-p bibliography of folksongs.

WILCOX, JOHN C.
The living voice: a study guide for song & speech; a presentation of vocal laws & theories, together with specific instructions for training voices. viii, 75 p, mus ex. C. Fischer (1935) rev enl ed 1945.   1.50

ZAY, W. HENRI
Practical psychology of voice and of life. xi, 139 p, illus, mus ex. G. Schirmer 1917 (1945).   2.00

Combining "the psychic & physical energies into a positive force," and requirements of "singing on the timbre."

VOLPE, Arnold
See also: America (music in).

VOLPE, MARIE
Arnold Volpe: bridge between two musical worlds. Forew Olin Downes. 230 p, 51 pl (pors, facs, etc). University of Miami Press, via Farrar Straus 1950.   3.50

A biography, by his widow, of the Russian-American conductor who pioneered in open-air concerts at the Lewisohn Stadium & in Florida.

Volpe, Marie. Author. See A. Volpe.

VOLUNTARY
See: Church Music, Organ Music.

Votaw, Lyravine. Author. See Children–6.
Vuillermoz, Émile. Author. See App Ia.

—W—

Wackernagel, Peter. Editor.
See Bach-2 (Kirkpatrick), App Ib (Bach).
Wadley, Fredericka. Author (with Allison).
See Children-3.

WAELRANT, Hubert
See: Medieval/Renaissance (esp Lowinsky).

Waesberghe, Josef Smits van. Author.
See Gregorian Chant.

WAGNER, Cosima
See:

History	F. Wagner
Liszt	R. Wagner
Romantic Era	Women

Note: Standard works apparently O/P (or not easily available) include several volumes of correspondence (in German), and biographies by Moulin-Eckert & Richardson.

WAGNER, Friedelind
WAGNER, FRIEDELIND & COOPER, PAGE
Heritage of fire: the story of Richard
Wagner's granddaughter. xv, 231 p,
8 photos. Harper 1945.   3.00
Bayreuth memoirs, stressing Hitler's attempt to take over the Wagnerian music drama as a symbol of Nazi ideology.

WAGNER, Richard

1. **Own Writings (Autobiography, Correspondence, etc)**
2. **Life & Theories (Biographies, etc)**
3. **Works (Collective & Individual Studies, Librettos, etc)**

General Note: More words have been written, more books have been published, about Wagner and his influence than on any other individual in all musical history. Yet ("sic transit gloria mundi"), comparatively few of these remain in-print today or are likely ever to be reprinted. The O/P notes below necessarily are confined to the more important works only and for the most part to those in English, for it is extremely difficult to obtain accurate availability—information on German & French publications.

For the benefit of specialists, however, it might be noted that many of the out-of-print

Wagner books still can be unearthed in the second-hand bookshops in larger cities, as well as consulted in larger music-libraries.

Except for specialized instruction books & "methods," most books on music include at least some reference to Wagner, his works, or his influence. For some of the more important references, see under the following subject-headings in particular—

Acting	Mann (essays)
Aesthetics	Modern Music
Appreciation	Opera
Autographs	Philosophy
Berlioz	Phonograph Records
Composers	Poetry & Music
Contemporary Music	Program Notes
Facsimiles	Romantic Era
Hanslick	Song(s)
History	Themes
Letters	Timing
Liszt	Vocal Music
Literature & Music	F. Wagner

WAGNER

(1. **Own Writings: Autobiography, Correspondence, etc**)

Note: Among the works apparently O/P (or not easily available) are those on Beethoven & Conducting, the 2-v "My life," Evans's translation of "Opera and drama," the collection of letters ed Altmann, collections of correspondence with Liszt, Nietzsche, Mathilde Wesendonck, Mina Wagner, etc; also many volumes of collected & individual works & correspondence in German.

Wagner's prose works. Tr William
Ashton Ellis. 8 v (Kegan Paul)
1892/9, via Reeves.   △
Note: Although v 5 & 6 are O/P, the others are still listed in the current Reeves catalogue (prices on application). The individual volume titles are:

V 1: The art-work of the future.
V 2: Opera and drama.
V 3: The theatre.
V 4: Art and politics.
V 5: Actors and singers (O/P).
V 6: Religion and art (O/P).
V 7: In Paris and Dresden.
V 8: Posthumous.

Judaism in music: being the original
essay together with the later supplement. Tr & ed Edwin Evans, Sr. xvi,   △
93 p. Reeves 1910.   (3.00)

The controversial 1850 article, together with the supplement of 1869.

(BURK, JOHN N., *ed*)
Letters of Richard Wagner: the Burrell collection.   xi, 665 p, 8 pl (pors), 3 b&ws, mus ex (facs).   Macmillan 1950.   10.50

A monumental collection, long shrouded in secrecy, of some 840 items; plus 25 additional letters included in Mrs Efrem Zimbalist's gift to the Curtis Institute of Music.   The translations are by Hans Abraham, Henry Lea, & Dr Richard Stoehr, and the editor contributes a chapter on Mrs Burrell & many illuminating notes.

SCHUH, WILLI, *ed.*   See App Ib (Judith Gautier correspondence, in German).

WAGNER (2.   Life & Theories)

Note: Standard works in English apparently O/P (or not easily available) include those by Bekker, Burrell, Chamberlain, Dannreuther, Ellis, Finck, Hight, Hueffer, Irvine, Kapp, Neumann, Newman, Nietzsche, Pourtylès (but see App Ia for a French version), Runciman, Steigmann, Wallace, Wolzogen, etc.
See also: App IIa (Burch juvenile).

BARZUN, JACQUES
Darwin, Marx, Wagner: critique of a heritage.   xii, 420 p, bibl refs.
Little Brown 1941.   3.50
Section III, "The artistic revolution," p 253/348, deals mainly with Wagner.

BEAUFILS, MARCEL.   See App Ia.

EVANS, EDWIN, *Sr*
Wagner's teachings by analogy: his views on absolute music & on the relations of articulate & tonal speech, with special reference to "Opera and Drama."   viii, 79 p.   Reeves n d △
(1915).   (2.40)
A series of papers intended as an introduction to the study of Wagner's prose works.

GLASENAPP, CARL F. & ELLIS, W. ASHTON
Life of Richard Wagner.   6 v.   (Kegan Paul 1900/8), via Reeves.   △
Still available in the Reeves catalogue (price on application).   V 1 & 2 are by Glasenapp, translated by Ellis; v 3 is partly a translation, partly Ellis's own work; v 4, 5, & 6 are by Ellis alone.
V 1: xiii, 400 p, mus ex. 1900.
V 2: ix, 436 p, mus ex. 1902.
V 3: ix, 528 p. 1903.

V 4: x, 537 p, mus ex, frontis. 1904.
V 5: vi, 460 p, mus ex. 1906.
V 6: x, 472 p, mus ex. 1908.

HADOW, W. HENRY
Richard Wagner.   256 p.   (Butterworth) 1934, via Oxford.   1.50
"Home University Library" series.

HELINE, CORINNE
Esoteric music: based on the musical seership of Richard Wagner.   274 p, illus.   New Age Press, Los Angeles, 1948.   3.00

HENDERSON, W. J.
Richard Wagner: his life & his dramas, a biographical study of the man & an explanation of his work. xiv, 504 p, mus ex.   Putnam (1901) 2nd rev ed 1923.   5.00
A standard American biography.

JACOBS, ROBERT L.
Wagner.   xii, 268 p, 8 pl, 11–p bibl. Dent (1935) aug repr 1947, via Pellegrini 1949.   2.50
"Master Musicians" series, with usual calendar, catalogue of works, etc, plus—in the 1947 ed—a synopsis of the "Ring".

LICHTENBERGER, HENRI.   See App Ia.

MALHERBE, HENRY.   See App Ia.

MANN, THOMAS.   See Mann (essays).

McNALLY, WILLIAM
Prelude to exile: a play in 3 acts. 183 p.   Putnam 1936.   2.00
A Theatre Guild, New York, production, based on an episode in Wagner's life (1858).

NEUMANN, ANGELO
Personal recollections of Richard Wagner.   Tr Edith Livermore.   v, 329 p, 5 pl (pors, fac).   (1908).   G. Schirmer 1915.   2.00
Memoirs of a singer & opera-manager: first published in German 1907.   The present translation is from the 4th German edition.

NEWMAN, ERNEST
(See also Wagner-3.)
The life of Richard Wagner.   4 v. Knopf 1933/46.   Complete: 25.00
V 1: 1813–1848.   xxviii, 509, xxxi p, 12 pl, 9–p bibl. 1933 (4th pr 1942).   7.50
V 2: 1848–1860.   xx 619, xxviii p, 13 pl, 6–p bibl. 1937 (2nd pr 1946).   7.50
V 3: 1859–1866.   xvi, 569, xxxvi p, 12 pl, 4–p bibl. 1941 (2nd pr 1948).   7.50
V 4: 1866–1883.   xvii, 729, lvi p, 12 pl, 3–p bibl. 1946.   7.50

The standard biography in English, immensely detailed insofar as Wagner's career is concerned, but laying little stress on purely musical analysis of his works.

Wagner. 30 p, cover por, paper. Novello n d (1940). .60
Miniature biography ("great musicians")
Wagner as man and artist. xv, 399 p, 7 pl. (1914) Knopf 1924. 5.00
Same, Tudor repr 1946. 1.98
A study of the man, the artist in theory & practice, with a "synthetic table of Wagner's life & works & synchronous events."

POURTALÈS, GUY DE. See App Ia.
Note: The English edition, 1932, of this French biography apparently is O/P.

REICH, WILLI. See App Ib.

STEIN, LEON
The racial thinking of Richard Wagner. xiv, 252 p, 2 pl, 6–p bibl. Philosophical 1950. 4.75
The sources of Wagner's "racial" ideas & their realization in Hitler's 3rd Reich.

TURNER, W. J.
Wagner. 143 p, frontis por. (1933) Wyn n d (1948). 1.00
"Great Musicians" series. A miniature biography by a non-idolator, originally published by Duckworth, London, 1933, in the "Great Lives" series.

WAGNER
(3. Works: Collective & Individual Studies, Librettos, etc)
See also: esp Opera, Program Notes.
Also: App IIa (Diller)
Note: Standard works in English apparently O/P (or not easily available) include those by Aldrich, Armour (tr), Buesst, Chamberlain, Cleather & Crump, Dickinson, Dry, Guerber, Hadden, Heintz, Hutcheson, Kilbourn, Kobbé, Krehbiel, Lavignac, Lawrence, Lewis, McSpadden, Newman, Shaw, Thompson, Winworth, Wolzogen, Young, etc.

(WAGNER, RICHARD)
The authentic librettos of the Wagner operas. vi, 470 p, music. Crown 1938 (11th pr n d). 2.50
V 1 of the "Opera Libretto Library" (see Opera–2).
Note: Individual libretto publications of Wagner's works are not listed.

BAGAR, ROBERT
Wagner and his music-dramas. 52 p,

12 illus (pors, facs, etc), bds. Grosset 1950. .50
"New York Philharmonic-Symphony Society Musical Biographies" series: mainly brief notes on the works. Originally published (1943) for the society's subscribers only.

BÉDIER, JOSEPH
The romance of Tristan and Iseult. Tr Hillaire Belloc; completed by Paul Rosenfeld. 254 p, 20–p illus (Joep Nicolas). (1913) Pantheon 1945. 2.50
Not strictly a Wagner book: a re-telling of the famous tale from its French sources.

BENOIT, CAMILLE
The typical motives of "The Mastersingers of Nuremberg" by Richard Wagner: a study for serving as a guide through the score, preceded by a review of the poetical work. Tr J. H. Cornell. 48 p, mus ex. G. Schirmer 1889. .50

GEISSMAR, BERTA
Wagner: The Rhinegold. 34 p + 4 pl, mus ex, 1–p bibl, paper. Boosey 1949. .60
Richard Wagner: The Valkyrie. 35 p + 4 pl, mus ex, paper. Boosey 1948 .60
Wagner: Siegfried. 40 p + 4 pl, mus ex, paper. Boosey 1948. .60
Wagner: The twilight of the gods. 61 p + 4 pl, mus ex, 1–p bibl. paper. Boosey 1949. .60
All four booklets above are in the "Covent Garden Operas" series.

GILMAN, LAWRENCE
Wagner's operas. xix, 268 p. Rinehart 1937. 2.75
The only book by the late N. Y. "Herald-Tribune" music critic currently available in-print and one of his most characteristic, dealing warmly not only with the music-dramas themselves, but with Flagstad & other foremost interpreters.

HALL, GERTRUDE
The Wagnerian romances. Intro Willa Cather. x, 414 p. (1907) Knopf 1925 (repr 1942). 2.50
Stories of the operas, originally published by Lane, London, 1907.

HEINTZ, ALBERT
"The Master-Singers of Nuremberg," by Richard Wagner: attempt at a musical explanation. Tr J. H. Cornell (from 2nd German ed). 128 p, 84 mus ex. G. Schirmer 1890. 1.00

NEWMAN, ERNEST
(*See also Wagner–2*)
The Wagner operas. xii, 724, v p,
frontis por, mus ex. Knopf 1949.　　　7.50

*V 1 of a projected 3–v series, completely
rewritten to replace the author's "Stories of
the famous operas" (See Opera–3). The
present volume deals exclusively with
Wagner's 10 best-known music-dramas; those
in preparation will deal with operas by other
composers.*

OVERHOFF, KURT.　See App Ib.

RAYNER, ROBERT M.
Wagner and "Die Meistersinger."
263 p, illus, mus ex, 5–p annot bibl.
Oxford 1940.　　　4.50

*A documented study of the sources and
detailed commentary on the score.*

REDLICH, HANS FERDINAND
Richard Wagner: Lohengrin.　38 p
+ 4 pl, mus ex, 1–p bibl, paper.
Boosey 1949.　　　.60
Richard Wagner: Tristan and Isolde.
34 p + 4 pl, mus ex, 1–p bibl, paper.
Boosey 1948.　　　.60

Both in the "Covent Garden Operas" series.

TERRY, EDWARD M.
A Richard Wagner dictionary.　186
p + 32–p mus ex (motives), 2 pl,
8–p bibl.　Wilson 1939.　　　2.25

*A dictionary of Wagnerian subjects, "Actors
& singers" to Zürich, plus an appendix of
the leading motives of the music-dramas.*

WELLESZ, EGON
Introduction to the music of Wagner.
Dobson 1950 in prep.　　　1.00
Richard Wagner: The Mastersingers.
31 p + 4–pl, mus ex, 1–p bibl, paper.
Boosey 1948.　　　.60

"Covent Garden Operas" series.

WINN, CYRIL
The "Master-Singers" of Wagner.
50 p, mus ex, paper. Oxford 1925.　　　1.00

"Musical Pilgrim" series of analyses.

WOLZOGEN, HANS VON
Thematic guide through the music of
"Parsifal:" with a preface concerning
the traditional material of the
Wagnerian drama. Tr J. H. Cornell.
100 p, mus ex, flex.　G. Schirmer
1891 (8th ed n d).　　　.90

Walcott, John.　Co-author (with Burch).
See App IIa (juveniles).

WALES (Music in)/WELSH MUSIC

See also:

Dances–2 (Mellor)	Folksongs–1
Facsimiles (Lewis)	History
Folklore	National Music

*Note: Pertinent works apparently O/P (or
not easily available) include those by Graham,
Griffith, Smith, etc.*

CROSSLEY-HOLLAND, PETER (*ed*)
Music in Wales.　147 p, frontis map,
mus ex, paper. Hinrichsen 1948.　　　2.00
*"Survey" series S–9, on Welsh composers and
the growth of music in Wales.*

WILLIAMS, W. S. GWYNN
Welsh national music and dance.　ix,
165 p, frontis fac, mus ex, 15–p
annot bibl (of music only).　Curwen
n d (1933?).　　　2.50

Walker, Ernest.　Author.
See England (music in).
*Note: A book of essays, "Free thought and
the musician" (1946) apparently is O/P.*

Walker, William.　Editor
See Songbooks.

Wallace, William.　Author.
*Note: Several books (on Psychology, Wagner,
etc) apparently are O/P (or not easily
available in this country).*

Waller, Judith Cary.　Author.
See Radio.

Walls, Robert B.　Co-author (with Jones &
Smith).　See Pronunciaton.

Walsh, Gertrude.　Author. See Speech.

WALTER, Bruno (B. W. Schlesinger)

See also:

Bruckner	Mahler
Conductors	Opera–1
History	Philharmonic
Interpreters	Phonograph Records
Lehmann	Vienna

*Note: Walter's own book on Mahler (1936) &
"Von den moralischen Kräften der Musik"
1935) apparently are O/P, as is a collection
of tributes to Walter (in German, ed Stefan).*

Theme and variations: an autobiography.　Tr James A. Galston.
xi, 244, xx p, 15 photos. Knopf 1946
(3rd pr 1947).　　　5.00
*Memoirs of the long career & many musical
associates of the noted conductor.*

Walters, Edward.　Co-author (with Haddon).　See Theory–3.

Walton, Thomas.　Author.
See Mozart–3 (ed Crozier).

WALTON, William

See also:

Appreciation	Contemporary Music
Chamber Music	English Music
Choir/Choral–3	Modern Music
(esp Manners)	Phonograph Records
Composers–2 & 3c	Program Notes
Concerto	Symphony

HOWES, FRANK
The music of William Walton. 2 v:
76, 75 p, mus ex, paper. Oxford 1942
(repr 1944) & 1943. 2,00
*"Musical Pilgrim" series of analyses. V 1:
Piano Quartet, Façade, Viola Concerto, In
Honor of the City of London, Violin Concerto.
V 2: Belshazzar's Feast, Symphony, Sinfonia
Concertante, Portsmouth Point Overture,
Siesta, Scapino, Crown Imperial March.*

WALTZ

See also:

Appreciation	Phonograph Records
Ballet	Program Notes
(The) Dance	Strauss Family
Dances–1. 2. 3	J. Strauss
History	Vienna

CARNER, MOSCO
The waltz. 72 p, 4 col pl. 31 b&ws,
mus ex. Chanticleer 1948. 2.50
*"World of Music" series No 5: historical
survey with emphasis on the 19th century.*

NETTL, PAUL
Birth of the waltz. ? p, illus, paper.
Auvergne in prep. .75
*Development of the waltz from court to the
ballroom.*

REESER, EDUARD
The history of the waltz. Tr W. A. G.
Doyle-Davidson. 60 p, 23 illus, mus
ex, 2–p bibl, bds. Continental n d
(1947?). 2.50
*"Symphonia" series of illustrated mono-
graphs.*

WAR (and Music)

See:

America (music in)	History
Community Music	Military Music
Contemporary Music	Psychology
English Music (esp	Queen's Hall
Meyers)	Songbooks (esp
Health	Adler, Palmer)

Warburton, Annie Osborne. Author.
See Harmony–2.
Ward, Arthur Edward. Author.
See School Music–1.
Ward, Sylvan Donald. Author.
See School Music–3.

WARFIELD, Frances

Cotton in my ears. 152 p, illus
(Eileen Evans), bds. Viking 1948. 2.75
*An autobiography illuminating the problems
and compensations of the hard-of-hearing.*

Waring, Fred. Author. See Diction.

WARLOCK, Peter

(Pseudonym of Philip Heseltine)
See:

Composers–2 & 3c	History
English Music	Phonograph Records

*Note: "Warlock's" "The English ayre" and
Heseltine's book on Delius both are O/P, as is
Cecil Gray's memoir of this extraordinary
dual personality.*

Warrack, Guy. Author.
See Holmes (Sherlock).
Warrington, Johnny. Author.
See Arranging–2.
Wasner, Franz. Editor. See Carols.
Waterman, Elizabeth. Author
See Organ Music.
Waterman, Richard A.
Compiler (with Lichtenwanger & others).
See Asiatic Musics (note).
Waters, Charles F. Author.
See Organ Music
Waters, Crystal. Author.
See Singing–1.

WATERS, Ethel

See also:

Jazz	Phonograph Records
Negro Music &	Popular Music
Musicians	

His eye is on the sparrow. Ed Charles
Samuels. 278 p. Doubleday 1951. 3.00
The great blues singer's autobiography.

Waters, Fred Elbert. Author.
See Baton–1.
Watkins, John Goodrich. Author.
See Interpretation.
Watson, Jack McLaurin. Author.
See Education.

WATTS, Isaac

See also:

Church Music	History
England (music in)	Hymns/Hymnody

DAVIS, ARTHUR PAUL
Isaac Watts: his life & works. xiii,
306 p, 25–p bibls. (1943) Independ- △
dent Press, London, 1948. (2.50)
*A standard study, originally published by
The Dryden Press, New York. There is an*

11-p bibliography of Watts's own works, plus a 14-p general bibliography.

WEBER, Carl Maria, Freiherr von

See also:

Appreciation	Phonograph Records
Ballet (ed Haskell)	Program Notes
Berlioz	Romantic Era
Composers-1	Themes
History	Timing
Opera	Vocal Music

Note: Standard works apparently O/P (or not easily available) include Weber's correspondence (in German), and books by Benedict, Moser (in German), Simpson, etc.

Also O/P, but probably only temporarily, is William Saunders's biography (1940) in the "Master Musicians" series.

COEUROY, ANDRÉ. See App Ia.

DENT, EDWARD J. (*tr*)
Der Freischütz (The Devil's Bullet): a romantic opera in 3 acts. Words by Friedrich Kind; music by Carl Maria von Weber. English version. 68 p, paper. Oxford 1948.   .80

GODDARD, SCOTT
Weber. 16 p, cover por, paper. Novello n d (1941/2).   .40
Miniature biography ("great musicians").

STEBBINS, LUCY POATE & RICHARD POATE
Enchanted wanderer: the life of Carl Maria von Weber. xi, 345 p, 15 pl, 17-p bibl. Putnam 1940.   3.50
A romanticized life-story.

WEBERN, Anton von

See: esp App Ia (Leibowitz)

Also:

Composers-2	Schoenberg
Contemporary Music	Twelve-Tone
History	Technique
Modern Music	

WECHSBERG, Joseph

The continental touch. 323 p. Houghton 1948.   3.00

Looking for a bluebird. 210 p, illus (F. Strobel). Houghton 1945.   2.50

Sweet and sour. viii, 268 p. Houghton 1948.   3.00

Three collections of humorous sketches & reminiscences (many of which first appeared in the "New Yorker"), by an ex-salon-fiddler.

Wedge, George Anson. Author. See:
Ear-training. Ear-training & sight-singing (1921).   3.00

—. Advanced ear-training & sight-singing (1922).   4.00
Harmony-2. Applied (1930). 2v.   5.00
Keyboard Harmony. (1924).   3.00
Rhythm. Rhythm in music (1927).   2.00
Theory-2. Gist of music (1936).   3.00

Weer, Robert Lawrence. Author.
See Voice.

Weigl, Bruno. Editor. See App Ib.

WEINGARTNER, Felix

See:

Conductors	Phonograph Records
History	Vienna
Interpreters	

Author. See Conducting, Symphony, App Ib (autobiography in German, & a Schubert biography in German by Weingartner & Studer).

Note: The English edition of Weingartner's autobiography apparently is O/P (or not easily available), as are a satirical comedy & a collection of essays in German.

Weinmann, Karl. Author.
See Church Music.

Weinstock, Herbert. Author.
Chopin-1. Biography (1949).   5.00
Handel-1. Biography (1946).   5.00
Tchaikovsky-1. Biography (1943).   5.00
Co-author with Brockway. See:
Composers-1. Men of music (1939).   5.00
Opera-1. The opera (1941).   3.75

Weirick, Paul. Author.
See Arranging-2.

Weitzmann, Karl Friedrich. Author.
See Theory-2.

Welch, Lucy M. Author.
See School Music-4.

Welch, Roy Dickinson. Author.
See Appreciation.

Wellesz, Egon. Author. See:
Beethoven-3. Introduction to the music of (1950) in prep.   1.00
Byzantine Music. Eastern elements in western chant (1947).   7.50
——. History of Byzantine music & hymnography (1949).   8.50
Opera-1. Essays (1949/50).   3.75
Wagner-3. Introduction to the music of (1950) in prep.   1.00
——. The Mastersingers (1948).   .60

Note: Other books by Wellesz, including a biography of Schoenberg (1925), apparently are O/P (or not easily available).

Wells, Amos Russel. Author.
See Hymns & Hymnody–2.
Wells, Evelyn Kendrick. Author.
See Ballad.
Wells, Howard. Author.
See Piano Playing–2.

WELSH MUSIC
See: Wales (Music in)/Welsh Music.

Werfel, Franz. Author. See Verdi–1.
Werner, Heinz. Co-editor (with Fabricant).
See Anthologies.
Werner, Jack. Author.
See Mendelssohn–2 & 3.
Werner, Wilt. Author. See Tempo.
Werth, Alexander. Author.
See Russia (music in).

WESLEY FAMILY
See:
Church Music   History
England (music in)   Hymns/Hymnody
*Note: Lightwood's biography of Samuel
Wesley (1937) and Rattenbury's study of
Charles Wesley's hymns (1941) both ap-
parently are O/P (or not easily available in
this country).*

West, John Ebenezer. Author.
See Organists.
Westbrook, Francis B. Author.
See Elgar.
Westerby, Herbert. Author. See:
Beethoven–3. Piano works (n d).   2.25
Liszt. Miniature biog (1939).   .40
——. Piano works (1936).   3.75
Organ Music. The complete organ
recitalist (n d).   5.00
Piano Music. How to study piano
works of great composers (n d).   3.00

Westerman, Kenneth Neville. Author.
See Singing–2, Voice.

WESTMINSTER ABBEY
See:
England music in)   Organ (esp Perkins)
History   Organists

WESTMINSTER CATHEDRAL
See: esp Terry.
Church Music   History
England (music in)   Organists

WESTRUP, Jack Allan
Sharps and flats. viii, 238 p.
Oxford 1940.   3.00

*Varied essays by the British historian,
musicologist, & critic.*
Author, editor. See also:
English Music. British music
(1943/9).   .50
Handel–1. Miniature biog (1938).   .40
History–1. Oxford (new series).   △
——. Introduction to (1950).   △
——. Meaning of (1946).   .50
Liszt. Miniature biog (1939).   .40
Purcell. Biography (1937).   2.50
Schubert–2. Introduction to the
music of (1950) in prep.   1.00

Wever, Ernest Glen. Author.
See Hearing.
Wheeler, Benson. Author (with Purdy).
See App IIa (Mozart juvenile).
Wheeler, Mary. Author. See Folksongs–2.
Wheeler, Opal. Author.
See App IIa (juvenile biographies):
Bach   Haydn
Beethoven   MacDowell
Chopin   Mozart
Foster   Paganini
Gilbert & Sullivan   Schubert
Handel   Schumann

Wheelwright, Mary C. Author.
See Indians (American).

WHISTLING
Woodward, Agnes
Whistling as an art: a method for
the development of tone, technique,
& style, with many musical selections
prepared for solo use. xvii, 142 p,
mus ex. C. Fischer (1923/5) rev aug
ed 1938.   2.50

Whitaker-Wilson, Cecil. Author.
See Schubert–1.
White, A. W. Author. See Violin.
White, Bernice. Author. See Dictation.
White, Donald F. Co-author (with
McHose). See Keyboard Harmony.
White, Ernest G. Author.
See Singing–1.
White, Eric Walter. Author.
See Britten (also App Ib), Stravinsky–2.
White, Herbert D. Author.
See Vocal Music.
White, Llewellyn. Author. See Radio.
White, Newman Ivey. Author.
See Negro Spirituals.
White, S. Young. Author
See Ultrasonics.
White, William Braid. Author.
See Piano.
White, William Carter. Author.
See Arranging–1, Military Music.

WHITEMAN, Paul
See:

America (music in)   Phonograph Records
Jazz   Popular Music

Author.   See Dance Band, Phonograph Records.

Note: Whiteman's "Jazz" (1926) is O/P.

Whiteside, Abby. Author.
See Piano Playing–2.
Whitfield, Irène Thérèse. Author.
See Folksongs–2.

WHITHORNE, Emerson
See also: American Music, Composers–3a.
HOWARD, JOHN TASKER
Emerson Whithorne. 42 p, frontis por, fac, mus ex, paper. C. Fischer 1929.   .25
"Studies of Contemporary American Composers" series; catalogue of works & brief analyses.

Whitlock, Ernest Clyde. Editor (with Saunders). See America (music in).
Whitlock, Virginia Bennett. Author.
See Dances–2.
Whitmer, Thomas Carl. Author.
See Improvisation.
Whittaker, Ruth W. Co-author (with Freeman). See App IIa (juvenile biographies).

WHITTAKER, William Gillies
Collected essays.   235 p, 3 pl + fold-out chart, mus ex.   Oxford 1939.   5.00
Scholarly studies of Bach cantatas, English folk music, Purcell's harmony, editing, etc.

Note: Several other books by Whittaker apparently are O/P (or not easily available).

Whittlesey, Walter R. Compiler (with Sonneck). See Foster.
Whitworth, Reginald. Author. See Organ.

WHO'S WHO (Musical)
See also:

Composers   History
Dictionaries of Music   Interpreters
Encyclopedias of   Yearbooks
  Music

Note: Pertinent works apparently O/P (or not easily available) include those by Key, Ronald, Saerchinger, Spaeth, etc.

MIZE, J. T. H. (ed)
Who is who in music: 5th ed, 1950.
Who is Who in Music, Chicago, in   △
prep.   10.00
Now announced for 1951 publication. The

previous edition (now apparently O/P) was that for 1941.

PINE, LESLIE G. (ed)
The musicians' international directory & biographical record 1950.
lxxxviii, 420 p.   Shaw Pub. Co.,   △
London, 1950.   (10.00)
The present title apparently is for exported copies only; in England the same book is titled "Who's who in music." It includes some 10,000 brief biographical entries, plus a section on "Legal information" by F. H. Cowper, & a list of music publishers, etc.

Widor, Charles-Marie. Author.
See Instrumentation.
Wier, Albert Ernest. Editor.
See Aesthetics–1.
Wierzynski, Casimir. Author.
See Chopin–1.
Wiese, Lucie. Co-editor (with Mellquist).
See Rosenfeld.
Wilcke, Eva. Author.
See German Language.
Wilcox, Ernest Harold. Co-author (with Smallman). See Choir/Choral–1.
Wilcox, John C. Author. See Voice.
Wiley, Lulu Rumsey. Author.
See Jewish Music.
Wilkins, Joseph Fellows. Compiler.
See Children–7.
Wilkinson, Charles W. Author.
See Bach–2, Piano Music.
Willaman, Robert. Author.
See Clarinet.
Williams, Albert Nathaniel. Author.
See Radio.
Williams, Charles Francis Abdy. Author.
See Song(s).

Note: Other books by Williams (including several in the "Music Story" series) apparently are O/P (or not easily available).

WILLIAMS, Ralph Vaughan. Catalogued under Vaughan Williams, Ralph.

Williams, Stephen. Author.
See Opera–3, Verdi–2.
Williams, William Sydney Gwynn.
Author. See Wales (music in).
Williams, Wyndham G. Author.
See Children–2.
Williamson, Audrey. Author.
See Ballet.

WILLSON, Meredith
And there I stood with my piccolo.
255 p. Doubleday 1948.   2.75
Humorous, anecdotal memoirs of a radio musician and composer.

Wilson, Don. Co-author (with Jones). See Operetta.

Wilson, Harry Robert. Author. See:
Arranging–1. Choral arr (1949). 3.50
Community Music. Lead a song! (1942). 1.50
School Music–1. Music in the high schools (1941). 3.50
Co-author (with Van Bodegraven). See: School Music–3. School music conductor (942). 2.00

Wilson, M. Emmett. Author. See History–3.

Wilson, Mortimer. Author. See Theory–4.

Wilson, Robert Barclay. Author. See Conducting.

Wilson, Steuart. Author. See Bach–2.

WIND INSTRUMENTS

See also:

Arranging	Instruments
Band	Military Music
Bassoon	Orchestra
Children–4	Recorder
Clarinet	Sax/Saxophone
Flute	School Music–3
French Horn	Trombone
History	Trumpet
Instrumentation	

Note: Not included in the works listed below are numerous privately printed booklets and the many "methods" or instruction books that consist mainly of musical exercises with little or no accompanying text.

CARSE, ADAM
Musical wind instruments: a history of the wind instruments used in European orchestras & wind-bands from the later middle ages to the present time. xv, 381 p, 30 photo pl, 41 b&ws, 11 fingering diagrs, 8–p △ bibl. Macmillan 1939. (7.50)
A standard scholarly work, companion to the author's various books on the orchestra & its instruments (see Orchestra).

DAUBENEY, ULRIC
Orchestral wind instruments, ancient and modern: being an account of the origin & evolution of wind instruments from the earliest to the most recent times. vi, 147 p, 61 illus, 1–p △ bibl. Reeves n d (1920?) (5.75)

DELAMATER, ERIC
Lip science for brass players. 20 p, illus, mus ex, paper. Rubank (1923) 1943. .75

GRUPP, M.
In the name of wind-instrument play-

ing: the first guide to natural & correct wind-instrument playing. 100 p, 1 por, bds, spir. Author, N. Y., 1939. 3.75
Inspirational notes & advice.

KOECHLIN, CHARLES. See App Ia.

LARSON, GLEN & BAXTER, HARRY
Oboe reed technique. ump (15 p), 8 illus, paper. Baxter-Northrup Co., Los Angeles, Calif., 1933 1.50
A practical treatise on making reeds & retouching finished reeds.

Wing, Herbert Daniel. Author. See Tests.

Winn, Cyril. Author. See:
Accompaniment. Do you accompany? (1939). 1.00
Mendelssohn–3. Analyses of music works (1927). 1.00
Wagner–3. Mastersingers (1925). 1.00

WINN, Edith Lynwood
The etudes of life. 105 p, frontis por (MacDowell). C. Fischer 1908. .75
Inspirational essays: "The Idealist," "Song Cycle," "Soul Technic," etc.
Author. See also:
Children–4. First steps in violin playing (1908/24). 2.50
Fiorillo. How to study (1910). 1.00
Gaviniés. How to study (1913). 1.00
Kreutzer. How to prepare (1910). 1.50
——. How to study (1910/26). 1.00
Violin Playing. Representative violin solos (1911). 1.00

Winter, Marion H. Author. See Minstrels/Minstrelsy.

Winternitz, Emanuel. Author. See Autographs.

Winwar, Frances. Author. See Sand.

Witherspoon, Herbert. Author. See Singing–1 & 2.

Withrow, Marie. Author. See Singing–2.

WITMARK, Isidore
Note: Witmark & Goldberg's "From ragtime to swingtime: the story of the house of Witmark" (1939) apparently is O/P.

Witzig, Louise. Author. See Dances–2 (ed Alford).

Wodell, Frederick William. Author. See Choir/Choral–2.

Wohlfahrt, Heinrich. Author.
See Melody-Writing.

WOLF, Hugo
See esp App Ib (Reich: "Hugo-Wolf-Rhapsodie"; Refardt: "Brahms, Bruckner, Wolf").
Also:

Appreciation	Program Notes
Composers–1	Song(s)
History	Song Translations
Phonograph Records	Vocal Music

Note: Standard works apparently O/P (or not easily available) include those by Decsey (in German), Newman (in English), & various writers in German.

For information on the Henry S. Drinker song-text translations (not generally available), see the note under the Drinker author entry.

Wolf, Johannes. Author.
See Medieval/Renaissance.
Wolfe, Bernard. Co-author (with Mezzrow). See Mezzrow.
Wolfe, Halley. Co-author (with Frayne).
See Sound Recording & Reproduction.
Wolfe, (Rev) Paul Austin. Author (with Dickinsons). See Church Music.
Wolff, Werner. Author.
See Bruckner, also App Ib.
Wolffheim, Werner. Co-editor (with (Springer). See App Ib.
Wolzogen (und Neuhaus), Hans von.
Author. See Wagner–3.

WOMEN (and Music)
See also:

Anderson	Joyce
Appreciation	Lawrence
Carreño	Lehmann
Chanler	Letters
Foldes	Sand
Galli-Curci	Smyth
Harding	Stein
Heiner	Swarthout
History	Thursby
Hughes	F. Wagner

Also: Composers, and under the names of individuals (for references to the women in their lives).

Note: Pertinent works apparently O/P (or not easily available) include those by Barnes, Elson, Upton, etc, as well as various books on Clara Schumann, Cosima Wagner, and others.

DRINKER, SOPHIE
Music and women: the story of women in their relation to music.
xv, 323 p, 67 pl, 14–p bibl refs.
Coward 1948. 5.00
A singular book, blending extensive historical

research with a spirited plea for women's musical rights.

RITTER, FANNY
Woman as a musician: an art-historical study. 18 p, paper. △
(Schuberth 1876) via Reeves. (.75)
An address before the U. S. Congress.

Wood, Alice L. Author.
See Children–7.
Wood, Benjamin. Author. See App Ia.
Wood, Carl Paige. Author.
See Harmony–2.
Wood, Clement (also Dubois, Alan, pseud).
Editor. See Songwriting.

WOOD (Sir) Henry Joseph
See also:

Conductors	Queen's Hall
England (music in)	Phonograph Records
(esp Russell)	

Author. See also Conducting.
Note: Wood's "Gentle art of singing" (1927/8) apparently is O/P (or not easily available in this country), as are books about him by Hill & Rees and Newmarch.

My life of music. Intro Sir Hugh
Allen. 384 p. Gollancz (1938) 1st △
cheap ed n d (1947). (2.00)
The autobiography of the famous conductor of the British "Proms."

Wood, James. Co-author (with Richards & Ogden). See Aesthetics–1.
Woodgate, Leslie. Author.
See Choir/Choral–2.
Woodhouse, George. Author.
See Interpretation.
Woods, Glen Howard. Author.
See School Music–3.
Woodside, James. Author.
See Singing–2.
Woodward, Agnes. Author.
See Whistling.

WOOD-WIND INSTRUMENTS
See:

Bassoon	Instruments
Clarinet	Orchestra
Flute	Wind Instruments
Instrumentation	

Wooldridge, H. Ellis. Author.
See History–1 (Oxford old series v 1 & 2, note only).

WORCESTER MUSIC FESTIVAL
See also: America (music in)

MORIN, RAYMOND
The Worcester music festival: its

background & history, 1858–1946.
xv, 189 p, illus (pors, facs, etc).
Worcester County Musical Assn,
Mass, 1946.   3.00

*A documented historical account of one of
the notable American musical festivals.*

Work, John Wesley. Compiler & arranger.
See Negro Spirituals.

Works Progress Administration (WPA).
See Children–7, Songbooks (ed Walker).

"(THE) WORLD OF MUSIC" Series

*Note: This is a novel series of music books
in uniform format, under the general editorship of Sir George Franckenstein & Otto
Erich Deutsch, published by Parrish, London, and (with the exception of Russell's
"The Proms") by Chanticleer, New York.
The books themselves are printed in Holland
by a rotographic process and include several
plates in color as well as numerous black-&-
white illustrations. For works already published or announced, see:*

Chamber Music	Military Music
(King)	(Farmer)
Church Music	Opera–1 (Cooper)
(Robertson)	Operetta/Opéra-
Concerto (Culshaw)	Comique (Cooper)
Covent Garden	Orchestra (Carse)
(Shawe-Taylor)	Program Music (Hill)
England (music in)	Song(s)
(Russell)	(E. Schumann)
Handel–2 (Herbage)	Vienna (Gál)
	Waltz (Carner)

Wörner, Karl H. Author. See App Ib.

Worthington, Robert Alfred. Co-author
(with Evetts). See Singing–1.

Wotton, Tom. Author. See Berlioz–2.

Wright, Anita Peters & Dexter. Authors.
See Dances–3.

Wright, Denis. Author.
See Conducting.

Wright, Frances. Author.
See School Music–1. Compiler (with
Lossing). See School Music–4.

Wright, Frank. Author.
See Counterpoint–2, Ear-Training.

Wrightson, Herbert James. Author.
See Theory–3.

Wyzewa, Théodore de. Co-author (with
Saint-Foix). See App Ia.

—X Y Z—

XYLOPHONE

See:

Africa (music in)	Instruments
(esp Tracey)	Java (music in)
Bali (music in)	Latin America
Children–4	Mexico (music in)
Instrumentation	Orchestra

Yasser, Joseph. Author.
See Jewish Music, Tonality/Atonality.

YEARBOOKS

*General Note: Only the few more important
recent books dealing with serious music are
listed below. Not included are most of those
in foreign languages (but for an exception
see App Ib, ed Barth), those dealing primarily with popular music (such as the "Bill-
board Encyclopedia"), special issues of
musical periodicals, and yearbooks of general
coverage (such as the "Writers' & Artists'
Yearbook"), as well as older publications
now O/P (or not easily available).*

See also:

America (music in)	Popular Music
(Whitlock)	(Burton)
Ballet (Haskell)	Song(s) (Mattfeld &
California (music in)	Davis)
(Saunders)	Who's Who

BARTH, HERBERT (*ed*). See App Ib.

EWEN, DAVID (*ed*)
The year in American music, 1948
edition. 551 p, 12–p bibl. Allen
Towne 1948, via Crown.   6.00

*Covering the period June 1947 through May
1948 in a day-by-day chronicle, plus extensive
lists of composers in America, orchestras &
companies, phonograph-record releases, world
& American first performances, awards,
obituaries, etc.*

*Note: The 1946–1947 edition, ed Julius
Bloom, apparently is O/P.*

HILL, RALPH (*ed*)
Music 1950. 253 p, paper. Penguin
1950.   .35

*Pelican Book A-225: first of a series of annual
surveys, succeeding the "Penguin Music
Magazine." There are brief articles by some
26 authors, including the editor's own "New
books about music" (p 147/65).*

HILL, RALPH & HINRICHSEN, MAX (*eds*)
Hinrichsen's musical year book, v
II/III, 1945–46. 404 p, photo, fac,
40–p bibl. Hinrichsen 1946.   5.00

HINRICHSEN, MAX (ed)
Hinrichsen's musical year book, v
IV/V, 1947–1948. xiv, 545 p, illus,
mus ex, 39–bibl. Hinrichsen 1948.   5.00
Hinrichsen's musical year book, v VI,
1949–1950. xiii, 416 p, illus, mus ex,
44–p bibl. Hinrichsen 1949.   4.50
*This unusual series (of which v 1, 1944, is
O/P), includes more than the usual chronicle.
Indeed each volume is more nearly a compact
encyclopedia, stressing but not exclusively
confined to British activities. The current
volume VI, for example, includes the Nelson-
Rubsamen film & radio bibliography, Lowen-
stein's article on Bernard Shaw as music
critic, Seeger's "Music & Musicology in the
New World", etc, as well as Jack Werner's
bibliographies of books & articles and published music.   It is announced that future
issues will drop the name of "year book" in
favor of the more appropriate "survey."*

HONEGGER, ARTHUR (& others). See App Ia.

MYERS, ROLLO H. (ed)
Music today: 1st annual issue,
Journal of the International Society
for Contemporary Music.   162 p,
2 photos, mus ex, paper.   Dobson
1949.   2.50
*Texts in English & French; includes an index
of ISCM Festivals composers, 1923/48, an
open forum on "Tonal or atonal," and
articles by Cooper, Dent, Goldbeck, Koechlin,
K. Mengelberg, de Paoli, Searle, Carleton
Sprague Smith, Stuckenschmidt, & J. Weissmann.*

Yocom, Rachel Dunhaven.   Co-author
(with Shurr).   See Dances–1.
Yoder, Paul.   Author.   See Arranging–1.
York, Francis Lodowick.   Author.
See Counterpoint–2, Harmony–2.
Yost, Gaylord.   Author.
See Violin Playing.
Young, Percy Marshall.   Author.
See   Handel–1 & 2,   Mendelssohn–3,
Vaughan Williams.
Young, Thomas Campbell.   Author.
See Instruments.   Co-author (with
Newton).   See School Music–3.

YOUTH (and Music)
See:

Amateur Music	Education
Children	School Music
Community Music	App II (juveniles)

YRIARTE (Iriarte), Tomas de
See: esp App Id (Subirá biog).
Also: History, Spain (music in).

YSAŸE, Eugène
See also:

Belgium (music in)	Violin Playing
History	Violinists

CHRISTEN, ERNEST.   See App Ia.

YSAŸE, ANTOINE & RATCLIFFE, BERTRAM
Ysaÿe: his life, work, & influence.
Pref Yehudi Menuhin.   xi, 250 p, 28 △
pl (pors etc).   Heinemann 1947.   (4.00)

YUGOSLAVIA (Music in)/YUGOSLAV-
IAN MUSIC
See:

Dances–2	Folklore (esp Bartók)
History	Folksongs–1

Zagiba, Franz.   Author.   See App Ib.
Zahn, Johannes.   Author.   See App Ib.
Zanzig, Augustus Delafield.   Author,
editor.   See:
Appreciation.   Roads to (1939).   .35
Children–4.   How to make & play
a shepherd's pipe (1939/42).   .35
Children–6.   Starting & developing
a rhythm band (1937).   .35
Community Music.   Community &
assembly singing (1933).   .75
——.   Music & men (1941).   .15
——.   Starting a community orches-
tra (1940).   .35
Songbooks.   Singing America (1946).   2.00
Teaching–2.   Concord teachers' guide
(1929).   .50
*Note: Zanzig's "Music in American life"
(1932) apparently is O/P.*

Zavadini, Guido.   Author.   See App Ic.
Zay, William Henri.   Author.
See Voice.
Zerkaulen, Heinrich.   Author.   See App Ib.
Zimmermann, Curt.   Author.   See App Ib.
Zoeller, Carli.   Editor.
See Modulation.
Zucker, Paul.   Co-editor (with Henderson).
See Almanacs.

ZWEIG, Stefan
See also: R. Strauss.
*Note: Zweig's book on Romain Rolland
(1921) & a biography by Friderike Maria
Zweig (1946) both apparently are O/P.*

The world of yesterday: an autobiography.   xiv, 455 p, illus.   Viking
1943.   4.00
*The novelist's memoirs, including consider-
able material on Richard Strauss, for whom
he wrote the libretto of the opera, "Die
schweigsame Frau."*

APPENDIX I

Warning: While all book-prices quoted in the GUIDE *are of course subject to change without notice, those for the following foreign publications are particularly likely to fluctuate, as affected by the international exchange, number of copies imported, etc. So while the prices given here are based on the best information available to us, they should be read as approximations only.*

Furthermore, it should be stressed that even the larger American dealers in imported books do not always stock all of those listed here or stock many of them in large quantities. Special ordering often is required and delays in shipment often may be expected. Indeed, it is only to avoid excessive repetition that we do not place our usual warning sign (△) beside every entry in Appendix I; however it is actually used here only for limited editions or publications available only on subscription, or where a definite U. S. A. price has not been set.

APPENDIX Ia: Books in French

(A selected list only—arranged in alphabetical order by authors' names)

A—

ARMA, PAUL & TIÉNOT, YVONNE
Nouveau dictionnaire de musique.
285 p, 365 illus & mus ex, bds.
Ouvrières, Paris, 1947.   3.50
Biographical notes & musical terms.

AUDA, ANTOINE
Les gammes musicales: essai historique sur les modes et sur les tons de la musique, depuis l'antiquité jusqu'à l'époque moderne.   xxxii, 393 p, 10 pl, charts, mus ex, 8-p bibl & bibl refs, paper.   Author, Woluwe-Saint-Pierre, Belgique (1939) rev ed 1947. △ 20.00
Limited edition of a scholarly study.

B—

BARTÓK, BÉLA
Pourquoi et comment recueille-t-on la musique populaire? (Législation du folklore musical).   Tr E. Latji. 21 p, paper.   Albert Kundig, Genève, 1948.   1.00

BEAUFILS, MARCEL
Wagner et le Wagnerisme.   381 p, mus ex, paper.   Aubier, Paris, 1946.   2.40

BECK, GEORGES
Darius Milhaud: étude suivie du catalogue chronologique complet de son oeuvre.   140 p, 4 photos (pors), paper.   Heugel, Paris, 1949, via Mercury.   2.00
A brief biographical sketch & general note on the works, followed by an analytical catalogue of the works published by Heugel (p 17/51), a tabular catalogue of all works to 1 November 1949 (p 52/129), a discography (p 130/5), and alphabetical list.

BECK, JEAN & LOUISE
Le manuscrit du roi. (Fonds français de la Bibliothèque Nationale.) 2 v. △
Pennsylvania 1938.   25.00
V 1:   Reproduction phototypique. xxxiv p + 468 pl.
V 2:   Analyse et description raisonnées du manuscrit restauré. 208 p.
Limited edition of a standard facsimile reproduction & scholarly study. This is the 2nd in a sereies, "Les chansonniers des troubadours et des trouvères,"—the 1st of which ("Le chansonnier Cangé," 1927) is O/P.

BEETHOVEN, LUDWIG VAN
See Prod'homme, ed: "Cahiers," below.

BELGODÈRE-JOHANNÈS, V.
Histoire de la musique de l'antiquité
à nos jours.   Pref Georges Migot.
375 p, mus ex, paper.   Renouard,
Paris, 1947.   2.00

BERBEROVA, NINA
Tchaikovsky: histoire d'une vie soli-
taire. Tr Berberova & Journot. 253
p + 6 photos (pors), paper. Egloff,
Paris, 1948.   2.00

BERNARD, ROBERT
Albert Roussel: sa vie—son oeuvre.
128 p, frontis fac, 3-p bibl, paper.
La Colombe, Paris, 1948.   1.50

BERTRAND, PAUL
Le monde de la musique: souvenirs
d'un éditeur. Pref Adolphe Boschot.
251 p, 8 photos (pors), paper. La
Palatine, Genève, 1947.   3.60

BOLL, ANDRÉ & DAMAIS, ÉMILE
Répertoire analytique de la musique
française des origines à nos jours.
299 p, paper.   Horizons de France,
Paris, 1948.   5.00
*Classified lists (by composers & categories)
of French works, plus lists of recordings &
film music.*

BORY, ROBERT (*ed*)
La vie et l'oeuvre de Wolfgang-
Amadeus Mozart par l'image.   225
p, illus, bds.   Editions Contemp-   Δ
oraines, Genève, 1948.   20.00
*Limited edition of a lavishly illustrated work,
the bulk of which consists (after a brief introduction, p 11/32) of plates (portraits,
facsimiles, etc).*

BOSCHOT, ADOLPHE
Hector Berlioz: une vie romantique.
3 v, paper.   Plon, Paris, (1906/13)
rev eds 1946/50).
V 1: La jeunesse d'un romantique
(1803–1831). 317 p. Rev ed 1946.   2.00
V 2: Un romantique sous Louis-
Philippe (1831–1842). 383 p. Rev
ed 1948.   3.00
V 3: Le crépuscule d'un romantique
(1842–1869). 451 p. Rev ed 1950.   3.50
*A standard work in revised & corrected edi-
tions embodying the latest documentation.*

Le Faust de Berlioz: étude sur la
"Damnation de Faust" et sur l'âme
romantique. 181 p, 4 illus, 3-p bibli,
paper.   Plon, Paris, (1910) 3rd ed
1945.   2.00

Mozart. 225 p, 10 illus, paper. Plon,
Paris, 1935 (1947).   3.60
Musiciens-poètes: Bach, Beethoven,
Schubert, Liszt, Chopin.   203 p, 11
pl (pors, etc), paper.   Plon, Paris,
1937.   2.75
La musique et la vie. xi, 244 p, paper.
Plon, Paris, 1931.   1.20
Portraits de musiciens.   2 v: viii,
229 p; vii, 224 p, 20 pl, paper.   Plon,
Paris, 1946/7.   6.00
Souvenirs d'un autre siècle.   178 p,
paper. Plon, Paris, 1946.   1.20
Memoirs of the period 1870 to 1900.

BOUCHER, JEAN
L'amateur d'art lyrique: un siècle
de Théâtre Lyrique Français—le 19e
siècle. 81 p, paper. Heugel, Paris,
1946.   1.50

BOUVET, CHARLES
Spontini.   99 p + 60 pl, 1-p bibl,
paper. Rieder, Paris, 1930.   1.20

BOZZA, E.
Tableau instrumental: indiquant
l'étendue, la notation écrite, et les
sons réels de tous les instruments
principaux des orchestres symphoniques et militaires, complétés par un
tableau annexe concernant les instruments divers ainsi que les claviers
et les instruments à percussion. 2
large charts, mus ex, paper. Leduc,
Paris, 1947.   2.70

BRAGARD, ROGER
Histoire de la musique belge.   2 v:
88 p; 91 p, 4 facs, paper.   Collection
Nationale, Office de Publicité, Brux-
elles, 1946/9.   2.50
V 1: Des origines au XVIe siècle.
V 2: De 1600 à 1750.
Further volumes are in preparation.

BRELET, GISÈLE
Esthétique et création musicale. 167
p, paper.   Presses Universitaires de
France, Paris, 1947.   1.50
Essai d'une esthétique nouvelle de
la musique. 2 v: 842 p. 1949.   Δ
*Later information gives the main title as
"Le temps musical: essai . . .", etc.*

BRINDEJONT-OFFENBACH, JACQUES
Offenbach, mon grand-père. viii, 311
p, 26 pl (pors, facs, etc), paper. Plon,
Paris, 1940 (1945).   2.20
*Biography (& catalogue of works) by the com-
poser's grandson.*

BRONARSKI, LUDWIK
Chopin et l'Italie.   Pref D. E.
Inghelbrecht. 149 p, paper. La Con-
corde, Lausanne, 1946.   2.50
Études sur Chopin.   Pref. Franck-
Louis Schoell. 2 v: 181, 174 p, paper.
La Concorde, Lausanne, 1944/6.   4.00

BRUYR, JOSÉ
La belle histoire de la musique.   455
p, mus ex, paper.   Corrêa, Paris,
1946.   2.50
Honegger et son oeuvre.   259 p,
illus, mus ex, 1–p bibl, paper. Corrêa, Paris, 1947.   3.00
Maurice Ravel: ou le lyrisme et les
sortilèges. xviii, 239 p, mus ex. Plon,
Paris, 1950.   2.00

BUENZOD, EMMANUEL
Musiciens. 223 p, paper.   Rouge,
Lausanne, 1945.   2.40
*Bach, Beethoven, Haydn, Mendelssohn,
Schumann, Berlioz, Brahms, Franck, Mus-
sorgsky, & Debussy.*
Musiciens: 2me série.   236 p, paper.
Rouge, Lausanne, 1949.   2.50
*Handel, Mozart, Schubert, Weber, Rossini,
Liszt, Wagner, Bizet, Ravel, Stravinsky.*
Pouvoirs de Beethoven.   222 p, 6 pl
(pors, facs, etc), paper.   (1936)
Rouge, Lausanne, rev ed 1947.   3.00
Franz Schubert.   181 p, paper.   Cor-
rêa, Paris, (1937), rev ed 1946.   1.25

C—

CABOS, FRANCINE
Le violon et la lutherie.   Pref. Émile
Français.   xi, 111 p, illus, 3–p bibl,
paper. Grund, Paris, 1948.   2.50

CALVÉ, EMMA
Sous tous les ciels j'ai chanté: sou-
venirs. 297 p, 16 pl, paper. Plon,
Paris, 1940.   1.50

CART, WILLIAM
J. S. Bach, 1685–1750: étude.   262
p, col frontis, por, paper.   Rouge,
Lausanne, 1946.   3.00

CELLIER, ALEXANDRE & BACHELIN, HENRI
L'orgue: ses éléments—son histoire
—son esthétique. Pref. C. M. Widor.
254 p, illus, tables, mus ex, 3–p bibl.
Delagrave, Paris, 1933.   12.50
*An extensive, standard work on the instru-
ment, its music, & its aesthetics.*

CHAILLEY, J. & CHALLAN, H.
Théorie de la musique.   Pref Claude
Delvincourt.   95 p, mus ex, paper.
Leduc, Paris, 1947.   1.40

CHALUPT, RENÉ
George Gershwin: le musicien de la
"Rhapsody in blue."   179 p, photos,
1–p bibl.   Amiot Dumont, Paris,
1948.   2.00

CHAMPIGNEULLE, BERNARD
L'âge classique de la musique fran-
çaise. 351 p, table, mus ex, 6–bibl,
paper.   Aubier, Paris, 1946.   2.00
Histoire de la musique.   128 p, paper.
Presses Universitaires de France,
Paris, (1941), 4th ed 1946.   .90

CHANTAVOINE, JEAN
Beethoven. 181 p, mus ex, 5-p, bibl,
paper. (1906) Plon, Paris, 1948.   2.00
Liszt.   180 p, mus ex, paper. Plon,
Paris, (1910, 3rd ed 1913), new ed
1950.   2.00
Mozart. 146 p, mus ex, paper. Plon,
Paris, 1949.   2.00
Mozart dans Mozart. 271 p, mus ex,
paper.   Desclée de Brouwer, Paris,
1948.   4.00
Mainly devoted to Mozart's operas.
Petit guide de l'auditeur de musique:
cent opéras célèbres, analyse du livret
et de la partition.   521 p, paper.
Plon, Paris, 1948 (1950).   3.00
Petit guide de l'auditeur de musique:
musique symphonique et religieuse,
compartant un avant-propos sur la
manière d'écouter la musique pour
la bien goûter et suivi de l'analyse de
plus de 300 oeuvres symphoniques
fréquemment exécutées.   Textes
choisis par Albert Malpas. li, 287 p,
paper. Plon, Paris, 1947 (1948).   2.00
Camille Saint-Saëns. 126 p, 6 illus
(pors & facs), 1 p, bibl, paper.   Richard Massé, Paris, 1947.   1.50
*Includes a 5-p catalogue of works & a 3-p dis-
cography.*

CHEVALIER, MAURICE
Ma route et mes chansons.   4 v,
paper.   Julliard, Paris, 1946/–.
V 1: La louque.   275 p. 1946.   2.25
V 2: Londres, Hollywood, Paris. 241
p. 1947.   2.25
V 3: Temps grises. 239 p. 1948.   1.75
V 4: Par ci, par là. 212 p. 1950.   Δ

The music-hall star's memoirs, for which we have no price yet on volume 4. See also the main Guide entry under Chevalier for an English version, probably abridged: "The man in the straw hat."

CHRISTEN, ERNEST
Ysaÿe. Pref Jaques-Dalcroze. 231 p, illus (pors & facs), paper. Labor et Fides, Genève, (1946) 2nd ed 1947. 3.25

CLERCX, SUSANNE
Le baroque et la musique: essai d'esthétique musicale. Pref E. de Bruyne. 243 p, mus ex, 4–p bibl, paper. Librairie Encyclopédique, Bruxelles, 1948. 2.50
Publications de la Société belge de Musicologie, 2me série, tome 1. A scholarly analysis of the baroque era's inner stylistic unity.

Grétry, 1741–1813. 139 p, frontis por, 10-p bibl, paper. La Renaissance du Livre, Bruxelles, 1944. 1.25

CLERCX, S. & VAN DER LINDEN, A. (*eds*)
Hommage à Charles van den Borren: mélanges. xi, 360 p, 16 pl, mus ex, paper. Nederlandsche Boekhandel, Anvers, 1945, via Musurgia. 6.00
A collection of tributes to the noted musicologist, including a chronological bibliography of his works, p 19/53, by R. Wangermée.

CLOSSON, ERNEST
L'élément flamand dans Beethoven. 279 p, 2 pors, 2–p bibl + bibl refs, paper. Editions Universitaires, Les Presses de Belgique, Bruxelles, (1927) 2nd rev aug ed 1946. 4.50
An English edition (Oxford 1936) is O/P.

Mélanges Ernest Closson: recueil d'articles musicologiques offert à Ernest Closson à l'occasion de son soixante-quinzième anniversaire. 201 p, frontis por, mus ex, 12-p bibl, paper. Société Belge de Musicologie, Bruxelles, 1948. 5.00
Introduction by Charles van den Borren; bibliography of Closson's works by Anne-Marie Regnier; articles by many other writers.

COEUROY, ANDRÉ
Les Lieder de Schubert. 89 p, paper. Larousse, Paris, 1948. .80

Weber. 188 p, 2–p bibl, paper. Presses Universitaires de France, Paris. 1925. 1.00

COLLAER, PAUL
Darius Milhaud. 239 p, illus, mus ex,

paper. Nederlandsche Boekhandel, Anvers, 1947. 6.00
With many illustrations & analyses of works.

COLLET, HENRI
Albéniz et Granados. 235 p, mus ex, 1–p bibl, paper. (1938) Plon, Paris, new ed 1948. 1.75

COPPOLA, PIERO
Les affres du Roi Marke: et autres variations en majeur et en mineur. 182 p, illus (L.Keiner), paper. Roth, Lausanne, 1945. 2.50
Includes a list of Coppola's musical works.

CORTE, ANDREA DELLA
Toscanini. Tr A. Jacquemard. 181 p, paper. Rouge, Lausanne, 1948. 3.00
Originally in Italian, 1946 (see App Ic).

CORTOT, ALFRED
Aspects de Chopin. 324 p, 8 pl (pors & facs), paper. Albin Michel, Paris, 1949. 2.00

La musique francaise de piano. 3 v, paper. (1930/2) Presses Universitaires de France, Paris.

V 1: Debussy, Franck, Fauré, Chabrier, Dukas. 252 p. (1930) 5th ed 1948. 1.80

V 2: Ravel, Saint-Saëns, d'Indy, Schmitt, de Séverac, Emmanuel. 252 p. (1932) 3rd ed 1948. 1.80

V 3: Les "Six" et le piano, Roussel, Stravinsky, Satie, Pierné, Samazeuilh. 292 p. (1932) 1944. 1.80
A standard work, originally written as essays for "La Revue Musicale." An English edition of v 1 (tr Hilda Andrews, Oxford, 1932) is O/P.

Note: See also (main Guide entry under Piano Playing-1): Cortot's "The rational principles of piano technique" (Salabert 1930), which also is available in the original French text, $3.50.

CRUSSARD, CLAUDE
Marc-Antoine Charpentier, 1634-1704: un musicien français oublié. 128 p, 3 pl, mus ex, paper. Floury, Paris, 1945. 2.50

CUVELIER, ANDRÉ
La musique et l'homme: ou, relativité de la chose musicale. viii, 287 p, bibl refs, paper. Presses Universitaires de France, Paris, 1949. 3.00
"Bibliothèque de philosophie contemporaine: morale et valeurs" series. With sections on acoustics, aural perception, aesthetics, images & music words & music, etc.

D—

DANHAUSER, ADOLPHE
Théorie de la musique. Édition
revue et corrigée par Henri Rabaud.
128 p, mus ex, paper. Lemoine,
Paris, 1929. 2.00

DEBUSSY, CLAUDE
Claude Debussy et Gabriele D'Annunzio: correspondance inédite, pré-
sentée par Guy Tosi. 129 p, 8 illus,
paper. Denoël, Paris, 1948. 6.00
Correspondance de Claude Debussy
et Pierre Louÿs (1893–1904). Recu-
eillié et annotée par Henri Borgeaud. Intro G. Jean Aubry. 206
p, mus ex, paper. José Corti, Paris,
1945. 2.00
Lettres à deux amis: 78 lettres inédites à Robert Godet et G. Jean
Aubry. 194 p, paper. José Corti,
Paris, 1942. 1.50

(DURAND, JACQUES)
Lettres de Cl. Debussy à son éditeur.
190 p, frontis por, paper. Durand,
Paris, 1927. 3.75

DOISY, MARCEL
Musique et drame. 262 p, mus ex,
6–p bibl, paper. Flament, Paris,
1949. 2.00
*A study of opera in general and of various
opera composers, Monteverdi to Dukas.*

DOUEL, JEAN
Précis d'harmonie expérimentale.
Pref Paul Le Flem. Basses et chants
donnés de Georges Hugon, Henri
Challan, Georges Dandelot, Pierre
Lantier, Paul Maurice. 100 p, mus
ex, paper. Gallet et Fils, Paris, n d
(1944?). 4.00

DUBOIS, THÉODORE
Traité de contrepoint et de fugue.
vii, 310 p, mus ex, paper. Heugel, Δ
Paris, 1901 (1928). 12.00

DUFOURCQ, NORBERT
J. S. Bach: le maître de l'orgue. 431
p, 32 pl (pors, facs, organs, etc),
some 300 mus ex, 3–p bibl + 2–p
bibl music editions, paper. Floury,
Paris, 1948. 12.50
*The detailed study of Bach's organ works is
preceded by a study of those of his most im-
portant forerunners. There is also a list of
French organs with stop specifications.*
Le clavecin. 128 p, bibl refs, paper.
Presses Universitaires de France,
Paris, 1949. .90

César Franck: le milieu, l'oeuvre,
l'art . . . l'oeuvre d'orgue de César
Franck. 128 p, mus ex, 2–p bibl,
paper. La Colombe, Paris. 1949. 1.00
Le grand orgue et les organistes de
St. Merry de Paris: pour un tri
centenaire, 1647–1947. 89 + 48–p
pl, paper. Floury, Paris, 1947. 2.50
La messe en si mineur de J.-S. Bach.
79 p, mus ex, paper. Larousse, Paris,
1948. .80
La musique, des origines à nos jours.
Pref Claude Delvincourt. 591 p, +
800 pl incl 6 col pl. Larousse, Mont- Δ
rouge, 1946. 15.00
*A large-size limited edition, lavishly illus-
trated with portraits, facsimiles, etc, and including articles by many authors under the
general editorship of Dufourcq.*

La musique française. 380 p + 96
pl, 15–p bibl refs, paper. Larousse,
Paris. 1949. 2.75
A detailed over-all historical survey.

La musique d'orgue française de Jehan
Titelouze à Jehan Alain: les instru-
ments, les artistes, et les oeuvres, les
formes, et les styles. 260 p, facs, 1–p
bibl + chap bibls, paper. Floury,
Paris, (1941), 2nd rev aug ed 1949. 3.00
L'orgue. 126 p, paper. Presses Uni-
versitaires de France, Paris. 1948. .90
Facture et facteurs; musique et musiciens.
Petite histoire de la musique en
Europe. 164 p, 32 pl (pors, facs, etc),
paper. Larousse, Paris, 1942 (1943). 1.60

DUKAS, PAUL
Les écrits de Paul Dukas sur la
musique. Pref G. Samazeuilh. 703
p, frontis por, paper. Société d'Éditions Françaises et Internationales,
Paris, 1948. 3.50
Collected writings & a catalogue of works.

DUMESNIL, RENÉ
L'envers de la musique: le monde
des musiciens et le monde de la
danse. 213 p, paper. La Nouvelle
Édition, Paris, 1948. 2.00
*Miscellaneous essays on the public, opera,
chamber & church music, recording & radio,
teaching, etc.*
La musique contemporaine en
France. 2 v: 216 p; 207 p, 2–p bibl,
paper. Armand Colin, Paris, (1930),
2nd rev ed 1949. 3.00
La musique en France entre les deux
guerres (1919–1939). 264 p, illus,

paper. Milieu du Monde, Genève, 1946.　2.60

La musique romantique française. 253 p, paper. Aubier, Paris, 1944.　2.00

L'opéra et l'opéra-comique. 128 p, paper. Presses Universitaires de France, Paris, 1947.　.90

Le rythme musical: essai historique et critique. 208 p, mus ex, 12-p bibl, paper. La Colombe, Paris, 1949.　2.00

DUPRÉ, MARCEL
Cours complet d'improvisation à l'orgue. 2 v, paper. Leduc, Paris, 1925/37.

V 1: Exercices préparatoires à l'improvisation libre. 60 p, mus ex. 1937.　4.00
V 2: Traité d'improvisation à l'orgue. 139 p, mus ex. 1925.　8.75

DURAND, JACQUES
(*See also Debussy letters above.*)

Abrégé de l'histoire de la musique. 40 p, paper. Durand, Paris, 1924.　.40
Abrégé historique et technique de l'édition musicale. 15 p, facs, paper. Durand, Paris, 1924.　.40
Quelques souvenirs d'un éditeur de musique. 136 p, paper. Durand, Paris, 1924.　1.00

D'ERLANGER, RODOLPHE
La musique arabe. 5 v. Geuthner, 1930/49.　△

V 1: xxviii, 329 p, diagrs, mus ex, paper. 1930.
V 2: 310 p, diagrs, mus ex, paper. 1935.
V 3: xiv, 618 p, diagrs, mus ex. 1938.
V 4: 530 p, diagrs, mus ex, paper. 1939.
V 5: Essai de codification des règles usuelles de la musique arabe moderne. xv, 426 p, diagrs, mus ex, paper. 1949.
A monumental, standard work, the first four volumes of which are French translations, with commentaries, of Islamic writings on music. (At the time the above entry was set in type we lacked full availability & price information, but more recently Musurgia has advertised complete sets for $25.00.)

F—

FAURE, GABRIEL
Gabriel Fauré. 129 p, illus, paper. B. Arthaud, Paris, 1945.　1.00

FERCHAULT, GUY
Faust: une légende et ses musiciens. 115 p, mus ex, paper. Larousse, Paris, 1948.　1.00
Introduction à l'esthétique de la musique (Essais sur les fondements psychologiques d'une esthétique musicale). ? p, paper? Orphys, Paris, 1947.　△

FÉVRIER, HENRY
André Messager: mon maître, mon ami. Pref Jean Messager. 250 p + 9 pl (pors, facs, etc), paper. Amiot-Dumont, Paris, 1948.　2.00

FLORAND, FRANÇOIS
Jean-Sébastien Bach: L'oeuvre d'orgue, suivi d'un essai sur l'expression musicale du sentiment religieux. Pref Marcel Dupré. 248 p, 4 pors, mus ex, paper. Éditions du Cerf, Paris, 1947.　2.50

G—

GAUDEFROY-DEMOMBYNES, J.
Histoire de la musique française. 431 p, 2–p bibl, paper. Payot, Paris, 1946.　4.00

GAVOTY, BERNARD
Jehan Alain: musicien français (1911-1940), avec un choix de lettres et de dessins inédits. 207 p, illus (pors, etc), paper. Albin Michel, Paris, 1945 (1950).　1.50
Louis Vierne: la vie et l'oeuvre. 325 p, 12 pl (pors, facs, etc), paper. Albin Michel, Paris, 1943.　1.60

GÉDALGE, ANDRÉ
Traité de la fugue: lre partie, De la fugue d'école. 379 p, mus ex. Enoch, Paris, n d (1901?).　17.50

GENEST, ÉMILE
L'opéra-comique: connu et inconnu. Pref Albert Carré. xi, 346 p, 12 pl, 2–p bibl, paper. Fischbacher, Paris, 1925.　2.50

GÉROLD, THÉODORE
Histoire de la musique: des origines à la fin du XIVe siècle. 436 p, 32 pl, 166 mus ex, 5–p bibl, paper. H. Laurens, Paris, 1936.　4.50
For a companion work, covering the 15th & 16th centuries, see Pirro below.

GEVAERT, FRANÇOIS-AUGUSTE
Histoire et théorie de la musique de l'antiquité. 2 v: xvi, 450; xix, 652 p,

mus ex (some col), bibl refs, paper.
Annoot-Braeckman, Gand, 1875/81, △
via Messagerie Musicali, Milan.   15.00

A standard 19th-century study in four sections: "Notions générales," "Harmonique et mélopée," "Rhythmique et métrique," "Histoire de l'art pratique."

GHÉON, HENRI
Promenades avec Mozart.   484 p,
20 pl (pors, etc), mus ex, 1–p. bibl,
paper.   Desclée de Brouwer, Paris,
(1932), 7th ed n d.   4.00

An English version, "In search of Mozart" (Sheed & Ward 1934), apparently is O/P.

GIDE, ANDRÉ
Notes sur Chopin.   131 p, mus ex,
paper.   L'Arche, Paris, 1948.   3.00

For an English edition, see the main Guide entry under Chopin–1.

GILBERT, J. M. & JACQUES, HENRY
Introduction à la discophilie.   151 p,
4–p bibl, paper.   Colbert, Paris, 3rd
ed 1946.   1.00

Notes on record-collecting, Charles Cros (true inventor of the phonograph), a basic discography of French music (p 75/112), the complete recordings of Berlioz's "Requiem" & Debussy's "Pelléas et Mélisande."

GIRDLESTONE, C. M.
Mozart: ses concertos pour piano.
2 v: 534 p, frontis por, mus ex, paper.
Fischbacher, Paris, 1939.   10.00

For an English edition, see the main Guide entry under Mozart–3.

GODET, ROBERT
(*See also Debussy letters above.*)
En marge de Boris Godounof: notes
sur les documents iconographiques
de l'édition Chester.   2 v: 551 p,
paper.   Alcan, Paris, 1926.   4.80

GRENIER, HÉLÈNE
La musique symphonique de Monteverde à Beethoven, 213 p, illus, 5–p
bibl, paper.   Éditions Variétés,
Montreal, 1947.   1.50

GROVLEZ, GABRIEL
L'initiation à l'orchestration.   Pref
H. Busser. 68 p, mus ex, paper.   Gallet et Fils, Paris, 1946.   3.00

GUILBERT, YVETTE
Autres temps, autres chants.   Pref
Bussane.   218 p, 32 illus, paper.
Lafont, Paris, 12th ed 1946.   1.75

La chanson de ma vie (mes mémoires).   260 p, frontis por, paper.
Grasset, Paris, 1927 (1945).   1.50

H—

HAHN, REYNALDO
Thèmes variés. 302 p, paper. Janin,
Paris, 10th ed 1946.   2.00

HANSEN, JULES
Les trois cahiers d'écriture musicale.
3 v: 16, 16, 24 p, music, paper.   Leduc, Paris, n d.   1.20

HÉVÉSY, ANDRÉ DE
Beethoven: vie intime.   241 p, 10 pl
(pors), 3–p bibl, paper.   Émile-Paul
Frères, Paris, (1926) 1949.   1.75

An English translation by Flint ("Beethoven the man", 1927) apparently is O/P.

HISSARLIAN-LAGOUTTE, PIERRETTE
Style et technique des grands maîtres
du piano. Henn, Genève, (1944), 2nd
aug ed 1948.   3.00

HOFMANN, ROTISLAV
Un siècle d'opéra russe: de Glinka
à Stravinsky. 255 p, paper. Corrêa,
Paris, 1946.   1.50

HONEGGER, ARTHUR (& others)
Almanach de la musique 1950.   Ed
Eric Sarnette. (xvi–p advts), 223 p
+ 4 pl + 424 pors, paper. Editions
de Flore et La Gazette des Lettres,
Paris, 1949.   1.75

A yearbook with contributions by Bernard, Bruyr, Dumesnil, Hoerée, Landowski, Migot, Samazeuilh, Vuillermoz, et al.; a dictionary of contemporary composers, professional groups, etc; and a section, "Pour une petite bibliothèque musicale," by Ghislaine Juramie, p 163/70.

HOROWICZ, BRONISLAW
Le théâtre d'opéra: histoire—réalisations scéniques—possibilités. 270 p,
illus, 7–p bibl, paper. Flore, Paris,
1946.   3.50

HOUSTON-PERET, ELSIE (ed)
Chants populaires du Brésil: première
série. Intro Philippe Stern. 27 p +
46–p music (tunes only), paper.
Geuthner, Paris, 1930.   4.75

HUYGENS, CHRISTIAAN
Musique et mathématique [etc].
(Oeuvres complètes, v XX). 624 p,
1 pl, facs (diagrs & mus ex), 16–p
bibl, paper. Société Hollandaise de
Sciences, Martinus Vijhoff, La Haye,
1940, via Musurgia.   7.35

The musical writings of the great Belgian scientist & mathematician (1629-1695).

I—

D'INDY, VINCENT
Cours de composition musicale. Rédigé avec la collaboration d'Auguste Sérieyx. 3 v, diagrs, mus ex, paper. Durand, Paris, 1902/33.

V 1: 228 p. 1902 (1912).	4.00
V 2, part 1: 500 p. 1909.	8.00
V 2, part 2: 340 p. n d (1933).	9.00

INGHELBRECHT, D. E.
Le chef d'orchestre et son équipe. 239 p, illus, diagrs, mus ex, paper. Julliard, Paris, 1949. 2.75

J—

JANKÉLÉVITCH, VLADIMIR
Debussy et le mystère. 152 p, mus ex, paper. La Baconnière, Boudry, 1949. 2.25

JAQUES-DALCROZE, ÉMILE
La musique et nous: notes sur notre double vie. 285 p, 2–p bibl, paper. Perret-Gentil, Genève, 1945. 3.00
Notes bariolées. 196 p, paper. Jeheber, Genève, 1948. 2.40
Jottings & day-by-day notes on music, travels, & pedagogical reforms.
Souvenirs: notes et critiques. 221 p, 2–p bibl, paper. Attinger, Neuchâtel, 1942. 3.00

JAROSY, ALBERT
Nouvelle théorie du doigté: Paganini et son secret. Tr S. Joachim-Chaigneau. 71 p, mus ex, paper. Eschig, Paris, 1924. 1.45
An English edition (1933/4) is O/P.

JOURDAN-MORHANGE, HÉLÈNE
Ravel et nous: l'homme, l'ami, le musicien. Pref Colette. 269 p, 26 pl (Luc-Albert Moreau & others), paper. Éditions du Milieu du Monde, Genève, 1945. 2.75

JOUVE, PIERRE JEAN
Le Don Juan de Mozart. 279 p, table analytique, paper. (1942) Egloff, Fribourg, 2nd rev ed 1944. 3.00

K—

KOECHLIN, CHARLES
Études sur les notes de passage. 77 p, mus ex, paper. Eschig, Paris, 1922 (6th ed n d). 1.20

Gabriel Fauré. 166 p, mus ex, 4–p bibl, paper. Plon, Paris, (1927), new ed 1949. 2.00
For an English edition, see the main Guide entry under Fauré.

Les instruments à vent. 127 p, mus ex, 2–p bibl, paper. Presses Universitaires de France, Paris, 1948. .90
Théorie de la musique. 105 p, mus ex, paper. Heugel, Paris, 1935. 2.20
Abrégé de la théorie de la musique. 38 p, mus ex, paper. Heugel, Paris, 1935. 1.25

KUNEL, MAURICE
La vie de César Franck: l'homme et son oeuvre. 259 p, illus, 3–p genealogy, paper. Grasset, Paris, 1947. 2.40

L—

LALO, PIERRE
De Rameau à Ravel: portraits et souvenirs. Forew Gustave Samazeuilh. 422 p, paper. Albin Michel, Paris, 1947. 2.00

LA LAURENCIE, LIONEL DE
Les créateurs de l'opéra français. 217 p, mus ex, 3–p bibl, paper. Alcan, Paris, (1920) 2nd ed 1930. 1.20
Rameau: biographie critique. 128 p, 13 pl (pors, facs, etc), 1–p bibl. Librairie Renouard, Paris, (1908) 1926. 1.50

LAMBOTTE, LUCIEN
L'éducation de la mémoire musicale. Pref I. Philipp. 123 p, paper. Eschig, Paris, n d (1937?). 1.45

LANDORMY, PAUL
Brahms. 185 p, mus ex, 4–p bibl, paper. Gallimard, Paris, 1948. 1.75
Histoire de la musique. 476 p, mus ex. Mellottée, Paris, (1910), new rev aug ed 1942 (1947). 2.50
La musique française de la Marseillaise à la mort de Berlioz. 302 p, mus ex, paper. Gallimard, Paris, (1944), 15th ed 1948. 2.00
La musique française de Franck à Debussy. 244 p, mus ex, paper. Gallimard, Paris, (1943), 18th ed 1948. 2.50
La musique française après Debussy. 382 p, mus ex, paper. Gallimard, Paris (1943), 14th ed 1948. 1.50

LANDOWSKI, W. L.
Histoire générale de la musique. 307
p, 6–p iconographie, paper. Aubier,
Paris, 1945.   1.50
Histoire universelle de la musique
moderne.   272 p, 2–p bibl, paper,
Aubier, Paris, new rev aug ed 1947.   1.50
L'oeuvre de Claude Delvincourt. 85
p, paper.   Plon, Paris, 1948.   1.20
Maurice Ravel: sa vie—son oeuvre.
136 p, frontis por, 1½–p bibl, paper.
Éditions Ouvrières, Paris, 1950.   1.50
Le travail en musique: le progrès de
la musique fonctionnelle. 85 p, 2–p
bibl, paper. Plon, Paris, 1949.   1.75
Functional music: its general, decorative, &
therapeutic applications.

LAWRENCE, LUCILE & SALZEDO, CARLOS
See main Guide entry under Modulation for
"The art of modulating", with text in Eng-
lish & French.

LEIBOWITZ, RENÉ
Introduction à la musique de douze
sons: les variations pour orchestre,
Op. 31, d'Arnold Schoenberg. 351 p,   △
mus ex, paper. L'Arche, Paris, 1949.   4.50
Limited edition.   A detailed analysis of the
Schoenberg Variations; analyses of other
works by Schoenberg, Berg, & Webern; plus
list of the 3 composers' works.
Qu'est-ce que la musique de douze
sons?: le concerto pour neuf instruments, Op. 24, d'Anton Webern. 63
p + 8–p mus ex, paper. Dynamo,
Liége, 1948.   2.75
Schoenberg et son école: l'étape
contemporaine du langage musical.
303 p, 3 pors, 116 mus ex, 1–p bibl,
paper. Janin, Paris, 1947.   2.50
For an English edition (1949 , see the main
Guide entry under Schoenberg.

LE ROUX, MAURICE
Introduction à la musique contemporaine.   Pref Claude Delvincourt.
132 p, mus ex, paper. Grenier, Paris,
1947.   1.50

LEVRON, JACQUES
Clément Jannequin: musicien de la
renaissance. 130 p, 8 pl, bibl notes,
paper. Arthaud, Paris, 1948.   1.50

LICHTENBERGER, HENRI
Richard Wagner: poète et penseur.
241 p, mus ex, 4–p bibl, paper.
Presses Universitaires de France,
Paris, (1931), 11th ed 1948.   2.40

LOCARD, PAUL
Le piano. 128 p, 1 diagr, 1–p bibl,
paper.   Presses Universitaires de
France, Paris, 1948.   .90
L'histoire et la technique; la musique.

M—

MACHABEY, ARMAND
Le bel canto. 124 p, mus ex, 5–p bibl,
paper. Larousse, Paris, 1948.   .80
Portraits de trente musiciens français. 169 p + 31 pors & facs (autographs).   Richard Masse, Paris,
1949.   3.50
Brief sketches of & abridged lists of works by
French musicians from Aubin to Tomasi.
Traité de la critique musicale: la
doctrine, la méthode: anthologie
justificative. 222 p, 7–p bibl. Richard Masse, Paris, 1947.   4.00
La vie et l'oeuvre d'Anton Bruckner.
237 p, pors, mus ex, paper. Calmann-
Levy, Paris, 1945.   3.00

MAGNAT, G. E.
Portraits de quelques musiciens.
Pref Alfred Cortot. 115 p, facs, pa-
per.   Foetisch Frères, Lausanne,
1948.   4.00
Graphological interpretations of the manu-
scripts & autographs of Monteverdi, Bach,
Mozart, Beethoven, Wagner, Debussy, Ravel.

MALHERBE, HENRY
Franz Schubert: son amour, ses
amitiés.   298 p, 8 pl, paper. Albin
Michel, Paris, 1949.   3.00
Richard Wagner, révolutionnaire.
348 p, 13 illus, paper. Albin Michel,
Paris, 1938.   2.00

MANUEL, ROLAND
Ravel. 190 p, 2 facs, mus ex, 5–p
bibl, paper. (1938) Gallimard, Paris,
2nd ed 1948.   2.00
See also main Guide entry under Ravel for
an English version (1947).

MANUEL, ROLAND & TAGRINE, NADIA
Plaisir de la musique. 2 v, paper.
Seuil, Paris 1947 (1949).
V 1: 333 p, mus ex, brief bibl.   1.75
V 2: 303 p.   1.75
Broadcast interviews & discussions with some
60 musicians: Auric, Bernac, Ibert,Pincherle,
Poulenc, etc (v 1); Bruyer, Honegger, Sau-
guet, etc (v 2).

MARCEL-DUBOIS, CLAUDIE
Les instruments de musique de
l'Inde ancienne. vii, 261 p + 56
illus (Jeannine Auboyer), 14–p bibl,
paper. Presses Universitaires de
France, Paris, 1941.   4.00

MASSON, PAUL-MARIE
L'opéra de Rameau. 595 p, 16 pl
(pors, etc), mus ex, 7–p bibl, paper.
Laurens, Paris, 1930.   5.00

MERCURE, GEORGES
Rythmique grégorienne. Édité par
les moines de Saint Benoît du Lac.
252 p, illus, mus ex. Les Presses de
l'Action Catholique de Québec, 1937
(1943).   2.50
*Originally issued in two volumes to accom-
pany a series of Gregorian phonograph recordings of the monks of St Benoît.*

MESSIAEN, OLIVIER
La technique de mon langage mu-
sical. 2 v: 71; 61 p, music, paper.
Leduc, Paris, 1944 (1947/8).   10.00
V 1: Texte. V 2: Exemples musicaux.

Vingt leçons d'harmonie: dans le
style de quelques auteurs importants
de "l'histoire harmonique" de la musique depuis Monteverdi jusqu' à
Ravel. 53 p, mus ex, paper. Leduc,
Paris, 1939.   2.70

MEYER, MARIE ANTOINE
J. Ph. Rameau; J. S. Bach. 90 p, bibl
refs, paper. Editions Lire, Cham-
bery, 1946.   .90

MICHAUT, PIERRE
Histoire du ballet. 128 p, paper.
Presses Universitaires de France,
Paris, (1945), 2nd ed 1948.   .90

MIGOT, GEORGES
Lexique de quelques termes utilisés en
musique: avec des commentaires
pouvant servir a la compréhension
de ce art. Intro Maurice Hendrio.
257 p, illus, mus ex, paper. (1935)
Didier, Paris, 1946 (1947).   4.00

MILHAUD, DARIUS
(*See also Beck catalogue above.*)

Notes sans musique. 336 p, frontis
por, paper. Julliard, Paris, 1949.   2.00
Autobiographical reminiscences.

MOCQUEREAU, R. P. ANDRÉ
Le nombre musical grégorien: ou,
rythmique grégorien, théorie et pratique. 2 v, paper. Desclée de Brouwer,
Paris, 1908/27, via J. Fischer.

V 1: 430 p, mus ex. 1908.   4.00
V 2: xxvii, 855 p, mus ex (some on
fold-out charts), 13–p bibl. 1927.   4.00
*An extensive, standard work. See the main
Guide entry under Gregorian for an English
edition of v 1, part 1, "L'origine du rythme."*

MOOSER, R.-ALOYS
Annales de la musique et des mu-
siciens en Russie au XVIIIe siècle.
V 1: Des origines à la mort de Pierre
III (1762). 456 p, illus (pors, facs,
etc), music, 6–p bibl. Les Éditions
du Mont-Blanc, Genève. 1948.   △ 22.75
A monumental standard work.

Opéras, intermezzos, ballets, can-
tates, oratorios joués en Russie durant le XVIIIe siècle: avec l'indication
des oeuvres de compositeurs russes
parues en Occident, à la même époque. Essai d'un répertoire alpha-
bétique et chronologique. xi, 173 p,
9–p bibl, paper. Kundig, Genève,
1945.   3.00

Regards sur la musique contemporaine: 1921–1946. Pref Arthur Honegger. 457 p, paper. Rouge, Lausanne, 1946.   6.00

MOREUX, SERGE
Béla Bartók: sa vie, ses œuvres, son
langage. Pref Arthur Honegger.
128 p, 4 pl (pors, fac, etc). Richard
Masse, Paris. 1949.   2.25

MULLER, DANIEL
Leoš Janáček. 94 p + 60-p illus
(pors, facs, etc), paper. Rieder,
Paris, 1930.   1.50

N—

NEWMARCH, ROSA
L'opéra russe. 312 p, paper. Alcan,
Paris, & Chester, London, 1922.   1.00
*The original English version of 1914 appar-
ently is O/P.*

O—

OPIENSKI, HENRYK
I. J. Paderewski: esquisse de sa vie et
de son œuvre. Pref Gagriel Hanotaux,
Gustave Doret, & Alfred Cortot.
148 p, 34 photos & facs, paper. Spes,
Lausanne, (1928), new ed 1948.   2.75

P—

PANASSIÉ, HUGUES
Louis Armstrong. 107 p + 11 photos, paper. Belvédère, Paris, 1947.   1.50
On the cover only: "L'homme, le style, l'œuvre; suivi d'une discographie complète établie par Charles Delaunay." This discography occupies p 89/103 of the book.

PANIGEL, ARMAND (& *others, comps*)
L'œuvre de Frédéric Chopin: discographie générale réalisée sous la direction d'Armand Panigel. Intro & notes Marcel Beaufils. 253 p + 8 pl (pors, facs), paper. Éditions de la Revue Disques, Paris, 1949.   5.00
The first volume in the series of "Archives de la Musique Enregistrée UNESCO." Co-compilers: Claude Galtat, Jean Germain, Antoine Goltea, & Henry-Jacques. See the main Guide entry under Chopin–2 for an English version.

PANZÉRA, CHARLES
L'art de chanter. Pref Arthur Honegger. 120 p, illus (M. P. P. Ogé), mus ex, paper. Éditions Littéraires de France, Paris, 1945.   3.00
The noted baritone discusses vocal études & disciplines, recording, & interpretation.

PARROT, LOUIS
Mozart. 198 p, paper. Laffont, Paris, 1945.   1.60

PEETERS, FLOR
See the main Guide entry under Gregorian for "A practical method of plain-chant accompaniment," with texts in English & French.

PERI, NOËL
Essai sur les gammes japonais. v, 70 p, illus, diagrs, mus ex, 8–p bibl, paper. Geuthner, Paris, 1934.   3.75
Bibliothèque musicale du Musée Guimet, 2. série, No 1. The revision of the manuscript, the bibliography, & the table of modes are by Serge Elissée & Philippe Stern.

PIGUET, J.-CLAUDE
Découverte de la musique: essai sur la signification de la musique. Pref Étienne Souriau. 221 p, mus ex, 14–p annot bibl, paper. Éditions de la Baconnière, Neuchâtel, 1948.   2.50

PINCHERLE, MARC
Les instruments du quatuor. 127 p, mus ex, 1–p bibl, paper. Presses Universitaires de France, Paris, 1948.   .90
With a chapter on other bowed instruments.

Musiciens peints par eux-mêmes: [160] lettres inédites de Piccini, Philidor, Grétry, Méhul, Spontini, Boieldieu, Hérold, Gounod, Berlioz, Liszt, Saint-Saëns, Wagner, Bizet, Chabrier, Borodine, Lalo, Debussy, etc. 251 p + 14 pl (facs) (also 21 facs in text), paper. Cornuau, Paris, 1939.   2.50

L'orchestre de chambre. 74 p, mus ex, 2–p bibl, paper. Larousse, Paris, 1948.   .80

Antonio Vivaldi et la musique instrumentale. 2 v, paper. Floury, Paris, 1948.   15.00
V 1: 318 p, 15 pl (pors, facs, etc), 9–p bibl.
V 2: Inventaire thématique. vi, 77 p, mus ex.
The first detailed, scholarly study of Vivaldi's instrumental works, with a complete thematic catalogue, concordances of printed & MS collections, and a list of modern transcriptions.

PIRON, CONSTANTIN
L'art du piano. Pref Marguerite Long. 318 p, paper. Arthème Fayard, Paris, 1949.   3.00

PIRRO, ANDRÉ
Jean-Sébastien Bach. Pref Jean Chantavoine. 224 p, mus ex, 7–p bibl, paper. (1906) Plon, Paris, new ed 1949.   1.50

Histoire de la musique de la fin du XIVe siècle à fin du XVIe. 370 p, 32 pl, mus ex, paper. Laurens, Paris, 1940.   4.50
For a companion work, covering the period up through the 14th century, see Gérold above.

Schütz. 243 p, mus ex, 2–p bibl, paper. (1913) Alcan, Paris, 1924.   1.20

PITROU, ROBERT
Musiciens romantiques: Beethoven, Weber, Schubert, Chopin, Mendelssohn, Schumann, Berlioz, Liszt, Wagner. 197 p, paper. Albin Michel, Paris, 1946.   1.50

POCHON, ALFRED
Musique d'autrefois: interprétation d'aujourd'hui. 72 p, paper. Henn, Genève, 1943.   1.25
Notes on musical evolution, arrangements, nuances, dynamics, & tradition.

Le rôle du point en musique: placé au-dessus ou au-dessous d'une note. 61 p, mus ex, paper. Rouge, Lausanne, 1947.   1.25

POTHIER, JOSEPH
Les mélodies grégoriennes d'après la tradition. 272 p, music (Gregorian notation), paper. Desclée de Brouwer, Paris, 1880, via J. Fischer.   3.00
A standard 19th-century work.

POUGIN, ARTHUR
Hérold: biographie critique. 124 p, 15 p, paper. Laurens, Paris, n d (1906).   1.20

POURTALÈS, GUY DE
Berlioz et l'Europe romantique. 382 p, frontis por, 3–p bibl, paper. Gallimard, Paris, 1939.   3.25
Chopin: ou le poète. 252 p, 2–p bibl, paper. Gallimard, Paris, (1927) 1946.   1.75
Wagner: histoire d'un artiste. 446 p, paper. Gallimard, Paris, (1932) rev aug ed 1942.   3.00

PROD'HOMME, J.-G.
Beethoven raconté par ceux qui l'ont vu: lettres, mémoires, etc. Ed & tr Prod'homme. vii, 266 p, paper. Stock, Paris, (1927), 13th ed 1947.   3.00
Les cahiers de conversation de Beethoven: 1819–1827. Ed & tr Prod'homme 477 p, mus ex, paper. Corrêa, Paris, 1946.   3.00
Gluck. Pref René Dumesnil. 447 p, 8 pl (pors), 2–p mus ex, 5–p bibl & iconography, paper. Société d'Éditions Françaises et Internationales, Paris, 1948.   3.50
François-Joseph Gossec, 1734–1829: la vie, les œuvres, l'homme, et l'artiste. 128 p, 2–p bibl, paper. Colombe, Paris, 1949.   1.25

R—

RAMUZ, C. F.
Souvenirs sur Igor Strawinsky: portraits et pages manuscrits. 165 p, 9 pl (pors & facs), paper. Mermod, Lausanne, 1946.   △ 2.50
Limited edition.

RAUGEL, FÉLIX
Le chant choral. 128 p, 2–p bibl, paper. Presses Universitaires de France, Paris. 1948.   .90
History, technique, repertory.
L'oratorio. 143 p, 2–p bibl, paper. Larousse, Paris. 1948.   1.00

REBER, HENRI
Traité d'harmonie. 287 p, mus ex, paper. Gallet et Fils, Paris, (1862), 1943.   6.00

REBOUX, PAUL
Liszt: ou les amours romantiques. 208 p, 1–p bibl, paper. Flammarion, Paris, 1940 (1946).   1.25

REUTER, EVELYN
La mélodie et le lied. 128 p, 2½–p bibl, paper. Presses Universitaires de France, Paris, 1950.   .90
Concise survey of 2 centuries, with special attention to French songs 1840-1940, & cross-index of French & German Lieder titles.

ROLLAND, ROMAIN
Histoire de l'opéra en Europe avant Lully et Scarlatti. 316 p + 15–p music, 6–p bibl, paper. (1895) Thorin, Paris, 3rd ed 1931.   4.00
Originally a thesis: "Les origines du théâtre lyrique moderne."
Musiciens d'aujourd'hui: Berlioz, Wagner, Saint-Saëns, d'Indy, Debussy, Wolf, R. Strauss, et le renouveau de la musique française. 281 p, paper. Hachette, Paris, (1908), 18th ed 1947.   2.30
An English edition (1915) is O/P.
Vie de Beethoven. viii, 152 p, 11–p bibl, paper. Hachette, Paris, (1903), 25th ed 1949.   1.00
An English edition (1924) is O/P.

ROSTAND, CLAUDE
L'œuvre de Fauré. 213 p, 16 pl (pors, facs, etc), paper. Janin, Paris, 4th ed 1945.   1.75
Petit guide de l'auditeur de musique: les chefs-d'œuvre du piano. Forew Alfred Cortot. 318 p, bibl refs, paper. Plon, Paris. 1950.   3.00
Program notes on piano works, classified by eras & composers. V 3 of a series (for v 1 & 2, see under Chantavoine above).
Richard Strauss: l'ambiance, les origines, la vie, l'œuvre, l'esthétique, et le style. 128 p, brief bibl, paper. Colombe, Paris, 1949.   1.25

S—

SAINT-FOIX, GEORGES DE
(*See Wyzewa & Saint-Foix below.*)

SAMSON, JOSEPH
Paul Claudel: poète-musicien; précédé d'un argument et d'un dialogue

de Paul Claudel. 279 p + 21 photos, paper. Milieu du Monde, Genève, 1947. **3.60**

SARNETTE, ERIC (*ed*)
(*See Honegger "Almanach" above.*)

SCHMID, WILLY
Concerts: notes sur la musique et sur quelques musiciens. Pref Ernest Ansermet. 248 p, paper. Delahaux et Niestlé, Neuchâtel, 2nd ed 1945. **2.40**
Concerts: nouvelle série. Ed René Gerber. 217 p, frontis por, paper. Delahaux et Niestlé, Neuchâtel, 1945. **2.40**

SÉNÉCHAUD, MARCEL
Le répertoire lyrique: guide des amateurs de théâtre, de musique, de disques, et de radio . . . 350 p, 1–p bibl, paper. Payot, Lausanne, 1945. **3.75**
Analyses of some 145 works by some 85 composers.
Concerts symphoniques: symphonies, oratorios, suites, concertos et poèmes symphoniques; guide à l'usage des amateurs de musique . . . 269 p, 1–p bibl, paper. Marguerat, Lausanne, 1947. **4.50**
Extremely detailed program notes.

SEROFF, VICTOR
Le groupe des cinq: Balakirev, Borodine, Moussorgsky, César Cui, Rimsky-Korsakoff. Tr André Vaudoyer. 315 p, paper. Plon, Paris, 1949. **2.75**
For an English edition, see the main Guide entry under Composers-3e.

STOECKLIN, PAUL DE
Grieg. 141 p, 1-p bibl, paper. Alcan, Paris, 1926. **1.20**

STRAWINSKY, THÉODORE
Le message d'Igor Strawinsky. 127 frontis, paper. Rouge, Paris, 1948. **2.40**
By the painter-son of Stravinsky.

T—

TAGRINE, NADIA
(*See Manuel & Tagrine above.*)

TANSMAN, ALEXANDRE
Igor Stravinsky. 314 p, 17 pl (pors, facs, etc), paper. Dumont, Paris, 1948. **3.00**
For an English version (1949), see the main Guide entry under Stravinsky-2.

TAPPOLET, WILLY
Arthur Honegger. Tr Hélène Breuleux; pref Arthur Hoerée. 315 p, some 11 pl (pors, fac, etc), mus ex, 14–p bibl, paper. Éditions de la Baconnière, Neuchâtel, 1939. **2.40**
La notation musicale et son influence sur la pratique de la musique du moyen-âge à nos jours. 112 p, 20 pl (facs, etc), paper. Éditions de la Baconnière, Neuchâtel, 1947. **2.40**
Especially notable for its fine illustrations.

TEMPLIER, P. D.
Erik Satie. 107 p + 60 pl (pors, facs, etc), 2-p bibl, paper. Rieder, Paris, 1932. **1.80**

THIBAUD, JACQUES
Un violon parle: souvenirs de Jacques Thibaud recueillis par Jean-Pierre Dorian. 301 p, paper. Éditions du Blé que Lève, Lausanne, 1947. **1.25**

TIERSOT, JULIEN
(*See also: Main Guide, Folksongs–1.*)
Les Couperin. 217 p, 6–p bibl, paper. Alcan, Paris, 1926. **1.20**
La musique aux temps romantiques. 186 p, 12 pl (pors, etc), mus ex, paper. Alcan, Paris, 1930. **1.50**

TOSI, GUY (*ed*)
(*See Debussy letters above.*)

TOURNEMIRE, CHARLES
Précis d'exécution, de registration, et d'improvisation à l'orgue. 118 p, music, paper. Eschig, Paris, 1936. **6.50**

V—

VAILLAT, LÉANDRE
Histoire de la danse. 190 p, 82 pl (pors, etc), paper. Plon, Paris, 1942 (repr 1949). **5.00**
A world-wide, over-all survey of the dance with many reproductions of old prints, etc. The text is dated 1939.

VALENSI, THÉODORE
Beethoven en trente-deux tableaux. 205 p, paper. La Bruyère, Paris, 1946. **1.60**

VALLAS, LÉON
Achille-Claude Debussy. 256 p, paper. Presses Universitaires de France, Paris, 1944. **2.00**
Vincent d'Indy: la jeunesse (1851-1886). 305 p, illus (pors, etc), mus ex, paper. Albin Michel, Paris, 1946. **3.50**

Vincent d'Indy: la maturité—la vieillesse. 394 p, illus, 8-p bibl, paper. Albin Michel, Paris, 1950. 4.00

VAN DEN BORREN, CHARLES
(See also Clercx & Van der Linden above.)
César Franck. 141 p, frontis por, 15–p bibl, paper. La Renaissance du Livre, Bruxelles, 1949. 1.25

Orlande de Lassus. 254 p, 8–p bibl, paper. Alcan, Paris, (1920), 3rd ed 1930. 1.20

Roland de Lassus. 117 p, frontis por, 2–p bibl, paper. La Renaissance du Livre, Bruxelles, 1944. 1.25
Despite the difference in Christian names (one of style only), both books are about the same composer. The bibliography of the former book is particularly valuable.

VANNES, RENÉ (comp)
Dictionnaire universel des luthiers. Pref Giovanni Iviglia; forew Ernest Closson. Some 500 p & 156 pl (facs, etc). (1932) Les Amis de la Musique, △ Bruxelles, 2nd rev aug ed 1950. (12.00)
Limited edition, on subscription only, of a monumental reference work (originally "Essai d'un dictionnaire," 1932), with some 15,000 biographical sketches of violin-makers & 2512 reproductions of labels & brand-marks.

VASSENHOVE, LÉON VAN
Anton Bruckner. 257 p, illus (pors. etc), mus ex, 2–p bibl, paper. Éditions de la Baconnière, Neuchâtel, 1942. 2.40

VUILLERMOZ, ÉMILE
Histoire de la musique. 479 p + 2 fold-out charts, paper. Arthème Fayard, Paris, 26th ed 1949. 3.75

W—

WOOD, BENJAMIN
L'art mysterieux du violon. 117 p, illus, mus ex, paper. Senart, Paris, 1927. 2.50

WYZEWA, TEODOR DE & SAINT-FOIX, G. DE
Wolfgang-Amédée Mozart: sa vie musicale et son œuvre, de l'enfance à la pleine maturité. Essai de biographie critique suivi d'un nouveau catalogue chronologique de l'œuvre du maître. 5 v, bibl refs, paper. Desclée de Brouwer, Paris, 1912/46.
Complete set: 24.00

V 1: L'enfant prodige (1756–1773). xiv, 527 p, 8 pors, 4 facs, mus ex. (1912) new ed 1936. 6.50

V 2: Le jeune maître (1773–1777) 459 p, 5 pors, 2 facs (1912) new ed 1936. 5.50

V 3: Le grand voyage (1777-1784). 425 p, 6 pors, 1 fac, mus ex. 1936. 5.50

V 4: L'épanouissement (1784-1788). 400 p, 10 pors, 2 facs, mus ex. 1940. 5.50

V 5: Les dernières années (1789-1791). 369 p, 9 pors, 3 facs, mus ex. 1946. 5.00
A monumental standard work, the last 3 volumes of which are by Saint-Foix alone.

APPENDIX Ib: Books in German

(A selected list only—arranged in alphabetical order by authors' names)

A—

ADAMI, GIUSEPPE (ed)
Giacomo Puccini: Briefe des Meisters. 259 p, 13 pl (pors, facs, etc), bds. Frisch & Perneder, Lindau-Bodensee n d (1948?). 2.50
Originally published in Italian (1928).

ADLER, GUIDO (ed)
Handbuch der Musikgeschichte: unter Mitwirkung von Fachgenossen; mit vielen Notenbeispielen und Abbildungen zur Geschichte der Notenschrift, der Musikinstrumente, der Operndarstellung, und mit Wiedergaben von Autographen. 2 v: xiv, 1294 p, 87 pl (facs, etc), 298 mus ex, subj bibls. (Keller, Berlin, 1924, rev enl 2nd ed 1930) Musurgia photolith repr pending. △
A standard collection of scholarly historical monographs by various musicologists. Publication of the reprint is not yet definite (see note under Musurgia below).

ALTMANN, WILHELM (comp)
Orchester-Literatur-Katalog. vii, 197 p, mus ex, bds. (Leuckart, Leipzig, 1919) E. C. Schirmer n d. 2.00
A standard reference work (also listed in the main Guide under Orchestral Music) to all types of orchestral works published since 1850. A second edition (1926) & a supplementary volume (1936) apparently are O/P (or not easily available).

Note: Unfortunately we do not have availability & price data on the various other Altmann catalogues of chamber music (1910, 1930), piano trios (1934), piano quintets (1936), string quartets (1928), viola & viola d'amore music (1937, with Borissowsky), violin music (1935), theatrical music (1935/6), etc.

APPENZELLER, ELSE
Harmonielehre. 240 p, mus ex. Atlantis, Zürich, 1947. 6.00

ARGINTEANU, SELDA (ed)
Reprints of periodicals in musicology. Series A: German periodicals 1869–1943. 9 v in 7 + sup. Musurgia photolith repr pending. △
V 1: Monatshefte für Musikgeschichte, 1869–1905.
V 2: Vierteljahresschrift für Musikwissenschaft, 1885–1894.

V 3 & 4: Sammelbände der Internationalen Musikgesellschaft, 1899–1914.
V 5: Zeitschrift der Internationalen Musikgesellschaft, 1899–1914.
V 6: Studien zur Musikwissenschaft, 1913–1934.
V 7: Archiv für Musikwissenschaft, 1918–1927.
V 8 & 9: Zeitschrift für Musikwissenschaft & Archiv für Musikforschung, 1918–1935, 1936-1943.
Sup: Acta Musicologica, 1928–1943.

A formidable project for the reprinting of complete periodical files, more than 50,000 pages in the originals, reprinted 6 pages on 1. (A 1951 report announces the abandonment of book-publication plans, but states the complete file will be made available instead on 10 spools of microfilm: price $93.00.)

AUER, MAX
Anton Bruckner: sein Leben und Werk. 2 v: 542 p, 86–p mus ex, 46 pl, bds. (1923, 3rd enl ed 1941) Amalthea, Zürich, 1947. 6.00
A standard work. See also Bruckner below for Auer's edition of the letters.

B—

BACH, JOHANN SEBASTIAN
Johann Sebastian Bach Briefe: Gesamtausgabe. Ed Hedwig & E. H. Müller von Asow. 228 p, 8 pl (pors, fac), mus ex, bds. Bosse, Regensburg (1938) 2nd enl ed 1950. 3.00
Some 73 letters, inscriptions, etc, plus 6 Albumblätter, 4 Anna Magdalena Bach letters, & the biographical sketch from Lorenz Mizler de Koloff's "Musikalische Bibliothek."

Fantasia super Komm heiliger Geist: Faksimileausgabe mit erläuternden Worten von Peter Wackernagel. Unp (5–p facs + 4–p text), col frontis por. Merseburger, Leipzig, 1950, via Peters. 6.50
For a facsimile edition of the Brandenburg Concertos, with notes by Wackernagel (in German & English), also of the 2- & 3-part Inventions, see main Guide entry under Bach-2 (Kirkpatrick).

BARTH, HERBERT (ed)
Jahrbuch der Musikwelt: 1. Jahrgang 1949–50. xvi, 696 p, illus, mus ex, 6–p-bibl. Steeger, Bayreuth, 1949. 7.50

First issue of a new yearbook, with an introduction also given in English & French. The work includes many articles, illustrations, obituaries, lists of festivals, first performances, contemporary composers, etc.

BEETHOVEN, LUDWIG VAN
Beethoven-Suite: aus Briefen.   Ed Willi Reich. 96 p. Classen, Zürich, 1948.   1.50
A selection from the letters.

Briefe. Ed Tilly Kopp. 77 p. Scherz, Bern, (1947), 2nd ed 1948.   1.00
A pocket edition of selected letters.

Briefe und Gespräche. Ed Martin Hürlimann. 260 p, mus ex, 1–p bibl. Atlantis, Zürich, (1944), 2nd ed 1946. 4.50
Note: See also under Hürlimann below for a collection of essays on Beethoven by his teachers, contemporaries, etc.

BERR, ALBERT
Geigengeschichten: Erinnerungen und Notizen. 192 p. Atlantis, Zürich, 1949.   2.50

Handbuch der Geige. Atlantis, Zürich, in prep.   △

BESCH, HANS
Johann Sebastian Bach: Frömmigkeit und Glaube. Band 1: Deutung und Wirklichkeit: Das Bild Bachs im Wandel der deutschen Kirchen- und Geistesgeschichte. 314 p, 1 fac, 7–p bibl, bds. (1937/8), Bärenreiter, Kassel, 2nd ed 1950.   5.00
The first volume of an extensive theological & philosophical study. No data are yet available on further volumes.

BESSELER, HEINRICH
See below: Bücken, ed, Handbuch der Musikwissenschaft, v 2.

BLUME, FRIEDRICH (ed)
Die Musik in Geschichte und Gegenwart: allgemeine Enzyklopädie der Musik. Bärenreiter, Kassel, in progress.   △
Lieferung 1: A-AK, 112 p, was issued in 1949 and succeeding sections are in the process of publication. The complete work is to contain some 6000 pages in six volumes and promises to be one of the most comprehensive music encyclopedias in any language.

BRANDL, WILLY
Richard Strauss: Leben und Werk. 88 p, frontis por, 1–p annot bibl. Breitkopf & Härtel, Wiesbaden, 1949. 1.50
A biographical & analytical sketch, with a catalogue of works & a chronology.

Der Weg der Oper. 120 p, ½–p bibl, bds. Schwab, Stuttgart, 1949.   2.25
Renaissance era to Pfitzner & Strauss.

BRUCKNER, ANTON
Gesammelte Briefe. Ed Max Auer. 408 p, pors, 5 facs. Bosse, Regensburg (1924), new ed n d.   5.00
See also Auer above for a standard Bruckner biography.

BÜCKEN, ERNST
  (*See also below: Bücken, ed, Handbuch der Musikwissenschaft, v 4, 5, & 7.*)
Don Juan: Roman. 251 p. Staufen, Köln, 1949.   2.75
Sinfonia Eroica: ein Beethoven-Roman. 205 p. Staufen, Köln, (1947), 2nd ed 1948.   2.75
Two novels, dealing with Mozart & Beethoven respectively.

BÜCKEN, ERNST (ed)
Handbuch der Musikwissenschaft. 13 v in 9. (Athenaion, Potsdam, 1929/31) Musurgia photolith repr △ 1949/50.   150.30
V 1, 11, 12, & 13. Sachs: Die Musik der Antike, 32 p. Heinitz: Instrumentenkunde, 160 p. Lachmann: Die Musik der aussereuropäischen Völker, 34 p. Panöff: Die altslavische Volks- und Kirchenmusik, 32 p, illus, mus ex.   18.50
V 2 & 8. Besseler: Die Musik des Mittelalters und der Renaissance, 338 p. Haas: Aufführungspraxis der Musik, 299 p, illus, mus ex.   18.50
V 3. Haas: Die Musik des Barocks. 291 p, illus, mus ex.   18.50
V 4. Bücken: Die Musik des Rokokos und der Klassik. 248 p, illus, mus ex.   18.50
V 5. Bücken: Die Musik des 19. Jahrhunderts bis zur Moderne. 320 p, illus, mus ex.   18.50
V 6. Mersmann: Die moderne Musik seit der Romantik. 228 p, illus, mus, ex.   18.50
V 7. Bücken: Geist und Form im musikalischen Kunstwerk. 196 p, illus, mus ex.   18.50
V 8. (See v 2 above.)
V 9. Ursprung: Die katholische Kirchenmusik. 312 p, illus, mus ex. 18.50
V 10.   Blume: Die evangelische Kirchenmusik. 172 p, illus, mus ex. 18.50
V 11, 12, 13. (See v 1 above.)

An outstanding work of German musical scholarship, made available again in the Musurgia series of photolithographic reprints. The numbering of the volumes is slightly different from the original publication and the original color plates now are reproduced in black & white, but otherwise the reprint contains the complete texts, musical examples, and all the original plates & facsimiles (over 1100). Available on subscription only (see the note under Musurgia below).

BUSCH, FRITZ
Aus dem Leben eines Musikers. 222 p, 8 photos. Rascher, Zürich, 1949. 5.00
The story of the conductor's life up to his exile from Hitlerian Germany.

C—

CHALIAPIN, (SCHALJAPIN), FEODOR
Meine Jugend: Erinnerungen. Tr Arthur Knüpffer. Nachwort von Edzard Schaper. 228 p, bds. Classen, Zürich, 1949. 3.00

CHERBULIEZ, ANTOINE-ELISÉE
Johann Sebastian Bach: sein Leben und sein Werk. 235 p, 7 pl (pors, fasc, etc), bibl refs. Walter, Olten, 1946. 2.75
Fryderyk Chopin: Leben und Werk. 208 p, 4 pl, 21 mus ex, 9–p bibl. Müller, Zürich, 1948. 3.75
Edvard Grieg: Leben und Werk. 191 p, 4 pl, 29 mus ex, 5–p bibl, Müller, Zürich, 1947. 2.50
Georg Friedrich Händel: Leben und Werk. 389 p, 8 pl, 2–p bibl + bibl notes. Walter, Olten, 1949. 4.00
Die Schweiz in der deutschen Musikgeschichte. 403 p + 47–p pl, 11–p bibl refs. Huber, Frauenfeld, 1932. 5.25
Tschaikowsky und die russische Musik. 208 p, 41 pl, 21 mus ex. Müller, Zürich, 1948. 3.75
Giuseppe Verdi: Leben und Werk. 219 p, 4 pl, 26 mus ex. Müller, Zürich, 1949. 3.75

CORRODI, HANS
Othmar Schoeck: eine Monographie. 335 p, 1 por, 1 fac, music, 157 mus ex, 2½–p bibl. Huber, Frauenfeld, (1931), 2nd aug ed 1936. 4.00
Includes 4 unpublished compositions, 1 song in MS facsimile, catalogue of works, etc.

CZECH, STAN
Franz Lehár: sein Weg und sein Werk. 260 p, 47 pl (pors, facs, etc),

5–p bibl. (1940) Scientia, Zürich, n d (1948/9?) 4.50

D—

DECSEY, ERNST
Johann Strauss: ein Wiener Buch. 288 p, 18 pl (pors, facs, etc), mus ex, 2–p bibl, bds. (1922?) Neff, Wien, 1948. 5.00

DIETRICH, FRITZ
Geschichte des deutschen Orgelchorals im 17. Jahrhundert. 106 p, mus ex, bibl refs, paper. Bärenreiter, Kassel, 1932. 5.00
Band 1 "Heidelberger Studien zur Musikwissenschaft," ed Heinrich Besseler.

E—

EHINGER, HANS
Klassiker der Musik (Bach, Händel, Haydn, Mozart, Beethoven): ihr Leben und Werk in kurzen Biographien. 211 p, illus, bds. Amerbach, Basel, 1946. 2.25
Meister der Oper (Gluck, Wagner, Verdi, Strauss): ihr Leben und Werk in kurzen Biographien. 151 p, 4 pors, bds. Amerbach, Basel, 1947. 2.25

EHMANN, WILHELM
Die Chorführung. 2 v: 116, 175 p, diagrs, mus ex, paper. Bärenreiter, Kassel. 1949. 5.00
V 1: Das umgangsmässige Singen. V 2: Das künstlerische Singen.

EITNER, ROBERT
Biographisch-Bibliographisches Quellenlexikon der Musiker und Musikgelehrten der christlichen Zeitrechnung bis zur Mitte des neunzehnten Jahrhunderts. 10 v: 480 to 484 p each. (Breitkopf & Härtel, Leipzig, 1900/4) Musurgia photolith repr 1947. △
A standard reference work, temporarily O/P in the present reprint (see note under Musurgia below), but scheduled for re-issue. See also Springer, et al., below for a supplementary work.

EITNER, ROBERT (& others, comps)
Bibliographie der Musik-Sammelwerke des XVI. und XVII. Jahrhunderts. ix, 964 p + ?–p sup. (Liepmannssohn, Berlin, 1877) Musurgia photolith repr 1950. △ 26.75

*A standard reference work to 16th & 17th
century music editions (chronologically by
titles, alphabetically by composers & works),
compiled by Eitner with F. X. Haberl, A.
Lagerberg, & K. F. Pohl. The forthcoming
reprint will include Eitner's own additions
& corrections, edited by George Berkovits.
Available on subscription only (see note
under Musurgia below).*

ERPF, HERMANN
Vom Wesen der neuen Musik. 144
p, 24 mus ex, 1–p bibl, bds. Schwab,
Stuttgart, 1949.   2.25
With detailed technical analyses.

F—

FARGA, FRANZ
Anton Bruckner: ein Lebensbild.
80 p, paper. Humboldt, Wien, 1948.   .75
Geigen und Geiger. 340 p, 154 pl
(pors, etc). Müller, Zürich, (1940)
3rd rev ed n d.   6.50
*For an English translation, by Egon Larsen,
see main Guide entry under Violin.*

Die Wiener Oper von ihren Anfängen
bis 1938. 324 p, 43 pl. Göth, Wien,
1947.   5.00
*Die Oper des Hofes, die Oper des Bürgertums,
und die Oper des Volkes.*

FAVRE-LINGOROW, STELLA
Der Instrumentalstil von Purcell.
116 p, bibl refs, + Anhang (20–p,
240 mus ex), paper. Haupt, Bern,
1950.   3.00
*A scholarly study, v 16 in the series "Berner
Veröffentlichungen zur Musikforschung,"
edited by Ernst Kurth.*

FISCH, SAMUEL
Goethe und die Musik: mit Lied-
beispielen. 106 p, music, bds. Huber,
Frauenfeld, 1949.   3.75

FISCHER, EDWIN
Johann Sebastian Bach: eine Studie.
40 p, flex. Scherz, Bern, 1948.   1.00

FISCHER, KURT VON
Die Beziehungen von Form und
Motiv in Beethovens Instrument-
alwerken. 274 p, mus ex. Heitz,
Strasbourg, 1948.   △
*A scholarly work of musical & psychological
analysis, v 30 in the series "Sammlung mu-
sikwissenschaftlicher Abhandlungen."*

FORKEL, JOHANN NIKOLAUS
   (See also: Neupert "Klavichord.")
Über Johann Sebastian Bachs Leben,
Kunst, und Kunstwerke: für patrio-
tische Verehrer echter musikalischer
Kunst. x, 69 p (facs), + 2–p ex,
paper. (Hoffmeister & Kühnel 1802)
Peters facs repr 1950.   3.50
*A facsimile reprint of the first edition, issued
in this country with an inserted 1-p foreword
(in English) by Ralph Kirkpatrick.*

Same: Bärenreiter, Kassel, 1950 cheap
reprint in prep.   △
*Note: The Haldimann reprint (1946) is O/P,
as apparently is the Terry English translation
(Constable 1920). However, the Stephenson
English translation is included in the David
& Mendel "Bach Reader" (see main Guide
entry under Bach–1).*

FRÖHLICH, JOSEPH
Joseph Fröhlich (1780-1862) über
Joseph Haydn: die älteste Haydn-
Biographie. Ed Adolf Sandberger.
Bosse, Regensburg, 1950/1, in prep.   △

FURTWÄNGLER, WILHELM
Gespräche über Musik. 139 p, paper.
Atlantis, Zürich, 1948.   2.40
*Essays by the noted conductor on conducting,
audiences, tonality, & music in general*

G—

GEORGII, WALTER
Klaviermusik von den Anfängen bis
zur Gegenwart: Geschichte der Musik für Klavier zu 2 und 4 Händen.
xv, 656 p, chart, 329 mus ex, 28-p
bibl. Atlantis, Zürich (1941), 2nd
rev enl ed 1950.   6.50
*An extensively annotated survey of piano
music, including 1-, 3-, 5-, & 6-hand works.*

GERSTBERGER, KARL
Kleines Handbuch der Musik. 252
p, mus ex, paper. Bärenreiter, Kassel, (1932), 5th aug ed 1949.   2.75
Concise subject & biographical dictionary.

GIEGLING, FRANZ
Giuseppe Torelli: ein Beitrag zur
Entwicklungsgeschichte des italien-
ischen Konzerts. 88 p + 36–p thematic index (mus ex), bibl, refs,
paper. Bärenreiter, Kassel, 1949.   2.50

GINZKEY, FRANZ KARL *(ed)*
Genius Mozart. 195 p + 8 pl.
Scientia, Zürich, 1949.   2.25
*Articles, lectures, poems, letters, etc, by the
editor, Grimm, Rossini, Viardot, Grillparzer,
Hoffmann, Wagner, et al.*

GREEFF, PAUL
E. Th. A. Hoffmann: als Musiker
und Musikschriftsteller. 261 p, frontis por, 126 mus ex, bds. Staufen,
Köln, 1948.   3.00

GREGOR, JOSEPH
Kulturgeschichte des Ballets: seine
Gestaltung und Wirksamkeit in der
Geschichte und unter den Künsten.
337 p 264 p, 20 col pl. Scientia, Zü-
rich, n d (1946).   10.00
*An over-all ballet history, particularly notable
for its wealth of photographs & reproductions
of prints.*

GREINER, ALBERT
Wegweiser durch die Stimmbildung.
96 p + 4-p pl (Bildermappe von
Karl Wünsch), mus ex, paper.
Schott, Mainz, 1949.   3.00
*An outline-guide to the author's 5-volume work
on voice cultivation.*

GRÜNINGER, FRITZ
Anton Bruckner: der metaphysische
Kern seiner Persönlichkeit und seiner
Werke. 304 p, frontis por, 4-p bibl.
Naumann, Augsburg, (1930) 2nd ed
1949.   4.75

GURLITT, WILIBALD
Johann Sebastian Bach: der Meister
und sein Werk. 86 p, frontis por, 1-p
bibl, paper. (1933) Reinhardt, Basel,
1936 (1947).   1.80

H—

HAAS, ROBERT MARIA
*See above: Bücken, ed, Handbuch der Musik-
wissenschaft, v 3 & 8.*

HABERL, FRANZ XAVER (co-comp)
See above: Eitner (& others, comps).

HADAMOWSKY, FRANZ & OTTE, HEINZ
Die Wiener Operette: ihre Theater-
und Wirkungsgeschichte. 427 p, 4
col pl, 34 pl (pors, facs, etc), tables,
bds. Bellaria, Wien, 1947.   5.50

HAMEL, FRED & HÜRLIMANN, MARTIN (eds)
Das Atlantisbuch der Musik. 931
p, illus (pors, facs, etc), mus ex, 8-p
bibl. Atlantis, Zürich, (1934) 6th ed
1946.   7.50
*An unusual, richly illustrated, combination
reference book & musical "companion," including articles by many writers, among them
Unger on teaching & theory, Tappolet on new
music, Schünemann on instrumental music,
Johannes Wolf on musicology, etc.*

HAMMA, FRIDOLIN
Meister deutscher Geigenbaukunst.
70 p + 66-p pl (violins, labels), col   △
frontis por. Schuler, Stuttgart, 1948. 16.00
*Limited edition of an unusually handsome
dictionary of violin makers.*

HANDSCHIN, JACQUES
Musikgeschichte im Überblick. 432
p, 22-p bibl. Räber, Luzern, 1948.   7.50
*A noted musicologist's general history of
music, with emphasis on earlier eras.*

Der Toncharakter: eine Einführung
in die Tonpsychologie. xvi, 436 p,
1 pl, mus ex, bibl refs. Atlantis, Zürich, 1948.   7.50
*A scholarly discussion of tonal-relationship
theories from Aristotle & Pythagoras to
Stumpf & von Hornbostel, but on the phenom-
enological level exclusively, with no reference
to recent researches in psychophysiology.*

HEINETZ, WILHELM
*See above: Bücken, ed, Handbuch der Musik-
wissenschaft, v 11.*

HENNING, LAURA
Die Freundschaft Clara Schumanns
mit Johannes Brahms: aus Briefen
und Tagebuchblättern. 147 p, 3
pors, 1-p bibl. Classen, Zürich, 1946. 3.00

HENSEL, WALTHER
Auf den Spuren des Volksliedes:
sprachliche und musikalische Betrachtungen als Beiträge zu seiner
Wesensschau (kleine Volksliedkunde).
103 p, mus ex, paper. Bärenreiter,
Kassel, 1944.   2.25

HEROLD, HUGO & NOATZSCH, RICHARD
Grundlagen allgemeiner Musikbild-
ung: Hilfs- und Nachschlagebuch
für Schüler und Musikfreunde. 114
p, illus, mus ex, paper. Hug, Zürich,
8th ed n d.   1.50
*A dictionary of musical terms: Musiklehre,
Formenlehre, Musikgeschichte, Instrumentenkunde.*

HIEBNER, ARMAND
Musikgeschichte im Querschnitt.
212 p, bds. Amerbach, Basel, 1947.   2.40
*From "Musiken der alten Kulturvölker" to
"19. Jahrhundert und Gegenwart."*

HIRSCH, PAUL & MEYER, KATHI (eds)
Katalog der Musikbibliothek Paul
Hirsch. Band 4: Erstausgaben, Chor-
werke in Partitur, Gesamtausgaben,
Nachschlagewerke, etc.   Ergän-
zungen zu Bd. 1/3. xxviii, 695 p.
University Press, Cambridge, Eng-   △
land.   20.00

Completing a series of catalogues of one of the most noted music libraries. The earlier volumes (published by Breslauer, Berlin, 1928, 1930, 1936), now apparently O/P or not easily available, dealt with Books on music published before 1800, Full scores of operas, Instrumental & vocal editions to c. 1830.

HOESLI, IRMA
Wolfgang Amadeus Mozart: Briefstil eines Musikgenies. 147 p, 4 pors, 1 fac, paper. Artemis, Zürich, 1948.　　3.00

HOFFMANN, E. T. A.
Autobiographische und musikalische und vermischte Schriften. Ed Martin Hürlimann. 543 p, illus, mus ex. Atlantis, Zürich, 1946.　　4.50
Volume 1 of a 5-v set of Selected Works. See also, for a book about Hoffmann, Greeff above.

HOFFMANN, HANS
Vom Wesen der zeitgenössischen Kirchenmusik. 112 p, mus ex, paper. Bärenreiter, Kassel, 1949.　　2.40

HOFMANNSTHAL, HUGO VON
Beethoven: eine Rede. Ed & Nachwort von Willi Schuh. 46 p, bds. (1938) Arche, Zürich, 1949.　　1.00
A lecture delivered 10 December 1920

HOLL, KARL
Verdi. 445 p, 31 pl (pors, etc), bibl refs. (1939) Scientia, Zürich, 1942.　　5.00

HUBER, ANNA GERTRUD
Bach als Meister der "Gemüths-Ergötzung." 72 p + 11 pl + foldout chart (mus ex), 1½-p bibl, paper. Speer, Zürich, 1948, via Peters.　　4.00
Johann Sebastian Bach als Meister der Farben: Beiträge zu der Entwicklungsgeschichte der musikalischen Dynamik. 48 p + 7 pl, mus ex, 2-p bibl, paper. Eulenburg, Zürich, 1949, via Peters.　　4.00

HÜRLIMANN, MARTIN (ed)
(See also above: Beethoven, ed Hürlimann; Hamel & Hürlimann; Hoffmann, ed Hürlimann.)
Besuch bei Beethoven: aus zeitgenössischen Berichten und den Konversationsheften. 215 p + 20 pl (pors, 1 fac, etc). Atlantis, Zürich, 1948.　　3.75
A collection of short pieces about Beethoven by his teachers & pupils (Ries, Czerny, Hirsch), painters (Höfel, Mähler, et al.), musical & other friends (Spohr, Moscheles, Brentano, Grillparzer, Unger, Sontag, et al.).

I—

ISTEL, EDGAR (ed)
E. T. A. Hoffmann: musikalische Aufsätze. Bosse, Regensburg, 1950/1, in prep.　　△

J—

JASPERT, WERNER
Johann Strauss: sein Leben, sein Werk, seine Zeit. 252 p, 11 pl (pors, etc), bibl refs. (1939) Scientia, Zürich, n d (1949).　　4.50

JEPPESEN, KNUD (ed)
Die italienische Orgelmusik am Anfang des Cinquecento: Die "Recerchari, motetti, canzoni, libro primo" des Marco Antonio (Cavazzoni) da Bologna (1523) in Verbindung mit einer Auswahl aus dem "Frottole intabulate da sonare organi" des Andrea Antico da Montona (1517). 130-p text + 82-p music, tables, mus ex, bibl refs, paper. Munksgaard, Kopenhagen, 1943.　　7.50
A standard, scholarly work.
See also main Guide entry under Organ Music for Rawski's English edition, in prep.

K—

KAHL, WILLI (ed)
Selbstbiographien deutscher Musiker des 18. Jahrhunderts. 349 p, facs, bibl refs, paper. Staufen, Köln, 1948.　　4.00
Facsimile reproductions (printed pages) of autobiographical writings by J. S. & C. P. E. Bach, J. W. Hässler, Haydn, J. P. Kellner, J. J. Quantz, J. H. Quiel, G. A. Stölzel, G. P. Telemann; with introduction & notes.

KELLER, HERMANN
Die Orgelwerke Bachs: ein Beitrag zu ihrer Geschichte, Form, Deutung, und Wiedergabe. 228 p, mus ex, tables, paper. Peters, Leipzig, 1948.　　5.00
A general discussion of Baroque & Bachian organ music, followed by detailed analyses, with lists of works according to the order of difficulty, and by Bach Gesellschaft & Peters edition numbering.

KLOTZ, HANS
Das Buch von der Orgel: Über Wesen und Aufbau des Orgelwerkes, Orgelpflege, und Orgelspiel. 148 p, 10 pl, 70 diagrs & mus ex, 5½-p bibl, paper. (1937) Bärenreiter, Kassel, 1949.　　2.75

Über die Orgelkunst der Gotik, der Renaissance, und des Barocks: die alten Registrierungs- und Dispositionsgrundsätze. xxiii, 415 p, tables, mus ex, 8–p bibl. Bärenreiter, Kassel, 1934.   10.00

KOBALD, KARL
Alt-Wiener Musikstätten. 400 + 4 p, 110 pl, bds. Amalthea, Zürich, 1923 (repr 1947).   5.00
Buildings & places associated with music in Vienna and with Gluck, Haydn, Mozart, Beethoven, & Schubert. The fascinating illustrations (12 of which are double-spread plates) include portraits, facsimiles, scenes, etc.

Beethoven: seine Beziehungen zu Wiens Kunst und Kultur, Gesellschaft und Landschaft. 426 + 4 p, 52 pl, 1–p bibl, bds. Amalthea, Zürich, 1927 (repr 1946).   5.00

Franz Schubert. 428 p, 137 pl (pors, facs, etc), 1–p bibl. Amalthea, Zürich, 1921 (repr 1948).   5.00
Marshall's English translation ("Franz Schubert and his times," Knopf 1928) apparently is O/P.

KÖCHEL, LUDWIG VON (*comp*) & EINSTEIN, ALFRED (*ed*)
Chronologisch-thematisches Verzeichnis sämtlicher Tonwerke Wolfgang Amade Mozarts. xlix, 1052 p, mus ex. Edwards repr of B & H 3rd ed 1937 + supplement 1947.   △   12.50
An indispensable reference work (also listed in the main Guide entry under Mozart-3). Köchel's original edition appeared in 1862; Einstein's 3rd ed in 1937 (Breitkopf & Härtel, Leipzig); the present version includes marginal notes & a supplement—"Berichtigungen und Zusätze", (p. 982/1052)—by Einstein.

KOLB, ANNETTE
Mozart. 318 p, 14 pl (pors, etc), 2 facs, mus ex. (1937) Rentsch, Zürich, 1947.   4.00
Franz Schubert: sein Leben. 256 p. (1941) Rentsch, Zürich, 1947.   3.25

KOMORZYNSKI, EGON
Der Vater der Zauberflöte: Emanuel Schikaneders Leben. 239 p, 8 pl (pors, etc). Neff, Wien, 1948.   3.50

KOPP, TILLY (*ed*). See Beethoven above.

KŘENEK, ERNST
Musik im goldenen Westen: das Ton-

schaffen der U. S. A. 74 p, 5 pors, bds. Hollinek, Wien, 1949.   2.50
Note: "Über neue Musik" (1936) apparently is O/P, as is the English translation, by Fles: "Music here and now" (1939).

Selbstdarstellung. 66 p, frontis por, paper. Atlantis, Zürich, 1948.   1.60
Autobiographical & analytical sketch, including a list of works.

KULL, HANS
Dvořáks Kammermusik. x, 203 p, diagrs, mus ex, 1–p bibl, typescript repro, paper. Haupt, Bern, 1943.   5.00
Extensive analyses. ("Berner Veröffentlichungen zur Musikforschung," herausgegeben von Ernst Kurth, Heft 15.)

KURTH, ERNST
Grundlagen des linearen Kontrapunkts: Bachs melodische Polyphonie. xx, 532 p, mus ex. Krompholz, Bern, (1917) 3rd ed 1927 (repr n d, 1948?).   7.50
Musikpsychologie. xii, 324 p, bibl refs. Krompholz, Bern, (1930) 2nd ed 1947.   6.00
Two standard works of musical & psychological analysis by the late founder of a special school of thought in "tone-psychology."

KWASNIK, WALTER
Die Orgel der Neuzeit. 206 p, 27 illus, bds. Staufen, Köln, 1948.   3.00

L—

LACHMANN, ROBERT
See above Bücken, ed. Handbuch der Musikwissenschaft, v 12.

LACROIX, JEAN (*ed*)
Die berühmten Musiker. Tr Hans Schweitzer. 358 p + many pl (some col). Mazenod, Genf, 1946.   17.50
A lavishly illustrated collection of biographical sketches by many authors.

LAGERBERG, A. (*co-comp*)
See above: Eitner (& others, comps).

LARSEN, JENS PETER
Die Haydn-Überlieferung. 335 p, tables, 2½–p bibl, paper. Munksgaard, Kopenhagen, 1939.   7.50
A standard work: a scholarly examination of all the available source materials (Haydn's MSS & catalogues, printed editions, contemporary catalogues, etc), with discussions of the authenticity of doubtful works, a suggested chronology of undated works, & a wealth of other factual information.

LARSEN, JENS PETER (*ed*)
Drei Haydn Kataloge in Faksimile:
mit Einleitung und ergänzenden
Themenverzeichnissen. 141 p (113–
p facs), mus ex, paper. Munksgaard,
Kopenhagen, 1941.   15.00
*A supplement to the work above: facsimile
reproductions of the Entwurf-Katalog, Katalog Kees, & Haydn-Verzeichnis; with thematic indices, notes, & source references.*

LAUX, KARL
Anton Bruckner: Leben und Werk.
89 p, frontis, mus ex, paper. Breitkopf & Härtel (1940), Wiesbaden
ed 1947.   1.50

LEICHTENTRITT, HUGO
Musikalische Formenlehre.   Pref
Xaver Scharwenka. xvi, 464 p, mus
ex, paper. Breitkopf & Härtel,
Leipzig, (1907) 4th rev ed 1948.   6.00
*A standard work on musical form. (An Eng-
glish, revised edition is in preparation:
Harvard Univ. Press 1951, $6.50.)*

LIESS, ANDREAS
Johann Joseph Fux: ein steirischer
Meister des Barock. 90 p, 4 pl (por,
facs, etc), mus ex, 1–p bibl, paper.
Doblinger, Wien, 1948.   3.00
*With a catalogue of works and catalogue of
newly discovered works & MSS.*

Die Musik im Weltbild der Gegenwart: Erkenntnis und Bekenntnis.
266 p, 45 mus ex, bibl refs. Frisch
& Perneder, Lindau im Bodensee,
1949.   3.75

Wiener Barockmusik.   236 p, bds.
Doblinger, Wien, 1946.   7.50

LISZT, FRANZ
Frédéric Chopin: nach der Urfassung
von 1852, übersetzt von Hans
Kühner.   187 p, illus. bds. Amerbach, Basel, 1948.   3.00
*For an English translation (by Broadhouse),
see the main Guide entry under Chopin–1).*

M—

MAHRENHOLZ, CHRISTHARD
Glockenkunde. 43 p, diagr, tables,
mus ex, paper. Bärenreiter, Kassel,
1948.   1.50

Die Orgelregister: ihre Geschichte
und ihr Bau. xvi, 324 p, 8 pl, 3–p
bibl, paper. Bärenreiter, Kassel,
1930.   10.00

MAINWARING, JOHN
G. F. Händel: nach Johann Matthe-
sons deutscher Ausgabe von 1761,
mit andern Dokumenten hrsg. von
Bernhard Paumgartner. 240 p, frontis por, 2–p bibl. Atlantis, Zürich,
1947.   4.00

MAINWARING, JOHN; MÜLLER VON ASOW,
HEDWIG & E. H. (*eds*)
Georg Friedrich Händel: Biographie
von John Mainwaring; Briefe und
Schriften, herausgegeben im Auftrage
des Internationalen Musiker-Brief-
Archivs von H. & E. H. Müller von
Asow. 219 p, 14 pl (pors, facs, etc).
Frisch & Perneder, Lindau am Bo-
densee, 1949.   3.50
Life, p 13/89; letters etc, p 93/207.

MATTHAEI, KARL
Vom Orgelspiel: eine kurzgefasste
Würdigung der künstlerisch orgelge-
mässen Interpretationsweise und
ihrer klanglichen Ausdrucksmittel.
vi, 283 p + 8 pl, mus ex, 9–p bibl,
paper. Breitkopf & Härtel, Leipzig,
(1936) 2nd rev enl ed 1949.   4.00

MATTHAEI, KARL (*ed*)
Bach-Gedenkschrift 1950: im Auftrag
der Internationalen Bach-Gesell-
schaft. 216 p, tables, mus ex, bibl
refs. Atlantis, Zürich, 1950.   4.50
*Articles (some in French, some in English)
by some 16 contributors, including Ausbacher,
Besch, Ferchault, Pfatteicher, Ramin,
Schrade, Schweitzer, Westrup, et al.*

MATZKE, HERMANN
Unser technisches Wissen von der
Musik: Einführung in die musikalische Technologie. 604 p, 204
illus. Frisch & Perneder, Lindau
am Bodensee, 1949.   10.00
*An extraordinary, detailed study of the
materials used in musical instruments,
acoustics & electroacoustics, & the technology
of various instruments.*

MENDELSSOHN-BARTHOLDY, FELIX
Denkmal in Wort und Bild. Ed Max
F. Schneider & Willi Reich. 150 p +
15–p music facs, 10 pl (pors & facs)—
1 in col. Amerbach, Basel, 1947.   5.00
*Excerpts from Mendelssohnian letters & docu-
ments, with a biographical introduction.*

Felix Mendelssohn-Bartholdy: sein
Leben in Briefen.   Ausgewählt &
eingeleitet von Reinhold Sietz. 273

p, 2 b&w pors, 2 facs, 2–p bibl, bds. Staufen, Köln, 1948.   2.50

MENKE, WERNER
Die Geschichte der Bach- und Händel-Trompete.   xiii, 233 p, 5 pl, 4 b&ws, 6-p mus ex, paper.   Reeves, London, n d (1934?).   3.75
German & English text—the latter is in Gerald Abraham's translation.

MERSMANN, HANS
(See also above: Bücken, ed, Handbuch der Musikwissenschaft, v 6.)
Neue Musik: in den Strömungen unserer Zeit.   59 p, paper.   Steeger, Bayreuth, 1949.   1.50

MEYER, KATHI (*co-ed*)
See above: *Hirsch & Meyer (eds).*

[MEYNELL, ESTHER]
Die kleine Chronik der Anna Magdalena Bach.   248 p.   Scherz, Bern, n d.   4.00
For the original English version, see the main Guide entry under Bach–2.   Although this is a fictitious biography of Bach, the German publishers consciously or unconsciously imply its authenticity by omitting (in their ambiguous preface) any mention of either the author's or the German translator's name.

MIES, PAUL
Der Charakter der Tonarten: eine Untersuchung.   228 p, tables, mus ex, 1–p bibl, paper.   Staufen, Köln, 1948.   3.50
A detailed, technical study.
Wege zur modernen Musik.   Some 190 p, mus ex.   Staufen, Köln, in prep.   Δ

MINGOTTI, ANTONIO
Maria Cebotari: das Leben einer Sängerin.   145 p, 25 photos.   Hellbrunn, Salzburg, 1950.   3.25
A memorial biography of the noted soprano, with a 3-p list of roles & films.

MÖRIKE, EDUARD
Mozart auf der Reise nach Prag: novelle.   79 p.   (1855) Scherz, Bern, 4th ed 1946.   1.00
For an English translation (by Walter & Catherine Alison Phillips) of this fictional episode in Mozart's life, see the main Guide entry under Mozart–2.

MOSER, HANS ALBRECHT
Über die Kunst des Klavierspiels. 128 p, bds.   Scherz, Bern, 1947.   2.75

MOZART, WOLFGANG AMADEUS
(See also above: Hoesli, Köchel & Einstein.)
Briefe.   Ed & Nachwort Willi Reich. 419 p.   Manesse, Zürich, 1948.   2.00
Pocket-size edition of selected letters.
Denkmal im eigenen Wort: Lebensdokumente.   Ed & intro Willi Reich. 79 p, bibl refs, bds.   Schwabe, Basel, (1945), 2nd ed 1947.   1.25
Wolfgang Amadeus Mozart: Briefwechsel und Aufzeichnungen.   Gesamtausgabe herausgegeben im Auftrage des Internationalen Musiker-Brief-Archivs von Hedwig & E. H. Müller von Asow.   4 v. Frisch & Perneder, Lindau im Bodensee, 1949/51.   Δ   24.00
V 1: Familienbriefwechsel, 1769-1775.   xxviii, 359 p, mus ex. (1942) new ed 1949.
V 2: Familienbriefwechsel, 1777-1779.   691 p, mus ex. (1942) new ed 1949.
V 3 & 4.   1951, in prep.
New edition (which will run to some 2000 pages in all) of a collection originally published (1942) in 2 volumes, edited by E. H. Müller von Asow alone.

MÜLLER, ERNST
Robert Schumann: eine Bildnisstudie.   209 p, 8 pl (pors, facs), ½-p bibl.   Walter, Olten, 1950.   2.75

MÜLLER VON ASOW, HEDWIG & E. H. (*eds*)
See above: *Bach, Mainwaring, Mozart; & below: Schütz.*

MÜLLER-BLATTAU, JOSEPH
Genealogie der musikalisch-Bachischen Familie: nach Ph. E. Bachs Aufzeichnungen   wiederhergestellt und erläutert von Joseph Müller-Blattau.   24 p, 1 b&w (genealogical tree by Lisa Hampe), paper.   Bärenreiter, Kassel, n d (1950?).   .80

MUSURGIA (*Reprints*)
Note: This is a series of photolithographic reprints of important musicological works, mostly German, that have been O/P or otherwise unavailable for many years.   Issued primarily for libraries, universities, etc (but often of great interest to individual specialists), they are sold on subscription only, usually at a lower rate if the subscription is entered before publication.   Some of these reprints are temporarily O/P, but re-

issues are pending; others are pending publication; and in each case, of course, actual publication, or re-publication, depends on the receipt of a sufficient number of subscriptions to cover printing costs. For detailed information & rates, address Musurgia Publishers, 4 East 41st Street, New York City 17.

See:

Adler (pending)	Eitner & others
Arginteanu (pending)	(pending)
Bücken	Springer & others
Eitner (temp O/P)	(temp O/P)
	Zahn (pending)

See also: App Ie (Coussemaker & Gerbert).

N—

NEF, KARL
Einführung in die Musikgeschichte. 328 p, mus ex, 4–p bibl. (1919), Atlantis, Zürich, 3rd ed (ed Walter Nef) 1945.   5.00

Geschichte unserer Musikinstrumente.   213 p, 75 pl, brief bibl. (1925?), Amerbach, Basel, 2nd ed rev Edgar Refardt) 1949.   3.50

NETTL, PAUL
Goethe und Mozart: eine Betrachtung.   45 p, 2 silhouettes, mus ex, paper. Bechtle, Esslingen, 1949.   1.00

NEUMANN, WERNER
Handbuch der Kantaten Joh. Seb. Bachs. 202 p, paper. Breitkopf & Härtel, Leipzig, 1947, via Associated 1950.   3.00

A detailed reference guide to all the sacred & secular cantatas, with titles, voice registers, instrumentation, Bach Gesellschaft references, etc, for each aria & chorus. The paper edition is available in the United States via Associated Music Publishers, with cover & title page (only) in English.   Also listed in the main Guide entry under Bach–2.

NEUPERT, HANNS
Das Klavichord: Geschichte und technische Betrachtung des "eigentlichen Claviers."   70 p, 12 illus, mus ex, bibl refs, paper.   Bärenreiter, Kassel, 1948.   2.00

With an appendix: "Von der wahren Güte der Clavichorde" (nach einem Manuskript von J. N. Forkel).

NIESSEN, CARL
Die deutsche Oper der Gegenwart.

Some 100 p + 400 illus.   Bosse, Regensburg, 1950/1, in prep.   Δ
A history of opera in the last 100 years, extensively illustrated with stage scenes & sets (9 in color), 63 composers' portraits & facsimiles, etc.

NIETZSCHE, FRIEDRICH
Randglossen zu Bizets "Carmen." ? p, mus ex. Bosse, Regensburg, 1950/1, in prep.   Δ
Probably a re-issue of H. Daffner's edition, published in 1912.

NIEVERGELT, EDWIN
Beethovens Sinfonien: Einführung in die neun Sinfonien. 40 p, paper. Apollo, Zürich, 1945.   .50

NOATZSCH, RICHARD
See above: Herold & Noatzsch.

NOHL, WALTHER
Goethe und Beethoven.   104 p, paper. (1929) Bosse, Regensburg, repr n d.   1.00

NOWAK, LEOPOLD
Joseph Haydn. 628 p, 230 illus, 40 mus ex, 5 p bibl, cloth.   Amalthea, Zürich, 1951.   6.50

O—

ODERMATT, HERMANN
Bruckners Sinfonien: Einführung in die neun Sinfonien. 40 p, bibl refs, paper. Apollo, Zürich, n d.   .50

OREL, ALFRED
Johannes Brahms: ein Meister und sein Weg. 270 p, 8 pl (pors, facs, etc), 1–p bibl. Walter, Olten, 1948.   2.75

OTTERSTRÖM, THORWALD
See the main Guide entry under Modulation: "A Theory" (1935), with text in German as well as English.

OVERHOFF, KURT
Richard Wagners Tristan Partitur: eine musikalisch-philosophische Deutung. 88 p, mus ex, bds. Steeger, Bayreuth, 1948.   1.80

P—

PANÒFF, PETR ASSÈN
See above: Bücken, ed, Handbuch der Musikwissenschaft, v 13.

PAUMGARTNER, BERNHARD
(See also above: Mainwaring "Händel.")

Mozart. 551 p, 7 pl (pors), 3–p annot bibl. (1927) Atlantis, Zürich, (1940) 3rd ed 1945.   6.00

Franz Schubert. 368 p, 1 por, 2 facs, 2–p bibl. Atlantis, Zürich, 2nd ed 1947.   5.00

PFISTER, KURT

Das Leben Rossinis: Gesetz und Triumph der Oper. 162 p + 36 pl (pors, facs, etc), 1–p bibl note. Scientia, Zürich, 1948.   4.50

Richard Strauss: Weg, Gestalt, Denkmal. 170 p + 87 pl (pors, fac, etc). Bergland, Wien, 1949.   4.75

PFROGNER, HERMANN

Von Wesen und Wertung neuer Harmonik. 45 p, mus ex, bibl refs, paper. Steeger, Bayreuth, 1949.   1.80
"Zur Wesensfrage der Harmonik" & "Von neufunktionaler Wertung der neuen Harmonik."

PIERSIG, JOHANNES

Das Weltbild des Heinrich Schütz. 91 p, 2–p bibl & bibl refs, paper. Bärenreiter, Kassel, 1949.   2.25

POPPEN, HERMANN

Max Reger: Leben und Werk. 103 p, frontis por, 1½–p bibl, paper. Breitkopf & Härtel, Leipzig, (1917), 2nd ed 1947.   1.00

PREUSSNER, EBERHARD

Die musikalischen Reisen des Herrn von Uffenbach: aus einem Reisetagebuch des Johann Friedrich A. von Uffenbach aus Frankfurt a. M., 1712-1716. 195 p, 25 pl (facs, etc). Bärenreiter, Kassel, 1949.   5.00

R—

RAUPACH, HANS *(ed)*

Das wahre Bildnis Johann Sebastian Bachs: eine Erstveröffentlichung mit Erläuterungen von Hans Raupach. 23 p (text) + mounted-insert por + fold-out sheet with 7 pors, paper. Möseler, Wolfenbüttel, 1950.   2.50
Handsome reproduction, with notes, of a hitherto-unknown Bach portrait by Elias Gottlieb Hausmann (1748).

REDLICH, HANS FERDINAND

Claudio Monteverdi: Leben und Werk. 232 p, 8 pl (pors, facs), mus ex, 5–p bibl. Walter, Olten, 1949.

REFARDT, EDGAR
(See also below: Schuh, ed: Schweizer Musikbuch; v 2 with Refardt as co-editor.)

Johannes Brahms, Anton Bruckner, Hugo Wolf: drei wiener Meister des 19. Jahrhunderts; ihr Leben und Werk in kurzen Biographien. 229 p. Amerbach, Basel, 1949.   4.00

REHBERG, WALTER & PAULA

Johannes Brahms: sein Leben und Werk. 655 p, 16 pl (pors, etc), 2 facs, 59 mus ex, 2–p bibl. Artemis, Zürich, 1947.   6.50

Frédéric Chopin: sein Leben und sein Werk. 567 p, 17 pl (pors, facs, etc) 67 mus ex, 1–p bibl. Artemis, Zürich, 1949.   6.50

Franz Schubert: sein Leben und Werk. 471 p, 4 pl (pors, etc), 92 mus ex, 2–p bibl. Artemis, Zürich, 1946.   5.00

REICH, WILLI

Richard Wagner: Leben, Fühlen, Schaffen. 232 p, 8 pl (pors, facs, etc). Walter, Olten, 1948.   2.75

REICH, WILLI *(ed)*
(See also above: Beethoven, Mendelssohn, Mozart; & below: Schumann, Spitteler, Widmann.)

Joseph Haydn: Briefe und Lebensdokumente. 264 p, 12 pl (pors, etc), bibl refs. Stocker, Luzern, 1946.   4.50

Bekenntnis zu Mozart. 318 p, 13 pl (pors, etc). Stocker, Luzern, 1945.   4.50
An anthology of pieces by various authors.

Musik in romantischer Schau. 2 v. Amerbach, Basel, 1946/7.

V 1: Visionen der Dichter. 118 p, bds, 1946.   1.35

V 2: Worte der Musiker. 128 p, bds, 1947.   1.35
Anthologies of writings on music by poets (Eichendorff, Goethe, Mörike, et al.) & musicians (Schumann, Liszt, Berlioz, et al.).

Schubert-Brevier: aus den Dokumenten seines Lebens. 91 p. Classen, Zürich, 1949.   1.50

Hugo-Wolf-Rhapsodie: aus Briefen und Schriften. 94 p. Classen, Zürich, 1947.   2.00

RÉVÉSZ, GÉZA
Einführung in die Musikpsychologie.
314 p, 30 pl, 27 tables, 47 mus ex, 5–p
bibl. Francke, Bern, 1946.   6.50
*"Gehör, Laut, und Ton;" "Grundprobleme
der Tonpsychologie & Musikpsychologie."*

RIEMANN, HUGO
Kleines Handbuch der Musikgeschichte: mit Periodisierung nach Stil-
prinzipien und Formen. viii, 296 p,
mus ex, 4–p bibl, bds. Breitkopf &
Härtel, Leipzig, (1907) 7th ed 1947.   4.00
Reprinted from the 5th rev edition.

ROLLAND, ROMAIN
Ludwig van Beethoven. Tr L. Lang-
nese-Hug. 160 p, 12 pl (pors, etc),
8–p annot bibl & iconography, bds.
Rotapfel, Zürich, (1936) new ed 1948.   3.75
*Originally in French (1928): see App Ia.
The English translation (1929) is O/P.*
Goethe und Beethoven. Tr Anton
Kippenberg. 105 p, 16 pl (pors, etc),
bds. Rotapfel, Zürich, new ed 1948.   2.75
Originally in French (1930).
Das Leben G. F. Händels. Tr L.
Langnese-Hug. 280 p, mus ex, 2–p
annot bibl, bds. Rotapfel, Zürich,
(1925) repr n d.   2.50
*Originally in French (1910). The English
translation by Hull (1916) is O/P.*

ROTH, ERNST
Vom Vergänglichen in der Musik:
ein Versuch. 119 p, bds. Atlantis,
Zürich, 1949.   1 75

RUTZ, HANS
Neue Oper: Gottfried von Einem und
seine Oper "Dantons Tod."   70 p,
4 photos, mus ex, paper. Universal,
Wien, 1947.   1.00
*With essays by Caspar Neher, Bernhard
Paumgartner, Schneditz, & Schuh.*
Oesterreichs grosse Musiker in Doku-
menten der Zeit: Haydn, Mozart,
Beethoven. 335 p, illus? Oesterrei-
chische Buchgemeinschaft, Wien,
1949.   △
Hans Pfitzner: Musik zwischen den
Zeiten. 160 p, frontis por, 2–p bibl.
Humboldt, Wien, 1949.   3.00

S—

SACHS, CURT
*See above: Bücken, ed, Handbuch der Musik-
wissenschaft, v 1.*

SANDBERGER, ADOLF (*ed*)
See above: Fröhlich (Haydn).

SCHAEFFNER, GEORG
Claude Debussy und das Poetische
(aus Igors Papieren).   420 p.
Francke, Bern, 1943.   3.00

SCHENK, ERICH
Kleine Wiener Musikgeschichte. 208
p, 16 pors, bds. Neff, Wien, 1946.   2.00

SCHERCHEN, HERMANN
Musik für Jedermann: ein Lernbuch
zum Selbstunterricht. 157 p, diagrs,
193 mus ex. Mondial, Winterthur,
1950.   4.00
*An important new elementary theory book by
a noted conductor.*
Vom Wesen der Musik. 215 p, mus
ex. Mondial, Winterthur, n d (1946). 6.50
*V 1 of "Das moderne Musikempfinden"
series, with studies of the works & influences
of Joseph Sauveur (the acoustician), Bach, &
Beethoven. (An English ed was pub by
Dobson in 1950; the U. S. A. Regnery publication—listed in prep on p 5—is not yet out.)*

SCHIEDERMAIR, LUDWIG
Musik am Rheinstrom: Entwicklung-
en und Wesenheiten, Gestalten und
Schicksale. 270 p + 4–p pl, 6 b&ws
(pors, facs, etc), mus ex, 4–p bibl.
Staufen, Köln, 1947.   3.00
Musikalische Begegnungen: Erlebnis
und Erinnerung. 231 p, frontis por,
bds. Staufen, Köln, 1948.   3.00
The memoirs of a noted musicologist.

SCHMIEDER, WOLFGANG (*ed*)
See below: Spitta; & main Guide: Bach-2.

SCHMID, GOTTFRIED (*ed*)
Musica aeterna: eine Darstellung des
Musikschaffens aller Zeiten und
Völker unter besonderer Berücksich-
tigung des Musiklebens der Schweiz
und desjenigen unserer Tage. 2 v:
vii, 367; 404 p, illus, mus ex. Metz,
Zürich, 1948.   24.00
*A lavishly illustrated miscellany, with con-
tributions by many authors, in four parts:
"Allgemeines & Historisches," "Unsere
Zeit," "Die musikalischen Gattungen," and
"Unsere Schweiz."*

SCHNEIDER, MAX (*ed*)
See below: Springer, Schneider, & Wolffheim.

SCHNEIDER, MAX FERDINAND (*ed*)
*See also above: Mendelssohn letters (ed
Schneider & Reich.)*

Alte Musik in der bildenden Kunst
Basels. 43 p + 78 pl, bibl refs, bds.
Holbein, Basel, 1941, via Musurgia. 3.75
Reproductions of old (up to the 16th century)
prints dealing with music & musicians, with
an introduction & detailed notes.

Musik der Neuzeit in der bildenden
Kunst Basels. 102 p + 120 pl, bibl
refs, bds. Holbein, Basel, 1944, via
Musurgia. 7.50
A companion volume covering the period from
around 1520 to the present. The reproduc-
tions are grouped by subjects: 1. Konzert- und
Hausmusik; 2. Militär- und Volksmusik; 3.
Musikerbildnisse.

SCHOPENHAUER, ARTHUR
Arthur Schopenhauer: Schriften über
Musik. Ed Karl Stabenow. Bosse,
Regensburg, 1950/1, in prep. △

SCHUH, WILLI
Über Opern von Richard Strauss. 157
p, paper. Atlantis, Zürich, 1947. 2.40
"Salome," "Elektra," "Rosenkavalier," "Ar-
iadne," "Frau ohne Schatten," "Ägyptische
Helena," "Schweigsame Frau," "Friedens-
tag," "Daphne," & "Capriccio."
Zeitgenössische Musik. 137 p, paper.
Atlantis, Zürich, 1947. 2.00
Debussy, Strauss, Pfitzner, Scriabin, Schoen-
berg, Bartók, Stravinsky, Kaminski, Berg,
Martinu, Hindemith, Gershwin, Křenek,
Shostakovitch, & Britten.

SCHUH, WILLI (ed)
(See also above: Hofmannsthal; and below:
R. Strauss, Wagner.)
Schweizer Musikbuch und Musiker-
Lexikon. 2 v: 421, 220 p, photos, mus
ex, bibl refs. Atlantis, Zürich, 1939. 7.20
V 1: "Geschichte der Musik in der Schweiz,"
with contributions by many authors and
lavishly illustrated. V 2: "Das schweizer
Musikleben," a biographical dictionary (no
illustrations), for which Edgar Refardt is
co-editor.

SCHUMANN, ROBERT
Aus Kunst und Leben. Ed & intro
Willi Reich. 136 p, frontis por, bds.
Schwabe, Basel, 1945. 1.50
Selected Schumann writings on music.

SCHÜNEMANN, GEORG (ed)
Lieder von Goethe komponiert von
Franz Schubert: Nachbildung der
Eigenschrift aus dem Besitz der
Preussischen Staatsbibliothek. 57 p,
21 illus (pors, facs, etc) mus ex, bibl

refs; + 31-p music facs, bds. Frisch,
Berlin, 1943. 15.00
Facsimile reproductions (with notes) of the
16 Goethe Lieder, including "Heidenröslein,"
"An Mignon," "Gretchen am Spinnrade,"
"Der Erlkönig," etc.

SCHÜTZ, HEINRICH
Heinrich Schütz: Briefe und Schrift-
en. Ed Hedwig & E. H. Müller von
Asow. Bosse, Regensburg, 1950/1,
in prep. △

SCHWEITZER, ALBERT
J. S. Bach. Forew Charles Marie
Widor. xvi, 843 p, 5 pl (pors, etc),
mus ex. Breitkopf & Härtel, Leip-
zig, (1908) 1947. 14.00
For an English translation by Ernest New-
man (1911/23), see main Guide entry under
Bach-1.

Albert Schweitzers Leben und Denken. Sel & ed Kurt Bergel. xviii,
104, lxvii p, frontis por, 3-p bibl.
Holt 1949. 1.90
A school textbook, with introduction in Eng-
lish, of selections from Schweitzer's auto-
biographical writings, plus a 67-p German
vocabulary at the back of the book.

SIETZ, REINHOLD
(See also above: Mendelssohn letters, ed
Sietz.)
Carl Loewe: ein Gedenkbuch zum
150. Geburtstag. 69 p, mus ex, 1-p
bibl, paper. Staufen, Köln, 1948. 1.00

SLEZAK, LEO
Meine sämtlichen Werke. Ed Roy
Temple House & Johannes Malth-
aner. vi, 138, lxxiv p, illus. Holt
1937. 1.75

A school textbook, with 36 pages of exercises,
& a 74-p German vocabulary at the back of
the book. For an English version of Slezak's
memoirs, see main Guide entry under Slezak.

SMEND, FRIEDRICH
Johann Sebastian Bach: bei seinem
Namen gerufen. Eine Notenin-
schrift und ihre Deutung. 36 p +
9 pl (pors, etc), mus ex + separate
sheet (Beilage) of mus ex, bds. Bärenreiter, Kassel, 1950. 1.80
Discussions & solutions of Bach canons.

SMOLLE, KURT
Beethovens "Unsterbliche Geliebte":
eine Studie. 39 p, 1½-p bibl, paper.
Europa, Wien, 1947. 1.00

SPITTA, PHILIPP
Johann Sebastian Bach. Gekürzte
(Volks-) Ausgabe mit Anmerkungen
und Zusätzen von Wolfgang Schmieder. xi, 388 p, frontis por, bibl refs.
Breitkopf & Härtel, Leipzig, (1935)
3rd ed 1949.   3.75
*A drastically abridged version of the famous
biography (originally 1873/80), which apparently is O/P both in German and in the English translation of 1884/5.*

SPITTELER, CARL
Musikalische Essays.   Ed & intro
Willi Reich. 115 p, bds. Schwabe,
Basel, 1947.   1.40

SPRINGER, HERMANN; SCHNEIDER, MAX &
WOLFFHEIM, WERNER (eds)
Miscellanea musicæ bio-bibliograph-
ica: Musikgeschichtliche Quellennach-
weise als Nachträge und Verbesserung-
en zu Eitners Quellenlexikon, in Verbindung mit der Internationalen
Musikgesellschaft herausgegeben ...
3 v in 1: 435 p. (Breitkopf & Härtel
1912/6), Musurgia photolith repr
1947.   △
*A standard reference work: the addendum to
R. Eitner's "Biographisch-Bibliographisches
Quellenlexikon" (see Eitner above). Both of
these works are temporarily O/P (see note
under Musurgia above), but are scheduled for
re-issue. The former subscription rate was
$9.75 for the "Miscellanea;" $117.35 for both
it & the "Quellenlexikon."*

STABENOW, KARL (ed)
See above: Schopenhauer.

STAIGER, EMIL
Musik und Dichtung. **119 p, paper.**
Atlantis, Zürich, 1947.   2.00
*Discussions of Bach's organ works, Gluck's
operas, Goethe & Mozart, "Deutsche Romantik," "Der Rosenkavalier," Schoeck, & Honegger.*

STEGLICH, RUDOLF
Wege zu Bach. 208 p, 5 pl (por, facs,
etc), mus ex, 2–p bibl note, bds.
Bosse, Regensburg, 1949.   2.75
*Notes on Bach's life & works, including com-
ments by Goethe, Zelter, Hoffmann, Schumann, Chopin, Berlioz, Schweitzer, et al.*

STRAUSS, RICHARD
Betrachtungen und Erinnerungen.
Hrsg. Willi Schuh. 206 p, 2–p bibl.
Atlantis, Zürich, 1949.   2.75
Interviews, speeches, & articles.

STROBEL, HEINRICH
Debussy. 296 p, 2 pors. **Atlantis,**
Zürich, (1940) 3rd ed 1943.   4.00
Paul Hindemith. 144 p + 4-p music,
por, tables, mus ex, paper. Schott,
Mainz, (1928) 3rd rev enl ed 1948, via
Associated.   2.40

T—

TENSCHERT, ROLAND
Salzburg und seine Festspiele. 424
p, 80–p photos, bds. Oesterreich-
ischer Bundesverlag für Unterricht,
Wissenschaft und Kunst, Wien, 1947. 3.50
*A detailed, extensively illustrated study, with
a list of stage works produced at the festival
up to 1947.*
Richard Strauss und Wien: eine
Wesensverwandtschaft, 174 p, 27 pl
(pors, facs, etc), 9 b&ws, mus ex, bds.
Hollinek, Wien, 1949.   3.75

THIELE, EUGEN
Die Chorfugen Johann Sebastian
Bachs. 223 p, mus ex, bibl refs,
paper. Haupt, Bern, 1936.   3.00
*"Berner Veröffentlichungen zur Musikfor-
schung," Heft 8.*

THOMAS, KURT
Lehrbuch der Chorleitung. **3 v.**
Breitkopf & Härtel, Leipzig, 1935/48.
V 1. 148 p + 8 pl, diagrs, mus ex,
1–p bibl, paper. (1935) 6th ed 1949. 2.75
V 2. 121 p, mus ex, paper. (1937)
4th ed 1949.   2.75
V 3. 73 p, mus ex, paper. (1948)
2nd ed 1949.   2.25
*An extremely comprehensive & detailed study
of both the theoretical & practical aspects
of choral conducting & choir-training, including program-building, the accompaniment of soloists, boys' choirs, & composition.*

TOBEL, RUDOLF VON
Pablo Casals. 140 p, 27 photos (Paul
Senn), 1–p bibl. Rotapfel, Zürich,
(1941) 2nd rev ed 1945.   3.00

U—

URSPRUNG, OTTO
*See above: Bücken, ed, Handbuch der Musik-
wissenschaft, v 9.*

V—

VALENTIN, ERICH
Mozart. 351 p, frontis por, bibl refs,
bds. Seifert, Hameln, 1947.   3.50

Georg Philipp Telemann, 1681–
1767: eine Biographie. 68 p, frontis
por & autograph + 2 b&ws, bibl refs,
paper. Seifert, Hameln. 1947.   1.50

VOGT, HANS
Pianistische Grundbegriffe: Vorbe-
merkungen zu einer Lehre des Kla-
vierspieles. 48 p, paper. Amerbach,
Basel, 1949.   1.50

W—

WACKERNAGEL, PETER (ed)
(See above: Bach, Fantasia).

WAGNER, RICHARD
Die Briefe Richard Wagners an
Judith Gautier. Mit einer Einleitung,
"Die Freundschaft Richard Wagners
mit Judith Gautier." Ed Willi Schuh.
197 p, 8 pl (pors, facs, etc), bibl refs.
Rotapfel, Zürich, n d (1936)   3.00

WEIGL, BRUNO (ed)
Handbuch der Orgelliteratur: voll-
ständige Umarbeitung des Führers
durch die Orgelliteratur, herausgegeben von Kothe-Forchhammer, neu-
bearbeitet von O. Burkert ... zusam-
mengestellt mit kritischen Erläuterungen und Angabe der Schwierig-
keitsgrade versehen von Bruno Weigl.
viii, 318 p, 5–p + 12–p annot bibls.
Leuckart, Leipzig, 1931 (repr n d).   5.00
The original "Führer," compiled by B. Kothe
& Th. Forchhammer, was published in 1890;
O. Burkert's revision in 1909. The present
version (a standard reference work), includes,
besides its immensely detailed lists of organ
music of all types (solo, 4-hands, with orch.,
with voices, etc), a Section XV, "Schriften
über Orgelbau, Orgelgeschichte," p 279/283,
and "Schriften über Musik," p 284/295.

WEINGARTNER, FELIX
Lebenserinnerungen. 2 v: 377, 464
p + 48 pl (pors, etc), 9 facs. Füssli,
Zürich, v 1 (1923) 2nd ed 1928; v 2
1929.   12.00
The noted conductor's memoirs. An English
translation by Wolff (1937) is O/P.

WEINGARTNER, FELIX & STUDER, CARMEN
Franz Schubert: sein Leben und sein
Werk.   230 p, 1–p bibl. Walter,
Olten, 1947.   2.75

WIDMANN, JOSEPH VIKTOR
Johannes Brahms in Erinnerungen.
133 p, 3 pl, bds. (1898) Amerbach,
Basel, new rev aug ed (ed Willi
Reich) 1947.   1.50

WOLFF, WERNER
Anton Bruckner: Genie und Einfalt.
288 p, illus (pors, facs), mus ex.
Atlantis, Zürich, 1948.   5.00
The revised German edition of a biography
originally published in English (1942).
(See the main Guide entry under Bruckner.)

WOLFFHEIM, WERNER (ed)
See above: Springer, Schneider, & Wolffheim.

WÖRNER, KARL H.
Musik der Gegenwart: Geschichte
der neuen Musik. 259 p, 28 pors,
mus ex, 8–p bibl, paper. Schott,
Mainz, 1949.   3.70
A discussion of contemporary composers of
the generations before & after 1890.

Robert Schumann.   371 p, 16 pl
(pors, facs, etc), mus ex, 4–p bibl.
Atlantis, Zürich, 1949.   4.50

Z—

ZAGIBA, FRANZ
P. J. Tschaikowskij.   Some 700 p,
50 illus & facs, 126 mus ex. Amalthea, Zürich, 1950 in prep.   △

ZAHN, JOHANNES
Die Melodien der deutschen evan-
gelischen Kirchenlieder: aus den
Quellen geschöpft und mitgetheilt.
6 v. (1888/93), Musurgia photolith
repr pending.   △
A standard reference work containing more
than 8000 hymn tunes, an extensive bibliography (v 5), & indices (v 6). Definite publication plans depend on subscriptions (see note
under Musurgia above).

ZERKAULEN, HEINRICH
Beethoven in Amsterdam: Eine Er-
zählung.   Ed T. A. Rattler.   76 p
(40 p text), paper.   Oxford 1938.   .65
A portrait of Beethoven as a child, designed
as a textbook for 2nd year college German
classes; with introduction (in English).

ZIMMERMANN, CURT
Alte Meister der Musik: Palestrina,
Monteverdi, Schütz, Purcell, A.
Scarlatti, Lully; ihr Leben und Schaf-
fen in kurzen Biographien. 253 p, 6
pors, 2½–p bibl, bds.   Amerbach,
Basel, 1948.   3.75

APPENDIX Ic: Books in Italian

(A selected list only — arranged in alphabetical order by authors' names)

A—

ADAMI, GIUSEPPE
Puccini: il romanzo della vita di Giacomo Puccini. 269 p, 16 pl (pors, facs, etc), paper. (1935, 2nd ed 1938) Rizzoli, Milano, 1942 (1944). 2.00

ALALEONA, DOMENICO
Storia dell' oratorio musicale in Italia. 382 p, mus ex, 12–p bibl (of oratorios), paper. (1908) Bocca, Milano, 1945. 4.00

B—

BACCHELLI, RICCARDO
Rossini. 339 p, 14 pl (pors, etc), 1–p bibl note, paper. Unione Tipografico, Torin, 1941. 3.00

C—

CAPRI, ANTONIO
Tartini. 581 p, 22 illus + thematic catalogue, 6–p bibl, paper. Garzanti, Milano, 1945. 2.75

CAVAZZUTI, PIETRO
Bellini: a Londra. 77 p, paper, Barbèra, Firenze, 1945. 1.20

CORTE, ANDREA DELLA
Gluck e i suoi tempi. vii, 213 p, some 28 pl (pors, facs, etc), paper. Sansoni, Firenze, 1948. 2.50

Toscanini. 145 p, paper. Pellicano, Vicenza, 1946. 2.00

For a French edition, see also App Ia.

F—

FAILONI, SERGIO
Senza sordina. Intro Renzo Rossellini. 187 p, paper. Piccinelli, Roma, 1946. 2.50

A conductor's collection of essays.

G—

GALILEI, VINCENZO
Dialogo della musica antica e della moderna. Intro Fabio Fano. 218 p, mus ex, paper. (1581, 2nd ed 1602), Minuziano, Milano, 1947. 2.00

A famous historical work by the father of the great astronomer and himself an important musician of his time (c. 1520–1591). The "dialogue" is in two parts: "Questioni di acustica e di estetica" & "Strumenti musicale e strumentisti."

GIAZOTTO, REMO
Tomaso Albinoni: musico di violino dilettanto veneto (1671–1750), con il catalogo tematico delle musiche per strumenti. 363 p + 14 pl (facs, por, etc), 197 mus ex, bibl refs, paper. Bocca, Milano, 1945. 3.00

The only extended study of a composer highly esteemed by Bach. The work includes analyses of Albinoni's chamber music (with thematic catalogue, p 325/51) and a significant general study of instrumental Italian music in the Baroque era.

M—

MALIPIERO, G. FRANCESCO
Strawinsky. 88 p + 12–p pl (pors, etc). Cavallino, Venezia, 1945. 2.25

N—

NARDI, PIERO
Vita di Arrigo Boito. 753 p, 52 illus (pors, etc), 10 facs, paper. Mondadori, Milano, (1942), 2nd ed 1944. 3.00

O—

OTTANI, GIANCARLO
Stradivari. 278 p, frontis, 4–p bibl, paper. Bocca, Milano, 1945. 2.50

P—

PAOLI, DOMENICO DE
Claudio Monteverdi. 357 p, 12 pl (pors, etc), music facs, 1–p bibl. Hoepli, Milano, 1945. 3.00
With 3 ariette inedite in facsimiles.

PIZZETTI, ILDEBRANDO
La musica italiana dell' ottocento. 331 p, bds. (1930) Pezzani, Torino, 1945 (1947). 6.00
Studies of Spontini, Rossini, Bellini, Donizetti, & Verdi.

R—

RONCAGLIA, GINO
Rossini: L'Olimpico.   557 p, 17 pl
(pors, fac, etc), mus ex, 11–p bibl,
paper. Bocca, Milano, 1946.   3.00

RUDGE, OLGA (ed)
Lettere e dediche di Antonio Vivaldi.
35 p, 1 fac, bibl refs, paper. Ticci,
Siena, 1942.   1.50

T—

(TEATRO DI SAN CARLO)
Cento anni di vita del Teatro di San
Carlo (1848–1948).   219 p, 5 col pl,
90 pl. Teatro di San Carlo, Napoli,
1948.   10.00

V—

VALABREGA, CESARE
Domenico Scarlatti: il suo secolo,
la sua opera.   335 p, 233 mus ex,
1½–p bibl, paper. Guanda, Modena,
1937.   3.00

Z—

ZAVADINI, GUIDO
Donizetti: vita, musiche, epistolario.
xx, 1017 p, 34 pl (pors, facs, etc), mus
ex. Istituto Italiano d'Arti Gra-
fiche, Bergamo, 1948.   8.50
*A handsomely illustrated work, largely de-
voted to Donizetti's letters, p 221/955.*

APPENDIX Id: Books in Spanish

**(A selected list only — arranged in
alphabetical order by authors' names)**

C—

CARRILLO, JULIÁN
Tratado sintético de harmonía.   Pref
Rubén M. Campos. v, 102 p + fold-
out score page, mus ex, bds. (1913)
G. Schirmer (1915), 7th rev ed
(1920?).   1.75

COOPERSMITH, J. M.
Música y músicos de la República
Dominicana.   Forew Charles Seeger;
Spanish tr María Hazera & Elizabeth

M. Tylor.   146 p, 5–p pl (pors,
photos, map), mus ex, 6–p bibl,
paper. Pan American Union 1949.   1.25
*Pan American Music Series No 15, with text
in English & Spanish. A history of Dominican music and a study of its folk music &
instruments based on a field trip made in
1944. A list of recordings is included.*

D—

DANHAUSER, A.
Teoría de la música.   Tr G. J. Llom-
part. 125 p, mus ex, paper. G. Schir-
mer new ed (1925?).   1.25
*Translation of a standard 19th-century
French textbook.*
Compendio de la teoría de la música.
Tr G. J. Llompart. 47 p. mus ex,
G. Schirmer n d.   .50
Abridgment of the above, for school use.

G—

GARIEL, EDUARDO
Nuevo sistema de armonía: basado
en cuarto acordes fundamentales. vii,
55 p, mus ex. G. Schirmer 1915.   1.00
*Spanish edition (see main Guide entry under
Harmony–2).*

M—

MARTI, SAMUEL
*See main Guide entry under String Playing:
"Basic violin-viola technique," 1937, with
text in Spanish as well as English.*

MAYER-SERRA, OTTO
El estado presente de la música en
México. Forew Charles Seeger. viii,
47 p, paper. Pan American Union
1946.   .50
*Pan American Music Series No 14, with
text in Spanish & English.*
Música y músicos de Latino América.
2 v: 1134 p, illus, mus ex, bibl refs.
Atlante, México, 1947, via W. M.
Jackson Inc, N. Y.   Δ
*A standard Latin American dictionary of
music & musicians. The exact price in the
U. S. A. depends on the current rate of exchange (at one time it was $30.00).*
Panorama de la música mexicana
desde la independencia hasta la
actualidad.   196 p, 4 facs, mus ex,
7–p bibl, paper. El Colegio de México
1941.   2.25

P—

PAHISSA, JAIME
Vida y obra de Manuel de Falla. 208
p, photos, facs, mus ex. Ricordi
Americana, Buenos Aires, 1947.   5.00

PEREIRA SALAS, EUGENIO
Notas para la historia del intercambio
musical entre las Americas antes del
año 1940. xx, 37 p, paper, mim. Pan
American Union 1943.   .25
*A Spanish edition of the Pan American
Music Series No 6, O/P in the English
edition.*

S—

SALAZAR, ADOLFO
La música en la sociedad Europea.
4 v, paper. El Colegio de México
1942/6.   △
V 1: Desde los primeros tiempos
cristianos. 504 p, mus ex, bibl refs.
1942.
V 2: Hasta fines del siglo XVIII.
478 p, mus ex, bibl refs. 1944.
V 3 & 4: El siglo XIX. 533, 517
p, 2 pl, mus ex, bibl refs. 1946.
*A comprehensive over-all history, the first
substantial work in its field to be written
from a Spanish point of view. A fifth volume,
"La música moderna" (1944), is available
in an English version: "Music in our time"
(see main Guide entry under Contemporary
Music).*

Música y sociedad en el siglo XX:
ensayo de crítica y de estetica desde
el punto de vista de su función social.
223 p, bibl refs, paper. La Casa de
España en México 1939.   1.00

SCHINDLER, KURT
Música y poesia popular de España
y Portugal. xxx, 370, 127 p, frontis
por, music (tunes only), paper. Hispanic Institute, N. Y., 1941.   10.00
*An extensive standard study: text in Spanish
& English; some 1000 musical examples.*

SUBIRÁ, JOSÉ
El compositor Iriarte (1750–1791):
y el cultivo español de melólogo. V
1: 254 p, illus?, paper? Instituto
Español de Músicología, Barcelona,
1949.   △
*The first extended study of a Spanish poet
& composer, who specialized in melodramas.
A second volume is in preparation.*

Historia de la música. 2 v.
Salvat, Barcelona, 1947.   △
V 1: Música antigua. xvi, 627 p.
V 2: Música moderna. xi, 744 p.
A richly illustrated over-all history.

V—

VIU SALAS, VICENTE
Músicos modernos de Chile. 26 p,
paper, mim. Pan American Union
1944.   .25
Pan American Music Series No. 11.

W—

WPA WRITERS, (comps)
*See the main Guide entry under Children–7:
"The Spanish-American song & game book,"
1942, with text in Spanish as well as in
English.*

APPENDIX Ie: Books in Latin

**(A selected list only — arranged in
alphabetical order by authors' names)**

C—

COUSSEMAKER, EDMOND DE (ed)
Scriptorum de musica medii aevi
novam seriem a Gerbertinam Alter-
am collegit nunque primum edidit.
Parisiis, 1864–1876. 4 v. Facsimile
repr (Bollettino Bibliographico Musicale, Rome, 1931) Musurgia photolith repr pending.   △
A supplement to the Gerbert work below.

G—

GERBERT, MARTIN (ed)
Scriptores ecclesiastici de musica
sacra potissimum. Ex variis Italiæ,
Galliæ, et Germaniæ codicibus manu-
scriptis collecti et nunc primum pub-
lica luce donati. Typis San-Blasianis
1784. 3 v. Facsimile repr (Bollettino
Bibliografico Musicale, Rome, 1931)
Musurgia photolith repr pending.   △
*The standard collection of medieval treatises
on music, supplemented by the Coussemaker
work above. Available only on subscription:
$126.00 for both works (7 volumes in all).*

APPENDIX II

APPENDIX IIa (Juvenile Biographies)

(1. Collective Biographies—arranged in alphabetical order by author)

See also (main Guide entries):

Appreciation	Interpreters
Children–2	Organists
Composers–1, 2, 3a	Pianists
(& under individual	Pictures/Portraits
names)	Program Notes
Dictionaries of Music	School Music–2
Encyclopedias of	Singers
Music	Violinists
History	

ACKER, HELEN
Five sons of Italy. 191 p, 2–p bibl.
Nelson 1950.   2.25
Including Paganini, Verdi, & Leonardo da Vinci; along with Michelangelo Buonarroti.

Four sons of Norway. 225 p, 8 illus
(Nils Hogner), 1–p bibl. Nelson
1948.   3.00
Ole Bull (p 12/72), Edvard Greig (p 132-198); also Henrik Ibsen & Fridtjof Nansen.

BAKELESS, KATHERINE LITTLE
Story-lives of American composers.
xiii, 287 p, 14 photo pors, 2–p bibl.
Lippincott 1941.   2.75
Foster, Sousa, Herbert, MacDowell, Nevin, Handy, Carpenter, Griffes, Kern, Taylor, Berlin, Harris, Gershwin, Copland.

Story-lives of great composers. 264
p, illus. Lippincott 1940.   2.75

BROWER, HARRIETTE
Story-lives of master musicians. x,
371 p, 22 pors. Lippincott 1922
(14th pr n d).   2.50

BURCH, GLADYS
Famous pianists for young people.
vii, 156 p, photos. (Barnes 1943)
Dodd Mead 1948.   2.50
Originally entitled "Famous pianists for boys and girls."

Famous violinists for young people.
viii, 232 p, photos. (Barnes 1946)
Dodd Mead 1948.   2.50

Modern composers for young people.
207 p, photos. (Barnes 1941) Dodd
Mead 1948.   2.50
Originally entitled "Modern composers for boys and girls."

BURCH, GLADYS & WOLCOTT, JOHN
Famous composers for young people.
184 p, photos. (Barnes 1939) Dodd
Mead 1948.   2.50
Originally entitled "A child's book of famous composers."

CRAWFORD, ALETHEA B. & REBEKAH
Pictured lives of great musicians.
191 p, illus, mus ex. Birchard 1924.   2.75

FREEMAN, W. S. & WHITTAKER, R. W.
The child's book of great composers.
128 p, illus. Durrell 1951, in prep.   △
18 biographical sketches: Bach to Gershwin.

OVERMYER, GRACE
Famous American composers. xiii,
210 p, illus (Constance Joan Naar),
2–p mus ex, 4–p bibl. Crowell 1944
(4th pr 1945).   2.50

SCHMITZ, MARY M.
Little life stories of the great masters:
in questions & answers for juvenile
clubs & young musicians. 98 p,
paper. Presser 1925.   .60
Pocket-size, catechism style.

SCHWIMMER, FRANCISKA
Great musicians as children. ix, 238
p. Doubleday (1929) 1938.   2.25

SCOBEY, K. L. & HORNE, O. B.
Stories of great musicians. 189 p,
illus, ex. American 1905.   O/P

SMITH, HANNAH
Founders of music: life-sketches for
young readers. 150 p, 13 pors. G.
Schirmer 1903 (8th pr 1930).   1.50

TAPPER, THOMAS
Child's own book of great musicians
(series). Each booklet 14 to 16 p,
illus (cut-out pictures), paper. Presser 1915/41.   Each: .20
The series includes booklets on:

Bach	MacDowell
Beethoven	Mendelssohn
Brahms	Mozart
Chopin	Nevin
Dvořák	Schubert
Foster	Schumann
Grieg	Sousa
Handel	Tchaikovsky
Haydn	Verdi
Liszt	Wagner

First studies in music biography.
316 p, illus, mus ex. Presser 1900.   1.75

From Palestrina to Grieg: 1st year
music biography. **v**, 247 p. Schmidt
(1929 rev ed 1946.   1.75

Pictures from the lives of great composers for children. 185 p. Presser
1899.   1.50

WHEELER, OPAL & DEUCHER, SYBIL
Curtain calls for Joseph Haydn &
Sebastian Bach. 103 p, illus (Mary
Greenwalt), music. Dutton 1939
(2nd pr 1945).   2.75

APPENDIX IIa (Juvenile Biographies)

(2. Individual Biographies, plus a few
miscellaneous works devoted to individual
composers—arranged in alphabetical order
by individual subjects)
See also: main Guide entries under individual names.

ANDERSON, Marian

ALBUS, HARRY JAMES
The "deep river" girl: the life of
Marian Anderson in story form. 85
p, frontis por, bibl refs. Eerdmans
1949.   1.00

BACH, Johann Sebastian

ALBUS, HARRY JAMES
Music maker: Johann Sebastian
Bach. 93 p, bds. Eerdmans 1950.   1.00

GOSS, MADELEINE
Deep-flowing brook: the story of
Johann Sebastian Bach. x, 289 p,
illus (Elinore Blaisdell). Holt 1938
(3rd pr, rev, 1945).   3.00

TAPPER, THOMAS. See col. biogs. above.

WHEELER, OPAL & DEUCHER, SYBIL
Sebastian Bach: the boy from Thur-
ingia. 126 p, illus (Mary Greenwalt),
music. Dutton 1937 (17th pr 1949).   2.75

BEETHOVEN, Ludwig van

GOSS, MADELEINE
Beethoven: master musician. 364 p,
illus (Karl Schultheiss), mus ex, 1–p
bibl. (1943) Holt rev ed 1946 (1949).   3.00
*With bibliography, lists of works & record-
ings, and chronology by Elizabeth C. Moore.*

TAPPER, THOMAS. See col. biogs. above.

WHEELER, OPAL
Ludwig Beethoven: and the chiming
tower bells. 140 p + 20–p music,
illus (Mary Greenwalt). Dutton 1942
(5th pr 1949).   2.75

BERLIN, Irving

EWEN, DAVID
The story of Irving Berlin. viii, **179**
p, illus (Jane Castle). Holt 1950.   3.00
*With lists of recordings, films, shows, & song
titles.*

BRAHMS, Johannes

DEUCHER, SYBIL
The young Brahms. 160 p, illus
(Edward & Stephani Godwin), music.
Dutton 1949.   2.75

GOSS, MADELEINE, & SCHAUFFLER, R. H.
Brahms: the master. 351 p, illus
(Frederic Door Steele), mus ex, 1–p
bibl. Holt 1943.   3.00
*With bibliography, lists of works & record-
ings, and chronology by Elizabeth C. Moore.*

TAPPER, THOMAS. See col. biogs. above.

BULL, Ole

See also: Col. biogs. above (Acker).

HEADLAND, HELEN
Ole Bull: Norwegian minstrel. 142
p + 12–p music, illus (Headland
drwgs & 3 photo pors). Augustana
1949.   1.75

CHALIAPIN, Feodor

ACKER, HELEN
Three boys of old Russia. 258 p,
illus (Zhenya Gay). Nelson 1944.   2.50
Chaliapin, Leo Tolstoy, & Maxim Gorky.

CHOPIN, Frédéric

TAPPER, THOMAS. See col. biogs. above.

WHEELER, OPAL
Frederic Chopin: son of Poland; early
years. 156 p, illus (Christine Price),
music. Dutton 1948.   2.75
Frederic Chopin: son of Poland; later
years. 160 p, illus (Christine Price),
music. Dutton 1949.   2.75

DEBUSSY, Claude

HARVEY, HARRY B.
Claude of France: the story of De-
bussy. 190 p, illus (Salcia Bahnc).
(Allen Towne 1948) via Lothrop 1950.   2.75
With lists of works & recordings.

DUKAS, Paul

COOKE, DONALD EDWIN
Sorcerer's apprentice: a story of
magic based upon the legend that
inspired the ballad by Goethe and
following close upon the program of

Dukas' famous musical fantasy, "L'Apprenti sorcier." 56 p, col illus (author). Winston 1947.   2.50

ROSTRON, RICHARD
The sorcerer's apprentice: the ancient story, from which Paul Dukas drew inspiration for his music. unp (79 p), illus, some col (Frank Lieberman). Morrow 1941.   2.50

DVOŘÁK, Antonín

JUDSON, CLARA INGRAM
The lost violin: they came from Bohemia. viii, 204 p (illus Margaret Bradfield). Houghton 1947.   2.50
In the "They came from . . ." series. Dvořák, among other Czechs, is discussed here.

PURDY, CLAIRE LEE
Antonín Dvořák: composer from Bohemia. 200 p, frontis por, mus ex, 3–p bibl. Messner 1950.   2.75
Including a list of works.

TAPPER, THOMAS. See col. biogs. above.

VAN STRAATEN, JAN
Slavonic rhapsody: the life of Antonín Dvořák. 231 p, illus (Marion R. Kohs). (Allen Towne 1948) via Lothrop 1950.   2.75
With lists of works & recordings.

FOSTER, Stephen

BARTLETT, ELLA HERBERT (*ed*)
Stephen Foster songs for boys and girls. 47 p, col illus (Stephen J. Voorhies), music (arr. Mario Agnolucci). Whittlesey 1945.   2.75
14 songs in simplified arrangements.

HIGGINS, HELEN BOYD
Stephen Foster: boy minstrel. 201 p, illus (silhouettes by Clothilde Embree Funk), mus ex. Bobbs-Merrill 1944.   1.75

PURDY, CLAIRE LEE
He heard America sing: the story of Stephen Foster. 236 p, illus (Dorothea Cooke), music. Messner 1940 (11th pr 1948).   2.75
Includes 27 songs (tunes only).

TAPPER, THOMAS. See col. biogs. above.

WHEELER, OPAL
Stephen Foster and his little dog Tray. 172 p, illus (Mary Greenwalt), music. Dutton 1941 (5th pr 1948)   2.75

GERSHWIN, George

EWEN, DAVID
The story of George Gershwin. ix, 211 p, illus (Graham Bernbach),

music, ex, 1–p bibl. Holt 1943 (7th pr 1946).   3.00
With list of recordings & a chronology.

GILBERT & SULLIVAN

BUSH, MARGARET (*ed*)
Gilbert & Sullivan songs for young people. Intro & notes J. R. de la Torre, jr. 72 p, col illus (Erna M. Karolyi), music. Whittlesey 1946.   O/P

PURDY, CLAIRE LEE
Gilbert & Sullivan: masters of mirth & melody. 276 p, illus (Eric Godal), mus ex, 2–p bibl. Messner 1946.   2.75
Including stories of the operettas & a catalogue of works.

WHEELER, OPAL
H. M. S. Pinafore: story & musical arrangements adapted from Gilbert & Sullivan. 96 p, col illus (Fritz Kredel), music. Dutton 1946.   3.75

GRIEG, Edvard

See also: Col. biogs above (Acker).

DEUCHER, SYBIL
Edvard Grieg: boy of the northland. 165 p, illus (Mary Greenwalt), music. Dutton 1946 (1947).   2.75

PURDY, CLAIRE LEE
Song of the north: the story of Edvard Grieg. viii, 274 p, illus (Susanne Suba), music, 3–p bibl. Messner 1941 (6th pr 1948).   2.75
Including a list of works.

TAPPER, THOMAS. See col. biogs. above.

HANDEL, George Frideric

TAPPER, THOMAS. See col. biogs. above.

WHEELER, OPAL
Handel at the court of kings. 135 p + 30–p music, illus (Mary Greenwalt). Dutton 1943.   2.75

HAYDN, Josef

EWEN, DAVID
Haydn: a good life. 245 p, illus (Marion Kohs), mus ex. Holt 1946.   3.00
With lists of works & recordings, and a chronology.

TAPPER, THOMAS. See col. biogs. above.

WHEELER, OPAL & DEUCHER, SYBIL
Joseph Haydn: the merry little peasant. 118 p, illus (Mary Greenwalt), music. Dutton 1936 (16th pr 1946).   2.75

HERBERT, Victor

BARTLETT, ELLA HERBERT (*ed*)
Victor Herbert songs for children.

46 p, illus, some col (Guy Edgar Fry), music (arr Margaret Bush). Whittlesey 1943. 3.25
12 songs, selected & edited, with a 3-p introduction, by the composer's daughter.

PURDY, CLAIRE LEE
Victor Herbert: American music-master. 271 p, illus (Everett Shinn), mus ex, 5–p bibl. Messner 1944 (4th pr 1948). 2.75
With lists of works and recordings.

HUMPERDINCK, Engelbert
GRIMM, WILHELM K. K. & JAKOB L. K. Hansel and Gretel: a story of the forest. Unp (31 p), col illus (Warren Chappell), music. Knopf 1944. 2.00
With 4 theme songs in simplified versions.

LAUDER, Harry
MALVERN, GLADYS
Valiant minstrel: Harry Lauder. 259 p, illus (Corinne Malvern). Messner 1943 (3rd pr 1946). 2.75

LIND, Jenny
BENÉT, LAURA
Enchanting Jenny Lind. viii, 452 p, illus (drwgs George G. Whitney, & photos). Dodd Mead 1939 (1948). 3.00

HEADLAND, HELEN
The Swedish nightingale: a biography of Jenny Lind. 145 p + 14–p music, illus (author), 1–p bibl. Augustana 1940 (4th pr 1946). 1.50

LISZT, Franz
TAPPER, THOMAS. See col. biogs. above.

MacDOWELL, Edward
TAPPER, THOMAS. See col. biogs. above.

WHEELER, OPAL & DEUCHER, SYBIL
Edward MacDowell: and his cabin in the pines. 144 p, illus (Mary Greenwalt). Dutton 1940 (9th pr 1945). 2.75

MENDELSSOHN, Felix
ERSKINE, JOHN
Song without words: the story of Felix Mendelssohn. xii, 205 p, illus (William Spielter). Messner 1941 (4th pr 1947). 2.75

HUMPHREYS, DENA
On wings of song: the story of Mendelssohn. 285 p, illus (Phyllis Coté), mus ex, 2–p bibl. Holt 1944 (4th pr 1945). 3.00

TAPPER, THOMAS. See col. biogs. above.

MOZART, Wolfgang
LINGG, ANN M.
Mozart: genius of harmony. viii, 331 p, illus (Helen Frank). Holt 1946. 3.00
With lists of works & recordings.

TAPPER, THOMAS. See col. biogs. above.

WHEELER, BENSON & PURDY, CLAIRE LEE
My brother was Mozart. 209 p, illus (Theodore Nadejen), mus ex, 3–p bibl. Holt 1937 (3rd pr 1946). 3.00
With a catalogue of works.

WHELLER, OPAL & DEUCHER, SYBIL
Curtain calls for Wolfgang Mozart: a musical play for children. 109 p, illus (Mary Greenwalt), music. Dutton 1941. 2.75

Mozart: the wonder boy. 127 p, illus (Mary Greenwalt), music. Dutton (1934) new enl ed 1941 (15th pr 1949). 2.75

NEVIN, Ethelbert
TAPPER, THOMAS. See col. biogs. above.

NILSSON, Christina
HEADLAND, HELEN
Christina Nilsson: the songbird of the north. 173 p, illus (author), music. Augustana 1943. 1.50

PAGANINI, Nicolò
See also: Col. biogs. above (Acker).
WHEELER, OPAL
Paganini: master of strings. 151 p + 8–p music, illus (Henry S. Gillette.) Dutton 1950. 2.75

PAVLOVA, Anna
MALVERN, GLADYS
Dancing star: the story of Anna Pavlova. 280 p, illus (Susanne Suba), 2–p bibl. Messner 1942 (5th pr 1946). 2.75

PROKOFIEV, Sergei
DEAKIN, IRVING
Peter and the wolf. Unp (45 p), col illus (Richard C. Jones). Oxford 1940. 1.75

(PROKOFIEV, SERGEI)
Peter and the wolf. Forew Serge Koussevitzky. Unp (32 p), illus, some col (Warren Chappell), mus ex, calligraphy (Hollis Holland). Knopf 1940. 2.00

RACHMANINOFF, Sergei
GRONOWICZ, ANTONI
Sergei Rachmaninoff. Tr Samuel

Sorgenstein & Edna Ruth Johnson. 153 p, illus (Woodi Ishmael), 3–p bibl. Dutton 1946.   2.75
With a catalogue of works.

SCHUBERT, Franz
Goss, MADELEINE
Unfinished symphony: the story of Franz Schubert. 330 p, illus (Karl M. Schultheiss), 1–p bibl. Holt 1941 (3rd pr 1945).   3.00
With list of works & a chronology.

TAPPER, THOMAS. See col. biogs. above.

WHEELER, OPAL & DEUCHER, SYBIL Curtain calls for Franz Schubert: a musical play for children. 103 p, illus (Mary Greenwalt), music. Dutton 1941.   2.75
Franz Schubert: and his merry friends. 124 p, illus (Mary Greenwalt), music. Dutton 1939 (10th pr 1943).   2.75

SCHUMANN, Clara & Robert
SPAETH, SIGMUND
Dedication: the love story of Clara & Robert Schumann. xii, 180 p, frontis (Fritz Kredel), 2–p bibl. Holt 1950.   3.00
With a list of recordings.

SCHUMANN, Robert
TAPPER, THOMAS. See col. biogs. above.

WHEELER, OPAL
Robert Schumann and mascot Ziff. 167 p, illus (Christine Price), music. Dutton 1947.   2.75

SCHWEITZER, Albert
GOLLOMB, JOSEPH
Albert Schweitzer: genius in the jungle. 249 p. Vanguard 1949.   2.75
A straightforward, non-romanticized account of Schweitzer's life and achievements.

SIBELIUS, Jean
ARNOLD, ELLIOTT
Finlandia: the story of Sibelius. 247 p, illus (Lolita Granahan). Holt (1941) rev ed 1950.   3.00
Includes a list of recordings.

SOUSA, John Philip
TAPPER, THOMAS. See col. biogs. above.

STRADIVARI, Antonio
TINYANOVA, HELEN
Stradivari: the violin-maker. Tr

& rewritten in English by Charles Angoff. 99 p, illus. Knopf 1938 (3rd pr 1946).   1.75

STRAUSS, Johann
EWEN, DAVID
Tales from the Vienna woods: the story of Johann Strauss. viii, 216 p, illus (Edgard Cirlin), mus ex, 1–p bibl note. Holt 1944 (4th pr 1946).   3.00
With lists of works & recordings, thematic index, and chronology.

TCHAIKOVSKY, Peter Ilyitch
GRONOWICZ, ANTONI
Tchaikovsky. Tr Joseph Vetter. 192 p, 6 illus (George Avison), 3–p bibl. Nelson 1946.   2.00
With a catalogue of works.

PURDY, CLAIRE LEE
Stormy victory: the story of Tchaikovsky. xiv, 248 p, illus (Vera Bock), mus ex (Rudolf W. Kohl), 4–p bibl. Messner 1942 (5th pr 1946).   2.75

TAPPER, THOMAS. See col. biogs. above.

VERDI, Giuseppe
See also: Col. biogs. above (Acker).
DILLER, ANGELA
The story of Verdi's "Aida": retold & illustrated with 51 musical excerpts from the opera. 44 p, music, paper. G. Schirmer 1937.   .75

HUMPHREYS, DENA
Verdi: force of destiny. viii, 341 p, 24 illus (Hans Alexander Mueller). Holt 1948.   3.50
With lists of works & recordings.

TAPPER, THOMAS. See col. biogs. above.

WAGNER, Richard
BURCH, GLADYS
Richard Wagner: who followed a star. xi, 577 p, illus (Robert Ball, 3–p bib.. Holt 1941 (2nd pr 1945).   3.00
With list of recordings & chronology.

DILLER, ANGELA
The story of "Lohengrin": retold & arranged with 21 motives from Wagner's opera & 4 easy piano transcriptions. 38 p, music, paper. G. Schirmer 1932.   .75

The story of "Siegfried": retold & arranged with 23 motives from Wagner's opera. 22 p, music, paper. G. Schirmer 1931.   .60

TAPPER, THOMAS. See col. biogs. above.

APPENDIX IIb (Miscellaneous Juveniles)

See also (main Guide entries): Children, School Music, Songbooks.

Note: The enormous literature of song, dance, game, piano, picture, & story books (most of which contain little if any text) is not included in the listings below, except in rare instances where there is considerable text dealing with a specific musical subject.

Among the works omitted, it might be well to signal out for special mention the popular series of songbooks, etc, for home & school use, by Inez Bertail, Lottie Ellsworth Coit & Ruth Bampton, Satis N. Coleman, Ethel Crowninshield, Angela Diller & Kate Stearns Page, William C. Hartshorn & Helen S. Leavitt ("World of Music" series), Osbourne McConathy & others ("New Music Horizons" series), A. A. Milne & Fraser-Simpson, Beatrice Perham ("Growing Up with Music" series), Lilla Belle Pitts & others ("Our Singing World" series), Ada Richter, Louise Robyn, Mother Georgia Stevens ("Tone & Rhythm" series), Janet E. Tobbitt & Alice M. G. White, Opal Wheeler, etc.

BAKELESS, KATHERINE LITTLE
Glory, hallelujah!: the story of "The Battle Hymn of the Republic." 100 p, illus (Edward Shenton). Lippincott 1944.   1.50

BALET, JAN
What makes an orchestra. Forew Deems Taylor. 48 p, illus (Balet). Oxford 1950.   2.50
Pictures, with simple, informative text.

BARBOUR, HARRIET B. & FREEMAN, W. S.
A story of music. x, 300 p, illus (Martha Powell Setchell & Arthur Lougee). Birchard (1937) rev ed 1950.   1.75
Key to "A story of music." iv, 84 p, paper. Birchard 1943.   .60

BARNE, KITTY
Musical honors. 207 p. Dodd Mead 1947. (*Fiction.*)   2.25

BUCHANAN, FANNIE R.
How man made music. 302 p, illus (Roby Ann Nelson), mus ex. Wilcox Follett (1935) rev enl ed 1941, 4th pr 1948, rev 1951.   2.75

BURCH, GLADYS, & RIPPERGER, HELMUT
The junior music quiz: a musical game. 134 p, illus, bds. G. Schirmer 1940.   1.00

COMMINS, DOROTHY BERLINER
Making an orchestra: descriptions of all the instruments by families, also a chart, with cut-outs, to set up a small orchestra on paper. 45 p, chart, illus (David T. Darling), mus ex (2 score pages). Macmillan 1931 (1949).   2.00
Perhaps the most popular "cut-out" book.

COOKE, JAMES FRANCIS
Young folks' picture history of music: with "cut-out" pictures to be pasted in each chapter. 82 p + 6-p blank staves, bds. Presser 1925.   1.25

DIKE, HELEN
Stories from the great Metropolitan operas. 247 p, illus, some col (Gustaf Tenggren), mus ex. Random 1943.   2.75
Stories of 25 operas, with biographical notes; sponsored by the Metropolitan Opera Guild.

DUSHKIN, DAVID
Fun with flutes. 28 p, illus (Alfred D. Sterges), music. Chicago 1934.   1.50

FREEMAN, WARREN S.
The child's book of musical instruments. 128 p, illus. Durrell 1951, in prep.   Δ

GERALTON, JAMES
The story of sound. 74 p, 65 illus (Joe Krush). Harcourt 1948.   2.00
Simple acoustics for ages 10 to 14.

GEST, ELIZABETH
Betty and the symphony orchestra. 16 p, illus, paper. Presser 1923.   .25

GRAHAM, ALBERTA POWELL
See main Guide entry under Dance Bands.

GRONOWICZ, ANTONI
Bolek. Tr Jessie McEwen. vi, 241 p, illus (Zhenya Gay). Nelson 1942.   2.50
Fiction: the story of a Polish village boy with a gift for music.

HUNTINGTON, HARRIET E.
See main Guide entry under Children–4.

KINSCELLA, HAZEL GERTRUDE (ed)
Stories in music appreciation. Forew Frances Elliott Clarke. 6 v, illus, some col (Ruth Mary Hallock). University 1939, 1951 revs in prep.
V 1: 2nd grade: Storyland. x, 134 p.   1.52
V 2: 3rd grade: The man in the drum. x, 212 p.   1.56
V 3: 4th grade: Folk tales from many lands. x, 246 p, mus ex.   1.64
V 4: 5th grade: Conrad's magic flight. x, 342 p, mus ex.   1.72
V 5: 6th grade: Tales of olden days. x, 406 p, photos.   1.80

V 6: 7th grade: Around the world in story. x, 502 p, photos. 1.92

Anthologies of stories & poems, by Miss Kinscella & many others, for collateral reading in music appreciation.

LAPRADE, ERNEST

See main Guide entry under Children–4.

LOOFBOUROW, REGINALDUS

All aboard for theoryland: an illustrated manual on the theory of music for elementary grades. 55 p + music staves, illus (Angelique Sabourin), paper. Beckley-Cardy Co, Chicago, 1946. .44

Let's go to theoryland: a book in the theory of music for the young beginner. 48 p + cut-out notes & keyboard, illus (Angelique Sabourin), paper. Beckley-Cardy Co, Chicago, 1946. .44

Elementary workbooks. No data are available on a companion booklet, "Adventures in theoryland."

LYONS, JOHN HENRY

Stories of our American patriotic songs. 72 p, illus (Jacob Landau), music, bds. Vanguard 1942. 2.50

MACY, JAMES C.

Young people's history of music: with biographies of famous composers. 147 p, pors, mus ex. Ditson (1886) rev ed 1914. 1.25

MARIE-JEANNE

Opera ballerina. v, 233 p, photos, Dodd Mead 1948. 2.50

Fiction ("career books" series), with photographs of the author & noted ballets.

MASON, GEORGE F.

Animal sounds. 94 p, illus (author). Morrow 1948. 2.00

Songs & cries of birds, insects, animals.

McPHEE, COLIN

A club of small men. 61 p, illus (photos & drwgs by the author). Day 1948. 2.00

A companion work to the author's books on Balinese music (see main Guide entry under Bali): the story of some 5-to-8-year-olds who formed their own gamelan orchestra.

POSELL, ELSA Z.

This is an orchestra. 96 p, illus (photos & b&ws). Houghton 1950. 2.50

A youngster's guide to the orchestra & its instruments, with pictures of Cleveland Orchestra members, and chapters on choosing & playing an instrument, building a record library, & famous string-instrument makers.

RUBEL, EDITH

The merry muse: heydays of music & art. viii, 144 p, illus (Harvey Peake), bds. G. Schirmer 1937. 2.50

Narrative music & art history in jingles.

RUSETTE, LOUIE E. DE

Dulcimer stories: music & stories. 61 p, music (tunes only), paper. Pitman 1932. 1.00

SCHAUFFLER, ROBERT HAVEN (ed)

The magic of music: an anthology for music weeks & days, musical memory contests, games, stories, plays, etc. xxii, 387 p. Dodd Mead 1935. 2.75

SIMON, GEORGE T.

Don Watson starts his band. Forew Benny Goodman. xii, 303 p. Dodd Mead 1940 (1946). 2.50

Fiction ("career books" series): the story of a young dance-band leader.

SKOLSKY, SYD

The music box book. 79 p, illus, some col (Roberta Paflin). Dutton 1946. 1.50

A companion to the author's appreciation books (see main Guide entry under Appreciation), including an introduction to the orchestra and stories of Shéhérazade, The Bartered Bride, Nutcracker Suite, Sorcerer's Apprentice, Midsummer Night's Dream, & Till Eulenspiegel.

STREATFEILD, NOEL

Ballet shoes. 294 p, illus (Richard Floethe). Random 1937. 2.50

Fiction ("shoes" series). Also published by Dent, London, illus Ruth Gervis.

TAYLOR, FREDERICK A.

So you're going to take music lessons. 31 p, illus (Richard K. Moll), paper. Humphries 1947. .75

Practical advice for children; a companion to "So we're going to have music lessons" (see main Guide entry under Children–1).

WHEELER, OPAL

Sing for Christmas: a round of Christmas carols & stories of the carols. 127 p, col illus (Gustaf Tenggren), music. Dutton 1943 3rd pr 1946). 3.75

Sing in praise: a collection of the best loved hymns; stories of the hymns & music arrangements. 94 p, col illus (Marjorie Torrey), music, bds. Dutton 1946. 3.75

WHITEMAN, PAUL & LIEBER, LESLIE

See main Guide entry under Dance Bands.

KEY TO PUBLISHERS

Genera. Note: In a reference work of this kind, it is extremely wasteful of space to give publishers' names and addresses in full every time one of their publications is listed, especially since this involves the frequent repetition of credits to a comparatively few "major" music-book publishers. The more economical method of using "code" initial-or-name schemes, on the other hand, has the great disadvantage of making annoying demands on the casual reader, who usually can identify a particular publisher only by taking time out to consult a key to the code employed.

Balancing these disadvantages, we have adopted a compromise scheme for these pages:

1. Publishers represented by only one or two entries in the Guide are identified by full name and city (but without street address) in the entries themselves.

2. "Major" music-book publishers (i.e., those represented by more than an occasional entry in these pages) are indicated in individual entries by short, *but identifiable forms of their full names, but without addresses. Hence, it is only when the latter are required that it should be necessary for the reader to consult the following "key," which lists all these publishers in alphabetical order by the short forms employed in the Guide, together with their full names and addresses. In some cases the names of controlling or distributing agencies, or the U. S. A. agents for British publishers, also are given. In the case of larger publishers, with branches in several cities or countries, the main office address is sometimes followed by that of a major branch, but no attempt is made to list the branches in full.*

Readers seeking additional information (street addresses of the publishers in group 1 above for example, or representatives of major publishers in various cities and countries) are advised to consult the H. W. Wilson Company, 950 University Avenue, New York City 22. We ourselves are indebted to the Wilson Company for information culled from its "Directory of Publishers," which appears at the back of each issue of its invaluable "Cumulative Book Index" series. But while we have tried to prepare and check our listings from this and other up-to-date sources, they are of course subject to change and correction. Not only addresses, but firm names, and even more agent-affiliations, trade distributors, etc., are in a constant state of flux and all information given in the following lists should be accepted with that in mind.

—A—

Abingdon
Abingdon-Cokesbury Press. 810 Broadway, Nashville 2, Tennessee; 150 Fifth Ave., New York City 11.

Ackerman
Bernard Ackerman Inc. New York City. *See Beechhurst.*

Alabama
University of Alabama Press. Drawer 2877, University, Alabama.

Allen
George Allen & Unwin Ltd. Ruskin House, 40 Museum St., London W C 1.

Allen Towne
Allen, Towne & Heath Inc. New York City. Now out of business, but most publications have been taken over and are distributed by Crown, except for a few that are handled by Lothrup and a few others by Merlin.

Allyn
Allyn & Bacon. 50 Beacon St., Boston 8; 11 East 36th St., New York City 16.

American
American Book Company. 55 Fifth Ave., New York City 11.

Anglobooks
Anglobooks. 475 Fifth Ave., New York City 17.

Appleton
Appleton-Century-Crofts Inc. 35 West 32nd St., New York City 1. (Former Appleton-Century and former Crofts publications now are included in the Appleton-Century-Crofts catalogue.)

Arco
Arco Publishing Company. 480 Lexington Ave., New York City 17.

Ascherberg
Ascherberg, Hopwood & Crew Ltd. 16 Mortimer St., London W 1.

Asia
Asia Press. New York City. *See Day.*

Associated
Associated Music Publishers Inc. 25 West 45th St., New York City 19. USA agent of Universal, Schott, etc.

Association
Association Press (National Council of the YMCA). 291 Broadway, New York City 7.

Augener
Augener & Company Ltd. 18 Great Marlborough St., London W 1. USA agent: Broude.

Augsburg
Augsburg Publishing House. 425 South 4th St., Minneapolis 15, Minnesota.

Augustana
Augustana Book Concern. Rock Island, Illinois.

Augustin
J. J. Augustin Inc. 445 West 41st St., New York City 18.

Auvergne
Auvergne Publishers. 63 Fifth Ave., New York City 3.

Avon
Avon Publishing Company. 119 West 57th St., New York City 19.

—B—

Baker
Walter H. Baker Company. 178 Tremont St., Boston 11, Mass.

Bantam
Bantam Books Inc. 1107 Broadway, New York City 10.

Barnes
A. S. Barnes & Company Inc. 101 Fifth Ave., New York City 3.

Barnes & Noble
Barnes & Noble Inc. 105 Fifth Ave., New York City 3.

Batsford
B. T. Batsford Ltd. 15 North Audley St., Grosvenor Square, Mayfair, London W 1; 122 East 55th St., New York City 22.

Baylor
Baylor University Press. Waco, Texas.

Beacon
The Beacon Press. 25 Beacon St., Boston 8.

Beaumont
Cyril W. Beaumont. 75 Charing Cross Road, London W C 2.

Beechhurst
Beechhurst Press Inc. 296 Broadway, New York City 7. (Formerly Ackerman.)

Bell
George Bell & Sons Ltd. York House, 6 Portugal St., Lincoln's Inn Fields, London W C 2. USA agent: British Book Centre.

Belwin
Belwin Inc. 43 West 23rd St., New York City 10. USA agent of Bosworth.

Benn
Ernest Benn Ltd. Bouverie House, 154 Fleet St., London E C 4.

B & H
Breitkopf & Härtel. Leipzig & Wiesbaden, Germany. USA agent: Associated (but currently for the Wiesbaden—American zone—B & H publications only).

Birchard
C. C. Birchard & Company. 285 Columbus Ave., Boston 16.

Bittner
H. Bittner & Company. 67 West 55 St., New York City 19.

Black
A. & C. Black Ltd. 4 Soho Square, London W 1. USA agents: Macmillan & Transatlantic.

Blakiston
The Blakiston Company, 1012 Walnut St., Philadelphia 5 (A subsidiary, scientific & medical books only, of Doubleday.)

Bloch
Bloch Publishing Company Inc. 31 West 31st St., New York City 1.

Blue Ribbon
Blue Ribbon Books. Garden City, New York. *See Doubleday and Garden City.*

Bobbs Merrill
The Bobbs-Merrill Company Inc. 730 North Meridan St., Indianapolis 7, Indiana.

Bonnier
Albert Bonnier's Publishing House. 605 Madison Ave., New York City 22. USA agent of Continental.

Boosey
Boosey & Hawkes Ltd. 295 Regent St., London W 1. Boosey & Hawkes Inc. 30 West 57th St., New York City 19; P O Box 418, Rockville Center, N. Y. (Rogers publications also are owned & distributed by Boosey & Hawkes.)

Boston
Boston Music Company. 116 Boylston St., Boston 16.

Bosworth
Bosworth & Company Ltd. 14 Heddon St., Regent St., London W 1. USA agent: Belwin.

Bowker
R. R. Bowker Company. 62 West 45th St., New York City 19.

Bregman
Bregman, Vocco & Conn Inc. 1619 Broadway, New York City 19.

(Breitkopf & Härtel)
See B & H above.

Briegel
George F. Briegel. 17 West 60th St., New York City 23.

British Book Centre
The British Book Centre Inc. 122 East 55th St., New York City 22. USA agents for some twenty British publishers, including Bell, Cape, Cassell, Chatto & Windus, Drummond, English Universities Press, Harrap, Hodder & Stoughton, Hogarth, Methuen, Phoneix, Rockliff, Wingate, etc.

Broadman
The Broadman Press (Sunday School Board, Southern Baptist Convention). 127 Ninth Ave., North, Nashville 3, Tennessee.

Broude
Broude Brothers. 56 West 45th St., New York City 19. USA agent of Augener, Heffer, etc.

Bruce
Bruce Publishing Company. 400 North Broadway, Milwaukee 1, Wisconsin.

—C—

California
The University of California Press. California House, Berkeley 4, California.

Cambridge
Cambridge University Press. Bentley House 200 Euston Road, London N W 1. American branch: 51 Madison Ave., New York City 10.

Cape
Jonathan Cape Ltd. 30 Bedford Square, London W C 1. USA agent: British Book Centre.

Cassell
Cassell & Company Ltd. 37 St. Andrew's Hill, London E C 4. USA agent: British Book Centre.

Caxton
Caxton Publishing Company Ltd. Clun House, 17 Surrey St., London W C 2.

Caxton Printers
Caxton Printers Ltd. Caldwell, Ohio.

Chanticleer
Chanticleer Press Inc. 41 East 50th St., New York City 22. USA associates of Adprint Ltd., 51 Rathbone Place, London W 1. (USA distributor 1951: Crown.)

Chemical
Chemical Publishing Company Inc. 26 St., Brooklyn 2, N. Y. Publications are distributed by Tudor.

Chester
J. & W. Chester Ltd. 11 Great Marlborough St., London W 1.

Chicago
University of Chicago Press. 5750 Ellis Ave., Chicago 37.

Church
John Church Company. Cincinnati, Ohio. Publications now owned and distributed by Presser.

Cole
M. M. Cole Company. 823 South Wabash Ave., Chicago 5.

Coleman
Coleman-Ross Company Inc. 25 West 45th St., New York City 19.

Collins
William Collins Sons & Company Ltd. 14 St. James Place, London S W 1. American branch: 425 Fourth Ave., New York City 16.

Columbia
Columbia University Press. 2960 Broadway, New York City 27. (Some publications are issued under the imprint of the King's Crown Press.) For books issued by the Bureau of Publications, Teachers College, Columbia University, see Teachers College.

Concordia
Concordia Publishing House. 3558 South Jefferson Ave., St. Louis 18, Missouri.

Congdon
C. H. Congdon. 508 West 28th St., New York City 1.

Conn
C. G. Conn & Compnay. 1101 East Beardsley Ave., Elkhart, Indiana. (Ludwig & Ludwig publications now are handled by Conn.)

Continental
Continental Book & Publications Distributing Company. Aktienbolag, Regeringsgatan 39, Stockholm, Sweden. USA agent: Bonnier.

Cosmos
Cosmos Publishing Company. 475 Fifth Ave., New York City 17.

Coward
Coward-McCann Inc. 210 Madison Ave, New York City 16.

Creative Age
Creative Age Press Inc. Taken over by Farrar in 1951.

Criterion
Criterion Music Corporation. RKO Building, Rockefeller Center, New York City 20.

Crofts
F. S. Crofts & Company. Publications now are included in the Appleton-Century-Crofts catalogue.

Crowell
The Thomas Y. Crowell Company. 432 Fourth Ave., New York City 16.

Crown
Crown Publishers.   419 Fourth Ave., New York City 16. (Some former Allen Towne and some Durrell publications now are handled by Crown, which is also the distributor for Chanticleer & Lear books.)

Curwen
J. Curwen and Sons Ltd.   24 Berners St., London W 1. USA agent: G. Schirmer.

—D—

Day
The John Day Company Inc.   62 West 45th St., New York City 19. (Asia Press publications are included in the Day catalogue.)

Dent
J. M. Dent & Sons Ltd. Aldine House, 10 Bedford St., Strand, London W C 2. USA agent: William Salloch (but some Dent publications are issued in this country by Dutton and the "Master Musicians" series, formerly handled by Dutton, now is issued here by Pellegrini).

Denver
University of Denver Press.   University Park, Denver, Colorado.

Devin-Adair
Devin-Adair Company.   23 East 26th St., New York City 10.

Dial
Dial Press Inc.   461 Fourth Ave., New York City 16.

Didier
Didier Publishing Company.   660 Madison Ave., New York City 21.

Ditson
Oliver Ditson Company. Boston. (Ditson publications now are owned and distributed by Presser.)

Dobson
Dennis Dobson Ltd. 12 Park Place, London S W 1. (Some Dobson publications now are being issued in the United States by Roy.)

Dodd Mead
Dodd, Mead & Company Inc. 432 Fourth Ave., New York City 16.

Dorrance
Dorrance & Company Inc.   364 Drexel Bldg., 5th & Chestnut St., Philadelphia 6.

Doubleday
Doubleday & Company Inc. 1951 address: 575 Madison Ave., New York City 22. Trade orders to Garden City, N. Y. Subsidiaries are the Garden City Publishing Company, Blue Ribbon Books, Halcyon House, Hartsdale House, Permabooks, etc.

Dover
Dover Publications Inc.   1780 Broadway, New York City 19.

Drummond
Lindsay Drummond Ltd. 2 Guilford Place, London WC 1. USA agent: British Book Centre.

Duckworth
Gerald Duckworth & Company Ltd.   3 Henrietta St., Covent Garden, London W C 2. USA agent: Macmillan (but some former Duckworth publications are issued here by Wyn.)

Duell Sloan
Duell, Sloan & Pearce Inc.   270 Madison Ave., New York City 16. (Includes Theatre Arts publications.)

Durrell
Oliver Durrell Inc.   257 Fourth Ave., New York City 10. (Formerly Smith & Durrell. Some Durrell publications are now distributed by Crown.)

Dutton
E. P. Dutton & Company Inc. 286 Fourth Ave., New York City 10.

—E—

Edwards
J. W. Edwards. 1745 South State St., Ann Arbor, Michigan. (Formerly Edwards Bros.)

Eerdmans
W. B. Eerdmans Publishing Company (Reformed Press). 255 Jefferson Ave., S E, Grand Rapids 3, Michigan.

Elkan
Elkan-Vogel Company Inc.   1716 Sansom St., Philadelphia 3. USA agent of Durant, Jaubert, Lemoine, & other French publishers.

Exposition
Exposition Press.   251 Fourth Ave., New York City 10.

Expression
The Expression Company.   Magnolia, Mass.

—F—

Faber
Faber & Faber Ltd.   24 Russell Square, London W C 1.

Fairchild
Fairchild Publications.   7 East 12th St., New York City 3. (Trade books are distributed by Wyn.)

Farrar
Farrar, Straus & Young Inc. 53 East 34th St., New York City 16.
(*See also Rinehart, formerly Farrar & Rinehart.*)

Fell
Frederick Fell Inc. 386 Fourth Ave., New York City 16.

C. Fischer
Carl Fischer Inc. 56 Cooper Sq., New York City 3. USA agent of Paterson.

J. Fischer
J. Fischer & Bro. 119 West 40th St., New York City 18. USA agent of Desclée et Cie., Tournai, Belgium, and for Rushworth & Dreaper, Liverpool, England.

FitzSimons
H. T. FitzSimons Company Inc. 615 North La Salle St., Chicago 10.

Flammer
Harold Flammer Inc. 251 West 19th St., New York City 11.

Florida
University of Florida Press. Room 202, Building G, Gainesville, Florida.

Follett
Follett Publishing Company. 1255 South Wabash Ave., Chicago. *For trade books, see Wilcox & Follett.*

Fox
Sam Fox Publishing Company. 1250 Ave. of the Americas, New York City 20.

Funk
Funk & Wagnalls Company. 153 East 24th St., New York City 10.

—G—

Galaxy
Galaxy Music Corporation. 50 West 24th St., New York City 10. USA agent of Stainer & Bell.

Gamble
Gamble Hinged Music Company. 218 South Wabash Ave., Chicago 4. (Now a division of the Music Publishers Holding Corporation 1250 Ave., of the Americas, New York City 20.)

Garden City
Garden City Publishing Company Inc. Garden City, New York. Trade distributors for Doubleday, Blue Ribbon, Halcyon House, Hartsdale House, Permabooks, etc.

Georgia
The University of Georgia Press. Athens, Georgia.

Ginn
Ginn & Company (Athenaeum Press). Statler Building, Park Square, Boston 17.

Gollancz
Victor Gollancz Ltd. 14 Henrietta St., Covent Garden, London W C 2.

GPO
Government Printing Office. Washington 25, D C. Address communications and make out checks to the Superintendent of Documents.

Grafton
Grafton & Company. Coptic House, 51 Great Russell St., London W·C 1.

Gray
H. W. Gray Company Inc. 159 East 48th St., New York City 17. USA agent of Novello.

Greenberg
Greenberg, Publisher. 201 East 47th St., New York City 22.

Greystone
Greystone Press. 100 Ave. of the Americas. New York City 13.

Grosset
Grosset & Dunlap Inc. 1107 Broadway, New York City 10.

—H—

Halcyon
Halcyon House. Garden City, New York. *See Doubleday and Garden City.*

Hall
Hall the Publisher Ltd. 2 Littlegate, Oxford, England.

Hall McCreary
Hall & McCreary Company. 434 South Wabash Ave., Chicago 5.

Harcourt
Harcourt, Brace & Company Inc. 383 Madison Ave., New York City 17. (Now owners & distributors of Reynal & Hitchcock Publications.)

Harper
Harper & Brothers, 49 East 33rd St., New York City 16.

Harrap
George G. Harrap & Company Ltd. 182 High Holborn, London W C 1. USA agent: British Book Centre.

Hartsdale
Hartsdale House. Garden City, New York. *See Doubleday and Garden City.*

Harvard
Harvard University Press. 44 Francis Ave., Cambridge 38, Mass.

Hastings
Hastings House, Publishers, Inc. 41 East 50th St., New York City 22.

Heath
D. C. Heath & Company. 285 Columbus Ave., Boston 6.

Heffer
W. Heffer & Sons Ltd. 3 Petty Cury, Cambridge, England, USA agent: Broude.

Heinemann
William Heinemann Ltd. 99 Great Russell St., London W C 1.

Herder
B. Herder Book Company. 15 South Broadway, St. Louis 2, Missouri.

Hermitage
Hermitage House Inc. 1 Madison Ave., New York City 10. (Formerly Hermitage Press.)

Hinds
Hinds, Haydn & Eldridge Inc. 105 Fifth Ave., New York City 3.

Hinrichsen
Hinrichsen Edition. 25 Museum St., London W C 1. American branch: 1209 Carnegie Hall, 881 Seventh Ave., New York City 19. Also C. F. Peters Corporation.

Hodder
Hodder & Stoughton Ltd. St. Paul's House, 20 Warwick Square, London E C 4. USA agent: British Book Centre.

Hogarth
Hogarth Press Ltd. 40 William IV St., London W C 2. USA agent: British Book Centre.

Holt
Henry Holt & Company Inc. 257 Fourth Ave., New York City 10.

Houghton
Houghton Mifflin Company (Riverside Press, Cambridge). 2 Park St., Boston 7; 432 Fourth Ave., New York City 16.

Howell
Howell, Soskin, Publishers, Inc. 11 East 45th St., New York City 17.

Humphries
Bruce Humphries Inc. 30 Winchester St., Boston 16.

Hutchinson
Hutchinson & Company (Publishers) Ltd. Stratford Place, London W 1. (*See also Jarrolds.*)

—I—

Illinois
University of Illinois Press. Urbana, Illinois.

International
International Universities Press Inc. 227 West 13th St., New York City 11.

Iowa
State University of Iowa, Department of Publications, Iowa City, Iowa.

Island
Island Press Co-operative Inc. 470 West 24th St., New York City 11. (Formerly Island Workshop.)

—J—

Jarrolds
Jarrolds, Publishers (London) Ltd. 47 Princes Gate, London S W 1. A subsidiary of Hutchinson.

Johns Hopkins
The Johns Hopkins Press. Homewood, Baltimore 18, Maryland.

Jones
L. R. Jones. 356 South Wilton Place, Los Angeles, California.

—K—

Kalmus
Edwin F. Kalmus, Music Publisher. 112 West 89th St., New York City 24.

Kamin
Kamin Dance Publications. 1365 Ave. of the Americas, New York City 19.

Kegan Paul
Kegan Paul, Trench, Trubner & Company. London. Now included under Routledge.

King
King Music Publishing Corp. 152 West 42nd St., New York City 18.

Kjos
Neil A. Kjos Music Company. 223 West Lake St., Chicago 6.

Knopf
Alfred A. Knopf Inc. 501 Madison Ave., New York City 22.

—L—

Laidlaw
Laidlaw Brothers Inc. 221 Fourth Ave., New York City 3.

Lane
John Lane, The Bodley Head, Ltd. 7 Bury Place, London W C 1. USA agents: Macmillan & Chanticleer.

Lawrence
Lawrence & Wishart Ltd. 81 Chancery Lane, London W C 2.

Lear
Lear Publishers Inc. 105 East 15th St., New York City 3. (Publications are distributed by Crown.)

Lehmann
John Lehmann Ltd. 6 Henrietta St., London W C 2.

Lewis
Warren F. Lewis. 707 South Broadway, Los Angeles 14, California.

Library of Congress
Library of Congress, Music Division. Washington 25, D. C. (Most Library of Congress publications must be ordered from the Superintendent of Documents, Government Printing Office, Washington 25, D. C.)

Lippincott
J. B. Lippincott Company. East Washington Square, Philadelphia 5. (Also owners and distributors of Stokes publications.)

Little Brown
Little Brown & Company. 34 Deacon St., Boston 6. (Includes Atlantic Monthly Press publications.)

Liveright
Liveright Publishing Corporation. 386 Fourth Ave., New York City 16.

Longmans
Longmans, Green & Company Inc. 55 Fifth Ave., New York City 3. Longmans, Green & Company Ltd. West End, 6 Clifford St., London W 1.

Lorenz
Lorenz Publishing Company. 501 East 3rd St., Dayton 1, Ohio.

Lothrop
Lothrop, Lee & Shepherd Company Inc. 419 Fourth Ave., New York City 16.

Louisiana
Louisiana State University Press. University Station, Baton Rouge 3, Louisiana.

Ludwig
Ludwig & Ludwig. Chicago. Now a division of Conn, Elkhart, Indiana.

Lyrebird
The Lyrebird Press (Editions de l'Oiseau-Lyre). Mrs. Louise B. M. Dyer, Les Ramparts, Monaco; 122 Rue de Grenelle, Paris VII.

—M—

Macmillan
The Macmillan Company. 60 Fifth Ave., New York City 11. Macmillan & Company Ltd. 10 St. Martin's St., Leicester Square, London W C 2.

McBride
Medill McBride Company. 200 East 37th St., New York City 16. (Successors to Robert M. McBride Company.)

McGraw
McGraw Hill Book Company Inc. 330 West 42nd St., New York City 18. (Includes Whittlesey House Publications.)

McKay
David McKay Company Inc. 225 Park Ave., New York City 17.

McLaughlin & Reilly
McLaughlin & Reilly Company. 45 Franklin St., Boston 10.

Mediaeval
The Mediaeval Academy of America. 1430 Massachusetts Ave., Cambridge 38, Massachusetts.

MENC
Music Educators National Conference. 64 East Jackson Blvd., Chicago 4.

Mentor
Mentor Books. Published by the New American Library, 501 Madison Ave., New York City 22.

Merlin
Merlin Press. 545 Fifth Ave., New York City 17.

Messner
Julian Messner Inc. 8 West 40th St., New York City 18.

Methuen
Methuen & Company Ltd. 36 Essex St., Strand London W C 2. USA agent: British Book Centre.

Michigan
University of Michigan Press. 311 Maynard St., Ann Arbor, Michigan.

Mills
Mills Music Inc. 1619 Broadway, New York City 19.

Minnesota
University of Minnesota Press. 10 Nicholson Hall, Minneapolis 14, Minnesota.

Minton
Minton, Balch & Company. *See Putnam.*

Modern Library
Modern Library Inc. 437 Madison Ave., New York City 22. (A subsidiary of Random House.)

Morrow
William Morrow & Company Inc. 425 Fourth Ave., New York City 16. (Includes Swallow Press Publications.)

Muhlenberg
Muhlenberg Press. 1228 Spruce St., Philadelphia 7.

Munksgaard
Einar Munksgaard Forlag. Nørregade 6, Copenhagen K, Denmark.

(Music Educators Nat. Conference)
See MENC above.

Musical Opinion
Musical Opinion Ltd. 13 Chicester Rents, Chancery Lane, London W C 2.

Musical Research
Bureau of Musical Research Inc. 3309 Barham Blvd., Hollywood 28, Califronia.

Musurgia
Musurgia Book & Music Publishers. 4 East 41st St., New York City 17.

—N—

National Recreation Assn
National Recreation Association. 315 Fourth Ave., New York City 10. (Includes publications originally issued by the National Bureau for the Advancement of Music.)

Nebraska
University of Nebraska Press. Lincoln 8, Nebraska.

Nelson
Thomas Nelson & Sons. 19 East 47th St., New York City 17.

Nelson-Hall
Nelson-Hall Company. 321 South Wabash Ave., Chicago 4.

New Directions
New Directions. Norfolk, Connecticut; 333 Ave. of the Americas, New York City 14.

New Mexico
University of New Mexico Press. Albuquerque, New Mexico.

North Carolina
University of North Carolina Press. Box 510, Chapel Hill, North Carolina.

Norton
W. W. Norton & Company Inc. 101 Fifth Ave., New York City 3.

Nostrand
D. Van Nostrand Company Inc. 250 Fourth Ave., New York City 3.

Novello
Novello & Company Ltd. 160 Wardour St., London W 1. USA agent: H. W. Gray.

—O—

Oklahoma
University of Oklahoma Press. Faculty Exchange, Norman, Oklahoma.

Organ Interests
Organ Interests Inc. Richmond, Staten Island, New York City 6.

Oxford
Oxford University Press Inc. 114 Fifth Ave., New York City 11; Amen House, Warwick Square, London E C 4.

—P—

Pacific
Pacific Books. Box 558, Palo Alto, California.

Paebar
The Paebar Company. 256 West 55th St., New York City 19.

Page
L. C. Page & Company. 53 Beacon St., Boston 8.

Pan American Union
Pan American Union, Division of Music & Visual Art. Washington 6, D. C.

Pantheon
Pantheon Books Inc. 333 Ave. of the Americas, New York City 14.

Paterson
Paterson Sons & Company Ltd. 152 Buchanan St., Glasgow, Scotland. USA agent: C. Fischer.

Pelican
Pelican Books. *See Penguin.*

Pellegrini
Pellegrini & Cudahy Inc. 41 East 50th St., New York City 22.

Penguin
Penguin (& Pelican) Books. Harmondshire, Middlesex, England. USA agent: Allen Lane Inc., 3300 Clipper Hill Road, Baltimore 11, Maryland. (Not all Penguin & Pelican books are available in the United States, owing to copyright restrictions.)

Pennsylvania
University of Pennsylvania Press. 3436 Walnut St., Philadelphia 4.

Permabooks/Perma-Giants
Permabooks. Garden City, New York. *See Doubleday and Garden City.*

Peters
C. F. Peters Corporation. *See Hinrichsen.*

Philosophical
Philosophical Library Inc. 15 East 40th St., New York City 16.

Phoenix
Phoenix House Ltd. 38 William IV St., London W C 2. USA agent: British Book Centre.

Pilot
Pilot Press Ltd.   45 Great Russell St. London W C 1.

Pitman
Pitman Publishing Corporation. 2 West 45th St., New York City 19.   Sir Isaac Pitman & Sons Ltd.   Pitman House, 39 Parker St., Kingsway, London W C 2.

Pittsburgh
The University of Pittsburgh Press. Bigelow & Parkman Sts., Pittsburgh, Pennsylvania.

Pocket Books
Pocket Books Inc.   18 West 48th St., New York City 19.

Porcupine
Porcupine Press Ltd. 26 Bloomsbury Way, London W C 1.

Prentice
Prentice-Hall Inc.   70 Fifth Ave., New York City 11.   (All Ziff-Davis book publications now are distributed by Prentice-Hall.)

Presser
Theodore Presser Company. Bryn Mawr, Pennsylvania. (Owner and distributor of Oliver Ditson and John Church publications.)

Princeton
Princeton University Press.   William & Charlton Sts., Princeton, N. J.

Pustet
Frederick Pustet Company Inc. 436 Main St., Cincinnati 1, Ohio.

Putnam
G. P. Putnam's Sons.   210 Madison Ave., New York City 16.   Putnam & Company Ltd., 42 Great Russell St., London W C 1. (Putnam's catalogue also includes the Minton, Balch & Company publications.)

—R—

Random
Random House Inc. 457 Madison Ave., New York City 22. (Also owner and distributor of the Modern Library publications.)

RCA Victor
RCA Victor Division, Radio Corporation of America, Educational Division. Camden, New Jersey.

Reeves
William Reeves Ltd. 83 Charing Cross Roas, London W C 2.

Regnery
Henry Regnery Company.   20 West Jackson Blvd., Chicago 4.

Revell
Fleming H. Revell Company.   158 Fifth Ave., New York City 10.

Reynal
Reynal & Hitchcock Inc. See Harcourt Brace.

Ricordi
G. Ricordi & Cia.   Via Berchet 2, Milan, Italy.   G. Ricordi & Company, RKO Bldg., New York City 20.

Rider
Rider & Company. 47 Prince's Gate London S W 7.

Rinehart
Rinehart & Company.   232 Madison Ave., New York City 16   (Formerly Farrar & Rinehart.)

Robbins
Robbins Music Corporation.   799 Seventh Ave., New York City 19.

Rockliff
Rockliff Publishing Corporation Ltd.   1 Dorset Bldgs., Salisbury Square. London E C 4. USA agent: British Book Centre.

Rogers
Winthrop Rogers Ltd.   London.   See: Boosey & Hawkes (owners & distributors of the Rogers publications.)

Ronald
The Ronald Press Company. 15 East 26th St., New York City 10.

Routledge
Routledge & Kegan Paul Ltd. Broadway House, 68 Carter Lane, London E C 4. (Formerly George Routledge & Sons Ltd and Kegan Paul, Trench, Trubner & Company Ltd.)

Roy
Roy Publishers.   30 East 74th St., New York City 21. (Some Dobson publications are issued in the USA under the Roy imprint.)

Rubank
Rubank Inc.   736 South Campbell Ave., Chicago 12.

Rushworth
Rushworth & Dreaper Ltd.   11 Islington, Liverpool, England. USA agent: J. Fischer.

Rutgers
Rutgers University Press.   New Brunswick, New Jersey.

—S—

Salabert
Editions Salabert.   22 Rue Chauchat, Paris 9.   Salabert Inc. 1 East 57th St., New York City. 22.

Sampson
Sampson, Low, Marston & Company Ltd. 25 Gilbert St., Oxford St., London W 1.

E. C. Schirmer
E. C. Schirmer Music Company. 221 Columbus Ave., Boston 16.

G. Schirmer
G. Schirmer Inc. 3 East 43rd St., New York City 17. USA agent of Curwen.

Schmidt
Arthur P. Schmidt Company. 120 Boylston St., Boston 12.

Schmitt
Paul H. Schmitt Music Company. 86 South 10th St., Minneapolis 2, Minnesota.

Schocken
Schocken Books Inc. 342 Madison Ave., New York City 17.

Schroeder
Schroeder & Gunther Inc. Rhinebeck, N.Y.

Schuberth
Edward Schuberth & Company Inc. 240 West 55th St., New York City 19.

Sci-Art
Sci-Art Publishers. Harvard Sq., Cambridge, Massachusetts.

Scribner
Charles Scribner's Sons. 597 Fifth Ave., New York City 17.

Secker
Martin Secker & Warburg Ltd. 7 John St., Bloomsbury, London W C 1.

Sentinel
Sentinel Books. 112 East 19th St., New York City 3. (Successors to The Leisure League.)

Sheridan
Sheridan House Inc. 257 Fourth Ave., New York City 10.

Sidgwick
Sidgwick & Jackson Ltd. 44 Museum St., London W C 1.

Signet
Signet Books. Published by the New American Library, 501 Madison Ave., New York City 22.

Silver
Silver, Burdett Company. 45 East 17th St., New York City 3.

(Simon & Schuster)
See S & S below.

Skelton Robinson
Skelton Robinson. 30 Cornhill St., London E C 3.

Sloane
William Sloane, Associates, Inc. 119 West 57th St., New York City 19.

Smith
Peter Smith. 321 Fifth Ave., New York City 16.

Southern
Southern Music Company. 830 East Houston St., San Antonio 6, Texas.

Southwest
Southwest Printing Company. 703 Browder St., Dallas 1, Texas.

Southworth
Southwork-Anthoensen Press. (Now Anthoensen Press.) 105 Middle St., Portland, Maine.

S & S
Simon & Schuster Inc. 1230 Ave. of the Americas, New York City 20.

Staff
The Staff Music Publishing Company. P. O. Box 37, Great Neck, New York.

Stainer
Stainer & Bell, Ltd. 58 Berne St., London W 1. USA agent: Galaxy.

Stanford
Stanford University Press. Stanford Calif.

Stewart
George W. Stewart, Publisher, Inc. 109 East 39th St., New York City 16.

Stokes
Frederick A. Stokes Company. See Lippincott.

Storm
Storm Publishing Inc. 507 Fifth Ave., New York City 17.

Strad
The Strad. 2 Duncan Terrace, London N 1.

Summy
Clayton F. Summy Company. 235 South Wabash Ave., Chicago 4.

Sylvan
Sylvan Press Ltd. 24 Museum St., London W C 1. USA agent: Transatlantic.

—T—

Teachers College
Bureau of Publications, Teachers College, Columbia University, 525 West 120th St., New York City 27. (See also Columbia University Press.)

Texas
University of Texas, University Publications. Austin 12, Texas.

Theatre Arts
Theatre Arts Books. 270 Madison Ave., New York City 16. (Now included in Duell, Sloan & Pierce.)

Transatlantic
Transatlantic Arts Inc.   Hollywood-by-the-Sea, Florida.   USA agents of Black, Sylvan, etc.   Transatlantic Arts Ltd.   29 Percy St., London W 1.

Tudor
Tudor Publishing Company (Harlem Book Company).   221 Fourth Ave., New York City 3.   (Also distributors of Chemical publications.)

—U—

Universal
Universal-Editions A. G.   6 Karlsplatz, Vienna I, Austria.   USA agent: Associated Music Publishers.

University of ——— Press
See under key word: California, Chicago, etc.   Also Columbia University Press, Harvard University Press, etc.

University
University Publishing Company.   1126 Q St., Lincoln 1, Nebraska.

Unwin
Arthur Unwin.   3 England's Lane, London N W 3

—V—

Valparaiso
Valparaiso University Press.   Valparaiso, Indiana.

Vanderbilt
Vanderbilt University Press.   Nashville 4, Tennessee.

Vanguard
Vanguard Press Inc.   424 Madison Ave., New York City 17.

Viking
The Viking Press Inc.   18 East 48th St., New York City 17.

Vincent
Vincent Music Company.   See Reeves.

Volkwein
Volkwein Brothers. 632 Liberty Ave., Pittsburgh 22, Pennsylvania.

—W—

Washburn
Ives Washburn Inc.   27 West 57th St., New York City 19.

Weekes
A. Weekes & Company.   13 Hanover St., Regent St., London W 1.

Westminster
Westminster Press.   Witherspoon Bldg., Philadelphia 7.

Whittlesey
Whittlesey House.   See McGraw.

Wilcox Follett
Wilcox & Follett Company.   1255 South Wabash Ave., Chicago 5.   (Trade-book publications; for text-books see Follett.)

Wilde
W. A. Wilde Company.   131 Clarendon St., Boston 16.

Wiley
John Wiley & Sons Inc.   440 Fourth Ave., New York City 16.

Williams
Joseph Williams Ltd.   29 Enford St., Marylebone, London W 1.   USA agent: Wood.

Williams & Norgate
Williams & Norgate Ltd.   36 Great Russell St., London W C 1.

Willis
The Willis Music Company.   124 East 4th St., Cincinnati 2, Ohio.

Wilson
The H. W. Wilson Company.   950 University Ave., New York City 52.

Winston
John E. Winston Company.   1006 Arch St., Philadelphia 7.

Wisconsin
University of Wisconsin Press.   811 State St., Madison 5, Wisconsin.

Wood
B. F. Wood Music Company.   24 Brookline Ave., Boston 15.   USA agent of Williams.

World
The World Publishing Company.   2231 West 110th St., Cleveland 2, Ohio.

Wyn
A. A. Wyn Inc.   23 West 47th St., New York City 19.

—Y—

Yale
Yale University Press.   143 Elm St., New Haven 7, Conn.

—Z—

Ziff-Davis
Ziff-Davis Publishing Company.   185 No. Wabash Ave., Chicago 1.   See Prentice.

Zondervan
Zondervan Publishing House.   815 Ottawa St., N. W., Grand Rapids 2, Mich.

ADDENDA

ADDENDA (May 1951)

(A selected list only—arranged in alphabetical order by authors' names)

General Note: The following addenda include: some of the more important releases of late 1950 and early 1951 (up to May 1st), on which information was not available in time for insertion in the main Guide; several books considered earlier to be O/P, but which currently have been re-issued or proved to be still available; and a few additional comments on books entered in the Guide before they were available for examination. These addenda do not include works in foreign languages, new books on "related" subjects (of minor musical interest), last-minute price-changes or O/P information.

A—

ABBOT, GEORGE J.
Instrumental music in the public schools. xii, 51 p, mus ex, paper. Birchard 1935. .75
Elementary manual, now available again.

B—

BACHARACH, A. E. (*ed*)
The music masters (including "Lives of the great composers"): v 2, After Beethoven to Wagner. 400 p. Cassell 1950. (4.00)
Biographical studies, by various authors, of some 38 composers. For v 1 in this series (now taken over by Cassell), see page 74.

BARBOUR, J. MURRAY
Tuning and temperament. Michigan 1951 in prep. △

BOUCHER, MAURICE
The political concepts of Richard Wagner. Tr Marcel Honoré. 222 p, 2-p bibl. M & H Pubs., N. Y., 1951, via Exposition. 4.00
Originally "Les Idées politiques de Richard Wagner," Paris, 1918.

BROOK, DONALD
Masters of the keyboard.
The Rockliff publication entered on page 237
now is issued in the U. S. A. by Macmillan at $3.00.

C—

CHING, JAMES
The amateur pianist's companion: a short, simple, & precise guide to greater progress & greater pleasure for all sorts & conditions of pianists. xiii, 114 p + 15 pl & fold-out chart, tables, mus ex. Hall 1950. (2.50)
The mental & emotional background; factual details & practical application of technical processes; the learning process; with repertory & analysis suggestions.

COHEN, HARRIET
Music's handmaid.
The 1950 Faber edition entered on page 240 now is issued in the U. S. A. by Transatlantic at $2.50.

COOK, KENNETH (*comp*)
The bandsman's everything within. Forew Denis Wright. 208 p, brief bibl. Hinrichsen 1950. 3.00
A directory & general reference work to British bands & band music. (The note to Cook's "Oh, listen to the band!" on page 27 of the Guide, erroneously confused that work with the present, separate publication.)

COOPER, MARTIN
French music: from the death of Berlioz to the death of Fauré. 238 p, frontis, mus ex. Oxford 1951 in prep. 4.00

D—

DAVIDSON, ARCHIBALD T.
Bach and Handel: the baroque in music. 85 p, 2-p bibl. Harvard 1951. 2.00

DE LORENZO, LEONARDO
My complete story of the flute: the instrument, the performer, the music. Intro Wesley La Violette. xvi, 493 p, 16-p pl (pors, etc), mus ex, brief bibl. Citadel 1951. 6.00
A short history with thumbnail biographies of famous flutists, notes on performance & music, and the author's reminiscences.

DOLPH, EDWARD ARTHUR
Sound off!: soldier songs from the
Revolution to World War II. xxvii,
621 p, illus (Lawrence Schick),
music (arr Philip Egner), 3-p bibl.
(1929) Rinehart 1942. 4.00
A songbook, originally published by Cosmopolitan in 1929.

DUCKLES, V. H. & NICEWONGER, H. S.
A guide to reference materials on
music. 31 p, paper, mim. California
1949. .70
Univ. of California Syllabus US.

DUNN, JOHN PETRIE
Student's guide to orchestration.
105 p, mus ex, paper. Novello
1928 (1950?). (1.50)
Novello Primer 107, again available.

DURÁN, GUSTAVO (comp)
Recordings of Latin American songs
and dances: annotated selective list
of popular & folk-popular music
(with bibliographies). xii, 92 p, illus,
paper. Pan American Union 2nd
ed (rev enl Gilbert Chase) 1950. 1.00

E—

ELKIN, ROBERT (ed)
A career in music.
*Incorrectly titled in the Guide entry (page 51)
as "Your musical career." Twelve articles
by various British writers on various musical
occupations, with photographs & autograph
signatures of the contributors.*

EVANS, EDWIN, Sr
How to accompany at the piano:
plain accompaniment, figurated accompaniment, practical harmony
for accompanists . . . 231 p, 172 mus △
ex. Reeves 1917. (3.00)
A standard work, again available.

F—

FELLOWES, EDMUND H.
Orlando Gibbons: a short account of
his life & work. Oxford (1925) 2nd
ed 1951 in prep. △
The standard biography.

FLOTHUIS, MARIUS
Modern British composers. Tr Olive
Renier. 60 p, illus, bds. Continental
(Stockholm) & Sidgwick (London)
1950. (2.50)
*"Symphonia" series of illustrated mono-
graphs; presumably to be made available in
U. S. A. via Bonnier, New York.*

FLOWER, (Sir) NEWMAN
(See also Sullivan & Flower below.)
Just as it happened. xi, 274 p, illus.
Cassell 1950; Morrow 1951. 4.00
*An autobiography by the noted publisher &
biographer of Handel & Schubert.*

G—

GARDEN, MARY & BIANCOLLI, LOUIS
Mary Garden's story. xii, 302 p
+ 32-p pl (pors, etc). S & S 1951. 3.75
Same, paper covers. 1.00
*Life-story of the noted soprano, with remi-
niscences of Debussy, the Chicago Opera
Company, etc.*

GOLDBECK, FREDERICK
The perfect conductor.
*The entry on page 12 of the Guide gives a
sub-title that appears on the jacket only.
The title-page sub-title now reads, "an
introduction to his skill & art for musicians
& music-lovers." One of the more notable
"appreciation" books, this includes discussions of The maestro & the score, The
score & the orchestra, The orchestra & the
maestro, The maestro & the baton.*

GRAF, HERBERT
Opera for the people. Minnesota
1951 in prep. △
*Note: Another opera work (correctly entered
on p 221) is erroneously included in the Max
Graf author entries on p 136 of the Guide.*

GRAHAM, PERCY
Vocal music in the elementary
schools. Ed Ruth L. Curtis. vii,
194 p, diagrs, mus ex, paper. △
Birchard 1950.

H—

HESELTINE, PHILIP ("Peter Warlock")
Frederick Delius. Intro & additions
Hubert Foss. 240 p, illus, bibl. △
Lane (1923) new ed 1951. (3.75)
*New edition of a standard work (listed O/P
on page 98 of the Guide), with a new intro-
duction & an added chapter on Delius's last
years by Hubert Foss, reminiscences by Percy
Grainger, & a catalogue of works.*

HILL, RALPH (ed)
Music 1951. 281 p, paper. Penguin
1951. .65
*Second in a series of surveys (see page 344
for "Music 1950"): review of the previous
year's activities and articles by various
authors on the music of India & South Africa,
the role of the accompanist, etc.*

HODGART, MATTHEW J. C.
The ballads. 184 p, illus, mus ex,
11-p bibl. Hutchinson (London)
1950, via Longmans. 2.00
A survey of the ballads included in the Child collection. Hutchinson's University Library, English Literature Series No. 38.

HOLMES, MALCOLM H.
Conducting an amateur orchestra.
Forew Archibald T. Davison. xii,
128 p, diagrs, mus ex. Harvard 1951. 2.50
A practical handbook, with lists of sources of orchestral repertory.

HORTON, JOHN
Some nineteenth century composers.
xi, 106 p. Oxford 1950. 1.50
Brief studies of Borodin Debussy, Elgar, Fauré, Franck, Grieg, Liszt, Mahler, Mendelssohn, Rimsky-Korsakov, Saint-Saëns, & Smetana.

HULL, A. EAGLEFIELD
Organ playing: its technique &
expression. viii, 263 p, 7 pl, 4
diagrs, mus ex. Augener 1911 (8th
pr, n d, via Broude). 6.00
A standard work, listed O/P on page 228.

I—

ILLING, ROBERT
A dictionary of music. 318 p, 10
diagrs, tables, mus ex, paper. Penguin 1950. .65
"Reference Book" series R-4, including some 1500 concise entries.

J—

JOHNER, (*Dom*) P. DOMINICUS
The chants of the Vatican gradual.
Tr monks of St. John's Abbey. xiii,
500 p, 3-p bibl. St. John's Abbey
Press, Collegeville, Minn., 1940,
via Gregorian Institute of America,
Toledo, Ohio. 4.85
With an introduction on the form of Gregorian pieces, notes on the liturgical interpretation of the proper mass chants, translations & sources of Latin texts.

K—

KARASOWSKI, MORITZ
Frédéric Chopin: his life & letters.
Tr Emily Hill. xiii, 479 p, 14 illus. △
Reeves (1879) 3rd ed 1938. (5.50)
A standard work, originally published in German 1877; in a 2-volume English edition

in 1879; listed O/P on page 65 of the Guide, but now made available again.

KATZ, ERICH
Recorder playing: a new & comprehensive method, with many original rounds & arrangements of folk tunes & other pieces. 64 p, diagrs, music, paper, spir. Clarke & Way Inc, N. Y., 1951. 2.50
Mostly music (some 71 progressive exercises & little pieces), with a 2-p introduction and 4 pages of general instructions.

L—

LAPIERRE, EUGÈNE
Gregorian chant accompaniment: a
new & simple approach according
to the theory of the basic modal
intervals. 103 p, music. Gregorian
Institute of America, Toledo, Ohio,
1949. 2.50
Twenty-one lessons with questions.

LAWS, GEORGE MALCOLM, *Jr.*
Native American balladry: a descriptive study & a bibliographical
syllabus. xii, 276 p. American Folk-
Lore Society, Univ. of Pennsylvania,
1950. 4.50
Bibliographical series, v 1; v 2 is Tristram P. Coffin's "The British traditional ballad in North America" (1950, $4.50).

LLOYD, LLEWELLYN S.
Music and sound. Forew Sir William
Bragg. 200 p, illus. Oxford (1937)
2nd ed 1951 in prep. 3.50
A standard work (listed O/P on page 2 of the Guide): written especially for musicians & music students.

LUPER, ALBERT T.
Music of Argentina. 10 leaves, paper.
Pan America 1942 (1949). △
Music of Brazil. 13 leaves, paper.
Pan American 1943 (1949). △
Pan American Union "Music Series" Nos 5 & 9 reprinted, the latter with revisions.

M—

MARTI, GERTRUDE AUSTIN
Teach your child music: with
suggestions for parents & teacher.
viii, 48, p, diagrs, mus ex, paper.
E. C. Schirmer 1951. 2.50
With references to songs in the Concord Series of folksong publications.

MENDL, ROBERT W. S.
The soul of music. Forew Ernest
Newman. xv, 2⁹1 p, 96 pl (pors,
facs, etc). Rockliff 1950; Macmillan 1951. 3.50
*The relationships between music and religion,
emotion, nature, etc.*

MOLDENHAUER, HANS
Duo-pianism: a dissertation. 400
p, 1 diagr, 13-p music, 11-p annot
bibl. Chicago Musical College Press,
Chicago, 1950. 4.90
*History of duo-pianism, with detailed studies
of the medium & its repertory.*

MONTELL, MARJORIE
Montell vocal technique. Pref J.
T. H. Mize. xii, 132 p, illus. Montell △
Foundation, Miami, Florida, 1950. 6.50
*Limited, signed edition of the self-proclaimed
"greatest book on singing of all time."*

MUNN, SHEPHERD
Playing the piano. 2 v: 27, 27 p,
photos, diagr, mus ex, paper. Novello
n d (1950 repr.) 2.40
Novello Primers Nos 116/7.

MUELLER, JOHN H.
The American symphony orchestra:
a history of musical taste. Indiana △
Univ. Press 1951 in prep. 6.00

N—

NETTL, PAUL
Forgotten musicians. Philosophical △
1951 in prep. 3.75
Announced for Nov. 1950, but not yet out.

O—

OWEN, H. GODDARD
A recollection of Marcella Sembrich.
79 p, some 80 illus (pors, facs, etc).
Marcella Sembrich Memorial Assn.
N Y.(?), 1950. 2.50
*A brief biographical sketch, with excerpts
from articles & many pictures.*

P—

PAPPOUTSAKIS, IPPOCRATES
Diagrams of basic movements in
conducting. Forew Francis Findlay.
Unp (12 single-sided pages), 28
diagrs, paper. Birchard 1942. .60
Baton-movement diagrams with captions.

PETTIS, ASHLEY
Music: then and now. Coleman 1951 △
in prep. 3.00

*Discussions of our musical heritage from the
Bible & music of our own time.*

PORTER, EVELYN
Concert-goer's guide. vi, 175 p, △
illus. Epworth Press, London, 1950. (2.50)
The story of music. Philosophical △
1951 in prep. 3.00
Announced for Nov. 1950, but not yet out.

POTIRON, HENRI
Practical instruction in plainsong
accompaniment. Tr Dom Gregory
Murray. 240 p, music. Society of
St. John the Evangelist, Desclée &
Co., Tournai, 1949. △
*Presumably to be made available in the
U. S. A. by J. Fischer & Bro.*

R—

RÉTI, RUDOLPH
The thematic process in music.
x, 362 p, mus ex. Macmillan 1951. 5.00

RICE, EDWARD & GLEASON, RALPH
Blue book of jazz. Duell Sloan
1951 in prep. 5.00
*Including some 300 illustrations. Originally
announced for 1948 publication.*

S—

SALTER, LIONEL
Going to a concert. 160 p, 23 photos,
b&ws, mus ex, 1-p bibl. Phoenix
1950. (2.25)
*"Excursions" series No 6: primarily for
children.*

SAUNDERS, ARETAS A.
A guide to bird songs: descriptions
& diagrams of the songs & singing
habits of landbirds & selected species
of shore birds. xiv, 307 p, 201 diagrs
(author). Doubleday 1951. 3.00
*An authoritative work with song-diagrams
in a musical shorthand indicating time, pitch,
quality, volume, & phonetics. Enlarged ed
of a work first published in 1935.*

SCHALLENBERG, EVERT WILLEM
Tchaikovsky. Tr M. M. Kessler-
Button. 60 p, illus, bibl, bds.
Continental (Stockholm) & Sidgwick
(London) 1950. (2.50)

*"Symphonia" series of illustrated mono-
graphs; presumably to be made available in
the U. S. A. via Bonnier, New York.*

SENDREY, ALFRED
Bibliography of Jewish music.
The Guide entry (page 176) omits comment

*on the unusual comprehensiveness &
importance of this remarkable reference work.
The bibliography itself includes some 11,000
items and the extensive introduction includes
a historical survey.*

SMITH, FLORENCE
Protestant church music: with an
account of its history & development.
158 p. Higley Press, Butler, Indiana,
1949.   1.50

SPAETH, SIGMUND
Opportunities in music.   128 p, 2-p
bibl, paper.   Vocational Guidance
Manuals, N. Y., 1950, via Grosset.   1.00
*A concise discussion of various types of
careers in music, with a chapter on prizes,
scholarships, & awards.*

STAINER, JOHN
The organ: a new edition critically
revised, with numerous addenda, &
adapted to the requirements of both
pneumatic & electric actions. Ed F.
Flaxington Harker. viii, 124 p, 45
illus, music, paper. (187?).   G.
Schirmer 1909 (1937).   1.50
*A standard 19th-century work (originally a
Novello "primer") in a revised edition.*

STANFORD, C. V. & FORSYTH, CECIL
A history of music. xii, 384 p, 34 pl,
mus ex.   Macmillan (1916) new ed
1925 (1947).   4.50
A standard work, re-issued 1951.

SULLIVAN, HERBERT & FLOWER, NEWMAN
Sir Arthur Sullivan: his life, letters,
& diaries.   306 p, illus.   Cassell   Δ
(1927) rev ed 1950.   (3.75)
New edition of a standard work long O/P.

T—

TAYLOR, COLIN
These music exams!: a general survey
teachers, parents, candidates & other
students.   Forew George Dyson.
xii, 96 p, mus ex, 1-p bibl, bds.
Curwen & G. Schirmer 1951.   (2.25)
A detailed study of British examinations.

THOMSON, VIRGIL
Music right and left. x, 214 p.
Holt 1951.   3.50
*A third collection of N. Y. Herald-Tribune
articles & reviews (1947/1950), many of which
deal with the special problems of modern music
and include memorials of Debussy, Ravel,
Weill, & Bartók.   For the two earlier
Thomson collections, see page 319 of the
Guide.*

TOBIN, J. RAYMOND
Music: background notes for schools,
colleges, discussion groups, etc. 185
p, brief bibl.   Evans Bros. Ltd.,
London, n d (1950).   (1.80)
"Appreciation" & lesson-outlines.

V—

VENNARD, WILLIAM
Singing: the mechanism & the
technic. v, 171 p, 29 diagrs (author),
mus ex, paper. Author, Los Angeles,
(1949) 2nd ed 1950.   3.50
With an extensive thesaurus of terms.

W—

WATERMAN, RICHARD A. (& others, comps)
Bibliography of Asiatic musics.
*The note on page 17 of the Guide should be
augmented with the information that the 14th
(& presumably final) installment of this
series appeared in "Notes" for March 1951
and was devoted to Addenda items.*

WILSON, HARRY ROBERT
A guide for choral conductors: with
interpretative suggestions for the
choral program series.   70 p, illus,
mus ex, paper.   Silver 1950.   1.00
*Concise notes on conducting with specific
interpretative notes for some 95 pieces.*

WOODHOUSE, GEORGE
A guide to the new way to piano
technique.   28 p, music, paper.
Schmidt 1949.   .75